International Relations Theories

International Relations Theories

Discipline and Diversity

Edited by Tim Dunne, Milja Kurki,
and Steve Smith

OXFORD
UNIVERSITY PRESS

OXFORD
UNIVERSITY PRESS

Great Clarendon Street, Oxford OX2 6DP

Oxford University Press is a department of the University of Oxford.
It furthers the University's objective of excellence in research, scholarship,
and education by publishing worldwide in

Oxford New York

Auckland Cape Town Dar es Salaam Hong Kong Karachi
Kuala Lumpur Madrid Melbourne Mexico City Nairobi
New Delhi Shanghai Taipei Toronto

With offices in

Argentina Austria Brazil Chile Czech Republic France Greece
Guatemala Hungary Italy Japan Poland Portugal Singapore
South Korea Switzerland Thailand Turkey Ukraine Vietnam

Oxford is a registered trade mark of Oxford University Press
in the UK and in certain other countries

Published in the United States
by Oxford University Press Inc., New York

© Oxford University Press 2007

British Library Cataloguing in Publication Data

Data available

Library of Congress Cataloging in Publication Data

Data available

Typeset by Newgen Imaging Systems (P) Ltd., Chennai, India
Printed in Great Britain
on acid-free paper by
Ashford Colour Press Ltd., Gosport, Hants.

ISBN 978–0–19–929833–4

10 9 8 7 6 5 4 3 2

Preface

When we invited our line-up of leading theoreticians to participate in the volume, we feared they would turn us down when they saw the details of our request. We asked them to provide a synopsis of the literature *and* their own original interpretation. We asked them to engage in the complexities of the theoretical underpinnings of the position in question *and* we asked them to show how and why their theories matter. Fortunately they not only agreed to come on board, in our view they met all of these aims with a great deal of rigour and creativity. The three editors have found it an enormous pleasure to work with such a professional group of collaborators.

The result of their endeavours is a book on *International Relations Theories* that will speak to International Relations students at all levels as well as stimulating debates in the academy about the state of International Relations theory today. Below we set out in more detail the rationale for the book as well as including a brief guide to the structure of each chapter.

Rationale for the book

Underpinning the ethos of the book are a number of thematics about theory and the nature of the discipline of International Relations (IR). When using this term, we are following the important convention that distinguishes between capital IR denoting the academic study of International Relations, and lower-case international relations which is shorthand for the object of the discipline's investigations (the actors, interests, institutions, and identities on a global scale). This distinction enables us to examine the sociology of knowledge of IR as a discipline: how and when it became a distinct subject, what kinds of topics get taught, where the subject is studied, what kinds of research get funded. If we were to do away with the distinction, we would end up assuming that there is a direct read-across from the discipline to the interactions that constitute the real world of international relations.

What thematics, then, underpin this book? Below we highlight seven:

1. **Theory is the discipline's centre of gravity.** Academic International Relations is a broad church. It includes a number of very active sub-fields, many of which are motivated by applied agendas. We would argue that the centre of gravity of the field is IR theory (a point made by Ole Wæver in the concluding chapter). It is no coincidence that histories of the discipline tend to map directly onto the major theoretical contestations or debates.

2. **Theory helps us to explain the world of international relations.** All contributors agree that theory is central to explaining the dynamics of world politics, whether one is interested in regionalism, identity, security, or foreign policy. To put it more graphically, there is no hiding place from theory, there is no alternative but to engage with issues

concerning causation, interpretation, judgement, and critique. The introduction and the opening two chapters deal at some length with what theory is, how it is interpreted differently, and what is at stake in applying theory to the world.

3. **Theoretical diversity is to be valued.** All books on IR theory include a variety of different theoretical positions, particularly the historically dominant traditions of realism, liberalism, and Marxism: latterly, it is commonplace, especially in US-based scholarship, to include constructivism in the mix. We go much further in terms of defending diversity. To these four we have added the English school (resurgent in the last decade), feminism and poststructuralism (powerful critical voices since the 1980s), and two relatively recent theories in the form of postcolonialism and green theory. The order of the chapters proceeds along a continuum, from established at the beginning of the book to the newer theories at the end. This does not mean, however, that we believe the established traditions ought to be discounted for being 'old': indeed, the fact that we allocate two chapters to realism and neorealism, and liberalism and neoliberalism, underscores the importance we attach to these two rich theoretical perspectives as well as recognizing the presence of a significant fault-line within each.

4. **Theoretical diversity is contested.** Related to the above, we are aware of the fact that the positive value we attach to theoretical diversity is not universally shared. Many established scholars think that the core of the discipline – the focus on inter-state dynamics of conflict and cooperation – is being undermined. We disagree. We think more is better, and that theoretical pluralism not only enables old issues to be addressed in new ways, but also opens up new agendas which speak more directly to changing threats and potentialities. As Steve Smith shows in his introduction, inside the thick walls of the academy, this debate has generated a great deal of anxiety. Those committed to a particularly narrow concept of theory as a set of propositions formulated as testable hypotheses have unnecessarily sought to *discipline* diversity.

5. **The limits to theoretical diversity.** The book does not have a clear answer to the question whether there are limits to theoretical diversity. On the one hand, the arguments we advance for letting new voices be heard must be extended into the future. Yet on the other, we agree with Ole Wæver that theoretical innovation *within* existing perspectives is more likely (hence the proliferation of different 'wings' within each overarching theory, discussed in the chapters themselves).

6. **Choosing between theories.** Those who advocate theoretical diversity need to confront the question – often posed by students – how to decide between them. The introduction goes into this issue in some detail. At this stage we remind our readers that each contributor is defending their particularly theory. As Milja Kurki and Colin Wight put it in the first chapter, it is important that we remember theorists are 'selling' their ideas. They may not always admit to the weaknesses in their own position which is why it is important for 'buyers' to read the alternatives.

7. **Diversity and the reinvention of the discipline.** The penultimate chapter by Colin Hay differs from the previous thirteen chapters in that it is not 'selling' a particular IR theory in the same sense as the others. Instead, the reader will find an analysis of the impact globalization is having on mainstream IR theories such as realism. Rather than

concluding that changes in global politics have brought the legitimacy of the entire discipline into question, both Hay and Wæver recognize that there are powerful structures at work which will ensure the ongoing resilience of International Relations.

How to use the book

We anticipate that students will read the book in different ways, and that course tutors will recommend the book for different purposes. With some certainty, we can predict that all IR theory courses will cover *some* of the ground contained in the volume. It is equally certain that only a few IR theory courses will cover *all* of the same ground.

The book has been compiled in such a way that tutors and students can read chapters as though they are free standing. However, for those courses that follow more closely the progression established throughout, we anticipate that there will be a pay-off in terms of cumulative learning. We think this is particularly true in the case of the introduction and the two opening chapters which cover contextual issues to do with the relationship between IR theory and the social sciences, and between IR theory and political theory. Furthermore, many similar themes are interwoven through various chapters – understanding constructivism is going to help the reader to comprehend what is meant by feminist constructivism in a later chapter.

Each chapter has followed the same format, and incorporates many of the learning aids which have proven to be highly successful in companion volumes such as John Baylis's and Steve Smith's edited textbook *Globalization of World Politics,* also published by Oxford University Press and now in its third edition.

Acknowledgements

We owe a significant debt to Ruth Anderson, our editor at Oxford University Press. She has been extremely positive about the book from the outset and her input has been invaluable. During the final stages of submitting the manuscript, Jodie Hobbs was a marvellous editorial assistant. She put her Ph.D. research on hold for several weeks so that she could compile a consolidated bibliography, as well as helping with other aspects of the manuscript.

Our final debt is to our students. It would be unthinkable to be involved in a project of this kind without the shared experience of talking about theory to excited (and sometimes frustrated) students. In a very particular sense, the three editors directly shared this experience in that Steve taught both Tim and Milja, the former at the University of East Anglia in the late 1980s and the latter at Aberystwyth in the early 2000s. This book will have succeeded if it can stimulate the minds of the next generation to engage critically with the ever changing discipline of International Relations.

Tim Dunne, Milja Kurki, Steve Smith
University of Exeter, April 2006

Brief Contents

Detailed Contents

About the Contributors

Chris Brown is Professor of International Relations at the London School of Economics and Political Science and the author of *International Relations Theory: New Normative Approaches (1992)*, *Understanding International Relations* (1997; 2nd edn 2001), *Sovereignty, Rights and Justice* (2002), as well as numerous book chapters and journal articles in internatinal political theory. He is editor of *Political Restructuring in Europe: Ethical Perspectives* (1994) and (with Terry Nardin and N. J. Rengger) *International Relations in Political Thought: Texts from the Greeks to the First World War* (2002).

David Campbell is Professor of Cultural and Political Geography at Durham University. His research deals with the visual culture of geopolitics, and international relations, political theory and global geopolitics, and US security policy. The author of *Writing Security: United States Foreign Policy and the Politics of Identity* and *National Deconstruction: Violence, Identity and Justice in Bosnia* – which won International Forum Bosnia's 'Bosnia-Herzegovina Book of the Year 1999' – he is working on a new manuscript about geopolitics and visual culture which explores the imaging of Sudan in the period after the Second World War.

Tim Dunne is Reader in International Relations and Head of the Department of Politics at the University of Exeter. Previously, he worked for ten years in the Department of International Politics at Aberystwyth. He is the author of *Inventing International Society* (1998) and has been associate editor of the *Review of International Studies*. He has edited six books, including *Human Rights in Global Politics* (with Nicholas J. Wheeler, 1998) and *Worlds in Collision: Terror and the Future of Global Order* (with Ken Booth, 2002).

Robyn Eckersley is Reader in the Department of Political Science, University of Melbourne, Australia. She is the author of *Environmentalism and Political Theory: Toward an Ecocentric Approach* (1992) and *The Green State: Rethinking Democracy and Sovereignty* (2004), and has edited five books, the most recent of which are *The State and the Global Ecologicial Crisis* (with John Barry, 2005) and *Political Theory and the Ecological Challenge* (with Andrew Dobson, 2006).

K. M. Fierke is Professor of International Relations at the University of St Andrews. She has previously held positions at Queen's University Belfast, Nuffield College, Oxford University, and Amsterdam School for Social Science Research, University of Amsterdam. She is author of *Critical Approaches to International Security* (2007), *Diplomatic Interventions: Conflict and Change in a Globalizing World* (2005), *Changing Games, Changing Strategies: Critical Investigations in Security* (1998), as well as co-editor of *Constructing International Relations: The Next Generation* (2001).

Siba N. Grovogui is Professor of International Relations theory and law at the John Hopkins University. He is the author of *Sovereigns, Quasi-sovereigns, and Africans* (1996) and *Beyond Eurocentrism and Anarchy* (forthcoming). These two books and other works by Grovogui examine disciplinary assumptions about international existence in the hope of bringing to the fore postcolonial actors, their intellectual resources, and their ideas of the moral order.

Colin Hay is Professor of Political Analysis at the University of Birmingham. He has held visiting posts at Harvard University, MIT, and the University of Manchester. He is the author, co-author or editor of a number of books. These include *Why We Hate Politics* (2007), *Developments in British Politics* 8 (2006), *The State: Theories and Issues* (2006), *Political Analysis* (2002), *British Politics Today* (2002), *Demystifying Globalization* (2000), *The Political Economy of New Labour* (1999), and *Re-stating Social and Political Change* (1996). He is co-founder and co-editor of the journals *Comparative European Politics* and *British Politics*.

Milja Kurki is Lecturer in International Relations at the University of Exeter. Her Ph.D. thesis on the concept of cause in International Relations theory was completed at the Department of International Politics at Aberystwyth and has been awarded prizes by the British International Studies Association and the Political Studies Association. She has recently been published in the *Review of International Studies*.

Lisa L. Martin is Clarence Dillon Professor of International Affairs in the Government Department at Harvard University. She works in the areas of international political economy and international institutions. Current research projects include a comparative analysis of the autonomy of international financial institutions and the strategic choice of the form of international agreements.

John J. Mearsheimer is the R. Wendell Harrison Distinguished Service Professor of Political Science at the University of Chicago, where he has taught since 1982. He has written extensively about security issues and international politics more generally. He has published three books: *Conventional Deterrence* (1983), which won the Edgar S. Furniss, Jr. Book Award; *Liddell Hart and the Weight of History* (1988); and *The Tragedy of Great Power Politics* (2001), which won the Joseph Lepgold Book Prize. He has also written many articles for academic journals such as *International Security*, and popular magazines such as *Foreign Policy* and the *London Review of Books*.

Richard Ned Lebow is the James O. Freedam Presidential Professor of Government at Dartmouth College. He is a Fellow of the Centre of International Relations and Wolfson College, both at Cambridge University. His most recent single-authored book is *The Tragic Vision of Politics: Ethics, Interests and Orders* (Cambridge, 2003). It won the Alexander L. George Award for the best book in political psychology.

Diana Panke graduated with an MA from the University of Mannheim, Germany, in 2003. Her thesis, 'Arguing and Bargaining in the EU Negotiation Systems' won the award of the Lorenz-von-Stein Foundation for the best MA thesis of 2002. She is currently a research associate at the Free University Berlin, where she is working on a Ph.D. project on state compliance and the European Court of Justice.

Thomas Risse is Professor of International Politics at the Otto Suhr Institute for Political Science of the Free University Berlin. He is also coordinator of the Research Centre for Governance in Areas of Limited Statehood at the Free University and has been associate editor of *International Organization*. His most recent publications include (as co-editor) *Handbook of International Relations* (2002), *Transnational Identities: Becoming European*

●

in the European Union (2004), and *Transforming Europe: Europeanization and Domestic Change* (2001).

Mark Rupert is Professor of Political Science at Syracuse University's Maxwell School of Citizenship and Public Affairs, and teaches in the areas of international relations and political economy. Mark's research focuses on the intersection of the US political economy with global structures and processes. He is the author of *Producing Hegemony* (1995), *Ideologies of Globalization* (2000), and *Globalization and International Political Economy* (with Scott Solomon, 2005).

Laura Sjoberg is Visiting Assistant Professor of Political Science at Duke University. Previously, she was a Research Fellow at the Kennedy School of Government at Harvard University. She is the author of *Gender, Justice, and the Wars in Iraq* (2006), and several articles on gender and international security. She has been awarded prizes and fellowships for her work on gender and war by the Center for the Study of Sexuality in the Military, Women in International Security, the Century Foundation, the Bannerman Foundation, and the International Studies Association.

Steve Smith is Vice-Chancellor of the University of Exeter and Professor of International Relations. He has written or edited fourteen books. His most widely read work is *Explaining and Understanding International Relations* (co-authored with the late Professor Martin Hollis, 1990). He was the editor of the prestigious Cambridge University Press / British International Studies Association series from 1986 to 2005. In 2003–4 he was President of the International Studies Association. He is an Academician of the Social Sciences (AcSS).

J. Ann Tickner is Professor of International Relations at the University of Southern California. She is the author of *Gender in International Relations: Feminist Perspectives on Achieving Global Security* (1992) and *Gendering World Politics: Issues and Approaches in the Post-Cold War Era* (2001). Her work has appeared in *International Studies Quarterly, International Political Science Review,* and *Millennium.* She was President of the International Studies Association in 2006–7.

Ole Wæver is Professor of International Relations at the University of Copenhagen. Before this, he was a researcher at the Centre for Peace and Conflict Research in Copenhagen (COPRI) from 1985 to 1999. He has written or edited twenty books and published in international journals such as *Journal of Peace Research, International Affairs, Cooperation and Conflict, Journal of International Affairs, Journal of Common Market Studies, Review of International Studies, International Organization,* and *Millennium.* His most recent book is *Regions and Powers: The Structure of International Security* (with Barry Buzan, 2003).

Colin Wight is Professor of International Relations at the University of Exeter. Prior to this he worked at the Department of International Politics at Aberystwyth and the Department of Politics in Sheffield. He is the author of *Agents, Structures and International Relations* (2006). He was Associate Editor of *International Relations* from 2002 to 2003. He has published articles in *International Studies Quarterly, European Journal of International Relations, Political Studies,* and the *Philiosophy of the Social Sciences.*

Guided Tour of Learning Features

This text is enriched with a range of learning tools to help you navigate the text material and reinforce your knowledge of International Relations theory. This guided tour shows you how to get the most out of your textbook package and do better in your studies.

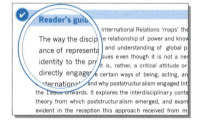

Reader's Guides

Reader's Guides at the beginning of every chapter set the scene for upcoming themes and issues to be discussed, and indicate the scope of coverage within each chapter topic.

Analysis

The main section of the chapter, where contributors examine the defining ideas of the theory in question, as well as the central fault-lines within each position.

Case Studies

Students frequently point to the abstract nature of a great deal of theoretical discussion. While this text recognizes that certain philosophical issues should not be sidelined, it also recognizes the value of showing the application of theory to concrete political problems. The case studies will facilitate class discussion and debate and will help you to bridge theory and practice in your assessments.

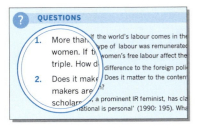

Questions

A set of carefully devised questions has been provided to help you assess your comprehension of core themes, and may also be used as the basis of seminar discussion and coursework.

Further Reading

To take your learning further, reading lists have been provided as a guide to find out more about the issues raised within each chapter topic and to help you locate the key academic literature in the field.

Important Websites

At the end of most chapters you will find an annotated summary of useful websites that are central to International Relations and that will be instrumental in further research.

Glossary Terms

Key terms are bold-faced in the text and defined in a glossary at the end of the text, to aid you in exam revision.

Guided Tour of the Online Resource Centre

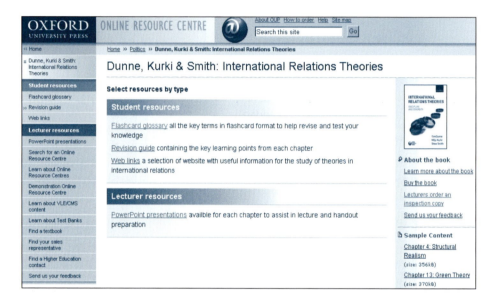

www.oxfordtextbooks.co.uk/orc/dunne/

The Online Resource Centre that accompanies this book provides students and instructors with ready-to-use teaching and learning materials. These resources are free of charge and designed to maximize the learning experience.

Revision Guide

Key points that summarize the most important arguments developed within each chapter topic.

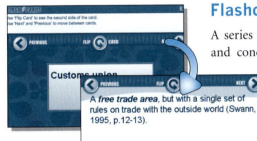

Important Websites

Annotated web links, organized by issue area, have been provided to point you in the direction of different theoretical debates, important treaties, working papers, articles and other relevant sources of information.

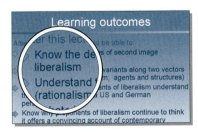

Flashcard Glossary

A series of interactive flashcards containing key terms and concepts has been provided to test your understanding of International Relations theory terminology.

PowerPoint Slides

These complement each chapter of the book and are a useful resource for preparing lectures and handouts. They allow lecturers to guide students through the key concepts and can be fully customized to meet the needs of the course.

Introduction: Diversity and Disciplinarity in International Relations Theory

STEVE SMITH

 Chapter Contents

- All these theories but the bodies keep piling up
- What do the theories share?
- Diversity and disciplinarity

Why did British Prime Minister Tony Blair support the decision of US President George W. Bush to attack Iraq in April 2003 in order to remove Saddam Hussein from power? This book is explicitly aimed at helping you think through how such a decision became possible. At first sight, you might think that surely we do not need theory to explain this decision: we just go and ask Tony Blair, and thus can dispense with academic theories. There are at least two main problems with this position: the first, and less important one, is that it requires us to believe what the Prime Minister said in reply to our question. Maybe, as many British people think, he lied about the reasons for going to war. According to this line of argument, there were never any weapons of mass destruction and he knew it: he used the argument that they existed simply to give legitimacy to his desire to support the USA in its war against Iraq. Therefore, the argument runs, he would simply reply to our question by repeating his earlier lie, and we would not get to the 'real' reason for his decision. The only way of working out the 'real' reason would be to deduce from the action what must have been his motivation for the decision. The second, and more fundamental, problem is that the world is rarely so simple that people can be completely aware of why they are acting in certain ways; perhaps the Prime Minister was looking for evidence of a clear and present danger to justify a feeling about what was 'right', what 'the international community' had to do to oust a dangerous dictator? Perhaps, like all of us, he could not be entirely aware of the many motives that triggered this course of action. We therefore have to locate his reasons in a wider context, one that he may not himself accept or recognize.

Each of these objections places us immediately in the realm of theory, since we have to make assumptions about the Prime Minister's behaviour and the extent to which he is either being truthful about his reasons or is fully aware of the context within which he is acting. This position could strike some readers as a bit harsh, since they might argue that surely the Prime Minister knew exactly what he was doing. My simple response is to ask each reader to think through their own behaviour: why is it that we feel what we feel, think what we think, say what we say, and do what we do? We know that in fact we are often not sure of our reasons, and sometimes catch a glimpse of ourselves acting in accordance with what is fashionable or what is consistent with a particular rationale which we hope will be publicly acceptable. In short, in the social world it is not enough simply to base our accounts of individuals solely on the reasons they give for their actions. The social world is one in which individuals exist within powerful economic, political, social, gendered, racial, linguistic, and moral structures. We might be able to *describe* action fairly easily (the Prime Minister said that he supported the US President in going to war against Iraq), but it is far more difficult to *explain* it (why was the action undertaken?). And, when it comes to explaining action, we are, whether we like it or not, in the realm of theory. Theories offer accounts of why things happened, and the fact that they offer a wide range of reasons for action reflects the fact that they have very different assumptions. Therefore, after reading this book, you may want to come back to my starting point and ask how the various theories in this book would answer the question about why Prime Minister Blair supported the Iraq War. Suffice it for now to say that you would get very different answers from the theories represented in this book. In fact, if you were to ask each of the authors of the chapters, I suspect that you would get a distinctly different answer from each of them. Some of the differences would result from the fact that the authors focused on different aspects of the issue: some might focus on political economy issues, such as the importance of oil; others might look at the role of international law and institutions; others might concentrate on notions of maximizing power, while still others would see this as an example of constructing an 'other' so as to reinforce existing internal power structures. Yet other differences would be because the authors saw the world in very different ways from one another: some would see a world of power and security; others would see a world of meaning and community; while others would see a world of economic forces capturing political actors.

These differences sometimes worry students new to the discipline of International Relations (IR), since they expect some kind of 'right' answer, and are often frustrated when teachers of the subject keep referring them back to a range of theories, each of which has a different take on the question. In my view, this is an absolutely central issue, and I hope in this introduction to show why, in the case of the social world, it is indeed interpretation all the way down. To be completely clear from the outset, I do not think that we can evaluate accounts of why people act as they do in a way that leads to one definitive story; in the social world there is always more than one story to tell.

As I write this chapter (April 2006), the press throughout the world is preoccupied with whether the USA will use military force against Iran in order to remove its capability to produce enriched uranium. This follows a leaked document, which talks of the preparations for such an attack. Yet there is no agreement at all over why the USA might act in this way: different commentators give different reasons. It is about President Bush's desire to divert attention from internal problems; it is part of a master plan to attack the new enemies of the USA; it is a defensive move to ensure the security of the USA; it is about oil; it is a leaked story to get the international community, especially the United Nations (UN), to pressurize the Iranian leadership to give up its nuclear programme; it is about the identity of President Bush, who is looking at his place in history; it is about influencing other possible opponents of the USA in the Middle East; it is about diverting attention from the failures of the 'war on terrorism'. I could go on, but hopefully the point is clear: in explaining why this action might take place, a variety of accounts offer very different reasons, each based on a different theoretical account of US foreign policy, and ultimately a distinctly different view of international relations.

In this introduction I want to do three main things: first I want to explain why we (the three editors) have chosen to cover the theories that we have, and to say something about our view of international theory and its relationship to the world, an important issue which features prominently in the text through the use of case-study analysis. Second, I want to look at the kind of assumptions about theory that underlie each of the approaches. Finally, I want to discuss explicitly the issue of how one might make a choice between the rival theories covered in this book.

All these theories but the bodies keep piling up[1]

The book includes nine chapters on distinct theories of International Relations – realism / structural realism, liberalism / neoliberalism, the English school, constructivism, Marxism and critical theory, feminism, poststructuralism, green theory, postcolonalism – alongside chapters that reflect on IR theory and social science, IR theory as a form of political theory, the effect of globalization on IR theory and on the diversity of IR as a discipline. The existence of so many theories of International Relations does lead to one obvious query, namely why such a range of contending positions? In the history of the discipline of IR there have always been debates between competing theories. Kurki and Wight cover the history of these debates in the following chapter, so I am not going to rehearse them here: suffice it to state that from the earliest days of its existence as a discipline, the main debate has been between forms of realism and liberalism. In recent years this debate has been between versions of realism and liberalism known as neorealism and neoliberalism. Although there are clear linkages between classical and 'neo' variants, we allocated them separate chapters because we think that the later versions contain distinctly different assumptions about the nature of theory. Marxism has been the other main approach to studying international relations, and by the 1980s it was commonplace to speak of the three approaches (realism, liberalism, and Marxism) as constituting an 'interparadigm debate'. This is how most of the textbooks of the 1980s and 1990s represented international theory and, as a consequence, this is how theory was taught.

From the vantage point of today, it seems that there were a number of problems with this way of thinking about IR theory. First, it exaggerated the amount of debate: what actually happened was that realism dominated the discipline given that it claimed to explain the bipolar structure of the international system, while liberalism was able to cover secondary issues to do with institutions and trade, with Marxism being invoked to explain relative economic power and structural inequality. This notion of an interparadigm debate hinted at a kind of intellectual pluralism, whereby there was a level playing field on which the theories competed. Yet, the priority accorded to explaining the military confrontation enabled realism to assume primacy. The key point to note is the power of assumptions about 'what' the world of international relations consisted of in determining the explanatory power of the rival theories. Thus, since international relations was defined as being about war, the theory that would appear to be most useful in explaining it, not surprisingly, would be the one that focused on war. I am not saying that war is not a feature of world politics, only that the dominance of realism and neorealism reflected often implicit, unstated, 'common-sense' assumptions about the content of world politics.

But it was another problem that caused most reflection among those who felt uneasy at the notion of intellectual pluralism implied by the idea of an interparadigm debate. The phrase suggested that the three approaches were all vying for attention in terms of their ability to explain *the same world*. The rather unsettling worry was that the three approaches were actually focusing on rather different features of international relations, and thus they were not in debate at all; what they disagreed about was which events should be the focus of the discipline. Thus whereas realism might focus on the Cold War, liberalism might concentrate on international economic relations between the leading capitalist economies, and Marxism might stress the patterns of world trade and investment that create divisions between the 'haves' and the 'have-nots'. If you accept this argument, then it follows that the dominance of one theory is the result of a prior assumption about the main things in world politics that need explaining. This leads to a rather destabilizing thought, which is that something as seemingly 'academic' and 'non-political' as deciding which theory is of most help in explaining international relations might in fact be a very political act, because which theory you see as being the most useful will depend on what you want to explain, and this, in turn, will depend on your values and beliefs about what international relations is all about. Put very simply, if you live in a wealthy part of the world, where there are no apparent military threats, you might think that the key features to be explained are those concerned with the economic relations between the main wealthy powers. If you live in a conflict zone, where the survival of your society is at issue, you might well want a theory that explains conflict. Finally, if you are in a very poor part of the world, you may see the central features of world politics as those related to the creation and support of differences between national levels of wealth.

This sense of dissatisfaction with the comforting notion of an interparadigm debate led to what many have called the fourth **great debate** in IR, between what can broadly be called **rationalist** and **reflectivist** theories. This debate was launched by Robert Keohane in his 1988 International Studies Association (ISA) presidential debate, and referred to the tensions then emerging between rationalist approaches such as neorealism and neoliberalism on the one hand and reflectivist approaches, such as feminism and poststructuralism on the other. To simplify things a bit, the chapters in this book dealing with neorealism and neoliberalism would be seen by Keohane as rationalist, whereas most of the others, with two main exceptions, would be seen by him as reflectivist; the two exceptions would be constructivism and the English school, both of which can best be understood as overlapping the rationalist / reflectivist divide. The key difference between rationalist and reflectivist approaches is that, broadly speaking, rationalist accounts are **positivist**, whereas reflectivist approaches oppose positivism. Again, the Kurki and Wight chapter discusses this distinction in detail; for now it is enough to note that the central difference between rationalist and reflectivist accounts is thus an **epistemological** and **methodological** one, rather than one about what the world is like (**ontology**). That is to say that the fourth debate is one about how we know what we claim to know. In this important sense, the main dividing line between the significant theories of IR for the last two decades has been their attitude towards positivist accounts of knowledge.

Since the interparadigm debate of the 1980s, there has been an explosion of theories about international relations. Most of these theories have opposed the dominance of rationalist approaches (neorealism and neoliberalism), primarily on epistemological grounds. Rationalist theories accept a notion of **foundationalism**, whereby there are secure grounds for making knowledge claims about a world that is separate from the theories commenting on it. Rationalist theories sometimes claim that their accounts are more accurate than others because, due to their systematic scientific approach they can capture the essence of the way the world is in an empirically justifiable way. By way of contrast, reflectivist approaches do not share a commitment to the form of foundational positivism found in rationalist approaches. This has caused a significant problem for reflectivist approaches, because they have been dismissed by leading rationalist scholars for not being legitimate social science. Keohane made this point in his ISA presidential address: he claimed that reflectivism's main weakness was the lack of a research programme:

> **"** Until the reflective scholars or others sympathetic to their arguments have delineated such a research program and shown in particular studies that it can illuminate important issues in world politics, they will remain on the margins of the field, largely invisible to the preponderance of empirical researchers, most of whom explicitly or implicitly accept one or another version of rationalistic premises. **"**

Keohane 1989: 173

What was needed, he went on to add, was for reflectivist scholars to develop 'testable theories' without which 'it will be impossible to evaluate their research programme' (1989: 173–4).

More recently, Stephen Walt, in a highly influential review of the state of IR theory, argues that although the key debate has been, and continues to be, that between realism and liberalism, there is a third approach which he sees as the main alternative to these two. But for Walt this alternative approach is not one of the main reflectivist approaches; instead it is constructivism, which concedes a great deal of philosophical ground to rationalism. But he goes further than this: Walt explicitly rejects reflectivism 'because these scholars focused initially on criticizing the mainstream paradigms but did not offer positive alternatives to them, they remained a self-consciously dissident minority for most of the 1980s' (1998: 32).

Walt sets out the main features of these three 'paradigms' (realism, liberalism, and constructivism) in a figure representing a classical Greco-Roman building with three pillars. Under the heading of constructivism he lists its 'unit of analysis' as 'individuals' and its 'main instruments' as 'ideas and discourse'. Its 'main limitation' is that it is 'better at describing the past than anticipating the future'. It is not just that this is a very thin account of constructivism but also that constructivism is portrayed as the only approach that deals with ideas, discourse, and identities, which a variety of reflectivist theorists would see as the core concerns of their approaches. Not only does Stephen Walt effectively silence more radical theoretical approaches, he understates the value of constructivism. This is evident in his belief that 'the "compleat diplomat" of the future should remain cognizant of realism's emphasis on the inescapable role of power, keep liberalism's awareness of domestic forces in mind, and occasionally reflect on constructivism's vision of change' (1998: 44). By way of contrast, Walt argues that 'realism is likely to remain the single most useful instrument in our intellectual toolbox' (1998: 43).

The current situation is one where there is a wide range of theories of International Relations. It is very important to stress that while some of these are trying to explain the same features of world politics as others, others are focusing on very different aspects. The problem is that many of the mainstream (rationalist) theorists deny the legitimacy of *both* sets of alternative theories. Those that are offering competing accounts of the same phenomena are usually deemed illegitimate, as not being 'proper' social science, while those focusing on other features of world politics (such as poverty, gender, race, international law, the environment, etc.) are dismissed as not dealing with the most important features of world politics (usually defined as inter-state war). In an important respect, the dismissal of work as illegitimate (in terms of epistemology) is in many ways more insidious than a dismissal on the grounds that the features focused on (that is to say, on grounds of ontology) are not central to international relations.

None of this means that the traditionally dominant mainstream approaches are outdated or peripheral to an explanation of international relations. Indeed, by giving each of the historically dominant traditions two chapters, we hope that we have made clear the importance that we place on these theories. In our view, they are absolutely central to explaining international relations but, equally importantly, we do not feel that they are sufficient on their own. We believe that there are other accounts that explain areas of international relations, and we feel that our job as editors is to offer as wide a range of accounts as possible in this book. We believe that the reader needs to understand both that the historically dominant approaches are vitally important for an understanding of international relations, and that these need to be complemented by other accounts that are equally legitimate.

Some established scholars in the discipline, such as Kal Holsti, regret this proliferation of theories, and the disappearance of a specific core to the field. As he puts it:

> **"** It is hard to say that there is any longer a particular core to the field . . . Our field should be basically concerned with the relations between states, and relations between societies and non-state actors to the extent that those relations impinge upon and affect the relations between states. When we go far beyond these domains, we get into areas of sociology, anthropology, and social psychology that are best dealt with by people in those disciplines. **"**

Holsti 2002: 621

He adds:

> **"** I am somewhat concerned that too many people may be spending time discussing great issues of epistemology and metaphysics . . . But beyond a certain point . . . concern with epistemology may lead us to lose sight of the subject matter. The greatest texts of our field were written by those who were deeply immersed in the subject, and not by epistemologists. **"**

Holsti 2002: 623

We disagree with Holsti. We believe that the field is now much healthier because of the proliferation of theories. Not only has this resulted in a significant rethink about what the field consists of, it has also led to a questioning of the main assumptions of the ontology and epistemology of the discipline. Together we see these developments as opening up space so as to allow for much more debate, and, crucially, to legitimize a wider variety of theories. On the one hand, then, the range of theories allows us to think about more aspects of international relations than before, and because they are often based on epistemological positions far removed from positivism they also allow us to think through just how we think about the world. This widening of theories has been achieved in part by a much closer engagement with other social sciences, so that sociological or anthropological accounts of international relations are every bit as worthy as conventional political or economic accounts. We see this situation as better than that of most of the last century, when one theory (realism) dominated the discipline, and one view of knowledge construction (positivism) reigned supreme. But, of course, there is no denying that this plurality of approaches does raise some significant problems, most obviously how to choose between theories.

What do the theories share?

Despite the very significant differences between the theories dealt with in this book, it is important to note that they share three significant assumptions. First, and chief among these, is their shared commitment to the importance of theory in understanding the world. In direct contrast to those who see theory as irrelevant or optional, all the authors in this book think that theory is central to explaining international relations. We need to stress the importance of this assumption, since many continue to believe that theory merely gets in the way of understanding the world, and at worst is simply a way of making things more complicated than they really are. In our view, the option of non-theoretical accounts of the world is simply not available. All observation of international relations has to be carried out in the language of some theory or other. The choice, then, is one of whether you are aware of the assumptions you are bringing to your study of the world or not. Indeed, texts that begin by saying that they are only looking at 'the facts' are theoretically laden: this is because what counts as 'the facts' is either something that is explicitly linked to a theory, or is instead the result of powerful and unstated assumptions.

Second, all the theories have a history, though not always within the discipline of IR. These histories mean that comparing theories is not easy, since they emerge from very different intellectual traditions. Therefore many of the chapters use the word 'theory' in specific ways: we need to stress this to the reader, since the different usage results directly from the historical and intellectual heritage of each approach. Thus, the chapters on feminism, poststructuralism, green theory, and postcolonialism are developed from work that has mainly appeared in other academic disciplines, mostly in the last fifty years. By way of contrast, the chapters on classical realism, liberalism, Marxism and critical theory, and the English school are each referring to a long-standing approach that goes back much further, in most cases at least a century. The debates on social science and international political theory – discussed in the first two chapters – also have a long history, if not explicitly within the confines of IR theory but rather within the disciplines of philosophy or political theory. Finally, the chapters on neorealism, neoliberalism, constructivism, and the effects of globalization are all focused on the main theoretical developments in IR over the last twenty years.

Third, each of the chapters makes claims about the linkages between theory and practice, though, again, they do this in a variety of ways. Some of the chapters that follow treat theory as something akin to a toolkit, whereby the reader can, by understanding certain key concepts, apply them to the world and thereby understand it better. The four chapters on classical realism, classical liberalism, neorealism, and neoliberalism are good examples of this notion of theory. Other chapters present theory as something that critiques the existing dominant order and offers ways of emancipating individuals from that dominant order: the chapters on green theory, Marxism and critical theory, and postcolonialism are good examples of this version of theory. Still other chapters, such as feminism, poststructuralism, international political theory, the English school, globalization, and constructivism, are more concerned with what gets presented as the core issues represented in the discipline, and how they relate to identity. Thus, the theories we cover in this book offer a variety of ways of approaching the relationship between theory and practice: the range varies from helpful toolkit all the way through to human emancipation, and this, again, raises the question of what is the role of theory.

For most of its history as a separate discipline, IR has been dominated by one specific answer to this question, which is that theory has the role of explaining a world that can be separated from the world of theory. That is to say that the job of theories is to report on the world – this is very much the 'toolkit' model of theory. According to this view, theories are devices to explain a world that exists apart from them. Such a belief was a very strong assumption of positivism. This view of theory is known as an 'explanatory' view. It means that theories explain a world that is 'out there', and explaining it means making sense of it. But there is another view of theory which is that theories 'constitute' the world that they are explaining. By this we mean only that theories can never be separate from the world, they are an intrinsic part of it, and thus they can never be neutral. Therefore, there can never be a 'view from nowhere', and *all* theories make assumptions about the world, both ontological ones (what features need explaining) and epistemological ones (what counts as explanation). The critically important point here is that whereas positivist theories claim that non-positivist theories are illegitimate because they are not neutral (i.e. they make explicit assumptions about ontology and epistemology, take for example the chapter on feminism) the problem is that positivist theories fail to recognize that they do exactly the same thing but this time by maintaining a separation between observer and observed, and between theory and the world. It is this claim that needs contesting. All theories are located in space, time, culture, and history, and, simply put, there is no possibility of the separation from these that positivism requires.

Therefore, we have compiled this book to start with two chapters that introduce the major debates in the discipline of IR with regards to both the philosophy of social sciences and those within political theory (IR and social science, and IR as political pheory). We then have four chapters dealing with the traditional mainstream of the discipline (classical realism, liberalism, structural realism, neoliberalism). These are followed by three chapters dealing with approaches that share much with the mainstream, but which have been seen as developments of it, or as significantly distinct enough to constitute separate intellectual traditions (the English school, Marxism and critical theory, and constructivism). Finally, we have a set of four chapters which are importantly 'critical' of the traditional mainstream (feminism, poststructuralism, postcolonialism, green theory). We end the book with two chapters, each of which serves as a conclusion. The chapter on globalization looks at contemporary international relations and discusses whether such a thing as globalization exists and whether the assorted phenomena of globalization make theories of International Relations redundant. The final chapter looks at the current nature of the discipline of IR and the ways in which the theories discussed in this book relate to the emerging structure of debate in the field. As you will see, these chapters have important things to say about the linkage between how the discipline has traditionally defined the subject matter of international relations and how then one might decide which theory was of most use in explaining that world.

Diversity and disciplinarity

The picture that emerges from this book is that the discipline of IR is, we believe, far more relevant to the world of international relations than it has been at any point in its history. We think that this is very much to be welcomed. For too long the theories discussed in the academic literature of the field were very restrictive. It is only in the last twenty years that it has become common to discuss more than rationalist accounts. The great debates of the discipline have mostly been debates within rationalism; it is only with the 'fourth debate' (or, as some following Lapid (1989) term it, 'third debate') between rationalism and reflectivism, that there has been an opening-up of the theoretical basis of the field to include approaches other than those found in the mainstream.

The existence of this growing body of distinctly different theories has given all students of international relations two main problems. The first is whether there can be said to be a discipline of IR at all after the proliferation of theories, many of which have their intellectual basis in different social sciences. The final chapter of this book deals with this question in detail, but, similarly, the penultimate chapter on globalization implies that if we start our analysis of international relations from an economic perspective we get a much altered view of what are the core features to be explained by any theory. In an important sense the editors of this book are relaxed about what the proliferation means for the identity of the discipline, since we believe that what matters most is the ability of theories to explain the world as it is seen from a variety of different cultural, economic, gendered, political, ethnic, and social locations. One problem of an insistence that the boundaries of the discipline should be clear, precise, and fixed, is that this absolutely determines what counts as acceptable scholarship. We prefer boundaries to a discipline that can alter, as our views of the political shift according both to our identity as observers and also according to the agenda that we wish to explain. In this light, we note that the discipline has played a role in recreating the realist world of great power dominance, simply because that is what generations of IR academics taught as 'reality' or the 'real world' to their students. In that sense, too much concern with maintaining the boundaries of an academic discipline look dangerously like a very conservative move to privilege the existing power distribution in the world. We feel that the current diversity in the discipline offers far more in the way of opportunity to examine a variety of policy concerns and issues than has ever been the case in the discipline's history. Taken together, the theories in this book create space for thinking about what international relations consists of and what are its most salient features. In this important sense, if the discipline is facing an identity crisis because the old certainties are no longer quite so secure, then we think that this is a positive and empowering development.

However, the second problem created by the proliferation of IR theories is much deeper. This is the question of how one chooses which theory to use. Traditionally, this has not been a problem for the discipline, since the answer was always a choice between realism and liberalism, with realism being dominant. This was largely the case because if the subject was defined by the presence of war, then realism seemed to be the best theory to explain war. If one's focus was international cooperation, then liberalism was appropriate; and the debate between these two theoretical strands constituted the founding debate within IR. Today, not only is there a set of well developed and powerful alternative theories, but these theories dispute the core assumptions about the content of the field.

This situation raises the question of the grounds on which we make a choice between theories. For many new undergraduate students of IR this is a major worry, since they want to be guided to the 'right' answer. And, of course, this is why realism has been so powerful, because it explicitly sees itself as the best account of the persistence of inter-state war and competition. We feel that there is much more at stake in answering this question. In my view, the first criterion involved in making a choice between theories has to be the issues you wish to explain. Thus, if you are interested in the future of the environment, it is likely that green theory will be as good a place to start as any. That does not mean that only green theory can offer explanations, but it does give the reader a place to start their thinking about which is the most appropriate theory. It would be tempting to leave the issue of theory choice here, since I could imply that the theories in this book are all dealing with different, discrete, aspects of the same world of international relations, and that you could adopt a kind of 'pick and mix' attitude towards theory. Accordingly you might think it sensible to use, say, green theory when discussing the environment, feminism when discussing global gender inequalities, and structural realism when looking at great power rivalry in the Asia–Pacific. But though this might seem comforting, I do not think that this move is possible. This is because the various theories are not like parts of a jigsaw that can be neatly combined together with each explaining one part of international relations. Rather I think that the theories in this book are like different coloured lenses: if you put one of them in front of your eyes, you will see things differently. Some aspects of the world will look the same in some senses, for example shapes, but many other features, such as light and shade of colour, will look very different, so different in fact that they seem to show alternative worlds.

In thinking about this you might like to visualize Martin Hollis's excellent example of a mobile hanging over a child's bed, a metaphor he regularly used in his teaching. The view that the various theories each explain part of the world of international relations is akin to the view that someone standing looking at the child's mobile will see the same mobile as the child lying on the bed, albeit from different angles. There is nothing incommensurable about their two perspectives; simple geometric analysis can show how their different views of the mobile can be combined together – they are just different views of the same mobile. Yet Hollis always argued, persuasively in my view, that the social world is not like this. The theories we use cannot simply be combined together so as to add up to different views of the same world of international relations; instead, they actually *see* different worlds. Thus a Marxist writer, though they will focus on power, will see a different form of power (ultimately economic) to that seen by a classical realist (ultimately political). Similarly, a classical liberal will not see cooperation over environmental issues in anything like the same way as a green theorist will see them. Finally, think of, say, a feminist writing about the global power structure, and compare it to a neorealist account. It is not possible simply to add up these various accounts of international relations to get one overarching theory. Theories are *part* of the social world, they can never be separate from it, and thus they constitute the social world in which we live. Each defines the problems to be examined differently, and may well define how we know things about those problems in different ways. Thus the social location of the observer will influence which theory they see as most useful, simply because that location will predispose that observer to define some features of international relations as key and others as less relevant.

But in putting forward this view of theory we need to be clear that we are not saying that each theory is equally good at explaining everything. It is not a case of 'anything goes'. Our view is that a variety of theories will claim to offer explanations for the same kinds of features of international relations. We believe that there are grounds for choosing between them, though we want to stress that these grounds are nothing like as restrictive as positivists claim. Thus while we do not think that theory choice is simply a matter of whatever appeals to a reader on a given day, we do think that the grounds cannot be those of one dominant view of epistemology and methodology.

All of this brings us back to where we started this chapter. There are many theories that offer explanations as to why British Prime Minister Tony Blair supported the USA's decision to invade Iraq. You will find some of them persuasive, others less so. Our argument is not that each of these theories should be deemed equally appropriate, or helpful, or valid. Decisions over which theories are tenable and which are not should be determined, respectively, by the reader of this book or the proponent of the theory concerned. The judgement cannot be made by advocates of another theory that its rivals are either irrelevant or illegitimate. We also want to point out that there are epistemological difficulties with combining different theories, although both critical realism and the English school attempt to provide theories which are a synthesis of more than one position.

Many treatments of IR avoid the problem of incommensurability by focusing only on those theories that share an epistemological grounding. That makes 'debates' relatively easy. We have not chosen to deal with theories of International Relations in that way. Instead we have tried to offer you a wide choice of theories and leave you with the somewhat unsettling task of having to decide which theory you find most useful in explaining and understanding international relations, and then answering the question why that is the case. We think that this gives you a real choice, and, although at first sight it may be a little disturbing to question whether it is possible to use theory as a toolkit to answer different issues and problems, we do think the fact of theoretical diversity in IR forces readers to confront questions about how to choose between theories. Such questions are unavoidable; previously they have been overlooked because of the tendency to present only compatible theories of International Relations. The diversity represented in this book offers more space to think about IR and thus offers the prospect of a discipline that is of more relevance to people in a variety of locations than has hitherto been the case. The editors of this book strongly believe that it is better to open up space for analysis and debate, even though that will lead to difficult ethical and philosophical questions about theory choice, than it is to close down debate and insist that the only theories that are 'right' are those which fit either into preconceived, and often hidden, assumptions about what international relations consists of, or into a fixed notion of what epistemological and methodological positions are acceptable. It is our strong view that this diversity is to be celebrated rather than disciplined (as some traditionalists would prefer).

Diversity may be unsettling because it leaves the reader facing some fundamental problems about how to make a choice between rival theories; but at the very least it does make it possible to confront orthodoxy, to develop theory relevant to a wider range of humanity, and, ultimately, to accept that our choice of theories to explain the world of international relations can never be a neutral act. Theory is always socially located, always has an unavoidable relationship to power, and can never be defended by resort to one foundational account of what is 'truth'. In this sense, our aim is not so much to provide the reader with one account of international relations but to offer a choice of International Relations theories that allow us to make sense of our multi-layered and cultural complex world, as well as to recognize the processes and difficulties involved in coming to understand them.

 Visit the Online Resource Centre that accompanies this book for lots of interesting additional material. www.oxfordtextbooks.co.uk/orc/dunne/

1 International Relations and Social Science

MILJA KURKI AND COLIN WIGHT

 Chapter contents

- Introduction
- The philosophy of social science in IR: an historical overview
- Contemporary IR theory: science and the fourth debate
- Case study
- Conclusion

Reader's guide

This chapter provides an overview of the key philosophy of social science debates within International Relations (IR) theory.[1] Often IR theorists do not address the philosophy of social science explicitly, but nevertheless philosophical issues are implicit in their claims. Since the mid-1980s 'meta-theoretical' debates surrounding the philosophy of social science have played an important and highly visible role in the discipline. This chapter explores both the implicit and explicit roles played by meta-theoretical assumptions in IR. It begins with a brief historical overview of the philosophy of social science within IR. We then examine the contemporary disciplinary debates surrounding the philosophy of social science. Finally, the case-study section highlights some of the key ways in which meta-theoretical positions shape theoretical approaches to the study of world politics.

Introduction

The philosophy of social science has played an important role in the formation, development, and practice of IR as an academic discipline. Often issues concerning the philosophy of social science are described as meta-theoretical debates. Meta-theory does not take a specific event, phenomenon, or series of empirical real world practices as its object of analysis, but explores the underlying assumptions of all theory and attempts to understand the consequences of such assumptions on the act of theorizing and the practice of empirical research. One way to think about this is in terms of theories about theories.

The role of meta-theoretical debates is frequently misunderstood. Some see meta-theorizing as nothing more than a quick precursor to empirical research. Others see it as a distraction from the real issues that should concern the discipline. However, it is impossible for research to proceed in any subject domain in the social sciences in the absence of a set of commitments embedded within positions on the philosophy of social science. In this sense, meta-theoretical positions direct, in a fundamental way, the manner in which people theorize and, indeed, 'see' the world.

To put this in philosophical terminology, all theoretical positions are dependent upon particular assumptions about ontology (theory of being: what is the world made of? what objects do we study?), epistemology (theory of knowledge: how do we come to have knowledge of the world?), and methodology (theory of methods: what methods do we use to unearth data and evidence?). On the basis of these assumptions researchers may literally come to 'see' the world in different ways: ontologically in terms of seeing different object domains, epistemologically in terms of accepting or rejecting particular knowledge claims, and methodologically in terms of choosing particular methods of study. Meta-theoretical positions have deep, if often unrecognized, consequences for social analysis. Being aware of the issues at stake in meta-theoretical debate, and of their significance in terms of concrete research, serves as an important starting point for understanding IR theory and facilitates a deeper awareness of one's own meta-theoretical orientation.

Meta-theoretical debates surrounding the philosophy of social science in IR have tended to revolve around two interrelated questions. Is International Relations a science or an art? What does the 'scientific' study of world politics entail? A position can be taken on the question of whether IR can be a science only on the basis of some or other account of what science is, and an account of what we think IR is. Hence, the questions of what science is, and what IR is, are prior to the question of whether IR can be a science. This inevitably takes the discussion into the terrain of the philosophy of science. This seems a long way from the concerns of a discipline focused on the study of international political processes, and the frustration of some within the discipline concerning meta-theoretical debate is understandable. Yet, there is no way to avoid these issues and at a minimum all contributors to the discipline should understand the assumptions that make their own position possible; as well as being aware of alternative conceptualizations of what IR theory and research might involve.

That the philosophy of science has played an important role in the history and development of the discipline is easy to demonstrate. For a large part of the history of the field a particular conception of science has dominated. The influence of positivism as a philosophy of science has shaped not only how we theorize about the subject, and what counts as a valid question, but also what can count as valid forms of evidence and knowledge. Moreover, the training in methodological techniques given to graduate students – particularly in the leading graduate schools in the USA – tends still to be deeply embedded within positivist assumptions. Indeed, so strong is the influence of positivism on the disciplinary imagination that even those concerned to reject a scientific approach to IR do so on the basis of a general acceptance of the positivist model of science. There are two points worthy of note in this respect. First, despite the acceptance of the positivist model of science by both advocates and critics alike, it is clear that the account of positivism that dominates the discipline is rudimentary. Second, within the philosophy of science positivism was long ago discredited as a valid account of scientific practice. Had the discipline been prepared to take the philosophy of social science, and by extension the philosophy of science, more seriously, a long and potentially damaging commitment to positivism might have been avoided. This does not mean that all research underpinned by positivist principles is invalid. Indeed, we believe that scholars, who might be considered to be working in the positivist tradition, have made some of the most important and lasting contributions to the discipline. Nonetheless, this view of science is highly contested and there is no reason to insist that all research should fit this model. Equally, a rejection of the positivist model of science need not lead to the rejection of science.

This chapter argues that social science debates within the discipline can be moved forward by a comprehensive re-examination of what science is. Hence, besides reviewing the historical and contemporary philosophy of social science debates in IR, the chapter also points towards new accounts of science that have been introduced to the discipline in the last decade or so; accounts that hold the promise of reformulating our understanding of the aims and methods of IR as a social science. Science, we argue, is not based on a dogmatic insistence on the certainty of its claims but, rather, rests on a commitment to constant critique.

The philosophy of social science in IR: an historical overview

The discipline of International Relations, in common with all the social sciences, has been deeply divided on many issues throughout its history. A common way of narrating this history is in terms of the great debates surrounding these key issues. In many respects debate is the wrong term to use, since in some of them a group of theorists situated their own approach as a direct counter to previous ways of thinking, without generating a substantial set of responses (Schmidt 1998). Some of the debates, however, were genuine and scholars within the discipline have often been prepared to engage with one another over substantial areas of disagreement. Although there is no consensus on the exact number of great debates four are generally accepted to have played an important role in shaping the discipline (Wæver 1996).

The first debate refers to the exchanges between the realists and idealists before, during, and immediately after the Second World War. This was primarily waged over the role of international institutions and the likelihood that the causes of war might be ameliorated. The second debate emerged in the 1960s. It pitted the traditionalists, who were keen to defend a more humanistic methodology, against the modernizers, who aimed to introduce a greater level of methodological rigour to the discipline. The interparadigm debate of the 1970s and 1980s focused on disagreements among the realist, pluralist, and Marxist perspectives on how best to understand and explain international processes. Finally, the most recent debate, which some IR theorists call the fourth debate, has centred on deep-seated disagreements about what the discipline should study and how it should study it. While these debates have often highlighted the paradigmatic divisions between different and distinct IR theoretical schools of thought, an often-unrecognized issue has cut across and underpinned all the debates. This is the issue of whether or not International Relations can be, or should be, a form of inquiry based upon scientific principles.

Science and the first debate

The first great debate in the discipline is said to have taken place between the idealists and the realists. The idealists were driven by a desire to develop a set of institutions, procedures, and practices that could eradicate, or at least control, war in the international system. They were motivated by the horrors of the First World War and they sincerely believed that there must be a better way to organize international affairs. The most visible, and historically important, aspect of their programme cohered in Woodrow Wilson's Fourteen-point Plan for a new postwar order. However, the most enduring contribution of the idealists in terms of disciplinary development was the idea of an academic discipline constructed to study the world of international politics. For the idealists, ignorance and lack of understanding was a primary source of international conflict. A better understanding of international processes was required if control of the system was to be achieved. The idealists believed progress was only possible if we could develop and use reason to control the irrational desires and frailties that infect the human condition. The pinnacle of human reason in the service of effective control was science. This thinking led to the establishment of an academic department of international politics located in Aberystwyth, Wales. The aim of this new discipline was the production of a body of knowledge that could be used in the furtherance of peace. Although the idealists never clearly articulated what they meant by science, they were committed to producing knowledge that was scientific.

The absence of a clear account of science in the early years of the discipline is understandable given that the philosophy of science was itself not yet fully established as an academic field of study. Science, to the Enlightenment mind, was self-evident. Yet the realist critique of the idealists was to challenge the extent to which the knowledge produced by the idealists was scientific. In particular, realists challenged the 'unsystematic' and value-driven idealist approach to IR. Both E. H. Carr (1946; 1987) and Hans Morgenthau (1947; 1948a; discussed in more detail in **Chapter 3**) accused the idealists of focusing their attention on how the world 'ought' to be, as opposed to dealing with how it objectively was. In a scathing attack Carr famously concluded that the difference between realism and idealism was analogous to that between science and alchemy (1946: 1–11).

Neither Carr, nor Morgenthau, however, can be said to have uncritically embraced a naive view of science. Carr was only too well aware of the problematic status of facts and associated truth claims. His celebrated notion of the 'relativity of thought' and his sophisticated treatment of historical method can hardly be said to constitute an uncritical commitment to science. Likewise, Morgenthau went to great lengths to distance his approach to political science from attempts to construct 'iron laws' comparable to those discovered in the natural sciences (Morgenthau 1947). Despite his belief that international politics was governed by 'objective laws' rooted in human nature, Morgenthau articulated a series of telling objections to any attempt to construct a science of international politics modelled on the natural sciences. After all, if international politics was governed by 'objective laws' rooted in human nature, then the true causes of war were to be found in biology, and any nascent science of IR could provide only suggestions for dealing with a realm of human activity that was to a great extent predetermined. Morgenthau's account of IR was not concerned to provide a series of depth explanations of the workings of the world but, rather, aimed at articulating a series of techniques and modes of operation for dealing with a world on the basis of a simple, but enticing, explanation. Nonetheless, despite these caveats, and the limited nature of debate surrounding understandings of science within the discipline, the status of science was clearly important in the early period of the development of the subject. In the second great debate, however, it was to take centre stage.

Science and the second debate

The second debate took the 'rhetorical' arguments about science and gave them methodological substance. Drawing on the behaviourist revolution in the social sciences a new breed of 'scientific' IR scholars, such as David Singer and Morton Kaplan, sought to define and refine systematic scientific methods of inquiry for the discipline of IR. The behaviourist research instigated fierce resistance from those committed to a more historicist, or interpretive, form of IR.

For the proponents of the behavioural revolution, IR could move forward only if it consciously modelled itself on the natural sciences. By the time the second debate had emerged in IR the philosophy of science was a well developed and institutionally located academic discipline. Moreover, within the philosophy of science one view had come to dominate; although ironically just as IR was to formalize its vision of science the consensus within the philosophy of science had already begun to unravel. The model of science that had dominated was called positivism, and the behaviouralists in IR embraced it enthusiastically. There are many versions of positivism and such was its promotion and reception in IR that it has come to be a synonym for science. This is a regrettable move since it effectively closes down all debate on what kind of science IR might be; if IR is to be a science, it must be modelled on positivist principles.

Positivism suggests that scientific knowledge emerges only with the collection of observable data. The collection of sufficient data, it was presumed, would lead to the identification of patterns that would in turn allow the formulation of laws. The importance of observable data for this approach cannot be over-stressed. The inscription on the Social Science Research Building façade, at the University of Chicago, reads, 'If you cannot measure it, your knowledge is meagre and unsatisfactory.' This stress on observable data and measurement led the proponents of the new scientific model to engage in a series of sharp criticisms of the account of science adhered to by many realists and other IR scholars. Many of the core concepts of 'classical' realism were deemed to be lacking in specificity and were not susceptible to measurement. Power and the national interest, for example, if they were to be studied according to the principles of the new science, needed increased levels of clarity and specification; anything that could not be rigorously measured and subject to testing was to be purged from the new ontology. New methods were developed and the mathematical modelling of international processes took pride of place. The behaviouralists hoped that through the relentless accumulation of data, knowledge would progress and control would follow.

The behaviouralist criticisms of the traditional approach did not go unchallenged. Many argued that the core concepts of the discipline were simply not susceptible to the kind of austere data collection procedures advocated by the new model of science. Chief among them was the English school theorist Hedley Bull, but the traditionalists also included some of the initial defenders of science in IR such as Morgenthau (see exchanges in Knorr and Rosenau 1969). For these theorists, systematic inquiry was one thing, the obsession with data collection and manipulation on positivist lines was another. Study of IR for Bull and Morgenthau involved significant conceptual and interpretative judgements, something that the behaviourist theorists in their focus on systematic data collection and scientific inference seemed not to adequately recognize. The dispute over science also developed a geographical aspect. Although there were some advocates of the new science in Britain and Europe it was largely a US-led development. Despite the fact that the austere version of science advocated by the behaviouralists was significantly watered down over the passage of time, the underlying principles of that approach remain deeply embedded within the account of science that continues to dominate the discipline. It was also to have a lasting affect on the methodological techniques taught in graduate schools, with hypothesis testing, statistical analysis, and data manipulation becoming indispensable requirements of all methodological training.

Science and the interparadigm debate

In the 1970s and 1980s the so-called interparadigm debate ostensibly moved IR away from the 'methodological' issues of the 1960s. The question of science was not an explicit component of this debate because to a large extent a consensus had emerged around a commitment to positivism. Indeed, it could be argued that this debate could take the form it did only as a result of a general shared commitment to the principles of science. All parties to the interparadigm debate accepted the validity of a broadly conceived positivist account of science. Certainly, the fascination with data collection, the insistence on measurement, hypothesis testing, and the statistical analysis of the early behaviouralists had been modified and toned down but, nonetheless, no one seriously attempted to argue that these were not important aspects of the study of international phenomena. Despite the consensus on science, however, issues surrounding the nature of scientific inquiry quickly resurfaced; in particular, the problem of theory choice and the alleged incommensurability of differing theoretical perspectives.

Much of this was indebted to Thomas Kuhn's (1962) ground-breaking study of the history of science. Kuhn had argued that science developed through two distinct phases. In its 'revolutionary' phase, science was marked by theoretical fragmentation. New modes of thought would arise and challenge traditional ways of thinking. Although the revolutionary phase ensured that theoretical innovation was always possible, Kuhn argued that such phases did not lead to a progression in terms of a body of cumulative knowledge. In a revolutionary phase, the theoretical protagonists expend their energy on attempting to gain theoretical dominance as opposed to increasing the overall stock of knowledge surrounding a subject domain. Knowledge could only progress, Kuhn argued, in periods of what he called normal science. In an era of normal science one theoretical school, or what Kuhn called a paradigm, would dominate. In such periods knowledge could progress because everyone was in agreement on the validity of the chosen paradigm and hence the vast majority of scholars were working in a particular subject using agreed methods and techniques and could compare their findings.

Kuhn's model of scientific development was enthusiastically embraced by the discipline. Since its inception the discipline had been attempting to develop a body of cumulative knowledge surrounding international processes. Yet, after decades of study there was still very little agreement on key issues. Despite the disagreements between them, the realists and behaviouralists had suggested that progress could be achieved only by adopting a more scientific mode of study. Kuhn's model suggested a different, more conservative, conclusion. The discipline needed the adoption of a single paradigm around which research could converge. In the mid-1970s three paradigms vied for theoretical dominance; realism, Marxism, and pluralism. The question was how to compare them. Which paradigm should the discipline adopt in order to move forward? Kuhn provided no answers. Indeed, he suggested that there was no answer; paradigms were incommensurable; they simply could not be compared. Theory choice became largely a matter of aesthetics; or what one of Kuhn's critics was to call 'mob psychology' (Lakatos 1970: 178).

It is ironic that although the interparadigm debate did not directly involve disputes over the nature of science it was the period of disciplinary development in which the philosophy of science began to play a substantial and explicit role. The conservative nature of Kuhn's model, and the fact that theory choice becomes a matter of taste, ensured that some scholars would look to alternatives. Karl Popper (1959) became an important influence, but it was the importation of Imre Lakatos's (1970) model of research programmes that was to have the greatest impact, and it is his model that is generally adopted by the more scientifically orientated 'positivist' wing of the discipline.

Contemporary IR theory: science and the fourth debate

What we call the 'fourth debate' emerged in the mid-1980s. (Note that this debate is somewhat confusingly also referred to as the 'third debate' by some IR theorists.)[2] This debate has most explicitly focused on the issue of science in the disciplinary history of IR. Since the discipline is still largely in the middle of this debate we will deal with it as a contemporary issue and discuss it in terms of the cleavages and divisions around which the discipline is currently organized. There are many ways to characterize the 'fourth debate'; as a debate between explaining and understanding, between positivism and postpositivism, or between rationalism and reflectivism. This section will examine these different terms and through them the key philosophical positions in contemporary IR.

Explaining and understanding

The terms explaining and understanding come from Max Weber's distinction between Erklären and Verstehen. Another way of describing this distinction is in terms of a scientific approach versus an interpretive or hermeneutic approach. While explanatory theorists seek to emulate the natural sciences in following scientific methods and in seeking to identify general causes, advocates of understanding focus on the analysis of the 'internal' meanings, reasons, and beliefs actors hold and act in reference to (Hollis and Smith 1990). For the advocates of understanding, social meanings, language, and beliefs are said to constitute the most important (ontological) aspects of social existence. Explanatory theorists do not generally disagree with this claim; however, they do not see how such objects can be incorporated into a scientific framework of analysis. Scientific knowledge, for the explanatory theorist, requires empirical justification; and meanings, beliefs, and ideas are not susceptible to validation by such techniques. Without such justifications knowledge claims can be nothing more than mere speculation. Advocates of an interpretive approach, on the other hand, argue that we should be guided in our analytical procedures by the most important factors impacting on human behaviour (beliefs, ideas, meanings, reasons), not by an a priori commitment to something called science.

Clearly, a particular vision of what science is frames this debate. The explanatory theorist reduces the ontological complexity of the social world to those aspects of it that can be observed and measured. Thus the ontology adopted by this approach is shaped by epistemological and methodological concerns. This leads to a sharp split between these two approaches in terms of methodology. Explanatory theorists privilege quantitative methods, or attempt to quantify qualitative data. Supporters of understanding adopt interpretive methods (qualitative, discursive, historical), shunning the generalizing approach of the explainers. This debate also has epistemological consequences insofar as explanatory theory emphasizes observation as perhaps the only way of generating valid knowledge, whereas the understanding side of the debate concentrates attention on the interpretation of unobservable, and hence immeasurable, contexts of action.

Positivism and postpositivism

Underpinning the explanatory framework is a positivist vision of science. This account of science has its roots in an empiricist epistemology. Often the terms positivism and empiricism are confused in the discipline. Positivism is a theory of science, and generally most positivists adopt an empiricist epistemology. However, not all empiricists embrace positivism, so it is important to maintain the distinction between the two terms. Equally, it is possible to accept the validity of empirical data without adopting a positivist account of science. As an epistemology, the empiricist approach to the acquisition of knowledge is premised on the belief that the only genuine knowledge we can have of the world is based on those 'facts' that can be experienced by the human senses. The implication of this empiricist epistemology for science is that scientific knowledge is secure only when based on empirical validation. This is why positivists privilege observation, empirical data, and measurement; what cannot be an object of experience cannot be scientifically validated.

The key assumptions of the positivist view of science and social explanation can be summarized as follows. First, for positivists, science must be focused on systematic observation. The aim of the philosophy of science is to produce a set of logically rigorous guidelines concerning appropriate methodological techniques and criteria for ensuring that knowledge claims are grounded in appropriate observations. Indeed, for positivists the validity of science rests on these rigorous methodological guidelines; it is these guidelines that allow us to distinguish between scientific knowledge and mere 'belief'. Second, all positivists believe that the collection of sufficient data, generated through repeated instances of observation, will reveal regularities, which are indicative of the operation of general laws. These general laws are only the expression of relationships between patterns among observable events and there is nothing more going on behind the data. Any attempt to introduce non-observable processes, mechanisms, and events as explanations of the data are considered inadmissible. This belief in the importance of regular patterns when linked to the insistence on empirical validation becomes important in terms of how positivists conceive of causal analysis. For the positivists, causal relations are discovered through the detection of regular patterns of observable behaviour.

Third, because positivists emphasize the importance of observation, they avoid talking about 'realities' that cannot be observed. This directs them away from developing 'deep ontological' conceptual systems that aim to grapple with unobservable entities such as 'discourses' or 'social structures'. This insistence on observation means that positivists are not, as they are sometimes described, naive realists.[3] Positivists do not believe in an external world independent of humanity (Kolakowski 1969). The positivist motto was *esse est percipi* (to be is to be perceived), which makes existence logically dependent upon perception (Hollis 1996). When non-observable entities are referred to, they are treated in wholly instrumental terms. These non-observables are useful fictions that help explain the data, but positivists refrain from giving them ontological significance. It follows that positivists emphasize the instrumental function of knowledge. Knowledge has to be useful not truthful (Waltz 1979). It is partly this commitment to the instrumental validation of knowledge that makes positivists some of the most vehement critics of the role of meta-theory within IR.

The positivist approach to social explanation has been modified in significant ways since the 1960s as the positivist philosophy of science has adapted itself as a result of a range of criticisms. The so-called 'soft' postbehaviourist form of positivism is still significant in contemporary IR. It underpins, for example, the influential contribution to social analysis of King, Keohane, and Verba (1994). They aim to build a unified logic of inference for both quantitative and qualitative inquiry, and foreground the role of observation and measurement. Indeed, they aim to rescue social science from speculative and unsystematic social inquiry by showing that the 'scientific logic of inference' can be applied in qualitative studies. By demonstrating how qualitative analysis can become 'scientific', King, Keohane, and Verba hoped to force qualitative approaches to 'take scientific inference seriously', hence allowing these approaches to start making 'valid inferences about social and political life' (King, Keohane, and Verba 1994: 3, ix).

Against the positivist insistence on a 'science' of human behaviour, a diverse range of postpositivist positions has emerged. It is tempting to categorize these postpositivists as articulating a version of the interpretive understanding position detailed above. However, whilst many postpositivists draw inspiration from interpretive thinkers, the term 'postpositivist' can be used to refer to approaches that draw on a wider range of intellectual traditions; what unites them all is a commitment to reject positivism as a valid approach to the study of social processes.

Some postpositivists are influenced by developments from within the philosophy of science and attempt to use these to articulate a non-positivist version of science (see the later section on scientific realism for more detail). These postpositivists reject both the positivist account of science and the hermeneutic alternatives. Importantly, for these post-positivists it is only a particular version of science that is rejected, not the idea of science itself. Many feminist theorists (discussed in more detail in Chapter 10), who would rightly be considered postpositivists, are also keen to develop more sophisticated versions of science. And many postpositivists are keen to repudiate the positivist account of science that has dominated the discipline and accept the importance of meanings, beliefs, and language without adopting a hermeneutic perspective. This is particularly the case in relation to postmodern, or poststructuralist, theories (discussed in more detail in Chapter 11). The interpretive approach rests on the conviction that meanings and beliefs are the most important factors in the study of social processes and that social inquiry could play an important role in uncovering the deep meanings that exist beneath the surface appearance of observed reality. This conviction relies on the belief that there are hidden meanings to be had. Poststructuralist theorists are sceptical of this viewpoint and have no wish to return to what they term the 'hermeneutics of suspicion'. Poststructuralists are also sceptical of the validity of all knowledge claims and reject the idea that science produces anything like true knowledge, even in terms of the natural sciences.

In many respects, the positivist/postpositivist designation represents a particular moment in the history of the discipline. It marks a particular period in time when the positivist orthodoxy had begun to crumble in the philosophy of science, and the effect of this was felt throughout the social sciences. It is an accident of history that this collapse occurred at the same time as a range of new social theories, and philosophies, was emerging. These new theories all rejected the positivist vision of science and, in particular, its application to the social sciences. Yet in many respects this rejection of positivism was all they shared in common and it is incorrect to infer that this necessarily requires them to adopt an interpretive philosophy and methodology.

Rationalism and reflectivism

The rationalist/reflectivist divide takes the explaining/understanding divide and the positivist/postpositivist debate and encapsulates them both under a single label. This terminology, utilized by Robert Keohane (1988) in his address to the International Studies Association, can be associated with the explanation/understanding and positivist/postpositivist divides, but also has particular additional connotations. Keohane takes his label of rationalism directly from rational choice theory. Rational choice theory is essentially a methodology constructed from a commitment to a positivist account of science. The rational choice theorist accepts the general complexity of the social world but ignores the majority of it in order to produce predictions based on a particular understanding of individuals. According to rational choice theorists we should treat individuals, and by extension states, as utility maximizers, and ignore every other aspect of their social being. This does not mean that rational choice theorists actually believe this is a correct description of what an individual is. However, they do believe that if we treat individuals in this manner we may be able to generate a series of well grounded predictions concerning behaviour on the basis of observed outcomes. Keohane accepts the limitations of this approach, but argues that it has been spectacularly successful in terms of knowledge production (Keohane 1988). This approach is deductive as opposed to the inductive bias of previous forms of positivism but, nonetheless, observation, measurement, and the attempt to specify general universal laws are still at the heart of this form of analysis. The approach is deductive because it begins with a theory of the individual and then utilizes observation and hypothesis testing to substantiate, or falsify, a set of claims relating to behaviour on the basis of this view. It is an approach to explanation that is compatible with the wider positivist tradition in IR, but it is not synonymous with it. It is for this reason that the term rationalism has been associated with both the explanatory and the positivist tradition in IR.

In his now (in)famous speech, Keohane (1988) also noted the emergence of a series of theories that were sharply critical of mainstream rationalist approaches to the discipline – critical theory, constructivism, poststructuralism, and feminism. He called these approaches reflectivist, due to the fact that they rejected the classical positivist/explanatory approach to IR theory and research, emphasizing instead reflexivity and the non-neutral nature of political and social explanation. He noted the potential of these approaches to contribute to the discipline but, in a direct reference to Lakatos's account of science, suggested that they could be taken seriously only when they developed a 'research programme'. This was a direct challenge to the new theories to move beyond criticism of the mainstream and demonstrate, through substantive research, the validity of their claims. Many of the so-called reflectivists have seen this as nothing other than a demand that they adopt the model of science to which Keohane and the mainstream are committed. On the other hand, the mainstream has been reluctant to take the knowledge claims of reflectivist scholars seriously, because they challenge the very status of the ontological, epistemological, and methodological assumptions upon which the mainstream depend.

Beyond the fourth debate? Rethinking International Relations as a science

The debates between explaining and understanding and rationalism and reflectivism have produced a dichotomous logic that has fashioned two wings of the discipline: a 'pro-science' viewpoint versus an 'anti-science' position. Typically, this debate has been framed around positivism as the dominant account of what science is. While positivism and its debate with the anti-science faction of the discipline has been the dominant issue in IR, recent developments in the philosophy of science and the philosophy of social science suggest that this way of framing the issues is unproductive. Significant strides have been taken in the philosophy of science to move beyond positivism: positivism is no longer seen to be a valid account of science and has been replaced by scientific realism. A comprehensive account of scientific realism is beyond the scope of this chapter; however, the important contribution it makes in terms of social science is to reject any attempt to arrive at a set of clearly defined procedures that fix the content of the scientific method. For scientific realists, each science must arrive at its own mode of operation on the basis of the object domain under study (see, for example, Roy Bhaskar 1978; 1979). Because object domains differ in fundamental ways, scientific realists claim it would be inappropriate to expect methods deployed in one science to have a universal application. Hence the social sciences should not be attempting to copy the natural sciences, not least because given the immeasurable distinctions within the various natural sciences it is impossible to identify a set of procedures and techniques that are adopted by all.

For scientific realists, what makes a body of knowledge scientific is not its mode of generation, but its content. Contra a positivist account of science, a body of knowledge is not declared scientific because it has followed a particular set of procedures based upon empirical 'facts' but, rather, because it constructs explanations of those facts in terms of entities and processes that are unknown and potentially unobservable. For scientific realists, scientific knowledge goes beyond appearances and constructs explanations that often run counter to, and even contradict, observed outcomes. Social science involves the study of the complex and interacting social objects that produce the patterns we observe. Because of their unobservable nature, most social objects have to be 'got at' through careful conceptualization. This is always a complex process that involves mutually constituted processes between agents and the objects of knowledge; yet social knowledge, however imperfect and embedded in conceptual and discursive frameworks, is knowledge of something – something called social reality.

Epistemologically, scientific realists are relativists; they argue that no epistemological position has priority in the acquisition of knowledge for there are always many ways in which to come to know the world. But this does not mean that all views are equally valid and they believe in the possibility of rationally adjudicating between competing knowledge claims. What is important to science is that any and every claim is open to challenge and, moreover, that all claims require epistemological support. This does not mean that these epistemological supports are always predicated on facts, or other such empirical data, but it does mean that those concerned to challenge particular claims make clear the evidential basis on which the challenge is made. Science, it is argued, rather than being committed to a dogmatic insistence on the certainty of its claims, rests on a commitment to constant critique.

Methodologically, it follows that scientific realists adopt a pluralist approach: contrary to the positivist emphasis on quantitative methods and the interpretive emphasis on qualitative methods, scientific realists emphasize methodological pluralism. Because the social world is ontologically highly complex, and there are many ways to come to know the world, it is better that one does not restrict methods a priori. A student of democratic peace, for example, should not study only regular patterns in history (positivist approach), nor simply interpret particular decision-makers' perceptions ('understanding' approach), but should make use of multiple ways of obtaining data. Because the social world is ontologically complex, it is better that one does not take an a priori position on either methodology or epistemology.

Scientific realism has already made major contributions to social theory and the development of research techniques in other social sciences, and it is now beginning to make an impact in IR. It has played a major role in the development of constructivism, although not all constructivists have embraced it. Alexander Wendt (1999) is perhaps the most notable theorist to embed his theory explicitly in a scientific realist framework, and it underpins his attempt to construct a *via media*, or middle ground, between rationalism and reflectivism. However, Wendt's adoption of scientific realism has been criticized by other scientific realists on the grounds that he has failed to move sufficiently beyond the parameters of the current debate and that he remains basically locked into a modified commitment to positivism. Another version of scientific realism has emerged which uses the label critical realism to differentiate itself from Wendt's account. Critical realists such as Patomäki and Wight (2000) take scientific realist ideas further in important respects. Notably, they argue that the dichotomy between rationalism and reflectivism is mirrored in the distinction between an approach that focuses on materialist issues, and one that concentrates on ideas. For critical realists, both ideas and material factors are important in producing social outcomes, and both need to be integrated into the research process. According to critical realists, the question of whether material factors or ideational issues are the most important in determining outcomes is an empirical matter that can be decided only on the basis of research that examines the relationship and interplay of both. So while critical realists agree that meanings and ideas matter they insist that ideas always emerge in a material context, and that the meanings we give to events are, in part, a consequence of how these events were materially constructed, composed, and represented.

The emergence of scientific and critical realism in IR is an important new trend in the discipline. It has opened up new potentially constructive avenues for meta-theoretical and theoretical debate in IR. By refusing to juxtapose explaining and understanding and causal and non-causal analysis, by rejecting an a priori commitment to either material or ideational factors, and by refusing to endorse either the positivist model of science, or the rejection of science advocated by some reflectivists, it has enabled the discipline to move forward from the fourth debate and allowed the non-positivist theoretical perspectives to be appreciated in a new light; as scientific contributors to the discipline.

Case study: exploring the key implications of meta-theoretical differences in IR theory

Since the focus in this chapter is on investigating the role of meta-theory, it follows that, rather than examining a particular political process, event, or phenomenon in world politics, our case study will examine the ways in which meta-theoretical differences play themselves out in theoretical positions in IR. We will see that, depending on their meta-theoretical leanings, IR theorists come to formulate very different understandings of certain issues. We examine just four such issues here: the nature of theory, the possibility of objectivity, the criteria to be used in theory-testing, and the relationship of theory and practice. In many respects these issues emerge out of the debates considered above, and in some cases they are constitutive of them. In the chapters that follow many of these issues will re-emerge, even if only implicitly. With this case-study section in mind, students should be able to keep their eyes open to the multiple ways in which meta-theoretical assumptions influence IR theory and research, even when theorists do not make their commitments to particular positions clear.

Types of theory

It is reasonable to assume that a book dealing with IR theory would provide a clear account of what theory is. Unfortunately there is not one but many. This makes a direct comparison between theoretical claims often difficult if not impossible; being aware of the many different types of theorizing means that comparison is not always possible and alerts us to the fact that different types of theories have different aims.

One of the most common types of theory is what we will term explanatory theory. This is probably the type of theory most students initially think of when they use the term theory. Explanatory theory attempts to 'explain' events by providing an account of causes in a temporal sequence. Thus, for example, we can think of theories that attempt to explain the end of the Cold War in terms of a series of connected events occurring over time. For positivists, this type of theory must produce verifiable (or falsifiable) hypotheses which can be subject to empirical test. Another common type of explanatory theory does not attempt to link particular events in causal sequences but, rather, attempts to locate the causal role played by particular elements in the chosen object domain and, on the basis of this analysis, draw conclusions and predictions aimed at exercising control. A good example of this type of explanatory theory is neo- or structural realism (see Chapter 4). According to neorealists such as Waltz (1979) theory can be considered a simplifying device that abstracts from the world in order to locate and identify key factors of interest. Once these factors are identified this type of theory aims at predicting a large range of outcomes on the basis of a few important causal factors. For this type of explanatory theory it is not important that the theory provides a realistic model of the world but, rather, that the theory is 'useful' in terms of its predictive capacity.

Explanatory theories are sometimes said to be 'problem-solving theories'. This distinction comes from Robert Cox (1981) who claims that this type of theory is concerned only with taking the world as given and attempting to understand its modes of operation. As such, problem-solving theories are often said to be concerned only with making the world work better within clearly defined, and limited, parameters. In opposition to explanatory theories Cox identified another type of theory which he called 'critical theory'. Cox's category of critical theory is confusing since the content of the term critical is dependent on a political context. What one theorist considers critical may be considered dogmatic by another. However, there is a form of theorizing that we think does merit the label 'critical'. By critical theory we mean that type of theory which begins with the avowed intent of criticizing particular social arrangements and/or outcomes. Hence a theory might be considered critical in this sense if it explicitly sets out to identify and criticize a particular set of social circumstances and demonstrate how they came to exist. We want to phrase it in this manner since it is highly probable that this type of critical theory builds its analysis on the basis of an examination of the causal factors that brought the particular unjust state of affairs about. On this account of critical theory there is no necessary conflict between the identification of an unjust state of affairs and a consideration of the causes of that state of affairs. Hence it is possible for a theory to be both explanatory and critical. Many feminist theories fit this model. They identify a particular set of social arrangements that are considered unjust and locate those social conditions in a set of particular causal circumstances. Interestingly, many feminists also take the additional step of indicating how an eradication of those causal factors might make the world better in some or other way.

Once a theorist takes the step of indicating alternative futures or social modes of operation that do not currently exist, but might be brought into being, they have entered the realm of normative theory. Normative theory examines what 'ought' to be the case. It comes in strong or weak versions. In the weak version the theorist is concerned only to examine what ought to be the case in a particular domain of interest. Theories of justice for example can be considered normative in that they debate not only what justice is, but also what it ought to be (for a further discussion of approaches to justice, see Chapter 2). The strong version of normative theory is often called 'utopian' in that it sets out to provide models of how society ought to be reorganized. Marxist theory can be considered strongly utopian in this manner. This type of theorizing has been neglected for some time now, mainly because the term utopian has negative connotations associated with 'unrealistic' expectations.

Another common type of theory is known as constitutive theory. Constitutive theory does not attempt to generate, or track, causal patterns in time, but asks, 'How is this thing constituted?' This type of theory can take many forms. In one sense constitutive theory entails the study of how social objects are constituted. State theory, for example, does not always ask how the modern state came to be, but can focus solely on questions, such as, 'What is a state?', 'How is a state constituted?', 'What functions does the state play in society?'. However, the term constitutive theory is also used in the discipline in another sense: to refer to those authors that examine the ways in which rules, norms, and ideas 'constitute' social objects. For these theorists, the social world (and perhaps the natural world) is constituted through the ideas, or theories, that we hold. For this type of constitutive theory, it becomes important to theorize the act of theorizing.[4]

The last type we wish to discuss is theory considered as a lens through which we look at the world. Many positivists would be unhappy at labelling this theory. It is certainly not theory in the sense of a coherent and systematic set of logical propositions that have a well formulated and specified set of relationships. However, many social theorists do not think that the ontology of the social world permits a view of theory that allows such clearly defined sets of relationships. Instead, they are concerned to explore how social actors navigate their way through social events and processes. In order to make sense of this we need to comprehend what these social processes mean to them, and we do this by understanding the varied ways they make sense of the social world. All social actors view the world in particular ways, and these views of the world do not always display as much coherence, or logic, as one might expect of a systematic and well defined theory. Yet, if the theorist is to grasp how social actors understand the world, they need to be aware of the lens through which those actors view, and act in, the world.[5]

Question of objectivity

Another important issue of contention that arises in meta-theoretical debates is that of objectivity. One of the key notions of Western thought, particularly since the

Enlightenment, has been the search for truth, and the ideas of truth and objectivity are closely related. It is important, however, to distinguish between truth and objectivity. There are many theories of truth, and some theories deny that there is, or can be, such a thing.[6] Philosophers have addressed the issue of truth in various ways and we cannot go into them at length here. The confusion of truth with objectivity arises due to the fact that the term objective has two closely related meanings. In the first sense, an objective claim can be said to be a statement relating to external facts as opposed to internal thoughts or feelings. Hence, it is possible to talk in this sense of something being objective independent of any belief or statement about it. It is easy to see how this can be confused with truth. Something that is said to be the way it is independent of any belief is a common-sense way of talking about truth. This is not, however, how most philosophers, or scientists, think about truth. Truth is typically understood by philosophers and scientists to express a relationship between the world (however defined) and a statement referring to that world; or to a set of beliefs or statements that can be said to be true if they have been arrived at through a given set of procedures. Truth expresses a relationship between language and the world, or a set of human conventions about what counts as 'true'. For many philosophers the idea of an external world having a 'truth' independent of any belief about it is nonsense. External objects may exist independent of theory but they could not be said to be true in any meaningful sense of the word. They have an existence, but to exist is not the same thing as to be true.

The second sense of objective is more interesting in terms of disciplinary debates. Objectivity in this sense relates to a statement, position, or set of claims that is not influenced by personal opinions or prejudices. Objectivity thus refers to the attempt by the researcher to remain detached, dispassionate, impartial, open-minded, disinterested, judicial, equitable, even-handed, fair, unprejudiced. Very few, if any, theorists in IR believe that we can ever produce a set of statements that can be said to be accurate in terms of representing the external world exactly as it is. The main lines of debate surround the extent to which we might aspire to knowledge that approximates this goal, how we might justify and provide evidential support to show how one claim fares better than another in this respect, and how objective, in the sense of impartial, we might be.

Positions on these issues deeply divide the discipline. Most positivists, for example, strive for objective knowledge by attempting to define methods and criteria for knowledge production that minimize the influence of value-biased judgements. This point of view seems persuasive in that striving for systematic and rule-governed procedures relating to knowledge production seems preferable to knowledge acquisition on the basis of an unsystematic and haphazard set of procedures. Positivists argue that, although knowledge is never perfect, through the observance of agreed-upon research criteria, we can aim to make some justifiable judgements between competing knowledge claims. Neoliberals (see Chapter 6), for example, might claim that while their account of the role of institutions is not the only one, nor necessarily an absolute truth, it is still empirically the most valid one in relation to a number of instances. Because this theory can be validated by empirical observations and patterns, and can be used to predict state behaviour, it can be considered more truth-approximating than many others.

For theorists informed by more interpretive approaches to knowledge, social knowledge is by definition always 'situated knowledge'; knowledge claims can never be formulated outside the influence of social and political context. It follows that we must accept that knowledge systems are always socially and politically informed and socially, politically, and ethically consequential. Poststructuralists take this view on knowledge to entail that claims about 'reality' are always constructions of particular discursive and social systems and are always implicated in power relations. They are also sceptical of truth claims due to the fact that such claims have often driven some of the most violent episodes of human interaction. When a group of people firmly believes that they alone possess the truth they can become dogmatic and attempt to implement policies on the basis of that truth, with little or no regard for alternative views. Being sceptical of truth claims then becomes not only a philosophical belief but a political position aimed at preventing totalitarian forms of politics.

Other interpretive theorists are concerned to maintain some notion of objectivity even if they reject the idea of truth. Constructivists, for example, recognize that there is no way to produce statements about the world that might be said to be true in the sense of providing complete and accurate accounts of the way the world is, but they do aspire to objectivity in the sense of attempting to remove bias and gaining support for claims by negotiation within the scientific community. In some respects this position can be said to resemble the position advocated by many positivist scholars. However, for constructivists, the overriding considerations for arriving at judgements relating to knowledge claims are intersubjective agreement as opposed to empirical evidence.

Scientific and critical realists accept large parts of the interpretivist position regarding objectivity, and argue that while we always interpret the world through our own socially positioned lenses, and while there is no easy way to prove the truth of a particular theory, not all theories are equal. Importantly for scientific realists, it is precisely because the world is the way it is independent of any theory that some theories might be better descriptions of that world, even if we do not know it. It then becomes a task of deciding which theory is the most plausible. In determining this scientific realists rule nothing out and privilege no one factor; they are epistemological opportunists. For scientific realists there is not one set of procedures for adjudicating between knowledge claims that covers all cases. Each case must be assessed on its own merits and on the basis of the evidence it supplies. For scientific realists, scientific and explanatory activity is rendered meaningless if we are not accounting for something real in more or less objective ways.

Theory testing and theory comparison

Related to the issue of truth and objectivity is the question of how to evaluate and compare our theoretical frameworks. Positivists argue that only systematic empirical observation guided by clear methodological procedures can provide us with valid knowledge of international politics, and that we must test theories against the empirical patterns in order to compare theories. Interpretivists, and many other postpositivists, on the other hand, insist that there is no easy or conclusive way of comparing theories, and some go so far as to suggest that theories are incommensurable; in other words, theories cannot be compared because either the grounds for their knowledge claims are so different, or they see different worlds (Wight 1996). Scientific and critical realists accept that theory comparison and testing always require recognition of the complexity of judgements that are involved, and an awareness of, and reflection on, the social and political context in which such judgements are formed, as well as analysis of the potential consequences of our judgements. They accept that positivist observational criteria are often a poor guide to choosing between theories if applied in isolation and without adequate critical reflection. Scientific and critical realists argue that theory comparison must be based on holistic criteria: not merely on systematic observation but also conceptual coherence and plausibility, ontological nuance, epistemological reflection, methodological coverage, and epistemological pluralism. They also accept that all judgements concerning the validity of theories are influenced by social and political factors and hence are potentially fallible.

The consequences of how we test and evaluate the validity of knowledge claims are fundamental to any theory. Depending on our different criteria of evaluation some approaches literally get legitimated while others are marginalized. These kinds of judgements have important theoretical and empirical consequences for the kind of world we see but, also, political consequences for the kind of world our theoretical frameworks reproduce. The important thing to note in engaging with the theoretical frameworks in the chapters to come and in comparing their validity is that there are multiple criteria for theory testing and comparison in IR. Although some social scientists have assumed that criteria regarding the predictive and instrumental empirical value of a theory provide superior criteria for theory testing, the interpretive and scientific realist positions on theory comparison also have their strengths. Indeed, having been dominated by the rather narrow criteria for theory comparison for some time, IR theory should, in our view, start to make more use of the holistic criteria. Science, after all, need not be defined by empirical methods alone but can also be seen to be characterized by ontological, epistemological, and methodological pluralism and reflectivity.

Theory and practice

Another key aspect at stake in meta-theoretical debate within the discipline has been a discussion over the purpose of social inquiry. For some the purpose of social inquiry is to gain adequate knowledge of social reality to ground and direct policy-making (Wallace 1996). Others argue that the relationship between theory and practice is more complex than this. Booth (1997) and Smith (1997), for example, argued that the role of theory is often practical in a different sense from what is understood by those who argue for a policy-relevant IR. Wallace and others, Booth and Smith argue, make too much of a separation between theory and practice: they assume that theory is not practice and that 'practice' entails 'foreign policy making' devoid of theoretical groundings. Booth and Smith, and alongside them many critical theorists, argue that theory can in itself be a form of practice, that is, if we accept that theory constitutes the world we live in, by advancing a theory one may either reproduce or change mindsets and, hence, social realities. Equally, all practice is predicated on the basis of some or other theory. As Booth and Smith point out, a policy-maker's view of the world is not necessarily untheoretical: it is actually deeply embedded in social and political points of view.

As the following chapters will reveal, theorists from different camps tend to hold different views on this issue. The traditionally dominant perspectives of realism and liberalism, along with their neo-variants, tend to lean towards Wallace's point of view, while many of the newer perspectives, especially feminism, poststructuralism, and postcolonialism, tend to put emphasis on the role of theorizing itself as a form of world political practice. Again, the key point advanced here is that there is no agreed-upon understanding of the relationship of theory and practice: a position on theory and practice is directed by a meta-theoretical and theoretical framework; and the way one conceives of the relationship of theory and practice has important consequences for how one views the purposes of IR theorizing itself.

Conclusion

This chapter has aimed to provide the reader with an understanding of the nature and importance of meta-theoretical, or philosophy of social science, debates within IR. We have examined the manner in which discussion concerning the nature of inquiry in the discipline has shaped both the history of the discipline and the contemporary theoretical landscape. We have argued that positivist models of science have dominated, but that recent engagements with the nature of science are creating possibilities for new kinds of understandings of IR as a social science. In the case study we examined a number of important issues that are at stake in the way in which theorists from different theoretical schools come to understand and study the world and how they propose to validate or reject knowledge claims. We would like to conclude by highlighting another aspect of debate within the discipline that students should be aware of.

All sciences are social environments with their own internal dynamics and modes of operation. As a set of social practices taking place within a structured social environment the discipline of IR has a unique internal political structure that is both shaped by the manner in which debate occurs, and which shapes the contours of that debate. In examining and evaluating the theoretical approaches outlined in the following chapters, students should be aware that all the theoretical schools of thought in IR and all meta-theoretical positions that underpin them – including ours – are attempting to get their audience to 'buy in' to the argument. In this respect IR theorists resemble salespeople, and what they are selling is their theory. Words such as 'critical', 'sophisticated', 'simplistic', 'naive', and 'dogmatic' are not neutral descriptions of theoretical positions but, rather, are deployed to either delegitimate alternative views, or prove the superiority of one approach over all others. However, much like any good customer, the student would be well advised to reflect critically on the limitations inherent in all the approaches presented to them, even the most persuasive. It is important to remember that all theoretical and underlying meta-theoretical positions are subject to criticism and dispute. Indeed, viewing IR through the philosophy of social science reminds us that all claims to knowledge are open to challenge from other perspectives. Recognizing this does not necessarily lead to relativism, but to a certain humility and degree of reflection with regard to the claims we make and reject in studying world politics.

Realizing that all theories are 'selling you' a perspective is also important in highlighting the politics of the theoretical and meta-theoretical decisions we make. Each theoretical and meta-theoretical avenue involves a number of judgements about what is an important object of inquiry and what is, or is not, a valid knowledge claim. These judgements have consequences for the kind of world we come to see, for how we account for processes within it, and for how we act in that world. Meta-theoretical and theoretical debates, then, are not abstract philosophical exercises but are also potentially politically consequential for the kind of world we live in. *Caveat emptor* (let the buyer beware).

? QUESTIONS

1. What is meta-theory? What role does meta-theoretical debate play in International Relations scholarship?

2. What role has the debate over science played in the discipline of IR historically?

3. Is IR a science or an art? What is at stake in this debate? What does 'scientific' study of world politics entail?

4. What is meant by the terms positivism/postpositivism, explaining/understanding, rationalism/reflectivism?

5. Should we think of the contemporary meta-theoretical debates in IR (between positivism and postpositivism, explaining and understanding and rationalism and reflectivism) as debates between mutually incompatible positions?

6. What are the key assumptions of scientific realism? What is the significance of scientific realism in disciplinary debates?

7. How should we conceptualize the role of theory in the discipline? What do different conceptions of theory have to offer?

8. Can we have value-neutral knowledge of world politics?

9. Can we judge some theories to be better than others? If so, what is involved in making such judgements?

10. What is the purpose of IR theorizing?

11. How significant is the fourth debate in the contemporary discipline of IR? Has it, and should it be, transcended? What is the significance of meta-theoretical debates for IR theory and research?

12. Which meta-theoretical leanings do you find persuasive? Why? How would you justify the validity of your position against your critics?

≋ FURTHER READING

■ **Hollis, M. and Smith, S. (1990),** *Explaining and Understanding International Relations* **(Oxford: Clarendon Press).** An influential account of the meta-theoretical debates over explaining and understanding in the context of IR.

■ **Smith, S., Booth, K., and Zalewski, M. (1996) (eds),** *International Theory: Positivism and Beyond* **(Cambridge: Cambridge University Press).** A collection of essays evaluating the contributions of the positivist/postpositivist debate in IR.

■ Nicholson, M. (1996), *Causes and Consequences in International Relations: A Conceptual Study* (London: Pinter). A positivist introduction to philosophy of social science in IR.

■ King, G., Keohane, R. O., and Verba, S. (1994), *Designing Social Inquiry; Scientific Inference in Qualitative Research* (Princeton NJ: Princeton University Press). A seminal work outlining a positivist approach to qualitative research.

■ Cox, R. (1981), 'Social Forces, States and World Orders: Beyond International Relations Theory', *Millennium: Journal of International Studies*, 10/2: 126–55. A seminal piece outlining a critique of 'problem-solving theory' in IR.

■ Knorr, K. E. and Rosenau, J. N. (1969) (eds), *Contending Approaches to International Politics* (Princeton NJ: Princeton University Press). A collection of key articles by the contenders in the second debate.

■ Wendt, A. (1999), *Social Theory of International Politics* (Cambridge and New York: Cambridge University Press). An important constructivist work with a strong philosophy of social science element. Notably, this book introduces scientific realist themes to IR theory.

■ Patomäki, H. and Wight, C. (2000), 'After Post-Positivism? The Promises of Critical Realism', *International Studies Quarterly*, 44/2: 213–37. This article outlines the contributions of a critical realist approach to theorizing science in IR.

■ Wallace, W. (1996), 'Truth and Power, Monks and Technocrats: Theory and Practice in International Relations', *Review of International Studies*, 22/3: 301–21.

■ Booth, K. (1997), 'Discussion: A Reply to Wallace', *Review of International Studies*, 23/2: 371–7.

■ Smith, S. (1997), 'Power and Truth: A Reply to William Wallace', *Review of International Studies*, 23/4: 507–16. These three articles constitute an interesting debate over the relationship of theory and practice in IR theory.

 Visit the Online Resource Centre that accompanies this book for lots of interesting additional material. www.oxfordtextbooks.co.uk/orc/dunne/

2 International Relations as Political Theory

CHRIS BROWN[1]

✔ **Reader's guide**

Political theory has always engaged with international issues although some modern political theorists, and some theorists of international relations, have denied that there is a close relationship between the two discourses. Here the contrary case will be made, and International Political Theory will be treated not as an optional extra but as, at least implicitly, an ever-present feature of both Political Theory and International Relations Theory. International Political Theory will be studied here via, in the first instance, a reading of the classics of political thought, and of modern political theory; this examination will employ three themes – inside/outside, universal/ particular, and, of especial importance in the study of modern 'Westphalian' inter- national relations, system/society. The case study will focus on international/global justice. Demands for justice on a world scale are an important part of contemporary international relations, and here the ramifications of these demands are explored via the writings of political theorists who have, of course, focused on the meaning of jus- tice for 2,000 years or more. Finally, the impact of globalization on International Political Theory will be examined.

Introduction

The core question posed by moral philosophy is, and always has been, 'How should we live?' Political philosophy poses the same question with specific reference to the common life of the community and its political institutions. What forms of rule are best? What is the basis of political obligation? What is involved in behaving justly to one another? In the West, these questions were first formulated and answered by the Greeks of the classical age, the fifth and fourth centuries BCE; similar questions have been posed in most other cultures and civilizations. The key point is that however these questions are posed, and whatever answers are offered, 'international relations' is always and necessarily involved, even though the term itself is a late-eighteenth-century invention. Political life is always lived in bounded communities. But what of those who live beyond our borders? Do we have obligations towards them, and if so how do they differ from our obligations to our fellow citizens, if at all? How should our community relate to others – by power, or law, or some mixture of the two? Here is the subject matter of International Political Theory (IPT).

If the connection between International Relations (IR) and Political Theory is, as suggested above, ubiquitous and obvious, why is it that the contrary impression is so widespread? Why is IPT generally seen as a new discourse, the product of the last two or three decades? The answer is to be found in the dominance, until comparatively recently, of 'realism' in IR theory, and the social contract tradition in Anglo-American political theory – and the latter qualifier is important here, since International Relations as an academic discourse has been heavily dominated by English-speaking scholars.

In its most uncompromising form, realism holds that international relations is governed by the pursuit of power defined in terms of interest, to employ Hans Morgenthau's formula (1948). In this world normative issues are irrelevant and the concerns of political theorists redundant. Less uncompromising classical realists (including, sometimes, Morgenthau himself) do acknowledge the existence of norms in international relations, but they see them as *sui generis* and associated with the notion of an international society. In this tradition, Martin Wight draws a distinction between political theory, which he sees as an essentially progressivist project, associated with the state, and international theory, which cannot be progressive because international relations is a realm of recurrence and repetition (1966). It may be possible to theorize the society of states (sometimes known as the Westphalian system) but not with the resources provided by 'domestic' political theory.

If the latter is understood in terms of social contract theory, this is a reasonable judgement. Contract theory holds that the political dimensions of the question 'How should we live?' can be encompassed by the terms of a contract, either between rulers and ruled (Locke) or between potential citizens in order to create a ruler or a system of laws (Hobbes, Rawls).[2] Either way the position of non-contractors poses serious problems; the most important modern contract theorist, John Rawls, explicitly assumes that he is providing a theory of justice for a self-contained polity, whose members enter by birth and leave by death (1971). In this picture of the world, there is little room for a political theory of international relations – thus, realist IR theory and the theory of the social contract reinforce the separation of the two discourses.

In the late twentieth century this mutual exclusion pact began to break down under the influence of events in the real world. The state-centric nature of IR theory came under attack from theorists of interdependence, transnationalism, and, later, globalization; the idea that international relations was simply synonymous with inter-state relations could no longer be sustained without difficulty and, as this identity crumbled, so the notion that international relations was a timeless realm of recurrence and repetition became equally difficult to defend. From the political theory side of things, much of the critical reaction to Rawls's masterwork focused on his assumption that communities were self-contained. The notion that one could have a theory of justice that dealt at length with inequalities within societies, but had virtually nothing to say about international inequality seemed perverse and unsustainable.

A new discourse of International Political Theory emerged from these two wreckages, with some genuinely original contributions from scholars such as Brian Barry (1998), Charles Beitz (1979/2000), Andrew Linklater (1990), Terry Nardin (1983), and Thomas Pogge (2002). But as this new discourse emerged it also became clear that IPT had much more of a past than that assigned to it by realist and/or contract theorists. Even during the so-called Westphalian era, some key political theorists had realized that the exclusion of international relations was unacceptable. Immanuel Kant, working mostly from within the contract tradition, understood that his conception of politics required the theorizing of the international 'right' (*Recht*) of states, and the cosmopolitan right of all sentient beings as well as the civil right of individuals within a nation. G. F. W. Hegel, working from outside the contract tradition and with a far stronger sense of the importance of the state than that tradition allows, still felt the necessity to theorize the international. Kantian cosmopolitanism, and Hegelian communitarianism are live doctrines to this day.

But, even apart from these Enlightenment and post-Enlightenment thinkers, premodern political theory has much to say about international concerns. It is customary to identify a canon of thinkers who define (Western) political theory – from Plato and Aristotle to Mill and Rawls – and most members of this canon had something to say about the international, even if sometimes it is necessary to read between the lines and take account of gaps and omissions in their thought if one wishes to grasp what they have to say about relations beyond the walls of the city or the bounds of the state. The international canon is, in fact, much the same as the domestic canon, although a few figures – especially the founders of the Law of Nations – play a somewhat more important role in the former.

Debates in International Political Theory

This chapter will examine both the historical roots of IPT, and some representative contemporary work in the field, with more emphasis on the latter in the case study that follows. As part of an examination of the former it is necessary to form a view on the importance of traditions – how should we read the classics of International Political Theory?

Is there a 'realist tradition'? For some writers the answer is, yes; they attempt to identify a genealogy of classical realism that usually begins with Thucydides, includes *en passant* Machiavelli and Hobbes, and ends with mid-twentieth-century figures such as E. H. Carr and Hans J. Morgenthau. Often this tradition is contrasted (usually favourably) with neo- or structural realism as practised by Kenneth Waltz, Robert Gilpin, or John Mearsheimer (see Chapter 3 on classical realism and Chapter 4 on structural realism). But is there actually a meaningful tradition here? Proponents of this view would say that there are certain problems, connected in this case to the management of power, that are effectively timeless. Thucydides' account of the moral dilemmas of empire in the 'Melian Dialogue' (where the Athenians explain to the Melians that the strong rule where they can and the weak must obey), Machiavelli's advice to the Prince, and Hobbes's notion of the state of nature illuminate issues which are still current in the twenty-first century; the account of the Athenians' disastrous Sicilian expedition in *The Peloponnesian War* has been very effectively employed to critique the USA's wars in Vietnam and Iraq – proof surely that Thucydides can be treated, in certain respects, as our contemporary?

Much modern thought on how to interpret texts would beg to differ.[3] In the first place, one needs to be able to reconstruct the context of a piece of writing in order to make sense of it. Thucydides, for example, lived in a world where ideas about human psychology, citizenship, the role of religion, and so on were radically different from ours; in his world, victorious generals could be executed for failing to recover the bodies of the dead, and the Sicilian expedition was largely rendered unsuccessful because of the fall-out from the mutilation of the *Hermae* (statues with exaggerated phalluses, found on every street corner in Athens) just before it sailed. Second, we need to try to establish what work particular texts were intended by their authors to do; with some moderns careful scholarship may take us almost there, but in many cases intention is not recoverable – we know what the Melian Dialogue means to us, but we can only guess what it meant to Thucydides.

Fortunately, the fact that the classical authors were not addressing our agendas or trying to answer our questions does not mean that we are completely cut off from making sense of their work – although deconstructionists such as Derrida come close to this position. There may be no common questions, but there are some core concerns which, suitably translated into particular historical circumstances, have generated themes which most authors relate to, one way or another. Three such themes can be identified; in shorthand, inside/outside, universal/particular, and system/society. The latter theme will be explored in greater depth later in this chapter in the context of the political theory of the Westphalian system – here the focus will be on inside/outside and universal/particular.

Inside/outside, universal/particular

In every political arrangement, whether empires, city-states, feudal ties of obligation, nation-states, non-state systems, there can be found a distinction between *insiders* and *outsiders* – indeed often several such distinctions. The modern nation-state makes the distinction on the basis of territory and formal citizenship – thus, say, the UK is a carefully delineated space on the surface of the earth, and its citizens are identifiable by means of a very complex set of legal rules, mostly introduced in the last fifty years – but even with such modern states there are complications involved; citizens of other European Union countries or of the Commonwealth are, for certain purposes, insiders in the UK, for other purposes outsiders.

Earlier political orders looked at things differently; in classical Greece, territory was less significant than lineage – classical authors refer to 'the Athenians' rather than 'Athens' and to be an Athenian it was necessary to be born of Athenian parents. At another level, and for certain purposes, all Greeks were to be distinguished from all non-Greeks; the latter were not allowed to attend the Olympic Games, or to share in various common religious rites – they were literally 'barbarians', people who didn't speak properly, whose language sounded like babble. To be considered part of the Greek world, *Hellas*, was politically enormously important to marginal cases; the Macedonians in particular spent a great deal of political capital establishing that they really were proper Greeks. In another era, in medieval Europe, the core insider category was based on religion. Christendom was the common name for medieval Europe and one's identity as a Christian was, for most people, more important than any local, territorial allegiance; the outsiders here were initially pagans, later Jews and Mohammedans; the latter were physically outsiders as far as most of Europe was concerned, while the Jews were physically inside.

As these three examples indicate, there are numerous ways in which the inside–outside distinction can be characterized, and in an era of globalization these ways will probably multiply. Moreover, any particular inside–outside formulation can be further broken down and is subject to disruption from the outside. One final example: the tribes of *Aotearoa* (New Zealand) were kin-groups for whom genealogy (*whakapapa*) was central; insiders were fellow descendants of particular mariners who made the original voyage from the ancestral homeland, *Hawaiki*, to *Aotearoa* in the same canoe and no collective term for the inhabitants of *Aotearoa* existed – until, that is, the arrival of the Europeans, at which point a core insider–outsider shift took place and the term *Maori* emerges to describe the original inhabitants; it means 'normal' as distinct from the *Pakeha* ('whites' or Europeans).

Political theorists of all ages have drawn the distinction between insiders and outsiders – but what is really interesting is what they have made of this distinction, and in particular what they have taken to be the normative implications of insider or outsider status. It is here that notions of *universalism* and *particularism* become highly relevant. Is the frame of reference for political obligation understood to be local, particular, based on the polity, or is some wider notion of obligation, a universalist element, present?

The contrast between the world of the classical Greeks and the world of medieval Christendom is instructive here. The Greeks drew a sharp cultural distinction between themselves and the barbarians, but this had little political significance. Leading cities were quite willing to make alliances with the Persians (the most powerful barbarians) against other Greeks – even at the time of the Persian invasion when the Athenians and the Spartans repulsed the empire of Xerxes at Salamis and Platea, many of the Greek cities, including one of the most important, Thebes, 'medized'. And, as the Melians discovered – and the Athenians later in Sicily – being a fellow Greek did not protect one from massacre or slavery. The point is that for the classical Greeks the key reference point was their own city; for Plato, Aristotle, and Thucydides it was important that some civilized standards in warfare were upheld, and the Athenian behaviour at Melos – killing all the men and boys, enslaving all women and children – was probably seen as disgraceful, but, nonetheless, political life was something lived in the city, and what went on between cities was of much lesser importance. The key political activity was self-rule, which was not necessarily democratic even in the restricted Greek sense, i.e. excluding women, slaves, and resident aliens; communal autonomy – the right to take part in the religious rites of one's own city and to experience one's form of rule as self-chosen – was central. It was only once the cities had lost their political independence, to the Macedonians and their successors, that a different approach emerged, and Diogenes the Cynic could announce that he was a 'cosmopolite' – a citizen of the world, a position most closely associated with Stoic thinkers such as the later Roman Emperor Marcus Aurelius.

This universalist position was adopted by the Christian Middle Ages in Europe. The most important Christian thinkers of the era all endorsed the proposition that the powers-that-be must be obeyed, but they also held that allegiance to these powers could not be at the expense of one's loyalty to Christendom as a whole. St Augustine established this position early in the era with the 'two cities' doctrine. The city of man had to deal with a corrupt human nature after the Fall from the Garden of Eden; only a strong authority capable of exercising power could handle this task and such an authority ruling justly (for without justice, he remarked, the state was simply a band of robbers) deserved our support – but we must never forget the existence of the City of God, uniting the saved of the past, present, and future; our hope that we are of this number must always take precedence over our loyalty to the secular city. Much later, as part of the medieval rediscovery of Greece, St Thomas Aquinas rested the authority of the secular city in an Aristotelian account of the importance of the political. Man is a political and a social animal said Aquinas – but he also developed a strong account of Natural Law; human beings have an essential nature which dictates that certain kinds of human goods are always and everywhere desired; because of this there are common moral standards, discernible by the application of reason, that govern all human relations.

The universalist element in Augustine and Aquinas led to the development of the most distinctive contribution of medieval thinkers to International Political Theory – the notion of the just war. For the classical world, war was simply something that cities did; etiquette required a nominal cause for a war (which could always be found if needed), and Greeks ought not to enslave or massacre other Greeks, but war was certainly not regarded as a pathological condition. For Christians, this approach was unacceptable and some, probably following Jesus himself, simply became absolute pacifists, but for Augustine and Aquinas this was not an option; political authorities deserved our support and they could not survive without occasionally resorting to violence. What these Christian thinkers did was to establish the proposition that peace (understood as representing social justice and not simply the absence of war) was the norm and that force could only be justified in order to restore a just peace that had been disrupted. Moreover, in Aquinas's formulation, the means employed had themselves to be proportionate and measured; force was to be a last resort.

It would be a mistake to think that the notion of just war had a great deal of impact on medieval international relations; when the Church was strong and was able to use excommunication as a credible threat, it could have some impact on the behaviour of secular princes, but, overall, restraints on violence were never particularly effective. Indeed, when the Church declared a 'Crusade' to liberate the Holy Lands from their Muslim rulers it actually contributed to high levels of violence as well as pogroms against Jews in Europe. It should be said that the crusade was not that far removed from the Muslim doctrine of *Jihad*; Islam had never been pacifist, and the Prophet himself was an effective war leader. Still, unlike the Catholic Church, Islamic rulers rarely went in for forced conversion, partly, no doubt, because it would reduce their tax base since only non-believers paid the poll tax.

Medieval Christendom slowly broke up from at least the fifteenth century onwards, and among the casualties of this fall were the ideas on politics sketched above. The Renaissance exposed educated Europeans to the thought of the classical world and, while some features of this thought were compatible with the Christian world-view, others were not. In the city-states of Italy, Roman patriotism struck a chord, and Machiavelli was able to make the extraordinary statement that he valued the interests of Florence higher than he valued his own soul. European voyages to the Americas shook up the world economy, but they also disrupted notions of inside and outside. It was difficult to fit the 'Indians' into pre-existing categories, unlike the Jews (who had rejected the Christian message) or the Muslims (who were essentially extreme heretics) these peoples had no biblical status. Were they human at all? Could they be conquered and enslaved at will? In a last gasp of the medieval natural law tradition the Salamanca school – Vitoria, Suarez – bravely resisted the secular powers and asserted the rights of the aboriginal inhabitants of the Americas, but to no great effect, partly because they also asserted the right of the Christian Spaniards to proselytize and trade even against the wishes of the locals.

Renaissance humanism, the proposition that man is the measure of all things, combined with the Reformation, which destroyed the unity of Christendom, and, with economic and military revolutions, brought to the fore a new relationship between inside and outside, and the universal and the particular. The territorial, sovereign state, legally autonomous and recognizing no internal equal or external superior, became the new political unit and generated a new kind of political theory recovering some of the classical heritage, albeit in a much changed form, **civic republicanism**.[4] The notion of just war changed to reflect this new reality, first, by incorporating the thought that both sides in a conflict had to be treated as just because we are not in a position to tell which one really is, and then by introducing a distinction, not present in the medieval era, between *ius ad bellam* (just resort to war) and *ius in bello* (just conduct of war), building up the latter at the expense of the former. For many writers, such as, in the twentieth century, both Carl Schmitt and Hans Morgenthau (in other respects bitter enemies), this transformation was to be welcomed (Schmitt 2003). Whatever the intent, just war thinking worked to legitimize total war. Just war theorists may have attempted to limit the role of violence in human affairs, and the Catholic Church in the Middle Ages certainly did try to use its influence to ban certain weapons and enforce truces, but these measures were always subverted by the basic logic of the just war. The latter, by inviting the judgement that one side in a conflict is 'just', involved identifying the other as 'unjust', with the concomitant that the unjust must be defeated whatever the cost, even if this involved using banned weapons or taking a conflict to extremes.

There is a logic to this critique – but the other half of the story for both Schmitt and Morgenthau was that the European order that replaced medieval Christendom introduced the principle that, as between European rulers within Europe, war could be 'bracketed' – rationalized and humanized. Rather than a divine punishment, war became an act of state. Whereas in the medieval order the enemy must necessarily be seen as unjust, the new humanitarian approach to war involved the possibility of the recognition of the other as *justi hostes*, an enemy but a legitimate enemy, not someone who deserves to be annihilated, someone in whom one can recognize oneself, which is always a good basis for a degree of restraint. This all sounds reasonably attractive, but one is entitled to ask whether the new European order actually worked in this way. To approach this question we need to introduce a third theme to accompany inside/outside and universal/particular – system/society.

System or society: the Political Theory of the Westphalian Order

Between the end of the fifteenth and the mid-seventeenth centuries – the peace treaties of 1648 are a conventional date here, hence the 'Westphalian order' – a political arrangement based on the sovereign territorial state emerged in Europe. This arrangement is now global, and has been affected in major ways by the Enlightenment, the rise of industrial society, of nationalism, of democracy, and, most recently, of globalization, but the essential elements remain in place – the key international actors are still legally autonomous territorial states, acknowledging no superior authority. Unlike the medieval order which had strong hierarchical, universal elements, this arrangement is an anarchy. What are the implications of this characterization?

Modern neorealists have an answer to this question, which they claim is also the answer offered by classical realists from Machiavelli and Hobbes to Carr and Morgenthau. Westphalia is a 'self-help system' in which each state attempts to ensure its own security by the exercise of power, and by forming temporary alliances. Order in this system – such as it is – is a by-product of the balance of power, a configuration of countervailing forces which sometimes emerges as a largely unintended consequence of the struggle for power. In this system, norms of conduct – 'logics of appropriate behaviour' – may have a shadowy existence, but they are rarely compelling; states make decisions on the basis of 'logics of consequences' overriding norms when they deem it to be necessary so to do (Krasner 1999).

This rather bleak vision receives some support from the historical record; there have indeed been many wars since 1648, and periods of stability rarely last. Still, the fact that the Westphalian order has survived and not collapsed into chaos or evolved into an empire does pose problems for this position. Can it really be the case that this achievement rests on purely fortuitous balances of power? The traditional self-understanding of European statecraft, as represented by, *inter alia*, the founders of the modern law of nations and many political thinkers, historians, and diplomatists would deny that this is so. They believe that rather than an international *system*, there exists – or at least has existed – an international *society*, an association of states that recognizes, and values, the existence of certain norms and common practices, in particular the practices of diplomacy and international law, and the norms of sovereign equality and non-intervention. Everyone agrees, of course, that such norms are frequently violated and practices misused, but the claim is that their very existence, and the inability of states to deny this existence without denying their own legitimacy, makes a genuine difference to the conduct of international relations.

In the recent history of International Relations, this view is particularly associated with the 'English school' – the subject of Chapter 7 in this book – but the core ideas predate Hedley Bull's *Anarchical Society* by several hundred years (1977/1995). Even Thomas Hobbes, allegedly an arch realist, acknowledges that in the state of nature, analogous to the international anarchy, there are principles of natural law which are discernible by reason and which ought to govern behaviour – although, of course, neither human beings nor states can be relied upon to act on these principles in the absence of Leviathan, and Hobbes did not believe the costs of international anarchy were so severe that it was necessary to break out of it at all costs, as is the case for him domestically. But, although a close reading of Hobbes is useful in order to dispel the idea that he was a forerunner of modern neo-realism, the main sources of thinking about international society come from elsewhere, in the first place from the international lawyers Grotius, Pufendorf, Wolff, and Vattel, and in the second place from a miscellany of commentators on international affairs in the eighteenth and nineteenth centuries, many of whose insights were repeated by the classical realists of the mid-twentieth century.

The arguments of these writers are too complex to be examined in detail within the scope of this chapter, but the essential notion common to all is that, while Westphalian international society is composed of sovereign states which are to be regarded as legally equal and autonomous, there is also a sense in which international society is a unified body – a 'supreme state' (*civitas maxima*) according to Christian Wolff, or 'one great republic' as both Edward Gibbon and Edmund Burke would have it. Just how much weight ought to be given to this *civitas maxima* was a matter of dispute and the trend among the international lawyers was towards minimizing its importance by comparison with the sovereign state but the core point is that although its existence made only a marginal difference to state practice, this was an important margin, something that made civilized life possible.

For many writers of the Enlightenment, this was not enough. The most famous figure of the Enlightenment, Immanuel Kant, refers to the international lawyers as 'sorry comforters' offering little to relieve the sufferings caused by inter-state war. Kant's critique of international society is very powerful and remains influential with the theorists of global justice who will be examined in the case study of this chapter. He both advocates and predicts the emergence of a new system of international relations to guarantee Perpetual Peace; this new order would not be based on the abolition of states, but it would involve the abolition of variations in political arrangements. The Definitive Articles of a Perpetual Peace, for Kant, are only three in number – all states must have republican constitutions, they must agree to abolish war, and they must support a cosmopolitan right of hospitality. It is the first of these principles that is the most revolutionary, and would have the greatest influence. Whereas in the Westphalian order the principle of non-intervention is designed as a kind of ethic of coexistence, allowing different states to pursue different conceptions of the good within the unifying framework of the *civitas maxima*, Kant's position holds that peace will be maintained only if there is a high degree of ideological uniformity. In twenty-first-century terminology, he stresses the importance of regime-type in determining foreign-policy behaviour, while realists regard regime-type as wholly unimportant, and theorists of international society are concerned only that, whatever regime exists, it acknowledges the authoritative practices of that society – it was because revolutionary France refused to make this acknowledgement that it was denounced so ferociously by Edmund Burke.

The most compelling response to Kant was offered by G. W. F. Hegel. Whereas Kant's 'sorry comforters' relied, to a greater extent than they were perhaps prepared to admit, on the medieval ancestry of their 'one great republic', Hegel builds his system on different principles; he regards the authority of the modern state as resting on its capacity to create a genuine community. In the modern world, civil society – the collective life of human beings beyond the notional warmth of the family, the associations we join, the economic activities we carry out in order to live – is a source of division, discord, and inequality; our chances of living a good life depend on the capacity of a constitutional state to bring together individuals as fellow citizens, equal in this respect if in no other. According to Hegel such states cannot accept any external authority without undermining their capacity to perform this unifying function – hence even the limited federalism proposed by Kant is unacceptable. The possibility of war cannot be eliminated, says Hegel, and, in any event, it can perform a positive function in allowing citizens to display their commitment to the common good; lest this seem too red-blooded a position, it should be said that Hegel sees war as the business of armies and argues strongly for the protection of civil society from the consequences of this contest between states.

Kant and Hegel have had a major impact on modern International Political Theory, but before moving on to the moderns and notions of justice in IR it is worth making one final point about the old European notion of international society. It was, explicitly, European. The *civitas maxima* was a European 'great republic'; in the eighteenth century the Ottoman Empire tried to be accepted as a member of European international society, but was rebuffed on essentially cultural grounds, only eventually to be allowed to join after the Crimean War in 1856. By then it was clear that the Westphalian order was ceasing to be European, but the terms under which it would spread to the rest of the world were less clear. This was an era when the 'standards of civilization' were imposed by European power on societies which had been civilized for millennia. In one of the great defences of the norm of non-intervention, the English philosopher J. S. Mill explicitly excludes uncivilized societies (including India and Ireland) from its benefits. In principle the uncivilized were uncivilized because of the absence of the rule of law and the protection of property, but since such criteria had not been applied in Europe (for example, to czarist Russia), the suspicion that international society was based on racist principles is difficult to dispel. This issue was not finally clarified until 1945 with the establishment of the UN, and the application of the norm of non-intervention to all its members including the future decolonized – but at this point a contradiction entered international society because the post-1945 order did not simply endorse universal non-intervention, it also introduced the idea of human rights, which, in the minds of some, represented a new, perhaps more insidious, form of the 'standard of civilization'.

Case study: justice and international relations

There is today a widespread perception that we live in an unjust world. The millions of young people, predominantly in Europe and North America, who listen to consciousness-raising pop concerts and wear plastic bracelets proclaiming their desire to 'Make Poverty History' reflect this perception. The UN's Millennium Development Goals have been adopted by all 191 UN members. In order to achieve this consensus the language of justice and injustice is used only sparingly, but there is no doubt that most of the peoples and governments of the poorest states are convinced that they live in a world characterized by unjust inequalities of wealth and power. The Trade Justice Movement and other parts of the broader global justice campaign are determined to bring this point of view home to the governments of the rich and powerful world when they come together in the G8, or at UN World Summit meetings.[5]

Such campaigns raise interesting questions for international political theorists. Who, exactly, is being instructed to make poverty history, and on what authority? How are we to reconcile the needs of distant strangers with our obligations to our fellow citizens? At its most basic, to behave justly towards someone means to give them their due – but who is the relevant 'someone' when it comes to justice and IR? And what is their due? The realist position, predictably, says that these are unanswerable questions; justice as a concept is simply inappropriate outside the context of domestic society. Enough has been said already to allow the reader to decide whether or not to accept this point of view, and, in any event, it has never been the dominant approach to the subject, which has, in fact, deemed international justice to be a desirable end and worthwhile object of study. However, this latter approach has defined justice in procedural terms, and taken the referent object of justice to be sovereign states – clearly this is not what campaigners for global justice usually have in mind. More recently, a literature on global distributive justice, or social justice, has emerged, taking the individual as the appropriate reference point, and here the academy is in tune with modern protesters.[6]

Justice between states

The distinction between 'procedural' and 'substantive' notions of justice is, in principle, clear enough; it is the distinction between following the right procedures and getting the right result – thus a fair trial (the paradigm of procedural justice) may still result in a wrongful verdict (which is substantively unjust). Generally, in conventional international law, justice is procedural, a matter of impartial rules, impartially applied; thus, for example, the law of the sea imposes obligations on all maritime and coastal nations, and the law on the expropriation of economic assets is the same for all states, rich and poor. Clearly such a procedural approach is not substantively neutral – the poor may be unable to pay the compensation that international law mandates for expropriations, countries with big navies and merchant marines benefit more from freedom of passage on the oceans than others – but this has been deemed defensible because of the assumption that the subjects of international law are states. Matters of substantive justice have been seen as essentially domestic, to be decided within the bounded community – justice as between such communities is about fair dealing rather than outcomes.

The fathers of modern international law – Grotius, Wolff, *et al.* – would have found this approach questionable. Although they were, of course, concerned with justice between states, they inherited from the medieval natural law tradition the idea that the ultimate subjects of all law are individuals; this thought was gradually eliminated as the international law of Westphalian international society became increasingly state-centric. Something similar has happened to the idea of just war: for medieval thinkers, the fate of individual souls was a central concern, hence their emphasis on 'right intention', while for modern writers, such as Michael Walzer, intention is unimportant – a Weberian ethic of responsibility demands that we look to the consequences of actions not intentions, which are, in any event, ultimately unknowable (Walzer, 2000). For Augustine and Aquinas, they are known by God, which is why they are so important. Still, although the founders of international law were concerned with the individual, they were not concerned with notions of global social justice in any substantive sense. Economic inequality as between communities was not something they were concerned with, and nor, for that matter, did Kantian cosmopolitanism in the hands of Kant himself lead in this direction. For Kant, cosmopolitan right is about hospitality to visitors, not global social justice. Modern theorists of justice, on the other hand, are concerned with this topic and wish to see issues of justice as between peoples and individuals in substantive terms. Before turning to their work, it is instructive to examine the thinking of John Rawls, who is both the founder of modern thinking about justice, and the last great defender of the position that social justice does not have an international dimension (Rawls 1971; 1999).

Rawls in his magisterial *Theory of Justice* develops a complicated apparatus to determine which social arrangements should be considered just.[7] Societies are understood to be schemes of cooperation for mutual advantage; because there is a social product greater than the sum of the products individuals alone could produce, principles of distributive justice are required. He posits a presocial 'original position' in which potential contractors choose the principles of social justice that would persuade them to enter society. They do so under a 'veil of ignorance' which requires them to choose these principles without knowing important facts about their position; under these conditions he suggests they will maximize political liberties, rejecting caste systems or slavery, and, crucially, they will accept only economic equalities which work for the benefit of the least advantaged (the 'difference principle'). These are radical notions because many of the most obvious inequalities in domestic societies could not be defended on this basis. However, some of the most obvious inequalities in our world are not to be found within but between societies – and here, Rawls argues, the difference principle does not apply.

In his world, societies are assumed to be self-contained. The society of states is not a cooperative scheme for mutual advantage; distributive justice is not possible between societies, because there is no social product to distribute. Instead, Rawls suggests the representatives of just societies would endorse the conventional rules of international society as set out in the final section of the main body of this chapter. In his later work, *The Law of Peoples* (1999), he elaborates a duty on the part of well ordered peoples to help 'burdened societies' to become part of international society but he specifically rejects the notion of developing principles of global social justice – from his point of view a world of socially just societies could still contain great, but legitimate, inequalities. Many of his followers regard this position as perverse in the extreme, and many, probably most, campaigners for global justice would agree.

Global social justice

The simplest argument against Rawls's position is that, under contemporary conditions of interdependence, national societies are not sufficiently discrete as to justify their being treated as separate, self-contained entities. Rather, the world has to be seen as, in certain respects, a single society and therefore the core Rawlsian idea that differences in outcome *vis-à-vis* the distribution of social and economic goods must be justified applies. Charles Beitz – one of Rawls's earliest critics – argues simply that the 'difference principle' should be applied globally (1979/2000). Apart from the obvious practical problems associated with such a position, there is a further difficulty which Beitz later acknowledged, namely that a Rawlsian society is to be understood as a cooperative scheme based on mutual advantage, and it is by no means clear that the current world economic order could be seen in this light. Straightforwardly Rawlsian principles of social justice may apply in areas where Rawls thought they did not – for example, it might be argued, as Beitz does, that contractors would not agree under a veil of ignorance to the principle that states own the raw materials found on their territory and thus resource-poor countries should be compensated by the equivalent of a global wealth tax – but a full-blown global difference principle seems to be taking the argument a step too far.

Unless, perhaps, existing international economic inequalities are actually created by, rather than reflected in, the international economic order, in which case a second argument in favour of global social justice kicks in – namely that rich countries are responsible for the poverty of poor countries and it is therefore right that they should acknowledge extensive obligations to the latter. This is a position that used to be associated with some post-Leninist theories of imperialism but the general argument has been taken up with great rhetorical force recently by Thomas Pogge, whose *World Poverty and Human Rights* is a seminal work (2002). Pogge argues that environmental degradation, mass poverty, malnutrition, and starvation are the price paid by the poor to support the life-style of all the inhabitants of the advanced industrial world; global redistribution via a tax on the use of natural resources is a requirement of global social justice. This is a powerful argument, although it is not simply neoliberal apologists for the International Monetary Fund (IMF) and World Trade Organization (WTO) who would wish to argue that the neomercantilism upon which Pogge's work is based, and in which he is joined by most modern campaigners for global justice, is ill-judged. Old-style liberals and unreconstructed Marxists can agree that genuinely free trade – that is, an end to industrial and agricultural protection in the advanced industrial world – would do more to help the poor than Pogge's global welfarism.[8]

Both of these arguments rest on questionable empirical propositions about how the world actually is; arguably the interdependence argument overstates the unity of global society while the dependency argument understates it. A third argument for global social justice is less dependent on facts about the world, resting on a priori moral principles which envisage all individuals as deserving of equal respect independent of national boundaries. The Kantian principle that a wrong done anywhere is felt everywhere comes into this category, as does his formulation of the categorical imperative, although, as noted above, his explicitly international writings offer little support for international redistribution. Peter Singer's utilitarian account of the obligations of the rich to the poor is, of course, different in form from the Kantian position, but leads to the same general result, as does Brian Barry's espousal of the principle that the basic needs of all should be met before the non-basic needs of anyone are satisfied, a cosmopolitan principle that he derives from the idea of justice as impartiality (Singer 1985; Barry 1998). These writers hold that the very existence of extremes of wealth and poverty in itself creates obligations on the rich to help the poor, regardless of the reasons why such extremes emerged.

However, all these approaches leave open the extent of such obligations, and whether they are necessarily best met by wholesale state-intervention to redistribute resources. As to the first of these points, most writers agree we have different and more extensive obligations towards those closest to us, family, friends, and, by extension fellow-citizens, than we have towards distant strangers; the key question is how different and how much more extensive. Rawls's proposition in *The Law of Peoples* is that our obligations extend only to helping societies that are not capable of sustaining internal schemes of social justice to reach the point at which they would be so capable. This would, as he acknowledges, leave many global inequalities in place, but it is not self-evident that impartiality, or Kantian/utilitarian principles actually require that we promote global equality. As to the means by which assistance is given, Rawls argues that burdened societies require the right kind of civil society and socio-political values, and that this does not require that wealth be transferred, or income redistributed. This may understate the importance of grinding poverty in keeping societies burdened, but Rawls is certainly on firmer ground when he argues that, in fact, it is very difficult to transfer wealth from rich to poor countries; making poverty history may, indeed, depend on changing attitudes in poor countries as much, if not more than, transferring resources.

International versus global justice

Defenders of a traditional conception of international justice are somewhat on the defensive in the face of the claims of global justice although, as noted above, the former have better arguments than they are often credited with. Still, the strongest case in favour of international as opposed to global justice perhaps rests on a *political* defence of pluralism, and the merits of communal autonomy. To a degree, this can be cast in terms of Kant versus Hegel, but this rather implies that the defence of pluralism is a conservative project and, although the supporters of global social justice consider themselves to be politically on the left, it is worth stressing that those societies where functioning and effective social democratic polities have existed have usually been strong defenders of the idea of national sovereignty – the Scandinavian social democracies being the obvious example. There seems to be a clear affinity between social democracy and the kind of moderate nationalism that is endorsed by theories of international as opposed to global justice.[9] It is striking that the Scandinavian social democracies, although good, law-abiding, international citizens with an excellent record of support for the UN and in the giving of development aid, have been very reluctant to surrender power to supranational institutions within Europe and have always enforced strict immigration controls. Domestic welfare states are impossible on any other basis. In short, the pluralism that international justice defends has a positive as well as a negative side. It provides the benefits of coexistence to both progressive and reactionary social systems and it is clear that the replacement of this pluralism by cosmopolitan principles of global justice would bring costs as well as benefits. It is understandable enough that the pop stars, church leaders, and political activists who campaign to make poverty history should disregard or underestimate these costs, but part of the role of the international political theorist is to insist that the benefits of a plural international order should not be ignored.

Conclusion

The purpose of this chapter has been to give the reader some sense of the kind of resources political theory – both the classical canon, and the work of modern analytical theorists – has to offer to the study of International Relations. Inevitably, this has been a highly selective survey, more so, perhaps, than any other chapter in this book, since it attempts to say something about the thought of two and a half millennia. If it were possible to treat the greats of political theory as our contemporaries addressing our agendas it would be much easier to package their ideas for current consumption, but this option is simply not available. There are no timeless traditions, with recurring questions and answers.

Still, if not a common agenda, some common themes have emerged; in the main body of the text three such were identified – the distinctions between inside and outside, universal and particular, and system and society. At an even more general level, it is possible to identify two families of dispositions towards International Political Theory, 'cosmopolitanism' and 'communitarianism'. But even at this level of abstraction caution is required. The cosmopolitanisms of Diogenes and Kant were very different one from another, although they can both claim the title 'cosmopolitan'. Perhaps even more subversive of such categories is the undoubted fact that all the thinkers discussed above to some degree or other straddled the categories employed here – for all his cosmopolitanism, Kant was a statist and an anti-Semite, while, for all his emphasis on the state, Hegel believed in an absolute morality and the moral unity of the human race; things are never as simple as we would like them to be.

If this were not enough complexity, there is one final consideration to be examined. Is it not possible that much of International Political Theory past and present will be rendered pointless by the development of globalization? The latter is a deeply contested term – some argue persuasively that 'internationalization' of the world economy is a more appropriate term – but whether or not one wishes to argue that a qualitative change has taken place, it seems difficult to deny that there has been a kind of transformation in recent years (the theoretical significance of this issue is considered in Chapter 14). This is partly a matter of an increasingly integrated global economy but also involves the emergence of a global society, with identities and social structures shaped increasingly by global forces. Also part of globalization is the emergence of resistance movements: fundamentalisms of all varieties, and the uneasy coalition who make up the anti-global capitalism movement that has been so effective in disrupting meetings on the WTO and other bodies in recent years and whose passion for global justice was discussed above.

How might globalization impact on International Political Theory? At one level it might seem to undermine communitarian perspectives; if the best defence of international as opposed to global justice is that it allows individual societies to set their own priorities, and develop their own projects, then this defence is vulnerable to the charge that the processes of globalization make such aspirations unattainable even for the most powerful states. On the other hand, globalization will not leave cosmopolitan approaches unscathed; much cosmopolitan thought presumes the existence of separate societies, even while arguing that resource transfers should take place between them, and the emergence of a genuinely global political order would challenge this assumption quite as effectively as it would challenge the communitarian ideal of national self-determination.

These challenges are, for the moment, still hypothetical. Globalization has not developed to such an extent that it undermines all national projects (although it does place some limits on what is possible) nor has it led to the emergence of a global polity (although there are signs in that direction). And it may never develop that kind of world-changing significance – indeed, some would argue that the most significant feature of contemporary world politics is not globalization but the emergence of a single power as a kind of world hegemon, a shift that, if carried to extremes, would also have great significance for all varieties of International Political Theory. In any event, there can be no guarantee that International Political Theory will play the same role in the future as it has in the past. But it is certain that, when we attempt to interpret these changes, we will, if we are wise, draw extensively upon the resources that Political Theory has to offer to International Relations.

? **QUESTIONS**

1. Why have scholars of International Relations so frequently assumed that the work of political theorists is irrelevant to their interests?

2. Why is 'context' regarded as important as 'text' when it comes to understanding the classics? Does it really matter that we do not know what the 'Melian Dialogue' meant to Thucydides?

3. Discuss the significance of the apparently universal distinction societies make between 'insiders' and 'outsiders'.

4. In what sense did Europe form 'one great republic' during the years of the Westphalian system?

5. Why is Kant generally considered the most important classical international political theorist?

6. Is Rawls right to think it impossible to develop principles of global social justice?

7. Why has the discourse of International Political Theory developed so rapidly over the last twenty-five years?

8. Why have realists sometimes understood international relations to be a realm of 'recurrence' and 'repetition'?

9. Do you agree that to contrast the universal and the particular is to set up a false dichotomy and that most great political theorists have held both positions at once?

10. Does just war thinking legitimize total war?

11. What are the core values of the Westphalian international order?

12. How has – or will – globalization change the basics of IPT?

■ Brown, C., Nardin, T., and Rengger, N. J. (2002) (eds), *International Relations in Political Thought: Texts from the Ancient Greeks to the First World War* (Cambridge: Cambridge University Press). Contains the most extensive collection of substantial extracts from the canon of International Political Theory. All the classical writers referred to in this chapter are represented here.

■ Williams, H., Wright, M., and Evans, T. (1992) (eds), *A Reader in International Relations and Political Theory* (Buckingham: Open University Press). Covers somewhat less of the ground and with shorter extracts.

■ Boucher, D. (1998), *Political Theories of International Relations* (Oxford: Oxford University Press). The most comprehensive textbook on classical International Political Theory, with extensive commentaries on all the major figures and theories.

■ Knutsen, T. (1992), *A History of International Relations Theory* (Manchester: Manchester University Press). Good, though less extensive than Boucher (1998).

■ Keene, E. (2005), *International Political Thought: A Historical Introduction* (Cambridge: Polity). Equally excellent, more thematic, less author-oriented than Knutsen (1992) or Boucher (1998).

■ Tuck, R. (2001), *The Rights of War and Peace: Political Thought and the International Order from Grotius to Kant* (Oxford: Oxford University Press) is an outstanding monograph, overturning much conventional wisdom on the authors covered.

■ Reiss, H. (1970) (ed.), *Kant's Political Writings* (Cambridge: Cambridge University Press). Kant's international thought is sufficiently important that it is desirable to go to the original works; see especially his pamphlet 'Perpetual Peace' reprinted in full here.

■ Frost, M. (1996), *Ethics in International Relations* (Cambridge: Cambridge University Press). By a modern neo-Hegelian, the best way to enter into Hegel's approach to International Political Theory.

■ Linklater, A. (1990), *Men and Citizens in the Theory of International Relations*, 2nd edn (London: Macmillan) links the work of the classical international lawyers Kant, Hegel, and Marx in a coherent narrative.

■ Nardin, T. (1983), *Law, Morality and the Relations of Nations* (Princeton NJ: Princeton University Press) restates the notion of an international society in modern, Oakeshottian, terms.

■ Nardin, T. and Mapel, D. (1992) (eds), *Traditions of International Ethics* (Cambridge: Cambridge University Press). Provides a good set of essays on International Political Theory, which is sometimes called 'international ethics'.

■ Rawls, J. (1999), *The Law of Peoples* (Cambridge MA: Harvard University Press) is a seminal work by the leading modern theorist of justice; the position set out here is contested by many Rawlsians.

■ Beitz, C. R. (1979/2000), *Political Theory and International Relations* 1st/ 2nd edns (Princeton NJ: Princeton University Press). Remains the best of these critiques.

■ **Walzer, M. (2000), *Just and Unjust Wars*, 3rd edn (New York: Perseus Publishers).** Has much wider importance than its title would suggest; it is still the most characteristic work of the most important modern international communitarian thinker although Walzer would contest this description of his work.

■ **Beitz, C. R., Lawrence, A., and Scanlon, T. (1985) (eds), *International Ethics* (Princeton NJ: Princeton University Press).** Although a little dated, contains a number of important essays and debates, with extensive contributions from Walzer, Beitz, O'Neill, and Singer.

■ **Shapiro, I. and Brilmayer, L. (1999) (eds), *Global Justice* (New York: New York University Press).** Is more up to date, but less balanced, with most contributors cosmopolitan in outlook.

■ **Hutchings, K. (1999), *International Political Theory: Rethinking Ethics in a Global Era* (London: Sage).** A good, modern overview with an emphasis on feminist and postpositivist approaches.

■ **Brown, C. (2002), *Sovereignty, Rights and Justice* (Cambridge: Polity).** Covers similar ground but with more emphasis on analytical political theory.

Visit the Online Resource Centre that accompanies this book for lots of interesting additional material. www.oxfordtextbooks.co.uk/orc/dunne/

INTERNATIONAL RELATIONS AS POLITICAL THEORY

3

Classical Realism

RICHARD NED LEBOW

Chapter contents

- Introduction
- Classical realism on order and stability
- Classical realism and change
- Classical realism on the nature of theory
- Case study
- Conclusion

Reader's guide

Classical realism represents an approach to International Relations that harks back to fifth-century BCE Greek historian Thucydides and his account of the Peloponnesian War. It recognizes the central role of power in politics of all kinds, but also the limitations of power and the ways in which it can readily be made self-defeating. It stresses sensitivity to ethical dilemmas and the practical implications and the need to base influence, wherever possible, on shared interests and persuasion. In the pages that follow, I examine the core assumptions of classical realism through the texts of ancient and modern writers, contrast their ideas with neorealism and other variants of modern realism, and analyse the Anglo-American intervention in Iraq in terms of the tenets of classical realism.

Introduction

There is widespread recognition that the realist tradition reached its nadir in neorealism (also referred to as structural realism; for a discussion of structural realism, see Chapter 4). In his unsuccessful effort to transform realism into a scientific theory, Kenneth Waltz, father of neorealism, denuded the realism of its complexity and subtlety, appreciation of agency, and understanding that power is most readily transformed into influence when it is both masked and embedded in a generally accepted system of norms. Neorealism is a parody of science. Its key terms like power and polarity are loosely and haphazardly formulated and its scope conditions are left undefined. It relies on a process akin to natural selection to shape the behaviour of units in a world where successful strategies are not necessarily passed on to successive leaders and where the culling of less successful units rarely occurs. It more closely resembles an unfalsifiable ideology than it does a scientific theory.

Like most ideologies, neorealism is unfalsifiable, and its rise and fall has had little to do with conceptual and empirical advances. Its appeal lay in its apparent parsimony and superficial resemblance to science; something that says more about its adherents than it does about the theory. Its decline was hastened by the end of the Cold War, which appeared to many as a critical test case for a theory that sought primarily to explain the stability of the bipolar world. The end of the Cold War and subsequent collapse of the Soviet Union also turned scholarly and public attention to a new range of political problems to which neorealism was irrelevant. For a contrasting view of the merits of neo- or structural realism, see Chapter 4 by John Mearsheimer.

The decline of neorealism has encouraged many realists to return to their roots. In doing so, they read with renewed interest the works of great nineteenth- and twentieth-century realists like Max Weber, E. H. Carr, and Hans Morgenthau in search of conceptions and insights relevant to contemporary international relations. Weber and Morgenthau in turn were deeply indebted to the Greeks – to the tragic playwrights and Thucydides – as is the broader tradition of classical realism.

Classical realism can be said to have displayed a fundamental unity of thought across a span of nearly 2,500 years. The writings of its principal adherents – Thucydides, Niccolò Machiavelli, Carl von Clausewitz, and Hans J. Morgenthau – are concerned with questions of order, justice, and change at the domestic, regional, and international levels. Classical realists have holistic understandings of politics that stress the similarities, not the differences, between domestic and international politics, and the role of ethics and community in promoting stability in both domains. In keeping with their tragic orientation, they recognize that communal bonds are fragile and easily undermined by the unrestrained pursuit of unilateral advantage by individuals, factions, and states. When this happens, time-honoured mechanisms of conflict management like alliances and the balance of power may not only fail to preserve the peace but may make domestic and international violence more likely. Like Greek tragedians, classical realists tend to regard history as cyclical, in the sense that efforts to build order and escape from fear-driven worlds, while they may succeed for a considerable period of time, ultimately succumb to the destabilizing effects of actors who believe they are too powerful to be constrained by law and custom.

This chapter explores the thought of two of the most important classical realists writers on international affairs: Thucydides (460– *c*.390 BCE.), a fifth-century Athenian general and author of an account of the Peloponnesian War between Athens and Sparta, and their respective allies; and Hans J. Morgenthau (1904–79), a German-born lawyer who migrated to the USA as a refugee during the Second World War, taught for many years at the University of Chicago, and was arguably the most influential postwar theorist of international relations.[1] I will show the many similarities in their writings, at least some of which derive from the tragic view of life and politics they both shared.

The importance of community for classical realists directs our attention to the ever present tensions between the interests of the community and those of its members, whether individuals or states. The first section explores the classical realist reflections on community. Thucydides and Morgenthau believe that the tensions between individuals and communities could be reconciled in part at a deeper level of understanding. This is because a well functioning community is essential to the intelligent formation and pursuit of individual interests. The principles of justice on which all viable communities are based also allow the efficient translation of power into influence. Membership in a community imposes limits on the ends and means of power. And failure to subordinate goals to the requirements of justice leads to self-defeating policies of overexpansion. Classical realists understand that great powers are often their own worst enemies because success and the hubris it engenders encourage actors to see themselves outside of and above their community, and this in turn blinds them to the need for self-restraint.

The second section of the chapter explores change and transformation. Classical realists think of political systems in terms of their principles of order, and the ways in which they help to shape the identities of actors and the discourses they use to frame their interests. For Thucydides and Morgenthau, changes in identities and discourses are often the result of modernization, and hegemonic war is more often a consequence than a cause of such a transformation. This different understanding of cause and effect has important implications for the kinds of strategies classical realists envisage as efficacious in maintaining or restoring order. They put more weight on values and ideas than they do on power.

The third section of the chapter shows the similarities in their understanding of the nature and purpose of theory. Thucydides constructed no theories in the modern sense of the term, but he is widely regarded as the first theorist of international relations. Morgenthau is explicitly theoretical. They are united in their belief that theoretical knowledge is not an end in itself, but a starting point for actors to work their way through contemporary problems and, in the process, come to deeper forms of understanding.

The fourth section of the chapter is a case study of the war in Iraq. It offers a classical realist analysis of Anglo-American intervention to overthrow Saddam Hussein. I argue that it is characterized by three features – really pathologies – that are well described by classical realism but to which modern realists are largely oblivious. The first has to do with the inability to formulate interests intelligently and coherently outside of a language of justice. The second is hubris, and how it can readily lead to tragic outcomes that are the very opposite of those intended. The third has to do with the choice of means, and the generally negative consequences of choosing those at odds with the values of the community.

I conclude the chapter with a brief discussion of tragedy. Thucydides should be considered the fourth great tragedian of fifth-century Athens. His account of the Peloponnesian

War (431–404 BCE) is constructed in the form and style of a tragedy. Morgenthau wrote no tragedies, but his thinking, like many educated Germans of the nineteenth and twentieth centuries, was deeply steeped in a tragic understanding of life and politics. It lay at the core of his theory, and the strategies he thought appropriate to reconstituting political order.

Classical realism on order and stability

Community, order, and stability

Most realists have a straightforward answer to the problem of order: effective central authority. Governments that defend borders, enforce laws, and protect citizens make domestic politics more peaceful and qualitatively different from international politics. The international arena remains an anarchical, self-help system, a 'brutal arena where states look for opportunities to take advantage of each other' (Mearsheimer 1994–5). Survival depends on a state's material capabilities and its alliances with other states (Waltz 1979: 103–4). Thucydides and Morgenthau are not insensitive to the consequences of anarchy, but do not make this kind of generic distinction between international and domestic politics. For classical realists, *all* politics is an expression of the same human drives and subject to the same pathologies. They see more variation in order and stability *within* domestic and international systems than they do between them, and explain it with reference to the cohesiveness of society, domestic or international, and the channels into which it directs human drives.

Thucydides devotes equal attention to internal developments in Athens and external developments in the diverse theatres of war. He describes parallel developments in both realms and encourages us to understand them as the outcomes of similar and reinforcing processes. His city-states run the gamut from highly ordered and consensual to those racked by the anarchy and civil war. These differences have nothing to do with the presence or absence of a Leviathan, but with the cohesiveness of the community (*homonoia*). When communal bonds are strong, as in Periclean Athens, and in Greece more generally before the Peloponnesian War, *nomos* (laws, rules, norms, conventions) restrain actors, whether individuals or city-states. When community breaks down, as in Corcyra in the 420s, so does order. Thucydides would have agreed with Aristotle's observation that law 'has no power to compel obedience beside the force of habit' (*Politics*: 1269a20).

Morgenthau's understanding of the relationship between domestic and international politics mirrors that of Thucydides. At the outset of his famous text, *Politics among Nations*, he introduces a sharp distinction between international and domestic politics which he then systematically undermines. *All* politics, he insists, is a struggle for power that is 'inseparable from social life itself' (1948a: 17–18). In many countries, laws, institutions, and norms direct the struggle for power into ritualized and socially acceptable channels. In the international arena, the struggle cannot so readily be tamed. The character of international relations nevertheless displays remarkable variation across historical epochs. In the eighteenth century, Europe was 'one great republic' with common standards of 'politeness and cultivation' and a common 'system of arts, and laws, and manners' (1948a: 159–66). Although Morgenthau did not make the analogy in print, he often spoke of the parallel between international relations in the eighteenth century and pre-Peloponnesian-War Greece. In both epochs, 'fear and shame' and 'some common sense of honor and justice' induced leaders to moderate their ambitions (1948a: 270–84). The sense of community was ruptured by the French Revolution, and only superficially restored in its aftermath. It broke down altogether in the twentieth century when the principal powers became divided by ideology as well as by interests. In the 1930s, four major powers – Germany, the Soviet Union, Japan, and Italy – rejected the very premises of the international order. The Soviet Union continued to do so in the postwar era, reducing international politics 'to the primitive spectacle of two giants eyeing each other with watchful suspicion' (1948a: 285).

Morgenthau recognized the same variation in domestic politics. In strong societies like Britain and the USA, norms and institutions muted the struggle for power but, in weak societies like Nazi Germany and Stalin's Soviet Union, they broke down. Politics in these latter countries was every bit as violent and unconstrained as in any epoch of international relations. For Morgenthau, as for Thucydides, communities and the identities and norms they help to create and sustain are the most critical determinants of order, at home and abroad.

Balance of power

Contemporary realists consider military capability and alliances the very foundation of security. The Greeks were by no means insensitive to the value of alliances. Aristotle observed that 'When people are friends, they have no need for justice, but when they are just they need friends as well' (*Nicomachean Ethics*: 1155a24–6). Thucydides, and classical realists more generally, recognize that military power and alliances are double-edged swords; they are as likely to provoke as to prevent conflict.

Book One of Thucydides' *History of the Peloponnesian Wars* leaves no doubt that Athenian efforts to obtain a favourable balance of power were an instrumental cause of war. The alliance with Corcyra (present-day Corfu) led to a violent encounter with the Corinthian fleet and raised the prospect of a wider war with Sparta. Athens then took peremptory action against Megara and Potidaea, and made war difficult to prevent. Sparta's alliance with Corinth dragged it in turn into a war with Athens that many Spartans would have preferred to avoid. Nowhere in his text does Thucydides provide a single example of an alliance that deterred war, and by the logic of the balance of power some of them should have. His narrative of the Mytilenean Debate and Melian Dialogue suggest several reasons for this unrelieved pattern of deterrence failure. Chief among them is the pursuit of unrealistic goals which encourage wishful thinking in the form of downplaying risks and exaggerating the likelihood of success. In the case of Sparta, this led to an almost total failure by the Spartan war party to appreciate Athenian invulnerability to invasion (1.86–8).

Deterrence was also defeated by the breakdown of community and the conventions it sustained. Athenians increasingly succumbed to the impulses of self-aggrandizement (*pleonexia*). In the Sicilian debate, the sensible and cautious Nicias tries to educate Athenians about the size and population of Sicily, the military readiness of its largest city, Syracuse, and warns of the dangers of sailing against an island so far away when there are undefeated enemies close to home. Alcibiades dismisses these risks out of hand and appeals to the greed of his audience. Recognizing that direct arguments against the expedition will not succeed, Nicias now tries to dissuade the assembly by insisting on a much larger force and more extensive provisions than were originally planned. To his surprise, the more he demands, the more eager the assembly becomes to support the expedition, convinced that a force of such magnitude will be invincible. Carried away by the prospect of gain, Athenians became immune to the voice of reason, and committed the second fateful misjudgement – the alliance with Corcyra being the first – that ultimately led to the defeat of Athens (6.10–26).

For Morgenthau, the universality of the power drive meant that the balance of power was 'a general social phenomenon to be found on all levels of social interaction' (1958: 49, 81). Individuals, groups, and states inevitably combined to protect themselves from predators. At the international level, the balance of power had contradictory implications for peace. It might deter war if status quo powers outgun imperialist challengers and demonstrate their resolve to go to war in defence of the status quo. But balancing could also intensify tensions and make war more likely because of the impossibility of assessing with any certainty the motives, capability, and resolve of other states. Leaders understandably aim to achieve a margin of safety, and when multiple states or opposing alliances act this way, they ratchet up international tensions. In this situation, rising powers may be tempted to go to war when they think they have an advantage, and status quo powers to launch preventive wars against rising challengers. Even when the balance of power failed to prevent war, Morgenthau reasoned, it might still limit its consequences and preserve the existence of states, small and large, that constitute the political system. He credited the balance with having served these ends for much of the eighteenth and nineteenth centuries (1948a: 155–9, 162–6, 172; 1958: 80).

For Morgenthau, the success of the balance of power for the better part of two centuries was less a function of the distribution of capabilities than it was of the existence and strength of international society that bound together the most important actors in the system. When that society broke down, as it did from the first partition of Poland through the Napoleonic Wars, the balance of power no longer functioned to preserve the peace or existence of the members of the system (1948a: 160–6). International society was even weaker in the twentieth century, and its decline was an underlying cause of both world wars. Morgenthau worried that its continuing absence in the immediate postwar period had removed all constraints on superpower competition. By the 1970s, he had become more optimistic about the prospects for peace. Détente, explicit recognition of the territorial status quo in Europe, a corresponding decline in ideological confrontation, the emergence of Japan, China, and West Germany as possible third forces, and the effects of Vietnam on US power had made both superpowers more cautious and tolerant of the status quo (1972: preface). But perhaps most importantly, their daily contacts, negotiations, and occasional agreements had gone some way towards normalizing their relations and creating the basis for a renewed sense of international community.

Thucydides and Morgenthau understood politics as a struggle for power and unilateral advantage. The differences between domestic politics and international relations were differences of degree, not of kind. Military capability and alliances were necessary safeguards in the rough-and-tumble world of international relations, but could not be counted on to preserve the peace or the independence of actors. Order, domestic and international, ultimately rested on the strength of the community. When states and their rulers were bound by a common culture, conventions, and personal ties, competition for power was restrained in its ends and its means. Under such conditions, a balance of power might prevent some wars and limit the severity of others. In the absence of community, military capability and alliances were no guarantee of security, and could provoke wars they were intended to prevent. States like Athens, and leaders like Napoleon and Hitler, could not be deterred. As Morgenthau recognized, the balance of power works best when needed least.

Interest and justice

Contemporary realists define interest in terms of power. For the most part, they equate power with material capabilities. According to Kenneth Waltz (1979:153) 'the political clout of nations correlates closely with their economic power and their military might'. Many contemporary realists also believe in the primacy of self-interest over moral principle, and regard considerations of justice as inappropriate, if not dangerous foundations on which to base foreign policies. At best, appeals to justice can serve to justify or mask policies motivated by more concrete material interests. Classical realists consider capabilities to be only one source of power and do not equate power with influence. Influence for them is a *psychological* relationship and, like all relationships, based on ties that transcend momentary interests. Justice enters the picture because it is the foundation of relationships and of the sense of community on which influence and security ultimately depend.

The first level of Thucydides' history depicts the tension between interest and justice and how it becomes more acute in response to the exigencies of war. It also reveals how interest and justice are inseparable and mutually constitutive at a deeper level. In his funeral oration, Pericles describes Athens as a democracy (*dēmokratia*), but Thucydides (2.37.1) considered the constitutional reforms of 462–461 to have created a mixed form of government (*xunkrasis*). Behind the facade of democracy, he tells us, lay the rule of one man – Pericles (2.37.1, 2.65.9–10). The democratic ideology, with which he publicly associated himself, moderated class tensions and reconciled the *dēmos* to the economic and political advantages of the elite. When the gap between ideology and practice was exposed by the behaviour of post-Periclean demagogues, class conflict became more acute and politics more vicious, leading to the violent overthrow of democracy by the regime of the Thirty in 404 and its equally violent restoration a year later. Justice, or at least a belief in justice, was the foundation for community.

Athenian imperialism underwent a similar evolution. The empire was successful when power was exercised in accord with the social conventions governing Greek speech and behaviour. Post-Periclean Athens consistently chose power over principle, lost its *hēgemonia*, alienated allies, and weakened its power base. In 425, during the Mytilenean Debate, Cleon tells the assembly to recognize that their empire (*archē*) is a despotism (*turannis*) based on military power and the fear it inspires (Thucydides 3.37.2). In 416, the Athenian commissioners in the Melian Dialogue divide people into those who rule (*archē*) and those who are subjects (*hupōkooi*) (5.95). To intimidate allies and adversaries alike, they acknowledge their need to expand. Runaway imperialism of this kind stretched their resources to breaking point. Interest defined outside of the language of justice is irrational and self-defeating.

Thucydides' parallel accounts of Athenian domestic politics and foreign policy indicate his belief that coercion is a grossly inefficient and ultimately self-defeating basis of influence. The sophist Gorgias (*c.* 430) personified *logos* (words) as a 'great potentate, who with the tiniest and least visible body achieves the most divine works' (Diels and Kranz 1956: frg. 82, B11). Employed in tandem with persuasion, it 'shapes the soul as it wishes'. Thucydides leads us to the same conclusion. Persuasion (*peithō*) can maintain the position of the 'first citizen' (*stratēgos*) of Athens *vis-à-vis* the masses and that of the hegemon *vis-à-vis* its empire and effectively mask the exercise of power. To persuade, leaders and hegemons must live up to the expectations of their own ideology. For Athens, this meant providing benefits to citizens and allies, and upholding the principles of order on which the polis and its empire were based.

Perhaps the most frequently quoted line from *Politics among Nations* is the assertion in its opening pages that 'the concept of interest defined in terms of power' sets politics apart 'as an autonomous sphere of action' and in turn makes a theory of politics possible (1960: 5). Morgenthau goes on to subvert this formulation to develop a more nuanced understanding of the relationship between interest and power. These contradictions can be reconciled if we recognize that Morgenthau distinguished between the realms of theory and practice. The former aspired to create an abstract, rational ideal based on the underlying and unchanging dynamics of international politics. Such a theory represented the crudest of templates. Policy, and its analysis, were concrete, not always rational, and had to take into account many considerations outside the sphere of politics.

The contrast between theory and practice is equally apparent in Morgenthau's conceptualization of power. He thought of it as an intangible quality with many diverse components, which he catalogues at some length. But, in the real world, the strategies and tactics leaders use to transform the raw attributes of power into political influence were just as important as the attributes themselves. Because influence is a psychological relationship, leaders need to know not only what buttons are at their disposal but which ones to push in any circumstance. There were no absolute measures of state power, because it was always relative and situation-specific. Levers of influence that A could use against B might be totally ineffectual against C. The successful exercise of power required a sophisticated understanding of the goals, strengths, and weaknesses of allies, adversaries, and third parties. But, above all, it demanded psychological sensitivity to the others' needs for self-esteem.

People seek domination but most often end up subordinate to others (Morgenthau 1947: 145). They try to repress this unpleasant truth, and those who exercise power effectively employ justifications and ideologies that facilitate this process. Whenever possible, they attempt to convince those who must submit to their will that they are acting in their interests or those of the wider community (Morgenthau 1958:59). 'What is required for mastery of international politics,' Morgenthau insisted, 'is not the rationality of the engineer but the wisdom and moral strength of the statesman' (1948a: 172).

Like Thucydides, Morgenthau understood that adherence to ethical norms was just as much in the interest of those who wielded power as it was for those over whom it was exercised. He made this point in his critique of US intervention in Indochina, where he argued that intervention would fail and erode the USA's influence in the world because the ends and means of US policy violated the morality of the age. There was a certain irony to Morgenthau's opposition. Two decades earlier, he had written *Politics among Nations*, in large part to disabuse an influential segment of the US elite of its naive belief that ethics was an appropriate guide for foreign policy and that international conflicts could be resolved through the application of law. Intervention in Indochina indicated to him that US policy-makers had 'over learned' the lesson; they had embraced Realpolitik and moved to the other end of the continuum. Morgenthau was adamant that morality, defined in terms of the conventions of the epoch, imposes limits on the ends that power seeks and the means employed to achieve them (1947: 151–68).

For classical realists – and Machiavelli counts as one in this regard – justice is important for two different but related sets of reasons. It is the key to influence because it determines how others understand and respond to you. Policy that is constrained by accepted ethical principles and generally supportive of them provides a powerful aura of legitimacy and helps to reconcile less powerful actors to their subordinate status. Influence can also be bought through bribes or compelled by force, but influence obtained this way is expensive to maintain, tenuous in effect, and usually short-lived. By contrast, a demonstrable commitment to justice can create and maintain the kind of community that allows actors to translate power into influence in efficient ways.

Justice is important in a second fundamental way. It provides the conceptual scaffolding on which actors can intelligently construct interests. Above all else, a commitment to justice is a powerful source of self-restraint, and restraint is necessary in direct proportion to one's power. Weak states must generally behave cautiously because of external constraints. Powerful states are not similarly bound, and the past successes that made them powerful breed hubris, encourage their leaders to make inflated estimates of their ability to control events, and seduce them into embracing risky ventures. As in Greek tragedies, these miscalculations often lead to catastrophe, as they did for Athens, Napoleon, and Hitler. Internal restraint and external influence are thus closely related. Self-restraint that prompts behaviour in accord with the acknowledged principles of justice both earns and sustains the *hēgemonia* that makes efficient influence possible.

Classical realism and change

Change and modernization

Modern realists differentiate systems on the basis of their polarity (uni-, bi-, and multi-polar). System change occurs when the number of poles changes. This is often the result of hegemonic wars, brought on in turn by shifts in the balance of material capabilities. Rising powers may go to war to remake the system in their interests, and status quo powers to forestall such change. For some realists, this cycle is timeless and independent of technology and learning. Others believe that nuclear weapons have revolutionized international relations by making war too destructive to be rational. In their view, this accounts for the otherwise anomalous peaceful transformation from bi- to multipolarity at the end of the Cold War (Mearsheimer 1990; Waltz 1993; Wohlforth 1994–5).

For classical realists, transformation is a broader concept, and one they associate with processes that we have come to describe as modernization. It brings about shifts in identities and discourses and, with them, changing conceptions of security.

Thucydides' language (1.15) encourages his readers to draw an analogy between individual pursuit of wealth and Athenian pursuit of power. The empire is based on the power of money. It generates revenue to build and maintain the largest navy in Greece. Athens is so powerful relative to other city-states that it can dominate them by force. Tyrants, for Greeks, were rulers without any constitutional basis who dispensed with reciprocity and took what they wanted. Gyges of Lydia was the first known tyrant and, not coincidentally, Lydia was thought to be the first city to have introduced money. Like a tyrant, Athens no longer needed to legitimize its rule or provide the kind of benefits that normally held alliances or city-states together. Wealth encouraged the 'orientalization' of Athens, a perspective common to Herodotus and Thucydides. It led to a deep shift in Athenian values, superficially manifested in an increasing reliance on force. This pattern of behaviour was a reflection of changing goals; the goal of honour (*timē*) increasingly gave way to that of acquisition. And *hēgemonia* – rule based on the consent of others – was replaced by control (*archē*) exercised through threats and bribes.

Thucydides' account of the Peloponnesian War is rich in irony. Athens, the tyrant, has jettisoned the traditional bonds and obligations of reciprocity in expectation of greater freedom and rewards only to become trapped by a new set of more onerous obligations. As Pericles recognizes in his funeral oration, Athens had maintained its *hēgemonia* by demonstrating *charis* to its allies. 'In generosity,' he told the assembly, 'we are equally singular, acquiring our friends by conferring not by receiving favours' (2.40.4) The post-Periclean empire must maintain its *archē* by constantly demonstrating its power and will to use it. It must keep expanding, a requirement beyond the capabilities of any state. Athenians would discover this bitter truth with their crushing defeat in Sicily.

Morgenthau's understanding of modernization is not dissimilar. It led to a misplaced faith in reason and undermined the values and norms that had restrained individual and state behaviour. Morgenthau drew more directly on Hegel and Freud. In his *Phenomenology of the Spirit* (1807) and *Philosophy of Right* (1821), Hegel warned of the dangers of homogenization of society arising from equality and universal participation in society. It would sunder traditional communities and individual ties to them without providing an alternative source of identity. Hegel wrote on the eve of the industrial revolution and did not envisage the modern industrial state with its large bureaucracies and modern means of communication. These developments, Morgenthau argued, allowed the power of the state to feed on itself through a process of psychological transference that made it the most exalted object of loyalty. Libidinal impulses, repressed by the society, were mobilized by the state for its own ends. By transferring these impulses to the nation, citizens achieved vicarious satisfaction of aspirations they otherwise could not attain or had to repress. Elimination of the Kulaks, forced collectivization, Stalin's purges, the Second World War, and the Holocaust were all expressions of the transference of private impulses onto the state and the absence of any limits on the state's exercise of power. Writing in the aftermath of the great upheavals of the first half of the twentieth century, Morgenthau recognized that communal identity was far from an unalloyed blessing: it allowed people to fulfil their potential as human beings, but also risked turning them into 'social men' like Eichmann who lose their humanity in the course of implementing the directives of the state.[2]

The intellectual transformation Morgenthau attributes to the Enlightenment bears striking similarities to the proto-Enlightenment of fifth-century Greece. In both epochs, the self-definition of human beings, widespread belief in the power of reason, and the triumph of secular over religious values had far-reaching political implications. The biggest difference between the two periods was in the area of technology; the modern Enlightenment made possible the industrial revolution and machine-age warfare. Nuclear weapons are an outgrowth of this process and, for Morgenthau, 'the only real revolution which has occurred in the structure of international relations since the beginning of history'. War between nuclear powers was no longer an extension of politics by other means but mutual suicide (1958: 76; 1960: 326).

Restoring order

Thucydides and Morgenthau wrote in the aftermath of destructive wars that undermined the communities and conventions that had sustained order at home and abroad. None of them thought it feasible to restore the old way of life, aspects of which had become highly problematic even before the onset of war. They searched instead for some combination of the old and the new that could accommodate the benefits of modernity while limiting its destructive potential.

Thucydides wanted his readers to recognize the need for a synthetic order that would combine the best of the old and the new, and avoid, as far as possible, their respective pitfalls. The best of the new was its spirit of equality, and the opportunity it offered to all citizens to serve their polis. The best of the old was its emphasis on excellence and virtue (*aretē*), which encouraged members of the elite to suppress their appetite for wealth and power, and even their instinct for survival, in pursuit of valour, good judgement, and public service. The Athenians displayed *aretē* at Marathon and Salamis where they risked their lives for the freedom of Greece (2.20, 25, 41, 43, 4.81.2). By the end of the fifth century, *aretē* had progressed through three stages of meaning: from its original Homeric sense of fighting skill, to skill at anything, to moral goodness. Thucydides uses all three meanings, and has Pericles (2.34.5) introduce a fourth in his funeral oration where *aretē* now describes the reputation a state can develop by generous behaviour towards its allies. Thucydides offers an idealized view of Periclean Athens as an example of the kind of synthesis he envisages. It is the very model of a mixed government (*xunkrasis*) that allowed the capable to rule and the masses to participate in government in meaningful ways. It successfully muted tensions between the rich and the poor and the well-born and men of talent, and stood in sharp contrast to the acute class tensions and near stasis of *fin de siècle* Athens.

Thucydides may have hoped that inter-city relations could be reconstituted on similar foundations. The same kinds of inequalities prevailed between poleis as within them. If the power of tyrants could give way to aristocracy and mixed democracy, and the drive for power and wealth be constrained by the restoration of community, the same might be done for inter-polis relations. Powerful states might once again see it in their interest to wield influence on the basis of *hēgemonia*. Power imbalances could be 'equalized' through the principle of proportionality; the more powerful states receiving honour in degree to the advantages they provided for less powerful poleis. His history was intended to educate the wealthy and powerful to the baneful consequences of acting like tyrants, on the individual or state level, and the practical benefits, indeed the necessity, of maintaining the appearance, if not the substance, of the older forms of reciprocity in the political arena.

Thucydides is a stern sceptic and rationalist, but one who supports religion because he considered it to be a principal pillar of morality and conventions. In his view, the radical sophists had done a disservice to Athens by arguing that laws and conventions (*nomos*) are arbitrary justifications for various forms of inequality. Thucydides wrote for a small, intellectually sophisticated elite, who, like himself, were unlikely to accept *nomos* as god given. He appeals to them with a more sophisticated defence of *nomos* that does not require rooting it in man's nature (*phusis*). By demonstrating the destructive consequences of the breakdown of *nomos* and the conventions it upheld, he makes the case for its necessity and the wisdom of those in authority to act *as if* they believed it derived from nature. For Thucydides, language and conventions are arbitrary but essential. His history, like a tragedy, provides an 'outside perspective' for elites to generate a commitment to work 'inside' to restore what is useful, if not essential, to justice and order.

For Morgenthau, the absence of external constraints on state power was *the* defining characteristic of international politics at mid-century. The old normative order was in ruins and too feeble to restrain great powers (1958: 60; 1947: 168). Against this background, the Soviet Union and the USA were locked into an escalating conflict, made more ominous by the unrivalled destructive potential of nuclear weapons. The principal threat to peace was nevertheless political: Moscow and Washington were 'Imbued with the crusading spirit of the new moral force of nationalistic universalism', and confronted each other with 'inflexible opposition' (1948a: 430). The balance of power was a feeble instrument in these circumstances, and deterrence was more likely to exacerbate tensions than to alleviate them. Bipolarity could help to preserve the peace by reducing uncertainty – or push the superpowers towards war because of the putative advantage of launching a first strike. Restraint was needed more than anything else, and Morgenthau worried that neither superpower had leaders with the requisite moral courage to resist mounting pressures to engage in risky and confrontational foreign policies.

Realism in the context of the Cold War was a plea for statesmen and, above all, US and Soviet leaders, to recognize the need to coexist in a world of opposing interests and conflict. Their security could never be guaranteed, only approximated through a fragile balance of power and mutual compromises that might resolve, or at least defuse, the arms race and the escalatory potential of the various regional conflicts in which they had become entangled. Morgenthau insisted that restraint and partial accommodation were the most practical *short-term* strategies for preserving the peace (1948: 169; 1958: 80). A more enduring solution to the problem of war required a fundamental transformation of the international system that made it more like well ordered domestic societies. By 1958, the man who twenty years earlier had heaped scorn on the aspirations of internationalists, would insist that the well-being of the human race now required 'a principle of political organization transcending the nation-state' (1958: 75–6).

Morgenthau's commitment to some form of supranational authority deepened in the 1970s. Beyond the threat of nuclear holocaust, humanity was also threatened by the population explosion, world hunger, and environmental degradation. He had no faith in the ability of nation-states to ameliorate any of these problems. But if leaders and peoples were so zealous about safeguarding their sovereignty, what hope was there of moving them towards acceptance of a new order? Progress would occur only when enough national leaders became convinced that it was in their respective national interests. The series of steps Europeans had taken towards integration illustrated the apparent paradox that 'what is historically conditioned in the idea of the national interest can be overcome only through the promotion in concert of the national interest of a number of nations' (1958: 73).

Thucydides and Morgenthau grappled with successive phases of modernization and their social, political, and military consequences. They understood these consequences, and modernization itself, as an expression of evolving identities and discourses. Human beings were never entrapped by their culture or institutions, but were constantly reproducing, changing, and reinventing them. The central problem for Thucydides and Morgenthau was that old procedures were being abandoned or not working, and being replaced by new and dangerous practices that had entered without much warning. They recognized that stable domestic orders, and the security they might enable, could be restored only by some synthesis that blended the old with the new. This synthesis had to harness the power of reason, but make allowance for the disruptive passions that often motivated individuals, classes, and political units. It had to build community, but could not ignore powerful centrifugal forces, especially self-interest at the individual, group, and national levels, that modernization had encouraged and legitimated. The biggest challenge of all was to construct the new order through the willing agency of representatives of the old order in cooperation with the newly empowered agents of modernity.

Given the nature of the challenge, it is not surprising that classical realists were better at diagnosis than treatment, to use Thucydides' medical metaphor. Thucydides was the most sophisticated of the two thinkers. Perhaps by design, he offered no explicit synthesis, but contented himself with identifying an earlier synthesis – Periclean Athens – that might serve as a model, or at least a starting point, for thinking about the future. Morgenthau addressed the problem of order at two levels: he sought stop-gap political measures to buy time for leaders to grasp the need to transcend the state system. Their works remain possessions for all time, not only because of their insights into war, politics, and human nature, but because of something they may never consciously recognize: unresolved tensions that indicate the necessity but, also, the great difficulty of reconciling tradition and modernity by conscious, rational designs.

Classical realism on the nature of theory

Aristotle (*Nicomachean Ethics*: 141a–b) thought it unlikely that human investigations could ever produce *epistēmē*, which he defined as knowledge of essential natures reached through deduction from first principles. Thucydides does not directly engage questions of epistemology, but one can readily infer that he shared this understanding of the limits of social inquiry. One of his recurrent themes is the extent to which human behaviour is context dependent; similar external challenges provoke a range of responses from different political cultures. As those cultures evolve, so do their foreign policies, a progression I documented in the case of Athens. There is also variation within culture. Thucydides' accounts of the Spartan decision to go to war, the plague in Athens, the Mytilenian Debate, and *stasis* in Corcyra all reveal that individuals respond differently to the same or similar situation.

Morgenthau explicitly denies the possibility of general laws and of predictions based on more limited kinds of generalization. Morgenthau conceived of the social world as 'a chaos of contingencies', but 'not devoid of a measure of rationality'. The social world could be reduced to a limited set of social choices of uncertain outcome because of the irrationality of actors and the inherent complexity of the social world. The best a theory can do 'is to state the likely consequences of choosing one alternative as over against another and the conditions under which one alternative is more likely to occur or to be successful than the other' (1966: 77).

Theōrie, *theōrein*, and *theōrōs* are all post-Homeric words having to do with seeing and visiting. The noun (*theōrōs*) meant 'witness' or 'spectator'. A *theōrōs* was dispatched to Delphi by his polis to bring back a full account of the words of the oracle. He might also be sent to religious and athletic festivals, and it is here that the word picked up its connotation of spectator. Over time, the role of the *theōrōs* became more active; a *theōrōs* was expected not only to describe what he had seen but to explain its meaning. Thucydides comes closest to the model of the *theōrōs*; he provides readers with a description of events that has interpretations of their meaning embedded in it. Morgenthau conducts independent theoretical inquiries in which brief historical accounts, more properly described as examples, are used for purposes of illustration. But, in the best tradition of the Greeks, he aspires to develop a framework that actors can use to work their way through contemporary problems. Morgenthau insisted that 'All lasting contributions to political science, from Plato, Aristotle, and Augustine to the *Federalist*, Marx and Calhoun, have been responses to such challenges arising from political reality. They have not been self-sufficient theoretical developments pursuing theoretical concerns for their own sake' (1966: 77). Great political thinkers, confronted with problems that could not be solved with the tools at hand, developed new ways of thinking to use past experience to illuminate the present. Beyond this, Thucydides and Morgenthau sought to stimulate the kind of reflection that leads to wisdom and, with it, appreciation of the need for self-restraint (*sophrosun*). For both classical realists history was the vehicle for tragedy and the teacher of wisdom.

Case study: classical realist analysis of Iraq

Anglo-American intervention in Iraq is not a subject that can be addressed easily in a short case study. Its origins, implementation, and consequences all warrant lengthy analysis, and are likely to be the subject of considerable controversy for decades to come. My goal here is something different: to use classical realism to devise a framework for analysing the case. In doing so, I characterize intervention as a tragedy in the Greek sense of the term, and concentrate on the USA because all the key decisions were made in Washington.

One of the principal themes of tragedy and classical realism is that people who act outside a community and, hence, outside a language of justice, are incapable of formulating interests in an intelligent and coherent manner. They are moved by passions and hope, not by reason and careful calculation. Thucydides, as we have seen, portrays the Athenian invasion of Sicily in this light. His paired speeches of Alcibiades and Nicias reveal the emotional nature of the decision and how poorly connected it was to any strategic logic or estimation of the likely costs. Bush engaged in no public debate, nor would he be able to, but accounts of the inner workings of his administration reveal similar dynamics at work (Hersh 2004; Mann 2004; Woodward 2004; Daalder and Lindsay 2005).

Our tragedy begins with the end of the Cold War and the collapse of the Soviet Union. American neoconservatives hailed what they called the 'unipolar moment', and revelled in the unrivalled power of the USA. Mistaking power for influence, they felt no reason why their country should be bound by treaties, agreements, and norms that constrained its pursuit of its interests. The move towards unilateralism began with the Clinton administration but accelerated under Bush (Lebow 2003: 310–23). One of the most striking features of US unilateralism is how often it was manifest in pursuit of goals that could not reasonably be said to be in the USA's interest. Good examples are opposition to the International Criminal Court and European negotiations with Iran, from both of which, in the judgement of most American analysts, the USA had much to gain.

US power: hubris and nemesis

In Greek tragedies, success and power are the principal causes of hubris. US intoxication with power and disregard, even contempt, for the USA's traditional allies and the wider international community led the Bush administration to hubris. This is most evident in its policy towards Iraq. There was evidence that sanctions against Saddam Hussein were working, albeit at considerable humanitarian cost, but the administration was not satisfied with mere containment. Vice-President Cheney, Secretary of Defense Donald Rumsfeld, Under-Secretary of Defense Paul Wolfowitz, and National Security Advisor Condoleeza Rice sought removal of Saddam, and made no attempt to hide their objective. Their conversations with other officials and the media indicate that they were deeply offended by the survival of the Saddam regime, and expected that his overthrow by force would allow Washington to remake the map of the Middle East and dramatically increase its influence world-wide. They assumed that Iraqis would welcome American 'liberators' with open arms, accept their émigré puppet Ahmed Chalabi as their new ruler, and at one fell swoop gain significant leverage over Saudi Arabia, Iran, and the Palestinians. They further expected that a successful high-tech military campaign that removed Saddam by 'shock and awe' with few American casualties would intimidate North Korea and encourage widespread bandwagoning, making other countries more intent on currying favour with Washington.

The available evidence indicates that this circle of self-styled 'Vulcans' rarely, if ever, consulted with acknowledged Middle East experts in the State Department or the Central

Intelligence Agency (CIA); ignored reports and estimates that ran counter to their expectations; and put great pressure on the CIA and other organizations within the US intelligence community to confirm their views. This has been well documented with regard to 'evidence' that Saddam had, or was developing, weapons of mass destruction (WMDs).

Trust in hope rather than reason also characterized military planning. Donald Rumsfeld insisted on invading on the cheap, and ordered the Joint Chiefs of Staff to jettison their war plan calling for 400,000 troops and to produce one requiring no more than 125,000. Contrary to wishes of field commander General Tommy Franks, he also insisted the army begin withdrawing forces thirty days after the fall of Baghdad. The CIA contributed to the rosy picture the administration had formed. It advised that principal opposition would come not from Saddam's Red Guard, but from paramilitary forces with money and ample diverse weapons caches. The National Intelligence Council's (NIC) thirty-eight-page assessment of postwar Iraq mentioned internal opposition only once *en passant* in conclusion. It did warn, however, that there would be trouble if the Americans were perceived as occupiers. The CIA's regional officers worried about insurrection, but George Tenet, Director of Central Intelligence who was keen to please the President, made sure their fears were not reported in the NIC estimate.

Giving in to pressure from Rumsfeld, the CIA exaggerated the effectiveness of Iraq's infrastructure. The air force and navy were accordingly instructed not to target the electrical grid, but the system collapsed anyway. Getting the lights back on and rebuilding hospitals, schools, and sewage facilities became a major struggle for which the occupying forces were initially unprepared. Rumsfeld and his planners thought the bureaucracy would remain intact and could merely be reformed, as was true in the occupations of Germany and Japan! The White House, Secretary of Defence, and military were working with inadequate intelligence because Iraq had long been treated as a 'Tier 2' threat, in contrast to Iran and North Korea. The USA had no more than a handful of agents on the ground, and relied on refugees, foreign intelligence, and excellent photo intelligence. Intelligence supplied by Chalabi and refugees associated with him was given credence by Rumsfeld and Rice despite repeated warnings from the CIA and State Department's Bureau of Intelligence and Research that it was exaggerated or entirely fabricated (Phillips 2005: 68–73). State Department planning for the occupation, a task force that drew in seventy-five experts on all aspects of the Arab world, was terminated by Rumsfeld on the grounds that they were not fully committed to transforming Iraq (Woodward 2004: 282–4). The Pentagon's occupation plans, based on Rumsfeld's most optimistic scenario, were designed only to secure the oil ministry and oil fields, and secondarily to search for WMD. None of the latter was ever found.

Inadequate plans and occupation forces alienated many Iraqis and allowed those who were disgruntled to loot arsenals and seize weapons, ammunition, and explosives that they would later use against US occupation forces and US-trained police. In the resulting chaos, looting took the place of shopping. US proconsul Jake Garner, relying on advice provided by Chalabi and other refugees, was totally detached from the local scene. His replacement, Paul Bremer, disbanded the Iraqi army of 400,000, unwisely let them keep their guns, and many promptly joined the insurgency (Diamond 2004: 9–22; Phillips 2005: 198–9). There was no effective dialogue with local forces until well after the insurrection was underway, and house-to-house searches, and other measures designed to nip the insurgency in the bud, only intensified it. US generals would repeatedly claim over the next two years that the insurgents were losing, and would even cite increases in the number of their attacks as evidence. By January 2006, when this chapter was written, the Bush administration was in a quagmire, not unlike Vietnam. None of the options open to it were promising, the US public had increasingly turned against the war and the President's popularity had reached an all-time low in the polls. The Bush administration's experience in Iraq drives home what is perhaps the most important insight of classical realism: that great powers are their own worst enemies.

Conclusion: the tragic vision

The chorus in *Antigone* praises human beings as the most inventive of all creatures who reshape the goddess earth with their ploughs, yoke horses, and bulls, snare birds and fish in the twisted mesh of their nets, and make paths through the turbulent seas with their ships. But they destroy what they create, kill what they love most, and seem incapable of living in harmony with themselves and their surroundings. The juxtaposition of man's achievements and transgressions is a central theme of Greek tragedy and classical realism. Like the chorus in *Antigone*, Thucydides and Morgenthau recognized the extraordinary ability of human beings to harness nature for their own ends, and their propensity to destroy through war and civil violence what took them generations to build. Their writings explore the requirements of stable orders, but they remained pessimistic about the ability of the powerful to exercise self-restraint. Like Aeschylus, they saw a close connection between progress and conflict. They understood that violent challenges to the domestic and international orders are most likely in periods of political, economic, social, and intellectual ferment.

Thucydides was a friend of Sophocles and Euripides, and the only classical realist who wrote what might be called a tragedy. In the late eighteenth century, German intellectuals turned to tragedy as a model for reconstituting ethics and philosophy. Morgenthau was deeply influenced by this latter development. He was intimately familiar with the corpus of ancient and modern literature and philosophy. His intellectual circle included his colleague and fellow émigré Hannah Arendt, who had studied with Heidegger, wrote about tragedy, and applied its lessons to contemporary politics, as did American-born theologian Reinhold Niebuhr.

Morgenthau came to understand tragedy, he wrote to his British colleague Michael Oakeshott, as 'a quality of existence, not a creation of art' (1948b). His postwar writings, beginning with *Scientific Man vs. Power Politics*, repeatedly invoke tragedy and its understanding of human beings as the framework for understanding contemporary international relations. The principal theme at which he hammers away is the misplaced faith in the powers of reason that have been encouraged by the Enlightenment. But he is equally wary of emotion freed from the restraints of reason and community. 'The *hybris* of Greek and Shakespearean tragedy, the want of moderation in Alexander, Napoleon, and Hitler are instances of such an extreme and exceptional situation' (1947: 135). Although he never used the Greek word *sophrosunē* (prudence and self-restraint) his German and English writings and correspondence make frequent use of its equivalents: *Urteilskraft* (sound judgement) and prudence. He offers them, as did the Greeks, as the antidotes to hubris. Tragedy, and its emphasis on the limits of human understanding, also shaped his approach to theory. Like politics, it had to set realistic goals, and recognize the extent to which its vision was shaped and constrained by its political and social setting. Political leaders and theorists alike would do well to dwell on this lesson of history.

? QUESTIONS

1. What are the principal ways in which classical realists differ from neo- or structural realists?

2. How do classical realists conceive of influence? What is its relation to power?

3. Has our understanding of international politics progressed at all beyond that of Thucydides?

4. In what ways does Thucydides' account of the Peloponnesian War bridge realism and constructivism?

5. To what extent do Thucydides and Morgenthau attribute the decline and downfall of great powers to their own policy choices versus foreign threats?

6. What other writers on political and international affairs might be considered classical realists? What about Sun Tzu, Machiavelli, Carl von Clausewitz, John Herz, and E. H. Carr?

7. When Thucydides and Morgenthau write about ethics, do they have in mind a particular ethical code?

8. How would classical realist analyses of the Cold War (including its beginning and end) differ from a neo- or structural realist account?

9. To what extent can ethical precepts guide foreign policy in a world where there are fundamental disagreements about what is ethical?

10. Describe the respective understandings Thucydides and Morgenthau had of theory. In what ways were they similar and different? How do they differ from the neopositivist understanding of theory that underlies most so-called 'mainstream' theory building in the social sciences?

11. Analyse the respective understanding Thucydides and Morgenthau have of the ability of the balance of power and deterrence to preserve the peace.

12. How would classical realists characterize the similarities and differences between US intervention in Vietnam and Iraq, and between both of those and Soviet intervention in Afghanistan?

≋ FURTHER READING

■ **Frost, Mervyn, Mayall, James, Rengger, Nicholas, and Lebow, Richard Ned (2003, 2005), Two Symposia on 'Tragedy, Ethics and International Relations', *International Relations* 17/4: 480–503 and 19/4: 324–36.** A useful debate on the relevance of tragedy to contemporary International Relations.

■ **Herz, John (1950), 'Idealist Internationalism and the Security Dilemma',** *World Politics* **2/12: 157–80.** A discussion of the prospects of international transformation by one of the great classical realists and originator of the concept of the security dilemma.

■ **Lebow, Richard Ned (2003),** *The Tragic Vision of Politics: Ethics, Interests and Orders* **(Cambridge: Cambridge University Press).** Develops the concept of classical realism and uses it to critique modern realism and its belief that foreign policies should not be based on ethical considerations.

■ **Morgenthau, Hans J. (1947),** *Scientific Man vs. Power Politics* **(London: Latimer House).** A classical realist critique of behaviouralism.

■ **Morgenthau, Hans (1960),** *Politics among Nations,* **3rd edn (New York: Knopf).** A foundational work of modern classical realism.

■ **Reus-Smit, Christian (1999),** *The Moral Purpose of the State: Culture, Social Identity, and Institutional Rationality in International Relations* **(Princeton NJ: Princeton University Press).** Explores the links between ethics, politics, and identity.

■ **Thucydides (1996),** *The Landmark Thucydides: A Comprehensive Guide to the Peloponnesian War,* **edited by Robert B. Strassler (New York: Free Press).** The original text of classical realism.

IMPORTANT WEBSITES

● Columbia International Affairs Online (CIAO). Access through subscriber university URLs. The best up-to-date website for articles and documents on foreign affairs and international relations.
  www.ciaonet.org/

● Text of Thucydides' *History of the Peloponnesian War.*
  http://classics.mit.edu/Thucydides/pelopwar.html

Visit the Online Resource Centre that accompanies this book for lots of interesting additional material. www.oxfordtextbooks.co.uk/orc/dunne/

4 Structural Realism

JOHN J. MEARSHEIMER

Reader's guide

This chapter examines a body of realist theories that argue states care deeply about the balance of power and compete among themselves either to gain power at the expense of others or at least to make sure they do not lose power. They do so because the structure of the international system leaves them little choice if they want to survive. This competition for power makes for a dangerous world where states sometimes fight each other. There are, however, important differences among structural realists. In particular, defensive realists argue that structural factors limit how much power states can gain, which works to ameliorate security competition. Offensive realists, on the other hand, maintain that the system's structure encourages states to maximize their share of world power, to include pursuing hegemony, which tends to intensify security competition. The subsequent analysis revolves around four questions. Why do states want power? How much power do they want? What causes war? Can China rise peacefully (the thematic of the case study)?

Introduction

Realists believe that power is the currency of international politics. Great powers, the main actors in the realists' account, pay careful attention to how much economic and military power they have relative to each other. It is important not only to have a substantial amount of power, but also to make sure that no other state sharply shifts the balance of power in its favour. For realists, international politics is synonymous with power politics.

There are, however, substantial differences among realists. The most basic divide is reflected in the answer to the simple but important question: why do states want power? For classical realists like Hans Morgenthau (1948a), the answer is human nature. Virtually everyone is born with a will to power hardwired into them, which effectively means that great powers are led by individuals who are bent on having their state dominate its rivals. Nothing can be done to alter that drive to be all-powerful. A more detailed treatment of classical realism can be found in Chapter 3.

For structural realists, human nature has little to do with why states want power. Instead, it is the structure or architecture of the international system that forces states to pursue power. In a system where there is no higher authority that sits above the great powers, and where there is no guarantee that one will not attack another, it makes eminently good sense for each state to be powerful enough to protect itself in the event it is attacked. In essence, great powers are trapped in an iron cage where they have little choice but to compete with each other for power if they hope to survive.

Structural realist theories ignore cultural differences among states as well as differences in regime type, mainly because the international system creates the same basic incentives for all great powers. Whether a state is democratic or autocratic matters relatively little for how it acts towards other states. Nor does it matter much who is in charge of conducting a state's foreign policy. Structural realists treat states as if they were black boxes: they are assumed to be alike, save for the fact that some states are more or less powerful than others.

There is a significant divide between structural realists, which is reflected in the answer to a second question that concerns realists: how much power is enough? Defensive realists like Kenneth Waltz (1979) maintain that it is unwise for states to try to maximize their share of world power, because the system will punish them if they attempt to gain too much power. The pursuit of hegemony, they argue, is especially foolhardy. Offensive realists like John Mearsheimer (2001) take the opposite view; they maintain that it makes good strategic sense for states to gain as much power as possible and, if the circumstances are right, to pursue hegemony. The argument is not that conquest or domination is good in itself, but instead that having overwhelming power is the best way to ensure one's own survival. For classical realists, power is an end in itself; for structural realists, power is a means to an end and the ultimate end is survival.

Power is based on the material capabilities that a state controls. The balance of power is mainly a function of the tangible military assets that states possess, such as armoured divisions and nuclear weapons. However, states have a second kind of power, latent power, which refers to the socio-economic ingredients that go into building military power. Latent power is based on a state's wealth and the size of its overall population. Great powers need money, technology, and personnel to build military forces and to fight wars, and a state's latent power refers to the raw potential it can draw on when competing with rival states. It should be clear from this discussion that war is not the only way that states can gain power. They can also do so by increasing the size of their population and their share of global wealth, as China has done over the past few decades.

Let us now consider in greater detail the structural realists' explanation for why states pursue power, and then explore why defensive and offensive realists differ about how much power states want. The focus will then shift to examining different structural realist explanations about the causes of great power war. Finally, I will illuminate these theoretical issues with a case study that assesses whether China can rise peacefully.

Why do states want power?

There is a simple structural realist explanation for why states compete among themselves for power. It is based on five straightforward assumptions about the international system. None of these assumptions alone says that states should attempt to gain power at each other's expense. But when they are married together, they depict a world of ceaseless security competition.

The first assumption is that great powers are the main actors in world politics and they operate in an anarchic system. This is not to say that the system is characterized by chaos or disorder. Anarchy is an ordering principle; it simply means that there is no centralized authority or ultimate arbiter that stands above states. The opposite of anarchy is hierarchy, which is the ordering principle of domestic politics.

The second assumption is that all states possess some offensive military capability. Each state, in other words, has the power to inflict some harm on its neighbour. Of course, that capability varies among states and for any state it can change over time.

The third assumption is that states can never be certain about the intentions of other states. States ultimately want to know whether other states are determined to use force to alter the balance of power (**revisionist states**), or whether they are satisfied enough with it that they have no interest in using force to change it (**status quo states**). The problem, however, is that it is almost impossible to discern another state's intentions with a high degree of certainty. Unlike military capabilities, intentions cannot be empirically verified. Intentions are in the minds of decision-makers and they are especially difficult to discern.

One might respond that policy-makers disclose their intentions in speeches and policy documents, which can be assessed. The problem with that argument is policy-makers sometimes lie about or conceal their true intentions. But even if one could determine another state's intentions today, there is no way to determine its future intentions. It is impossible to know who will be running foreign policy in any state five or ten years from now, much less whether they will have aggressive intentions. This is not to say that states can be certain that their neighbours have or will have revisionist goals. Instead, the argument is that policy-makers can never be certain whether they are dealing with a revisionist or status quo state.

The fourth assumption is that the main goal of states is survival. States seek to maintain their territorial integrity and the autonomy of their domestic political order. They can pursue other goals like prosperity and protecting human rights, but those aims must always take a back seat to survival, because if a state does not survive, it cannot pursue those other goals.

The fifth assumption is that states are rational actors, which is to say they are capable of coming up with sound strategies that maximize their prospects for survival. This is not to deny that they miscalculate from time to time. Because states operate with imperfect information in a complicated world, they sometimes make serious mistakes.

Again, none of these assumptions by themselves says that states will or should compete with each other for power. For sure, the third assumption leaves open the possibility that there is a revisionist state in the system. By itself, however, it says nothing about why all states pursue power. It is only when all the assumptions are combined together that circumstances arise where states not only become preoccupied with the balance of power, but acquire powerful incentives to gain power at each other's expense.

To begin with, great powers fear each other. There is little trust among them. They worry about the intentions of other states, in large part because they are so hard to divine. Their greatest fear is that another state might have the capability as well as the motive to attack them. This danger is compounded by the fact that states operate in an anarchic system, which means that there is no nightwatchman who can rescue them if they are threatened by another country. When a state dials the emergency services for help, there is nobody in the international system to answer the call.

The level of fear between states varies from case to case, but it can never be reduced to an inconsequential level. The stakes are simply too great to allow that to happen. International politics is a potentially deadly business where there is the ever-present possibility of war, which often means mass killing on and off the battlefield, and which might even lead to a state's destruction.

Great powers also understand that they operate in a self-help world. They have to rely on themselves to ensure their survival, because other states are potential threats and because there is no higher authority they can turn to if they are attacked. This is not to deny that states can form alliances, which are often useful for dealing with dangerous adversaries. In the final analysis, however, states have no choice but to put their own interests ahead of the interests of other states as well as the so-called international community.

Fearful of other states, and knowing that they operate in a self-help world, states quickly realize that the best way to survive is to be especially powerful. The reasoning here is straightforward: the more powerful a state is relative to its competitors, the less likely it is that it will be attacked. No country in the Western Hemisphere, for example, would dare strike the USA, because it is so powerful relative to its neighbours.

This simple logic drives great powers to look for opportunities to shift the balance of power in their favour. At the very least, states want to make sure that no other state gains power at their expense. Of course, each state in the system understands this logic, which leads to an unremitting competition for power. In essence, the structure of the system forces every great power – even those that would otherwise be satisfied with the status quo – to think and act when appropriate like a revisionist state.

One might think that peace must be possible if all of the major powers are content with the status quo. The problem, however, is that it is impossible for states to be sure about each other's intentions, especially future intentions. A neighbour might look and sound like a status quo power, but in reality is a revisionist state. Or it might be a status quo state today, but change its stripes tomorrow. In an anarchic system, where there is no ultimate arbiter, states that want to survive have little choice but to assume the worst about the intentions of other states and to compete for power with them. This is the tragedy of great power politics.

The structural imperatives described above are reflected in the famous concept of the security dilemma (Herz 1950; see also Glaser 1997). The essence of that dilemma is that most steps a great power takes to enhance its own security decrease the security of other states. For example, any country that improves its position in the global balance of power does so at the expense of other states, which lose relative power. In this zero-sum world, it is difficult for a state to improve its prospects for survival without threatening the survival of other states. Of course, the threatened states then do whatever is necessary to ensure their survival, which, in turn, threatens other states, all of which leads to perpetual security competition.

How much power is enough?

There is disagreement among structural realists about how much power states should aim to control. Offensive realists argue that states should always be looking for opportunities to gain more power and should do so whenever it seems feasible. States should maximize power, and their ultimate goal should be hegemony, because that is the best way to guarantee survival.

While defensive realists recognize that the international system creates strong incentives to gain additional increments of power, they maintain that it is strategically foolish to pursue hegemony. That would amount to overexpansion of the worst kind. States, by their account, should not maximize power, but should instead strive for what Kenneth Waltz calls an 'appropriate amount of power' (1979: 40). This restraint is largely the result of three factors.

Defensive realists emphasize that if any state becomes too powerful, balancing will occur. Specifically, the other great powers will build up their militaries and form a balancing coalition that will leave the aspiring hegemon at least less secure, and maybe even destroy it. This is what happened to Napoleonic France (1792–1815), Imperial Germany (1900–18), and Nazi Germany (1933–45) when they made a run at dominating Europe. Each aspiring hegemon was decisively defeated by an alliance that included all, or almost all, of the other great powers. Otto von Bismarck's genius, according to the defensive realists, was that he understood that too much power was bad for Germany, because it would cause its neighbours to balance against it. So, he wisely put the brakes on German expansion after winning stunning victories in the Austro–Prussian (1866) and Franco–Prussian (1870–1) Wars.

Some defensive realists argue that there is an **offence–defence balance**, which indicates how easy or difficult it is to conquer territory or defeat a defender in battle. In other words, it tells you whether or not offence pays. Defensive realists maintain that the offence–defence balance is usually heavily weighted in the defender's favour, and thus any state that attempts to gain large amounts of additional power is likely to end up fighting a series of losing wars. Accordingly, states will recognize the futility of offence and concentrate instead on maintaining their position in the balance of power. If they do go on the offensive, their aims will be limited.

Defensive realists further argue that, even when conquest is feasible, it does not pay: the costs outweigh the benefits. Because of nationalism, it is especially difficult, sometimes impossible, for the conqueror to subdue the conquered. The ideology of nationalism, which is pervasive and potent, is all about self-determination, which virtually guarantees that occupied populations will rise up against the occupier. Moreover, it is difficult for foreigners to exploit modern industrial economies, mainly because information technologies require openness and freedom, which are rarely found in occupations.

In sum, not only is conquest difficult but, even in those rare instances where great powers conquer another state, they get few benefits and lots of trouble. According to defensive realism, these basic facts about life in the international system should be apparent to all states and should limit their appetite for more power. Otherwise, they run the risk of threatening their own survival. If all states recognize this logic – and they should if they are rational actors – security competition should not be particularly intense, and there should be few great power wars and certainly no **central wars** (conflicts involving all or almost all the great powers).

Offensive realists do not buy these arguments. They understand that threatened states usually balance against dangerous foes, but they maintain that balancing is often inefficient, especially when it comes to forming balancing coalitions, and that this inefficiency provides opportunities for a clever aggressor to take advantage of its adversaries. Furthermore, threatened states sometimes opt for **buck-passing** rather than joining a balancing coalition. In other words, they attempt to get other states to assume the burden of checking a powerful opponent while they remain on the sidelines. This kind of behaviour, which is commonplace among great powers, also creates opportunities for aggression.

Offensive realists also take issue with the claim that the defender has a significant advantage over the attacker, and thus offence hardly ever pays. Indeed, the historical record shows that the side that initiates war wins more often than not. And while it may be difficult to gain hegemony, the USA did accomplish this feat in the Western Hemisphere during the nineteenth century. Also, Imperial Germany came close to achieving hegemony in Europe during the First World War.

Both defensive and offensive realists agree, however, that nuclear weapons have little utility for offensive purposes, except where only one side in a conflict has them. The reason is simple: if both sides have a survivable retaliatory capability, neither gains an advantage from striking first. Moreover, both camps agree that conventional war between nuclear-armed states is possible but not likely, because of the danger of escalation to the nuclear level.

Finally, while offensive realists acknowledge that sometimes conquest does not pay, they also point out that sometimes it does. Conquerors can exploit a vanquished state's economy for gain, even in the information age. Indeed, Peter Liberman argues that information technologies have an 'Orwellian' dimension, which facilitates repression in important ways (1996: 126). While nationalism surely has the potential to make occupation a nasty undertaking, occupied states are sometimes relatively easy to govern, as was the case in France under the Nazis (1940–4). Moreover, a victorious state need not occupy a defeated state to gain an advantage over it. The victor might annex a slice of the defeated state's territory, break it into two or more smaller states, or simply disarm it and prevent it from rearming.

For all of these reasons, offensive realists expect great powers to be constantly looking for opportunities to gain advantage over each other, with the ultimate prize being hegemony. The security competition in this world will tend to be intense and there are likely to be great power wars. Moreover, the grave danger of central war will arise whenever there is a potential hegemon on the scene.

The past behaviour of the great powers has been more in accordance with the predictions of offensive rather than defensive realism. During the first half of the twentieth century, there were two world wars in which three great powers attempted and failed to gain regional hegemony: Imperial Germany, Imperial Japan, and Nazi Germany. The second half of that century was dominated by the Cold War, in which the USA and the Soviet Union engaged in an intense security competition that came close to blows in the Cuban Missile Crisis (1962).

Many defensive realists acknowledge that the great powers often behave in ways that contradict their theory. They maintain, however, that those states were not behaving rationally, and thus it is not surprising that Imperial Germany, Imperial Japan, and Nazi Germany were destroyed in those wars they foolishly started. States that maximize power, they argue, do not enhance their prospects for survival; they undermine it.

This is certainly a legitimate line of argument but, once defensive realists acknowledge that states often act in strategically foolish ways, they need to explain when states act according to the dictates of their structural realist theory and when they do not. Thus, Waltz famously argues that his theory of international politics needs to be supplemented by a separate theory of foreign policy that can explain misguided state behaviour. However, that additional theory, which invariably emphasizes domestic political considerations, is not a structural realist theory.

The theories of defensive realists such as Barry Posen, Jack Snyder, and Stephen Van Evera conform closely to this simple Waltzian template. Each argues that structural logic can explain a reasonable amount of state behaviour, but a substantial amount of it cannot be explained by structural realism. Therefore, an alternative theory is needed to explain those instances where great powers act in non-strategic ways. To that end, Posen (1984) relies on organizational theory, Snyder (1991) on domestic regime type, and Van Evera (1999) on militarism. Each is proposing a theory of foreign policy, to use Waltz's language. In essence, defensive realists have to go beyond structural realism to explain how states act in the international system. They must combine domestic-level and system-level theories to explain how the world works.

Offensive realists, on the other hand, tend to rely exclusively on structural arguments to explain international politics. They do not need a distinct theory of foreign policy, mainly because the world looks a lot like the offensive realists say it should. This means, however, that they must make the case that it made strategic sense for Germany to pursue hegemony in Europe between 1900 and 1945, and for Japan to do the same in Asia between 1931 and 1945. Of course, offensive realists recognize that states occasionally act in strategically foolish ways, and that those cases contradict their theory. Defensive realists, as emphasized, have a fall-back position that is not available to offensive realists: they can explain cases of non-strategic behaviour with a separate theory of foreign policy.

What causes great power war?

Structural realists recognize that states can go to war for any number of reasons, which makes it impossible to come up with a simple theory that points to a single factor as the main cause of war. There is no question that states sometimes start wars to gain power over a rival state and enhance their security. But security is not always the principal driving force behind a state's decision for war. Ideology or economic considerations are sometimes paramount. For example, nationalism was the main reason Bismarck launched wars against Denmark (1864), Austria (1866), and France (1870–1). The Prussian leader wanted to create a unified Germany.

Wars motivated largely by non-security considerations are consistent with structural realism as long as the aggressor does not purposely act in ways that would harm its position in the balance of power. Actually, victory in war almost always improves a state's relative power position, regardless of the reason for initiating the conflict. The German state that emerged after 1870 was much more powerful than the Prussian state Bismarck took control of in 1862.

Although isolating a particular cause of all wars is not a fruitful enterprise, structural realists maintain that the likelihood of war is affected by the architecture of the international system. Some realists argue that the key variable is the number of great powers or poles in the system, while others focus on the distribution of power among the major states. A third approach looks at how changes in the distribution of power affect the likelihood of war. Finally, some realists claim that variations in the offence–defence balance have the greatest influence on the prospects for war.

The polarity of the system

A longstanding debate among realists is whether bipolarity (two great powers) is more or less war-prone than multipolarity (three or more great powers). It is generally agreed that the state system was multipolar from its inception in 1648 until the Second World War ended in 1945. It was only bipolar during the Cold War, which began right after the Second World War and ran until 1989.

It is tempting to argue that it is clear from twentieth-century European history that bipolarity is more peaceful than multipolarity. After all, there were two world wars in the first half of that century, when Europe was multipolar, while there was no shooting war between the USA and the Soviet Union during the latter half of that century, when the system was bipolar.

This line of argument looks much less persuasive, however, when the timeline includes the nineteenth century. There was no war between any European great powers from 1815 to 1853, and again from 1871 to 1914. Those lengthy periods of relative stability, which occurred in multipolar Europe, compare favourably with the 'long peace' of the Cold War. Thus, it is difficult to determine whether bipolarity or multipolarity is more prone to great power war by looking at modern European history.

Proponents of these rival perspectives, however, do not rely on history alone to make their case; they also employ theoretical arguments. Realists who think bipolarity is less war-prone offer three supporting arguments. First, they maintain that there is more opportunity for great powers to fight each other in multipolarity. There are only two great powers in bipolarity, which means there is only one great power versus great power dyad. In multipolarity, by contrast, there are three potential conflict dyads when there are three great powers, and even more as the number of great powers increases.

Second, there tends to be greater equality between the great powers in bipolarity because, the more great powers there are in the system, the more likely it is that wealth and population, the principal building blocks of military power, will be distributed unevenly among the great powers. And, when there are power imbalances, the stronger often have opportunities to take advantage of the weaker. Furthermore, it is possible in a multipolar system for two or more great powers to gang up on a third great power. Such behaviour is impossible, by definition, in bipolarity.

Third, there is greater potential for miscalculation in multipolarity, and miscalculation often contributes to the outbreak of war. Specifically, there is more clarity about potential threats in bipolarity, because there is only one other great power. Those two states invariably focus on each other, reducing the likelihood that they will misgauge each other's capabilities or intentions. In contrast, there are a handful of great powers in multipolarity and they usually operate in a fluid environment, where identifying friends from foes as well as their relative strength is more difficult.

Balancing is also said to be more efficient in bipolar systems, because each great power has no choice but to directly confront the other. After all, there are no other great powers that can do the balancing or can be part of a balancing coalition and, although lesser powers can be useful allies, they cannot decide the overall balance of power. In multipolarity, however, threatened states will often be tempted to pass the buck to other threatened states. Although buck-passing is an attractive strategy, it can lead to circumstances where aggressors think they can isolate and defeat an adversary. Of course, threatened states can choose not to pass the buck and instead form a balancing coalition again the threatening state. But putting together alliances is often an uncertain process. An aggressor might conclude that it can gain its objectives before the opposing coalition is fully formed. These dynamics are absent from the simple world of bipolarity, where the two rivals have only each other to think about.

Not all realists, however, accept the claim that bipolarity facilitates peace. Some argue that multipolarity is less war-prone. In this view, the more great powers there are in the system, the better the prospects for peace. This optimism is based on two considerations. First, deterrence is much easier in multipolarity, because there are more states that can join together to confront an especially aggressive state with overwhelming force. In bipolarity, there are no other balancing partners. Balancing in multipolarity might be inefficient sometimes, but eventually the coalition forms and the aggressor is defeated, as Napoleonic France, Imperial Germany, Imperial Japan, and Nazi Germany all learned the hard way.

Second, there is much less hostility among the great powers in multipolarity, because the amount of attention they pay to each other is less than in bipolarity. In a world with only two great powers, each concentrates its attention on the other. But, in multipolarity, states cannot afford to be overly concerned with any one of their neighbours. They have to spread around their attention to all the great powers. Plus, the many interactions among the various states in a multipolar system create numerous cross-cutting cleavages that mitigate conflict. Complexity, in short, dampens the prospects for great power war.

With the end of the Cold War and the collapse of the Soviet Union many realists argue that unipolarity has arrived (Wohlforth 1999). The USA, in other words, is the sole great power. It has achieved global hegemony, a feat no other country has ever accomplished. Other realists, however, argue that the post-Cold War system is multipolar, not unipolar. The USA, they maintain, is by far the most powerful state on earth, but there are other great powers, such as China and Russia.

What are the consequences for international stability if the international system is unipolar? Such a world is likely to be more peaceful than either a bipolar or multipolar world. Most importantly, there can be neither security competition nor war between great powers in unipolarity, because it includes just one great power. Furthermore, the minor powers are likely to go out of their way to avoid fighting the sole pole. Think about the Western Hemisphere, where the USA clearly enjoys hegemony. No state in that region would willingly start a war with the USA for fear of being easily and decisively defeated. This same logic would apply to all regions of the world if the USA was a global hegemon.

There are two caveats to this line of argument. If the hegemon feels secure in the absence of other great powers and pulls most of its military forces back to its own region, security competition and maybe even war is likely to break out in the regions it abandons. After all, the sole pole will no longer be present in those places to maintain order. On the other hand, the hegemon might think that its superior position creates a window of opportunity for it to use its awesome military power to reorder the politics of distant regions. A global hegemon engaged in large-scale social engineering at the end of a rifle barrel will not facilitate world peace. Still, there cannot be war between great powers in unipolarity.

Balanced or imbalanced power

Rather than look to the number of great powers to explain the outbreak of war, some realists argue that the key explanatory variable is how much power each of them controls. Power can be distributed more or less evenly among the great powers. Although the power ratios among all the great powers affect the prospects for peace, the key ratio is that between the two most powerful countries in the system. If there is a lopsided gap, the number one state is a preponderant power, simply because it is so much more powerful than all the others.[1] However, if the gap between numbers one and two is small, there is said to be a rough balance of power, even though power might not be distributed equally among all the great powers. The key point is that there is no marked difference in power between the two leading states.

Some realists maintain that the presence of an especially powerful state facilitates peace. A preponderant power, so the argument goes, is likely to feel secure because it is so powerful relative to its competitors; therefore, it will have little need to use force to improve its position in the balance of power. Moreover, none of the other great powers is likely to pick a fight with the leading power, because they would almost certainly lose. However, war among the lesser great powers is still possible, because the balance of power between any two of them will at least sometimes be roughly equal, thus allowing for the possibility that one might defeat the other. But, even then, if the preponderant power believes that such wars might upset a favourable international order, it should have the wherewithal to stop them, or at least make them unusual events.

The historical case that proponents of this perspective emphasize is the period between Napoleon's defeat in 1815 and the outbreak of the First World War in 1914. There were only five wars between the great powers during these hundred years (1853–6, 1859, 1866, 1870–1, 1904–5), and none was a central war like the two conflicts that bracket the period. This lengthy period of relative peace – sometimes called the *Pax Britannica* – is said to be the consequence of Britain's commanding position in the international system. Conversely, the reason there were central wars before and after this period is that Napoleonic France and Imperial Germany, respectively, were roughly equal in power to Britain.

Other realists take the opposite view and argue that preponderance increases the chance of war. Indeed, central wars are likely when there is an especially powerful country in the system. A preponderant power, according to this perspective, is a potential hegemon. It has the wherewithal to make a run at dominating the system, which is the best guarantee of survival in international anarchy. Therefore, it will not be satisfied with the status quo, but instead will look for opportunities to gain hegemony. When there is rough equality among the great powers, no state can make a serious run at hegemony, ruling out deadly central wars. Great power wars are still possible, but the fact that power tends to be rather evenly distributed reduces the incentives for picking fights with other great powers.

Proponents of this viewpoint argue that the Napoleonic Wars were largely due to the fact that France was a potential hegemon by the late eighteenth century. The two world wars happened because Germany was twice in a position during the first half of the twentieth century to make a run at European hegemony. The long period of relative peace from 1815 to 1914 was not due to the *Pax Britannica*, because Britain was not a preponderant power. After all, no balancing coalition ever formed against Britain, which was hardly feared by Europe's continental powers. The reason there were lengthy periods of peace in Europe during these hundred years is that there was a rough balance of power in multipolar Europe. Unbalanced multipolarity, not balanced multipolarity, increases the risks of great power war.

Power shifts and war

Other realists maintain that focusing on static indicators like the number of great powers or how much power each controls is wrongheaded. They claim that instead the focus should be on the dynamics of the balance of power, especially on significant changes that take place in the distribution of power (Copeland 2000). Probably the best known argument in this school of thought is that a preponderant power confronted with a rising challenger creates an especially dangerous situation, because a central war usually results. The dominant state, knowing its days at the pinnacle of power are numbered, has strong incentives to launch a preventive war against the challenger to halt its rise. Of course, the declining state has to act while it still enjoys a decided power advantage over its growing rival. Some scholars argue that the rising power is likely to initiate the war in this scenario. But that makes little sense, because time is on the side of the ascending power, which does not need a war to catch up with and overtake the leading state.

The origins of the two world wars are said to illustrate this line of argument. Germany was the dominant power in Europe before both conflicts, but each time it faced a rising challenger to its east: Russia before 1914 and the Soviet Union before 1939. To forestall decline and maintain its commanding position in the European balance of power, Germany launched preventive wars in 1914 and 1939, both of which turned into devastating central wars.

The offence–defence balance

As noted, some defensive realists argue that there is an offence–defence balance which almost always favours the defence, and thus works to dampen security competition. As such, that balance is a force for peace. Some defensive realists, however, allow for significant variation in the balance between defence and offence, and argue that offensive advantage is likely to result in war, while defence dominance facilitates peace. For example, the Second World War occurred because the tank and the dive bomber, when incorporated into a blitzkrieg doctrine, markedly shifted the offence–defence balance in the offence's favour. On the other hand, there was no shooting war between the USA and the Soviet Union during the Cold War, because the coming of nuclear weapons sharply shifted the balance in the defence's favour.

In sum, a variety of structural arguments attempt to explain when great power war is more or less likely. Each has a different underlying causal logic and each looks at the historical record in a different way.

Case study: can China rise peacefully?

The Chinese economy has been growing at an impressive pace since the early 1980s, and many experts expect it to continue expanding at a similar rate over the next few decades. If so, China, with its huge population, will eventually have the wherewithal to build an especially formidable military. China is almost certain to become a military powerhouse, but what China will do with its military muscle, and how the USA and China's Asian neighbours will react to its rise, remain open questions.

There is no single structural realist answer to these questions. Some realist theories predict that China's ascent will lead to serious instability, while others provide reasons to think that a powerful China can have relatively peaceful relations with its neighbours as well as the USA. Let us consider some of these different perspectives, starting with offensive realism, which predicts that a rising China and the USA will engage in an intense security competition with considerable potential for war.

The rise of China according to offensive realism

The ultimate goal of the great powers, according to offensive realism, is to gain hegemony, because that is the best guarantor of survival. In practice, it is almost impossible for any country to achieve global hegemony, because it is too hard to project and sustain power around the planet and onto the territory of distant great powers. The best outcome that a state can hope for is to be a regional hegemon, which means dominating one's own geographical area. The USA's 'Founding Fathers' and their successors understood this basic logic and they worked assiduously to make the USA the dominant power in the Western Hemisphere. It finally achieved regional hegemony in 1898. While the USA has grown even more powerful since then, and is today the most powerful state in the system, it is not a global hegemon.

States that gain regional hegemony have a further aim: they seek to prevent great powers in other geographical regions from duplicating their feat. Regional hegemons do not want peer competitors. Instead, they want to keep other regions divided among several major states, who will then compete with each other and not be in a position to focus on them. Thus, after achieving regional dominance, the USA has gone to great lengths to prevent other great powers from controlling Asia and Europe. There were four great powers in the twentieth century that had the capability to make a run at regional hegemony: Imperial Germany (1900–18), Imperial Japan (1931–45), Nazi Germany (1933–45), and the Soviet Union (1945–89). In each case, the USA played a key role in defeating and dismantling those aspiring hegemons. In short, the ideal situation for any great power is to be the only regional hegemon in the world.

If offensive realism is correct, we should expect a rising China to imitate the USA and attempt to become a regional hegemon in Asia. China will seek to maximize the power gap between itself and its neighbours, especially Japan and Russia. China will want to make sure that it is so powerful that no state in Asia has the wherewithal to threaten it. An increasingly powerful China is also likely to try to push US military forces out of Asia, much the way the USA pushed the European great powers out of the Western Hemisphere in the nineteenth century. China can be expected to come up with its own version of the Monroe Doctrine.

From China's perspective, these policy goals make good strategic sense. Beijing should want a militarily weak Japan and Russia as its neighbours, just as the USA prefers a militarily weak Canada and Mexico on its borders. All Chinese remember what happened in the last century when Japan was powerful and China was weak. Furthermore, why would a powerful China accept US military forces operating in its backyard? US policy-makers, after all, become incensed when other great powers send their military forces into the Western Hemisphere. They are invariably seen as a potential threat to US security. The same logic should apply to China.

It is clear from the historical record how US policy-makers will react if China attempts to dominate Asia. The USA does not tolerate peer competitors, as it demonstrated in the twentieth century; it is determined to remain the only regional hegemon. Therefore, the USA will work hard to contain China and ultimately to weaken it to the point where it is no longer a threat to control the commanding heights in Asia. In essence, the USA is likely to behave towards China much the way it behaved towards the Soviet Union during the Cold War.

China's neighbours are also sure to fear its rise, and they too will do whatever they can to prevent it from achieving regional hegemony. In fact, there is already evidence that countries like India, Japan, and Russia, as well as smaller powers like Singapore, South Korea, and Vietnam, are worried about China's ascendancy and are looking for ways to contain it. In the end, they will join a US-led balancing coalition to check China's rise, much the way Britain, France, Germany, Italy, Japan, and even China, joined forces with the USA to contain the Soviet Union during the Cold War.

The rise of China according to defensive realism

In contrast to offensive realism, defensive realism offers a more optimistic story about China's rise. For sure, defensive realists recognize that the international system creates strong incentives for states to want additional increments of power to ensure their survival. A mighty China will be no exception; it will look for opportunities to shift the balance of power in its favour. Moreover, both the USA and China's neighbors will have to balance against China to keep it in check. Security competition will not disappear altogether from Asia as China grows more powerful. Defensive realists are not starry-eyed idealists.

Nevertheless, defensive realism provides reason to think that the security competition surrounding China's rise will not be intense, and that China should be able to coexist peacefully with both its neighbours and the USA. For starters, it does not make strategic sense for great powers to pursue hegemony, because their rivals will form a balancing coalition and thwart – maybe even crush – them. It is much smarter for China's leaders to act like Bismarck, who never tried to dominate Europe, but still made Germany great, rather than Kaiser Wilhelm or Adolf Hitler, who both made a run at hegemony and led Germany to ruin. This is not to deny that China will attempt to gain power in Asia. But structure dictates that it will have limited aims; it will not be so foolish as to try to maximize its share of world power. A powerful China with a limited appetite should be reasonably easy to contain and to engage in cooperative endeavors.

The presence of nuclear weapons is another cause for optimism. It is difficult for any great power to expand when confronted by other powers with nuclear weapons. India, Russia, and the USA all have nuclear arsenals, and Japan could quickly go nuclear if it felt threatened by China. These countries, which are likely to form the core of an anti-China balancing coalition, will not be easy for China to push around as long as they have nuclear weapons. In fact, China is likely to act cautiously towards them for fear of triggering a conflict that might escalate to the nuclear level. In short, nuclear weapons will be a force for peace if China continues its rise.

Finally, it is hard to see what China gains by conquering other Asian countries. China's economy has been growing at an impressive pace without foreign adventures, proving that conquest is unnecessary for accumulating great wealth. Moreover, if China starts conquering and occupying countries, it is likely to run into fierce resistance from the populations which fall under its control. The US experience in Iraq should be a warning to China that the benefits of expansion in the age of nationalism are outweighed by the costs.

Although these considerations indicate that China's rise should be relatively peaceful, defensive realists allow for the possibility that domestic political considerations might cause Beijing to act in strategically foolish ways. After all, they recognize that Imperial Germany, Imperial Japan, and Nazi Germany made ill-advised runs at hegemony. But they maintain that the behaviour of those great powers was motivated by domestic political pathologies, not sound strategic logic. While that may be true, it leaves open the possibility that China might follow a similar path, in which case its rise will not be peaceful.

There are other structural realist perspectives for assessing whether or not China's rise will be peaceful. If the world is unipolar, as some structural realists argue, then the growth of Chinese power will eventually put an end to unipolarity. When it does, the world will be a more dangerous place, since there cannot be war between great powers in unipolarity, while there certainly can be if both China and the USA are great powers. Furthermore, if Japan acquires nuclear weapons, Russia gets its house in order, and India continues its rise, there would be a handful of great powers in the system, which would further increase the potential for great power conflict.

Of course, one might argue that China's ascendancy will lead to bipolarity, which is a relatively peaceful architecture, even if it is not as pacific as unipolarity. After all, there was no shooting war between the superpowers during the Cold War. Indeed, the security competition between them was not especially intense after the Cuban Missile Crisis. It was more dangerous before then, mainly because the USA and the Soviet Union had to come to grips with the nuclear revolution and also learn the rules of the road for dealing with each other under bipolarity, which was then a new and unfamiliar structure. China and the USA, however, would have the benefit of all that learning that took place during the Cold War, and could deal with each other from the start much the way that Moscow and Washington dealt with each other after 1962.

Not all structural realists accept the argument that bipolarity is more prone to peace than multipolarity. For them, a return to bipolarity would be a cause for pessimism. However, if the rise of China was accompanied by the emergence of other great powers, the ensuing multipolarity would give these realists more cause for optimism.

Finally, for structural realists who believe that preponderance produces peace, the rise of China is ominous news. They argue that US power has had a pacifying effect on international politics. No other great power, and certainly no minor power, would dare pick a fight with the USA as long as it sits at the pinnacle of world power. But that situation would obviously change if China reached the point where it was almost as powerful as the USA. Preponderance would disappear, and without it the world would be a much more dangerous place. Indeed, these realists would argue that the USA would have strong incentives to launch a preventive war against China to forestall decline.

In sum, there is no consensus among structural realists about whether China can rise peacefully. This diversity of views is not surprising since these same realists disagree among themselves about how much power states should want as well as what causes war.

The only important point of agreement among them is that the structure of the international system forces great powers to compete among themselves for power.

Conclusion

It was commonplace during the 1990s for pundits and scholars to proclaim that the world was rapidly becoming more peaceful and that realism was dead. International politics was said to have been transformed with the end of the Cold War. Globalization of the economic sort was supposedly tying the state in knots; some even predicted its imminent demise. Others argued that Western elites were for the first time thinking and talking about international politics in more cooperative and hopeful terms, and that the globalization of knowledge was facilitating the spread of that new approach.

Many argued that democracy was spreading across the globe and, because democracies do not fight each other, we had reached the 'the end of history' (classical liberalism is discussed in Chapter 5). Still others claimed that international institutions were finally developing the capacity to cause the major powers to act according to the rule of law, not the dictates of realism.

In the wake of September 11, that optimism has faded, if not disappeared altogether, and realism has made a stunning comeback. Its resurrection is due in part to the fact that almost every realist opposed the Iraq War, which has turned into a strategic disaster for the USA and UK. But, more importantly, there is little reason to think that globalization or international institutions have crippled the state. Indeed, the state appears to have a bright future, mainly because nationalism, which glorifies the state, remains a powerful political ideology. Even in Western Europe, where there has been unprecedented economic integration, the state is alive and well.

Furthermore, military power is still a critical element in world politics. The USA and the UK, the world's two great liberal democracies, have fought five wars together since the Cold War ended in 1989. Both Iran and North Korea remind us that nuclear proliferation remains a major problem, and it is not difficult to posit plausible scenarios where India and Pakistan end up in a shooting war that involves nuclear weapons. It is also possible, although not likely, that China and the USA could get dragged into a war over Taiwan, or even North Korea. Regarding China's rise, even the optimists acknowledge that there is potential for serious trouble if the politics surrounding that profound shift in global power are handled badly.

In essence, the world remains a dangerous place, although the level of threat varies from place to place and time to time. States still worry about their survival, which means that they have little choice but to pay attention to the balance of power. International politics is still synonymous with power politics, as it has been for all of recorded history. Therefore, it behoves students of International Relations to think long and hard about the concept of power, and to develop their own views on why states pursue power, how much power is enough, and when security competition is likely to lead to war. Thinking smartly about these matters is essential for developing clever strategies, which is the only way states can mitigate the dangers of international anarchy.

? QUESTIONS

1. Why do states in international anarchy fear each other?

2. Is there a reliable way to determine the intentions of states?

3. Is China's rise likely to look like Germany's rise between 1900 and 1945?

4. Does it make sense for states to pursue hegemony?

5. Why was the Cold War not a hot war?

6. Does it make sense to assume that states are rational?

7. Is balancing a reliable deterrent against aggressive states?

8. What is the security dilemma and is there a solution to it?

9. Is the USA a global hegemon?

10. Is unipolarity more peaceful than bipolarity or multipolarity?

11. Is realism relevant in contemporary Europe?

12. What is the tragedy of great power politics?

FURTHER READING

■ **Brown, M. E., Coté Jr, O. R., Lynn-Jones, S. M., and Miller, S. E. (2004) (eds),** *Offense, Defense, and War* **(Cambridge MA: MIT Press).** Contains key articles by structural realists, including Robert Jervis's seminal article, 'Cooperation under the Security Dilemma', *World Politics*, 1978.

■ **Copeland, D. C. (2000),** *The Origins of Major War* **(Ithaca NY: Cornell University Press).** Sophisticated brief for the claim that major wars are caused by sharp changes in the balance of power.

■ **Dickinson, G. L. (1916),** *The European Anarchy* **(New York: Macmillan Company).** Short, but brilliant book which introduced the concept of international anarchy.

■ **Dunne, T. and Schmidt B. (2004), 'Realism', in J. Baylis and S. Smith (eds),** *The Globalization of World Politics*, **3rd edn (Oxford: Oxford University Press).** An accessible chapter which charts the major debates within and about realism.

■ **Mearsheimer, J. J. (2001),** *The Tragedy of Great Power Politics* **(New York: Norton).** The most comprehensive statement of offensive realism.

■ **Posen, B. R. (1984),** *The Sources of Military Doctrine* **(Ithaca NY: Cornell University Press).** A smart book that explains the limits of structural realism for explaining military doctrine.

■ **Schmidt, B. C. (1988),** *The Political Discourse of Anarchy* **(Albany NY: State University of New York Press).** A history of the early years of the discipline of International Relations which shows the dominance of realism.

■ **Snyder, J. (1991),** *Myths of Empire: Domestic Politics and the International Ambition* **(Ithaca NY: Cornell University Press).** Excellent case studies on how the great powers behaved in the twentieth century from a defensive realist perspective.

■ **Van Evera, S. (1999),** *Causes of War: Power and the Roots of Conflict* **(Ithaca NY: Cornell University Press).** An important study which argues that the offence–defence balance explains much of international history.

■ **Walt, S. M. (1987),** *The Origins of Alliances* **(Ithaca NY: Cornell University Press).** Influential work on the prevalence of balancing behaviour in international politics.

■ **Waltz, K. N. (1979),** *Theory of International Politics* **(Reading MA: Addison-Wesley).** Seminal book that lays out the fundamentals of structural realism but with a defensive realist bent.

IMPORTANT WEBSITES

● Interviews with Robert Jervis, John Mearsheimer, Stephen Walt, and Kenneth Waltz.
http://globetrotter.berkeley.edu/conversations/alpha.html

● Introduction to realism.
www.geocities.com/virtualwarcollege/ir_realism.htm

● Coalition for a Realistic Foreign Policy attempts to push US foreign policy in a realist direction.
www.realisticforeignpolicy.org/

Visit the Online Resource Centre that accompanies this book for lots of interesting additional material. www.oxfordtextbooks.co.uk/orc/dunne/

Liberalism

DIANA PANKE AND THOMAS RISSE

Chapter contents

- Introduction
- Varieties of liberal approaches
- Case study
- Conclusion

Reader's guide

This chapter provides an overview of liberal theories of International Relations (IR). It identifies the importance of domestic politics and polities for the international behaviour of states as the common core of all liberal theories. While their intellectual roots can be traced back at least to Immanuel Kant's writings, 'second image' approaches – as they have also been called – have mushroomed in the discipline from the 1970s on. To make sense of the variety of liberal second-image theories in contemporary IR, this chapter categorizes them according to two dimensions. We distinguish between liberal theories that focus either on domestic actors or on domestic structures, and those that follow either rationalist or constructivist meta-theoretical assumptions. We illustrate their empirical usefulness with regard to the Second Iraq War of 2003. How do the various liberal theories explain why the USA went to war against Saddam Hussein, while Germany opted for peace?

Introduction

All classical liberal theories of International Relations rest on the core assumption that domestic actors or structures strongly influence the foreign-policy identities and interests of states as well as their actual behaviour in international relations. In theorizing identities, interests, and behaviour from the 'inside-out', liberal approaches consider domestic properties (actors, institutions, practices) as crucial explanatory variables (also referred to as 'independent variables'). In the terminology of Waltz's 'three images', or 'levels of analysis', through which to theorize international politics (Waltz 1959: 12f.), we argue that liberal theories of IR tend to be second image approaches. By second image, we mean explanations for international outcomes that are located at the level of the state. This is significantly different to third-image approaches to liberalism which focus on the impact of regimes and international organizations on unit-level behaviour. (This strand is known as neoliberalism and is dealt with in Chapter 6.)

The most prominent contribution of classical liberalism to International Relations theory is probably the proposition that democratic states keep the peace among each other. This proposition goes at least back to the eighteenth century and to the German philosopher Immanuel Kant who explicated the foundations of liberal thinking in 1795:

> **"** If the consent of citizens is required in order to decide that war should be declared . . . nothing is more natural than they would be very cautious in commencing such a poor game, decreeing for themselves all the calamities of war. Among the latter would be: having to fight, having to pay the costs of war from their own resources, having painfully to repair the devastation war leaves behind, and, to fill up the measure of evils, load themselves with a heavy national debt that would embitter peace itself that can never be liquidated on account of constant wars in the future. **"**

Kant 1795: 94–5

In linking the decision of waging war or maintaining peace to domestic structures instead of pressures emanating from the international level itself, Kant laid the foundations for what is now called the democratic peace. In liberal republics, elected decision-makers are held responsible for all decisions (including foreign policy) by their constituencies. Assuming that citizens are cost- and risk-averse, the shadow of electoral sanctions would prevent republican governments from going to war too easily. Yet, the number of democracies was very limited until the middle of the twentieth century. So was the number of international organizations, on which the second causal mechanisms of the hypothesis on perpetual peace rest (Kant 1795; see also Russett and Oneal 2001). Last but not least, the ideas of liberal economic theory according to which trade and economic interdependence contribute to peace (see e.g. Angell 1913) were put to rest by the First World War which was fought among economically interdependent states. Against this background, and especially after the failure of the League of Nations in the inter-war period, liberal approaches on peace among democracies or among liberal economies were regarded as utopian. Scholars such as E. H. Carr labelled and denounced them as 'idealist' contrasting them to realism as the proper way to theorize about the international system (Carr 1946).

The end of the Second World War and the ensuing wave of democratization could have brought back Kant's ideas on peace among democratic republics. Indeed, foreign-policy analysis had always included second-image assumptions and James N. Rosenau's work in particular adopted many of their themes (see e.g. Rosenau 1967; Rosenau 1969; overview in Carlsnaes 2002). Yet, in the wake of the Cold War, international politics was overwhelmingly conceptualized as responding to the pressures of the anarchic international system and the power rivalries between the Communist East and the Capitalist West. Realist balance of power theories of international relations were in vogue once again (see e.g. Waltz 1979).

This changed with the détente period of the 1970s and with the rise of the European Community as a supranational organization of liberal states. Scholars empirically explored and theorized the emergence of international cooperation in international organizations and regimes 'after hegemony' (Keohane 1984; Keohane and Nye 1977) as well as the increasing importance of non-state actors on the international level (Keohane and Nye 1971, 1974; see also Risse-Kappen 1995a). This period was also conducive to a renaissance of liberal thinking. Kant's basic argument fitted well to the perceived change of international reality in the 1970s: economic interdependence increased; international cooperation and international organizations spread; and democratization continued. Since all three developments facilitate perpetual peace according to Kant's hypothesis (Kant 1795; see Russett and Oneal 2001), democratic peace approaches became integral parts of various research programmes (e.g. Czempiel 1986b). In 1982 already, Jack Levy called the 'democratic peace' proposition the only 'law' we have found so far in international relations (Levy 1982; see also Doyle 1983).

In addition, the renewed interest in international cooperation, which gave rise to regime analysis (Krasner 1983; Keohane 1989; see also **Chapter 6** by Lisa Martin) soon abandoned the idea of states as unitary actors and facilitated the opening up of 'black box' states assumed by the realists (see **Chapter 4** by Mearsheimer for a structural realist 'black box' view of states). Robert Putnam's **two-level game** metaphor in particular reintroduced a research programme into the field which brought domestic politics back into the study of international negotiations (see Putnam 1988; Evans, Jacobson, and Putnam 1993; Moravcsik 1993a; Moravcsik 1997). While democratic peace approaches refer to domestic structures as independent variables, negotiation theories and foreign-policy analysis put emphasis on domestic actors and processes of national interest formation.

Varieties of liberal approaches

There is no such thing as a single theory of 'classical liberalism' in International Relations as a discipline. Rather, there is a multitude of liberal approaches. All second-image theories share the core assumption that the crucial variables in explaining the behaviour of states at the international level relate to the domestic level. Yet, there are more differences than similarities. Some approaches regard domestic actors, or the dynamics of their interactions in the societal, economic, and political spheres, as the most important explanatory factors, while others focus on political constitutions, on dominant ideologies, or on economic systems as domestic structures. There are also different dependent variables in second-image approaches: foreign-policy decisions of single states and dynamics of interactions between states. Taken together, we suggest that liberal theories can be distinguished alongside two dimensions (see Figure 5.1): theories of action and interaction, on the one hand, and the choice between structures and agents as ontological prior, on the other hand.

The first dimension distinguishes between rationalist and constructivist approaches. Rationalism and constructivism are no substantial theories of international relations (Adler 2002; Risse 2003b; see also Chapters 1 and 9). Rather they are meta-theories, resting on different assumptions on the nature and constitution of actors (Wendt 1999). At its core, rationalism is based on methodological individualism according to which the actor is prior to and can be studied independently of social structures. Actors' substantial interests are conceptualized as exogenously defined and fixed during interactions and it is presumed that human beings act according to a strategic rationality (Tsebelis 1990; Zangl and Zürn 1994). They calculate ends and means and act to maximize (or optimize) their given interests. Preferences over strategies of how substantial interests are best pursued can change, when new ideas on external constraints alter means–ends calculations. In line with these assumptions, institutions are regulative in nature. As opportunity structures, they do not shape actors' identities or interests but influence strategic choices and enable, sanction, or prevent certain actions.

Social constructivism, by contrast, is based on the ontological assumption that intersubjective meaning is constitutive for intentional action (Wendt 1987). The actor is not the ontological prior, but agent and structure are mutually constitutive (Wendt 1987, 1999). Intersubjective meanings influence and are constitutive for the selection and development of actors' substantial policy interests. They are created and change through, for example, communicative action. The possibility of changing intersubjective meaning, in turn, requires that substantial policy interests and identities are conceptualized as endogenous. They are not taken as given, but can change in the process of action and interaction itself. Unlike rationalism, constructivism regards institutions not as regulative but as constitutive in nature. Accordingly, institutions influence actors' identities and policy interests.

The second dimension for distinguishing different types of liberal approaches relates to the relevance attributed to different domestic features. While some liberal theories are actor-centred and emphasize domestic politics, others put stronger emphasis on domestic structures (the polity). Actor-centred approaches theorize the relevance of *domestic politics* for the foreign policy of states. In this perspective, states are not treated as unitary actors with interests determined by the structure of the international system (e.g. neorealism: security). Rather, state interests can vary across time and policy, because they are shaped by the interests, beliefs, or identities of domestic groups. Accordingly, actor-centred liberal theories analyse interest and ideational constellations of domestic groups and the processes through which they influence substantial policy interests of national decision-makers. In pluralist regimes, interests or beliefs of domestic actors are most often conflictual. Hence, different societal interest groups (such as business associations, trade unions, grass-root organizations, or domestic NGOs) compete for influence over the positions a state represents on the international level. This includes various lobbying processes such as arguing and framing ('constructivist mechanisms') or bargaining

Figure 5.1 The variety of liberal approaches

	Rationalism	Constructivism
Actor-centred ('domestic politics matters')	Liberal intergovernmentalism (Moravcsik 1993b, 1998)	Actor-centred constructivism (Checkel 1998; Sikkink 1993)
	Utilitarian liberalism (Freund and Rittberger 2001)	Ideational liberalism (Moravcsik 1997)[1]
	Two-level games (Putnam 1988; Evans, Jacobson, and Putnam 1993)	
Structure-centred ('domestic polity matters')	Rationalist democratic peace and interdependence theories (Rummel 1983; Bueno de Mesquita and Lalman 1992; Russett 1993;[2] Russett and Oneal 2001)	Constructivist democratic peace theories (Czempiel 1986a; Doyle 1983; Russett 1993; Risse-Kappen 1995b)

('rationalist mechanisms'). In sum, actor-centred liberal theories endogenize interests and beliefs of national foreign-policy-makers by highlighting interest and ideational constellations within the respective state.

Unlike actor-centred approaches, structure-centred theories focus not on domestic politics but on the *domestic polity*. The basic assumption is that the conduct of a state in interaction with other states is not guided by the structure of the international system, but strongly influenced by domestic structures, i.e. their social, economic, and political institutions. States are regarded as the most important actors in international affairs. Yet, they are not like-units behaving similarly in responding to international pressures and opportunities. Rather, states are differentiated by properties of their polity which influence state behaviour in their interaction with others. We can distinguish three structural dimensions. Besides the political structure (regime types such as democracy versus autocracy; type of democracy), domestic polities encompass economic and social structures. Economic structures are types of economic systems (e.g. capitalism versus command economy) and domestic social structures are commonly shared convictions on truth, rightfulness, or appropriateness (e.g. the commitment to human rights, different ideologies, identities).

The two dimensions are orthogonal to each other. Assumptions about rationalist or constructivist theories of action are independent from emphasizing domestic actors or structures as the major explanatory factors. Combining both dimensions generates a two-by-two matrix (see Figure 5.1).

Upper-left box: actor-centred rationalist liberalism

Liberal theories in the upper-left box are based on a rationalist theory of action and presume domestic politics as crucial for endogenizing, or 'internalizing', foreign-policy interests. The basic claim of these approaches is that domestic actors influence how states define their foreign-policy interests and how they behave in the international arena (Moravcsik 1993b: 480–5; see also Milner 1997, 1998; Freund and Rittberger 2001; Putnam 1988). Theorizing proceeds in two steps: (1) the formation of states' interests, and (b) the behaviour of states on the international level. Moravcsik's liberal intergovern-mentalism and Putnam's two-level game approach constitute prime examples of this approach.

In a first step, rationalist and actor-centred liberal approaches theorize in a bottom-up perspective how policy interests and 'win sets' of national actors (i.e. the extent to which an international agreement will be accepted by domestic constituencies) are shaped by domestic groups as strategic rational actors. Liberal approaches of International Relations assume that there is no basic distinction between domestic and foreign policy, whereby the latter would become the realm of 'high politics' left to the discretion of national leaders. Whenever the interests of societal actors are at stake, which is when they expect concrete benefits or costs, societal actors have incentives for self-organization and for influencing and shaping the interests of states. In pluralist systems societal actors compete with each other for access to and influence on national decision-makers. Domestic groups draw on existing channels of access and lobby politicians, in order to capture the state as agent for their particular interests (Moravcsik 1997: 519). Such aggregation processes require that national decision-makers are responsive to societal demands. In democracies, decision-makers have an incentive to be responsive to interest group lobbying. Since politicians are dependent on getting re-elected, they aim at avoiding electoral sanctions through responding to the demands of their constituencies. In the absence of competing societal groups and free elections, i.e. democratic political systems, liberal theory is less able to explain the domestic origins of state interests and preferences. At least, one would have to focus on the ruling groups in autocratic regimes in order to theorize foreign-policy interests 'from the inside out'.

In a second step, rationalist and actor-centred liberalism brings constraints of the international level back in. After interest formation, states turn to the international level. Here, state negotiators are faced with external constraints, since other states are likely to pursue different interests. Such constraints influence means–ends calculations of states as strategic rational actors and facilitate behavioural adaptations (e.g. changes in negotiation strategies such as coalition building, issue linkage, side payments, package deals). Some variants of liberalism assume that transaction costs are low, transparency is high, and information on the interests of others is more or less complete (Moravcsik 1997).

Others, such as the two-level game model (Putnam 1988), assume that the transparency of state interests is restricted, that the level of information is low, and that getting addi-tional information is expensive. This creates a dual 'veil of uncertainty' for international negotiations. First, national decision-makers are not familiar with the domestic politics of other states and do not know their margin of manoeuvre ('win-sets' in Putnam's model). Since each government must rely on the information signalled regarding win-sets of others, there is uncertainty over which concessions, demands, and compromises might be truly acceptable to others. Every government can cheat and signal false information on the restriction of its win-set ('tying hands-strategy', see Putnam 1988; Evans 1993). In referring to a particular domestic interest constellation, national actors might refuse unfavourable demands or concessions and push for compromises that more strongly reflect their win-sets. The second aspect of the veil of uncertainty relates to the assumption of incongruent interests of domestic actors and state actors. Especially if the transparency of international negotiations is low and domestic groups are excluded, incongruence matters. International negotiations empower state actors to the disadvantage of domestic actors. In cases in which international negotiations take place behind closed doors, domestic actors must rely on the information regarding possible compromises that is disseminated by their governments. Governments can use information asymmetry in order to pursue their own interests. They can justify negotiation outcomes in pointing to the distribution of other states' interest and bargaining dynamics. Thus, state actors can play a strategy of 'cutting slack' (Putnam 1988; see also Moravcsik 1993a) in order to increase their win-set *vis-à-vis* domestic interests.

In a nutshell, in two-level bargaining state actors can benefit from the 'strength of weakness' resulting either from domestic or from international constraints in order to strategically optimize interests.

Upper-right box: actor-centred constructivist liberalism

The upper right box of Figure 5.1 consists of actor-centred constructvist approaches. Unlike their rationalist counterparts, constructivist theories emphasize not only the importance of ideas, norms, and worldviews for actors' identities and interests, but also that decision-makers' perceptions, identities, and interests are shaped in domestic processes of social learning and norm diffusion (Diani 1996; Fischer 2003; Kodré and Müller 2003; Surel 2000). Social learning is the mechanism by which actors acquire new substantial policy interests (Checkel 1999: 548). In rationalist liberal accounts, domestic actors shape state interests via bargaining dynamics. Domestic groups can highlight potential electoral sanctions if national decision-makers are not responsive to their demands. In constructivist accounts, domestic actors and state actors participate in processes of mutual persuasion and arguing (see Risse 2000), while electoral sanctions and other threats are less relevant. In interactions between domestic groups and political actors, different perceptions of problems, ideas on solutions, and policy interests compete with each. Accordingly, constructivist liberal approaches focus on which argument of which societal group will ultimately be convincing and shape the outcome of social learning processes and national policy interests. In particular, they emphasize norm-entrepreneurs such as advocacy coalitions (Keck and Sikkink 1998) who engage in moral persuasion, but also knowledge-brokers and 'epistemic communities' (Haas 1992) who have privileged access to authoritative knowledge and use this authority to push forward certain political agendas.

In answering the question who wins the argumentative competition, actor-centred constructivist liberalism inquires into the conditions facilitating successful persuasion. In general, there are two different possibilities of approaching this question. First, one could analyse conditions under which agents are open for social learning (Risse 2000; Deitelhoff and Müller 2005; Elster 1992). The novelty and uncertainty of the environment might be conducive for learning, for example (Checkel 1999: 550; Elster 1992). In a rapidly changing environment, political decision-makers would have fewer prior beliefs and clearly defined substantial policy interests than in an environment that is largely settled. Second, the emphasis could be on which type of arguments and which type of ideas might be persuasive in different contexts. For example, constructivist studies on 'framing' highlight that social learning is facilitated when arguments resonate well with existing ideas, interests, and identities (Rein and Schön 1993: 161; Payne 2001: 39; Snow and Benford 1992: 138).

Lower-left box: rationalist democratic peace and interdependence theories

Democratic peace theories have probably become the most significant and also most politically influential version of liberalism in International Relations. The starting point is a dual empirical puzzle. First, democracies rarely go to war against each other (Russett 1993; Russett and Oneal 2001; Bueno de Mesquita *et al.* 1991; overview in Levy 2002). Second, democracies are not *per se* more peaceful than any other regime type, because they are frequently involved in wars with authoritarian regimes. Moreover, democracies tend to win the wars which they are fighting (Lake 1992). Thus, empirically speaking, the 'democratic peace' refers to a zone of peace among democracies which was more or less predicted by Immanuel Kant back in 1795 (Kant 1795/1983).

Yet, the empirical finding is one thing, a causal theory of the democratic peace is quite a different endeavour, since it has to deal with the dual puzzle and, thus, has to link the domestic with the international level. Rationalist democratic peace theories start from polity variables and highlight how a democratic constitution prevents rational decision-makers from going to war (at least against other democracies). There are two causal pathways on how governments are constrained by the democratic institutions.

First, the institution of free and fair elections prevents democratic governments from going to war against other democracies. Already Kant assumed that rational citizens privilege welfare and are generally cost-sensitive and risk-averse. He argued that they oppose wars not least because they ultimately bear the costs of wars (see quote on p. 90). Dissatisfied citizens might then impose electoral sanctions upon its governments. In order to avoid electoral losses, governments as strategic rational actors seek to satisfy citizens' demands. As a consequence, strategic rational governmental decision-makers avoid starting wars (Kant 1795; Owen 1996; Doyle 1983).

Second, power-dividing institutions prevent democracies from waging war (Morgan and Campbell 1991: 190–1; see Bueno de Mesquita and Lalman 1992 in particular). In this line of argumentation, rationalist democratic peace approaches highlight institutional and functional horizontal systems of checks and balances. The basic assumption is that regimes go to war, if they manage to build a domestic winning coalition. In authoritarian regimes, control mechanisms between the executive, the legislative, and the judicative branch are lacking. There are also no strong opposition parties offering alternative policies to the electorate and they do not systematically grant societal groups access to political arenas. Compared with authoritarian regimes, democracies require broader winning coalitions. Constructing winning coalitions under democratic institutional constraints is time-consuming. This prevents democracies from aggressive foreign-policy responses in international affairs and from going to war (Bueno de Mesquita and Lalman 1992; Morgan and Campbell 1991). When faced with other democracies that are equally constrained by their institutional set-up, they can observe these constraints because of the openness and publicity of democratic systems. This facilitates the democratic peace.

There are two problems with these explanations, though (see Müller 2002). First, the 'rational citizens in democracies' account is ultimately based on the cost-sensitivity of citizens. What about 'cheap wars' that can be fought by democracies because of profound power asymmetries? How do we explain the democratic peace when two democracies with vastly asymmetric power resources face each other (say, the USA and Canada)? Second, the 'democratic constraints' explanation fails to account for cases in which democracies were rather fast in deciding to go to war, particularly against authoritarian systems (e.g. several US military interventions during the Cold War).

More recently, scholars have taken up again arguments by Adam Smith and others formulated in the nineteenth century, namely that economic interdependence also leads to peace. The basic argument concerns the proposition that states that are interconnected through a high level of trade, capital flows, and foreign direct investment are also unlikely to go to war against each other, because war would disrupt interdependence and, thus, mutually beneficial welfare gains. While this argument has been dismissed because of the First World War which had been fought among economically interdependent states, it has gained some ground more recently (see Russett and Oneal 2001). But it remains controversial. At least, the findings pertaining to economic interdependence and peace do not seem to be as robust as the data on the democratic peace. There are also some indications that economic interdependence adds to peace among democracies rather than constituting a stand-alone finding (Barbieri 2002).

Lower-right box: constructivist democratic peace theories

Just like their rationalist counterparts, constructivist democratic peace theories seek to explain the dual puzzle of mutually peaceful, but generally warlike democracies. The basic argument of this branch of approaches is that democracies do not fight each other, because they perceive each other as friendly rather than hostile.

One set of arguments rests on the assumption that democratic norms facilitate peaceful conflict resolution in the domestic realm. Democratic regimes act from the presumption that other democracies are as peaceful as them. At the same time, democracies assume that autocratic regimes are as aggressive on the international level as they are towards their own citizens (Doyle 1986; Russett 1993: 31). As a consequence, democracies are thought to be aggressive against authoritarian systems but peaceful among themselves.

A second approach takes the above line of argumentation a step further. It adds a causal mechanism of how the perception of friends and foes develops and how it becomes institutionalized. The starting point is Wendt's observation that 'anarchy is what states make of it' (Wendt 1992). Accordingly, democracies do not just know that like-minded regimes are more peaceful than others – they learn it over time. A democratic polity matters, because public debate and democratic decision-making induce streams of communication (domestically and on the international level). Democracies recognize common norms and shared ideas on the appropriateness of peaceful conflict resolution (Risse-Kappen 1995b: 508). This facilitates a pattern of cooperative interaction, which in the longer run furthers the development of a common identity of democracies as 'part of us' (in-group) and as distinct from authoritarian regimes as 'them' (Risse-Kappen 1995b: 504–7; see also Owen 1997 on the significance of mutual perceptions as peaceful). These mechanisms of democratic norms leading to peaceful conflict resolution on the domestic level, and streams of communication and publicity on both domestic and international levels leading to a mutual perception as peaceful, are all absent when democracies face autocratic regimes. The latter are then constructed as 'out-group' leading to a vicious circle of hostile perceptions that are self-reinforcing.

The constructivist variant of democratic peace theory might also be able to explain a more recent empirical finding that challenges overly optimistic assumptions about a peaceful world order if only all states were democratic. Scholars working on democratic peace have always pointed out that it pertains only to stable democracies that have been around for a while (e.g. Russett 1993; Ray 1995). Mansfield and Snyder have shown recently that the democratic peace proposition does not hold in cases of democratic transitions. Many democratizing states actually fight wars, and the likelihood of militarized disputes increases rather than decreases when countries in transition to democracy are involved (Mansfield and Snyder 2002). Constructivist democratic peace theory offers an explanation for this finding. Since social learning takes time, newly democratizing states have not yet developed the mechanisms to perceive their neighbours as equally peaceful, and the neighbours might not yet be able to recognize the democratic character of democratizing states.

Case study: the Iraq War 2003 – probing liberal hypotheses

This section develops propositions taken from each of the four liberalisms described above. It then illustrates these propositions empirically with regard to one case, namely the US (and UK) decision in 2003 to wage war against Iraq, and the German opposition against the war (for a classical realist view on Iraq, see Chapter 3). Before we start, a short description of the case is in order.

The context of the war[3]

In 2003, the USA – together with the UK and other selected partners – invaded Iraq and replaced the authoritarian regime of Saddam Hussein by an occupation regime that was supposed to introduce democratic rule to the country. The USA had been in a long conflict with Saddam Hussein, dating back to the autumn of 1990 when Iraq had invaded Kuwait. At the time, and supported by the international community, another US-led coalition had driven Iraq out of Kuwait, thus restoring the status quo. Iraq had been placed under strict UN sanctions. These included intrusive inspections of its military and industrial facilities, which were found to have produced (nuclear) weapons of mass destruction. In 1998, Iraq threw the international inspectors out of the country. In 2002 and in the aftermath of 9/11, the USA pushed for another UN Security Council resolution in order to force Iraq to accept inspections once again – or else! Such a resolution was passed in the autumn of 2002, and Iraq complied. At the time, there was no consensus in the UN Security Council on what would follow. The USA, the UK, and others argued that force should be used in order to punish further non-compliance by the Iraqi regime. France, Russia, China, and Germany (as a non-permanent member of the Security Council at the time) were opposed. The Iraq case led to a major conflict between allies such as the USA and the UK, on the one hand, and France and Germany, on the other, who led the coalition against President George W. Bush's foreign policy. In the end, the USA and the UK decided to go ahead without a further legitimation by the UN, and invaded and conquered Iraq. How can we explain the different decisions by the USA and the UK (in favour of the war), on the one hand, and by France and Germany (against it), on the other? We use this case in the following, concentrating on the USA and Germany to illustrate empirically the four types of liberal approaches to International Relations introduced above.

Liberalism I: actor-centred and rationalist

As argued above, actor-centred rationalist liberalism theorizes international relations including foreign-policy decisions from the bottom up assuming instrumentally rational domestic actors that raise demands to their governments. Utilitarian liberalism argues, therefore, that actors pursue given material interests including (domestic) power maximization, but also economic gains (Freund and Rittberger 2001). Thus, political leaders seek power and want to remain in power, while societal actors pursue – above all – economic interests. Moravcsik has called the latter 'commercial liberalism' (Moravcsik 1997). Whenever domestic actors expect economic advantages or disadvantages resulting from domestic or international developments, they aim to shape their respective states' foreign-policy interests accordingly. Responsive governments pursue foreign policy in accordance with the economic interests of domestic actors.

Actor-centred rationalist liberalism would explain the decision by the USA to go to war against Iraq as well as the opposition of the German government as follows. As to the US, 'commercial liberalism' would probably argue that there was a strong domestic coalition in favour of the war composed of US conservatives in the Republican party, backed by business interests and the US military–industrial complex. In the aftermath of 9/11, the USA has, once again, become a national security state as a result of which the power of business interests related to the military vastly increased. But there were also strong business interests in gaining access to oil and other resources in Iraq and to lessen US dependence on Saudi oil. As to Germany, one would point to the strong opposition against the war in public opinion. Moreover, Chancellor Schröder was facing general elections in Germany at the time and exploited the anti-war opposition for electoral reasons. From this perspective, it was almost impossible to compromise at the international level (second step), in this case the UN Security Council. The domestic win-sets of the two opposing coalitions were simply too far apart and there was no 'zone of possible agreement' (see Putnam 1988). As a result, the USA and its allies went to war without international backing.

At first glance, this account goes a long way to explain the US decision to wage war against Iraq as well as the German opposition to it. There are two critical points to be made, though. First, it remains unclear whether, in fact, there was such a strong business coalition in favour of the war in the USA. While the oil industry, for example, is interested in gaining access to Middle East oil reserves, there is a sense in which the industry is agnostic about where the reserves are located. Moreover, to blame the military–industrial complex for the war against Iraq overlooks the substantial political and ideological interests in favour of the war. Second, it might well be that Chancellor Schröder exploited the opposition to the war for electoral purposes. However, this does not explain why there was such a strong resistance against waging war on Iraq on the European continent. In both cases, the explanation remains incomplete, unless we bring in ideational and ideological factors.

Liberalism II: actor-centred and constructivist

Actor-centred constructivism highlights the argumentative competition of various domestic actors in shaping national interests. Societal ideas are not just aggregated by states. In principle, social learning is a two-way street, because neither governmental *nor* societal interests are treated as given, but emerge out of the processes of societal interaction and communication. The liberal branch of actor-centred constructivism primarily focuses on how the perceptions, interests, and identities of national decision-makers are socially constructed and shaped by argumentative interactions with and among domestic groups. In addition, 'ideational liberalism' assumes that societal identities and values are essential in shaping states' interests regarding borders or issues related to citizenship (Moravcsik 1997: 525). In exchange for acting according to domestic identity-based interests and creating legitimate institutions, society supports the government (Moravcsik 1997: 525). Actor-centred constructivist liberalism assumes that domestic norm-entrepreneurs and knowledge-brokers promote normative and causal ideas. Especially under conditions of uncertainty their arguments are likely to shape state interests.

If we apply this argument to the Iraqi case, we would focus on the ideational and norm-ative reasons for the decision to go to war against Iraq as well as for the opposition against it. With regard to the USA, there was a strong 'neo-conservative' group with access to the highest level of decision-makers in the US administration. This group held strong ideo-logical views combining a liberal agenda of democracy promotion worldwide with sup-port for unilateralism and the use of US (military) power to further these 'liberal' goals (for details see e.g. Mead 2001; Risse 2003a). In particular, the neo-conservatives – among them Paul Wolfowitz, Deputy Secretary of Defense at the time – were convinced that lack of democracy and authoritarianism were at the root of the problems which the USA faced in the Middle East. They also thought that the USA should reduce its economic and political dependence on Saudi Arab oil. Finally, they accused the administration of President Bush Senior for not having 'finished the job' of getting rid of Saddam Hussein and his brutal regime back in 1991. Thus, we can use ideational liberalism in order to explain their motives and beliefs.

Moreover, this group can be regarded as norm-entrepreneurs, as odd as this might sound to European ears. But they did act as an 'advocacy group' for Iraqi regime change inside the US administration. They had access to the highest levels in Washington, includ-ing Vice-President Cheney, Secretary of Defense Rumsfeld, and President George W. Bush himself. 9/11 provided a 'window of opportunity' for the neo-conservative group. The terrorist attacks on the World Trade Center and their aftermath created the type of uncertainty that is necessary to make arguments carry the day (see above). As Woodward has shown in detail (Woodward 2004), the 'neo-cons' wasted no time, and immediately started lobbying for the use of force against Iraq. Their arguments resonated well with the President, since they combined a liberal agenda with strong moral and even religious beliefs. Moreover, President Bush did not need much persuasion to regard Saddam Hussein as an almost personal enemy of the Bush family. In sum, actor-centred and constructivist liberalism offers a plausible account for both the ideological beliefs of the neo-cons, but also of the process of persuasion inside the US administration that ultimately led to the decision to attack Iraq.

As for the Europeans, constructivist liberalism fills the gap in the actor-centred rationalist account presented above. Among the German public, for example, an aversion to war is deeply embedded in the national culture and the country's collective identity. As a result, German foreign policy has been characterized frequently as that of a 'civilian power' (Harnisch and Maull 2001). While the use of force is not excluded (cf. the German participation in the military interventions in the Balkans in the late 1990s as well as in Afghanistan in 2001), unilateralism is anathema and almost constitutes a national taboo. To override this deeply embedded sentiment, the German government would have had to mount a major campaign of persuasion against a huge opposition in public opinion – in an election year! No wonder that Chancellor Schröder quickly decided to exploit the anti-war sentiment for his political purposes (see above).

Liberalism III: rationalist democratic peace theories

As argued above, there are two branches of rationalist democratic peace theory, which we can quickly recapitulate here. One emphasizes democratic elections as a potential domestic sanctioning mechanism; the other highlights power sharing and dispersing institutions, and their impact on the size of winning coalitions necessary for waging war. The first line of reasoning states that the causal mechanism, which prevents democratizers from going to war too often, rests on the democratic institution of free and fair elections. Citizens are assumed to be cost-sensitive and risk-averse. Since they would bear the costs of wars, they oppose them and prefer a peaceful foreign policy. Democratic elections hold democratic governments accountable for their policy. Therefore, elections generate incentive-structures for governmental actors inducing greater responsiveness towards their citizens' demands. Due to a cost-averse and peace-minded constituency, strategic rational democratic governments avoid wars in order to circumvent electoral ex-post sanctions (Kant 1795).

The second line of reasoning focuses on the constraining effects of democratic institutions and the system of 'checks and balances' between the various branches of government that democracies have instituted (see above). As a result, it is exceedingly difficult to form the winning coalitions necessary to wage war in democratic political systems.

If we apply democratic peace theory in general and its rationalist version in particular to the Iraqi case, we face a number of hurdles. First, like all structural theories, democratic peace theory in general is indeterminate with regard to explaining specific foreign-policy decisions. It accounts for one strong finding – that democracies almost never wage war against each other – but it is rather weak when it comes to explaining specific foreign-policy decisions. Since Iraq under Saddam Hussein was an authoritarian regime, democratic peace theory only predicts that the prohibition against war does not hold in this case. Whether or not democracies then fight a war of aggression against autocratic regimes, is beyond the scope of 'dyadic' democratic peace theory (focused on understanding whether democratic states are less violent towards other democratic states).

Second, if we assume for a moment that the rationalist version of the democratic peace argument holds on the 'monadic' level (democratic states are less violent towards all other states) and, hence, can explain individual decisions to go to war out of the institutional characteristics of democratic systems, we are faced with some further problems. The German 'no' against the war would be consistent with both the Kantian electoral argument and with the 'institutional constraints' hypothesis. As argued above, German public opinion was strongly opposed to the war against Iraq, and the electoral sanctioning mechanism was, of course, very salient in 2002 when the government faced national elections. However, if the German case is consistent with the rationalist version of democratic peace theory on the monadic level, the US decision certainly is not. At least, we would have to explain how the George W. Bush administration managed to overcome all domestic hurdles against invading Iraq. If the US government faced any constraints before going to war, it was at the UN Security Council, not in the domestic arena. Congress in fact had given a *carte blanche* to the administration already in the autumn of 2002 and public opinion was essentially split on the issue. Thus, if the electoral sanction and the institutional constraints mechanisms are supposed to put a brake on decisions by democracies to go to war in each and every case (on the monadic level), these brakes were absent here. Rationalist democratic peace theory offers little guidance here and is not of much help.[4]

Liberalism IV: constructivist democratic peace theories

Constructivist democratic peace theories highlight how polity variables facilitate processes of communication, mutual learning, and identity creation. Since the causal mechanism of how polity translates into dyadic state behaviour is elaborated in Risse's version of constructivist democratic peace theories, we focus on this approach in greater detail (Risse-Kappen 1995b; see also Owen 1997; Müller 2002; Wendt 1999). The basic argument is that democracies learn through experience that similar polities abstain from violent conflict resolution. Democratic values and features such as transparency of decision-making, free elections, a political opposition with alternative policy-programmes, and a free press allows democracies to observe each other in greater detail. Through observing communicative streams, democracies can convince themselves of each other's capabilities and willingness of peaceful conflict resolution in domestic affairs.

None of these mechanisms of mutual observation and communication is present when liberal democracies deal with authoritarian regimes. As a result, they are perceived as members of the 'out-group', since they do not share the polity characteristics of democracies that gave rise to mutual learning processes in the first place. Consequently, democracies are more sceptical in interactions with authoritarian regimes. Perceptions of authoritarian regimes as potentially violent can facilitate alliance formation within the democratic 'in-group' and even aggressive foreign policies of democracies towards authoritarian states. If the mutual perception of peacefulness among democracies serves as a 'virtuous circle' and becomes a self-fulfilling prophecy when democratic systems deal with each other, a 'vicious circle' can develop when they face autocratic regimes. 'Othering' including the construction of enemy images might occur that helps democratic leaders to overcome potential opposition against war-making and the institutional constraints against the use of force built into democratic polities.

If we apply this line of reasoning to the Iraq case, the above disclaimer concerning the weakness of structural theories to explain single foreign-policy cases applies, too. However, since constructivist democratic peace theory is based on a structurationist ontology, it emphasizes the mutual constitution of agency and structure. Social structures do not fall from heaven, but they are reproduced, activated, and also changed by the daily practices of social actors (see Giddens 1984; Wendt 1987). Thus, it is easier to relate this argument to our particular case than applying rationalist democratic peace theory.

With regard to the US decision to invade Iraq, the constructivist version of democratic peace theory offers an account that adds to the points made above in the sections on actor-centred liberalism. What we need to explain in this case is how President George W. Bush's administration managed to overcome the electoral sanctions mechanisms and institutional constraints built into democratic polities as a brake on decisions to go to war. Saddam Hussein is almost a showcase for the 'othering' mechanism mentioned above leading to a vicious circle that removes the democratic restraints on war-making. The Iraqi leader had already been constructed as *the* enemy of the USA and of the free world in general back in 1990 when he had invaded Kuwait. It was George Bush Senior who had used the ultimate analogy to construct an enemy in post-Second World War democratic systems, by comparing Hussein to Hitler. Since Hussein had used chemical weapons ('gas') against Iran, the Kurds, and his own people, the Auschwitz analogy could be used, too. Public opinion in the USA largely shared that view of Saddam Hussein as thoroughly evil. When 9/11 occurred, US President Bush immediately framed the meaning of the event as 'war'. As a result, the US public perceived the country at war against terrorism. The final link in the social construction of enmity was the (false) claim that Hussein's Iraq was somehow linked to transnational terrorism (constituting part of the 'axis of evil'). If Hussein is Hitler, if he is linked to Al Qaeda, and if the USA is at war against terrorism, the constraints on a liberal democracy to wage war against such an enemy are all removed.

In contrast, none of these social constructions was available to policy-makers in Germany even if they had supported US policy. First, the Hussein = Hitler analogy never worked in the collective psyche of German public opinion. Post-Second World War democratic Germany had been built on the 'never again Nazism, never again war' supposition. Hitler and Auschwitz had been constructed as the ultimate evil that would be diminished as evil when compared to other evils. While Hussein was certainly regarded as one of the world's remaining tyrants (and a particularly bad one), comparing him to Hitler would have meant that Hitler and Auschwitz would not have been uniquely evil events, but could be compared to other crimes against humanity. Second, the post-9/11 framing of 'war against terrorism' did not resonate well in Germany. Given German experiences with its own domestic terrorism of the 1970s (the Red Army Faction), the frame available for Al Qaeda was one of fighting terrorism as a (particularly vicious) crime. In other words, fighting terrorism was constructed as an issue of domestic security rather than international security (for details see Katzenstein 2003). The 'securitization' of terrorism, therefore, had its limits.

Thus, German policy-makers (even if they had wanted to) could not frame war against Iraq the same way as the Bush adminstation was able to. Moreover, the US President's construction of 'counter-terrorism as warfighting' and Hussein = Hitler served only to strengthen opposition against the war in Germany. In sum, constructivist democratic peace theory can not only explain the variation in outcomes between the US decision and the German opposition, it also adds important elements to the more actor-centred

Figure 5.2 Theoretical propositions and empirical applications

Variant of liberal theory	Independent variables	Propositions	Empirical case scorecard: US choice for war German opposition
1. Actor-centred rationalist	Domestic power interests; economic interests	If economic and political interests of significant domestic actors regard war more beneficial than peace, governments most likely wage war.	USA: yes, but insufficient Germany: yes, but insufficient
2. Actor-centred constructivist	Normative ideas; arguing; norm entrepreneurs; and advocacy groups	If arguments of moral authorities support war and resonate well with prior beliefs of decision-makers, social learning facilitates decisions to go to war.	USA: yes, complements 1 Germany: yes, complements 1
3. Rationalist democratic peace theories	Electoral sanctions; institutional constraints	Risk-averse citizens will oppose costs of war and punish belligerent policy-makers. Institutional constraints impede domestic winning coalitions to go to war.	Problems with applicability because of structural focus: USA: no Germany: yes
4. Constructivist democratic peace theories	Mutual observation and communication leading to 'virtuous circle' among democracies and 'vicious' circle' with regard to authoritarian regimes	The more democratic polities regard other countries as part of the 'out-group', the more the democratic restraints on war-making fail.	Applicable because of structurationist ontology: USA: yes, complements 1 and 2 Germany: yes, complements 1 and 2

account mentioned above by emphasizing discursive structures and constructions available to decision-makers.

Figure 5.2 summarizes the four theoretical arguments used above and the application to the empirical case.

Conclusion

This chapter has introduced four variants of liberal theories of International Relations according to two dimensions. Actor-centred liberalism focuses on domestic actors and explains how their identities and interests shape foreign policies of states as well as international outcomes. Structure-centred liberalism emphasizes institutional features of, in particular, liberal states, in order to explain international behaviour. The most significant variant of such liberalism is democratic peace theory. Both actor- and structure-centred liberalisms can be further sub-divided according to their underlying ontologies, namely rationalism and constructivism. Rationalist liberalism explains behaviour on the basis of given interests of instrumentally rational actors that seek to maximize or optimize their utilities. Constructivist liberalism endogenizes identities and interests and also emphasizes mechanisms such as discursive constructions, framing, and arguing leading to social learning that results in shaping the interests of actors.

After introducing the four variants of liberal theories, we deduced their most important propositions suitable to empirical testing. We illustrated their usefulness with regard to an empirical case, namely the US decision to invade Iraq in 2003 as well as the German opposition to the war. We found that three of the four theories offer plausible accounts of these decisions that complement each other. Actor-centred rationalism highlights the power of domestic interest groups and provides a good starting point in explaining the differences between the USA and Germany. Yet, it overstates the coherence and power of economic interests and neglects the role of normative ideas and identies. Actor-centred constructivism nicely complements its rationalist counterpart. It shows how narratives were developed and how they were used to influence foreign-policy decisions in Germany and in the USA. Unlike actor-centred approaches, structure-centred democratic peace theories are best suited to explain patterns of war and peace rather than single foreign-policy decisions. If democratic peace theory is applied to the Iraq War, the rationalist variant cannot explain why the USA as a democracy waged war. The constructivist branch, by contrast, highlights the role of collective identites and historical memories in constructing in- and out-groups. It complements the actor-centred explanations in highlighting the interplay of framings and collective identities. The USA framed the war as a war against terrorism and constructed Hussein as enmity, while this frame did not resonate well with the German identity.

Liberal theories of International Relations are second-image accounts that theorize international politics from the bottom up. This chapter illustrated that these approaches provide fruitful explanations of International Relations. The variety of liberal approaches indicates that classical liberalism widely attracts attention and has constantly been refined.

DIANA PANKE AND THOMAS RISSE

Recently, two upshots have become prominent. The first concerns transnational relations and politics, defined as cross-boundary relations in which societal (non-state) actors such as multinational companies or civil society organizations are involved (see Keohane and Nye 1971; review in Risse 2002). While focusing on transnational relations had led to the study of interdependence in the 1970s and 1980s (e.g. Keohane and Nye 1977), the most recent scholarly developments in this area concern the study of globalization processes, but also of transnational social movements and advocacy groups (see e.g. Held *et al.* 1999; Keck and Sikkink 1998).

Second, back in 1978, Peter Gourevitch proposed to study second image reversed processes, i.e. the impact of international structures and processes on domestic institutions and processes (Gourevitch 1978). Second image reversed studies have become rather prominent recently in work on Europeanization, i.e. the domestic effects of European integration (see e.g. Cowles, Caporaso, and Risse 2001; Featherstone and Radaelli 2003; Börzel 1999). Moreover, globalization has also led to a renewed interest in the effects of global processes on the domestic fabric of political systems (see e.g. Milner and Keohane 1996; Rieger and Leibfried 2003; Scharpf and Schmidt 2000). Given the usefulness of the liberal second image theorizing examined in this chapter, and the increasing interest in globalization and second image reversed inquiry, liberal international theory focused on the examination of the nature of states and domestic politics, and their interaction with international processes, is set to remain central in International Relations theorizing and research.

? QUESTIONS

1. What is the defining core characteristic of liberal approaches to IR? Why is there no such thing as a single theory of 'classical liberalism'?

2. How did historical developments influence the evolution and prominence of liberal theories?

3. What is the difference between 'classical' liberal approaches and neoliberalism?

4. What is the common core of democratic peace approaches? What are the differences between rationalist and constructivist democratic peace theories?

5. What is the major criticism democratic peace theories pose to structural theories of IR (e.g. neorealist approaches)?

6. Why is the 'dual finding' of democratic peace puzzling? How can it be explained? Which democratic peace approach fits best?

7. What are the defining characteristics of two-level game approaches, and why are they in the same box as commercial liberalism?

8. Which two-level game hypothesis could explain the German position on the second Iraq War?

9. How would ideational liberalism explain the war in Iraq? Which foreign policy of which states can it explain best?

10. How would commercial liberalism and actor-centred constructivism explain the democratization of Eastern European and of Latin American states? Which theory offers a better account and why?

FURTHER READING

■ **Brown, M. E., Lynn-Jones, S. M., and Miller, S. E. (1996) (eds),** *Debating the Democratic Peace* **(Cambridge MA: MIT Press).** This reader brings together contemporary democratic peace research combining theoretical approaches and empirical illustrations.

■ **Bueno de Mesquita, B. and Lalman, D. (1992),** *War and Reason* **(New Haven CT: Yale University Press).** This book is a comprehensive work on rationalist democratic peace theory.

■ **Checkel, J. T. (2001) 'Why Comply? Social Learning and European Identity Change',** *International Organization,* **55/3: 553–88.** An important example of actor-centred constructivism, that explains how processes of social learning shape interests and identities.

■ **Doyle, M. (1997)** *Ways of War and Peace* **(London: Norton).** This book explains constructivist democratic peace theory and highlights how constructivist explanations add value to their rationalist counterparts.

■ **Kant, I. (1795/1983) 'To Perpetual Peace: A Philosophical Sketch', in** *Immanual Kant. Perpetual Peace and Other Essays on Politics, History, and Morals,* **edited by T. Humphrey (Indianapolis IN: Hackett Publishing, 107–43).** The earliest defence of the idea that democracies are less war-prone, a claim that has been popularized by many contemporary second-image liberal thinkers.

■ **Moravcsik, A. (1997), 'Taking Preferences Seriously: A Liberal Theory of International Politics',** *International Organization,* **51/4: 513–53.** This work provides a good overview of actor-centred rationalist approaches and develops liberal intergovernmentalism, a theory very prominent in European integration research.

■ **Putnam, R. (1988), 'Diplomacy and Domestic Politics. The Logic of Two-level Games',** *International Organization,* **42/2: 427–60.** This article is the classical and most prominent work on two-level games.

■ **Risse-Kappen, T. (1995) 'Democratic Peace – Warlike Democracies? A Social Constructivist Interpretation of the Liberal Argument' in** *European Journal of International Relations* **(special issue), edited by Nils Petter Gleditsch and Thomas Risse-Kappen: 489–515.** This article highlights explanatory gaps of rationalist democratic peace approaches and develops a constructivist variant of democratic peace theory.

IMPORTANT WEBSITES

● Correlates of War project. Provides several databases on inter- and intra-state wars. The project is hosted by several institutions, which collect and disseminate issue-specific data. The periods of the data covered vary among the single projects. Using the databases is free of charge.
www.correlatesofwar.org

● Index of International Governmental Organizations. The Northwestern University offers an extensive list of international governmental organizations (IGOs) including web links.
www.library.northwestern.edu/govpub/resource/internat/igo.html

● Freedom House database on domestic regime types. Contains information on the degree to which regimes are democratic.
www.freedomhouse.org

● Domestic Veto Player Index. The website of George Tsebelis (University of Carolina) provides free access to the veto player index. This index measures the composition of government in advanced industrial states. Besides the number of parties in government, the database contains information on the ideological position of the parties.
www.polisci.ucla.edu/tsebelis/

● The Comparative Political Data Set: pluralism and corporatism. This dataset is funded by the Swiss National Science Foundation and contains institutional and political data, including degrees of pluralism and corporatism for twenty-three democracies. It covers the period between 1960 and 2003.
www.ipw.unibe.ch/mitarbeiter/ru_armingeon/CPD_Set_en.asp

● Database on national elections in democratic countries (Lijphardt archive). Collects election results for twenty-six democracies until 2003. It contains information on more than 350 national legislative elections.
http://dodgson.ucsd.edu/lij/

 Visit the Online Resource Centre that accompanies this book for lots of interesting additional material. www.oxfordtextbooks.co.uk/orc/dunne/

6 Neoliberalism

LISA L. MARTIN

Chapter contents

- Introduction
- The development of neoliberal theory
- Rules versus power
- Principal-agent approaches
- Case study
- Conclusion

Reader's guide

This chapter presents the neoliberal approach to the study of international relations, some challenges to it, and how neoliberal theorists have responded. I focus on two significant themes in relation to the role played by international organizations. First, an understanding of how international organizations work requires that we specify the fundamental strategic problems they address. These problems include balancing potential gains from cooperation with short-term temptations to defect from agreements and encouraging beneficial exchange while limiting moral hazard dilemmas. International organizations also constantly balance political and economic interests. A second major theme, therefore, is the balance between rule-based interaction and the unconstrained exercise of economic and political power. I illustrate the approach with a case study on the International Monetary Fund's use of conditionality.

Introduction

Neoliberalism is a theoretical approach to International Relations that draws on concepts of rationality and contracting, and focuses our attention upon the central role of institutions and organizations in international politics.[1] The international political and economic environment is highly institutionalized, and international organizations (IOs) play an important role in the international distribution of wealth and power. Neoliberalism is a prominent approach to studying IOs and patterns of international cooperation more generally. This chapter presents the neoliberal framework while also noting some challenges to it, and the kinds of responses these have provoked among neoliberals.

Two major themes are discussed below. First, to understand the causes and consequences of IOs we must begin by specifying the fundamental strategic problems they address. In some issue-areas, for example international trade, states face large potential gains from reducing barriers to exchange, but also constant political pressures to renege on liberalizing agreements. Thus, IOs that address such issues confront dilemmas at the bargaining, monitoring, and enforcement stages. For other IOs, such as the international financial institutions, the basic problem is to encourage beneficial exchanges while avoiding moral hazard problems. As a result, these organizations constantly balance political and economic interests, and much research has treated IOs as principals of their state agents. A second major theme, therefore, is the balance between rule-based interaction and the unconstrained exercise of economic and political power.

I begin the chapter by providing some background on the development of neoliberalism. This discussion shows how neoliberalism developed out of older intellectual paradigms in the study of International Relations. Then I turn to focus on the rules versus power struggle, then the application of principal-agent approaches. The final section provides a case study of International Monetary Fund (IMF) conditionality, showing how the neoliberal approach can be applied.

The development of neoliberal theory

Intellectual background

The roots of neoliberalism can be traced to the early 1980s. Prior to this time, the study of international institutions and IOs was quite policy-oriented and descriptive, lacking an overarching analytical framework (Martin and Simmons 1998). This lack of a theoretical foundation meant that, although individual studies generated strong insights, they did not cumulate to create a coherent picture of, or debate about, the role of IOs in the world economy. This situation changed with the publication of an edited volume called *International Regimes* (Krasner 1983) and of Robert O. Keohane's book *After Hegemony* (1984). These books cast international institutions in a new light and suggested a novel explanatory framework for studying them and patterns of international behaviour more generally.

The puzzle that motivated this research began with two observations: that international economic cooperation in the 1970s was stable in spite of substantial shifts in the distribution of international economic power, and that organizations such as the Bretton Woods institutions and the General Agreement on Tariffs and Trade (GATT) were prominent features of the economic landscape. Keohane and others argued that these two observations were connected to one another, and that the existence of institutions and IOs explained the persistence of economic cooperation. In intellectual terms, neoliberals reacted to two well established theoretical traditions: neo- or structural realism and transnationalism. Neorealists (Waltz 1979) saw the international distribution of power as the dominant explanatory factor driving patterns of international cooperation (see Chapter 4). Those concentrating on transnational relations (Keohane and Nye 1971) rejected the neorealist assumption that states were the sole important actors on the international stage, suggesting that actors such as nongovernmental organizations might also have systematic effects on patterns of international behaviour. Neoliberals accepted a central empirical observation of the transnational school, that levels of international cooperation were much higher than could be explained by neorealist theory. However, they undertook to answer this empirical challenge by conceding to neorealism the claim that states were in fact the dominant actors, and that states made decisions in a rational and strategic manner. In effect, neoliberals were able to make intellectual progress by adding a focus on institutions onto the neorealist framework (for other liberal approaches in IR, see Chapter 5).

The fundamental logic of neoliberalism is summarized in Keohane 1982.[2] In order for states to cooperate, they must overcome a range of collective-action problems, many of which are rooted in transaction costs. No external enforcement exists in the international system, so any agreements must be self-enforcing. This means that states must find ways to avoid temptations to cheat, for example by reneging on agreements to encourage trade by erecting protectionist barriers. Avoiding such temptations requires high-quality information about the actions and preferences of other states, and about the likely consequences of cheating on agreements. In addition, states must coordinate their actions, for example agreeing on common technological and public-health standards. IOs provide forums in which states can mitigate collective-action problems that threaten stable patterns of cooperation. IOs can perform monitoring functions, providing assurance that others are living up to the terms of their commitments. They are forums for negotiating to resolve coordination problems, and to learn about the preferences and constraints facing other governments. They create structures for enforcement and dispute resolution, although actual enforcement powers typically remain in the hands of member states.

Through these functions, IOs become a valuable foundation for international cooperation. Thus patterns of cooperation can be more resilient in the face of underlying shifts in power and interests. The initial work applying this neoliberal or contractual view of institutions concentrated on international regimes, defined as sets of principles, norms, rules, and decision-making procedures (Krasner 1982). One advantage of examining regimes, as compared to the earlier focus on individual IOs, is that this shift allowed researchers to consider informal institutions as well as formalized bodies. While in more recent years much attention has shifted back to formal IOs, such as the Human Rights

Commission or the World Trade Organization, there is an implied relationship between the informal norms which sustain cooperation in the global economy and the work on individual organizations today.

The neoliberal perspective relies on the assumption of rationality. That is, a core assumption of neoliberal theory is that states calculate the costs and benefits of different courses of action and choose the course of action that gives them the highest net pay-off. The assumption of rationality is a powerful one, allowing theorists to develop clear models and predictions about patterns of behaviour. It is also flexible enough to allow for substantial variation in the considerations that go into state decisions. For example, rational decision-making can encompass very different sorts of preferences: some states might put great weight on economic benefits, while others are driven more by security concerns. It also allows actors to put different weights on immediate versus long-term pay-offs, depending on their circumstances. The rationality assumption leads us to focus on strategizing, as actors take into account how their actions will lead to reactions by others, and recognize that their ultimate pay-off will depend on the interaction of multiple state strategies.

There are certainly limits to the reliance on rationality as a core assumption, and these limits have given rise to alternative theoretical perspectives such as constructivism. The assumption of rationality does not tell us what state preferences are. Specifying the content of preferences typically requires a specific complementary model (which may focus on material benefits or other sources of costs and benefits). At times extremely complex situations may mean that pure strategizing does not accurately characterize the process of decision-making; then alternative models such as those relying on bounded rationality may be superior. If actions are not driven by calculation of expected costs and benefits, but instead by role-playing or affective considerations, the rationality assumption will be a poor guide to actual behaviour. These alternative core assumptions are discussed in other chapters in this volume, particularly Chapter 9 on constructivism.

Critiques of neoliberalism

While neoliberal research on international regimes represented a major step forward in the analysis of international institutions, it was subject to criticism from a number of alternative perspectives. Friedrich Kratochwil and John Ruggie (1986) worried that neoliberal regime analysis was moving too far from the analysis of specific IOs, thus missing some important internal organizational dynamics. Stephan Haggard and Beth Simmons (1987) surveyed a number of weaknesses from the perspective of those undertaking positive empirical research on regimes. Because the concept of regimes was broadly defined and regimes are difficult to observe independent of their effects, much effort went into determining whether or not regimes actually existed in various issue-areas, and whether changes in patterns of behaviour reflected changes *within* regimes or *of* regimes. It is not clear that these descriptive debates about changes *within* versus *of* added a great deal to our understanding of the causes and consequences of institutions in the international environment.

Another weakness in the neoliberal literature is its state-centric focus, reflecting a neglect of domestic politics. In their desire to respond directly to neorealists, neoliberals accepted their assumptions that states were the dominant actors in international politics and that domestic politics did not have systematic effects on patterns of international cooperation. Amending this assumption to introduce domestic politics in a rigorous manner has been one of the challenges facing neoliberal theorists in recent years.

In another critique, Giulio Gallarotti (1991) argued that IOs systematically failed in their attempts to manage difficult problems in international relations. The inability of IOs to resolve serious conflict, in his analysis, reflected not just random mistakes, but a systematic pattern of failure. IOs could even have perverse effects, exacerbating conflict rather than mitigating it. For these reasons, Gallarotti argued against relying too heavily in formal IOs to manage international relations.

One of the most telling critiques of the neoliberal regimes literature came, perhaps paradoxically, from the editor of the *Regimes* volume, Stephen Krasner (1991). He charged that the work on regimes was too focused on market failures: instances where all could potentially benefit from mutual cooperation, but where collective-action problems such as high transaction costs prohibited states from reaching the 'Pareto frontier', the set of arrangements from which it is not possible to make any one actor better off without harming others. In his survey of efforts to cooperate in the field of communication, Krasner found that states had little trouble reaching the Pareto frontier. Instead, they found themselves trapped by distributional conflict, having to choose among bargains that benefited some while harming others. Thus the most significant problem plaguing efforts at international cooperation was not providing a good contractual environment to overcome transaction-costs problems such as informational limitations, but a coordination problem. Krasner's insight has led to a revision of early work on regimes, which claimed that coordination problems would be relatively easy to solve (Stein 1982). A new focus on how institutions might help in resolving coordination problems has added depth to our understanding of the functions of IOs (Morrow 1994; Oatley and Nabors 1998).

Neoliberal responses

In the 1990s, the neoliberal theory of international institutions became deeper and richer, partly in response to such critiques. Keohane (1990) brought the concept of multilateralism back into the study of institutions. He defined multilateralism simply, as cooperation among three or more states. This work served to redirect attention to variation among types of institutions, a highly productive move for the field.

Another debate arose regarding the problem of compliance with the rules of IOs and with international agreements more generally. A managerial school, representing primarily the views of legal scholars, argued that states generally wanted to comply with international rules, and that variation in compliance was therefore not a compelling puzzle (Chayes and Chayes 1993). Neoliberals responded by noting that the managerial argument was plagued by selection bias: if states almost always complied with the rules, it was likely because they would only accept rules that demanded minimal changes in their patterns of behaviour. The appropriate question, therefore, was not so much compliance as how different structures of rules would promote far-reaching changes in behaviour that left states open to exploitation, or 'deep cooperation' (Downs, Rocke, and Barsoom 1996). Interestingly, both the managerial and neoliberal schools agreed on the conclusion that variation in patterns of compliance was not a terribly important or interesting question, although they came to this conclusion by different paths. The managerial school argued that little variation in compliance could be observed because states are obliged to comply. The neoliberal analysis of compliance argued that minimal observed variation in compliance simply reflected the fact that states are unlikely to make commitments on which they intend to renege. Nevertheless, empirical research on variation in compliance has continued, leading to some intriguing findings (Brown Weiss and Jacobson 1998; Simmons 2000).

Other theoretical developments within neoliberalism focus on the form and design of IOs. One body of work asks why IOs are becoming more 'legalized': they more often incorporate legalistic features such as third-party dispute settlement (Goldstein *et al.* 2000). Researchers have begun to explore the advantages and possible disadvantages of legalization for promoting international cooperation. Another body of work focuses on design principles for IOs. Starting from the assumption that IOs are designed to resolve collective-action problems, analysts have derived a number of hypotheses about the form of IOs (Koremenos, Lipson, and Snidal 2001). For example, if states design an IO to reduce the transaction costs of monitoring members' behaviour, we would expect the organization to have relatively centralized monitoring capacities. Using logic like this, dimensions of IOs such as their centralization and autonomy from member states can be explained.

Overall, these developments suggest that one of the first questions to be asked when studying a particular organization is about the problems it was designed to address. An understanding of these issues then leads to predictions about the form and functioning of the organization, and about its effects on political outcomes. In practice, application of this neoliberal framework has directed attention to the relative influence of rules versus power in institutionalized settings, and to the role of IOs as agents. The next two sections elaborate these two perspectives.

Rules versus power

Bargaining

In general terms, the story of the institutionalization of international relations can be described as a continuing struggle between attempts to negotiate and enforce consistent norms and rules, and the desire of powerful states to exert their influence over outcomes. Whether we consider the process of bargaining, of dispute resolution, or the use of institutional loopholes, what we see is a struggle over the terms of political and scholarly debate. As the works discussed in this section suggest, while there are large potential benefits to be gained from consistently enforced rules evidence suggests that many political outcomes continue to be heavily influenced by power politics.

As the neoliberal framework described above suggests, the first step in analysing an IO is to identify the fundamental problems it needs to address. Many political issues, such as international trade, present a classic strategic problem and can be modelled as a **Prisoners' Dilemma** (PD). Using trade as an example, we know that impediments to trade are costly, decreasing the aggregate welfare of states by increasing costs to consumers, depriving exporters of markets, and generally distorting the allocation of economic resources. Thus, decreasing impediments to trade offers aggregate welfare benefits for states. Jointly moving away from a situation of high levels of protection for domestic producers is a mutually beneficial move for states as aggregate entities. However, this does not mean that every individual within these states will benefit from freer trade. In particular, domestic producers who will be forced into increased competition from imports will not benefit from trade liberalization, and will lobby their government for continued protection (Grossman and Helpman 1994). Thus, governments face continual pressure to renege on the terms of trade agreements, providing protection for injured domestic actors. Similar considerations apply when we look at other issues, such as environmental negotiations, regulation of financial relations, or alliance politics.

IOs that address PD situations thus have to face two fundamental problems. First, they must structure and facilitate international bargaining. By creating a framework in which negotiators can agree on the specifics of politics, institutions can do much to enhance international cooperation. Second, they must set up mechanisms to encourage states to live up to the terms of these agreements – I will focus on this problem in the next section.

Consider first an example of the bargaining problem. Kyle Bagwell and Robert Staiger (1999) offer a general economic theory of the structure of the World Trade Organisation (WTO) which structures the global trade regime, based on an analysis of the bargaining problem. Their analysis provides a good example of how a neoliberal analyst would approach bargaining problems. The authors begin from the observation that the only feasible and self-enforcing bargains on international trade are those that preserve the existing terms of trade: if deals change the terms of trade, at least one of the parties to the bargain will refuse to live up to it.[3] The structure of the WTO is thus designed to promote liberalization – reduction in barriers to exchange – while maintaining existing terms of trade.

From a neoliberal perspective, a major question about bargaining is whether the institutional structure itself influences the outcomes. Compared to unstructured, ad hoc bargaining, does the WTO structure lead to outcomes that protect the interests of smaller states, for example? Does it encourage greater liberalization? Both could well be true. The fact that small states are engaged in various ways in each negotiating round, and have to approve the final agreement, could give rise to more respect for their interests. One advantage of multilateral, structured negotiations is that they enhance the scope for mutually beneficial deals, compared to bilateral bargaining.

These neoliberal hypotheses have been subjected to empirical investigation. On the outcomes of bargaining, Richard Steinberg (2002) finds that the WTO structure (and its forerunner, the General Agreement on Tariffs and Trade) has not demonstrably promoted the interests of developing countries. He argues that each bargaining round begins with a law-based process designed to give account to the interests of all participants. However, the conclusion of a round involves tough deal-cutting, and has generally been dominated by powerful states. Thus, the USA and European Union (EU) have dominated the agenda, in spite of the attempt to use rules to craft a more equitable consensus. A contrasting view is presented by Christina Davis (2003) who finds substantial support for the proposition that multilateral bargaining leads to greater liberalization than a bilateral setting.

Concentrating on agriculture – one of the toughest trade issues – she demonstrates that trade conflict between the USA and EU or Japan is resolved in a manner that promotes liberalization when bargaining takes place in a multilateral setting. Davis attributes this outcome to the potential for issue-linkage as well as legal framing and reputation.

Enforcement

The other major problem to be resolved by an IO addressing a PD is to assure that states will uphold the agreements they reach. Because of the constant political pressure to deviate from the terms of cooperative agreements, governments are tempted to renege or simply fail to fully implement the measures agreed on. As the neoliberal framework suggests, we are unlikely to see institutions directly empowered to enforce agreements in order to overcome these temptations. However, they can nevertheless play a substantial role in facilitating decentralized enforcement. We see institutions developing strong monitoring and dispute-resolution mechanisms, and standards for punishment of those who defect from agreements, in response to these challenges.

On the one hand, information must be widely available about whether states are living up to the terms of their commitments. Here, institutions face a relatively easy challenge if many private (and public) actors are highly motivated to monitor what other governments are doing. This is often the case in trade for example, because if an exporter is finding it more difficult than expected to sell to a particular country or is losing market share, this actor has high incentives to discover any violations of international agreements by competitors. In addition, the structure of punishment procedures creates incentives for producers for the domestic market to uncover violations as well. Thus, the rather ingenious but simple punishment scheme typically used in trade agreements facilitates 'fire-alarm' monitoring mechanisms; little direct oversight by the organization itself would appear necessary (McCubbins and Schwartz 1984).

However, in other issues observation of compliance is more difficult, as private actors may not be able to play this fire-alarm role. In such cases, governments must play a more intrusive monitoring role. This is most prominently true in areas like arms-control agreements, which include extensive provisions for government monitoring. In addition, governments have become adept at non-obvious forms of reneging from agreements. As a result, we see that as the trade regime has developed over time it has gained enhanced monitoring capacities, now undertaking regular systematic reviews of members' practices.[4]

Both economists and political scientists have focused on dispute-resolution mechanisms of IOs. Economists, like lawyers, typically ask whether a dispute-resolution mechanism is optimal from the perspective of global welfare (Bütler and Hauser 2000; Hudec 1993; Jackson 1998). They also ask whether, as structured, it is effective in reaching this goal. Studies of the WTO, the most widely studied dispute-resolution mechanism, generally find that, while the WTO mechanisms are not fully optimal, over time the development of these mechanisms has been moving in the right direction. Rules that allowed the blatant exercise of state power, such as the ability to veto panel decisions, have been phased out. It has become easier for states without extensive legal and administrative capacities to initiate the dispute process. Overall, as the system has become more institutionalized and legalized, in normative terms it has come closer to meeting the demands of economic efficiency. However, the evidence on whether these new rules are in fact operating as intended remains quite mixed.

Political scientists, in contrast to the normative focus of economists, tend to focus on the distributional effects of dispute-resolution mechanisms, for example whether they tend to favour larger or smaller states. This leads them to consider questions such as which states bring complaints more often and against whom. They also focus on the patterns of settlement, asking which cases are resolved early and which go through the full process, and attempt to make judgements about which states most often prevail in these disputes. Marc Busch (2000) has focused on the formation of dispute-settlement panels in the WTO, asking which cases actually escalate to the panel stage as opposed to being settled at an earlier stage. This question is fundamental, because the evidence shows that the threat of future legal proceedings tends to generate larger levels of concessions if disputes are settled early; states are threatened as much by the process itself as by the actual decision (Reinhardt 2001). However, Busch finds that changes in procedures have not substantially altered panelling outcomes. Busch and Reinhardt (2003) similarly find that improved WTO procedures have not, in fact, allowed poor countries to achieve better outcomes. Instead, wealthier countries have tended to do better, suggesting that the capacity to litigate is an important component of success. Overall, the theoretical and empirical studies of the GATT/WTO suggest that the demands of politics and power continue to strongly influence international trade outcomes, in spite of higher levels of institutionalization over time.

Institutional design and effects

Issues of institutional design and its effects have dominated studies of bargaining and dispute resolution. One specific issue of institutional design, across both global and regional institutions, is the conditions under which states can 'legally' evade IO rules, at least on a temporary basis. Downs, Rocke, and Barsoom (1996) developed a general model of international cooperation in the face of domestic political uncertainty that provides great insight into this problem. When governments negotiate agreements, they know they will face political pressure to renege on these agreements. However, they do not know with certainty how intense these pressures will be or from which sectors they will come, because these pressures are subject to exogenous shocks and shifting patterns of political mobilization. If unexpectedly intense demands to renege emerge, governments may find that they are better off acceding to these demands and withdrawing entirely from deals. However, if they were instead allowed the option of temporarily backing out of their commitments in the face of unusually high political pressures, the regime could survive and make all better off than if these 'pressure valves' did not exist. Thus, the authors argue that a certain level of 'optimal imperfection' should be observed in agreements that have this political structure.

From a neoliberal perspective, this analysis suggests that the design of escape clauses and related loopholes is of vital importance to the success of many IOs. Scholars have picked up on this idea and developed arguments about the appropriate design of such loopholes. Rosendorff and Milner (2001) show that escape clauses enhance the durability and stability of trade institutions in the face of domestic political uncertainty. However, to prevent the abuse of these clauses, states must bear a cost for using them. This 'self-enforcing penalty' appears to be reflected in various dimensions of the WTO, for example, requiring offsetting concessions for the use of escape clauses. Barbara Koremenos (2001) considers the flexibility built into agreements in more general terms. She sees the fundamental problem as one of assuring a certain distribution of gains across states, rather than a response to unexpected domestic pressures. This sort of uncertainty explains the incidence of renegotiation provisions in many agreements, among other institutional features.

In many ways, the design and functioning of IOs reflects the basic strategic dilemmas they face. Promoting beneficial exchanges requires that institutions structure bargaining, monitor compliance with commitments, and provide enforcement mechanisms. We also see that the ongoing struggle between rule-based interaction and the exercise of power plays out continually. While rules attempt to constrain the processes of bargaining and dispute resolution, the best empirical studies confirm that the actual functioning of institutions reflects continuing realities of power politics. I next turn to consider another major theme of the recent neoliberal literature, the application of principal-agent approaches.

Principal-agent approaches

Consideration of the fundamental strategic problems that IOs confront has led many analysts to use a principal-agent framework to study them. Scholars ask about the relative freedom of manoeuvre available to IOs, given patterns of state interests. This problem is played out in an ongoing battle between rules that attempt to constrain state behavior and the continual exercise of state power.

A common strategic problem that IOs confront is to provide assistance to allow states to overcome short-term problems, while not providing an 'easy out' that will allow states to avoid adopting responsible policies. An example of this dynamic may be seen in peacekeeping, where the immediate advantages of having peacekeepers on the scene to reduce levels of violence are obvious, but at the same time the presence of peacekeepers may allow the conflicting parties to put off tough negotiations for a settlement. The tension between providing assistance and encouraging **moral hazard** is prominent in financial interactions. In any financial transaction, institutions need to walk a fine line between encouraging the provision of funding that will be beneficial for both the borrower and the lender and encouraging moral hazard. Consider the typical case addressed by the IMF. A country has fallen into a financial crisis, either through poor policy or exogenous shocks. The government finds itself unable to make good on its commitments to make payments on its outstanding debt, and the value of its currency is collapsing. If the roots of the crisis will pass, the provision of temporary financing will both benefit the country that receives the financing and lenders, who will be likely to recover more of their assets once the crisis has passed. However, a government that knows that it will be bailed out of such crises is likely to behave more recklessly, adopting inappropriate policies and overborrowing. This is the moral hazard dilemma.

IOs can address the moral hazard problem by imposing conditions on their assistance, attempting to force states to adopt more responsible policies. How this logic works in the IMF case will be explored more fully in the next section. Conditionality itself is contentious and subject to the battle between rules and power described above. This basic strategic problem – potential benefits from assistance, but a moral hazard problem – has led many scholars to use a principal-agent framework to study IOs. This approach is appropriate and useful because it allows us to ask about the likelihood that an IO will err on one side or the other. Will it follow the demands of powerful states and provide 'too much' assistance, thus exacerbating the moral hazard problem? Will it be autonomous enough to find an optimal path between moral hazard and assistance? Or will it be autonomous, but driven by its own bureaucratic logic?

In a principal-agent framework, the members of an IO, especially the most powerful states, are treated as the principals that use the IO to implement their preferred policies. IOs, as agents, have their own interests. Usually these are assumed to be relatively 'techno-cratic' interests, not as driven by politics as those of member states. The question is then the extent to which IOs can pursue their own agenda, as opposed to responding to the specific demands of their principals. The ongoing tug-of-war between rules and power describes the dynamics of most IOs. The general principal-agent literature gives rise to a number of propositions that can be applied to IOs. For example, greater divergence of interest among principals tends to increase agent autonomy; and greater agent expertise or access to information also tends to increase their autonomy.

Applications

Many applications of a principal-agent approach attempt to trace patterns of member-state influence on IOs. Strom Thacker has argued that the IMF's patterns of lending respond to the geopolitical interests of the USA, its dominant member (Thacker 1999). The 'public choice' school has studied the IMF as a self-interested organization attempting to assert itself in the face of constant political demands from its powerful member-states. This work, like Thacker's, illustrates that these states are often able to exert substantial influence over the IMF's activities. Thus, while the IMF is an agent with some autonomy, it has a hard time escaping its political confines. Dreher and Vaubel (2004) apply this analysis to examine the evolution of conditionality over time, asking about the content and number of conditions imposed. They demonstrate that the IMF can usefully be studied as a bureaucracy with its own internal rules and interests. In this sense, they posit that it has more autonomy than others have recognized. They reason that an autonomous IMF should impose stringent conditionality on states that have a poor record of living up to past commitments, and find evidence to support this argument. Overall, the evidence suggests that the IMF is an agent constrained by the political interests of its principals, but one that is able to exert autonomy under certain conditions.

Other scholars, working within the same general principal-agent framework, focus on the delegation of authority to IOs. They ask why states would choose to allow IOs what appears to be a substantial degree of autonomy. Some analysts find that delegation has not undermined the interests of the most powerful member-states, as delegation is itself a strategy for promoting these interests. For example, Daniel Nielson and Michael Tierney

(2003) demonstrate that the World Bank's environmental policies correlate highly with measures of the environmental interests of the USA. (For a discussion of environmental issues and theories from a green theory perspective in IR, see Chapter 13.) On the other hand, Erica Gould (2003) is more sceptical about the ability of member-states to maintain control over IO actions once they delegate authority. She argues that the IMF, in its use of conditionality, often responds to private financial actors rather than state interests.

Some argue that the autonomy of the IMF, which wishes to loan large amounts of money, causes conditions not to be enforced and undermines programmes (Vaubel 1986). Randall Stone (2004), however, has presented persuasive evidence that the fundamental problem is the reverse: that the Fund's principals frequently intervene to promote leniency towards favoured states. This persistent influence of political pressures means that the conditions the IMF so painstakingly negotiates are rarely imposed with any consistency or credibility. Thus, the problem with IMF programmes is not that they are poorly designed or based on an inappropriate economic ideology. It is that even well designed programmes are not enforced. Thus, we find that the struggle between political influence and rule-based behaviour defines the impact of the IMF on the world economy.

The neoliberal perspective has given rise to insights about the design of the IOs, particularly focusing on issues of delegation and influence. Some have critiqued this view of the IOs, arguing that it underestimates the autonomy of their staff. Through the exercise of authority that is perceived as legitimate, especially if it has the veneer of science, IOs may in fact be able to pursue agendas that have little relationship to the interests of either major donors or borrowers (Barnett and Finnemore 2004). This is likely to be especially true in areas that require high levels of technical expertise, such as financial, health, or environmental issues. This line of analysis presents a potentially strong threat to the entire neoliberal framework, as it conceives of a very different relationship between states and institutions. For example, it suggests that we should spend much more time analysing processes of socialization within institutions (see Johnston 2001).

Case study: IMF conditionality

The IMF was created at the end of the Second World War at the Bretton Woods conference. Initially, the main purpose of the IMF was to oversee the functioning of a fixed exchange-rate regime. In order to make this regime work, the IMF was to organize short-term support for members that were facing balance-of-payments crises. Over time, the exchange-rate regime fell apart. However, by then the IMF had proven itself valuable at providing relief for states facing balance-of-payments crises, and has continued to play the central role in these situations. This section will briefly illustrate how one would apply the neoliberal framework to the use of IMF conditionality, showing how the balance between rules and power, and the application of a principal-agent approach, lead to important insights.

While initially some IMF members opposed the use of conditionality in its lending, arguing that the organization's role was to provide funding as needed, the major creditors (especially the USA) have insisted on imposing conditions. The number and types of conditions has expanded substantially over the years. Governments wishing to conclude a programme with the IMF must typically commit to reduce public spending, increase collection of taxes, liberalize their international economic relations, and even improve other areas of governance. Even if they are economically justified, there are occasions on which the major creditor states would prefer looser conditions for purely political reasons. For example, it is widely understood that the USA opposed the imposition of tough conditions on Russia in the early 1990s, wishing to assure Russia's political stability. In addition, states that are home to private creditors with substantial exposure in the crisis country are likely to prefer looser conditions and flows of capital.

To illustrate how one would apply a neoliberal approach, assume a simple one-dimensional space over which member-states make decisions. In the case of the IMF, we could think of this continuum as ranging from loose conditions on drawings to rigorous conditions. States' preferred outcomes will array themselves along this continuum. I assume that the IMF staff also has a preference on this spectrum. States' preferences will be influenced by both economic and political factors. They will be concerned about the economic consequences of programmes for the international financial system, but also about their political relationship with borrowers. As the IMF staff are not directly responsible to any particular member-state, being made up of international civil servants, I assume their preferences are driven primarily by economic considerations.

In order to generate some explanatory leverage from this set-up, assume that the staff have a right to make a proposal and that it is approved by majority vote. In the IMF case, the states are represented by executive directors who make up the Executive Board (EB). One important question is whether states can amend staff proposals, or whether they are presented with a take-it-or-leave-it offer. Technically speaking, the Board has the right to do whatever it wants, and so could amend proposals. But, in practice, amendments would be controversial and cumbersome, subject to charges of political interference. Because conditions have been agreed in prior negotiations with the borrowing country, attempts to amend would mean sending the staff back for renegotiation. These considerations mean that, in practice, the Board almost never considers amending staff proposals. It therefore seems a reasonable simplification to assume that proposals to the Board are essentially take-it-or-leave-it offers (Gold 1984: 392; Garritsen De Vries 1985: 987).

Given this decision-making framework, on any individual programme the staff can have substantial influence over the content finally approved. The staff can propose the programme closest to their own preference that is able to muster majority support. States will only veto a staff proposal if a majority finds the status quo – i.e. no programme – more to its liking than the proposal.

This simple set-up leads to some propositions about staff autonomy, understood as the staff's ability to influence the content of programmes. First, we can observe that staff influence is likely to grow when the status quo is strongly disliked by most states. In this case, nearly any proposal will be able to gain a majority, so the staff can present something close to their ideal point. This observation could lead us to suggest, for example, that in times of crisis that threaten the international financial system, IMF staff will have substantial influence, as executive directors will be anxious to move away from the status quo. On the other hand, when dealing with relatively minor borrowing countries, or with chronic problems that do not pose any immediate threat to the international system, executive directors are more willing to live with the status quo. In this case, the staff will have to be more attentive to the executive directors' preferences, effectively limiting its autonomy.

A second observation is that the distribution of preferences among states will have implications for staff influence. When state preferences diverge, stretching along the entire policy continuum, there is more likely to be a wide range of proposals that could gain majority approval. This gives the staff room for manoeuvre, as they can choose the proposal within this space that comes closest to their ideal point. In contrast, when state preferences converge, the staff will have less flexibility. Now a smaller set of proposals is likely to gain approval, constraining the staff to make a proposal within this smaller space. Staff autonomy will therefore be greater when there is disagreement among states about the desired policy (the degree of conditionality in the IMF case). Such disagreement allows the staff to play states off against one another.

The propositions that follow from a simple neoliberal perspective help us to understand the evolution of IMF conditionality over time. The initial decision to attach conditions to IMF drawings in itself conferred some autonomy on staff and management. As the exact content of conditions would inevitably be subject to staff input, any use of conditionality provides it with authority. Therefore, understanding the Fund's early decisions to use conditionality and the procedures it developed to set conditions illuminates important aspects of the agency issue. These early decisions are also important because the procedures have changed surprisingly little over the last fifty years, in spite of massive change in the content of conditions, the scale of lending, and the variety of countries involved.

The Articles of Agreement negotiated by John Maynard Keynes and Harry Dexter White at Bretton Woods left the issue of conditionality intentionally vague. The positions of Keynes and White, and the politicians they represented, were predictable as Britain was certain to have to draw on Fund resources, while the USA would be the major source of these resources. The debate between automaticity, favoured by Keynes, and conditionality, favoured by White, played out over the first few years of the Fund, and was settled in the USA's favour by 1952.

The early signals indicated that automaticity would prevail (Robichek 1984: 67). Keynes was anxious to avoid giving the Fund the 'wide discretionary and policing powers' that he believed the USA wanted (Dell 1981: 1). His preferences were shared by virtually the entire membership other than the USA. Internal Fund memos and congressional hearings affirm that the USA wanted the Fund to be able to limit access to its resources. The USA settled for the requirement that governments make representations as to their intentions for using resources (Dam 1982: 117).

The USA opened the door to conditionality by assuring that the Articles of Agreement required that Fund resources could be used only for purposes consistent with the Fund's principles. If the EB could question members' representations, 'then there was the possibility that it might be able to exercise some discretion under cover of an assessment of need' (Dam 1982: 117). By 1947, the Executive Board decided that it had the right to challenge a member's representation about the purposes to which it would put Fund resources. This wedge allowed the principle of conditionality to develop.

However, the first managing director, Camille Gutt, expressed views consistent with automaticity (Dell 1981: 8), while the USA continued to insist on the Board's right to scrutinize requests for drawings. Between 1949 and 1951, drawings from the Fund nearly came to a halt, due to a combination of Marshall Fund aid substituting for IMF resources and deadlock about mechanisms for using them. No drawings occurred during 1950, and the entire amount drawn from October 1949 until September 1951 was only $76.8 million, while repayments of earlier drawings to the Fund during this period were $67.7 million (Garritsen De Vries and Horsefield 1969: 276).

During this period, the Executive Board as well as the staff and management paid a great deal of attention to developing procedures that would allow an increase in drawings. The concept of automaticity disappeared during these discussions. New managing director, Ivar Rooth, presented a plan in November 1951, known as the 'Rooth Plan', that finally broke the deadlock between those who wanted more staff autonomy and those who wanted direct executive director oversight. This plan became the basis of stand-by arrangements, the current tool for extending IMF financing. After extensive discussions and some modifications by a staff working party, the Rooth Plan was approved in February 1952. The basic idea of the plan was that drawings of greater resources would result in greater stringency of conditions. Members would agree with the Fund on a plan to assure policy changes and repayment of the drawing within a specified time before the executive board would approve the stand-by arrangement.

The development of the principle of conditionality went hand-in-hand with a shift in responsibility from the Board to the staff. In the first two years of the Fund, the executive directors played an active role in negotiations, heading field missions (Archives S1720, Meeting 170, 20 May 1947). The Board initially attempted to maintain tight constraints on staff autonomy. At times, executive directors questioned staff judgements on particular policy issues, such as advice to Iran on its exchange rate, or to Colombia on fiscal issues. Such questions continually raised the issue of staff autonomy, and executive directors attempted to delegate enough authority to the staff to allow them to do their jobs, but to maintain control.

The practice of directors participating in missions stopped in 1948 but, from 1948 until the early 1950s, the Board continued to keep a tight rein on staff missions. The 'composition of each staff mission was subject to Board approval, and the Board outlined detailed instructions for them' (Garritsen De Vries and Horsefield 1969: 11). Furthermore, members routinely discussed their prospective requests for drawings directly with the US executive director prior to submitting a formal request. This practice ended by 1956. Susan Strange sees this as an 'important shift of responsibility from the United States to the Fund' (1973: 279). Board oversight of staff missions also became less stringent. As staff members conducted missions, they had to make a number of immediate decisions that were only subject to review afterwards, indicating their agenda-setting function. As a result, Fund historian, Keith Horsefield, concluded that 'in later years the influence of the staff tended to grow' (Garittsen De Vries and Horsefield 1969: 471).

Horsefield draws attention to the conflict of interest among executive directors that the neoliberal framework suggests should give rise to staff autonomy. He argues that 'the principle reason for the strengthening of the staff's position was that it had opportunities for exercising initiative, and took them' (Garritsen De Vries and Horsefield 1969: 472). For example, the staff sent an important report on international reserves and liquidity to Fund members without Board review. Horsefield identifies 'a clash of views amongst Executive Directors, . . . which might have made it impossible to present an agreed Board report' as the permissive condition for this exercise of staff autonomy (Garritsen De Vries and Horsefield 1969: 472).

This brief discussion can provide only a taste of how one would go about applying a neoliberal perspective to the study of a particular institution. It first requires specification of the underlying pattern of interests and attention to how those interests interact in an institutionalized setting. We can draw inferences from this simple analysis, in this case about variation in the level of institutional autonomy from member-state interests. The early years of IMF conditionality suggest that this perspective provides substantial insight. There are, of course, alternative approaches to understanding the use and evolution of IMF conditionality. Those who concentrate on the IMF as a bureaucracy would consider how bureaucrats at the IMF could use conditionality to enhance their power, legitimacy (Barnett and Finnemore 2004), or monetary payoffs (Vaubel 1986). This approach, unlike neoliberalism, has a hard time explaining variation in IMF autonomy over time. A neorealist might see IMF conditionality as merely an unmediated response to the wishes of the USA. This approach underestimates the influence of other states, including developing countries, on IMF autonomy. Overall, the evidence suggests that neoliberalism provides a more powerful account of the pattern of behaviour that we observe over time and across cases.

Conclusion

The international polity and economy are highly institutionalized. The neoliberal approach to international politics provides a powerful explanation of this pattern and of the consequences of institutionalization. Neoliberals adopt a contractual view that sees institutions as solutions to collective-action problems. Thus, the neoliberal study of IOs begins by identifying the underlying strategic problems they address. These problems involve overcoming obstacles to bargaining, monitoring compliance with commitments, and enforcing agreements. At times, the fundamental problem is to provide flows of needed assistance while avoiding moral hazard problems. This tension sets up IOs as agents of their state principals who frequently have conflicting interests. Thus, the neoliberal approach with its emphasis on principals and agents has been a powerful tool.

The neoliberal study of IOs consistently shows that their dynamics, design, and effects reflect an ongoing struggle between the exercise of power and the rule of law. While some authors find more evidence for the weight of one side in this battle than the other, careful empirical research reveals that neither side triumphs. IOs will continue to have a major influence on the global creation and distribution of wealth and power. The neoliberal approach is a powerful way to understand the dynamics of IOs and of international conflict and cooperation more generally.

? **QUESTIONS**

1. What are the implications of treating states as the units of analysis, as neoliberals do?
2. What are the advantages of assuming rational state behaviour, as neorealists do? What costs are incurred with employing the rationality assumption?

3. What are the primary observable implications of neoliberalism for the activities of international organizations?

4. What are the primary observable implications of neoliberalism for patterns of cooperation among states?

5. What are the challenges of applying principal-agent models developed in other contexts to relations between international organizations and their member-states?

6. What are the intellectual roots of neoliberalism?

7. For what substantive issues is neoliberalism an appropriate approach? Is it more applicable, for example, to security or economic issues?

8. Do neoliberals deal adequately with the role of power or coercion in international politics?

9. What role does information play in a neoliberal analysis?

10. What are the primary theoretical challenges to neoliberalism?

11. What are the primary empirical challenges to neoliberalism?

12. With which empirical methods is neoliberalism consistent? Is it inconsistent with any particular empirical methods (e.g. statistical analysis, process tracing, comparative case studies, discourse analysis)?

FURTHER READING

■ Downs, G. W., Rocke, D. M., and Barsoom, P. N. (1996), 'Is the Good News about Compliance Good News about Cooperation?', *International Organization*, 50/3: 379–406. The authors explain the apparent high rate of compliance with international agreements by pointing out that rational states are unlikely to commit themselves to agreements that require large changes in state behaviour, thus challenging a more legalistic approach to compliance issues.

■ Keohane, R. O. (1984), *After Hegemony: Cooperation and Discord in the World Political Economy* (Princeton NJ: Princeton University Press). Keohane's book is the classic statement of the neoliberal approach.

■ Koremenos, B., Lipson, C., and Snidal, D. (2001), 'The Rational Design of International Institutions', *International Organization*, 55/4: 761–99. This is the introductory chapter to a special issue of the journal that focuses on the design of international institutions and organizations from a contractual perspective.

■ Krasner, S. D. (1983), *International Regimes* (Ithaca NY: Cornell University Press). This edited volume launched the neoliberal study of international regimes and institutions, although it also contains important contributions from scholars who do not adopt a neoliberal approach.

■ Krasner, S. D. (1991), 'Global Communications and National Power: Life on the Pareto Frontier', *World Politics*, 43/3: 336–56. Krasner challenges the standard neoliberal claim that the major challenge to international cooperation is overcoming transaction costs that prevent states from realizing mutual gains.

■ Martin, L. L. and Simmons, B. (1998), 'Theories and Empirical Studies of International Institutions', *International Organization*, 52/4: 729–57. A review article that surveys the study of international institutions and organizations from the 1940s until the 1990s.

IMPORTANT WEBSITES

- International Monetary Fund.
  www.imf.org

- An introduction to the principal-agent problem.
  http://en.wikipedia.org/wiki/Principal-agent_problem

Visit the Online Resource Centre that accompanies this book for lots of interesting additional material. www.oxfordtextbooks.co.uk/orc/dunne/

7 The English School

TIM DUNNE[1]

Chapter contents

- Introduction
- The interpretive mode of inquiry
- International society
- International society: between system and world society
- Case study
- Conclusion

Reader's guide

The principal alternative to mainstream North American theorizations of International Relations (IR) is the English school. I begin with an account of what the English school is and how it emerged. Thereafter, the chapter provides a reconstruction of its methodology before embarking on a substantive discussion of its master-concept of international society. I argue that the social order established by states and embodied in the activities of practitioners must be understood alongside the dynamics of the system and world society. The interplay of these three concepts is the primary theoretical contribution of the English school. In the case-study section, I look at the issue of human rights as it has become central to the occupation of many contemporary English school theorists. Human rights represent a significant transformation in our understandings of justice in international relations: at the same time, they pose a challenge for international order as Hedley Bull, a leading English school theorist, predicted over two decades ago.

Introduction

Writing in the mid-1990s, I began a book on the history of the English school[2] with the claim that the discipline of IR had either ignored or misunderstood the writings of its leading figures (Dunne 1998). Stanley Hoffmann's widely cited historiography of the field up until the 1970s illustrated how the English school had been ignored. Hoffmann claimed there was no systematic study of the discipline outside the USA, 'only the occasional brilliant contribution such as that by Hedley Bull', but his work had been 'unconnected and unsupported' (Hoffmann 1977: 37). In making this claim, Hoffmann overlooked the systematic research programmes undertaken by the British Committee on the Theory of International Politics. While being ignored in the USA, the work of the English school was misunderstood by leading IR thinkers outside the school who viewed it as a straightfor-ward variant of realism (Banks 1984).

Over a decade after *Inventing International Society* was published (Dunne 1998), the English school is no longer ignored: the inclusion of the English school in influential textbooks is one indicator, as is the number of discussions about it that have appeared in leading journals (including *Review of International Studies* 2001; *Millennium* 2005). Without overstating the impact of the English school on IR today, it is probably reasonable to claim that in Britain at least the English school has once more become the dominant theoretical voice. Beyond its heartland, there is significant interest in its work in contin-ental Europe as well as the USA, Canada, Australia, China, and India. Contrary to what is implied by the name, the English school was never very English and is even less so today. Despite the resurgence of interest in English school theory, there remain many detractors who view the enterprise as being conceptually underdeveloped; still others who regard it as being overly complacent about the political and social conditions which afflict the vast majority of peoples in the world. Even if the English school is regarded as flawed, it is at least being taken seriously as a distinctive approach to IR – this was not the case during the successive great debates between the three dominant paradigms in the 1970s (realism, pluralism, and structuralism) followed by the debate between neorealism and its critics in the 1980s.

Those who identify with the English school today see it as occupying the middle ground in IR alongside constructivism: this location is preferable to the dominant mainstream theories of neorealism and neoliberalism and the more radical alternatives (such as critical theory and poststructuralism). They are drawn to an English school perspective because it offers a synthesis of different theories and concepts. In so doing, it avoids the either/or framing of realism (*versus*) idealism, as set out in the writings of many great figures during the 1930s and 1940s. It also avoids the explanatory (*versus*) interpretive dichotomy which generated so much heat during the 'fourth debate' in the 1990s. In place of these dichotomies, the English school purports to offer an account of IR which combines theory *and* history, morality *and* power, agency *and* structure.

One obvious consequence of this level of theoretical ambition is that the boundaries of the English school often appear to be unclear, which in part explains the ongoing debate about who belongs in the school and how it differs from other theoretical accounts of world politics. To shed light on these questions, it is helpful to consider some contextual issues about what exactly defines the English school and who its principal contributors are. To begin with, it is useful to reflect on why it makes sense to speak of the English school as a distinct tradition of inquiry. First, there are the personal ties that grow when colleagues share institutional affiliations and belong to the same academic field – this is particularly relevant to the 1950s and 1960s when IR as a subject was in its infancy. Second, the main protagonists believed themselves to be part of a collective enterprise, and consciously sought to carry its debates forward. The emergence of a self-conscious research programme, with an open yet distinct agenda, can be seen in the writings of early post-1945 writers working in leading UK universities. Charles Manning developed a curriculum in which the idea of international society played a prominent role. In the 1950s, his colleague Martin Wight developed an approach to the subject that drew on 'three traditions' (Wight 1991) – one that was resigned to international relations being a state of war (realism), one that sought to reform its basic structure (the Grotian tradition), and one that strove to dismantle it (what Wight called 'revolutionism').

Beyond realism versus idealism

Many leading figures of the next generation attended to Wight's lectures on international theory (they were not published until two decades after his death). Wight's most famous protégé was Hedley Bull who was invited by Manning to join the staff in the IR Department at the London School of Economics in 1955. These lectures, Bull later wrote, exerted 'a profound impression on me' (Dunne 1998: 138). Like many other writers in the late 1950s, Bull was increasingly dissatisfied with the either/or choice between realism and idealism. He singled out E. H. Carr for severe criticism. His *Twenty Years' Crisis 1919–1939* (Carr 1946) was effective at undermining spurious claims to universality, such as free trade and national self-determination, yet at the same time it was flawed because Carr 'jettisons the idea of international society itself' (Dunne 1998: 143). Bull went on to conclude that this had to be the main idea out of which 'a new analysis of international relations should now begin'. In truth, it was already well underway.

The search for a new analysis of international relations was what drove Herbert Butterfield to set up the British Committee on the Theory of International Politics. The inaugural meeting was in January 1959 and the Committee persisted until the early 1980s – long after the parallel committee in the USA had broken up due to divisions between theorists and practitioners. Early discussions of the British Committee revolved around founding issues to do with the nature of IR theory, and the possibilities of establishing order given the condition of international anarchy. The best essays from this period were published in *Diplomatic Investigations*, including classic contributions from Butterfield and Wight on the balance of power, Bull on international law, and Bull and Wight on international society (Butterfield and Wight 1966). In the second phase of their research programme, the Committee looked at comparative states systems, leading eventually to Martin Wight's book *Systems of States* (1977) and Adam Watson's *Evolution of International Society* (1992). The third and final project of the Committee developed organically out of the second in that it focused on the emergence of European international society and the impact colonization and decolonization had on the rules and institutions of the newly globalized international society (Bull and Watson 1984).

By the time of Bull's death in 1984, the work inaugurated by the Committee and those sympathetic to it was increasingly seen as being out of step with the emergence of new theories and sub-disciplines (such as foreign-policy analysis and international political economy). Unsurprisingly, we find that in reflections on the 'state of the discipline' in the 1980s, the English school was nowhere to be seen (Banks 1984; Smith 1987); nor did it figure in early representations of the debate between neorealism and its critics. Yet within a decade, interest in the English school had begun to rekindle. Many influential textbooks began to include it as an alternative approach to the subject, placing it alongside realism, liberalism, and various critical approaches (Brown 1997; Der Derian 1994; Jackson and Sørensen 1999). Added to these, original contributions to the history and theory of international society have proliferated, all taking the English school as their point of departure (*inter alia*, Almeida 2000; Armstrong 1993; Buzan and Little 2000; Clark 2005, Gonzalez-Palaez 2005; Jackson 2000; Keene 2002; Korman 1996; Neumann 1996; Osiander 1994; Welsh 1995; Wheeler 2000).

This sense of a resurgent paradigm was prompted in part by the recognition that it represented a distinct position that was inhospitable to the rationalist assumptions underpinning both neorealism and neoliberalism. Moreover, in terms of substantive research questions, the English school had long focused on the kind of cultural questions and normative contestations that were rising to the top of the international agenda in the 1990s. Such momentum prompted Barry Buzan – along with Richard Little – to seek to invigorate English school theorizing by pulling the diverse strands together and forging a coherent research programme. This new phase was marked by the publication of Buzan's agenda-setting paper 'The English School: An Under-exploited Resource in IR' in 2001 (Buzan 2001: 471–88) and culminated in two major new theoretical works (Buzan 2004; Linklater and Suganami 2006).

The previous paragraphs have provided some historical and sociological context for the emergence of the English school. What follows will be a focused analysis of their key claims. A good place to begin the remainder of the chapter is to reflect on Kenneth Waltz's dismissal of the contribution made by writers such as Martin Wight and Hedley Bull. Waltz intimated that their work was valuable but it was not really theory, at least not in a sense that would be recognized by philosophers of science (Waltz 1998). Underlying Waltz's argument is his particularly positivist view of what counts as theory, an issue dealt with comprehensively in Chapter 1 of this volume. Nevertheless, if the English school is to appeal more widely it needs a rigorous account of exactly what it means by 'theory' and how knowledge is generated. What follows is an initial discussion on methodology, followed by an analysis of the school's conception of how the world political system ought to be understood in terms of the dynamic interplay of system, society, and community (or world society).

The interpretive mode of inquiry

The most infamous intervention into 'methodology' was Hedley Bull's 1996 paper in *World Politics* called 'the case for a classical approach'. As has often been remarked, it was more a case *against* the rigid application of scientific methods which he felt would not generate knowledge of any significance. By contrast, a classical approach was defined as 'that approach to theorizing that derives from philosophy, history and law, and that is characterized by explicit reliance upon the exercise of judgement' (Bull 2000: 255). One irony with regard to Bull's position in the article is that he had previously spent a good deal of time berating his colleagues in the British Committee for their disinterest in the new wave of scientific writing being developed in the USA in the early 1960s.

Bull's case for a classical approach was obscured by the polemical style he chose to adopt. Some years later, he wrote a much more considered account of what an interpretive methodology ought to involve (2000). His claims in this piece (written in 1972) serve as a good guide to the English school view of the field of International Relations and how to study it:

1. The subject matter of IR. Bull argued that the appropriate frame for IR was not 'inter-state relations' or the interactions of any other 'units'. Rather, IR was about establishing a body of general propositions about 'the global political system' by which he meant states and also regions, institutions, NGOs, transnational and subnational groups, individuals, and the wider community of human kind. In tracing the connections between these actors, and the patterns generated by their interactions, Bull placed a high premium on the role of IR theory to define concepts and theorize relations between them. This emphasis upon concepts constitutes a particular kind of theorizing, one which is designed to illuminate complex changes in world order. Such an interpretive understanding of theory is at odds with the positivist pursuit of the formulation of 'testable hypotheses' (King, Keohane, Verba 1994).

2. The importance of historical understanding. Academic knowledge needs to have historical depth. Bull gives a pertinent example: it is insufficient simply to know the facts about the strategic superiority of the USA over its competitors; what is preferable is to understand how and why the USA regards itself as an exceptional power. Institutions of international society, such as law and the balance of power, must also be understood in historical context. It matters, for example, whether human rights are as seen by a child of the Enlightenment, or whether they are believed to be a twentieth-century interpretation of the natural rights tradition. These different historical understandings are vital to the diplomacy of human rights and the rationale for promoting rights beyond borders.

3. There is no escape from values. It is important to be aware of one's values and for these to be subjected to critical scrutiny. Values will inform the selection of topics to be studied, and the writings and statements of academics will in turn have an impact on the political process. Despite denying the possibility of separating facts about the world and our values, academicians ought to aim at a position of detachment. By this, Bull was targeting those who were obsessed with policy relevance: he believed that the pursuit of political influence was likely to significantly diminish the prospects of generating research that would be of interest to practitioners. In the other camp, the pursuit of political causes is likely to undermine the integrity of the subject and the wider academic enterprise.

4. IR is fundamentally a normative enterprise. Values matter not just in terms of the relationship between the researcher and their subject but are central to the subject of IR, properly studied. The central problem in world politics was, according to Bull, how to

construct a form of international society that was both orderly and just. His answer to the Weberian question 'What shall we do, and how shall we live?' was not to enter the realm of 'ideal theory' with fictional assumptions and make-believe states (Rawls 2005). Unlike moral philosophers, Bull believed that the IR theorist doing normative inquiry needed to stay close to state practice. What mattered were not normative ideas *per se* but the ideas that practitioners believed in and sought to implement (Wight 1991). This involves elaborating the context within which actors takes decisions as well as understanding that in politics values are often irreconcilable and that terrible choices have to be made.

Throughout the 1970s and early 1980s, the English school's commitment to an interpretive mode of inquiry rendered it marginal to developments inside the North American heartland of IR. Such a position of marginality was further underscored by the fact that the English school was silent during the normative and interpretive assault on positivism that began in the mid-1980s (despite having opposed positivism for over three decades). At the vanguard of this movement were Gramscian critical theorists, feminists, poststructuralists, and constructivists. Of these, constructivism emerged as a mainstream alternative to neorealism and neoliberalism. Constructivism enabled IR to cling onto its claim to have a distinctive subject matter – broadly around the interaction of sovereign actors and institutions – without buying in to neorealism's obsession with material power and immovable international structures. As noted above, constructivists began to appreciate the overlaps between their approach to IR and that of the older English school (Finnemore 1996: 17; Wendt 1999: 31). For a much more extensive discussion of constructivism, see Chapter 9.

Were writers such as Manning, Wight, and Bull constructivists before their time? Read Manning's *Nature of International Society* (Manning 1962), or indeed Bull's *Anarchical Society*, and it is apparent that there is a degree of convergence with conventional constructivists such as John Ruggie and Alexander Wendt (Dunne 1998). Both regard the inter-state order as a fundamentally social sphere which constitutes states as agents and socializes them into following its rules and conventions. And both view norms and institutions as expressions of shared knowledge and shared values. Despite these overlaps, one could argue that as the two research programmes have evolved significant differences have emerged. Take the example of the basic 'unit' of analysis. Wendt believes that states are the key actors and they are 'like people too' (1999: 215–24). While English school scholars sometimes attribute agency to states as a form of shorthand, they believe that the real agents in international society are the diplomats and leaders who think and act on behalf of the state and its institutions.

Knowledge of how diplomats and leaders understand 'their' world can be enhanced by being attentive to the language they use and the justifications they employ. Two important inferences can be drawn from this relationship between language and social action. First, an action will be constrained 'to the degree that it cannot be legitimated' (Skinner 2002: 156). Second, the range of possible forms of innovative action is limited by the prevailing morality of international society. Actors 'cannot hope to stretch' the application of existing rules and meanings 'indefinitely' (2002: 156).[3] International law provides a testing ground for these intrepretive insights. What ostensibly appears to be an act of aggression is invariably justified as an act of self-defence. Whether this is condoned or not depends on how much 'stretch' is being demanded of the normative vocabulary. When Israel described its attack on Iraq's nuclear reactor in terms of self-defence, this was not accepted by the majority of states in international society. Yet the UN accepted the US government's argument that the use of force against the Taliban government in 2001–2 was acceptable given the attacks on New York and Washington on September 11 2001. The key difference was a change in the normative context of international relations such that the stretch to self-defence was thought to be that much smaller after 9/11. As has already been demonstrated by new thinking in the English school, identifying and tracking the constraining power of rules and norms is a fruitful direction for an interpretive methodology (Wheeler 2000).

Reading exchanges between Waltz and his critics in the 1980s, one could be forgiven for thinking that the scientific revolution in IR is a relatively recent occurrence. Yet, as early as the late 1950s, the British Committee on the Theory of International Politics was deeply sceptical that such methods could ever generate knowledge about world politics. Almost five decades later, the English school continues to offer an alternative way of studying IR which is rooted in the history of current and past states systems, and guided by moral questions about the adequacy of the current inter-state order. The more recent challenge posed by constructivism has brought a greater conceptual clarity to many implicit assumptions in English school theorizing. For instance, the work of Wendt provides a sophisticated account of how actors are constituted by normative structures while at the same time allowing for a certain degree of material determination of the system. Such a combination of ideas and material forces is also evident in Bull's thinking, albeit in his case it is more a matter of common sense than meta-theoretical application. Such overlaps offer mutual gains. The collective works of the English school have a great deal to say about the intersection of history, morality, and agency. What actors say, how they learn or adapt, under what conditions they act rationally, whether (and how do we know) they are speaking truthfully, and what possibilities they had to act differently. These questions can be answered using an interpretive methodology that borrows from constructivism although is not entirely reducible to it.

International society

Having reflected on the issue of the English school's approach, the main body of the chapter will delve deeper into the idea that states form an international society, a claim that has been said to distinguish it from other theories of IR. Following Barry Buzan's recent work (2004), I now hold the view that the school must not only provide a powerful account of how and why states form a society; it must also show how this domain relates to world society. While Buzan has brought world society back into the English school's ontology, he continued to consign the system to the margins: as argued below, it is time to bring the system back in.

What is the status of the categories system, society, and world society? As Bull reminded us, these are 'elements' that exist 'out there' in world politics but can be known to us only through interpretive designs. The sociologist Max Weber referred to these schemas as ideal-types. In order to show the relationship between capitalism and Christianity, Weber argued, it was first necessary to distil them into a conceptual form that made it possible to speak about certain values and institutions being shared by different peoples or successive generations. So it is with system, society, and world society. All are bundles of properties that highlight certain important features while minimizing that which is thought to be less relevant. By seeking to clarify the concepts which reveal patterns in world history, the English school is working with a very different notion of 'theory' to that which is found in the dominant American approaches. Rather than 'operationalizing' concepts and formulating 'testable' hypotheses, the emphasis upon contending concepts is driven by a search for defining properties which mark the boundaries of different historical and normative orders.

Before proceeding, it is important to consider one objection to representing English school theory as a conversation between three overlapping domains: while classical English school theorists alluded to 'three traditions' (Wight) or 'three elements' (Bull), they nevertheless privileged the domain of international society in their account. Therefore, to treat the three as being of equal significance is to misunderstand the distinctive character of English school thought. I do not doubt that one of the intellectual drivers propelling the English school into existence was a rejection of realism and idealism in favour of a middle way that recognizes institutions can moderate the dreaded dangers that are associated with life in the international anarchy. I also recognize that many publications by English school advocates in the 1990s continued to privilege the societal domain, in part due to the desire to show that the English school was not just a polite form of realism as many in the 1980s had assumed. Neither of these points undermines the claim set out in this chapter that the most persuasive case in defence of the English school is that it is potentially more illuminating than mainstream alternatives because it seeks to provide a synthetic account of global politics that avoids the series of false dichotomies thrown up by the alternatives such as power versus norms, materialism versus idealism, anarchy versus hierarchy, reasons versus causes. To do so, we need not only to think about international society as the defining marker of the English school, but also to include the other two ideal types to illustrate its boundaries and constraints. After discussing the properties and types of international society, the chapter will discuss how this domain is subjected to downward pressure generated by the system and upward pressure generated by transnational forces in world society.

International society: definition, properties, variations

According to Bull's classical definition, international society comes into being when 'a group of states, conscious of certain common interests and common values, forms a society in the sense that they conceive themselves to be bound by a common set of rules in their relations with one another, and share in the working of common institutions' (1977: 13).[4] The discussion which follows scrutinizes each component of this definition.

The first key element of international society is the unique character of the membership which is confined to sovereign states. What is significant here is that actors both claim sovereignty and recognize one another's right to the same prerogatives (Wight 1977). Clearly the act of mutual recognition indicates the presence of a social practice: recognition is fundamental to an identity relationship. Recognition is the first step in the construction of an international society. If we were to doubt for a moment the social nature of the process of recognition, then this would quickly be dispelled by those peoples in history who at some time have been or continue to be denied membership of the society of states. The history of the expansion of international society (Bull and Watson 1984) is a story of a shifting boundary of inclusion and exclusion. China was denied sovereign statehood until January 1942 when Western states finally renounced the unequal treaties. Why was this the case? Membership became defined, particularly in the nineteenth century, by a 'standard of civilization' which set conditions for internal governance that corresponded with European values and beliefs. What we see here is how important cultural differentiation has been to the European experience of international society. China was not recognized as a legitimate member of international society and, therefore, was denied equal membership. If the West and China did not recognize each other as equal members, then how should we characterize their relations? Here we see how the system–society dynamic can usefully capture historical boundaries of inclusion and exclusion. There was a great deal of 'interaction' between China and the West during the nineteenth and early twentieth centuries but this was driven by strategic and economic logics. Crucially, neither side believed themselves to be part of the same shared values and institutions: China, for example, long resisted the presence of European diplomats on its soil along with their claim to extra-territorial jurisdiction which has been a longstanding rule among European powers. In the absence of accepting the rules and institutions of European international society, it makes sense to argue that from the Treaty of Nanking in 1843 to 1942 China was part of the states system but was not a member of international society (Gong 1984).

Once it has been established who is entitled to claim the identity of a rightful member of international society, the next consideration involves thinking about what it means for a state to 'act'. Here the English school encounters criticism from empiricists who argue that collective constructs cannot have agency. What does it mean to attribute agency to collectivities like states? One straightforward answer is that states act through the medium of their representatives or office-holders. Every state employs officials who act externally on its behalf, from the lowly consulate dealing with 'nationals' who have lost their passports to the 'head of state'. In a narrowly empirical sense, therefore, this diplomatic and foreign-policy elite are the real agents of international society. This is the original sense in which the term 'international society' came into existence in the eighteenth century: in 1736, Antoine Pecquet argued that the corps of ministers formed an 'independent society' bound by a 'community of privileges'. If we are looking for the real agents of international society, then it is to the diplomatic culture that we should turn, that realm of 'ideas and beliefs held in common by official representatives of states' (Der Derian 2003).

While sovereign states are the primary members of international society, it is important to note that they are not strictly the only members. Historical anomalies have always existed, including the diplomatic network belonging to the Catholic church and the qualified sovereign powers that were granted to non-state actors such as the rights to make war and annex territory which were transferred to the great trading companies of the imperial era. One might also argue that influential international non-governmental organizations (INGOs) are members in so far as they give advice to institutions such as the UN and on occasions participate in the drafting of significant multilateral treaties. The other important anomaly with the membership of international society is the fact that sovereign rights are often constrained for economic or security reasons. Robert Jackson, a leading writer in the English school, pointed to the fact that post-colonial states are 'quasi' sovereigns in that they are recognized by international society but are unable to maintain an effective government internally (Jackson 1990). A related development is the temporary suspension of sovereign prerogatives by an international institution or occupying authority, a practice that follows from a period of civil conflict or external military intervention. In the colonial period this was often described as trusteeship (Bain 2003); in contemporary international society it goes under the less politically sensitive label of a 'transitional authority'.

While the element of mutual recognition is highly significant for English school understandings of international society, it is not a sufficient condition for its existence. The actors must have some minimal common interests such as trade, freedom of travel, or simply the need for stability. Here we see how aspects of the system impinge on the possibilities for a society to develop. The higher the levels of economic interdependence, the more likely it is that states will develop institutions for realizing coming interests and purposes. The independence of sovereign states, however, remains an important limiting factor in the realization of common goals. For this reason, the purposes states agreed upon for most of the Westphalian era have had a fairly minimal character centred upon the survival of the system and the endurance of the dominant units within it. The condition of general war is an example of the breakdown of order, but Bull was quick to point out that even during the Second World War certain laws of war were respected and, perhaps more significantly, the period of total war triggered an attempt to construct a new order based largely on the same rules and institutions that had operated in the pre-war era. It was this that led him to claim that 'the element of society had always existed' in the modern states system. Such a claim prompts disquiet among IR scholars trained in sophisticated social science methods. If 'society' explains the existence of order, how can it be a permanent presence in the world political system? One answer, which the English school needs to develop more fully, is to provide clearer benchmarks which enable an evaluation of how much 'society' is present in the inter-state order.

Types of international society

This criticism of the tendency in English school writings to treat international society as an unchanging entity is rebutted in part by the attempt to set out different kinds of international society. At the more minimal end of the spectrum of international societies, we find an institutional arrangement that is restricted solely to the maintenance of order. In a culturally diverse world, where members-states have different traditions and political systems, the only collective venture they could all agree on was the maintenance of international order. Without order, the stability of the system would be thrown into doubt and with it the survival of the units. Yet, the extent to which states formed an international society was limited and constrained by the fact of anarchy. For this reason, international society was not to be equated with a harmonious order but, rather, a tolerable order that was better than a realist would expect but much worse than a cosmopolitan desires (Linklater 1995: 95).

In a pluralist international society, the institutional framework is geared towards the liberty of states and the maintenance of order among them. The rules are complied with because, like rules of the road, fidelity to them is relatively cost free but the collective benefits are enormous. A good example is the elaborate rules to do with ambassadorial and diplomatic privileges. Acceptance that representatives of states are not subject to the laws of their host country is a principle that has received widespread compliance for many centuries. This is one instance among many where the rules of coexistence have come to dominate state practice. Pluralist rules and norms 'provide a structure of coexistence, built on the mutual recognition of states as independent and legally equal members of society, on the unavoidable reliance on self-preservation and self-help, and on freedom to promote their own ends subject to minimal constraints' (Alderson and Hurrell 2000: 7). To fully comprehend the pluralist order, one needs only to be reminded that great powers, limited war, and the balance of power, were thought by the English school to be 'institutions'. By this term, Bull and his colleagues were pointing to the practices which helped to sustain order, practices which evolved over many centuries. For example, if the balance of power was essential to preserve the liberty of states (an argument the English school shared with classical realists, see Chapter 3), then status quo powers must be prepared to intervene forcefully to check the growing power of a state that threatened the general balance.

To what extent are pluralist rules and institutions adequate for our contemporary world? This is a question that has provoked widely differing responses within the English school. On one side, traditionalists like Robert Jackson believe that a pluralist international society is a practical institutional adaptation to human diversity: the great advantage of a society based on the norms of sovereignty and non-intervention is that such an arrangement is most likely to achieve the moral value of freedom (Jackson 2000).

Critics of pluralism charge that it is failing to deliver on its promise. The persistence of inter-state wars throughout the twentieth century suggest that sovereignty norms were not sufficient to deter predatory states. Moreover, the rule of non-intervention that was central to pluralism was enabling statist elites to violently abuse their own citizens with impunity. For these reasons, both Bull and Vincent were drawn to a different account of international society in which universal values such as human rights set limits on the exercise of state sovereignty. The guiding thought here, and one that is captured by the term solidarism, is that the ties that bind individuals to the great society of humankind are deeper than the pluralist rules and institutions which separate them.

What does a solidarist international society entail? Bull originally defined it as the collective enforcement of international rules *and* the guardianship of human rights. It differs from cosmopolitanism in that the latter is agnostic as to the institutional arrangement for delivering universal values: some cosmopolitans believe a world government is best and others would want to abandon formal political hierarchies altogether. By contrast, solidarism is an *extension* of an international society not its transformation. Like pluralism, it is defined by shared values and institutions and is held together by binding legal rules. Where it differs is in the content of the values and the character of the rules and institutions. In terms of values, in a solidarist international society individuals are entitled to basic rights. This in turn demands that sovereignty norms are modified such that there is a duty on the members of international society to intervene forcibly to protect those rights. At this point, Bull was hesitant about what was implied by solidarism. He believed that there was a danger that the enforcement of human rights principles risked undermining international order. Until there was a greater consensus on the meaning and priority to be accorded to rights claims, attempts to enforce them – what he described as 'premature global solidarism' – would do more harm than good.

It is only in the last few years that international society has legitimized armed intervention on humanitarian grounds. According to the Commission on State Sovereignty's report *The Responsibility to Protect*, states have not only a duty of care to their citizens, they also have a responsibility to come to the aid of other peoples suffering a humanitarian emergency. As Wheeler convincingly shows, this is a significant change from the Cold War period when states could not appeal to humanitarian principles as an acceptable rationale for intervention (2000). Even though intervention for the protection of human rights has been accepted as a just cause, the danger of 'premature global solidarism' is evident in the US-led war against Iraq in 2003. In the absence of a consensus on whether constitutional democracy is the right form of government for non-Western states, the result of the war is likely to be the progressive weakening of United Nations use-of-force prohibitions. What is to be done if coalitions of willing Arab states decide to selectively enforce UN Security Council resolutions without proper authority? In this hypothetical case, an indignant response from Western states to the effect that Arab countries ought to respect the non-intervention principle will seem terribly hollow.

International society: between system and world society

Bull and Wight recognized that a sophisticated analysis of world politics required a systemic component. Yet their discussion of Hobbesian dynamics in the 'system' is inconsistent and unpersuasive. In my view, this vital element of the English school's theorization of world politics ought to be refined rather than discarded as some have claimed (see Buzan 2004). Bull defined the system as being an arena where there was interaction between communities but no shared rules or institutions. In order for a system to come into being, there has to be sufficient intensity of interactions to make 'the behaviour of each a necessary element in the calculations of the other' (Bull 1977: 10).

The concept of a system plays three important roles in the English school's theory of world politics. First, as discussed above, the system–society distinction provides a normative benchmark for addressing the question how far international society extends (Wight 1991: 6). Second, by looking at the formation of the system it is possible to discern mechanisms which shape and shove international and world societies. Third, the category of the system can usefully be used to capture the basic material forces in world politics – flows of information and trade, levels of destructive capability, capacities of actors to affect their environment. Let me examine each of these briefly in turn.

This view of an international system – or more accurately an inter-state system – shares a great deal with the use of systems theory in realist thought, both classical (Chapter 3) and structural (Chapter 4). What sets them apart is that the English school was interested in the system primarily for what it tells us about the history of international society. If one takes Bull's developmental insight into the relationship between system and society, then it is clear that the existence of a society presupposes the existence of a system. This can open up into an intriguing series of discussions as to when a system becomes a society. What level and type of interactions are required in order for the units to treat each other as ends in themselves? And under what circumstances might a society lapse back into a systemic order in which actions impact upon one another but there is no mutual recognition or acceptance of a common framework of rules and institutions? In the British Committee's writings on decolonization, the emphasis is placed on the gradual inclusion of the non-Western world into a globalized society of sovereign states. It is also important to realize that systemic interactions remain a possible future arrangement if the dominant actors in international society cease to comply with the rules and act in ways which undermine the international security. The hypothetical case of a major nuclear confrontation could become a reality only if the great powers acted in ways that were catastrophic for international society. As a result, the society collapses back into the system.

The idea of a states system is also useful to identity the current boundaries between members and those states who find themselves shunned by international society. It is in the dark recesses of the states system that pariah states and failed states find themselves. This does not mean pariahs are outside the framework of the rules and institutions entirely, only that their actions are subjected to far greater scrutiny. Actors in the states system can have structured interactions with members of international society – they may even comply with treaties and other rules – but these interactions remain systemic unless the parties grant each other mutual respect and inclusion into international society.

Thinking about the systemic domain also alerts us to the downward pressure exerted by the distribution of material power. In Bull's work we can find two important instances where the system impinges upon the society. First, he notes how general war is 'a basic determinant of the shape the system assumes at any one time' (1977: 187). Even in the Cold War, where the massive nuclear arsenals of the NATO and Warsaw Pact countries were not unleashed, the presence of these weapons was a crucial constraint on the two superpowers' room for manoeuvre. If the Soviet Union had had only conventional weapons, would the USA and its allies have tolerated the 'fall' of central European countries into the Soviet sphere of influence? Closely related to the phenomena of general war and destructive capacities as basic determinants of the system, one can find in the English school the view that there is a logic of balancing in the states system. Under conditions of anarchy, where there is no over-arching power to disarm the units and police the rules, it is in the interests of all states to prevent the emergence of a dominant or hegemonic power (Watson 1992). Those who take the balance of power seriously point to repeated instances in modern history where states with hegemonic ambition have been repelled by an alliance of powers seeking to prevent a change in the ordering principle of the system. Even if this tendency requires states to 'act' in order to uphold the balance of power, it can still be persuasively argued that the survival of the states system *demands* balancing behaviour from states such that it becomes an inbuilt feature of the system. This is contrasted with the institution of the balance of power in international society which is not mechanical but is rather the outcome of a deliberate policy of pursuing a strategy of self-preservation in the absence of world government (Wight 1978: 184).

Looking through the systemic lens shows not only the ordering of the units; it also directs our attention to the levels of technology, the distribution of material power, and the interaction capacity of the units. Together, these factors tell us a great deal about the ability of units to act and particularly their 'reach'. (Are actors local, regional, or global?) Levels of technology can be thought of as attributes of the units; an obvious case in point is whether a state has nuclear weapons technology or not. However, it is also useful to think about technology in systemic terms, particularly in areas such as communication, transportation, and levels of destructive capacity. Compare, for example, a states system in which the dominant mode of transportation is a horse-drawn wagon, as opposed to a system in which individuals and goods can be transported by supersonic jets, high-speed rail, and ships the size of several football fields placed end-to-end. As these technologies spread, 'they change the quality and character of what might be called the *interaction capacity* of the system as a whole' (Buzan *et al.* 1993).

What make these attributes 'systemic'? They are systemic in that for the most part they fall outside the institutional arrangement developed by states to regulate order and promote justice. By way of illustration, take the example of the place of Britain in the world from the early 1940s to the beginning of the Cold War. Throughout the war, Britain was one of the 'big three' great powers who were the architects of the postwar order. By 1948, the country was increasingly a policy-taker on the world stage and not a policy-maker despite the fact that its diplomatic network remained global, its language remained dominant, and its values ascendant. None of these soft power advantages were enough to configure the system in multipolar terms. Without wanting to imply over-determination, it is nevertheless useful to invoke the system to characterize those factors that appear immovable from the perspective of the actors, such as their geographic location, population base, and technological/economic capacity. Of course they are not immovable over the long term – even geographical 'distance' can change over time, as globalization has demonstrated in recent decades.

The third element in the English school triad is world society. This concept runs in parallel to international society albeit with one key difference – it refers to the shared interests and values 'linking all parts of the human community' (Bull 1977: 279). Vincent's definition of world society is something of a menu of all those entities whose moral concerns traditionally lay outside international society: the claim of individuals to human rights; the claim of indigenous peoples to autonomy; the needs of transnational corporations to penetrate the shell of the sovereign states; and the claim to retrospective justice by those who speak on behalf of the former colonial powers. It is undeniable that human rights are at the centre of the classical English school's conception of world society. An account of the development of human rights is presented in the case study. For now, it is important to give a brief account of how the cosmopolitan culture of late modernity is shaping a new institutional arrangement in world society.

One indicator of an evolving world society is the emergence of international humanitarian law. The UN Charter represented an important stage in this evolution, thus indicating the dynamic interplay between the inter-state and the world society domains. Justice, rights, fundamental freedoms, were all given prominence in the

Charter; subsequently, universal norms of racial equality, the prohibition on torture, and the right to development have been added (among others). Various changes in international criminal law have significantly restricted the circumstances in which state leaders can claim immunity from humanitarian crimes committed while they were in office. Similarly, the Rome Statute of the International Criminal Court adds another layer of international jurisdiction in which agents of states can be held accountable for alleged war crimes. Taken as a whole, one authority on the English school argued that they 'may be interpreted as involving a clear shift from an international society to a world society' (Armstrong 1999: 549). Such a claim, however, understates the extent to which the development of world society institutions is dependent on the ideational and material support of core states in international society.

World society is not just about the growing importance of transnational values grounded in liberal notions of rights and justice. Transnational identities can be based upon ideas of hatred and intolerance. Among a significant body of world public opinion, the strongest identification is to the faith and not to the state. This generates countervailing ideologies of liberation on the part of fundamentalist Christians and holy war on the part of Muslim extremists. In English school thinking, such dynamics can usefully be considered in the context of earlier 'revolts' against Western dominance that were apparent during the struggle for decolonization.

Case study: human rights[5]

The extension of international law from the exclusive rights of sovereign states towards recognizing the rights of all individuals by virtue of their common humanity is one of the most significant normative shifts in the history of world politics. To put it into the conceptual vocabulary used earlier, human rights are the most obvious indicator of a move beyond a pluralist international society and its exclusive interest in the pursuit of order and the limitation of justice claims to demands by sovereign states to be treated equally. Yet, as this case study suggests, for much of the post-1945 period human rights have been as much a source of division as a marker of the emergence of a solidarist international society. During the springtime of liberalism in the 1990s, human rights established an institutional presence that matched its rhetorical power: the winter of the post-9/11 era has illustrated that systemic and societal forces have reversed many previous gains as governments alter the priority accorded to national security over individual liberty. Before unpacking this argument further, let us remind ourselves of the journey human rights have taken in the modern era.

On 10 December 1948, the UN General Assembly adopted the Universal Declaration of Human Rights (UDHR). Eleanor Roosevelt, one of the main advocates, said that it had 'set up a common standard of achievement for all people and all nations' (Risse, Ropp, and Sikkink 1999: 1). The UDHR should be seen as a normatively ambitious document that was brought into being because of the realization of the horrendous destructive capacity of modern states. The document sought to establish a standard of civilized conduct which applied to all governments, irrespective of their ideology or the ethnicity of their citizens. It contains thirty articles, including basic rights (such as the right to life) and more aspirational rights (such as the right to rest and leisure). Despite the normative revolution signalled by the claim that all individuals should have rights by virtue of their common humanity, the institutionalization of human rights principles has been a long and incomplete journey.

Human rights advocates had to wait a further three decades before such principles began to significantly constrain the behaviour of states. In the intervening period, the siren call for states to live up to respecting universal rights was muted by two factors: first, the priority accorded to national security by the leading protagonists (and their allies) during the Cold War; and, second, the fact that states did no multilateral monitoring of their human rights practices. In other words, right at the outset, human rights were overshadowed by systemic factors to do with great power rivalry and the preference by members of international society to view human rights as standards and not as enforceable commitments.

Several factors converged in the mid-1970s which together signalled a step-change in the power of the human rights regime. These can be grouped into the following themes (examined in turn below): the growing legalization of human rights norms; the emergence of human rights international non-governmental organizations (INGOs); and the increased priority accorded to human rights in the foreign policies of key Western states. In terms of legalization, in 1976 the two international human rights covenants came into force. With no little historical irony, the Czechoslovak parliament ratified the two covenants in the knowledge that this would mean the treaty had enough support for the International Covenant for Civil and Political Rights (ICCPR) to come into effect. Over and above the internationalization of what Jack Donnelly calls 'an international bill of rights', other institutional changes had an important impact. The UN Human Rights Commission (UNHRC) became more active, in part helped by its expanded membership and the inclusion of states committed to make a difference. While the work of the Commission is largely that of information gathering and sharing, its role raises the status of human rights in the UN system. The appointment of a UN High Commissioner for Human Rights in 1993 took the profile to an even higher level.

Liberal states and INGOs as change agents

The 1970s also saw the emergence of international non-governmental organizations (INGOs) committed to deepening state compliance with human rights law. Dismissed by Soviet diplomats in 1969 as 'weeds in the field' (Foot 2000: 38), INGO activity was beginning to have a significant impact on state–society relations in all corners of the globe. Amnesty International (AI) is a good example. Its mission is to cajole governments into complying with human rights standards, such as freedom from torture and the preservation of human dignity. Originally set up around a clutch of activists in 1961, it had over 150,000 members in more than 100 countries by 1977 (it now has 1.8 million members). INGOs like Amnesty perform two vital functions. They act as information networks with a capacity to communicate evidence of human rights violations to their membership and the global media. If INGOs are believed to be authoritative and independent, as Amnesty is, then this information is taken seriously both by UN bodies entrusted with monitoring human rights and by other actors in global civil society. In 1977, Amnesty won the Nobel Peace Prize and, seven years later, it was highly influential in the drafting of the 1984

Convention Against Torture. The second key role of human rights INGOs in world politics is one of criticizing governments for failing to uphold the standards they sign up to. INGOs make up the most important institution in world society.

Of the three dynamics for change, probably the most significant was the intrusion of human rights into the diplomacy of Western states. In the USA, Congress was increasingly minded to pass legislation linking aid and trade to human rights. And when Jimmy Carter became President, the cause of human rights found a passionate advocate, in sharp contrast to the Nixon–Kissinger era when they were thought to complicate the achievement of more important goals in the economic and security domains. In Western Europe, Norway and the Netherlands were becoming more activist in promoting human rights in their own foreign policy. Within the European Community (EC) and, after 1993, the European Union (EU), respect for human rights had always been a condition for membership. Individuals in EC states could also bring cases against their governments, indicating a much higher level of institutionalization than is the case in the UN system.

The signing of the Helsinki Final Act of 1975 illustrates each type of agency at work. This treaty was the culmination of three years of negotiation among thirty-five states involved in the Conference on Security and Cooperation in Europe (CSCE). The Eastern Bloc countries were desperate to normalize relations with the rest of Europe and have the postwar division of Europe recognized in an international treaty. The West Europeans were pushing hard for shared commitments to fundamental human rights: while this was resisted by communist states, they eventually yielded in order to realize their gains in other issue-areas. The Final Act set out ten 'guiding principles for relations among European states', including 'respect for human rights and other fundamental freedom of thought, conscience, religion or belief'.[6] While the communist elites chose to emphasis other articles in the final declaration which underscored the principle of non-intervention in their internal affairs, activists inside their societies began a period of intense mobilization which did untold damage to the stability of communist rule. Within a year of the Helsinki Final Act, the normative context had become inhospitable to the status quo in Eastern Europe – the opposite of what the communist governments had hoped for when they called for a security conference (Thomas 1999: 214). Human rights had exposed, in the words of R. J. Vincent, 'the internal regimes of all the members of international society to the legitimate appraisal of their peers' (1986: 152).

Countervailing forces in the human rights regime

By the mid- to late 1990s, there was a process of 'norm cascade' underway as the influence of international human rights norm diffused rapidly (Risse, Ropp, and Sikkink 1999: 21). The cascade is complete when the norms acquire a common-sense quality such that they become unchallenged (even if they are not unbroken). The 1993 World Conference on Human Rights was an important signifier of the unchallenged status of the standard, as was the signing of the ICCPR by China in 1998. These tipping points illustrate the progressive socialization of states into a framework where their internal behaviour is subject to the scrutiny of other states as well as international public opinion. As the example of the Helsinki process illustrates, the effect of the diplomacy of human rights reinforced by civil society actors and transnational networks was to delegitimize the communist system. Such a process provides a powerful counter to hard-headed realists who believe that human rights are 'just talk'.

The embedding of human rights principles and the development of institutions in world society such as Amnesty, CARE, Oxfam, the International Committee of the Red Cross, and countless others, represents a significant change in our moral sensibilities. This, however, must be checked by the realization that the diplomacy of human rights in the inter-state order presents defenders of solidarism with a number of awkward challenges. The ongoing structural human rights violations in China suggest that its motivation for participating in the regime is primarily strategic – there is little to suggest the state believes in the ideas or the treaties. Perhaps more shocking for advocates of human rights is their marginalization in the liberal heartland by those states who see themselves fighting a global war on terror. The most graphic representation of the retreat of human rights is the haunting images of naked Iraqi prisoners, first aired on CBS news in April 2004.

The official reaction of the Bush administration to the Abu Ghraib scandal was that these incidents were committed by 'a few bad apples'. Such complacency ought to be countered by the argument that the USA has, since 9/11, systematically sought to reinterpret key articles of the international bill of rights, specifically in relation to the treatment of prisoners. The US Secretary of Defense called for stronger interrogation techniques to be used against so-called high-value detainees. Far from refraining from cruel and degrading treatment, the US administration raised the bar for what counts as torture such that it was equated with the infliction of lasting pain commensurate with 'serious physical injury such as death or organ failure' (Bybee 2002).

The context of the threat posed by Islamist suicide bombers prompted voices inside the liberal establishment to question whether certain human rights commitments were in tension with national security. In relation to the convention banning torture, both Michael Ignatieff and Alan Derschowitz have argued that 'mental' torture might be permissible in clearly prescribed circumstances. While liberal intellectuals slug it out, governments around the world are quickly curtailing the rights of terror suspects – often so widely defined as to include political opposition movements. The general relegation of human rights down the agenda of core states reminds us that compliance to human-rights norms is contingent and reversible: human wrongs – such as torture in the name of anti-terrorism – can 'cascade' throughout global politics just as quickly as human rights-enhancing norms can be diffused. As Ken Booth has powerfully argued, there is a growing disjuncture between the development of a human rights culture in world society as against the unwillingness of statist elites in international society to act as protectors of a universal community of humankind (Booth 1995).

Conclusion

The case study has illustrated a dimension of international relations that has been of growing importance during the late modern period. By way of an overall conclusion to the chapter, the following paragraphs situate human rights more directly in the frames of system, society, and world society. The claim here is that the three ideal types provide clarity with respect to the sources of agency pushing for change and the impact this has on the rule structure. As intimated in the opening section of the chapter, a revived classical approach enables the discussion of normative questions without abandoning the quest to explain 'how it all hangs together' (Searle 1995: xi).

In relation to human rights, an English school analysis reminds us that even during the high-water mark of colonialism, the rights of individuals were never entirely distinguished. Hence the attraction of historical figures such as Hugo Grotious who believed that the law of nations was a subset of the law of nature in which the right to liberty and self-defence were universal. In the post-Enlightenment period, changes inside core states, such as the abolitionist movement in Britain in the early nineteenth century, affected change internationally in so far as the hegemonic power used its naval supremacy to end the trade in slaves. Arguably what prevented the evolution of an effective human rights regime prior to the mid-1970s were systemic factors: the condition of general war from 1914 to 1945; great power rivalry until the period of détente; and the absence of institutions in world society with the capacity to lobby and cajole states into rule-compliance.

The retreat of human rights after 9/11 also has a systemic quality that makes the challenge more than simply the product of neo-conservative ideology. Here we are driven back to the thought that there is a centripetal momentum to power such that it concentrates around a single source. Once the centralization reaches a tipping point, the conditions exist to challenge the pluralist rules and institutions upon which the post-Westphalian order has been built. This line of thought goes to the heart of debates about the role of the USA (and its allies in the West) in building a world order in its own image. Arguably this is a greater threat to international society than the destabilizing potential posed by decolonization, a concern that consistently reappeared in the later work of the British Committee. Aside from the emergence of an unbalanced power with global economic and military reach, the other significant systemic logic is that of 'new terrorism'. The willingness of coordinated networks of Islamists to use violence against Western targets undermines international society's claim to monopolize violence and regulate its use.

Running these two tendencies together – the appearance of an imperial power seeking to wage pre-emptive war and a non-state actor wielding violence outside the framework of the laws of war – we might conclude that Bull was right to be concerned that the element of international society was in drastic decline. Set against this, just as the bell has tolled for the state many times before, it is possible that the element of society is resilient enough to resist the power of US hegemony and the challenge of transnational nihilists. Whichever pathways history proceeds down, the categories of system, society, and world society will retain their relevance as explanatory tools and normative benchmarks.

? **QUESTIONS**

1. What are the core elements of the English school's approach to IR? How, if at all, does it differ from realism?

2. Are English school writers correct in pointing to the gradual diffusion of human rights norms throughout the system? Answer the question with reference to dominant actors in both international society and world society.

3. What is the relationship between order in international society and justice claims advanced by actors in world society?

4. Do you agree with Hedley Bull's comment that 'international society has always been present' in the world political system?

5. Does the English school have an implicit theory of progress in human history?

6. When journalists report on gross human rights violations, they often claim that the international community ought to 'do something'. How would an English school theorist respond to this plea?

7. Is the USA, under the Bush presidency, part of the system but outside international society? Do these categories help or hinder an account of the USA's role in world affairs after 9/11?

8. Was R. J. Vincent right to argue that how a government treats its populations has become the subject of legitimate scrutiny? Answer with reference to the 'Responsibility to Protect' document (listed under Important Websites).

9. Analyse Prime Minister Blair's speech 'Doctrine of International Community'? Does this suggest that international rules matter for state leaders?

10. Use the concepts of system, society, and world society (or community) to illustrate the evolution of human rights. What explanatory power do these concepts have?

11. Do you agree with Bull that international order will be undermined by solidarism?

12. Does Hedley Bull's later work signify a shift away from pluralism towards solidarism? Would he be a solidarist today?

FURTHER READING

Bull, H. (1977/1995), *The Anarchical Society: A Study of Order in World Politics* **(London: Macmillan).** Probably the best single work by a member of the English school. It is a defence of international society while at the same time recognizing that other historical orders have existed, and future orders are not only perceptible they may also be normatively more desirable.

Bull, H. and Watson, A. (1984) (eds), *The Expansion of International Society* **(Oxford: Oxford University Press).** A collection of essays representing the last phase of the British Committee's work. Contributors trace the system/society boundary through various case studies: underpinning the work is a question about whether the rules and institutions of European international society can be sustained in a deeply divided world.

Buzan, B. (2004), *From International to World Society* **(Cambridge: Cambridge University Press).** Starts out as a bold reworking of the 'world society' category; in the process, reworks international society too.

Butterfield, H. and Wight, M. (1966) (eds), *Diplomatic Investigations: Essays in the Theory of International Relations* **(London: Allen & Unwin).** A collection of British Committee essays, including classics by Martin Wight on 'Western Values' and Hedley Bull on 'Society and Anarchy'.

Clark, I. (2005), *Legitimacy in International Society* **(Oxford: Oxford University Press).** A book of historical and sociological depth which puts legitimacy back at the centre of the English school's understanding of international society.

■ **Linklater, A. (2001), 'The English School', in S. Burchill, A. Linklater, *et al*. *Theories of International Relations* (London: Macmillan), 93–118.** The best chapter on the English school written for upper-level undergraduates and postgraduate students.

■ **Vincent, R. J. (1986), *Human Rights in International Relations* (Cambridge: Cambridge University Press).** Vincent shows how the post-1945 world has given us a different vocabulary for thinking about the relationship between the rights of states and the rights of individuals. He makes a persuasive argument in defence of the inviolability of basic rights.

■ **Wheeler, N. J. (2000), *Saving Strangers: Humanitarian Intervention in International Society* (Oxford: Oxford University Press).** Looking at a series of Cold War and post-Cold War case studies, Wheeler shows how a new norm of humanitarian intervention emerged after 1989. In this and other work, the author sets out criteria for evaluating when interventions are legitimate.

■ **Wight, M. (1991), *International Theory: The Three Traditions* (Leicester: Leicester University Press for the Royal Institute of International Affairs).** Lectures delivered at the London School of Economics in the 1950s. Wight shows how the history of IR can be 'read' as a debate between realist, rationalist, and revolutionist positions.

IMPORTANT WEBSITES

● The English school website. This website was pioneered by Barry Buzan and has subsequently been taken on by Jason Ralph. The site is a documentation centre, including an excellent bibliography and a collection of reading lists written by leading figures in the English school. It also has information on English school papers presented at national and international conferences.
www.leeds.ac.uk/polis/englishschool/default.htm

● Responsibility to Protect. The document produced by the independent International Commission on Intervention and State Sovereignty (established by the Government of Canada in September 2000). After twelve months of deliberation, it was submitted to the UN Secretary-General and the UN General Assembly.
www.iciss.ca/menu-en.asp

● Amnesty International (AI). A worldwide movement of people who campaign for internationally recognized human rights. It claims to be independent of ideology, religion, government, or economic interest.
http://web.amnesty.org/pages/aboutai-index-eng

● 'Doctrine of International Community', Prime Minster Tony Blair's speech to the Economic Club of Chicago on 28 April 1999. Readers interested in the English school will find this speech engaging as it sets up a tension between Westphalian conceptions of rules and institutions with late-twentieth-century ideas about the primacy of inalienable human rights. For all its flaws, the speech illustrates the clear connections between how leaders and practitioners view the world, and the lenses offered to us by the English school.
www.number10.gov.uk

Visit the Online Resource Centre that accompanies this book for lots of interesting additional material. www.oxfordtextbooks.co.uk/orc/dunne/

8

Marxism and Critical Theory

MARK RUPERT

✔ **Reader's guide**

In discussions of world politics, it is not uncommon for Marxism to be dismissed out of hand as being preoccupied with economics rather than politics, and concerning itself with domestic rather than international social relations. In this chapter I will suggest to the contrary that Marxist theory aims at a critical understanding of capitalism as an historically particular way of organizing social life, and that this form of social organization entails political, cultural, and economic aspects which need to be understood as a dynamic ensemble of social relations not necessarily contained within the territorial boundaries of nation-states. Viewed in this way, Marxism can yield insights into the complex social relationships – on scales from the workplace and the household to the global – through which human beings produce and reproduce their social relations, the natural world, and themselves. The case-study section delves deeper into the insights that can be gained from Marxism in understanding the so-called 'War on Terror'.

Introduction

Marxism and critical theory[1] may be fundamentally distinguished from both the liberal and the realist traditions. Liberalism generally constructs its view of social reality in terms of individuals pursuing their private self-interest. These individuals may be led by self-interest into a social contract to create a government which will protect their lives, liberty, and property (John Locke), or to specialize and exchange with one another so as to create the germ of a market-mediated social division of labour (Adam Smith). With such contractual theories, liberalism purports to have resolved the problem of social order and cooperation among self-interested individuals. But the question of relations among these contractually constituted political communities remains problematic. Accordingly, the modern structural realist theory of International Relations has defined its field of inquiry in terms of a fundamental distinction between 'international' and 'domestic' politics (evident in Chapter 4). While the latter is held to be governed by a sovereign authority and hence allows for the authoritative resolution of disputes, the former is distinguished by the absence of these. In such an insecure 'anarchic' environment, sovereign states encounter one another with diffidence, suspicion, and, potentially, hostility. On this view, the 'high politics' of national security and power struggle necessarily dominate the horizon. Neoliberalism has sought to reintegrate into this state-centric world the liberal concern with contractual relations of cooperation, suggesting that international interdependence can create a demand for more cooperative forms of interaction which are facilitated by regimes and international organizations (as set out by Lisa Martin in Chapter 6). Thus can the 'low politics' of interdependence and routinized cooperation tame the 'high politics' of power struggle.

Viewed from the perspective of Marxism and critical theory, both liberalism and realism (and their neo variants) are profoundly limited, and limiting, for each takes as its premise a world of preconstituted social actors (whether self-interested individuals or security-seeking states) and is therefore unable to understand the social processes through which these kinds of actors have been historically constructed, and implicitly denies the possibilities for alternative possible worlds which may be latent within those processes of social self-production. In addition to the analytical blinders which this entails, the presuppositions of liberalism and realism are exposed as embodying political commitments which are profoundly conservative in effect. In order to recover the analytical and political possibilities denied by liberalism and realism, Marxism and critical theory have sought to illuminate processes of social self-production and the possibilities they may entail.

Marxism constitutes a huge and varied tradition of scholarship and practical political activity which is probably impossible to catalogue adequately. Therefore, rather than attempting to map this extensive and varied terrain, I will instead sketch out a particular interpretation which I believe builds upon the strengths of the dialectical social philosophy developed by Karl Marx, and shows how those strengths can yield insights into the politics of global production as well as the production of global politics. I will relate this tradition of dialectical theory to strains of thought sometimes characterized as 'Western Marxism' (to distinguish them from the official state Marxisms of the twentieth-century 'East') – including the critical theory associated with the so-called Frankfurt school, and the political theory of Antonio Gramsci. The Western Marxist encounter serves to highlight the many ways in which humans are socially self-productive, and suggests important critical insights which include the cultural and political, as well as the economic, aspects of that process. These conceptual tools, then, enable a much richer and politically nuanced interpretation of the politics of globalizing capitalism, and the role of imperial power within that process.

Historical materialism and the purposes of critical theory

While it may not be possible to provide a simple or straightforward definition of Marxism which would comfortably encompass all its different variants and divergent strains, one fundamental commonality is the desire to provide a critical interpretation of capitalism, understood as an historically produced – and therefore mutable – form of social life, rather than as the ineluctable expression of some essential human nature. To the extent that the ways in which we live our lives, the kinds of persons that we are, and our social relations, are all seen as historical social products, the critical question arises as to whether, and how, we might organize ourselves differently. Given the historically specific social context in which we find ourselves, are there tensions or possibilities for change which might enable us to produce a different, conceivably more equitable and democratic, future possible world? Before any such questions can be posed, however, it is necessary to exert some critical leverage on the prevailing view that social life in commodity-based society is a necessary outgrowth of the natural characteristics of individual human beings.

Contrary to Adam Smith's world of self-interested individuals, naturally predisposed to do a deal, Marx posited a *relational* and *process-oriented* view of human beings. On this view, humans are what they are not because it is hard-wired into them to be self-interested individuals, but by virtue of the relations through which they live their lives. In particular, he suggested that humans live their lives at the intersection of a three-sided relation encompassing the natural world, social relations and institutions, and human persons. These relations are understood as *organic*: each element of the relation is what it is by virtue of its place in the relation, and none can be understood in abstraction from that context. Insofar as humans are material beings, we must engage in some kind of productive interchange with the natural world in order to secure our survival. Insofar as we are social beings, this productive activity will be socially organized, necessarily involving thinking, talking, and planning together. And in the process of this socially productive activity, Marx believed, humans continuously remake their world (both its natural and social aspects) and themselves. If contemporary humans appear to act as self-interested individuals, then, it is a result not of our essential nature but of the particular ways we have produced our social lives and ourselves. On this view, humans may be collectively capable of recreating their world, their work and themselves in new and better ways, but only if we think critically about, and act practically to change, those historically peculiar social relations which encourage us to think and act as socially disempowered, narrowly self-interested individuals.

The meaning of dialectic: social relations in process

This view of human social life as *relations in process* forms the core of Marx's famous dialectical understanding of history: humans are historical beings, simultaneously the producers and the products of historical processes. In one of his more justly famous aphorisms, Marx summarized his view of history in the following terms: 'Men [*sic*] make their own history, but they do not make it just as they please; they do not make it under circumstances chosen by themselves, but under circumstances directly encountered, given, and transmitted from the past' (2000: 329).[2]

This process is sometimes described as a dialectic of agents and structures. Agents are social actors, situated in the context of relatively enduring social relations or structures, often embodied in institutions. Structures generate the possibility of certain kinds of social identity and corresponding forms of action (i.e. roles which actors may play in the context of those structures), but the structures are not themselves determinative or automatic. They require human agents continuously to re-enact their structural roles. Actors or agents may enact structural roles in ways which reproduce, alter, or potentially even transform social structures in which they are embedded. 'This interplay between individual actions and the institutions that form the framework for individual action is what Marx means by dialectic' (Schmitt 1997: 50).

This dialectical, or process-oriented approach has important implications for the way in which we study social life. As Marx himself put it, 'as soon as this active life-process is described, history ceases to be a collection of dead facts as it is with the empiricists' (2000: 181). On this view, causal explanations which posit objective 'laws' of social life may be misleading insofar as they distract us from the ways in which our world has been produced by historically situated human social agents. For if we understand history as an open-ended process of social self-production under historically specific circumstances, then we are led to inquire about the historical context of social relations in which social action takes place, to ask about the historical processes which generated that kind of social context, and to look for structured tensions in those historically specific forms of life, tensions which could open up possibilities for historically situated actors to produce social change. Further, we are encouraged to ask how our own social situation in the present relates to that of those whom we are studying. Might our own inquiries have implications for the ways in which contemporary people know and (re-)produce our own social world?

Marx's dialectical framework of relations in process also has important implications for the ways in which we think about politics, freedom, and unfreedom. Traditionally understood in terms of authoritative processes of rule (based upon an official monopoly of the means of coercion), or the authoritative allocation of values (who gets what, etc.), from a Marxian perspective these understandings of politics seem remarkably limited, and *limiting*. In the context of a dialectical view of history, politics appears as struggle over processes of social self-production, the ability to steer those processes in one direction or another and thus to shape the kind of world in which we will live and the kinds of persons we will become in that world. Politics, in short, concerns future possible worlds. And freedom may correspondingly be understood in terms of social self-determination – our collective ability to shape ourselves and our world. This is an expansive understanding of freedom, much broader and potentially more empowering than the traditional liberal understanding of freedom as individual choice (often expressed in a market context where the object of choice is the maximal satisfaction of the individual's private wants and needs). Based on the dialectical approach to understanding history, with its expansive conceptions of politics and of freedom, Marx developed a powerful and enduringly relevant critique of capitalist social life.

Marx and the critique of capitalism

Marx was one of the most incisive critics of a peculiarly modern form of social life – capitalism. For Marx, capitalism was not to be confused with markets or exchange, which long predated capitalism. Rather, capitalism represented a form of social life in which commodification had proceeded to such a degree that human labour itself was bought and sold on the market. One of Marx's central insights was that this situation presupposed the development of historically specific class-based relations and powers: the concomitant development of capital – socially necessary means of production reconstituted as the exclusive private property of a few – and wage labour as the compulsory activity of the many. Under the class relations of capitalism, direct producers are not personally tied to their exploiter, as were slaves in bondage to their master or feudal serfs bound to the lord's estate. In a real historical sense, then, capitalism frees workers to treat their labour as their own property. However, this freedom is complemented by a peculiarly capitalist kind of unfreedom. Insofar as means of production are under the ownership and control of a class of private owners, workers are *compelled* to sell their labour to members of this owning class in order to gain access to those means of production, engage in socially productive activity, and secure through their wages the material necessities of survival.

Marx's critique of capitalism hinged upon the claim, intelligible within the context of his dialectical theory of social self-production, that capitalism simultaneously involves historically unique forms of human freedom and unfreedom, empowerment and disem-powerment. Marx believed that although capitalism develops the productive powers of human societies to historically unprecedented heights, it does so in ways which are also disabling, exploitative, and undemocratic.

Capitalism is *disabling* insofar as this way of organizing social life distorts and obscures real historical possibilities for social self-determination. Socially empowered as never before to remake their world and themselves, people under capitalism are simultaneously prevented from realizing the full implications of their socially productive powers and the fuller forms of freedom these powers might make possible. Within the context of capital-ist commodification and the ideology it supports, historically specific forms of social organization and activity take on the appearance of objective, necessary, natural, universal conditions. Marx referred to this kind of disabling mystification as 'alienation' or 'fetishism'. Insofar as these appearances involve abstracting particular elements out of the constitutive relations through which they are produced, and representing them as if they were self-subsistent, preconstituted entities, this ideological mystification may be under-stood as a sort of reification – the practice of conflating abstractions with reality.

One of the reified forms of appearance generated by capitalist social life is the abstract individual. When we understand ourselves as monadic persons pursuing private wants and needs via our interactions with others, our social practices reproduce our identity as abstract individuals. These individuals are abstract insofar as they are understood to embody certain attributes (propensities, preferences, aptitudes, rights, etc.) which 'are assumed as given, independently of social context' (Lukes 1973: 73). For persons understood in this way all social relations appear 'external', that is, as either an instrument or an obstacle for the realization of already given private purposes. The practices which might be seen as specific to a particular historical or social context (and hence to be potentially changeable along with that context) are instead presumed to be hard-wired into individuals as such. Thus the self-interested behaviour which Adam Smith observed among private producers in the context of a commodity society is represented as a universal human attribute, a natural 'propensity to truck, barter, and exchange' (Smith 1993: 21).

Further, to the extent that we understand ourselves as isolated individuals, we confront our social environment not as our collective social product, but as an objective constraint on our individual choices. Social life becomes something which happens to us, rather than a collective way of being in the world. This is an instance of a powerful critical insight derived from Marxian theory: to the extent that people understand existing social relations as natural, necessary, and universal, they are prevented from looking for transformative possibilities, precluded from imagining the social production of alternative possible worlds. In short, they may abdicate their collective powers of social self-production. Ironically, then, the unprecedented development of productive capacity under capitalism has as its historical correlate the disempowerment of collective human producers.

A second strand of Marxian critique holds that capitalism is exploitative. Often couched in the arcane language of the labour theory of value which Marx adopted for the purposes of his critical engagement with classical political economy, the theory of exploitation is a complex and controversial topic (Brewer 1990: 26–36; and Schmitt 1997: 100–13), but it may be more readily understandable when expressed as an instance of the disabling unfreedom discussed above. On Marx's view, capital is the *result* of socially productive activity, the creation of value by labour. Viewed as a 'thing', capital itself has no productive powers. But viewed as a social relation, capital is productive only as accumulation of previously expended labour power, set in motion by newly expended labour power. Yet, because capitalism is characterized by private ownership of the means of production, as owner the capitalist controls the production process and expropriates its product – the *surplus value* created by labour (i.e. the product of labour above and beyond that required to sustain the workers themselves). The process and product of socially organized labour are subordinated to private property and incorporated into the accumulation of capital.

Of course, the capitalists' ability to control the production process and expropriate its product depends upon the successful reproduction of their class-based powers, and the insulation of these powers from more democratic, collective forms of decision-making. The third strand of Marxian critique thus highlights the degree to which capitalism creates *private social powers* located in a separate 'economic' sphere of social life, effectively off limits from explicitly 'political' public deliberation and norms of democratic accountability. This is perhaps best understood in terms of an historical contrast. Pre-capitalist modes of production such as feudalism involved the direct coercive expropriation of surplus labour by the dominant class, a landed nobility whose social powers were simultaneously economic and political. Should serfs fail to yield surplus labour to their lord, the social significance of this was not simply a private deal gone bad but rather a direct challenge to the political–economic order upon which the lords's social position rested. That the lord would respond with coercive force would not have seemed extraordinary in a social context where economic and political aspects of social life were fused in this way.

In a modern capitalist context, however, it is relatively unusual (although certainly not unheard of) for employers to use direct coercive force as an integral part of their extraction of surplus labour. Rather, workers are compelled to work, and to submit to capitalist control of the workplace, by what Marxists often refer to as the 'dull compulsion of economic life', the relentless daily requirement to earn enough to pay the rent and put food on the table. The direct intervention of explicitly political authority and directly coercive force within the capitalist workplace is the exception rather than the rule. The social powers of capitalist investors and employers are ensconced in this depoliticized and privatized economic sphere, understood not as intrinsically political powers but as individual prerogatives attendant upon the ownership of private property. By virtue of being understood as attributes of 'private property', these powers are made democratically unaccountable (it is, after all, nobody else's business what each of us does with our own private property). Further, because of the state's structural dependence on private investment, government is effectively compelled to serve the long-term interest of the capitalist class (not necessarily congruent with that of individual capitalists). Failure to create the political conditions perceived by capitalists as a business-friendly climate would result in capitalist investors sending their capital after higher profits elsewhere and leaving the government to preside over economic crisis which could well be politically catastrophic for incumbent office holders. Insofar as politicians of all major parties are acutely aware of this structural dependence upon maintenance of a business-friendly climate, a range of possible policy orientations (which might be perceived as threatening to the profitability of private investment) are effectively precluded. This implicit veto power over public policy is yet another sense in which Marxists have argued that capitalism is undemocratic.

In these ways, then, capitalism effectively privatizes the social powers of investors and employers, lodging these in a privatized economic sphere, understood to be separate from the sphere of politics, public affairs, or the state. None of this is uncontestable in principle or uncontested in fact. A system of social organization premised upon *privatized social powers* is a system fraught with contradictions and tensions. Historical materialism highlights these powers, along with their structural and ideological defences, in order to subject them to critical scrutiny. The purpose of this critical analysis of historical structures is to enable identification of historically real possibilities for progressive social change.

Capitalism as a system of social organization, as a way of life, presupposes as part of its structure both a privatized and depoliticized economic sphere and, correspondingly, a public, political state. Further, this separation is embodied in a variety of cultural practices and representations in which we appear to ourselves as private individuals, workers, consumers, rights-bearing citizens, confronting a pre-given world in which we must choose the most efficient means for the realization of our private purposes. To identify capitalism narrowly with the economy – and therefore Marxism with economic analysis – is to miss the crucial point that particular forms of political and cultural organization and practice are bound up with capitalist social reality, and are implicated in political struggles over the reproduction – or transformation – of that entire way of life.

Classical theories of imperialism

Among the most influential contributions of the Marxist tradition to the study of world politics have been theories of imperialism. According to Anthony Brewer's authoritative text (1990: 25), Marx himself never actually used the term 'imperialism'. Further, Brewer's interpretation of Marx's relatively few discussions of the topic suggests that colonialism is not essential to capitalism: 'capitalism does not need a subordinated hinterland or periphery, though it will use and profit from one if it exists' (Brewer 1989: 57). Although he had relatively little to say about imperialism as such, regarding the expansionary dynamics of capitalism which we would nowadays associate with globalization Marx was prescient:

> The bourgeoisie, by the rapid improvement of all instruments of production, by the immensely facilitated means of communication, draws all, even the most barbarian, nations into civilization. The cheap prices of commodities are the heavy artillery with which it batters down all Chinese walls, with which it forces the barbarians' intensely obstinate hatred of foreigners to capitulate. It compels all nations, on pain of extinction, to adopt the bourgeois mode of production; it compels them to introduce what it calls civilization into their midst, i.e., to become bourgeois themselves. In one word, it creates a world after its own image.

Marx 2000: 248–9[3]

The conventional wisdom of some mainstream IR theorists notwithstanding, capitalism for Marx was clearly not a purely 'domestic' phenomenon, hermetically contained within the territorial vessels of modern nation-states. Its expansionist dynamics (rooted in the imperatives of competitive accumulation) overflowed those boundaries and outdistanced the geographical scope of state-based political authority. For Marx, the privatized social powers of capital have long had global horizons. Marx thought that the international activities of industrial capital (as distinct from the trading of merchant capital) were potentially transformative for the social organization of production on a world scale, spreading and intensifying the capitalist organization of production and greatly expanding socially productive powers. Consistent with his dialectical analysis of capitalism, Marx believed this process would entail both progressive and retrogressive aspects, generate massive suffering as well as the potential for qualitative and, he hoped, progressive social change.

In the early twentieth century, as the First World War loomed, a generation of Marxist writers emerged who are most appropriately associated with the theory of imperialism. Including Rosa Lumemburg, Rudolf Hilferding, Nicolai Bukharin, and most famously Vladimir Lenin, these writers argued that advanced processes of capitalist accumulation were driving the major capitalist countries into colonial expansionism. Although the precise mechanisms driving capitalism toward imperialism varied (e.g. the quest for raw materials, overproduction requiring a search for new markets, or over-accumulation compelling the export of capital), their thinking converged on the notion that advanced capitalist countries would be driven by the imperatives of capital accumulation to support the international expansion of their great monopolistic blocs of industrial–financial capital. In a finite world where much of the globe had already been colonized by one or another of the great imperialist powers, 'inter-imperialist rivalry' was seen as an overwhelmingly likely source of conflict, and the First World War would have appeared as confirmation of this.

Classical theories of imperialism have been subjected to sharp criticism insofar as they represent species of economic determinism – the idea that processes intrinsic to the economy are the primary determinants of social and political life. In the following section, I will discuss the evolution of dialectical theory in the form of Western Marxism and critical theory, and explain how these theoretical developments provide important conceptual resources for recasting Marxian theories of global power in more dialectical, and enabling, forms.

Western Marxism and critical theory

The Bolshevik revolution and the rise of Official Soviet Marxism in the 'East' provided the backdrop for the development of 'Western Marxism' – a family of innovative theories which both built upon, and reacted against, aspects of the classical Marxist tradition. The Marxist expectation that proletarian revolution, once ignited, would sweep the advanced capitalist world was bitterly disappointed in the early twentieth century. The Russian revolution gave birth to socialism in one nation and Marxists in the West were left to ponder the reasons why working-class revolution had failed to materialize in their own countries and, subsequently, why fascism had triumphed in some Western countries. Official Soviet Marxism soon solidified into a rigid Stalinist dogma in the service of a one-party state, stifling rather than enabling critical discourse and social self-determination. It is in this historic context that we may understand Western Marxism and critical theory not just in terms of a critique of capitalism but also a corresponding critique of positivism and economic determinism as ways of understanding social life. In the apt summary of critical theorist Douglas Kellner, 'those individuals who became known as "Western Marxists" saw the need to concern themselves with consciousness, subjectivity, culture, ideology and the concept of socialism precisely in order to make possible radical political change' (1989: 12). I will highlight the core contributions of two major strands of the Western Marxist tradition: the critical theory associated with the Frankfurt school, and the dialectical Marxism associated with Antonio Gramsci and his followers (among whom I count myself).

The term Frankfurt school refers to a group of theorists originally associated with the Institute for Social Research at Frankfurt University beginning in the 1920s. In some regards, these theorists worked within the spirit of the Marxian critique of the disabling effects of capitalist modernity, but in other ways they diverged from more mainstream forms of Marxism. Two of the early leading lights of the Frankfurt school, Horkheimer and Adorno, began 'to lose faith in the revolutionary potential of the working class in the face of the triumph of fascism and the integration of labour into the capitalist system in the democratic capitalist countries' (Kellner 1989: 105). Further, they saw how, in the Soviet Union, Marxism was being transformed into rigid doctrine of economic determinism sanctified as objective 'science'. In the face of these developments, they wanted to retain a critical and potentially progressive role for social theory, but were wary of orthodox Marxism's preoccupation with production (narrowly understood) and the corresponding emphasis on the historic role of the proletariat. Critical theorists were deeply suspicious of the idea that objectively valid forms of knowledge could be arrived at independent of social context, innocent of prevailing practices and norms. They questioned the dichotomization of is and ought, fact and value, known object and knowing subject, which underpinned 'positivist' forms of scientific knowledge claims and associated constructs. Horkheimer and Adorno, in particular, were sharply critical of 'instrumental reason' – a technical rationality of means (choosing the most efficient instrument to pursue a pre-given goal) which claims neutrality as to ends. Rather, the construction of knowledge claims is no less a purposive social practice than any other, and theory is permeated with social values and norms, fraught with political implications for the future, whether these are explicit or implicit. Theories which claim objective truth are then profoundly misleading: on the one hand, mystifying the normative commitments which underpin their own truth claims; and, on the other, denying that alternative normative values and future possible worlds are at stake in knowledge claims which the theory offers up as fact. Underlying bureaucratically administered societies of both East and West, twentieth-century cultures permeated by positivism and instrumental reason stifled critical discourse.

The Italian Marxist Antonio Gramsci, incarcerated in Mussolini's fascist prisons for the last decade of his life, was likewise sharply critical of economistic and positivistic forms of knowledge, including forms of Marxism based on economic determinism. Gramsci insisted on situating the process of human knowledge construction in particular historical social contexts and, in a devastating critique of the economistic and scientistic Marxism of Bukharin, he derided as 'metaphysical materialism . . . any systematic formulation that is put forward as an extra-historical truth, as an abstract universal outside of time and space' (Gramsci 1971: 437). For Gramsci, Marxism was not the objective truth of history, but was rather a way of telling the story of history from *within* a capitalist historical context, a story which could lead people to consider possible post-capitalist futures and ask themselves how, together, they might get there from here.

Accordingly, Gramsci developed a theory of **hegemony** as a form of political power which relied more strongly upon consent than coercion. In a hegemonic social situation, dominant groups (classes, class fractions, and their various allies) articulate a social vision which claims to serve the interests of all, and they use selective incentives to recruit junior partners into their coalition and to divide and disable opposition. Gramsci believed that in advanced capitalist societies, in which civil society was highly developed, hegemonic power might be promoted and contested in fora of popular culture, education, journalism, literature, and art, as well as in political parties and unions. Under conditions of hegemony, subordinate social groups might be led to consent to the power of dominant groups, making the widespread use of direct (and obviously oppressive) coercive power unnecessary. However, Gramsci argued, hegemony was not seamless, a dominant ideology which simply foreclosed any possibility of critique. On the contrary, hegemony could be and should be continuously challenged throughout civil society. In this way, Gramsci hoped, an atomized and depoliticized capitalist culture might be challenged by a counter-hegemonic political culture, people might be led to think of their economic lives as having political significance, and they might begin to question capitalism's structured separation of the economic from the political aspects of social life. This latter he saw as the necessary precondition for the concurrent democratization of economic, cultural, and political life, a gateway to a variety of possible postcapitalist futures (see Rupert 2005).

Contemporary critical analysis of global power

The forms of critical theory developed by the Frankfurt school and by Gramsci might lead us to regard with some scepticism claims of scientific objectivity associated with positivistic forms of International Relations theory, and the economic determinism underlying classical theories of imperialism. And, indeed, contemporary theorists have drawn upon these and related intellectual resources to begin to construct critical theories of world politics. Pioneering contributions were made in the early 1980s by scholars such as Richard Ashley, Robert Cox, and Andrew Linklater.

Ashley (who initially drew heavily on the contemporary critical social theorist Jurgen Habermas, but later became more closely associated with poststructuralism) began to develop a critique of Waltzian neorealism which, he argued, reframes classical realism (with its emphasis on actively interpreting the pragmatic, artful, and creative practices of statecraft) into a positivist theory in which world politics is itself depoliticized, reduced to an economic logic which takes as given the world it confronts, and inquires only as to 'the efficient achievement of whatever goals are set before the political actor' (Ashley 1986: 292). Questions regarding political ends are evacuated from the study of world politics, and the ability of theory critically to contemplate alternative possible worlds is effectively denied. The result, according to Ashley, is 'the impoverishment of political imagination and the reduction of international politics to a battleground for the . . . clash of technical reason against technical reason in the service of unquestioned ends' (1986: 297). Also, drawing on Habermas, critical IR theorists such as Linklater (1996) have sought to dereify the state, and to reincorporate processes of social reasoning and 'discourse ethics' into an explicitly normative account of the construction of political community at various levels. As Devetak (1995: 172) explains, 'discourse ethics promotes a cosmopolitan ideal where the political organization of humanity is decided by a process of dialogue in which participation is open to all who stand to be affected by the decision'.

Robert Cox (1986) also drew on the idea of critical theory to call into question prevailing modes of theorizing world politics: as a species of positivist or 'problem-solving' theory, 'Neorealism implicitly takes the production process and the power relations inherent in it as a given element of national interest, and therefore as a part of its parameters' (1986: 216–17). Assuming what needs to be explained, neorealism describes patterns in the operation of power among states without inquiring as to the social relations through which that power is produced. Moreover, those relations themselves have a history, a process of production, and they need not remain forever as we see them now. Accordingly, Cox adopts what he calls a method of 'historical structures' in which 'state power ceases to be the sole explanatory factor and becomes part of what is to be explained' (1986: 223):

> " The world can be represented as a pattern of interacting social forces in which states play an intermediate though autonomous role between the global structure of social forces and local configurations of social forces within particular countries. . . . Power is seen as emerging from social processes rather than taken as given in the form of accumulated material capabilities, that is as the result of these processes. (Paraphrasing Marx, one could describe the latter, neo-realist view as the 'fetishism of power'.) "

Cox 1986: 225

A critical theory approach to global politics would then take a relational, process-oriented perspective, and seek to show how social forces (classes, social movements, etc.), states, and world orders are bound up together in particular constellations of historical structures. It would inquire as to the ways in which those historical structures – entailing political, cultural, and economic aspects – had been socially produced, the ways in which they differentially empower various kinds of social agents, and the kinds of resistances which those power relations engender. It would seek to highlight tensions and possibilities within the historical structures of the present in order to open up political horizons and enable social agents situated within those structures to imagine, and potentially begin to realize, alternative possible worlds. The view of theory defended by Cox – and his characterization of 'problem-solving theory' – is discussed in Chapter 1.

Case study: War on Terror or twenty-first-century imperialism?

Within eighteen months of the horrible events of 11 September 2001, the USA, the UK, and an assortment of junior partners were engaged in a massive military invasion of Iraq. Despite the fact that Iraq had no demonstrable connection with the attacks, in its public justifications of the war the Bush administration associated the invasion of Iraq with its 'War on Terror'.

How can the dialectical approach to explanation associated with Marxism and critical theory help us to make sense of these vexing developments? From this perspective, a satisfactory account would need to incorporate not just the historical structures of global capitalism (with their economic, political, and cultural aspects) but also the ideologies and actions of human agents situated within these structures. The resulting multi-layered explanatory account would resemble a sort of dialectical layer cake seeking to explain: (1) how the structures of capitalist modernity create the possibility of particular kinds of world politics; (2) how those possibilities were realized in the particular forms of the twentieth-century capitalist world order; (3) within those historical structures, the key relationship between capitalism, Fordism, and the geopolitics of petroleum; and (4) the ideologies of 'economic security' which have animated US policy-makers from the Cold War to the Bush administration. I will be able to do no more in this context than to sketch out the broad outlines of what such an explanation might look like. That should be enough, however, to show how this kind of analysis differs from other approaches to the study of world politics.

Recall that at the heart of capitalism is a class relation between those who own means of production and those who must sell their labour-power in order to gain access to those means of production. One of Marx's most important insights was that this class relationship presupposes a broader set of social relationships, a set of social structures which make this kind of relation possible. One of these enabling structures involved the constitution of social means of production as private property, and hence presupposed the privatization and depoliticization of economic life (recall, by way of contrast, how economic and political life had been fused under feudalism). The creation of a privatized and depoliticized economy implies the exclusion of public, political concerns from the economy, and their assignment to a separate sphere of society, one which we have come to associate with the modern state. The political states which have developed within capitalist modernity are understood to be sovereign within their territory, and thus are enabled to legislate and regulate 'domestic' affairs. Yet, the activities of private economic actors continuously overflow those boundaries – in no small measure because of the dynamics of capitalism as a system of accumulation without limits, driven by the compulsions of relentless market competition. The structural contours of capitalist modernity, then, involve a system of territorially limited political authority and flows of economic activity which are not similarly limited. This structure represents a condition of possibility for imperialism – the exercise by states of coercive power in the service of capital accumulation – as well as systems of global hegemonic power in which coercive force is less evident and the ideological politics of consent come into the fore (Rosenberg 1994; Wood 2003; Cox 1986).

The productive power of Fordist capitalism

These structures of capitalist modernity are not automatically self-perpetuating, but rather are continuously (re-)produced, challenged, or changed by human agents under particular historical circumstances. Thus, these structures may assume distinct forms during identifiable historical periods. During the twentieth century, Fordist industrial capitalism in the USA was setting global standards of dynamism and productivity (this itself was not simply an historical datum but the result of long and complex political struggles – see Rupert 1995). After the Second World War a transnational coalition, centred on Fordist industrial capital, emerged and promoted a hegemonic world-order project which envisioned a global economy of free trade, but one in which state managers would be able to use macroeconomic policy to sustain economic activity and levels of consumption, and in which labour unions might be tolerated or even encouraged as brokers of industrial consent, securing the cooperation of workers within the framework of Fordist mass-production industry in exchange for real wages which would grow along with productivity. In the USA and across much of the industrial capitalist world, organized labour was integrated into a hegemonic coalition which sought to rebuild the world economy along the lines of this 'corporate–liberal' model (van der Pijl 1984; Rupert 1995). Securing a measure of political stability and institutionalizing a rough correspondence between mass production and consumption, this set of historical structures enabled a period of unprecedented economic growth and capital accumulation, and institutionalized a culture of mass consumerism, especially in the wealthy global 'North'. The political economy of Fordist capitalism played a central role in the great global order struggles of the twentieth century: arguably, it was the unparalleled productive power of Fordist capitalism which enabled the geopolitical triumph of the allies over the autarkic and authoritarian capitalism of the axis powers, and subsequently of the reunified West over the Soviet bloc in the Cold War.

Fordist capitalism depended not only on politically quiescent industrial labour and predictable levels of consumer demand for the products of mass production industry; it also required fuel and lubricants for its machines, raw material for its pervasive petrochemical industry, and inputs for its increasingly mechanized and chemical-intensive agriculture. Oil, in short, was indispensable to the energy-intensive form of Fordist capitalism at the heart of the twentieth-century world order. Although the US oil industry was able to provide from domestic production the great bulk of the oil consumed by the allies during the Second World War, by the end of the war it was clear that US reserves were not sufficient to fuel the reconstruction of the capitalist world economy or its growth in subsequent decades.

US foreign policy in the pursuit of capitalist interests

Framed in terms of 'economic security', US global strategy after the Second World War aimed not just at 'containing' the power of the Soviet Union, but also at creating a world which would be hospitable to the growth of US-centred capitalism (Pollard 1985). US strategists explicitly envisioned a symbiotic relationship between the vitality and robustness of the capitalist 'free world' and globally projected US military power (May 1993). Viewed through the lenses of this strategic vision, protecting the free world was closely identified with promoting a vigorous US-centred capitalist world economy, and it was this world-view which appeared to justify US interventions in order to counter political forces which might inhibit the growth of US-dominated global capitalism. Insofar as the Fordist world order depended upon ample and cheap supplies of oil which the USA could not itself provide, US strategists sought to establish predominance in the oil-rich Persian Gulf region.

Pivotal to postwar US strategic dominance in the Gulf were its relations with Iran and Saudi Arabia. Franklin Roosevelt had established a strategic partnership with the Saudi ruling family in 1945: 'Roosevelt forged an agreement with Abdul-Aziz ibn Saud, the founder of the modern Saudi dynasty, to protect the royal family against its internal and external enemies in return for privileged access to Saudi oil' (Klare 2004: 3). In Iran, US influence was secured for a quarter-century by the 1953 CIA-sponsored coup in which the democratically elected Prime Minister, Mohammad Mossadegh, was overthrown by forces who re-established the autocratic power of the Iranian monarch, the reliably pro-American Shah. In light of this history, it is little wonder that the Iranian Revolution which finally ended the Shah's rule in 1979 fused a Shiite Islamic theocracy with bitter anti-Americanism (Kinzer 2003). Nor should it be surprising that the USA–Saudi relationship is deeply ambivalent, with widespread resentment of US influence (and, for the last decade, military presence) in the Kingdom finding expression through the fundamentalist Wahhabi brand of Sunni Islam which predominates there. It is against this backdrop of global geopolitics and the ideology of economic security that we can reinterpret the invasion of Iraq under the guise of the War on Terror.

The most hawkish elements in the administration of George W. Bush exploited the atmosphere of jingoism and fear in the USA following the terrorist attacks of 11 September 2001 to put into effect their long-cherished vision of US global military supremacy, unilateral action, and the pre-emptive use of military force deployed to create a world in which the US model of capitalist democracy is unquestioned – a strategic vision now known as the Bush Doctrine. Building on 'a position of unparalleled military strength and great economic and political influence' – a unipolar condition to which Bush refers as 'a balance of power that favors freedom' – '[t]he United States will use this moment of opportunity to extend the benefits of freedom across the globe. We will actively work to bring the hope of democracy, development, free markets, and free trade to every corner of the globe' (White House 2002: 1–2). Iraqi leader Saddam Hussein's continuing defiance of US power in a region of such enormous strategic significance effectively mocked the Bush administration's pretensions to unquestioned global supremacy. That removing Saddam was a high priority for those who formulated the Bush Doctrine should not then be surprising. The administration also hoped that a postwar client regime in Iraq would provide the USA with a base of operations in the heart of the Gulf region more reliably open to US forces than Saudi bases. Further, among the so-called neoconservatives in the administration and their intellectual guides (such as the Arabist Bernard Lewis), it was believed that a forcefully 'democratized' Iraq would lead to the spread of liberal democracy throughout the Middle East, 'drain the swamp' of authoritarianism and poverty which was believed to be the breeding ground of terrorism, and lessen the perceived threats posed to Israel. Speaking just before the invasion of Iraq began, Vice-President Cheney suggested that the 'War on Terror' might be won by a forceful display of power and resolve in the heart of the Arab Middle East: 'I firmly believe, along with men like Bernard Lewis, who is one of the great students of that part of the world, that strong, firm U.S. response to terror and to threats to the United States would go a long way, frankly, toward calming things in that part of the world' (Cheney quoted in Waldman 2004).

But the Iraq War cannot be properly understood in abstraction from questions of world order following in the wake of Fordist capitalism. Iraq sits atop oil reserves estimated as second only to those of Saudi Arabia, so US dominance in postwar Iraq might promise a reliable source of petroleum supply as well as significant leverage over the Organization of Petroleum Exporting Countries (OPEC) and global oil prices. US dependence on imported oil continues to grow – as does the petroleum consumption of Europe, Japan, and rapidly industrializing countries like India and China – and no other petroleum reserves are as vast, or as significant for the future of global strategic power in a post-Fordist world, as those of the Gulf region. The Bush administration's National Energy Policy task force, chaired by Vice-President Cheney, estimated that the Gulf region will be supplying around two-thirds of the world's oil needs by the year 2020 (Dreyfuss 2003: 44). In their quest for global supremacy and a capitalist world order favourable to US interests, Bush administration officials may well have believed that militarily-based strategic dominance in the Middle East, and an American hand on the world's oil tap, would represent a bargaining chip of incalculable value when dealing with potentially incompliant allies and emergent rivals (especially China) even more dependent upon imported oil than the USA itself (Everest 2004).[4] On this view, the War on Terror is inextricably bound up with US attempts to achieve strategic dominance in the oil-rich Persian Gulf region, and this latter is deeply entangled with the historical structures of US-centred global Fordist capitalism.

Conclusion

Marxism is neither solely preoccupied with the economy, nor with domestic relations. Rather it aims at a critical understanding of capitalism as an historically particular way of organizing social life, one which entails political and cultural as well as economic relations and practices, which has never been containable within the boundaries of territorial states, and which has crucial implications for processes of social self-production on scales from the workplace and household to global order. Conceived by Marx as a dialectical theory of relations in process, the enabling implications of Marxist theory were substantially vitiated by interpretations which cast it as a form of economic determinism. Seeking to recover its ability to illuminate dialectical tensions and possibilities, Western Marxism and critical theory formulated sharp critiques of economic determinism and positivistic forms of knowledge more generally. These currents led toward a re-emphasis of politics, culture, and ideology within a broadly materialist understanding of social life, pointing towards an approach which Cox (1986) described as a 'method of historical structures'. Employing an analytic approach similar to the one Cox suggests, we may understand the Iraq War as the product of a confluence of social relations and processes which traverse and interrelate social forces, states, and world orders. The structures of capitalist modernity, the historical forms they assumed in the epoch of Fordism and the hegemonic world order which emerged out of that context, strategic ideologies of economic security, and the culture of Fordist consumerism are all implicated in this story.

But what of the political potential of Marxist theory, its ability to illuminate tensions and possibilities in the present which could open up alternative possible worlds and modes of social life? This is, in one sense, the perennially deferred question of Marxist theory. In the absence of a unitary revolutionary agent – the famous 'workers of the world' – how can a materialist theory talk about transformative politics? Some Frankfurt school theorists became deeply pessimistic about this. Certainly, from the perspective of an anti-determinist, non-teleological 'marxism without guarantees' (Hall 1996), no straightforward *a priori* answer to this question is possible. But twenty-first-century global politics is not without hope. As the century turned, a confluence of diverse social forces and movements – a 'movement of movements', radically decentralized yet strategically coordinated, sharing not so much a coherent ideological vision as a vigorous opposition to capitalist globalization – began through its collective resistance to enact new kinds of global politics. In a series of dramatic, globally visible protests, they called into question the reified representations of capitalist global hegemony and asserted that 'another world is possible'. They explicitly connected globalizing capitalism with US imperial power and, just prior to the invasion of Iraq, used their transnational activist networks to call forth and coordinate simultaneous anti-war demonstrations in hundreds of cities around the world, involving many millions of participants – an unparalleled achievement of grass-roots global politics. While some of these social movements embraced heterodox forms of Marxism such as 'Autonomism' (on which, see Tormey 2004: 114–17), most were probably non-Marxist in their political orientation. Yet, these movements were united in a kind of dialectical self-understanding: they represented themselves as contesting historically specific constellations of capitalist or corporate social power in order to open up the possibility of alternative future worlds. In this, I would suggest, they were true to the spirit if not the letter of Marx's dialectical theory of politics in the modern, capitalist world (see Rupert 2005). In such a world, where dialectics of power and resistance are continually re-enacted in various ways, I would argue that the central insights of Marxism and critical theory retain their relevance.

QUESTIONS

1. What do Marxists mean when they talk about a *dialectical* understanding of history?

2. How does such a view shed critical light on liberal individualist theories, such as that of Adam Smith?

3. What are the implications of a dialectical understanding of history for the way in which we think about *politics* and *freedom*? When we see the world in terms of dialectical theory, how do we need to redefine these terms?

4. Why do Marxists believe that capitalism cannot be adequately understood as a 'domestic' phenomenon? How has this belief been reflected in the theories of imperialism?

5. What do Marxists mean when they talk about capitalism as more than just an economy? In what ways are politics and culture integral to capitalism as a way of life?

6. How do the insights of Western Marxism shed critical light on more 'economistic' forms of Marxism?

7. What is the purpose of critical theory? How does it differ from 'positivist' or 'problem-solving' theory?

8. On what grounds has 'neorealist' IR theory been criticized by contemporary proponents of critical theory? What are the analytical and political limits of neo- or structural realism which critics highlight? What would a critical theory of world politics do which structural realism or other positivist theories cannot?

9. How does a critical understanding of capitalism as a way of life encompassing economic, political, and cultural or ideological aspects help us to make sense of US global strategy since the Second World War?

10. How does such an understanding enable us to reframe the War on Terror as an instance of twenty-first-century imperialism?

FURTHER READING

■ **Brewer, A. (1990), *Marxist Theories of Imperialism: A Critical Survey*, 2nd edn (London: Routledge).** A comprehensive explication and critique of the various theories of imperialism to which the Marxian tradition has given rise.

■ **Cox, R. and Sinclair, T. (1996), *Approaches to World Order* (Cambridge: Cambridge University Press).** Collected in this book are some of the most seminal essays by a leader in the neo-Gramscian tradition of international studies.

■ **Isaac, J. (1987),** *Power and Marxist Theory* **(Ithaca NY: Cornell University Press).** This innovative book uses a 'critical realist' view of the relation between agents and structures to reinterpret the concept of social power at the heart of Marxian theory.

■ **Kellner, D. (1989),** *Critical Theory, Marxism and Modernity* **(Baltimore MD: Johns Hopkins University Press).** Interprets the critical theory associated with the Frankfurt school as an outgrowth of a strongly Marxian-inflected critique of capitalist modernity, but one which diverged from increasingly orthodox Marxism over the course of the twentieth century.

■ **Robinson, W. I. (2004),** *A Theory of Global Capitalism* **(Baltimore MD: Johns Hopkins University Press).** Robinson posits the emergence of a globalized process of capital accumulation, a transnational capitalist class, and a nascent transnational state.

■ **Rosenberg, J. (1994),** *Empire of Civil Society* **(London: Verso).** Rosenberg critically situates the theory and practice of *Realpolitik* within the relations and processes of capitalist modernity.

■ **Rupert, M. and Smith H. (2002) (eds),** *Historical Materialism and Globalisation* **(London: Routledge).** Essays from a variety of scholars broadly sympathetic to historical materialism but understanding in very different ways its significance in a world of globalizing capitalism.

■ **Shannon, T. (1992),** *An Introduction to the World-system Perspective,* **2nd edn (Boulder CO: Westview).** A schematic overview and sympathetic critique of world-system theories.

■ **Tormey, S. (2004),** *Anti-Capitalism: A Beginner's Guide* **(Oxford: Oneworld).** Informed by a post-communist sensibility, this book offers a critical overview of theories and practices of contemporary anti-capitalism from Autonomism to Zapatismo.

■ **Wood, E. M. (2003),** *Empire of Capital* **(London: Verso).** A contemporary reinterpretation of imperialism theory from an influential Marxian political theorist.

IMPORTANT WEBSITES

● Marxists.org Internet Archive. A massive electronic resource including extensive selections of texts (in a variety of languages) from many major Marxist theorists, articles on the history of Marxism, and an encyclopedia of Marxism.
www.Marxists.org

● The Socialist Register. Web page of a leading socialist annual containing Marxian analyses of globalizing capitalism, US imperialism, and a variety of other topics.
http://socialistregister.com

● Dialectical Marxism. The writings of political philosopher Bertell Ollman, one of the world's leading scholars of dialectical theory. Check out 'Class Struggle', Ollman's Marxist board-game.
www.nyu.edu/projects/ollman/index.php

 Visit the Online Resource Centre that accompanies this book for lots of interesting additional material. www.oxfordtextbooks.co.uk/orc/dunne/

9 Constructivism

K. M. FIERKE

Reader's guide

This chapter will examine the key debates that have shaped the development of constructivism in International Relations (IR). The introduction will explore the general notion that international relations is a social construction, as it emerged from the critique of more traditional theories of IR. The second and third sections will examine the demarcations that have come to distinguish various constructivisms, focusing in particular on the contrast between those who seek a 'better' social science, and therefore better theory, as opposed to those who argue that constructivism is an approach that rests on assumptions at odds with those of positivist method. The fourth section will analyse the significance of this difference for undertaking research, including questions about the role of language and causality. The final section will bring these insights to bear in relation to the problem of NATO enlargement, which is an interesting case study because it so clearly defies several claims of realist theory.

Introduction

In the 1980s, when the Cold War was raging with renewed force, social movements concerned about the prospect of nuclear war emerged on both sides of the Atlantic. They shared roughly the same objective, that is to bring an end to the nuclear arms race, but approached the challenge in different ways. One movement, the US Nuclear Weapons Freeze Campaign came to the conclusion, given lessons from the Vietnam War protests, that achieving its objectives required moderation in behaviour and message. Rather than dressing like hippies, they would dress in suits, appeal to Middle America, and mobilize citizens to pressure their congressmen (*sic*). Their proposals were formulated in a measured way that would minimize alienating people and appeal to the wider spectrum. In another political context, across the water, the critique was somewhat more hard hitting and diverse. Rather than calling on the USA and Soviet Union to simply stop the development, testing, and deployment of nuclear weapons, they demanded actual disarmament and in some cases unilateral disarmament. While loose cooperation existed at the European level, in the form of European Nuclear Disarmament, movements in the Netherlands, Germany, or Italy, had a distinctive character.

These critical movements shared the aim of changing the nuclear status quo, and each was shaped by the politics of its respective locations, as well as the larger context of the Cold War. I start with this example from the political world for two reasons. First, against this background, that is the mid-to-late 1980s, questions began to be raised about the theories and scientific methods of IR and the extent to which they were implicated in the production of international power (see Cox 1981; Ashley 1981, 1984; Walker 1987). Challenges to the assumptions underpinning the study of IR emerged against the backdrop of a historical context where political actors were challenging the assumptions of the Cold War. As the end of the Cold War was ushered in, further questions about these changes and the social construction of IR were formulated. The failure of IR scholars to predict or initially explain the end of the Cold War, on the basis of the dominant theories of IR, reinforced the importance of these questions.

Second, the two social movements are a useful metaphor for thinking about the construction of constructivism within IR. Constructivists, broadly defined, have shared a critique of the static material assumptions of traditional IR theory. They have emphasized the social dimensions of international relations and the possibility of change. They have, however, differed in their approach. Some have been more conscious of their broader audience and have shaped their critique in a language that would open a space for dialogue with mainstream scholars. Others have been harder hitting in stating the problem and more far reaching in their critique. The two together have shaped the place of constructivism in IR. The main point – and, I might add, a very constructivist point – is that academic debate, no less than political, emerges in historically and culturally specific circumstances.

This is evident in other debates that have shaped IR theory. The debate between realism and idealism was a reflection on the weaknesses of idealism after the First World War against the background of Hitler's expansion across Europe (see Carr 1946). Attempts to solidify the scientific status of realist IR were led by European émigrés to the USA, following the Second World War. The debate between behaviouralists and traditionalists pitted scholars in the USA, who wanted to make International Relations into a science, against the international society theorists of the English school (see Knorr and Rosenau 1969). The postpositivist debate in the late 1980s was a reaction against the dominant place of scientific method in the American context (see Lapid 1989; see Chapter 11). The 'dialogue' over constructivism was a reaction to the third debate, or, as some prefer to call it, the fourth debate (see Chapter 1), and an attempt to speak across the barricades it had constructed, while addressing problems raised by the end of the Cold War.

The idea that international relations is a social construction can be thought about in quite simple terms. To construct something is an act which brings into being a subject or object that otherwise would not exist. For instance, a material substance, such as wood, exists in nature, but it can be formed into any number of objects, for instance the beam in a house, a rifle, a musical instrument, or a totem pole. Although these represent material objects in and of themselves, they do not exist in nature but have come about through acts of human creation. Once constructed, each of these objects has a particular meaning and use within a context. They are social constructs in so far as their shape and form is imbued with social values, norms, and assumptions rather than being the product of purely individual thought or meaning. Similarly, explicitly social phenomena, such as states or alliances or international institutions, that is the collective subjects of international relations, may build on the basic material of human nature, but they take specific historical, cultural, and political forms that are a product of human interaction in a social world.

Constructivists have highlighted several themes. First, the idea of social construction suggests difference across context rather than a single objective reality. Constructivists have sought to explain or understand *change* at the international level. Traditional theories of IR, which have often assumed the sameness of states, for instance, across time and space, have prioritized the identification of regularities for the purpose of generalization and theory construction. The dramatic changes with the end of the Cold War and in its aftermath revealed the importance of historical context and raised questions about the transition from conflict to cooperation or from peace to war.

Second, constructivists have emphasized the *social* dimensions of international relations, and have demonstrated the importance of norms, rules, and language at this level. The importance of Gorbachev's 'New Thinking' in bringing an end to the Cold War, the increasing importance of norms of humanitarian intervention, and the spread of liberal democratic values raised critical questions about the exclusive emphasis of realist theory on material interest and power. Constructivists emphasized that the latter were unable to account for some of the key issues of post-Cold-War international politics and sought to provide a more complete or 'better' explanation, based on an analysis of how material and ideational factors combine in the construction of different possibilities and outcomes.

Third, constructivists have argued that, far from an objective reality, international politics is 'a world of our making' (Onuf 1989). In response to the over-determination of 'structure' in neorealist and neoliberal theory, constructivists introduced the possibility of agency and have emphasized *processes of interaction*. It is not that actors are totally free to choose their circumstances, but rather that they make choices in the process of interacting with others and, as a result, bring historically, culturally, and politically distinct 'realities' into being. In this respect, international relations is a social construction rather than existing independent of human meaning and action. States and other actors do not merely react as rational individuals but interact in a meaningful world.

The central themes of change, sociality, and processes of interaction point to the added value of constructivism within a field that has emphasized generalization across time, materiality, and rational choice. However, as already suggested, constructivists have not sung from a single hymn sheet and the meaning of constructivism in IR has been transformed over time. In what follows I deepen discussion of the themes above by examining how the meaning of constructivism has been shaped by specific debates within IR.

Constructivism and rationalism

Most constructivists have presented some kind of critique of rationalism. However, unlike poststructuralism (see Chapter 11), this critique has not involved a wholesale rejection of scientific method. Below I examine how the meaning of constructivism has been shaped out of the dialogue with rationalists. Four central points will be discussed, including the nature of being, the relationship between structures and agents, the constitution of the material world, and the role of cognition.

Social being

Ontology is a word originating with metaphysics, which refers to the nature of being and focuses on the types of objects the world is composed of. Rationalist theories of IR have an individualist ontology insofar as the basic unit of analysis is the individual (whether human or state). Neorealist theory, for instance, treats states as if they were individuals who try to maximize their ultimate aim of survival. Neorealists, such as Kenneth Waltz (1979), present individual states as the prior condition for a structure of anarchy, which then constrains their character and behaviour. In a competitive environment, generated by multiple states acting in their self-interest, to follow a different logic of action, it is argued, would be suicide. While emphasizing the individual state and the distribution of power, his theory does contain an element of 'socialization', insofar as the effects of structure are produced 'through socialization of the actors and through competition among them' (Keohane 1986: 63).

Arguments by neoliberals, such as Goldstein and Keohane (1993), who focus on the role of ideas, contain a similar tension between the individual and the social. Ideas are treated as causal factors that are exchanged by fully formed individuals. As Ruggie comments:

> " The individuals featured in [Goldstein and Keohane's] story are not born into any system of social relationships that helps shape who they become. When we first encounter them, they are already fully constituted and poised in a problem-solving mode. "

Ruggie 1998: 866.

Constructivists have questioned the individualist ontology of rationalism and emphasize instead a social ontology. As fundamentally social beings, individuals or states cannot be separated from a context of normative meaning which shapes who they are and the possibilities available to them. Indeed, the concept of sovereignty is first and foremost a social and constitutive category insofar as the prior condition for *recognizing* the sovereignty of individual states is a *shared understanding* and acceptance of the concept.

The relationship between the individual and the social structure is important for both rationalism and constructivism, but is conceived in different ways by each. For rationalists, structure is a function of competition and the distribution of material capabilities. Structures first and foremost constrain the actions of states. The subjects of rationalism are guided by a **logic of consequences**, that is a rational act is one that will produce an outcome that maximizes the interests of the individual unit.

Constructivists focus more on the norms and shared understandings of legitimate behavior, although material factors also play a role. In their view, structures not only constrain; they also constitute the identity of actors. The subjects of constructivism are guided by a **logic of appropriateness** (March and Olson 1989). What is rational is a function of legitimacy, defined by shared values and norms within institutions or other social structures rather than purely individual interests. As Ole Jacob Sending (2002: 449) states, the self, in this logic, becomes social through acquiring and fulfilling an institutional identity. In this respect, norms not only constrain behaviour; they also constitute the identities of actors. Human rights norms, for instance, constrain less because of power considerations than because human rights are a constitutive feature of liberal democratic states, in particular, and increasingly, at the international level, the identity of legitimate states. The emphasis on norms and rule following can be distinguished from instrumentally rational behaviour in that actors try to 'do the right thing' rather than maximizing or optimizing their given preferences (Risse 2000: 4).

Mutual constitution

A social structure leaves more space for **agency**, that is for the individual or state to influence their environment, as well as to be influenced by it. The title of Alexander Wendt's famous article (1992), 'Anarchy Is What States Make of It', captures this idea. It is not that states in anarchy can, on a whim, change their circumstances. Rather, relationships evolve over time. They are not characterized, across the board, by enmity and egoism. The USA and Britain have evolved as friends, while other states are enemies. Many states within the European Union are former enemies who have learned to cooperate. Relationships are a product of a historical process and interactions over time. Wendt (1992: 404–5) illustrates this in his example of Alter and Ego, two space aliens who meet for the first time, and who, through a series of gestures, determine whether the other is hostile or friendly. Each exercises an element of choice, and thus agency, in how this relationship develops. Choice is not, however, unlimited. Alter and Ego coexist in a social relationship, and their choices are partially dependent on the response of the other. The space for choice can thus be said to be **mutually constituted**.

Rather than emphasizing how structures constrain, as rationalists do, constructivists focus on the constitutive role of norms and shared understandings, as well as the relationship between agency and structure (Wendt 1987). The subjects of international politics are not uniformly and universally rational egoists but have distinct identities shaped by the cultural, social, and political – as well as material – circumstances in which they are embedded. They are not static but ever evolving as they interact with each other and their environment.

Social facts

Rationalists assume a static world of *apriori* and asocial egoists who are primarily concerned with material interests. While constructivists would not deny the importance of interests, they would tie them more directly to the identity of the subject. Neither identity nor interests can be detached from a world of social meaning. As suggested in the last section, identity as a liberal democracy cannot be detached from an interest in complying with human rights norms. Identity as a capitalist cannot be separated from an interest in generating profit. Likewise, identities may be formed in conflict, for example, as enemies who have an interest in self-protection. Far from being detached from the material world, identity, and subsequent interest, may constitute a world populated by particular kinds of object. Missiles, for instance, are not created in a vacuum. The mass production of nuclear weapons by the USA, after the Second World War and during the Cold War, was a response to the emerging conflict with the Soviet Union. These weapons were bound up in the constitution of the Soviet Union as an enemy, defined by a distinction between capitalist and communist, among others, and related to an interest in containing that enemy.

Most objects of international relations, unlike trees, rocks, or glaciers, exist only by virtue of human acts of creation which happen in a cultural, historical, and political context of meaning. They are social facts, rather than purely material ones, that exist because of the meaning and value attributed to them. John Searle (1995: 2) argues that social facts depend on human agreement and typically require human institutions for their existence. Without the attribution of value, and the existence of financial institutions, a dollar bill or euro note would be nothing more than a piece of paper. As already suggested, sovereignty or the borders dividing states exist only by virtue of human agreement. Likewise, a nuclear weapon does not exist in nature, although objects in nature, such as sticks, can be used as weapons. It is human design and intent that shapes the material object into one with a specific meaning and use within a context, where specific identities and interests are at stake.

Social cognition

The question of intent in designing material objects or institutions raises a further issue about the role of human reasoning. Many constructivists have built on a Weberian concept of *Verstehen* or understanding, which refers to the hermeneutic theme that 'action must always be understood from within', and thus, that social meaning is a function of 'what is in people's heads' (Adler 1997: 326). The constructivist emphasis on Verstehen is interesting in so far as Weber was also one early source of the rational actor model. While rationalists highlight the rationality of decisions in terms of self-interest, thereby minimizing the role of context, constructivists have brought the social dimension back in.

Intersubjective meanings are not merely the aggregation of individual beliefs but have some independent status as collective knowledge, based on the notion that although 'each of us thinks his own thoughts, our concepts we share with our fellow men' (Toulmin 1972: 35). Verstehen is the 'collective interpretations, practices and institutions of the actors themselves' (Adler 1997: 326).

The emphasis on Verstehen highlights a similarity and difference between rationalists and constructivists. The difference is that the former emphasize the individual while the latter emphasize the social. However, looking more closely at the role of individual cognition and rationality in constructivism, the difference appears to be less stark. The logic of appropriateness emphasizes the individual (Sending 2002). The rational thought processes of Wendt's (1992) Alter and Ego are prior to social interaction. Verstehen emphasizes cognition and what is 'in the head' (Adler 1997: 326).

Constructivism, as outlined above, clearly adds a social dimension that is missing from rationalist approaches. However, it also contains some inconsistencies, which will be explored in the next section. These inconsistencies arise from the combination of a social ontology with an epistemology that rests on a separation between an external world and the internal thought processes of individuals. Constructivism, in this depiction, is cast in the positivist language of causality and hypothesis testing, complemented by a focus on the rationality of individuals, although more deeply embedded in a social context. The emphasis on the individual unit, whether human or state, fails to sufficiently problematize how the individual unit is constituted. Given the emphasis on ontology, the autonomy of the social and the role of language is obscured, both in their relation to the material world and individual cognition.

Constructivism as middle ground

Constructivism, as discussed above, has occupied a 'middle ground' between rationalist and poststructuralist approaches to IR (a ground it shares with the English school, as argued in Chapter 7). Initially, when the word was introduced to IR by Nicholas Onuf (1989), it referred broadly to a range of postpositivist perspectives, which shared a critique of the static assumptions of mainstream IR theory. Since that time, constructivism has become a subject of contention, with scholars making a distinction between 'conventional' constructivism, which is said to occupy the middle ground, and more critical variations (Adler 1997; Hopf 1998; Campbell 1998a), including poststructuralism. Conventional constructivists have not rejected the scientific assumptions of positivist science to the extent that more explicitly postpositivist approaches have. As Jeff Checkel (1998: 327) argues, the quarrel with rationalists is not epistemological but ontological (see also Katzenstein, Keohane, and Krasner 1998: 675).

Epistemology is a branch of philosophy that deals with the origin and nature of knowledge and begins with a question about how we come to have knowledge of the world. Constructivists embrace an intersubjective ontology, emphasizing norms, social agents, and structures, and the mutual constitution of identity, but accept an epistemology indebted to positivism,[1] which includes hypothesis testing, causality, and explanation. Ted Hopf (1998: 171) argues that emphasis on the ontological is part of an effort to overcome some of the scepticism about constructivism – arising from a conflation with postmodern approaches – and a scepticism because constructivists are assumed to be ambivalent towards mainstream social science methods. Hopf distinguishes 'conventional' constructivism by its distance from critical theory. He refers to conventional constructivism as a 'collection of principles, distilled from social theory but without the latter's more consistent theoretical and epistemological follow through' (Hopf 1998: 181). Both rationalists and constructivists claim that no great epistemological or methodological differences divide them (Wendt 1998: 116; Katzenstein, Keohane, and Krasner 1998: 675).

By accepting a positivist epistemology, constructivists have gained considerable legitimacy, such that the debate with rationalists has come to occupy an important place in the discipline (Katzenstein, Keohane, and Krasner 1998: 683). At issue in these debates is the nature of social science itself and therefore the discipline of IR, that is the claim to a 'naturalist' conception of science (associated with the positivists) or a social one (Adler 1997: 320). The primary concern of the conventional constructivists is one of bringing the social back into a discipline that has been undersocialized (Wiener 2003: 256). The constructivist emphasis on causality, hypothesis testing, and objective (intersubjective) truths, is distinguished from poststructuralists who are 'not especially interested in the meticulous examination of particular cases or sites for purposes of understanding them in their own distinctive terms' (Ashley 1989: 278). As Adler (1997: 334) states, constructivists are interested in providing a better explanation, rather than emancipation *per se*.[2]

Shifting the middle ground

As Kurki and Wight argue in **Chapter 1** the discipline of IR has failed to take philosophy of social science questions seriously and has far too often embraced an otherwise discredited 'positivism'. The key issue here is whether the combination of a constructivist ontology and a positivist epistemology is a consistent position. This question is implicit in Hopf's (1998) claim that critical constructivists have a 'more consistent theoretical and epistemological follow through'. Several scholars (Kratochwil 2000: 74; Onuf 1989; Fierke and Jorgensen 2001), have examined constructivism as part of a longer lineage outside IR and with a genealogy that intersects with, but is distinct from, poststructuralism. Constructivism is, from this perspective, first and foremost an epistemological position, heavily indebted to the so-called 'linguistic turn'.[3] If, following on the linguistic turn, constructivism raises fundamental questions about the natural connection between word and thing or between symbol and the symbolized (Palan 2000: 4), is it consistent to marry a social ontology to a positivist epistemology?

Positivist epistemology rests on a correspondence theory of language, that is objects are assumed to exist independent of meaning and words act as labels for objects in this reality. Hypothesis testing represents one expression of this assumption about language. It is a method of comparing scientific statements about the world with the world to see whether they correspond. By contrast, a constructivist epistemology, as a product of the linguistic turn, builds on the notion that we cannot get behind our language to compare it with that which it describes (Wittgenstein 1958). Language is bound up in the world rather than a mirror of it. The language of a knight in chess cannot be separated from the material object; it is by this language that we distinguish the knight, and the rules applying to it, from a piece of wood.

The distinction between conventional and critical constructivists often rests on an assumption that the former accept the existence of an objective world, while the latter emphasize 'merely' language. However, as Kratochwil (2000: 91) notes, 'hardly anyone doubts that the "world" exists "independent" from our minds. The question is rather whether we can recognize it in a pure and direct fashion . . . or whether what we recognize is always already organized and formed by certain categorical and theoretical elements'. The either/or designation of objective world versus interpretive relativism is too stark. A more nuanced position understands language as rule-based. This issue will be discussed in more detail in the next section.

Approach or theory

The ontology/epistemology issue is related to a further concern regarding constructivism's status as an approach or a theory. Onuf (1998: 1) argues that constructivism is not a theory but a way of studying social relations. Alexander Wendt's book, *Social Theory of International Politics* (1999), builds a constructivist *theory*. Wendt accepts certain tenets of mainstream methodology, although his is a modified commitment to positivism within a scientific realist framework (see Chapter 1). The problem with his approach is two-fold. On the one hand, if constructivism and positivism rely on differing assumptions about the nature of 'reality', then building a constructivist theory on a positivist epistemology is inconsistent. On the other hand, to treat constructivism as a theory in the same sense as realism is misleading: comparing realism with constructivism is like comparing apples and oranges. Realism is a substantive theory, which in IR theory has been married to positivist assumptions, but could also, arguably, be rethought on the basis of constructivist assumptions. It is not, in this line of thought, that constructivism is fundamentally incompatible with theory, but rather it necessarily raises a question about the nature of theory.

The constructivist label is now most often used to designate a middle ground between rationalist and poststructuralist approaches. This middle ground has emphasized a social ontology, a common epistemology with the mainstream, and a focus on the development of constructivist theory. Another constructivism shifts this middle ground, highlighting the inseparability of a social ontology *and* epistemology. Both accept the 'possibility of a reality to be constructed', which distinguishes them from poststructuralists who problematize this possibility (Zehfuss 2002).

In the next section, I argue that the second constructivism is more consistent than 'conventional' constructivism. I use the label 'consistent constructivism' to highlight that its assumptions correct the inconsistency at the core of conventional constructivism. This contrasts with the more common distinction between conventional and critical constructivism. The latter term often includes poststructuralism, while the idea of consistent constructivism presented here does not.

Consistent constructivism

Constructivists and rationalists have engaged in dialogue but method has not been on the agenda. There is a tension between a school of constructivism that sees no fundamental differences with mainstream methods and another which understands constructivism as an approach with roots in the linguistic turn. The inconsistency is most evident in relation to the role of language and rules, on the one hand, and the question of causality, on the other.

Language and rules

The role of language has been largely ignored in the debate between rationalists and constructivists. The avoidance of language is in part a reflection of the effort to create distance from poststructuralists, who are associated with interpretive relativism. It is also a reflection of the middle ground's focus on ontology. An approach to language that is consistent with the social ontology of constructivism should also occupy an epistemological middle ground. In between a view of language as either a mirror of the world or pure interpretation, is an understanding of language and action as rule-based. It is a small step from a focus on the role of norms and rules in international relations, to an acknowledgement that these only find expression and are constituted only in a language and action that is rule-based and itself infused with norms.

This conception of language rests on a distinction between rules (the concern of constructivists) and interpretation (the emphasis of poststructuralists). Following a rule is different from an interpretation. As Wittgenstein states,

> there is a way of grasping a rule which is *not* an *interpretation*, but which is exhibited in what we call 'obeying a rule' and 'going against it' in actual cases. Hence there is an inclination to say: every action according to the rule is an interpretation. But we ought to restrict the term interpretation to the substitution of one expression of the rule for another.

Wittgenstein 1958: para. 201

The unitary view of science rests on a dichotomy between the objective and the subjective. In this view language operates as a set of labels for the objective reality or for the mental processes of individuals. A consistent constructivist approach to language challenges this dichotomy. In this view, language use is fundamentally social. We are socialized into it and in the process we do not simply learn words but how to act in the world – what it means to promise, threaten, and lie, the types of context in which these speech acts are appropriate or meaningful, or even what it means to formulate a hypothesis, vote, or deploy a missile. Language use is part of acting in the world. Without language we could not begin to communicate with one another, attribute meaning to objects or acts in the world, think individual thoughts, or express feelings.

Hypothesis testing in positivist science rests on an assumption that labels will be either true or false. An approach to language as rule-based requires that we 'look and see' how language is put to use by social actors as they construct their world. In a situation of change, categories of identity or action are not likely to be static. For instance, the dominant categories defining identity in communist Yugoslavia were different from those that emerged along with the conflict between Serbs, Croats, and Muslims. The category Yugoslavia subsumes all of the latter under a common identity as 'southern slavs'. By contrast, the ethnic categories construct clear historical, religious, and political distinctions between the different groups. These categories may have begun as interpretations, in that they substituted one rule of identity for another, but they became rule-like in their designation of identity and the actions that followed from this. In the transition from Yugoslavia to violent conflict, neighbours, who had lived together in peace, became the objects of ethnic cleansing.

A consistent constructivist approach to language shifts emphasis to the generation of meaning, norms, and rules, as expressed in language, by the subjects of analysis. It is also concerned less with the intentions of individuals, as suggested by conventional constructivists (March and Olson 1989; Sending 2002; Adler 1997), than the intention expressed in social action. As Wittgenstein (1958: para. 337) said, 'An intention is embedded it its situation, in human customs and institutions.'

In the prior example, the 'intention' of individuals engaged in ethnic cleansing could not be separated from a social world in which neighbours had become 'dangerous others', defined as Chetnik, Ustasa, or Ottoman – terms with deep historical resonance – who had to be eliminated because of the threat they posed. Intention and action were defined in a public language by socially constituted actors. Questions of intention relate to a second category of inconsistency.

Reasons and causes

The other seeming inconsistency in the construction of constructivism *vis-à-vis* rationalism is the frequent emphasis on causality (Checkel 1997, 1998; Finnemore 1996: 28; Adler 1997: 329). On the surface, this appears to be merely a matter of word use. But the conflation of reason and cause raises a more serious issue, which is illustrated by the following example. Take a question about US President Bush's reasons for invading Iraq or the cause of the US invasion. Multiple possible reasons/causes have been identified: from oil, to the desire to complete unfinished business from the Gulf War, to concerns about Saddam's weapons of mass destruction, to human rights.

An hypothesis focusing on Bush's individual reasons or the cause of the invasion seeks an explanation that corresponds with the world. But truth and falsity are ultimately slippery insofar as we cannot get inside individual minds, and the competition to identify the 'true' cause or intention usually devolves into a battle of interpretations. The question can be asked in a different way, however, focusing less on the ultimate truth of why Bush or the USA undertook the invasion, and more on the social fact that the invasion happened and how it became possible. We might pose this 'how possible' question, as Howard (2004) has, in terms of the puzzle that Iraq actually posed less of a threat than North Korea yet became the object of invasion, while the latter was the subject of negotiations. He traces how the historical pattern of interaction between the two laid the groundwork for different policies towards these two 'Axis of Evil' states.

The 'how possible' question reveals the importance of public language and the intentionality embedded in it. It is now known that intelligence communities on both sides of the Atlantic got it wrong, in (falsely) believing that Iraq had weapons of mass destruction.

An explanation that the invasion was caused by Iraq's weapons of mass destruction is more accurately stated in the following terms. The reason for the invasion of Iraq, given by foreign-policy elites, was the threat posed by Saddam Hussein's weapons of mass destruction. Whether these actors believed the intelligence or manufactured it, this 'reason' made the invasion possible. The reason was the means for persuading the US public, and US soldiers, that this was a legitimate act by their government. The reason was strengthened by the link made in political discourse between Saddam and the attackers on 9/11. The premise that Saddam had weapons of mass destruction, although based on false data, established the context for making a justification, that is giving a reason for the invasion. This reason was publicly accessible in political language. It constituted an action and a 'reality', that is the invasion. The intention to invade was embedded in these language games and in the act of invasion itself.

To refer to a reason as a cause is an interpretation, that is it takes the rule by which 'giving a reason' has meaning and gives it a different meaning. However, a **reason** has a different logic than a cause. While X may give a reason for their action to Y, in doing so X explains their action. This may have an influence on Y, but, if so, it is less as a cause, in the sense that the impact of one stone on another may propel the latter in forward motion. It rather is part of a conversation where X is trying to persuade Y, and thereby legitimate their own actions in terms that can be understood and accepted by the other.

To give a reason, or to engage in many other speech acts, from promising to threatening, opens a space for the other to be engaged and respond. As a two-way relationship, this interaction is not merely a question of who has the greater material power; it is dependent on some degree of common language (the other must be able to understand what is being said and what constitutes a reason, promise, or threat), which incorporates standards of legitimacy (that is what will suffice as a good reason, as well as conditions, relating to past words and actions, which make a promise or threat credible). Power is a factor, since, particularly in the case of threats, material capability is one, although not the only, condition of credibility. Power may also be a factor insofar as the legitimacy of a reason may be tied to social role or position. For example, Western states may give reasons for maintaining a large nuclear arsenal, which are accepted as legitimate, while the desire for even one nuclear weapon by a small Middle Eastern nation, such as Iraq or Iran, may be widely viewed as illegitimate.

To call a reason a cause is to transform the meaning of the former. Obviously, the meaning of words can change over time. However, in this case, the two words are in conflict. We can replace the rule by which 'a reason' is given meaning with an interpretation that it is a 'cause', but this is like changing the direction of a signpost, which has constituted a regular use or custom (Wittgenstein 1958: para. 158).

Case study: the construction of NATO expansion

The purpose of this final section is to discuss the relevance of these distinctions in relation to an empirical context of international relations. The expansion of the North Atlantic Treaty Organization (NATO) has generated a literature that is explicitly constructivist in its orientation which grows out of a critique of more materialist or rationalist explanations. Two questions in particular have guided the constructivist critique. The first is how to explain not only the persistence but the expansion of the alliance after the demise of its Cold War enemy. Neorealists argue that alliances will disband in the absence of a threat. They assume that the state is the ultimate unit of analysis and that the benefits of cooperation will wane in the absence of a shared threat. The second question is how to explain the expansion of NATO in the absence of any obvious material, that is economic or military, interest in doing so.[4] From a realist perspective, NATO would only expand if it were a necessary and efficient way to balance against perceived threats (Schimmelfennig 1999: 203).

Non-constructivist accounts of NATO expansion

Competing versions of neorealism predicted, for different reasons, that NATO would at best be obsolete and at worst would collapse, given the demise of the Soviet Union eliminated NATO's *raison d'être*. Some neorealists have dodged the issue of subsequent enlargement, arguing either that NATO survival or enlargement is unimportant or that insufficient time has lapsed for the predictions to come true (Rauchhaus 2001: 12). Others have conceded that questionable assumptions led towards inaccurate conclusions. Waltz (Rauchhaus 2001) for instance, argued that it was a mistake to treat NATO purely as a military alliance, given its high degree of institutionalization and the range of issues it deals with. While this institutionalization provides a partial explanation of why NATO is surviving and expanding, Waltz focuses on how the USA used NATO to advance its own agenda, an argument that I will later return to.

Neoliberals have focused their explanations more explicitly on institutional questions, emphasizing, for instance, the institutional goals of promoting stability between member-states and preventing competition between them. While providing a clear explanation for NATO's survival, arguments of this kind are more ambiguous on the question of expansion. For instance, an institutional argument might have predicted that the Organization for Security and Cooperation in Europe (OSCE) (Conference on Security and Cooperation in Europe (CSCE) when the Cold War ended) would become the institutional cornerstone of post-Cold-War Europe, given it already incorporated states in the East and West.

Organizational theory, which emphasizes the internal dynamics of organizations, might assume that NATO had a momentum of its own, independent of its member-states or any specific objective, such as defence against the Soviet Union. In this line of thought, NATO would use the resources at its disposal to generate new goals that would justify the organization's continuation (Rauchhaus 2001: 16). From this perspective, one might argue that the desire of the Central and Eastern European countries (CEECs) to join NATO became a justification for its continuing existence. As will be discussed later, this overlaps with a constructivist analysis insofar as justification, which is a part of 'giving reasons', happens in an interaction. However, as Haas (Rauchhaus 2001: 17) argues, organizational analysts have failed to recognize that international organizations are fundamentally different from domestic ones. While domestic justification had a role, the international justification *vis-à-vis* the CEECs and Russia arguably did as well.

Foreign-policy approaches to NATO enlargement have highlighted the role of justifications to the US public. Kuchan (Rauchhaus 2001: 13), for instance, argues that key figures in the Clinton White House, inspired by pressure from heavy weights such as Kissinger and Brezinski, or fears of the electoral consequences of ignoring the influence of Eastern leaders, such as Lech Walesa or Vaclav Havel, on ethnic communities in the USA, were the motor behind the expansion process. This type of analysis largely ignores the rest of the world, including the NATO member-states – like the neorealist argument – and assumes the domestic and, in particular, electoral considerations of the White House were the most important factor. It isolates a decision of the Clinton administration in 1993 as the beginning point and fails to problematize the reluctance on the part of NATO, as well as the Clinton administration itself, to initially consider enlargement.

Contributors to a volume on NATO enlargement (Rauchhaus 2001: 19), representing diverse theoretical perspectives, agreed that the one area of consensus in this debate is the driving role of the USA and its preponderance of power. This consensus is very similar to Waltz's neorealist argument that enlargement is explained in terms of the advancement of US interests. NATO, in these analyses, is largely an arm of the USA, and the rest of the world is invisible. Constructivist analyses have focused more explicitly on the dynamics within NATO itself and have highlighted and accounted for many of the explanations mentioned above, in a more complex framework. They have focused on the interaction of different actors, and not simply US interests. They go beyond the institutional focus of neoliberals, to examine the role of NATO's shared values and norms of liberal democracy in propelling expansion.

Constructivism and NATO enlargement

Frank Schimmelfennig (1999: 210), for instance, argues that the identities, interests, and preferences of actors are products of intersubjective social structures, such as culture, institutions, and social interaction. It is not merely the cost–benefit analysis that determines an actor's behaviour, but rather their values and norms, and standards of legitimacy – in other words, a logic of appropriateness. In this respect, the enlargement of an international organization represents a process of international socialization. He hypothesizes that a state will seek and be granted NATO membership if it demonstrates that it shares liberal values and the multilateralist norms of the Western community. He explains NATO's decision to expand to the east as motivated by a desire to promote and strengthen liberal values, peace, and multilateralism in the area. The Czech Republic, Hungary, and Poland were chosen first because they were more advanced than other CEECs in adopting and internalizing Western values and norms.

NATO expanded in order to spread its liberal values. Schimmelfennig concludes that both values and material interests are important. In fact, the process was in part driven by threat, for instance the perception that undemocratic governments are a threat to the world order NATO prefers. The democratic socialization of members on its borders would promote the security needs of existing NATO members. Values and norms are more important, in his view, because the liberal democratic identity of NATO is driving the process and provides a framework for instrumental action.

While Schimmelfennig provides an explanation for NATO expansion, and a better explanation than neorealist accounts in particular, it is limited in two respects. First, he does not adequately address the question of why spreading its values would be *more* important for a military alliance than material interests. Second, in presenting the process as driven by NATO he ignores a further puzzle: that is, NATO was initially reluctant to consider expansion, yet over several years made gradual steps in this direction. Analyses that focus on a more dialogical process involving NATO, the CEECs, and Russia more squarely address these questions.

From a consistent constructivist perspective, NATO enlargement was mutually constituted out of an ongoing process in which actors occupying different positions gave reasons for their actions. These reasons are accessible through a public language. The method of language analysis is akin to that used by Thucydides (1954) – although far more modest – in constructing his narrative of the Peloponnesian War. Recurring categories used by NATO, the CEECS, and Russian elites provided the basis for pinpointing changes in the definition of their identities and interests over time (Fierke 1999: 29). The method begins with a recognition that it is all too easy for analysts, or political actors, to interpret the past through their current location in historical or geographical space. In this respect, the consensus among US scholars about the central role of the USA, for instance, is not surprising. By tracing changes in the language of actors in multiple locations, and the reasons given over time, the gradual construction of outcomes becomes evident.

It is impossible in this short space to outline the various changes in any detail.[5] Instead I make a few points that are salient to the argument of this chapter. First, dialogue itself was a part of the language of the unfolding process of NATO expansion. Following the collapse of the Eastern bloc and Warsaw Pact, 'dialogue' was presented as an alternative to NATO expansion. At the time, neither the CEECs nor NATO itself assumed that the organization would enlarge, particularly in light of public questions about the continuing relevance of NATO. The CEECs focused on the potential for a reconstituted CSCE as the framework for a pan-European security system. The US Bush administration, while stressing a commitment to democracy in Eastern Europe, was reluctant to discuss its security needs (Rodman 1995: 5).

In December 1991, NATO presented the North Atlantic Cooperation Council (NACC) as an alternative to extending military protection and as a forum for political dialogue and cooperation with the East, which would prevent the formation of competing alliances. Through 1992, NATO expressed clear opposition to enlargement 'for the foreseeable future'. Reasons ranged from the potential Russian response to fears it would weaken the alliance or become a source of division. The Clinton administration had, at the time, made the relationship to Russia a policy priority (Crawford in Rauchhaus 2001: 41). In 1993, Germany began to call for opening the European integration process, and NATO shifted towards a position of enlargement 'at an appropriate time'. This happened against the background of an increasing suspicion on the part of the CEECs that Western countries, which had challenged the Eastern bloc dissidents to tear down the wall dividing East and West, appeared to be constructing barriers to keep the CEECs out. In 1994, faced with increasing pressure from the CEECs to join NATO, and the prospect that a decision to enlarge would mobilize nationalist forces in Russia, NATO mapped a middle course. The clear opposition to enlargement 'in the foreseeable future' was replaced by 'no immediate enlargement', but agreement to the principle that the Alliance should be opened to new members. The result was the Partnership for Peace (PfP) which was designed to enhance dialogue and cooperation with the East, and reflected a desire to avoid 'new divisions of Europe'. The PfP provided a means to delay the expansion decision while allowing CEECs to prepare for the possibility of future membership by taking on a clearer military dimension. After Clinton's visit to Poland in mid-1994, when he stated that enlargement was a matter of 'when rather than if', the process gained momentum. The actual decision to enlarge, in December 1994, was accompanied by a commitment to deepen dialogue with Russia.

It is tempting to view these layers of dialogue as a vehicle for the USA or NATO to realize its interests or inculcate the CEECs with its values. While clearly in part true, this claim fails to recognize the extent to which the dialogue transformed all the participants and made enlargement possible. NATO's identity and interests were shaped by the process no less than Russia or the CEECs. The enlargement decision emerged out of the tension between CEEC demands for inclusion and Russian claims that expansion would recreate the division of Europe. NATO, in each of its moves, manoeuvred between these two positions.

Second, when the analysis is set up as a three-way dialogue, rather than the disciplining by NATO of the CEECs, an answer to the further question of why a military alliance would be primarily concerned about spreading its values comes into sight: NATO, confronted with the discrepancy between past promises to dissidents in the East during the Cold War, and its actions following the end of the Cold War, could not discount future enlargement, even though its members gave plenty of reasons for doing so. Maintaining its identity, against the backdrop of questions about its continuing relevance, required aligning its actions with its ideals. This element was evident in the analysis of another form of language, that is the speech act.

A speech act is a category of language that does not simply describe or convey information but is an act in and of its self. To promise or to threaten are not words referring to objects in the world but acts *vis-à-vis* others with language. Speech acts are dependent on a context. Fierke and Wiener (1999) analyse how, in a context of change, NATO's past 'promises' to the CEECS came back to haunt it as 'threats' to its identity, thereby transforming its institutional interest in enlargement.

Amid the dramatic changes of the early 1990s, past promises became one of the stable features of an otherwise uncertain situation. NATO had, in the 1980s, encouraged human rights initiatives in the CEECs to act in accordance with democratic ideals in resisting totalitarianism. Once the containment of the Soviet Union was no longer necessary, the CEECs argued that Western institutions had a responsibility to assist the CEECs in their recovery, in helping them to uphold these values. The threat was not merely one of instability in the East or, as suggested by Schimmelfennig, authoritarian neighbours. Rather, the failure to fulfil the promise, and the exposure of this failure, presented a threat to the identity of NATO. The threat contributed to a change in the structure of its institutional interests. The decision about NATO expansion unfolded *over time* and became NATO's *raison d'être*, against the backdrop of arguments that it was obsolete.

In order to maintain its identity, NATO had to act in a manner that was consistent with the ideals it had espoused during the Cold War, particularly in the face of claims that it was failing to do so. As Williams (2001: 532) notes, recognition involves not only recognition of the other but a judgement that it represents a *certain kind*, that is that it is worthy of respect. While Williams focuses on recognition of the CEECs by NATO, and, like other constructivist analyses, emphasizes the disciplining influence of NATO's norms on the CEECs (Schimmelfennig 1999; Rasmussen 2001); a dialogical analysis reveals that NATO identity also required recognition. Recognition depended on a consistency between words and actions, which eventually dictated enlargement to the East. This argument more clearly brings out the importance of the *process of interaction* between East and West in making the outcome of enlargement possible.

When language is connected to epistemology and method, a space is opened for greater attention to this process as an interaction or a dialogue in which each side is changed as a result of its engagement with the other. In this line of argument it is not merely the desire of the CEECs for recognition as NATO members that is at stake, but also the recognition of NATO identity in the face of widescale assumptions that it had become obsolete in the absence of any visible threat from the former Soviet Union. The desire of the CEECs to join NATO became proof of its continuing relevance. This type of analysis is also more equipped to address the question of why NATO expanded in the absence of any apparent interest in doing so and why liberal democracy, rather than military considerations, would be the driving force.

Conclusion

Constructivism was introduced to IR as the Cold War was ending. The central themes of change, sociality, and processes of interaction made it possible to examine dimensions of international relations that had been ignored, given the emphasis by dominant theories on generalization across time, material interest, and a notion of structure that was overly determined. The dialogue between constructivists and rationalists focused on ontological questions, contrasting the individual ontology of the former with the social ontology of the latter. In this dialogue, questions of epistemology and method were largely ignored, as many constructivists accepted the basic tenets of 'positivist' social science and adopted the language of causality and hypothesis testing. In a disciplinary context where this view of science was understood to be the mark of legitimacy, conventional constructivism has made important inroads. It is a small further step to recognize the inconsistencies generated by this dialogue. These inconsistencies are reinforced by the anomalies raised by the end of the Cold War and NATO expansion. While generating inconsistencies, the engagement with the mainstream over constructivism has also opened a space for broadening the dialogue to ask further questions about the methods most appropriate to a constructivist approach. A more consistent constructivism rests not only on a social ontology but also a social epistemology, which has the analysis of language and processes of interaction between multiple actors at its core. The importance of these tools was illustrated in a brief analysis of NATO expansion, which demonstrated the added value of approaching the context as a dialogue between NATO, Russia, and the CEECs that unfolded over time. From this perspective, not only the disciplining role of NATO's liberal norms was important in the process of enlargement, but the pressure placed on NATO to act in a manner consistent with its own promises and the principles it had exposed.

Both the construction of constructivism within IR, and the construction of NATO enlargement in international relations, emerged out of a dialogue between contextually bound actors occupying different positions. As such they both are examples of the constructivist point, originally made by Nicholas Onuf (1989) that we occupy a 'world of our making'.

? QUESTIONS

1. Constructivism was a response to changes in the world of international relations. Discuss.
2. Is it more important to generalize about international relations across time or to account for processes of change?
3. Discuss the idea that international relations is a social construction.
4. How have the central themes of constructivism contributed to the discipline of IR?
5. What are the central differences between rationalists and constructivists?
6. What does it mean to say that identities and interests are mutually constituted?
7. What was at stake in the distancing of 'conventional' constructivists from poststructuralists?
8. What is the significance of thinking about constructivism as an approach or a theory?
9. Is language important in a constructivist analysis? Why or why not?
10. Discuss the merits of different explanations of NATO enlargement.
11. What is the added value of a constructivist analysis of NATO expansion?

≈ FURTHER READING

■ **Fierke, K. M. and Jorgensen, Knud Erik (2001), *Constructing International Relations: The Next Generation* (Armonk NY: M. E. Sharpe).** A transatlantic dialogue over the meaning of constructivism.

■ **Finnemore, Martha (1996), *National Interests and International Society* (Ithaca NY: Cornell University Press).** An exploration of the role of norms in international relations.

■ **Katzenstein, Peter (1996), *The Culture of National Security: Norms and Identity in World Politics* (New York: Columbia University Press).** An edited collection of a range of empirical studies that apply a constructivist analysis.

■ **Kratochwil, Friedrich (1989), *Rules, Norms and Decisions: On the Conditions of Practical and Legal Reasoning in International Relations and Domestic Affairs* (Cambridge: Cambridge University Press).** A seminal work on the role of rules in international relations.

■ **Onuf, Nicholas (1989), *World of Our Making: Rules and Rule in Social Theory and International Relations* (Columbia SC: University of South Carolina Press).** The work that introduced constructivism to International Relations.

■ **Wendt, Alexander (1999), *Social Theory of International Politics* (Cambridge: Cambridge University Press).** The most comprehensive effort to build a constructivist theory of international relations.

IMPORTANT WEBSITES

- A Second Image: A Constructivism Resource
  http://home.pi.be/%7Elazone/

- NATO
  www.nato.int

Visit the Online Resource Centre that accompanies this book for lots of interesting additional material. www.oxfordtextbooks.co.uk/orc/dunne/

10

Feminism

J. ANN TICKNER AND LAURA SJOBERG

 Chapter contents

- Introduction
- Gender in International Relations
- Typology of IR feminist theories
- Gender, security, and global politics
- Case study
- Conclusion

Reader's guide

This chapter introduces feminist perspectives on international relations. It provides a typology of feminist International Relations (IR) theories, outlining their major tenets with illustrations from specific authors. Feminist theories of IR use gender as a socially constructed category of analysis when they analyse foreign policy, international political economy, and international security. This chapter focuses on feminist perspectives on international security. Feminist security research takes two major forms: theoretical reformulation and empirical evaluation. This chapter chronicles developments in feminist reanalyses and reformulations of security theory. It illustrates feminist security theory by analysing the case of United Nations Security Council sanctions on Iraq following the First Gulf War. It concludes by discussing the contributions that feminist IR can make to the discipline of IR specifically, and to the practice of international politics more generally.

Introduction

Feminist theories entered the discipline of International Relations in the late 1980s and early 1990s. The beginnings of IR feminism are associated with a more general ferment in the field – often referred to as the 'third debate' (or sometimes as 'fourth debate', see Chapter 1). Early IR feminists challenged the discipline to think about how its theories might be reformulated and how its understandings of global politics might be improved if gender were included as a category of analysis and if women's experiences were part of its subject matter. Feminists claimed that only by introducing **gender** analysis could the differential impact of the state system and the global economy on the lives of women and men be fully understood. IR feminists critically re-examined some of the key concepts in the field – concepts such as sovereignty, the state, and security. They began to ask new questions – such as whether it makes a difference that most foreign-policy leaders, military personnel, and heads of international corporations are men and why women remain relatively disempowered in matters of foreign and military policy.

IR feminists have also sought to make women visible as subjects in international politics and the global economy. They draw attention to women's invisibility and gender subordination in the theory and practice of international politics. Less than 10 per cent of the world's heads of state are women. IR feminists ask why this is the case and how this might affect the structure and practice of global politics. More recently, 'second generation' IR feminist empirical case studies have focused on hitherto understudied issues such as military prostitution, domestic service, diplomatic households, and home-based work, much of which is performed by women.[1] Through these studies feminists have sought to demonstrate how vital women are to the foreign policies of states and to the functioning of the global economy. Since most women speak from the margins of international politics, their lives offer us a perspective outside the state-centric focus of conventional Western international theories and broaden the empirical base upon which we build these theories. Feminist scholars suggest that if we put on **gendered lenses** we get quite a different view of international politics (Peterson and Runyan 1999: 21).

Feminists define gender as a set of socially constructed characteristics describing what men and women ought to be. Characteristics such as strength, rationality, independence, protector, and public are associated with masculinity while characteristics such as weakness, emotionality, relational, protected, and private are associated with femininity. It is important to note that individual men and women may not embody all these characteristics – it is possible for women to display masculine ones and vice versa. Rather, they are ideal types; the ideal masculine type (in the West – white and heterosexual) is sometimes referred to as 'hegemonic masculinity'. These characteristics may vary over time and place but, importantly, they are relational, meaning they depend on each other for their meaning. They are also unequal. Men, women, and the states they live in generally assign more positive value to masculine characteristics than to feminine ones – at least in the public sphere. The foreign policies of states are often legitimated in terms of hegemonic masculine characteristics; a desirable foreign policy is generally one which strives for power and autonomy and which protects its citizens from outside dangers. Appeals to these gender dualisms also organize social activity and divide necessary social activities between groups of humans; for example, since women are associated with the private sphere, it is seen as 'natural' for women to be caregivers while men's association with the public space makes them 'natural breadwinners' (Harding 1986: 17–18). While feminists rightly question the naturalness of these dichotomized distinctions, they have consequences – for women, for men, and for global politics. We will be discussing these consequences throughout the chapter.

In this chapter we trace the history of the development of feminist IR. We outline a typology of IR feminist theories which build on, but go beyond, a variety of IR approaches, such as liberalism (Chapters 5 and 6), constructivism (Chapter 9), critical theory (Chapter 8), poststructuralism (Chapter 11) and postcolonialism (Chapter 12) – theories which are discussed in other chapters. We offer some redefinitions and reanalyses of security as an illustration of how feminists are reformulating some of the key concepts in IR. We have chosen to focus on security because it has been central to the discipline since its founding in the early twentieth century. It has also been an important issue for feminist scholars because women have largely been absent – as security providers in the traditional state/military security sense and also as security scholars in the IR discipline. We will illustrate our feminist analysis of security through an examination of United Nations economic sanctions against Iraq in the 1990s. We propose that feminist IR offers some insights into this case that other sanctions theories do not. We conclude by suggesting the contributions of feminist IR to the discipline specifically and to global politics more generally.

Gender in International Relations

The 'third debate' of the late 1980s was a time when many scholars in the discipline began to debate its ways of knowing (Lapid 1989). Certain scholars began to question both the epistemological and ontological foundations of a field which, in the USA especially, had been dominated by positivist, rationalist, and materialist theories. Postpositivist scholarship, which includes critical theory, some forms of constructivism, poststructuralism, and postmodernism, questions positivists' beliefs about the possibility of creating universal, objective knowledge. Rejecting rationalist methodologies and causal explanations, postpositivists advocate more interpretive, ideational, and sociological methods for understanding global politics. They ask in whose interests and for what purpose is knowledge constructed. For a more detailed account of the different kinds of theorizing in IR, see Chapter 1.

Many feminists share this postpositivist commitment to examining the relationship between knowledge and power. They point out that most knowledge has been created by men and is about men.[2] Although IR postpositivists have been as slow as positivists to introduce gender into their research, their epistemological critiques created space for feminist analyses in a way that other IR scholarship had not. Conventional IR relies on generalized rationalist explanations of asocial states' behaviour in an anarchic international system. IR feminist theories focus on social relations, particularly gender relations;

rather than anarchy, they see an international system constituted by socially constructed gender hierarchies which contribute to gender subordination. In order to reveal these gender hierarchies, feminists often begin their examinations of international relations at the micro-level – attempting to understand how the lives of individuals (especially marginalized individuals) affect and are affected by global politics.

IR feminist research can be divided into two complementary but distinct generations: first generation, which largely focused on theory formulation, and second generation, which approached empirical situations with 'gendered lenses'. First-generation IR feminist theory was primarily concerned with bringing to light and critiquing the gendered foundations of IR theories and of the practices of international politics. Second-generation IR feminists have begun to develop their own research programmes – extending the boundaries of the discipline, investigating different issues, and listening to unfamiliar voices. These feminists use gender as a category of analysis in their studies of real-world events in global politics, incorporating feminist conceptual critiques into their analyses of specific situations. They have studied the gendered nature of the global economy, foreign policy, and security by examining specific political and economic situations in concrete historical and geographic contexts.

Typology of IR feminist theories

As in IR more generally there is a wide variety of feminist theoretical perspectives. Many of them build on, but go beyond, some of the IR perspectives discussed in other chapters – such as liberalism, constructivism, critical theory, poststructuralism, and postcolonialism. While they may disagree about the reasons, all of them are trying to understand women's subordination. IR feminists share an interest in gender equality or what they prefer to call gender emancipation. But what feminists mean by gender emancipation varies greatly, as does their understanding of the appropriate paths to reach it. We will now briefly outline the assumptions and methodological preferences of some of these approaches and refer to some exemplary writings in each. We note that there is significant overlap between these perspectives and that our typology is somewhat of a simplification, but useful for analysis.

Liberal feminism

Liberal feminism calls attention to the subordinate position of women in global politics but remains committed to investigating the causes of this subordination within a positivist framework. Liberal feminism challenges the content but not the epistemological assumptions of conventional IR. Liberal feminists document various aspects of women's subordination. For example, they have investigated the particular problems of refugee women, income inequalities between women and men, and human rights violations incurred disproportionately by women such as trafficking and rape in war. They look for women in the institutions and practices of global politics and observe how their presence (or lack thereof) affects and is affected by international policy-making. They ask what a world with more women in positions of power might look like. Liberal feminists believe that women's equality can be achieved by removing legal and other obstacles that have denied them the same rights and opportunities as men.

Liberal feminists also use gender as an explanatory variable in foreign-policy analysis. Using social scientific methods, Mary Caprioli and Mark Boyer (2001) employ quantitative social science data and statistical measures to test a variant of the democratic peace hypothesis – namely, whether there is a relationship between domestic gender equality and states' use of violence internationally. According to their measures of gender inequality, their results show that the severity of violence used by states in international crises decreases as domestic gender equality increases. Caprioli and Boyer are using gender as a variable to explain certain policies and policy results.

Many postpositivist IR feminists are critical of liberal feminism. They see problems with measuring gender inequality using statistical indicators. Caprioli and Boyer use national indicators, such as numbers of women in parliament and years since women gained the vote, to measure gender equality. Postpositivist feminists claim that such measures are inadequate for understanding gender inequality which is associated with gender role expectations that keep women out of positions of power; as we mentioned earlier, gender-laden divisions between public and private spheres consign women to certain socially accepted roles. Postpositivist feminists point out that gender inequalities continue to exist in societies that have long-since achieved formal equality so we must go deeper into our investigations of gender hierarchies if we are to explain these inequalities. All these feminists use gender (as we defined it earlier) as a category of analysis to help them understand these inequalities and their implications for global politics.

Critical feminism

Critical feminism goes beyond liberal feminism's use of gender as a variable. It explores the ideational and material manifestations of gendered identities and gendered power in global politics. Many critical feminists build upon, but go beyond the work of IR scholar Robert Cox. Cox (1981) portrays the world in terms of historical structures made up of three categories of reciprocal interacting forces: material conditions, ideas, and institutions. These forces interact at three different levels: production relations, the state–society complex, and historically defined world orders. While ideas are important in legitimating certain institutions, ideas are the product of human agents – therefore, there is always the possibility of change. Critical theory is committed to understanding the world in order to try to change it.

Sandra Whitworth is a feminist critical theorist who builds on Cox's framework. In her book *Feminism and International Relations* (1994) she claims that understandings about gender depend only in part on real material conditions of women and men in particular circumstances. She suggests that gender is also constituted by the meaning given to that reality – *ideas* that men and women have about their relationships to one another. Her research examines the different ways gender was understood over time in the International Planned Parenthood Federation (IPPF) and the International Labour Organization (ILO) and the effects that these changing understandings had on both institutions' population policies at various times in their history.

Christine Chin's *In Service and Servitude* (1998) also uses a critical feminist approach to study female domestic workers. Chin examines the increasing prevalence of underpaid and often exploited foreign female domestic workers in Malaysia during the 1970s – a time when the state was modernizing the economy. She rejects a traditional economic explanation of wage differentials to explain the importation of Filipino and Indonesian female domestic labour because, in this case, economic theory does not account for state involvement or the social dynamics around the employment of foreign domestic workers. Adopting a critical approach, Chin argues that the Malaysian state supported the importation and employment of foreign female domestic workers, who were often working in conditions not much better than slavery, as a part of a strategy to co-opt and win the support of middle-class families and decrease ethnic tensions. Her study shows that the Malaysian state, like other states, is not neutral, but an expression of class, race, and gender-based power which won support by co-opting certain citizens while repressing others. Consistent with critical theory more generally, Chin sees her study as emancipatory – to identify existing power relations with the intention of changing them.

Feminist constructivism

IR social constructivists called for rethinking the ways we see and understand international politics by adding a social layer to IR's analyses. They emphasize the ideational rather than the material elements of global politics. Constructivist approaches range broadly – from positivist versions that treat ideas as causes to a postpositivist focus on language. All agree that international life is social and that agents and structures are co-constituted. They challenge realist assumptions about states as unitary actors; instead, they see states as the dynamic results of the social processes that constitute their existence. States and other international actors' perceptions of their own and others' identities shape their behaviour in global politics.

Constructivist feminism focuses on the way that ideas about gender shape and are shaped by global politics. Elisabeth Prügl's book *The Global Construction of Gender* (1999) uses a linguistically based feminist constructivist perspective to analyse the treatment of home-based work in international negotiations and international law. Since most home-based workers are women, the debate about regulating this type of employment is an important one from a feminist perspective. Low wages and poor working conditions have often been justified on the grounds that home-based work is not 'real work' since it takes place in the private reproductive sphere of the household rather than the more valued public sphere of waged-based production. Prügl shows how ideas about womanhood and femininity contributed to the international community's debates about institutionalizing these workers' rights, a debate which finally culminated in the passage of the ILO's Homework Convention in 1996 due, in large part, to the lobbying of a variety of women's non-governmental organizations (NGOs). She sees gender as an institution that codifies power at every level of global politics, from the home to the state to the international system. She argues that gender politics pervades world politics, creating a set of linguistically based rules about how states interact with each other and with their own citizens. Prügl and other constructivist feminists study the processes whereby ideas about gender influence global politics as well as the ways that global politics shapes ideas about gender.

Nevertheless, as her study shows, political spaces created by negotiations do provide openings for alternative interpretations; therefore, they can be sites for emancipation.

Feminist poststructuralism

Poststructuralists focus on meaning as it is codified in language. They claim that our understanding of reality is mediated through our use of language. They are particularly concerned with the relationship between knowledge and power; those who construct meaning and create knowledge thereby gain a great deal of power. Feminists point out that men have generally been seen as the knowers – what has counted as legitimate knowledge in the social sciences has generally been based on knowledge about men's lives in the public sphere; women have been marginalized both as knowers and as the subjects of knowledge.

Poststructuralist feminism is particularly concerned with the way dichotomized linguistic constructions, such as strong/weak, rational/emotional, and public/private, serve to empower the masculine over the feminine. In international relations, dichotomous constructions, such as civilized/uncivilized, order/anarchy, and developed/underdeveloped, have been important in how we divide the world linguistically. Poststructuralists believe that these distinctions have real-world consequences. Dichotomous constructions denote inferiority and even danger with respect to those on the outside – they are also gendered and have racial implications. Feminist poststructuralists seek to expose and deconstruct these hierarchies – often through the analysis of texts and their meaning. They see gender as a complex social construction and they emphasize that the spoken meaning of gender is constantly evolving and changing with context. Deconstructing these hierarchies is necessary in order for us to see them and construct a less hierarchical vision of reality.

Charlotte Hooper's book *Manly States* (2001) is an example of poststructural textual analysis. One of her central questions is what role does International Relations theory and practice play in shaping, defining, and legitimating masculinities. She claims that we cannot understand international relations unless we understand the implications of the fact that it is conducted mostly by men. She asks how international relations might discipline men as much as men shape international relations. Hooper sets about answering this question through an analysis of theories of masculinity together with a textual analysis of *The Economist*, a prestigious British weekly newspaper that covers business and politics. She follows the practice of intertextuality – 'the process by which meanings are circulated between texts through the use of various visual and literary codes and conventions' (Hooper 2001: 122). Through an examination of texts, graphs, photos, and advertising material, she concludes that *The Economist* is saturated with signifiers of hegemonic masculinities and that gendered messages are encoded in the newspaper regardless of the intentions of its publishers or authors. She aims to show that gender politics pervades world politics and that gender is a social construction that results from practices that connect arguments at all levels of politics and society including the international.

Postcolonial feminism

Many postcolonial writers are poststructuralists. Their particular concern is colonial relations of domination and subordination established under imperialism. They claim that these dominance relationships have persisted beyond the granting of independence to formerly colonized states and that they are built into the way the colonized are represented in Western knowledge. Arguing that the colonized must represent themselves, postcolonial scholars aim to 'speak back', a task made harder by the erasure of their history and culture. Like poststructuralist scholars more generally, postcolonial scholars argue that, in international relations, constructions of 'self' and 'other' foster racial and cultural stereotypes that denote the other – in their case ex-colonial subjects – as inferior.

Postcolonial feminism makes similar claims about the way Western feminists have constructed knowledge about non-Western women. Just as feminists have criticized Western knowledge for its false assumptions about universality when, in reality, it is knowledge constructed mainly from men's lives, postcolonial feminists see false claims of universalism arising from knowledge which is based largely on the experiences of relatively privileged Western women. Chandra Mohanty (1988) critiques some Western feminists for treating women as a homogeneous category which does not acknowledge their differences depending on their culture, social class, race, and geographical location. This ethnocentric universalism robs women of their historical and political agency. Postcolonial feminists, such as Mohanty, are concerned that Western feminists assume that all women have similar needs with respect to emancipation when, in fact, their realities are very different. Postcolonial feminists challenge Western portrayals of Third World women as poor, undereducated, victimized, and lacking in agency. They see gender subordination as sitting at the intersection of gender, race, and culture. Recognizing this, they seek to redress these subordinations within their own cultural context, rather than through a universal understanding of women's needs.

Gender, security, and global politics

In this section we focus on how the theoretical perspectives we have outlined and how the scholarship we have discussed contribute to our understanding of security and insecurity. Feminist definitions of security, explanations of insecurity, and suggestions as to how to improve security are very different from those of conventional IR. We begin this section by offering some feminist redefinitions of security and insecurity. Then we suggest some feminist reanalyses of security and outline some empirical evidence that feminists are using to formulate their reanalyses.

Redefining security and its subjects

Conventional IR scholars, notably realists, define security primarily in terms of the security of the state. A secure state is one that can protect its physical and moral boundaries against an 'anarchic' international system. Neorealists focus on the anarchic structure of the international system, where there is no sovereign to regulate state behavior. They portray states as unitary actors whose internal structures and policies are less important than this anarchic condition for explaining their security and insecurity. The power-seeking behaviour and military capabilities of states are seen as ways to increase their security; many security specialists believe that power-seeking in order to promote security explains much of the international behaviour of states.

In the 1980s, certain IR scholars began to challenge these explanations and to articulate broader definitions of security. Noting that most wars since 1945 have been fuelled by ethnic and nationalist rivalries and have not been fought across international boundaries, they began to examine the interrelation of military threats with economic and environmental ones. Most of the world's poorest states have active military conflicts within their boundaries. These conflicts contribute to high numbers of civilian casualties, to **structural violence** – the violence done to people when their basic needs are not met – and to environmental destruction. Critical security scholars, as they are called, began to define security in terms of threats to human well-being and survival – security of the individual and their environment, as well as that of the state.

Like critical security scholars, many IR feminists define security broadly in multidimensional and multilevel terms – as the diminution of all forms of violence, including physical, structural, and ecological. According to IR feminists, security threats include domestic violence, rape, poverty, gender subordination, and ecological destruction as well as war. Feminists not only broaden *what security means* but also *who is guaranteed security*. Most of their analyses of security start at the bottom, with the individual or the community, rather than with the state or the international system. IR feminists have demonstrated how the security of individuals is related to national and international politics and how international politics impacts the security of individuals even at the local level.

Feminist research is demonstrating how those at the margins of states may actually be rendered more insecure by their state's security policies. The Malaysian case, discussed earlier, demonstrates that the exploitation of foreign domestic servants, often thought of as a 'private' issue, was permitted by the Malaysian state in order to win support of its middle class, thereby diminishing ethnic tensions – tensions that were causing threats to the security of the state. In *Sex Among Allies* (1997), a study of prostitution around US military bases in South Korea in the 1970s, Katharine Moon shows how prostitution became a matter of top-level US–Korean security politics. Clean up of prostitution camps, effected by imposing health standards and monitoring sex workers, was directly related to establishing a more hospitable environment for US troops at a time when the USA was pulling troops out of South Korea. Both these cases show how considerations of national security translated into insecurity for marginalized vulnerable women. Redefinitions of security and rethinking about the subjects of security prompt feminists to ask different questions, particularly about whose lives are being secured and whose are not.

Challenging the myth of protection

Our earlier definition of masculinity and femininity defined men as 'protectors' and women as 'protected'.[3] It is a widespread myth that men fight wars to protect 'vulnerable people' usually defined as women and children. Yet, women and children constitute a majority of casualties in recent wars as civilian casualties have risen from about 10 per cent at the beginning of the twentieth century to almost 90 per cent by its close. In 1999 about 75 per cent of refugees were women and children, many of them fleeing from wars. Wars make it harder for women to fulfill their caregiving responsibilities; as mothers and family providers, women are particularly hurt by the economic consequences of wars. Feminists have also drawn our attention to wartime rape; often rape is not just an 'accident' of war but, as in the case of the war in the former Yugoslavia in the 1990s, a deliberate military strategy. Instead of seeing military power as part of a state's arsenal to defend against security threats from other states, feminists see that militaries are often threats to the security of individuals (particularly women) and competitors for scarce resources on which women may depend more than men.

Looking at the effects of war through gendered lenses, we find that war is a cultural construction that depends on myths of protection. Such myths have been important in upholding the legitimacy of war. They also contribute to the delegitimation of peace which is often associated with feminine characteristics, such as weakness, concession, and idealism. Looking at these gendered constructions may deepen our understanding of the causes of war and allow us to see how certain ways of thinking about security have been legitimated while others have been silenced.

Understanding economic insecurity

Feminist analyses of military security have looked at the gendered impacts of war, particularly as they relate to the security of individuals. Feminist research on economic security highlights women's particular economic vulnerabilities. While there are obviously enormous global differences in women's socioeconomic status, depending on race, class, and geographic location, women are disproportionately located at the bottom of the socioeconomic scale in all societies. In order to explain this, feminists have drawn our attention to a gendered division of labour that had its origins in seventeenth-century Europe, where definitions of male and female were becoming polarized in ways that were suited to a growing division between work and home required by early capitalism. The notion 'housewife' began to place women's work in the private domestic sphere as opposed to the public world of production inhabited by men. Even though most women do work outside the home, the association of women with gendered roles, such as housewife, caregiver, and mother, came to be seen as 'natural'. Consequently, when women do enter the workforce, they are disproportionately represented in the caring professions or 'light' manufacturing industries, occupations that are chosen because of values that are often emphasized in female socialization. Women provide an optimal labour force for contemporary global capitalism because, since they are defined as housewives rather than workers, they can be paid lower wages on the assumption that their wages are supplemental to family income. Elisabeth Prügl's study of home-based labour, discussed earlier, talks about the low remuneration of home-based work which is grounded in this assumption. Nevertheless, in actual fact, about one-third of all households are headed by women.

Even when women do benefit from entry into the workforce, they continue to suffer from a double or even triple burden since women carry most of the responsibility for household labour and unpaid community work. Unremunerated labour plays a crucial role in the reproduction of labour necessary for waged work, yet it has rarely been of concern to economic analysis. A narrow definition of work as work in the waged economy, one that is used in economic accounting, tends to render invisible many of the contributions that women make to the global economy. The disproportionate poverty of women cannot be explained by market conditions alone; gendered role expectations about the economic worth of women's work and the kinds of tasks that women are expected to do contribute to their economic insecurity.

Like critical security scholars, feminist have broadened their definitions and analyses of security. But they go further by showing how important gender as a category of analysis is to our understanding of security and insecurity. Using our gendered lenses we will now examine in more detail the UN sanctions policy on Iraq during the 1990s, a case which supports this proposition.

Case study: UN sanctions on Iraq

In 1991 Iraq invaded and conquered Kuwait, claiming a right to Kuwaiti territory. The United Nations (UN) declared Iraq's invasion illegal and ultimately used military force to eject Iraq from Kuwait. This conflict is known as the First Gulf War. At the end of the First Gulf War, UN Security Council Resolution 687 left Iraq under a strict import and export embargo. According to the Resolution, the embargo would remain in place until Iraq met a list of demands imposed by the Security Council. These demands related to Kuwaiti independence, Iraqi weapons, terrorism, and liability for the Gulf War.[4] This sanctions regime, originally intended to last about a year, stretched over thirteen. It was marked by confusion, fits and starts, partial compliance, and ulterior motives. Iraq's cooperation was inconsistent at best and Saddam Hussein, the president of Iraq, often openly defied the sanctions. Throughout the 1990s, Iraq remained under one of history's longest and most strict economic sanctions regimes.

In the mid-1990s, international popular opinion turned against the sanctions because of the tragic humanitarian consequences. Many states that favoured the overthrow of the Saddam Hussein regime became critical of the sanctions. A number of UN Security Council member-states, including France and Russia, turned against the sanctions. Still, a Security Council vote to lift the sanctions was never taken because such a vote would have faced certain veto from the USA. The USA, but not the UN, insisted on regime change in Iraq as a condition for lifting sanctions. Meanwhile, pictures of malnourished children were publicized by activist organizations fighting the sanctions. The USA and the UN Security Council blamed Saddam Hussein for Iraq's non-compliance, while the Iraqi government blamed the UN.

The sanctions regime was a humanitarian disaster. The impacts of a thirteen-year-near-total embargo on the Iraqi economy were extensive. Before the First Gulf War, Iraq had an export-based economy, exporting oil. Iraq imported almost all of its food and other basic necessities. The Iraqi gross national product (GNP) fell by 50 per cent during the first year of sanctions, and declined to less than $500 in the following years. By 2000, Iraq was the third poorest country in the world. Economic decline caused a sharp decline in real wages and widespread unemployment.

These adverse economic impacts caused most Iraqis serious material problems. Often, women had less secure jobs than men because their job tenure had been shorter and they were not seen as the primary income-earners for their families. Iraq had neither the money to buy, nor the means to produce, essential supplies; before the sanctions it had imported most of its food. With no income, a crippled infrastructure, and an international law against both imports and exports, Iraq had a difficult time acquiring food. The result was catastrophic malnutrition. Households rarely had enough food and women were often the last to eat. Iraqis also lacked clean water, baby milk, vitamins, health-care supplies, and adequate electricity. The oil-for-food programme implemented by the UN Security Council allowed some needed supplies to enter Iraq by permitting limited oil exports. While the programme did result in some food entering Iraq, its provisions failed to provide for the restoration of Iraq's oil infrastructure which had been badly damaged in the First Gulf War. As a result, the oil-for-food programme did not meet the basic needs of Iraqi citizens. It was not until certain members of the international community began to trade with Iraq in the late 1990s despite the sanctions that the worst humanitarian impacts dissipated.

These deprivations had severe medical impacts. Finding adequate prenatal care was next to impossible for Iraqi women; even if their children were born healthy, the lack of vitamins and baby milk meant that child mortality skyrocketed. The cancer rate rose by 400 per cent. It is estimated that the sanctions led to the deaths of about 1 million Iraqis, half of them children and another 30 per cent women (Mueller and Mueller 1999). In a country that had previously possessed a world-class medical system, curable diseases and starvation were the leading causes of death. The education systems also plummeted. Crime rates and prostitution rose while culture, the arts, and religious activity decreased. Joy Gordon (1999) claimed that sanctions sent Iraq back to the stone age.

Some IR analyses of sanctions

Following the success of limited sanctions on South Africa in the 1980s, which contributed to the ending of Apartheid, economic sanctions were seen as a powerful but humane tool. IR analyses of the effectiveness of sanctions are informed by a variety of theoretical perspectives. Realists view sanctions as a way of raising the cost of non-compliance for the country on which sanctions are imposed until it becomes unacceptable (Baldwin 1985). Liberals explain sanctions as a way of depriving the target country of the means to commit a violation of international norms (Martin 1992). In other words, sanctions take away the resources an errant state would use to defy international will. Constructivists argue that sanctions are a socializing phenomenon, communicating a message of disapproval through the combination of negative consequences and international shame (Crawford and Klotz 1999). Scholars who focus on language see sanctions as discourse – as tools of argumentation which allow actors to demonstrate the importance of their point to other actors reticent to agree (Morgan and Schwebach 1997). Within each of these schools of thought, there are disagreements about which (if any) sanctions have worked, and how frequently they should be used. A feminist theory of sanctions draws from all these perspectives but goes beyond them, using gender as a category of analysis.

Feminists interpret sanctions on Iraq

Economic sanctions do not appear to be a security issue in the narrow sense: they are not fought with guns on a battlefield, or with bombs on airplanes. The UN Security Council did not declare war on Iraq and the sanctions on Iraq did not *look like* a conventional war. However, as we mentioned earlier, IR feminists who study war pay attention to structural and physical violence, and to what is happening on the ground – to individuals and communities. From this perspective, economic sanctions on Iraq not only looked like a war; they looked like a war on Iraq's most vulnerable citizens.

As we have shown, the UN Security Council's sanctions regime deprived most Iraqi citizens of their basic everyday needs. The aim of the sanctions was to stir up popular discontent against the Iraqi government and its policies. In other words, sanctions tried to *hurt civilians* so they would change their government. If sanctions were a war, they were a war against non-combatants. The civilians who were hurt the most were not the rich and powerful or the decision-makers, since they had the ability to buy food and supplies on the black market. Instead, it was Iraq's most vulnerable population that suffered most – low-income people, women, children, and the elderly. Economic sanctions against Iraq constituted both physical and structural violence. *Physical* violence was incurred though frequent bombings intended to communicate the unhappiness of UN member-states with Iraq's non-compliance. *Structural* violence was incurred through the destruction of the economic infrastructure and the lack of nutrition and medical care that had supported Iraq's poorest citizens. By these measures feminists would conclude that economic sanctions constitute war. This being the case, we will now suggest some research questions that feminists might ask and what we might learn from their analyses.

A liberal feminist study of sanctions might ask how many women participated in the sanctions decision-making process; they might also measure the varying effects of sanctions on individuals, focusing on gender differences. From this they might conclude that, while few women were involved in constructing and implementing the sanctions policy, women suffered more than their male counterparts, both through direct deprivation and through the effects of sanctions on their homes, families, and jobs.

Feminists from all postpositivist theoretical perspectives would introduce gender as a category of analysis and investigate the role that gender played in the politics of the sanctions regime. They might investigate how both the Iraqi government and the advocates of the sanctions regime used gender as a public relations argument against their opponents.

Along those lines, feminists might investigate the political appropriation of gender categories by both sides of the conflict. IR feminists emphasize the gendered social hierarchy in global politics that fosters an atmosphere of coercive competition by valuing traits associated with masculinity (bravery, strength, and dominance) over traits associated with femininity (compromise, compassion, and weakness). Feminists might investigate the gendered discourses of competitive masculinity that each side of the sanctions war used to legitimize their actions and delegitimize the enemy's; such discourses are often manifested in times of inter-state conflict. Specifically, they might point to instances where US CIA Director George Tenet talked about penetrating Saddam Hussein's 'inner sanctum', where US President George H. W. Bush talked about protecting Iraqi women as a justification for sanctions and war, and where Saddam Hussein countered with the threat of showing the USA what a 'real man' he was. It is often the case, particularly in times of conflict, that we personify enemy states in gendered ways, referring to them by their leaders' names. This hides the negative impacts of war on the lives of individuals – individuals who may not be responsible for the conflict in the first place. Feminists might also explore the punitive relationship between the UN Security Council and Iraq as an example of a hegemonic masculinity feminizing a weaker enemy.

Towards a feminist theory of sanctions

We suggest three major insights that feminists contribute to the theory of sanctions. First, feminists look for where the women are in sanctions regimes. They see that women are disproportionately affected by comprehensive sanctions. Women and children are the most likely to be malnourished. When women are malnourished, every stage of the child-bearing process becomes more difficult. Pre-natal and infant health care is often the first facet of the health-care system to suffer when a sanctioned economy begins to decline. Women lose their jobs and are charged with running households deprived of basic goods. An international policy of economic deprivation is felt most heavily at the level of individual households. While women suffer disproportionately from sanctions regimes, very few women are present in the decision-making process. When the sanctions on Iraq were enacted, there were no female heads of UN Security Council member-states. Feminists see the sanctions regime on Iraq as an example of the systematic exclusion of women's voices from decisions about international policies that disproportionately affect them. State and inter-state security policy can cause women's (and other individuals') insecurity.

The second insight feminists have is a critique of the gendered logic of sanctions as a policy choice. Sanctions are enacted by stronger actors in an attempt to force the weaker actor to submit to their will. They are coercive in nature – comply, or you starve. Feminists criticize the adversarial nature of international politics because it valorizes masculine values, such as pride, victory, and force, over feminine ones, such as compromise, compassion, and coexistence – values that are often seen as signs of weakness by most states and many of their citizens, women and men alike. This results in confrontational policies, policies that often hurt those at the margins of international political life the most. Sanctions demonstrate coercive, masculine policy logic. Postcolonial feminists would add a criticism of the assumption that the UN Security Council members somehow knew *better than Iraq* what was good for Iraqis. It is often the case that powerful people, many of whom are men, claim to know what is best for subordinate people (and often for women). IR feminists critique the gendered logic and gendered impacts of sanctions.

The third insight that IR feminists have to offer a theory of sanctions is a critical re-examination of the question of responsibility. Feminists look not only for the problems with hierarchical gender relationships in global politics, they also look for solutions. Having seen the tragic, gendered humanitarian consequences of the sanctions regime, feminists might ask why no one was fixing them. The Iraqi government used people's suffering to advance its political position at the expense of its most vulnerable citizens. Saddam Hussein showed no flexibility which could have saved lives. Whether or not the international community truly believed that the goal of sanctions was worth the catastrophic loss of life in Iraq, many governments in the international arena let people die. Feminists draw attention to the construction of state borders as a way to separate 'self' from 'other' and distance ourselves from the suffering of others. Feminists encourage states and their citizens to reflect on the false perception of separateness and the global hierarchies thereby created. Deconstructing these hierarchies might lead people to care for, rather than compete with, those others outside state boundaries.

Feminists would conclude that economic sanctions are not isolated areas of conflict within an otherwise peaceful system. Acts of coercion, physical or economic, put in place by both sides to win international competitions are not only violent, but part of a system that is condoning violence, both physical and structural. The sanctions regime on Iraq contributed to the perpetuation of a violent international system in which the most vulnerable people are rarely secure. Feminist IR highlights these gendered insecurities as central to global politics.

Conclusion

We believe that feminist IR has contributed substantially to our understanding of global politics over the last twenty years. Feminists have restored women's visibility, investigated gendered constructions of international concepts and policies, and questioned the naturalness of the gendered categories that shape and are shaped by global politics. First-generation feminist IR scholars have offered theoretical reformulations while second-generation scholars have applied these theoretical reformulations to concrete situations in global politics.

We have provided a brief overview of a number of different IR feminist theories, including liberal, critical, constructivist, poststructuralist, and postcolonial. While we realize it may be an over-simplification, we created this typology to illustrate one of the major goals of feminist IR – to demonstrate that gender relationships inhere in all IR scholarship. Gender relationships are everywhere in global politics; whenever they are not recognized, the silence is loud. IR feminists suggest that all scholars and practitioners of international politics should ask gender questions and be more aware of the gendered implications of global politics. Scholars should ask to what extent their theories are constructed mainly by men and from the lives of men. Practitioners should ask how their policies impact women and whether a lack of women's voices influences their policy choices. Recognizing gender and other hierarchies of power and their implications for the lives of both women and men allows us to begin to degender global politics – from inside the United Nations to inside the home.

In this chapter, we focused on feminist interpretations of security. Security is so important to states that sometimes they pursue sanctions and wars and cause structural violence in the name of preserving or enhancing security. However, in preserving state security members of the international community may violate the security of their own and others' most marginal citizens, notably women, children, the elderly, the poor, and the sick. IR feminists study security at the individual and community level; they notice the differential impacts of security policies on women and marginalized people more generally and interrogate the gendered nature of concepts such as war, security, and the state. The insights they produce reveal some new causes of insecurity at the global level, including gender subordination.

Gender subordination is visible at every level in the Iraq sanctions case. Individual women were disproportionately impacted by the sanctions; gendered states exploited that disparate impact by engaging in gendered discourses of masculine competition. From the policy logic to the effects, sanctions on Iraq were an example of a gendered international security policy. We have laid out a few paths feminists have used in reformulating IR's understandings of sanctions in order to make women and gender relationships visible, and thereby suggest some new ways to enhance security. These suggestions offer IR scholars of all perspectives some new insights into the feminist claim that gender is not just about women but also about the way that international policies are framed, studied, and implemented.

? QUESTIONS

1. More than half the world's labour comes in the form of the unpaid, home-based labour of women. If this type of labour was remunerated, labour costs in the global economy would triple. How does women's free labour affect the global economy?

2. Does it make any difference to the foreign policies of states that a vast majority of policy-makers are men? Does it matter to the content of IR scholarship that most of its leading scholars are men?

3. Cynthia Enloe, a prominent IR feminist, has claimed that 'the personal is international and the international is personal' (1990: 195). What does she mean by this?

4. Sanctions against Iraq were a case of extreme humanitarian suffering and political intransigence, but other sanctions have been more successful. Do gendered lenses have anything to say about economic coercion more generally? If so, what?

5. What about the men? How does gender affect men's experiences in everyday life? In global politics?

6. Once we realize that gender plays a pervasive role in global social and political interactions, we begin to ask what we can do about it. Could global politics be degendered?

7. One of the major claims that IR feminists make is that individual lives *are* global politics. How might your trip to the grocery store, choice of television programming, or choice of internet sites be global politics?

8. The debate about whether or not women should get the vote was a contentious one in most countries. Do women have something different from men to say about global politics? If so, what?

9. Many scholars who work on the humanitarian consequences of war talk about the effect of war on innocent women and children. How might women experience war differently from men?

10. Since feminist insights stretch across different perspectives on IR, this chapter raises the issue as to whether feminism belongs in one chapter of a book about IR theories. How might gendered lenses see the cases in other chapters?

11. Following the war in the former Yugoslavia in the 1990s, a number of scholars and activists argued that the international laws of war should include a prohibition against genocidal rape. What might a feminist perspective on IR contribute to the discussion of the problem of wartime rape?

12. In his 2002 State of the Union Address to the US Congress, President George W. Bush claimed that 'brutality against women is always and everywhere wrong', implying that brutality against women might justify war. Would a feminist perspective on IR agree?

FURTHER READING

■ **Peterson, V. Spike and Runyan, Anne Sisson (1999),** *Global Gender Issues,* **2nd edn (Boulder CO: Westview).** Peterson and Runyan introduce and apply 'gendered lenses' to global politics.

■ **Tickner, J. Ann (2001),** *Gendering World Politics: Issues and Approaches in the Post-Cold War Era* **(New York: Columbia University Press).** The author of the first singly authored book in feminist IR lays out a foundation for feminist IR in the twenty-first century.

■ **Enloe, Cynthia (2000),** *Maneuvers: The International Politics of Militarizing Women's Lives* **(Berkeley: University of California Press).** Enloe finds the relationship between gender and security in political phenomena as different as a military base and a can of soup, and weaves a framework for feminist security theories from these observations.

■ **Marchand, Marianne H. and Runyan, Anne Sisson (2000) (eds),** *Gender and Global Restructuring: Sightings, Sites, and Resistances* **(London and New York: Routledge).** This book addresses genderings in the global economy, going beyond the narrow limits of conventional approaches to globalization to reveal the complexities of global restructuring based on gendered economic and social disparities.

■ **Chin, Christine (1998),** *In Service and Servitude: Foreign Female Domestic Workers and the Malaysian 'Modernity' Project* **(New York: Columbia University Press).** Chin uses gendered lenses to show that the very private phenomena of home-based labour interacts with and *is* international relations in important, gendered ways.

■ **Moon, Katharine H. S. (1997),** *Sex Among Allies: Military Prostitution in U.S.–Korea Relations* **(New York: Columbia University Press).** Moon demonstrates that international security policy takes place at the level of regulating individual women's lives in Korean prostitution camps.

■ **Prügl, Elisabeth (1999),** *The Global Construction of Gender: Home-based Work in the Political Economy of the 20th Century* **(New York: Columbia University Press).** Prügl examines the social, political, and economic dynamics of home-based work in the twentieth century from a feminist constructivist perspective.

■ **Robinson, Fiona (1999),** *Globalising Care: Ethics, Feminist Theory and International Relations* **(Oxford: Westview Press).** Robinson derives an ethic of care from feminist theories and applies her theoretical insights to the empirical study of care for health and welfare around the world.

■ **True, Jacqui (2003),** *Gender, Globalization, and Post-socialism: The Czech Republic after Communism* **(New York: Columbia University Press).** True applies the insights of feminist theories of international political economy and international security to post-socialist Eastern Europe.

J. ANN TICKNER AND LAURA SJOBERG

IMPORTANT WEBSITES

- Council of Women World Leaders
  www.womenworldleaders.org

- UN Division for the Advancement of Women
  www.un.org/womenwatch/daw

- Women in International Security
  wiis.georgetown.edu

- MADRE, an international women's human rights organization
  www.madre.org

- Global Fund for Women
  www.globalfundforwomen.org

Visit the Online Resource Centre that accompanies this book for lots of interesting additional material. www.oxfordtextbooks.co.uk/orc/dunne/

11

Poststructuralism

DAVID CAMPBELL[1]

✔ **Reader's guide**

The way the discipline of International Relations 'maps' the world shows the importance of representation, the relationship of power and knowledge, and the politics of identity to the production and understanding of global politics. Poststructuralism directly engages these issues even though it is not a new paradigm or theory of International Relations. It is, rather, a critical attitude or ethos that explores the assumptions that make certain ways of being, acting, and knowing possible. This chapter details how and why poststructuralism engaged International Relations from the 1980s onwards. It explores the interdisciplinary context of social and political theory from which poststructuralism emerged, and examines the misconceptions evident in the reception this approach received from mainstream theorists. The chapter details what the critical attitude of poststructuralism means for social and political inquiry. Focusing on the work of Michel Foucault, it shows the importance of discourse, identity, subjectivity, and power to this approach, and discusses the methodological features employed by poststructuralists in their readings of, and interventions in, international politics. The chapter concludes with a case study of images of humanitarian crises that illustrates the poststructural approach.

Introduction

Interpretation, mapping, and meta-theory

Every discussion and every understanding of international politics depends upon abstraction, representation, and interpretation. That is because 'the world' does not present itself to us in the form of ready-made categories, theories, or statements. As the French philosopher-historian Michel Foucault (1984b: 127) has argued, 'the world does not provide us with a legible face, leaving us merely to decipher it; it does not work hand in glove with what we already know'. This means whenever we write or speak of 'the realm of anarchy', the 'end of the Cold War', 'gendered relations of power', 'globalization', 'humanitarian intervention', 'finance capital' – indeed, when we employ any term to grasp the meaning of events and issues – we are engaging in abstraction, representation, and interpretation. No matter what particular perspectives claim, even the most 'objective' theory that claims to offer a perfect resemblance or mirror image of things does not escape the inevitability and indispensability of interpretation (Bleiker 2001).

Political leaders, social activists, scholars, and students are all involved in the abstraction, representation, and interpretation of 'the world' whether they engage in the practice, theory, or study of international relations. This does not mean, however, that anyone can simply make things up and have the products of their imagination count as legitimate knowledge. That is because the dominant understandings of world politics are both *arbitrary* and *non-arbitrary*: arbitrary in the sense that they are but one possibility among a range of possibilities, and non-arbitrary in the sense that certain social and historical practices have given rise to dominant ways of making 'the world' that have very real effects upon our lives.

The dominant interpretations of 'the world' have been established by the discipline of International Relations, which traditionally talks of states and their policy-makers pursuing interests and providing security, of conflict and the need to balance power, of stability and the danger of anarchy, of economic relations and their material effects, of the rights of those who are being badly treated. The 'we' who talk in this way do so from a particular vantage point. 'We' are often white, Western, affluent, and comfortable. These representations, then, are related to our identities, and they establish a discourse of identity politics (primarily organized around the state) as the favoured frame of reference for world politics.

This highlights the relationship between knowledge and power. It is commonplace to say that 'knowledge is power', but this assumes they are synonymous rather than related. The production of maps illustrates the significance of the relationship between knowledge and power and the inevitability of interpretation. Maps are not simply inert records or passive reflections of the world of objects. They are selective in their content, particular in their styles, and limited in their subjects. They favour, promote, and influence specific sets of social relations (Harley 1988).

Consider the commonly used Mercator projection (Figure 11.1). Drafted in 1569 in order to provide the direct lines necessary for navigation, it placed Europe at the centre and put two-thirds of the world's landmass in the Northern Hemisphere. This representation

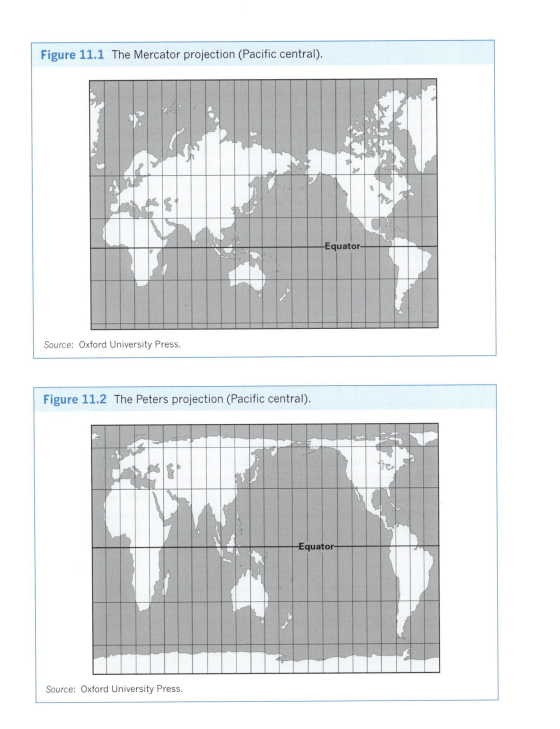

Figure 11.1 The Mercator projection (Pacific central).

Source: Oxford University Press.

Figure 11.2 The Peters projection (Pacific central).

Source: Oxford University Press.

supported the British Empire, and later reinforced Cold War perceptions of the Soviet threat (Monmonier 1996). Contrast this to the Peters projection, developed in the 1970s (Figure 11.2). This was based on equal-area projection which de-emphasized Europe and the North, and gave greater prominence to the South. Although not the first equal-area projection (which had been available since 1772) it was technically more accurate.

The Peters projection was significant because it came to prominence at a time of Third World political assertiveness in the United Nations, and was promoted by UN agencies keen to secure more resources for development. The Peters projection is, therefore, a manifestation of the power relations that challenged the two superpowers in the 1970s, and a form of knowledge which promoted the global South.

International Relations as a discipline 'maps' the world. However, it is only the critical perspectives – and poststructuralism in particular – which put the issues of interpretation and representation, power and knowledge, and the politics of identity at the forefront of concerns. Because of this poststructuralism is not a model or theory of international relations. Rather than setting out a paradigm through which everything is understood, poststructuralism is a critical attitude, approach, or ethos which calls attention to the importance of representation, the relationship of power and knowledge, and the politics of identity in the production and understanding of global affairs.

This means poststructuralism does not fit easily with the conventional view that International Relations is a discipline characterized by a diverse set of paradigms competing in 'great debates' (discussed in Chapter 1). Instead of being regarded as another school with its own favoured actors and issues to highlight, poststructuralism needs to be understood as promoting a new set of questions and concerns. This function – as a critical attitude rather than theory – means poststructuralism has a different perspective on the relationship between theory and practice. Instead of seeing a distinction *between* theory and practice, it sees theory *as* practice. This comes about because, in the first instance, poststructuralism poses a series of meta-theoretical questions – questions about the theory of theory – in order to understand how particular ways of knowing, what counts as knowing, and who can know (which includes other theories and theorists), have been established over time. In this context, poststructuralism is part and parcel of a wider group of critical social theories. It is an approach which comes from prior and extensive debates in the humanities and social science, in a manner akin to critical theory (Chapter 8), feminism (Chapter 10), and postcolonialism (Chapter 12). Like those perspectives, poststructuralism enters the study of international relations once the possibility of posing meta-theoretical questions within the discipline has been established.

Poststructuralism and International Relations

Poststructuralism's entrance into International Relations came in the 1980s through the work of Richard Ashley (1981, 1984), James Der Derian (1987), Michael Shapiro (1988), and R. B. J. Walker (1987, 1993). Two important collections (Der Derian and Shapiro 1989; Ashley and Walker 1990) brought together the early studies. These focused mostly on articulating the meta-theoretical critique of realist and neorealist theories to demonstrate how the theoretical assumptions of the traditional perspectives shaped what could be said about international politics. What drove many of these contributions was an awareness of how other branches of the social sciences and humanities had witnessed significant debates about how knowledge of the world was constructed. Recognizing that the dominant approaches to International Relations were unaware, uninterested, or hostile to such questions, the above authors sought to connect International Relations to its interdisciplinary context by introducing new sources of theory. The motivation for the turn to poststructuralism was not purely theoretical, however. Critical scholars were dissatisfied with the way realism – and its revivification at that time through neorealism – remained powerful in the face of new global transformations. These scholars felt that realism marginalized the importance of new transnational actors, issues, and relationships and failed to hear (let alone appreciate) the voices of excluded peoples and perspectives. As such, poststructuralism began with an ethical concern to include those who had been overlooked or excluded by the mainstream of International Relations.

In focusing on the conceptual and political practices that included some and excluded others, poststructural approaches were concerned with how the relations of inside and outside were mutually constructed. For realism, the state marked the border between inside/outside, sovereign/anarchic, us/them. Accordingly, poststructuralism began by questioning how the state came to be regarded as the most important actor in world politics, and how the state came to be understood as a unitary, rational actor. Poststructuralism was thus concerned at the outset with the *practices of statecraft* that made the state and its importance seem both natural and necessary. This approach is not anti-state, it does not overlook the state, nor does it seek to move beyond the state. In many respects, poststructuralism pays more attention to the state than realism, because – instead of merely asserting that the state is the foundation of its paradigm – poststructuralism is concerned with the state's historical and conceptual production, and its political formation, economic constitution, and social exclusions.

After the first wave of meta-theoretical critiques, subsequent studies employing a poststructural approach – while continuing to develop the theoretical basis for their alternative interpretations – engaged political events and questions directly. This research includes analyses of state identity and foreign policy in Korea, Bosnia, and the USA (Bleiker 2005; Campbell 1992, 1998b, 2005); studies of the gendered character of state identity in the context of US intervention (Weber 1994, 1999); studies of the centrality of representation in North–South relations and immigration policies (Doty 1993, 1996) a deconstructive account of famine and humanitarian crises (Edkins 2000); interpretive readings of diplomacy and European security (Constantinou 1995, 1996); the radical rethinking of international order and security (Dillon 1996); critical analyses of international law and African sovereignties (Grovougi 1996); a recasting of ecopolitics (Kuehls 1996); the rearticulation of the refugee regime and sovereignty (Soguk 1999); a problematization of the UN and peacekeeping (Debrix 1999); a semiotic reading of militarism in Hawaii (Ferguson and Turnbull 1998); investigations of contemporary warfare, strategic identities, security landscapes, and representations of sovereignty (Coward 2002, Der Derian 1992, 2001; Dillon 2003; Dillon and Reid 2001; Klein 1994; Lisle and Pepper 2005); a reinterpretation of area studies (Philpott 2001); and a rethinking of finance and the field of international political economy (de Goede 2005, 2006).

This list is not exhaustive, nor is it the case that all the authors cited would willingly accept the label 'poststructural' for their work. Nonetheless, their work intersects with, and would not have been possible without, an interdisciplinary debate that called into question the authority of the positivist meta-theoretical assumptions which secured realist and other traditional perspectives in International Relations. Before detailing what a poststructuralist perspective involves, it is necessary, therefore, to outline the key elements of this interdisciplinary debate.

The interdisciplinary context of poststructuralism

Positivism and science in question

International Relations has been shaped by the influence of science and technology in the development of the modern world. The potential for control and predictive capacity that the natural sciences seemed to offer provided a model that social scientists sought to emulate. This model, **positivism**, was founded on the empiricist theory of knowledge, which argued that sensory experience provides the only legitimate source of knowledge. 'Experience' refers to direct sensory access to an external reality comprising material things. As an epistemology (a meta-theory concerning how we know), the empiricist conception of knowledge understands knowledge as deriving from a relationship between a given subject (the person that knows) and a given object (that which is known).

These theoretical developments were central to a major historical transformation – the intellectual clash in the Renaissance period between the church and science which challenged the dominance of theology for social order. These intellectual developments, named as the Enlightenment, included making 'man' and 'reason', rather than 'god' and 'belief', the centre of philosophical discourse, and the construction and legitimation of the state, rather than the church, as the basis for political order. It was a moment in which knowledge intersected with power to lasting effect. Although the Enlightenment conception of knowledge was intended to free humanity from religious dogma, it was eventually transformed into a dogma itself. By the end of the nineteenth century, its dominance meant that knowledge was equated with science and reason limited to scientific reason. This dogmatization of science meant that social life is centred on technical control over nature and administrative control over humans, so that political issues became questions of order and efficiency.

The positivist account of science at the base of Enlightenment thought is founded upon three empiricist assumptions. First, **epistemic realism**: the view that there is an external world, the existence and meaning of which is independent of anything the observer does. Second, the assumption of a *universal scientific language*: the belief that this external world can be described in a language that does not presuppose anything, thereby allowing the observer to remain detached and dispassionate. Third, the **correspondence theory of truth**: that the observer can capture the facts of the world in statements that are true if they correspond to the facts and false if they do not. We can see these assumptions in Hans Morgenthau's classic text when he writes that a theory must 'approach political reality with a kind of rational outline' and distinguish 'between what is true objectively and rationally, supported by evidence and illuminated by reason, and what is only a subjective judgement,

divorced from the facts as they are and informed by prejudice and wishful thinking'
(Morgenthau 1978: 3–4).

Post-empiricism in science

A number of intellectual developments have demonstrated that the positivist understanding of scientific procedure that the social sciences have tried to model does not actually represent the conduct of scientific inquiry. The 'linguistic turn' in Anglo-American philosophy was a move away from the idea that language is a transparent medium through which the world can be comprehended – a view that suggested it was possible to get 'behind' language and 'ground' knowledge in the world itself – towards an account of language that understood it as embedded in social practice and inseparable from the world (Rorty 1967). Allied with the development of hermeneutic thought in continental philosophy – a tradition originally concerned with the reading of biblical, classical, and legal texts which developed into an account of the importance of interpretation to being human – these shifts contributed to a new understanding of the relationship between language and reality (see George 1994). Developments in the philosophy of science itself – especially what are called the postpositivist and **post-empiricist** debates (see Hesse 1980) – have also challenged the validity of the positivist account. These developments have also contributed to a reappraisal of science through social studies that question the value of 'facts' and the meaning of 'objectivity' for social inquiry (Megill 1994; Poovey 1998). Finally, the development of complexity science (including chaos theory and other new approaches to regularity) extends even further the challenge to 'common sense' assumptions of what counts as science and how it is conducted, and links contemporary understandings of science with poststructuralism (Dillon 2000). Given this, poststructuralism is in no sense anti-science.

In the philosophy of science, the post-empiricist debates focused on the core of the contention between positivists and anti-positivists: the Enlightenment conception of knowledge. For the Enlightenment the search for truth meant the search for foundations, facts that could 'ground' knowledge. The post-empiricist perspective is thus concerned with the rejection of such *foundational* thought (such as the claim that the state is the organizing principle of international relations, or that ethical theory requires established rules of justice as grounds for judging right from wrong), which it achieves through a new understanding of the subject/object relationship in theories of knowledge. Post-empiricists conceive of this relationship as one in which the two terms construct each other rather than the fundamental opposition of two pre-given entities. This undermining of the separation of subjects and objects means any claim to knowledge that relies on dichotomies analogous to the subject/object dualism (e.g. facts against values, objective knowledge versus subjective prejudice, or empirical observation in contrast to normative concerns) 'is . . . epistemologically unwarranted' (Bernstein 1979: 230; Bernstein 1983).

The end result is that in place of the basic assumptions of epistemic realism, a universal scientific language and the correspondence theory of truth that lay behind positivist understandings of science and the Enlightenment conception of knowledge, all inquiry – in *both* the human sciences and the natural sciences – has to be concerned with the social constitution of meaning, the linguistic construction of reality, and the historicity of knowledge. This reaffirms the indispensability of interpretation, and suggests that all knowledge involves a relationship with power in its mapping of the world.

The reaction of International Relations to poststructuralism

Critical anxiety

As we shall see, these dimensions are present in and help make possible the poststructuralist accounts of politics and international relations introduced above, even as those accounts go beyond the priority given to language in the constitution of reality that marks constructivist approaches to international politics. We need to be clear, then, about the similarities and differences in the critical approaches to International Relations. An awareness of these distinctions, however, is something that has been absent from the responses the critical approaches have provoked in the field.

Those who have objected to the meta-theoretical critiques of realism, neorealism, and the like, particularly the way those critiques have called into question the reliance on external reality, foundations, objectivity, and the transparency of language, have often called those critiques 'postmodern', even though there are few if any scholars who use that label, and many who explicitly reject it (see Campbell 1992: 246–7).

In one of the first assessments of the meta-theoretical critiques, Robert Keohane (1988) dichotomized the field into 'rationalists' versus 'reflectivists' and castigated the critical approaches of the latter position for lacking social scientific rigour. Keohane faulted the critical approaches for failing to embrace the empiricist standards concerning research agendas, hypothesis construction, and testing that would (in his eyes) lend them credibility. However, in making his claims, Keohane failed to demonstrate an awareness or understanding of the challenge posed by post-empiricist developments in the philosophy of science for his supposedly objective criteria (see Bleiker 1997). Subsequently accused of 'self-righteousness' (Wallace 1996), lambasted as 'evil' and 'dangerous' (Krasner 1996), castigated for 'bad IR' and 'meta-babble' (Halliday 1996), misread as 'philosophical idealism' (Mearsheimer 1994/5), and considered congenitally irrational (Østerud 1996), those named as 'postmodernists' have been anything but welcomed by the mainstream of International Relations (see Devetak 2001 for the best review using this term). Aside from their unwillingness to engage ways of thinking they regarded as 'foreign', these critics reacted as if the questioning of critical approaches meant that the traditional containers of politics (especially the state) and the capacity to judge right from wrong were being rejected. In so doing, they mistook arguments about the historical production of foundations for the claim that all foundations had to be rejected.

When theoretical contests provoke such vehemence, it indicates that there is something larger at stake than different epistemologies. As Connolly (2004) has argued, different methodologies express in one way or another deep attachments – understood as metaphysical commitments or existential faith – on behalf of those who advocate them. For those who take such intense objection to the critical perspectives they herd together and brand as 'postmodern', their faith is a particular understanding of science. Their attachment to that faith in science – despite the debates in the philosophy of science that demonstrate how their understanding of science cannot be supported through reason – in turn derives from an anxiety about what the absence of secure foundations means for ethics and politics. Bernstein (1983) has named this the 'Cartesian Anxiety', because in the philosophy of Descartes the quest was to find a secure ground for knowledge. The Cartesian Anxiety is the fear that, given the demise of objectivity, we are unable to make judgements that have been central to the understanding of modern life, namely distinguishing between true and false, good and bad. The challenge, though, is to escape from the straightjacket in which intellectual understanding and political life has to be organized by recourse to either one option or the other. The post-empiricist debates in the philosophy of science have demonstrated that dualistic or dichotomous frameworks are unstable. We need, in Bernstein's (1983) words, to move beyond objectivism and relativism. We need to develop modes of interpretation that allow judgements about social and political issues at home and abroad while accepting, first, that such judgements cannot be secured by claims about a pre-existing, external reality and, second, such arguments cannot be limited by invoking dichotomies such as fact/value or objective/subjective.

Poststructuralism misunderstood as postmodernism

By labelling the critical perspectives which deal with interpretation and representation in international politics as 'postmodern', the critics are suggesting that it is modernity which they believe to be under threat. If we are to understand what is meant by this label of postmodernism, we also have to be concerned with modernism. What is meant by this term?

'Modernism' refers to the predominant cultural style of the period from the 1890s to the outbreak of the Second World War, encompassing the ideas and values in the painting, sculpture, music, architecture, design, and literature of that period. Modernism was part of the great upheavals in political, sociological, scientific, sexual, and familial orders in Europe and the USA. It was also part of colonialism and imperialism, in which these aesthetic and technological transformations radically affected the political, sociological, scientific, sexual, and familial orders of non-Western societies. Modernism had much to do with large technological and scientific transformations which made the early twentieth century a time of both infectious optimism and unsettled fear. It was an era which saw the industrial revolution produce mass railways, the first aircraft, automobiles, light bulbs, photography, films, and a host of other mechanical inventions. These machines offered the hope of improved social conditions, increased wealth, and the possibility of overcoming human limitations. But their impact on pre-mechanized ways of life made people fear for the existing social order, at the same time as they compressed time and space in the global order. Modernism was the cultural response to this change, evident in the abstract art of the Cubists (like Picasso and Braque) whose work distorted perspectives and favoured manufactured objects over natural environments (see Hughes 1991; Kern 1983). Its aim was to represent, interpret, and provide critical commentary on modern life.

The faith in technology of the early modernists was soon extinguished in the First World War. The great machines of promise turned into technologies of mass slaughter. The future lost its allure, and art became full of irony, disgust, and protest. In the imperial domain of Europe the questioning of modernism fuelled anti-colonial nationalism. In this context, 'modernism' was a political intervention in a specific cultural context that had global affects. But, after fascism in Europe, another world war, the Holocaust, and the process of decolonization, the critical edge of modernism was spent. Modernist cultural forms lost any sense of newness and possibility.

It is against this background that 'postmodernism' emerged during the period after the Second World War, representing and interpreting the indeterminate, pluralistic, and ever more globalized culture of the Cold War world. In literature, art, architecture, and music the term 'postmodern' designated a particular, often eclectic, approach to this cultural context. (Examples here include the painting of Andy Warhol, the intermingling of styles in the architecture of Charles Jencks, and the music of Madonna.) In this context, 'postmodernism' refers to cultural forms inspired by the conditions of accelerated time and space and hyper-consumerism that we experience in the globalized era some call 'postmodernity'.

Many of the problems associated with the concept of 'postmodernism' come from the misleading periodization associated with the prefix 'post'. Many critics of postmodernism attack it by arguing that it assumes a temporal break with modernity. They argue that the term 'postmodernity' assumes that we live in an historical epoch that is quite distinct from, and in some way replaces, 'modernity'. However, as Jameson (1991) has argued, the structure of postmodernity that critical, interpretive approaches seek to engage historically is not a new order that has displaced modernity. It is, rather, a cultural, economic, social, and political problematic marked by the rearticulation of time and space in the modern world (see also Harvey 1989). It is evident in developments such as financial speculation and flexible accumulation that depart from the modern, industrial forms of capitalism rooted in the exploitation of labour in the production process.

Much of the confusion and hostility surrounding the concept of 'postmodernism' in International Relations stems from the mistaken idea that those deploying an interpretative analytic to critically understand the transformations in modernity are celebrating the apparently shallow and accelerated cultural context that has challenged many of modernity's certainties. While 'postmodernity' is the cultural, economic, social, and political formation *within* modernity that results from changes in time–space relations, poststructuralism is one of the interpretative analytics that critically engages with the production and implication of these transformations.

The critical attitude of poststructuralism

Political context

In philosophical terms a number of the scholars who resist the mistaken label of 'post-modernism' are more comfortable with the term 'poststructuralism'. 'Poststructuralism' is a distinct philosophical domain which has a critical relation to structuralism, modernity, and postmodernity. The 'structuralist' philosophical movement is associated with 'modernist' cultural forces. Structuralism was a largely French philosophical perspective associated with linguist Ferdinand de Saussure and cultural critic Roland Barthes.[2] Structuralists aimed to study the social and cultural construction of the various structures that give meaning to our everyday lives. Poststructuralism is equally concerned to analyse such meaning-producing structures, but in a manner consistent with transformations in the social order of the late twentieth century.

The events that influenced poststructuralism were associated with the resistance struggles against established and imperial power blocs, such as the Algerian and Vietnam wars, the Prague Spring of 1968, the May 1968 movement in France, cultural expression in Yugoslavia, demands for Third World economic justice and the civil rights, and environmental and women's movements in the USA and elsewhere. According to the French philosopher Giles Deleuze (1988: 150) these events were part of an international movement which 'linked the emergence of new forms of struggle to the production of a new subjectivity'. In other words, these struggles, unlike the revolutionary movements of the early twentieth century, were not concerned with freeing a universal 'mankind' from the chains imposed upon it by society, but with reworking political subjectivity given the globalizing forms of late capitalism. This context means poststructuralism has important things to say about the concept of identity in political life.

Michel Foucault: limits, ethos, and critique

The critical attitude of poststructuralism can be found in the writing of numerous thinkers.[3] For the purposes of simplicity, this chapter will focus on the work of Michel Foucault. Thinking the present historically involves an ethos of what Foucault has called 'the limit attitude'. It involves considering the limits that give meaning to our thought and practice – for example reason and rationality is given meaning by the establishing of limits at which unreason and irrationality are said to begin. Moreover, a 'limit attitude' involves interrogating those limits, not by getting rid of, escaping, or transcending them, but by contesting and negotiating them through argumentation.

This critical attitude is consistent with the Enlightenment project to critically interrogate the conditions of human existence and is animated by an emancipatory ideal. The critical attitude is emancipatory insofar as it draws out the limits that shape existence and in so doing gives the conditions under which such limits – and the exclusions they entail – can be challenged. Although those dismissive of 'postmodernism' claim that it is an anti-modern and anti-Enlightenment position, to talk in those terms (anti- versus pro-Enlightenment) is to replicate the either/or exclusionary logic that Foucault terms the 'blackmail of the Enlightenment'. Rather than succumbing to such gestures of rejection, Foucault argues that the attitude of modernity has had from its beginnings an ongoing relationship with attitudes of 'counter-modernity'. This agonism is itself characteristic of and inherent in the Enlightenment, for, in Foucault's terms, what connects us with the Enlightenment 'is not faithfulness to doctrinal elements but rather the permanent reactivation of an attitude – that is, of a philosophical ethos that could be described as a permanent critique of our era' (Foucault 1984a: 42). Poststructuralism, then, is first and foremost an approach rather than a theory. As Foucault argues:

> " The critical ontology of ourselves has to be considered not, certainly, as a theory, a doctrine, nor even as a permanent body of knowledge that is accumulating; it has to be conceived as an attitude, an ethos, a philosophical life in which the critique of what we are is at one and the same time the historical analysis of the limits that are imposed on us and an experiment with the possibility of going beyond them. "

Foucault 1984a: 50

As an approach, attitude, or ethos, poststructuralism is inherently critical. Critique, though, is a positive rather than negative attitude. It is about disclosing the assumptions and limits that have made things as they are, so that what appears natural and without alternative can be rethought and reworked. Critique is thus also inescapably ethical, because it is concerned with change. As Foucault writes:

> " A critique is not a matter of saying that things are not right as they are. It is a matter of pointing out on what kinds of assumptions, what kinds of familiar, unchallenged, unconsidered modes of thought the practices that we accept rest. We must free ourselves from the sacralization of the social as the only reality and stop regarding as superfluous something so essential in human life and in human relations as thought . . . It is something that is often hidden, but which always animates everyday behavior. There is always a little thought even in the most stupid institutions; there is always thought even in silent habits. Criticism is a matter of flushing out that thought and trying to change it: to show that things are not as self-evident as one believed, to see what is accepted as self-evident will no longer be accepted as such. Practicing criticism is a matter of making facile gestures difficult. "

Foucault 1988: 154–5. See Campbell 1992: ch. 9

Taking these arguments into account, we can see that poststructuralism has a lot in common with the attitude of Frankfurt school critical theory (see Chapter 8). Indeed poststructuralism also has much in common with the post-empiricist debates outlined earlier. It has a similar disdain for foundationalism (ideas of grounding thought on universal rules that exist independently of the observer), shares the view that language is central to the constitution of social life, and agrees that the historicity of knowledge (the historical production of knowledge in socio-cultural structures and, hence, the refutation of the idea of universal/timeless knowledge) is a major concern.

Subjectivity, identity, and power

However, poststructuralism differs from Frankfurt school thought in ways that are important to the analysis of international relations. Most importantly, poststructuralism takes a different conception of the human subject. Whereas much of Frankfurt school critical theory takes critique to involve the uncovering or emancipation of a 'humanity' whose autonomy and freedom is bound by ideology, Foucault's work involves creating 'a history of the different modes by which, in our culture, human beings are made subjects'

(Foucault 1982: 208). For Foucault, the modern individual is an historical achievement. This is to say that there is no 'universal person' – a human-being that has been the unchanging basis for all history – on whom power has operated throughout all time. Rather, the individual human is an effect of the operations of power. Similarly, there is no 'human nature' shared by all members of the species – the nature of individuals, their humanity, is produced by certain power structures. Foucault's poststructuralism is thus offering the most thoroughgoing questioning of foundations around. That is because it is a questioning of foundations that includes the category of 'man' as well as the bases upon which social and political order is constructed. Foucault is thus concerned with forms of subjectivity. What are the subjects of politics? If they are 'humans', in what way is the 'human' subject constituted historically? How have the identities of women/men, Western/Eastern, North/South, civilized/uncivilized, developed/underdeveloped, mad/sane, domestic/foreign, rational/irrational, and so on, been constituted over time and in different places? All of which means that *identity*, *subjectivism*, and *power* are key concepts for poststructuralism.

Foucault's focus on the constitution of the subject is in accord with poststructuralism's concern with the dualisms which structure human experience. In particular, it is concerned with the interior/exterior (inside/outside) binary according to which that which is inside is deemed to be the self, good, primary, and original while the outside is the other, dangerous, secondary, and derivative. French philosopher Jacques Derrida has approached this issue through his strategy of deconstruction – reversing the original order of the binary pair of terms to demonstrate how the exclusion of the second term is central to the first (Culler 1982). In this argument, the outside is always central to the constitution of the inside; the insane is central to the constitution of what it is to be sane or rational; the criminal is central to the constitution of the law-abiding citizen; and the foreign is pivotal in understanding the domestic. In *Discipline and Punish*, Foucault (1979) demonstrates how what the prison confines is as much the identity of society outside the walls as it is the prisoners on the inside. The good, civilized society is constituted by the bad, barbaric prisoners it confines. When drug abuse and prostitution are made pathological by being criminalized, the effect is to normalize a moral order in which certain behaviours are excluded.

The critique of inside/outside dualisms leads poststructuralist thinkers to emphasize the importance of studying cultural practices. Instead of claiming that reality is understood by isolating the internal nature of the object studied (e.g. states and their desire to maximize power) poststructuralism studies the cultural practices through which the inclusions and exclusions that give meaning to binary pairs are established. This shift to cultural practices means that poststructuralist thinkers refuse to take any identity – individual or collective – as given and unproblematic. Rather, they see identity as culturally constructed through a series of exclusions. The particular events, problems, actors that are recognized in history are thereby understood as constituted by an order always dependent upon the marginalization and exclusion of other identities and histories. This means there are considerable affinities between poststructuralism and postcolonialism.

The emphasis on practices of exclusion in poststructural accounts involves a different understanding of power. For Foucault power is not simply *repressive* (i.e. imposing limits and constraints on the infinite possibilities of the world) but is *productive* because of the imposition of limits and constraints. Relations of power establish the limitations of self/other, inside/relation to outside, but without those limitations those notions of self/inside, other/outside would not exist. The limitations are therefore productive: we know what that thing *is* by knowing what it is *not*. Foucault calls this productive power 'disciplinary power', power that disciplines in order to produce a certain political subject. The aim of poststructural analysis is, therefore, not to eliminate exclusion (since that is what makes meaning possible) but to understand the various forms of exclusion that constitute the world as we find it, understand how they come to be and how they continue to operate, and make possible interventions that can articulate alternatives.

Understanding discourse

Language, reality, and performance

The operations of disciplinary power, and the conceptions of subjectivity and identity to which it gives rise, takes place within **discourse**. Discourse refers to a specific series of representations and practices through which meanings are produced, identities constituted, social relations established, and political and ethical outcomes made more or less possible. Those employing the concept are often said to be claiming that 'everything is language', that 'there is no reality', and, because of their linguistic idealism, they are unable to take a political position and defend an ethical stance abounds.

These objections demonstrate how understandings of discourse are bedevilled by the view that interpretation involves only language in contrast to the external, the real, and the material. These dichotomies of idealism/materialism and realism/idealism remain powerful conceptions of understanding the world. In practice, however, a concern with discourse does not involve a denial of the world's existence or the significance of materiality. This is well articulated by Laclau and Mouffe (1985: 108): 'the fact that every object is constituted as an object of discourse has *nothing to do* with whether there is a world external to thought, or with the realism/idealism opposition . . . What is denied is not that . . . objects exist externally to thought, but the rather different assertion that they could constitute themselves as objects outside of any discursive condition of emergence.' This means that while nothing exists outside of discourse, there are important distinctions between linguistic and non-linguistic phenomena. There are also modes of representation which are ideational though strictly non-linguistic, such as the aesthetic and pictorial. It is just that there is no way of comprehending non-linguistic and extra-discursive phenomena except through discursive practices.

Understanding discourse as involving both the ideal and the material, the linguistic and the non-linguistic, means that discourses are performative. Performative means that discourses constitute the objects of which they speak. For example, states are made possible by a wide range of discursive practices that include immigration policies, military deployments and strategies, cultural debates about normal social behaviour, political speeches, and economic investments. The meanings, identities, social relations, and political assemblages that are enacted in these performances combine the ideal and the material. As a consequence, appreciating that discourses are performative moves us away from a reliance on the idea of (social) *construction* towards *materialization*, whereby discourse 'stabilizes over time to produce the effect of boundary, fixity and surface' (Butler 1993: 9, 12). Discourse is thus not something that subjects use in order to describe objects; it is that which constitutes both subjects and objects.

Discourse, materialism, and meaning

Within International Relations, there has been much misunderstanding of discourse in these terms. Even some constructivists (Wendt 1999) maintain a strict sense of the material world external to language as a determinant of social and political truth. When faced with poststructural arguments, they will maintain that no discursive understanding can help you when faced with something as material as a bullet in the head (Wendt 1999: 113; Krasner 1999: 51; cf. Zehfuss 2002). At first glance, this appears irrefutable. So how would a poststructuralist respond? First, they would say that the issue is not one of the materiality of the bullet or the reality of death for the individual when struck by the bullet in a particular way. The undeniable existence of that world external to thought is not the issue. Second, they would say that such a world – the body lying on the ground, the bullet in the head, and the shell casing lying not far away – tells us nothing itself about the meaning and significance of those elements. They would say that the constitution of the event and its elements is a product of its discursive condition of emergence, something that occurs via the contestation of competing narratives. Did the body and the bullet get to be as they are because of suicide, manslaughter, murder, ethnic cleansing, tribal war, geno-cide, a war of inter-state rivalry, or . . . ? Each of those terms signifies a larger discursive formation through which a whole set of identities, social relations, political possibilities, and ethical outcomes are made more or less possible. Whichever figuration emerges as the accepted or dominant one has little to do with the materiality of specific elements and much to do with power of particular discourses materializing elements into comprehens-ible forms with political effects. Therefore, focusing specifically on the bullets that riddled their bodies tells us very little about those circumstances beyond the fact people died, something that occurs in many other dissimilar circumstances. Not least it fails to tell us how people, knowing full well the likely futility of their actions in the face of overwhelm-ing force, nonetheless sacrifice themselves. That is an explanation which is going to require, among other things, that attention be paid to discourses of loyalty, pride, and the nation. If in International Relations we limit ourselves to the immediate cause and context of material events we will be unable to understand the larger ethical and political issues.

Discourses of world politics

Theory as the object of analysis

Understanding discourse as performative materialization, rather than linguistic construction, takes us beyond the idea that it is just a practice employed by the subjects of international relations (be they states, institutions, or trans-national actors). We need to consider not only the international relations discourse various actors are involved in but also the discourse of International Relations – the modes of representation that give rise to the subjects of international relations and constitute the domain to which International Relations theory is purportedly only responding.

This means poststructural accounts – in addition to the concern with the representations invoked by the actors of world politics – investigate the practices that constitute entities called 'actors' capable of representation. This includes the cultural, economic, social, and political practices that produce particular actors (e.g. states, non-government organizations, and the like). It also includes investigating the role of theorists and theory in representing some actors as more significant than others. In this latter sense, this means that instead of theory being understood as simply a *tool for analysis* poststructuralism treats theory as an *object of analysis*. This reorientation, which derives from poststructuralism's status as an approach to criticism rather than a critical theory *per se*, is no less practical in its implications. It asks, for both theorists and practitioners of international relations, how do analytic approaches privilege certain understandings of global politics and marginalize or exclude others?

This approach is evident in arguments that offer historical, theoretical, and political rereadings of the traditional concerns of International Relations. For example, Walker (1993) has investigated the way that many realist questions and answers have been produced via a particular reading of Machiavelli. His conclusion is that the dominant tradition in International Relations has endorsed a narrow ahistorical reading of the paradigmatic realist which has given us the slogans of power over ethics, ends justifying means, and the necessity of violence. Similarly, in identifying anarchy as integral to realist thought, Ashley (1984, 1988) demonstrated that its status as a 'given' is a matter not of factual observation but part of a particular discursive strategy which disciplines our understanding of the multiple and ambiguous events of world politics through hierarchies such as sovereign/anarchic, domestic/international, objective/subjective, real/ideal, is/ought, and masculine/feminine. This means that the problematization of 'reality' offers two possible solutions of which only one can be chosen: e.g. sovereignty or anarchy. The operation of this 'anarchy problematique' results in world politics being mapped into zones of sovereignty and zones of anarchy with sovereignty being normatively superior to anarchy.

From subjects to subjectivity

One of the most important functions of these historical and theoretical critiques has been to demonstrate that what we take to be real, timeless, and universal in both the domain of international relations and field of International Relations is produced through the imposition of a form of order. A poststructural approach seeks, therefore, to make strange and denaturalize taken-for-granted perspectives. Important here are the discourses of danger we consume as citizens of a modern state. In an argument examining US foreign policy towards Central America, Shapiro (1988: ch. 3) shows that foreign policy can be understood as the process of making 'strange' the object under consideration in order to differentiate it from 'us'. In the case of the construction of the 'Central American Other', the moral and geopolitical codes of US foreign policy discourse make US intervention in the region seem necessary, both in terms of US interests and the subject state's own good. Campbell (1992) developed this account to show that US foreign policy generally should be seen as a series of political practices which locate danger in the external realm – threats to 'individuality', 'freedom', and 'civilization' – thereby constructing the boundary between the domestic and the international, which brings the identity of the USA into existence. Together these arguments examine the practices of statecraft that produce 'the state' as an actor in international relations and the practices of statecraft that produce the identity of particular states. As such, these arguments are directly concerned with the state so they cannot be understood as being against the state or its importance. They focus on the production and meaning of the state rather than simply assuming or asserting that states exist naturally as particular identities.

These examples build upon poststructuralism's concern with subjectivity, identity, and power. In general, they shift analysis from assumptions about pre-given subjects to the problematic of subjectivity and its political enactment. This is achieved through three methodological precepts, which can be understood by contrasting them to the basic assumptions of the traditional approaches to International Relations.

Methodological precepts: interpretation, representation, politics

The most common meta-theoretical discourse among mainstream theories is committed to an epistemic realism, whereby the world comprises objects the existence of which is independent of ideas or beliefs about them. This commitment sanctions two other analytic forms common to the field: a narrativizing historiography in which things have a self-evident quality that allows them to speak for themselves; and a logic of explanation in which the purpose of analysis is to identify those self-evident things and material causes so that actors can accommodate themselves to the realm of necessity they create.

Contrary to the claims of epistemic realism, a poststructural approach maintains that because understanding involves rendering the unfamiliar in the terms of the familiar, interpretation is unavoidable and such that there is nothing outside discourse, even though there is a material world external to thought. Contrary to a narrativizing historiography, a poststructural approach employs a mode of historical representation which self-consciously adopts a perspective, a perspective grounded in the view that identity is always constituted in relationship to difference. Because of this, poststructural approaches need to be understood as interventions in conventional understandings or established practices. And, contrary to the logic of causal explanation, a poststructural approach works with a logic of interpretation that acknowledges the improbability of cataloguing, calculating, and specifying the 'real causes', and concerns itself instead with considering the manifest political consequences of adopting one mode of representation over another. As such, poststructural approaches identify and explain how actors, events, or issues have been problematized. This means poststructuralism examines the 'problematizations' which make it possible to think of contemporary problems, and then examines how that discourse has emerged historically to frame an understanding of problems and solutions (Campbell 1998a: preface).

DAVID CAMPBELL

Case study: images of humanitarian crises

As an approach that adopts a critical stance in relation to its objects of concern, poststructuralism differs from other theoretical perspectives in International Relations. Because it does not seek to formulate a theory of international relations, it does not outline a detailed scheme of international politics in which some actors, issues, and relations are privileged at the expense of others. As such, poststructuralism can therefore concern itself with an almost boundless array of actors, issues, and events. The choice of actor, issue, or event is up to the analyst undertaking a poststructural analysis. Because of this, there is no one set of actors, issues, or events that would illustrate poststructuralism better than others.

The case study chosen to illustrate poststructuralism here concerns visual images of humanitarian disaster, especially famine. Visual imagery can be approached from a range of theoretical positions, but in the way it calls attention to questions of interpretation, perspective, and their political effects, it is well suited to demonstrate aspects of a poststructural account. It also reminds us that discourse should not be confined to the linguistic (Rose 2001: chs 6, 7).

Visual imagery is of particular importance for international politics because it is one of the principal ways in which news from distant places is brought home. Indeed, ever since early explorers made a habit of taking cameras on their travels, photographs have provided much basic information about the people and places encountered on those travels. Much like cartography, these images contributed to the development of an 'imagined geography' in which the dichotomies of West/East, civilized/barbaric, North/South, and developed/underdeveloped have been prominent (Said 1979; Gregory 1995). Since the advent of technology for moving images (i.e. film, television, and video), much of the news from abroad centred on disaster, with stories about disease, famine, war, and death prominent (Moeller 1999). In the post-Cold War era, news about humanitarian emergencies has become increasingly prominent.

Humanitarian emergencies are matters of life and death. But they do not exist for the majority of the people in the world unless they are constructed as an event. This construction, which materializes these issues of life and death in particular ways, is achieved in large part through media coverage. These media materializations create a range of identities – us/them, victim/saviour – and are necessary for a response to be organized. This argument is consistent with poststructuralism's reorientation of analysis from the assumption of pre-given subjects to the problematic of subjectivity because it maintains that the event (the emergency or disaster) and the identities of those involved are the effects of discursive practices through which they are brought into being. As the development consultant Jonathan Benthall argues (thereby illustrating that one does not have to cite Foucault *et al.* to formulate a poststructural analysis):

> the coverage of disasters by the press and the media is so selective and arbitrary that . . . they 'create' a disaster when they decide to recognise it. To be more precise, they give institutional endorsement or attestation to bad events which otherwise have a reality restricted to a local circle of victims. Such endorsement is a prerequisite for the marshalling of external relief and reconstructive effort.

Benthall 1993:11

Pictures, especially those imprinted as photographs or frames of film, are especially apt for a poststructural analysis because they foreground questions of representation. Such pictures have been culturally produced as authoritative documents that witness atrocity and injustice, in large part because they are accepted as transparent windows on an already existing world. Through the photograph we are said to be able to view things as they are. However, technologically generated images are anything but objective records of an external reality. They are necessarily constructions in which the location of the photographer, the choice of the subject, the framing of the content, the exclusion of context, and limitations on publication and circulation unavoidably create a particular sense of place populated by a particular kind of people.

Famine images remain powerful and salient in modernity because they recall a precarious pre-modern existence industrialized society has allegedly overcome. Understood as a natural disaster in which there is a crisis of food supply, famine is seen as a symptom of the lack of progress that results in the death of the innocent (Edkins 2000). It is for this reason that famine images are more often than not of women and children, barely clothed, staring passively into the lens, flies flitting across their faces (Figure 11.3). Content analyses of newspaper photos during the Ethiopian famine of 1984 (which gave rise to the Live Aid phenomenon) found that mothers and children featured more than any other subject (Figure 11.4). As one study noted:

> All these pictures overwhelmingly showed people as needing our pity – as passive victims. This was through a de-contextualised concentration on mid- and close-up shots emphasising body language and facial expressions. The photos seemed mainly to be taken from a high angle with no eye-contact, thus reinforcing the viewer's sense of power compared with their apathy and hopelessness. The 'Madonna and Child' image was particularly emotively used, echoing the biblical imagery. Women were at the same time patronised and exalted.

van der Gaag and Nash 1987: 41

Content analyses of news images through time reveals that regardless of the context, time, or place in which famine has been observed, the same images recur (Moeller 1999: ch. 3) (Figure 11.5). They recur because they are the icons of a disaster narrative, in which complex political circumstances are interpreted through an established journalistic frame of reference. In this discursive formation, outsiders come from afar to dispense charity to victims of a natural disaster who are too weak to help themselves (Benthall 1993: ch. 5). Instead of this discursive formation having to be explained in full each time, the recurrence of the iconic image of the starving child triggers this general and established understanding of famine, thereby disciplining any ambiguity about what is occurring in famine zones.

This discursive formation has effects on 'us' at the same time as it gives meaning to 'them'. Indeed, it establishes a series of identity relations that reproduce and confirm notions of self/other, developed/underdeveloped, North/South, masculine/feminine, sovereignty/anarchy, and the like. Given that most contemporary famine imagery comes from one continent, it reproduces the imagined geography of 'Africa', so that a continent of 900 million people in fifty-seven countries is homogenized into a single entity represented by a starving child (Figure 11.6). In doing this, a stereotypical famine image is not creating

Figure 11.3 Famine victims with aid workers, Idaga Hamus, Northern Ethiopia, 1984.

Source: Camerapix.

Figure 11.4 Mohamed Amin and Michael Buerk filming in Ethiopia, 1984.

Source: Camerapix.

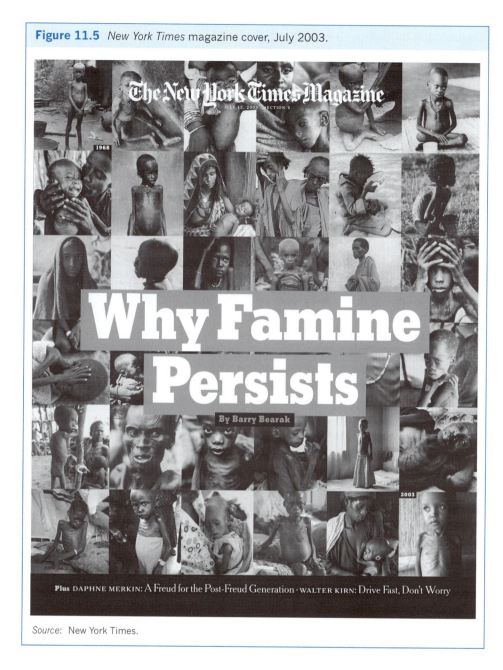

Figure 11.5 *New York Times* magazine cover, July 2003.

Source: New York Times.

something from nothing. It is drawing upon established modes of representation, bringing into the present something that has been historically significant for European identity – that since the first colonial encounters 'Africa' has been understood as a site of cultural, moral, and spatial difference populated by 'barbarians', 'heathens', 'primitives', and 'savages'. This attention to the historical emergence of particular modes of representation is a feature of poststructural analysis. Understood as genealogy, this concern with history

Figure 11.6 *Daily Mirror* cover image, 21 May 2002, 'Africa's Dying Again'.

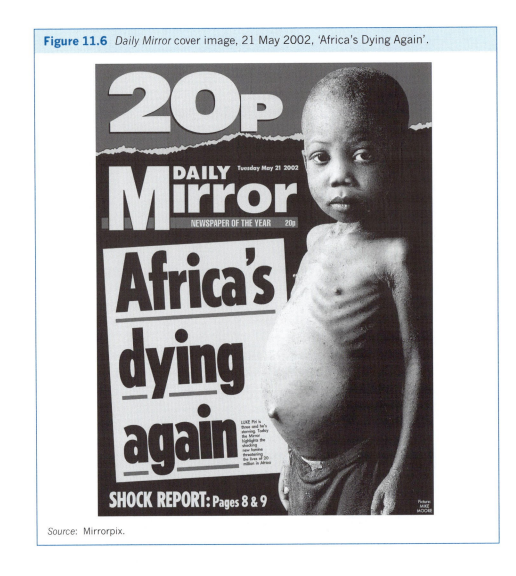

Source: Mirrorpix.

dispenses with the search for origins and deals with how dominant understandings have come to work in the present (see Foucault 1977; Ashley 1987).

As detailed above, the logic of interpretation that marks a poststructural analysis is concerned with the manifest political consequences of adopting one mode of representation over another. In terms of this case study, this focus would note two impacts. First, that the discursive production of 'Africa' means the majority of outsiders (more than 80 per cent of UK respondents in one survey) view the continent in wholly negative terms as a place of disease, distress, and instability.[4] Second, such representations establish the conditions of possibility for state and non-state action with regard to humanitarian crises, especially as they depoliticize the issues and render them best dealt with by humanitarian aid. Significantly, this logic of interpretation encompasses a notion of causality. But, rather than claiming a direct cause–effect relationship between pictures and policy (as in some arguments about the 'CNN effect' in international politics), this focus on the conditions of possibility posits an 'emergent causality' in which elements infuse and resonate across cultural and social domains, creating real effects without being able to specify a direct, causal link (see Connolly 2004).

The overall purpose of a poststructural analysis is ethical and political. Its emphasis on how things have been produced over time seeks to denaturalize conventional representations so as to argue that they could have been different. By repoliticizing dominant representations, poststructural analyses call attention to the inclusions and exclusions involved in producing that which appears to be natural, fixed, and timeless, and argue that the political action which follows from naturalized understandings could be pursued differently. In the context of humanitarian crises, especially famines, this would establish the following: the modern understanding of famine as starvation has been secured by visual representations of women and children as innocent victims, marginalizing in the process indigenous notions of famine as social catastrophe (Edkins 2000). Understanding famine as starvation leads to international action as humanitarian aid, directed towards the condition of individuals, whereas understanding famine as social catastrophe could lead to international action as conflict resolution, directed towards the state of the community. If followed, the consequence of this would be a complete overhaul of humanitarian action in the post-Cold War world.

Conclusion

From a poststructural perspective, interpretation and representation are indispensable and unavoidable when it comes to engaging both the domain of international politics and the field of International Relations. This claim is supported by the developments in philosophy and science which have undermined empiricist and positivist accounts of knowledge and theory. With its emphasis on the importance of language, culture, and history, the interdisciplinary context that has made critical perspectives like poststructuralism possible has challenged the 'common sense' and 'taken for granted' assumptions about reality which many traditional theories of International Relations have relied upon.

In assessing poststructuralism, it is important to be clear about the purpose of this body of thought. Poststructuralism is different from most other approaches to international politics because it does not see itself as a theory, school, or paradigm which produces a single account of its subject matter. Instead, poststructuralism is an approach, attitude, or ethos that pursues critique in particular ways. Because it understands critique as an operation that flushes out the assumptions through which conventional and dominant understandings have come to be (suppressing or marginalizing alternative accounts in the process), poststructuralism sees critique as an inherently positive exercise that establishes the conditions of possibility for pursuing alternatives. It is in this context that poststructuralism makes other theories of International Relations one of its objects of analysis, and approaches those paradigms with meta-theoretical questions designed to expose how they are structured.

Although it does not outline a specific theory of international relations, poststructuralism nonetheless offers a number of general and constructive arguments that can be used to approach the study of international politics in a different manner. Poststructuralism reorients analysis away from the prior assumption of pre-given subjects to the problematic of subjectivity. This involves rethinking the question of power and identity, such that all identities are understood as effects of the operation of power and materialized through discourse. While poststructuralism rejects empiricist understandings of knowledge, its critical approach is often empirical, using archives, images, survey data, content analysis, and the like as evidence in understanding the relationship between power and knowledge. The result of a poststructuralist analysis is itself an interpretation of international politics, and as such can (and should) be subject to the same ethos of critique that gave rise to it.

Poststructuralism has often found itself marginalized within International Relations. That is largely because those critical of it have misunderstood many of its central claims (especially with regard to the relationship between language and reality) and have been anxious about the effect of following its meta-theoretical questioning to its logical conclusion. Others have sought to confront poststructuralism with criticisms founded on positions that poststructuralism has questioned – arguing, for example, poststructuralism fails to accept the existence of material reality when it has questioned the idealism/materialism dualism on which that objection depends (Laffey 2000; cf. de Goede 2003). Poststructuralism is, like all perspectives, certainly open to question. But, to be effective, critiques need to engage poststructuralism in its own terms. The starting point for an effective critique of poststructuralism involves recognizing that, instead of seeking to establish a social science, it embodies an ethical and political attitude driven by the desire to make all facile gestures difficult.

? QUESTIONS

1. What does it mean to say that abstraction, interpretation, and representation are indispensable and unavoidable?

2. How does the discipline of International Relations 'map' the world?

3. How are power and knowledge related? What does it mean to say they are related rather than synonymous with each other?

4. What are the key features of the positivist meta-theoretical discourse which have underpinned traditional approaches to international politics, and how have developments in the philosophy of science challenged these features?

5. What are some examples of foundational thought in International Relations, and what critiques have been directed at foundational thought generally?

6. What is the relationship between modernity and postmodernity, modernism and postmodernism, and why do many scholars express an anxiety about what they (mistakenly) call 'postmodernism' in International Relations?

7. What is the critical attitude of poststructuralism as expressed in the work of Michel Foucault, and how does it differ from traditional conceptions of social scientific theory?

8. What is meant by the claim that poststructuralism reorients analysis from pre-given subjects to the problematic of subjectivity?

9. What are the main features of Foucault's conception of power and how does it differ from traditional perspectives in International Relations?

10. If there is 'nothing outside discourse', does this mean that language is all there is and reality is only a product of the imagination?

11. How can poststructuralism's concern with subjectivity, identity, power, and discourse be connected to the categories and concerns of International Relations?

12. Should poststructuralism be viewed as a paradigm in International Relations? How can we assess its impact on the discipline?

FURTHER READING

■ **Bleiker, R. (2000),** *Popular Dissent, Human Agency and Global Politics* **(Cambridge: Cambridge University Press).** Theoretically and empirically sophisticated demonstration of how exploring questions of identity, agency, and subjectivity widens the understanding of politics and permits a conception of resistance.

■ **Campbell, D. (1998a),** *Writing Security: United States Foreign Policy and the Politics of Identity,* **revised edn (Minneapolis: University of Minnesota Press).** One of the first book-length studies that works with a poststructural attitude to rethink international politics, with an epilogue in the revised edition reviewing the discipline's debates around identity.

■ **Der Derian, J. and M. J. Shapiro (1989) (eds),** *International/Intertextual Relations: Postmodern Readings of World Politics* **(Lexington KY: Lexington Books).** The first collection of poststructural work, for which the publisher insisted on having 'postmodern' in the title.

■ **Der Derian, J. (2001),** *Virtuous War: Mapping the Military–Industrial–Media–Entertainment Network* **(Boulder CO: Westview).** Based on theoretical readings and empirical fieldwork, this monograph, written before 9/11, offers a prescient recasting of the nature of contemporary war.

■ **Edkins, J. (1999),** *Poststructuralism and International Relations: Bringing the Political Back In* **(Boulder CO: Lynne Reinner).** Provides a good introduction to the work of Derrida and Foucault, amongst others, emphasizing questions of subjectivity and politics.

■ **Edkins, J., Pin-Fat, V., and Shapiro, M. J. (2004) (eds),** *Sovereign Lives: Power in Global Politics* **(New York: Routledge).** Offers recent work focusing on the issue of sovereignty, and introduces the idea of biopolitics to International Relations.

■ **George, J. (1994),** *Discourses of Global Politics* **(Boulder CO: Lynne Reinner).** Important discussion of the interdisciplinary debates in the social sciences that make a poststructural account possible.

■ **Shapiro, M.J. and Alker, H. R. (eds),** *Challenging Boundaries: Global Flows, Territorial Identities* **(Minneapolis: University of Minnesota Press).** A collection that demonstrates the wide range of events, issues, and topics involving the concept of identity that can be examined with a critical ethos.

■ **Walker, R. B. J. (1993),** *Inside/Outside: International Relations as Political Theory* **(Cambridge: Cambridge University Press).** Seminal discussion that critically examines International Relations as political theory, thereby establishing the possibility for poststructural analyses.

IMPORTANT WEBSITES

Although neither of these sites is self-consciously poststructuralist, the critical approaches to their objects of concern embodies the ethos of critique described above:

● The Imaging Famine project. Examines media coverage of famine from the nineteenth century to the present day. Focusing on photographic images, it contains background documents, reports as well as historic and contemporary photo essays.
www.imaging–famine.org

● The Information Technology, War and Peace project. At Brown University's Watson Institute, it covers the impact of information technology on statecraft and new forms of networked global politics.
www.watsoninstitute.org/infopeace/index2.cfm

Visit the Online Resource Centre that accompanies this book for lots of interesting additional material. www.oxfordtextbooks.co.uk/orc/dunne/

12 Postcolonialism

SIBA N. GROVOGUI

Chapter contents

- Introduction
- International morality and ethics
- Orientalism and identities
- Power and legitimacy in the international order
- Case study
- Conclusion

Reader's guide

Without impugning the eloquence and character of our precursors, any student of international relations may legitimately ask whether the likes of Thucydides, Machiavelli, Hobbes, and Kant give accurate accounts of the complex, varied, and unpredictable events that characterized their times. One may also ask whether their maxims of war-making and peace-making hold lessons for the present; and, importantly, whether their representations of human nature, power, and interest correspond to the experiences of societies conquered by Europe. Postcolonialism highlights that the views of politics held by these figures may not correspond to the experiences of non-Western societies. It offers new ways of knowing and thinking about the complex and fluid events that have shaped relations around the world by stressing the varying contexts of power, identity, and value across time and space. This chapter will, first, explore the morality and ethics in postcolonialism before moving on to discuss Said's work on 'Orientalism'. The chapter will then discuss notions of power and legitimacy in reference to the issue of nuclear proliferation. Finally, the case-study section discusses the issue of the nationalization of the Suez Canal from a postcolonial perspective.

Introduction

In 1961, a book appeared in France under the title of *The Wretched of the Earth* (Fanon 1968). Its author was Frantz Fanon: a black Frenchman born in Martinique and a psychiatrist by training, who had joined the anti-colonial Algerian struggle for independence from France. Needless to say, the book unsettled many who viewed its tone as 'angry'. Still, Jean-Paul Sartre, co-founder of French existentialism, noted in his introduction to Fanon's book the central reality that forms the backdrop to the book. Having once conquered and colonized other regions, an entity self-identified as 'Europe'[1] (later, the 'West') stipulated that the world contained 'Man' and 'native' (at the time 'five hundred million men' and 'one thousand five hundred million natives'). The European collectives, associated with the image of Man, believed themselves to be uniquely endowed with reason, science, and technology. As such, they aspired to dictate the direction of world affairs and to write the history of humanity as they willed and according to their own self-image (Trouillot 1995). This act was not merely hubris. It was accompanied by the degrading of the markers of culture, arts, and science in non-European societies to the status of folklore, myths, shamanism, and the like. Academic subjects such as Literature, Philosophy, History, and Anthropology – and now International Relations – contributed to this endeavour.

Now upon decolonization, Sartre reckoned, formerly native writers, artists, and scientists proclaimed themselves 'Men' of distinct will, conscience, and agency (Pillay 2004). Their advent as communities of citizens and free agents and actors did mean that the 'West' could no longer aspire to legislate and execute the 'will' of the entire world. It could still do so because it possessed the required political, military, and economic means. But the West could no longer aspire to such a position with legitimacy. Fanon's point was that others had never given permission to the West to be the ultimate judge of the propriety of values, desires, and interests. Like Fanon, formerly colonized entities everywhere imagined themselves as equal citizens of the world, equally unbound by place and time. They too aspired to reflect on international law and morality and to judge and be judged on the basis of actions and behaviours and their base systems of values, interests, and institutions.

In noting that decolonization required profound transformations in global values and institutions, Sartre summed up the ambition of postcolonialism, a phenomenon that figures in all former colonial expanses. In this chapter, I will use the term postcolonialism, with the obvious risks of anthropomorphizing, in order to provide an introduction to a multiplicity of perspectives, traditions, and approaches to questions of identity, culture, and power. Indeed, postcolonialism has multiple points of origination in Africa, Asia, Australia, Latin America, and the New World (see Gilroy 2005; Memmi 1965; Guha, Spivak, and Said 1988; Spivak 1987). These regions were subjected across time to different forms of governance and political traditions that account for the diversity of approaches to society, science, and knowledge (Mignolo 1995). Colonial histories also explain the overture of postcolonialism to a variety of theories, including liberalism, Marxism, postmodernism, and feminism and their applications to History, Philosophy, Sociology, Psychology, and Political Science. This diversity has led to confusions compounded by the academic confinement of postcolonial studies to ethnic, cultural, and regional studies programmes or departments. Yet, postcolonialism does not limit itself to a single region or discipline (Bhabha 1994; Said 1979; Mignolo 1995; Appadurai and Breckenridge 1990).

Postcolonialism thus offers new ways for thinking about techniques of power that constrain self-determination, whether they emanate from within or without. Consistently, postcolonialism contests the views of Western rationalists, humanists, and other universalists that their modes of signification (or ways of making sense of the world) were superior and that 'Europe' possessed the finer forms of reason, morals, and law. Second, postcolonialism aspires to participate in the creation of 'truths', based on distinct modes of signification and forms of knowledge (or the manners of representations) that advance justice, peace, and political pluralism. It applies so-called local memories, arts, and 'sciences' to the subjects of History, Literature, and Philosophy among others. Third, post-colonialism rejects 'native essentialism', or the idea that the 'natives' bore essential and timeless features. This idea has been (ab)used by Western powers and postcolonial elites to opposite ends, both connected to the acquisition and retention of power. Finally, postcolonialism also highlights the precarious relations between 'freedom' and politics. In this regard, postcolonialism elucidates the persistence of the colonial intellectual legacy in the supposedly neutral and universal settings of knowledge production and policy-making. In short, postcolonialism entertains the possibility of alternative conceptions and imaginaries of society, law, and morals.

This chapter has two aims. The first is to highlight the insufficiencies of current international norms as means to international justice. The second is to illustrate the postcolonial ambition to undo the legacies of European imperialism (when Europe unilaterally projected power abroad) and colonialism (European settlement or rule over other regions) in order to transform the international order and associated notions of community, society, and morality. The chapter is divided in four sections. The first explores the prospect of international morality and ethics in postcolonialism (Fanon 1968; Césaire 2000; Said 1979; Ashcroft *et al.* 1990; Chatterjee 1986). This section touches upon Kantian notions of international morality and pacific union under republicanism. The second section discusses Edward Said's *Orientalism* as one stream of postcolonial discussions of political subjectivity and identity (Bhabha 1994; Anzaldúa 1999; Moreiras 2001). This leads to the third section about power and international legitimacy, focusing on the recurrent themes in the debates over nuclear weapons proliferation. The case-study section shows how a postcolonial perspective might orient understandings of international relations. It focuses on Gamal Abdel Nasser's 'nationalization' of the Suez Canal and the crisis that ensued.

International morality and ethics

Postcolonialism associates the development of international order and society and its political economies with specific kinds of violence (Hulme 1992; Cheyfitz 1997). This association is not new; nor does it imply that one should give up on the idea of global orders. In the first instance, postcolonial critics find inspirations from a vast community of ecclesiastic, ethical, and moral thinkers worldwide who believed in the idea of common society or 'brotherhood' but expressed misgivings about the methods chosen by Europe to bring about this common society. Beginning with the conquest of the Americas, upon Christopher Columbus's 'discovery', Friars Antonio de Montesinos and Bartolomé de Las Casas initiated the first protests against the treatment of native populations (Galeano 1985: 57, 84). The protests of Montesinos and Las Casas were aimed at Spain but they reverberated later in other contexts where Christian powers conquered non-European lands. The methods of European conquest and expansion varied across time and space. While conquest led to European settlement or colonization in the New World, Europe's means of control elsewhere involved political control through multiple forms of colonial administration. They varied from protectorates (based on treaties of protection), to indirect rule (dual control by a colonial administration and native rulers), to direct rule (total administrative control). In any case, protests were heard everywhere whenever European imperial powers subjected new political entities to their own will through warfare and unfavourable political compacts – some of which were aptly named treaties of concession and capitulation while others were disingenuously categorized as protection and trusteeship.

In another instance, postcolonialism is cognizant that protests by the likes of Las Casas, although significant, did not prevent modern European imperialism, colonization, and colonialism. It also acknowledges that the institutions of modern European empires, settlements, and colonies laid the foundations for what the discipline of IR also calls international order, community, and/or society. In short, the coming together of the world as a single unit is one of the hallmarks of the modernity instigated by Europe. Postcolonialism perceives an irony in this event where others might not. In any case, postcolonialism does not take it for granted that the received world is preordained and given by force of nature: the world cannot be disentangled but its base institutions and systems of value and interest can be refashioned to reflect today's communities. In this regard too, postcolonialism has antecedents in revolts and revolutions by slave and colonial populations that sought justice in their particular locales by rejecting the moral, legal, and cultural foundations of their enslavement.

Postcolonialism and knowledge

Brought to the level of academic practice, postcolonialism today holds the motives and intentions of advocates of global institutions and systems of values separate from discussions of the systems of truths, values, and institutions that must shape the international or global order. Beginning with 'truths', postcolonialism notes that knowledge, or what is said to be, is never a full account of events. Gaps between what is said to have happened and what actually happened can be understood frequently by examining how imperial and colonial structures shaped such institutions as seemingly neutral as academic research. For instance, we can ascertain that colonial structures of power delivered the whole world to European and Western scholars as object of study. Among them, rationalists, humanists, and other cosmopolitans had 'universal' access to the whole world to which they applied the available scientific instruments, or methods of analysis, which allowed them to reach certain conclusions or 'truths' about themselves and native peoples everywhere. However, as observed by Talal Asad (1983) and Edward Said (1979), this enterprise was not a collaborative undertaking that involved 'natives' in the conceptions and implementation of its objectives. The knowledge resulting from 'observations' of and about 'natives' was neither constitutively 'native' knowledge nor based on native concerns. Even when Western theorists and scientists were generous and sympathetic to native populations, they could not wilfully escape the structures of empires and colonies and the political and cultural instruments that excluded colonial populations from the processes of decision-making and research. Finally, imperial knowledge was not universally accessible to natives. Not even the most dedicated metropolitan observers could make up for the political and economic processes that left vast majorities of colonial populations in abject poverty and illiteracy.

For these reasons and others, postcolonialism disputes the validity of ideas and commonplaces that today figure authoritatively in academic and public discourses as 'expert knowledges' about the former colonial expanses. These ideas and commonplaces include understandings of the inherence of labour and property, enterprise and capacity, in race, culture, and the environment – understandings which once served as justifications of imperialism and its distribution of value (Cohn 1996). Postcolonialism also disputes propositions by rationalists and critical theorists that Western methods, particularly rationalism and humanism, can adequately critique imperialism and colonialism and, by this token, offer the way to comfort and salvation for others (Césaire 2000; James 1989; Du Bois 1999). This conceit is combined with obstinacy in the belief that the West has sole responsibility for charting the course of human history (Prakash 1999). In addition, postcolonialism is sceptical of the prevailing rationalities and historical justifications for and of empire (Chakrabarty 2000). More often than not, related representations of the ends of imperialism and colonialism are self-serving (Prakash 1994). Finally, postcolonialism is suspicious of colonial ethnography and its accounts of cultures, rituals, and their significations. More often than not, the social structures and rituals 'discovered' by colonial ethnographers reflected their own castes of mind which were frequently at odds with what existed (Dirks 2001). Colonial understandings were deeply steeped in alternate forms of natural history and/or scientific racism that divided humanity into races, ethnic groups, heathens, and barbarians (Bensmaïa 2003). In short, colonial ethnography was mapped onto a cartography of morals, temperaments, and human capacities that helped to justify imperial political economies, and their systems of laws and morals (van der Veer 2001).

A postcolonial critique of the Western tradition

Postcolonial examinations of reason, history, and culture are necessary steps to re-envisioning the future (Scott 1999) and global designs (Mignolo 2000). Their aim is not, as has been argued (Hopkins 1997), to reject the principle of identifying and codifying international law and morality. To this end, postcolonialism forwards omitted or devalued *forms, ways of knowing* and their base-practices, or institutions, as possible expressions of valid moral concerns and, therefore, as the bases for valid formulations of value and interest. The postcolonial approach to this question upholds the principle of coexistence while rejecting erroneous ideas. In the first instance, postcolonialism recognizes the intrinsic merits of Western attempts and the intellectual prowess of the iconic figures that stand behind them – from Herodotus to Machiavelli, Kant, and beyond. Nor does postcolonialism impugn on the credentials of Europe and the West as purveyors of civilization. In the second instance, most postcolonial readers take Western iconic texts with degrees of irony – and depressing bemusement. Take Immanuel Kant, for instance. Kant has been lauded recently by an assortment of liberals who praise his republican ideas as the foundation for a pacific union of democratic states abiding by 'cosmopolitan law' (Doyle 1997; Russett 1993). Postcolonialism does not scorn such praises, but asks questions about the logic of an international order founded upon Kant's ideas. Specifically, they always return to gaps in Kant's representations of the eighteenth century and the implications of such gaps for the validity of his theory. This return to the source then serves as a metaphor and a point of criticism for today's liberals and institutionalists who would change the present world without due attention to its complexity and the diverse stakes involved in change.

Irrespective of whether they hold that Kant was 'racist' like many of his contemporaries, postcolonial scholars generally take issue with today's readings of Kant. There are complex arguments here that cannot be exposed fully in an introductory text. But imagine, if you will, writing about moral commands, ethics, and pacific union. Imagine that you live in an era when slavery was both the reality and the most potent metaphor for the absence of liberty (Trouillot 1997). Imagine also living in an era marked by three revolutions (in the USA, France, and Haiti), one of which arose from demand by actual slaves for freedom. Would you omit actual slavery and the aspiration of slaves for freedom from three major treatises on love for humanity and the related moral sentiments of solidarity and hospitality? Would you expect the slave or former slave to take resulting speculations about peaceful coexistence at face value? You might, but it will not be as easy to dismiss Kant's 'gaps' as mere historical perspectives.

We can now begin to understand postcolonial suspicions about dimensions of Kant's notions of moral imperatives – the sublime and the picturesque that underpin his vision of international order. In one postcolonial perspective, Kant's accounts of the picturesque omitted the actual scenes of enactment of the pacific union extending beyond Europe as it was in actuality. When imperialism and concerns about race and masculinity transformed landscapes in the New World, Africa, and elsewhere, the picturesque was more like an assemblage of scenes of intended and unintended crimes, including the vanishing of native populations in the New World and the African slave trade. The places of enactment of European agendas of universal salvation, emancipation, protection, and modernization were therefore scenes of crimes. When read against the background of global events, the picturesque quickly loses its lustre and reveals itself as imperial cartography in which the cosmopolitan sentiment of love or empathy (or colonial trusteeship) is inserted into a poetics or landscape of conquest, repression, and expropriation through broken treaties and shared violence. This conclusion raises question about the nature of the sublime or love itself. After all, the enactment of European trusteeship over others brought about social decay in the zones of enactment (Dirks 2001).

I do not propose an indictment of Kant's view of slavery. I merely wish to ask whether the omission of such an important institution as slavery and enslavement from moral thought diminishes the moral reach of resulting theories of republicanism and cosmopolitanism. I am therefore asking for a pause before proposing Kant as the prophet of ethics and pacific union. Although I personally favour the idea of global norms, questions remain about the origin of the norms; the manners by which they are attained; and their purpose. In these connections, postcolonialism draws three conclusions. The first is that it is not sufficient for theorists to simply embrace categories such as international order, international society, and international ethics. Because these concepts recall the era of European expansion and colonialism, they are not devoid of political effects. In fact, they exude a colonial anthropology in which a mythical righteous West poses as teacher for others, regardless of the context and purpose of engagement and the nature of behaviour.

Second, there is a double movement in Western moral thought involving 'presence' (when European authorship matters to the legitimacy and purpose of discourse) and 'erasure' (when European identity is necessarily concealed). There is strategy behind each mode of reasoning. For instance, the proposition that human rights are a universal value depends on a de-emphasis of their Western origins and the invocation of human rights by victims groups throughout the world. On the other hand, when Western intellectuals and politicians need to underscore European superiority, and the 'duty' or 'right to lead', they stress that human rights are civilizational markers of the West. The accentuation of Western origination of universal values then bolsters the position that the West may legitimately pose as moral teacher for others on value, morality, and ethics. Postcolonialism does not merely object that such debates close off inquiry on the merits and limits of related formulations of value, interest, and morality. Critics also note that discussions of Western universalism and moral rectitude obscure the Western origins of modern forms of political violence, including Nazism, Fascism, and Stalinism. These and the practices of total war witnessed in the two world wars of the twentieth century are thus relegated to recessive moments in the long Western march to emancipate Man. In short, there is political utility in the notion of the West as a modern, democratic, and prosperous province of the globe – just as other dimensions of the European trajectory are suppressed as a matter of political expedience.

Third, postcolonialism does not dispense with reason and universalism when practitioners propose that imperial Europe was self-interested and liable to historical follies. Nor would postcolonial critics claim that reason and pragmatism are not human faculties. However, postcolonialism is unmoved by the insistence in institutional narratives on the objectivity and neutrality of goals and methods of inquiry. These disciplinary narratives exude the sort of colonial hubris that mistakes one's desire for reality and one's own aspiration for universalism. Indeed, the related disciplinary perspectives are unable to speak to the world as a whole. They are the product of the kind of intellectual and moral presumptuousness that continues to lead to unpredictable (and at times dangerous) adventures disguised as liberation (like the Anglo-American invasion of Iraq) or humanitarian interventions (for instance in Somalia).

These comments are part of the suspicion that postcolonialism harbours toward today's institutional approaches to international relations. These approaches see regimes and 'international morality' as sublime (Kantian) settings for the enactment of value, without prior identification of value or deliberations on the nature or origin of the proposed institutions. Specifically, liberal and neoliberal discourses often appear as rationalizations of hegemony disguised as universal humanism. For its part, cosmopolitanism risks becoming a tangle of self-serving mis-representations of reason, solidarity, and the common good. Finally, constructivist notions of mutuality and co-constitution of norms appear to the postcolonial ear as an ironic attempt to embellish the resigned entry of constitutionally weakened and politically defeated postcolonies into existing international regimes.

Orientalism and identities

In the English-speaking world, postcolonialism has been associated with the study of identities and cultures. This is because the concept brings to mind such writers and works as Edward Said, *Orientalism* (1979); Gayatri Spivak, *In Other Worlds* (1987); Ngugi wa Thiong'o, *Decolonizing the Mind* (1986); Homi Bhaba, *The Location of Culture* (1994); Bill Ashcroft *et al.*, *The Empire Writes Back* (1989); and Gloria Anzaldúa, *Borderlands/La Frontiera* (1987). These authors and their texts have equivalencies in the French, Spanish, and Chinese-speaking worlds. Collectively, they have generated and supported scholarly genres and journals, including *Subaltern Studies*, *Presence Africaine*, and more recently *Nepantla*. Yet, contrary to what has been charged (Hopkins 1997; Todorov 1993), the post-colonial attention to identity and culture is neither chauvinism nor an endorsement of essentialism – the idea that identities and culture have their own essential features which are impermeable to others. Rather than proclaim fixity for identity and/or authenticity for culture, postcolonialism appropriates their historical representations for their legitimate uses in more fluid postcolonial contexts.

In most of Africa, for instance, few postcolonial theorists would use the idea of nation without a degree of dread. This is because the colonial populations that now form African 'nations' cannot be said to be linguistically or culturally coherent entities. Frequently, African states brought together under the umbrella of 'nation' are groups that speak different languages and that a mere century ago lived in separate political spaces under their own rules. Thus, the state provides a container for separate groups engaged in exercises of self-invention and self-determination. Likewise, the citizens of Latin American states have to formulate nationhood in fluid dynamics and symbolic competitions between and among the descendants of native Indians and the descendants of European settlers. The processes of self-invention and self-determination produced real effects in these contexts as they do in Africa. They allowed formerly colonial populations to divest themselves of colonial subjectivity, for instance tribes in Africa, in favour of new institutions, including nations. It follows that, in these contexts, notions of authenticity, indigeneity, and the like are embraced anew but not for their prior implications which suggested inherent and fixed qualities. They are embraced because they give historical credibility and legitimacy to political or ethical projects on account of authorship (Warrior 1994; Memmi 1965).

Postcolonialism acknowledges that there are dangers and opportunities contained in these rapid transformations in identity and culture even as it strives to divest science and politics of Western vestiges of identity and culture. This is particularly the case with historical Western views of 'natives' as the modern 'barbarians'. To illustrate these points, let us return to Said's most celebrated and controversial book: *Orientalism*. The title describes its object, the Oriental and the study of 'his' habits, as a phenomenon born of Europe's dominance of the world, including the Middle East. According to Said, Orientalism does not merely account for the reality of a geo-cultural space called the Orient because it is situated east of Europe. Rather Orientalism is a technique of power based in language and processes of translation of the identities, cultures, and religion of the Middle East. Through these techniques, European (and Western) intellectuals and public officers created a mythical space that only partially bore resemblance to the place it described. Through readings of English texts, Said illustrates how colonial representations of the (formerly) colonized are institutionalized as instruments and/or features of cultural dominance. Accordingly, Orientalist texts have material existence that can be detected only if one places such texts in the context of actual strategies of textual production.

Said helped to develop propositions about the cultural and political impact of European conquest of other regions and thus colonization and colonialism. In the tradition of the French philosopher Michel Foucault, Said claims that the histories revealed in texts are not unearthed from fixed 'burial grounds' of the past. Orientalist histories highlight the terms and stereotypes that formed the foundations of Europe's policies towards this region and linger today in policy-making circles as bases for current policies. In this light, *Orientalism*, first, illustrates cultural and political struggles in all colonies and postcolonies between imperial societies and colonial ones; struggles over **knowledge and power** and their respective ends. Second, Said provides useful methods for analysing imperialism and post-imperial cultural engagements. In this instance, he deconstructs authoritative – that is politically and culturally salient – Western discourses of self and others with an eye to their utility and instrumentalities. In another instance, Said lays the foundations for alternative discourses of self and others. Said also provides empirical and methodological frames for queries about identity and culture. For instance, he highlights how humanism counte-nanced colonial violence (which may be found in Fanon); how liberal constitutional orders in the USA and elsewhere underwrote racism (Du Bois 1999); and who was 'Man' and who spoke on 'his' behalf and about what subjects (Morrison 1993).

It is an understatement to say that Said provides useful tips for understanding Western political discourses about others. From Said's perspectives, the present terms and Western public understanding of Arab regimes as despotic, traditional, and irredeemable reiterate today yesterday's images of 'Oriental despotism' (Mill, 1806–73) and of the everyday of Bedouins and others as cave-dwelling (Montesquieu, 1689–1755). One can also detect echoes of Orientalism in the now declared long war on terrorism. The war on terrorism, it must be recalled, began with the identification of the terrorist, a specific type of individual or groups of individuals, and not any denunciation or call for the renunciation of the use of violence as a means to an end. The war on terrorism is in actuality a war on pre-assigned terrorists who hold identified beliefs and inclinations. In Western policy circles, the terrorists practise a sordid brand of Islamic fundamentalism; exude moral intolerance and hatred for the West and Western way of life; and are the product of social and political decay in the Muslim world. The war on terrorism dispenses therefore with the political rationality of the terrorists in that it has been determined in advance that the terrorists have no just cause that warrants the use of force or violence. Because terrorists do not have legitimate or just cause, civilized societies (the 'victims') have the right to violently combat terrorism and, yes, kill the terrorists with all available means – now, we understand, irrespective of international conventions and norms.

Regardless of one's views of current events, one can detect ideological slippages in the Orientalist continuum from actual reactions to actual events to invocations of a dubious cartography of region, religion, and culture. These slippages have caused many critics (and not just postcolonialists) to ask themselves about the interchangeability of Pakistan, Afghanistan, and Iraq; or wonder what it means that Bin-Laden and Saddam Hussein are indistinguishable in political standing; how it became legitimate to advocate the overthrow of the Afghan Talibans and Iraqi Ba'athist for the real sins of Al Qaeda; and, finally, how a majority in the USA and a minority in the UK can still believe in a collusion between Saddam Hussein and Bin-Laden – two men who belong to antagonist political movements.

One explanation might be that discourses on terrorism have found an easy entry point into three tenets of Orientalism: (1) the existence of separate, unequal, and hierarchical spheres of civilizations; (2) the need to maintain the boundaries between them by defending Western civilization's goods or values against corrupt ones without; and (3) the necessity for moderate or secular Arab groups to join the West in introducing progressive values in their region. Again, these ideas are not new. They go as far back as the end of the Crusades. Still, it is untrue that Europe has an original civilization, formed over an unbroken time-span within a homogenous space. Nor is it possible to draw a boundary or a straight line between 'civilized Europe' and the violent cultures without, including a place called the Orient. One would have to negate historical co-dependencies between Europe (and the West) and other regions: for instance, Byzantium and vast expanses beyond it. One would also have to argue that Russians and Bosnian Muslims do not share ethnographic traits with, say, the Franks. Finally, one would have to expunge Moorish Spain from memory as the cultural antecedent of contemporary Spain.

It is somewhat mystifying therefore that international theorists, from Hugo Grotius, in seventeenth-century Netherlands, to James Lorimer, in nineteenth-century England, would erect metaphysical boundaries between Europe and others (Grovogui 1996). They were not alone. The Berlin Africa Conference (1884–5), which finalized colonial boundaries in Africa, was also derivative of Europe's civilizational discourse that masked actually violent processes with humanitarian disguises (Fetter 1979). Today, pretentious civilizational discourses provide sustenance to the belief that Muslim émigrés within the gates of Europe would work in tandem with Muslim barbarians beyond to destroy Europe (Huntington 1998). These views are mistaken about the pervasiveness of political corruption and violence in modern life. Indeed, it is near fictitious to maintain an opposition between 'total European virtue' against 'total Oriental barbarism'. For this opposition to hold, one would have to negate that Nazism and Fascism were manifestations of modern European ideologies and practices. The photographs of atrocities taking place in Abu Ghraib and other US detention centres provide sufficient evidence that techniques of torture and barbarism are not the sole province of Middle East states.

It is beside the point that the 'facts' of the phenomenon of Orientalism are wrong. It functions to sow the seeds of antipathy to the Orient and its religion and culture in the

West. One view is that the European anxiety of being overtaken by Muslims has persisted because Islam does not easily lend itself to translation by the state, at least not by a democratic state. Further, individual European Muslims have remained on the margins of European societies and it is not yet clear how they and the collectives in which they exist will convey their 'gratitude' for the privileges of European citizenship. As the French 'Affaire du Foulard' (or Head Scarf Affair) showed, multitudes of European Muslims are not ready to divest themselves of their prior Islamic traditions as a condition of their entry into European political processes. On this and other scores, Orientalism has succeeded in generating great antipathy towards Islam and Muslims. Would-be defenders of secular Western norms may plead innocent as they help to proliferate mistaken views on the nature of European society and Islam as a religion and practice (Asad 1993). They may also point to the antipathies towards the West among Muslims and by people in the Middle East, with their equal share of unfounded beliefs. But, in a context of power, Orientalism has greater political effects.

It is not exaggerating to suggest that Western anxieties and antipathies towards Muslims are exerting considerable influences on debates about terrorism. For instance, outraged denunciations of Palestinian terrorism might rightly point out the cowardliness of would-be liberators and the devastating psychological toll of suicide bombing on non-combatant Israelis. The latter are cast as innocent victims who are violated in their legitimate expectation of security everywhere. All these concerns are real in that they are pertinent to the ability of people to function in society. But, in the West, few express equally emphatic outrage about the toll of daily violence on Palestinians due to military occupation by Israel. Fewer still ask themselves whether Palestinian children may be psychologically scarred by bombs that slam into any Palestinian building, any time of day, without notice, on the sole Israeli suspicion of an adverse activity in the abode. It would seem that the ethical reflex that demands that bus riders feel safe on their way home to their families, relatives, and friends, would demand that fathers and mothers be able to ensure the safety of their children at home – away from the streets and the riots. Due partly to Orientalism, the Western war on terrorism depends upon moral injunctions (the equivalent of fatwa) against total violence upon civil populations on one side of the civilizational-cum-political divide. By contrast, Western foreign policies most of the time countenance total violence against Palestinian civilians (Muslims and Christians alike) caught on the other side of the civilizational divide.

Power and legitimacy in the international order

Postcolonialism requires some degree of dexterity in thinking. It begins with views of empire and imperialism that contrast with the existing disciplinary common sense. To go back to Kant, Europeans might have experienced imperialism as a positive enterprise. Even a simple expression like *Pax Britannica* suggests that those involved in constructing empire believed that imperialism met metropolitan needs and desires – and therefore approval.

These and similar Western expressions of power, dictums about the use of power, and moral commands are now encoded as international morality. Approaches such as those of the English school remind us that empire and imperialism are the genetic ancestors of international order and morality. Postcolonialism begins with the truism that European institutions have occupied a central place in the development of such concepts as 'international order', 'international morality', and 'international law'. But, postcolonialism asks questions about the international order and international law and morality that do not comply with disciplinary verities or received notions of critique and judgement. Again, the key to postcolonial difference rests in the fact that the experiences of the conquered and colonized contrast with those of the conquerors and colonizers. Whereas the latter might recall *Pax Britannica* among other events as the flawed beginnings of a positive enterprise, the former might recall it as a quilt of nightmarish scenarios lived across time and space.

Non-proliferation from a postcolonial perspective

By way of illustration, I wish to sketch postcolonialism's response to supposed violations of the Nuclear Non-proliferation Treaty. So-called Third World countries universally greeted the idea that the spread of nuclear weapons must be prevented. However, they expressed concerns at the drafting of the treaty that led to two separate but complementary sets of prohibitions: one, against vertical proliferation (or the increase of nuclear capabilities within declared nuclear states), and another, against horizontal proliferation (from country to country). The ban on vertical proliferation has largely been ignored in public debates today in favour of the illegitimacy of the quest by so-called rogue states for nuclear weapons. Organizations such as the Wisconsin Project and the Carnegie Foundation for International Peace have on occasion noted the irregularity of omitting vertical proliferation, but they mostly attribute the danger of nuclear weapons to their possession by small albeit 'mal-governed' postcolonial states. However, if you were an African imbued in the history of arms control, it might occur to you that the political instrumentalization of the ban on weapons of mass destruction under the non-proliferation treaty has a kin in the Brussels Treaty in 1890. That treaty prohibited the sale of breechloaders to Africans between the 20th Parallel North and the 22nd Parallel South (Headrick 1981). The cartography of the ban allowed white regimes in Southern Africa and colonial powers to arm themselves with weapons inaccessible to Africans during the crucial period of formal colonization upon the 1885 Berlin Conference that delineated European colonial expanses in Africa.

From this perspective, political subjectivity in international theory and modern international regimes depends upon the use of violence by the few who monopolize the means of violence against the many who must be denied those means domestically (for national security) or internationally (in the national interest). Paired with the uses of modern weapons in the former colonial expanses subsequent to the two world wars, it is not paranoid to maintain the following belief: international regimes of arms control have largely kept the peace among the great powers but they have permitted ruinous wars against other peoples from Indochina to Africa to the Middle East. What should one make of the omission of such ruinous wars by disciplinary fields like realism and neoliberalism, particularly given their immodest claims to objectivity? There are many answers in postcolonial circles. For instance, realist propositions that mandate the defence of the national interest through the monopoly of the means and use of violence by the state seem to the postcolonial theorist to be nothing more than a compendium of narratives of salvation without ends and purposes, except for states able and willing to engage in arms races and the extra-territorial pursuit of national interests.

On such matters as nuclear non-proliferation, postcolonialism is at best ambivalent about enforcement under the current conditions – that is an arbitrary adjudication by the few about who should or should not get nuclear weapons.[2] On this particular matter, the postcolonial critic is caught between two untenable positions (Roy 1998). On the one hand, postcolonialism endorses a compelling international regime that would ensure human survival in peace and dignity. In this instance, one must oppose Third World attempts to acquire nuclear weapons. On the other hand, postcolonialism does not condone hegemony and unilateralism disguised as reason. Here, one must combat hegemonic reflexes on the part of so-called rationalists and universalists who would disguise parochial interests as the common good. The resolution of this dilemma can come only if and when the ethico-political language of great powers is exposed as obsolete and illegitimate. Until then, formerly colonial entities and weaker powers will try to secure their own place in the global economy of power. In the meantime, it would be difficult for postcolonialism to fully endorse solutions to global problems that are in no way universal.

Case study: the Suez Canal Crisis

As I have argued, postcolonialism arises from a temporal rupture in European modernity following the end of formal colonial rule. It is preceded by anticolonialism, or opposition to colonial occupation or administration, and other anti-imperialist movements, including resistance to the so-called colonial penetration. In short, postcolonialism signals the demise of the European colonial order and associated truth claims. It makes sense of this postcolonial moment by inviting re-examinations of the intellectual, political, and moral foundations of colonialism. In the political instance, postcolonialism insists on a new international order free of the legacies of colonialism or colonial institutions. As actualized today, postcolonialism has distinct goals that can be traced to the 1955 Bandung Conference, the 1961 Non-Aligned Movement, and Cuba's Tricontinentalism, among others. The Bandung Conference assembled leaders of Africa, Asia, and Latin America under the stewardship of Chou En Lai of China, Jawaharlal Nehru of India, and Sukarno of Indonesia. Its purpose was to decolonize international practices on questions of foreign policy and development. The Non-aligned Movement complemented the spirit of Bandung by underscoring the need for a community of interest to advance the single objective of equality, free association, and mutuality in international affairs. Finally, the idea of Tricontinentalism was to develop a new ethos of power and subjectivity for the three concerned continents through foreign policy.

These and antecedent agendas and demands were partly inspired by the United Nations Charter proclamation of self-determination as one of the cornerstone of the international order. They motivated decisions by Gamal Abdel Nasser and other so-called Third World leaders, including the decision to nationalize the Suez Canal in 1956. Still, most accounts of the Suez Canal Crisis tell a story of a superpower balance of power, uneasy Cold War alliances, and the 'recklessness' of Third World 'nationalism'. They might even refer to the event as the 'Suez Canal War'. This is because Nasser's ambition to nationalize the Canal resulted in a war of aggression against Egypt by the UK, France, and Israel. The prevailing Western narrative of events leading to the war is based upon simple axioms. To summarize a long story, the Canal was realized under the direction of Ferdinand de Lesseps, between 1854 and 1856, on concessions from Said Pasha, the viceroy of Egypt. It became operational on 15 December 1858 and, under agreement, was to be managed by the Suez Canal Company (also *Compagnie Universelle du Canal Maritime de Suez*) for ninety-nine years. Under European and US agreement, the Canal was to be open to ships of all nations under a plan drafted by Austrian engineer Alois Negrelli. Come 1956, Nasser, a left-leaning Arab Nationalist, if not Pan-Arabist, decided to annul the regime governing the Suez Canal. Nasser was then cast as an ally of the Soviet Union. He was said to be recklessly ambitious with little regard for the subtleties of international law. This narrative takes it for granted that the UK and France were obligated to pre-empt Nasser's actions, if only to deter similar actions by other Third World activists. Thus, the UK and France took umbrage at Nasser's decision to take over the Canal. Israel was worried about the 'right of passage' of ships bound for the port of Eilat.

The above narrative also poses the reactions of the world's two major powers – then, the USA and the Soviet Union – as logical and delicate balancing acts. Accordingly, the USA was a NATO ally of France and the UK but, on the geopolitical schemes of the Cold War, the Hungarian Crisis was a more efficacious terrain to fight Soviet power. The USA also faced a potential public relations embarrassment in the Third World if it criticized the Soviet Union's military intervention in Hungary while condoning military intervention by former colonial powers in one of their former provinces. The Soviet Union was allied with Egypt but had greater worries for the Hungarian Crisis, which threatened the very idea of communism. To show consistency in projecting its powers in defence of its allies, the Soviet Union had also promised to defend Egypt. In the end, the Franco-UK-Israeli oper-ation to take the Canal was highly successful from a military point of view. But, from a geopolitical perspective, it proved a diplomatic and ideological disaster for the UK and France. So too was the Israeli occupation of the Egyptian Sinai.

Questioning conventional accounts of the Suez 'crisis'

This widely circulated reading satisfies realists and others, but it is a bit removed from the primary issues underlying the takeover of the Suez Canal by Egypt. To postcolonialism, the letter of the Suez agreements is not unimpeachable, and the decision by Britain, France, and Israel to wage war on Egypt was illogical, absurd, and reckless in its own way. For explanation, imagine this writer in his introductory course in international law on the topic of international regimes of waterways. Guinea, his country of birth, had been inde-pendent from France for less than two decades. The professor, a Frenchman, wrote on the board the name of three canals: the Suez Canal, the Panama Canal, and the Kiel Canal (Kaiser-Wilhelm-Kanal). He then proclaimed confidently that, although entirely within Egyptian territory, Suez was an international passageway. The Panama Canal, which cuts across the state of Panama, was actually an American canal. The Kiel Canal, on the other hand, was German property because it was located in Germany. You can imagine that, if the professor intended to communicate respect for international law, he was not successful. While the professor perceived normative certainty, this student and his friends perceived colonial hubris and arrogance. We could not make sense of the argument that Germany claimed proprietorship of the Kiel Canal due to its location but Egypt could not claim Suez on accounts of colonial understandings. We were particularly incensed when, through an indiscretion, the law professor mentioned that the excavation of the Suez Canal was due mostly to the forced labour of poor Egyptians. Every student in the class could recall that unequal treaties, forced or slave labour, and discriminatory international regimes had in fact been the hallmark of colonialism!

The internationalization of the Suez Canal under private European management appeared to us to be a throwback to European notions of 'imperial sovereignty'. Thus, whereas we were supposed to be outraged by Nasser's 'adventure', we wished we had been there for the cheers. Nasser was in fact right that the letter and spirit of colonial agreements were inconsistent with postwar notions of self-determination. In this postcolonial contest, Nasser was not alone. Nor was it unique to this circumstance that former colonial powers attempted to preserve colonial privileges against Egyptian claims. Nasser was preceded by Mohammed Mossadegh in Iran (1953) who was removed from power by Mohammad Reza Pahlavi, the Shah of Iran, and pro-monarchy forces in a coup orchestrated by UK and US intelligence agencies. His sin: the desire to renegotiate turn-of-century oil deals that gave control of Iranian oil to UK firms. Mossadegh and Nasser were nonetheless followed by many more Third World leaders and movements from Africa to Asia and Latin America. However corrupt it may appear today, the Organization of Petroleum Exporting States (OPEC) was partly connected to postcolonial insurgency against such 'residual colonial forms' as reflected in the international regimes on waterways.

You might wonder why a simple lecture would offend anyone. But you would be mistaken in thinking that the justifications of unequal treaties, forced or slave labour, and discriminatory international regimes were mere political acts undertaken as a matter of expediency. This is not the case. Such actions were steeped in specific ways of thinking and relating to the world that were common among European and Western elites. Philosophers and political theorists condoned such actions and their processes through proprietary articulations of society and law; labour and property; and reason and moral sentiments. From the seventeenth century, European thinkers, including French *philosophes* and British utilitarians, developed historical understandings of societies and their institutions as bases for merits and entitlements. These understandings were complex and at times contradictory, and outside of the aims of this introduction. But, to elaborate on an earlier theme, they were grounded in presumed relationships of peoples to territory and economy, leading to conclusions that 'natives' had no firm moral connections to land that may result in property. The central view was that natives were less industrious and lacked reason to properly perceive the collective good. In contrast, Europeans were assumed to be endowed with reason to manage industry, to aspire to property, and to be nobly motivated. They were thus to bring science and value to the less fortunate, including through coercion. One could therefore extract concessions from a subservient viceroy, enlist forced labour to dig a canal, make money on it, and call it the common good. In this light, Nasser's action annulled in one stroke centuries-old European assumptions about the relationships of 'native' populations to nature (or their environment) by reclaiming Egyptian rights to the Canal. These assumptions, eloquently framed by the likes of John Locke (1632–1704) and Montesquieu (1689–1755), had been the bases for Europe's extra-regional claims to sovereignty and property.

These justifications have not disappeared from disciplinary narratives today. When it is convenient, the discipline of International Relations has embraced past 'imperial follies' and their rationalizations as 'state practice'. It is not uncommon to come across the axiom that great powers have the greatest influence in the world and, as such, should be willing to use their capabilities to nudge international order in particular directions. This assertion is made without questions about how particular great powers use their influence and the means and ends to which they apply their capabilities. Fortunately, considerable minorities among the citizens of great powers are somewhat sceptical of the implied wisdom.[3] From a postcolonial perspective, such truisms reflexively evoke memories of prejudices, discriminations, and privations. In such instances, the discipline appears more like an instrument of empire than a science.

Conclusion

Postcolonialism does not merely seek out points of convergence on formal planes of understanding of already-existing norms. Postcolonialism aspires to produce new political forms based on contingent and empathetic understandings of the trajectories of human societies. In this sense, postcolonialism conveys a sense of ethical and political possibilities after colonialism. It favours an ethos of egalitarianism, social justice, and solidarity. It has faith in its own reasonableness and decency (Scott 1999). Postcolonialism is also certain of its responsibility and duty towards other members of the international community. Postcolonialism, in fact, aspires to a different kind of universalism, one based on deliberation and contestations among diverse political entities, with the aim of reaching functional agreements on questions of global concern. This kind of universalism differs from one resulting from universal injunctions by self-assured subjects.

In these ends, postcolonialism maintains consistent positions on politics that do not distinguish between the domestic, national, and international spheres. In the international instance, postcolonialism is mindful of the failure of hegemonic powers to integrate postcolonial states into the decision-making processes of the international system. Yet, postcolonialism's ambivalence on these and other questions of international morality does not flow from outright rejection of systems of thought, whether rationalism, universalism, humanism, liberalism, and the like. Postcolonial antipathy is directed at the imperial desire for hegemony, or the aspiration to set the terms and rules of politics and culture unilaterally; to adjudicate international outcomes singly; and/or to manage knowledge and the memory of international relations. In the domestic instance, postcolonialism also denounces, with equal vigour, the failure of postcolonial elites to integrate co-citizens – and/or domestic social and cultural formations – into democratic structures of governance within the state. Postcolonialism, thus, is a broad commentary on present models of politics, economy, and ethics.

In both instances, postcolonialism must confront anxieties of survival that arise among subjects in any fluid and uncertain context. Again, postcolonialism embraces fluxes and the resulting opportunities, including the hybridity of culture and identity (Bhabha 1994). To do so, postcolonialism must rethink the boundaries between self and others (Anzaldúa 1987) as well as recognize transculturation as an inevitable historical process (Moreiras 2001). Thus, postcolonialism seeks to connect with progressive elements at home and in the former metropolises in order to productively engage the fields of culture and identity to eliminate violence and/or escape the problematic legacies of class hegemony, gendered exclusion, colonial domination, and capitalist exploitation (Scott 1999). All these themes are present in postcolonialism as articles or declarations of faith. The postcolonial order envisaged by postcolonialism would be more inclusive and solicitous. This future world would be based on tolerance toward self-criticisms and criticisms of the self by others; reverence for contingency and historical flows; and more fluid understandings of values, ethics, and the common good. You would not object to such a world, would you? If not, then you must always open your mind to new (and just) possibilities!

? QUESTIONS

1. Why is 'postcolonialism' as a phenomenon difficult to define and pinpoint as a single theoretical tradition?
2. What is the author's definition of postcolonialism?
3. What are some of the goals and agendas of postcolonialism?
4. How does postcolonialism approach 'truth' and 'knowledge'?
5. Discuss the postcolonial critique of Immanuel Kant and subsequent theories based upon the work of this theorist.
6. What is the postcolonial objection to 'human rights' as a 'universal value'?
7. How does Said's book *Orientalism* illustrate and elucidate the relationship between Europe and the East?
8. Describe the relationship between Orientalism and the discourses on terrorism including the 'war against terror'.
9. How does postcolonialism's response to the Non-proliferation Treaty illustrate its opinion about Western ideas of international morality and law?
10. What is the significance of the internationalization of the Suez Canal for postcolonialism?
11. What is the postcolonial approach to the future?
12. Compare the approaches of liberal internationalism, constructivism, and postcolonialism.

≋ FURTHER READING

■ **Darby, Phillip (2000), *At the Edge of International Relations: Postcolonialism, Gender and Dependency* (Cambridge: Continuum International Publishing Group).** Examines how a postcolonial perspective contributes or challenges traditional conventions in International Relations theory.

■ Spivak, Gayatri Chakavorty (1999), *A Critique of Postcolonial Reason: Toward a History of the Vanishing Present* (Cambridge MA: Harvard University Press). Divided between Philosophy, Literature, History, and Culture, this work gives extensive insight into the colonial and postcolonial paradoxes in the Western intellectual tradition and its viability for contemporary politics and ethics.

■ Nevzat, Soguk (1999), *States and Strangers: Refugees and Displacements of Statecraft* (Minneapolis: Minnesota University Press). An important work on the ways refugee and refugee law challenge traditional concepts in International Relations such as the state and the citizen.

■ Chowdry, G. and Nair, S. (2002) (eds), *Power, Postcolonialism and International Relations; Reading Race, Gender and Class,* Routledge Advances in International Relations Global Politics (London and New York: Routledge). This collection covers a wide range of contemporary topics in International Relations from questions of the secular to recent debates over the future of human rights.

■ Grovogui, Siba N. (2006), *Beyond Eurocentrism and Anarchy: Memories of International Order and Institutions* (New York: Palgrave Macmillan). Revisits a postwar encounter between a group of French-African intellectuals and Western elites as evidence of the importance of a genuinely global and equivocal perspective on International Relations.

■ Krishna, Sankaran (1999), *Postcolonial Insecurities: India, Sri Lanka, and the Question of Nationhood,* Borderlines series (Minneapolis: University of Minnesota). Addresses the question of nation and state formation as a political and ethical project.

■ Biswas, Shampa (2001), ' "Nuclear Apartheid" as Political Position: Race as a Postcolonial Resource?', *Alternatives: Global, Local, Political, 26/4*: 485–522 (38). Continues the discussions about the colonial legacy of the Nuclear Non-proliferation Treaty.

■ Lynn Doty, Roxanne (1996) *Imperial Encounters: The Politics of Representation in North–South Relations,* Borderlines Series (Minneapolis: Minnesota University Press). Engages how policy-making is informed and even proceeded by cultural and racial representations. Doty takes the position that politics is fundamentally interpretative.

IMPORTANT WEBSITES

● Postcolonial studies at Emory websites
http://www.english.emory.edu/Bahri/contents.html

● Edward W. Said
http://sun3.lib.uci.edu/~scctr/wellbeck/said/index.html

 Visit the Online Resource Centre that accompanies this book for lots of interesting additional material. www.oxfordtextbooks.co.uk/orc/dunne/

13 Green Theory

ROBYN ECKERSLEY

Chapter contents

- Introduction
- The emergence of green theory
- The transnational turn in green theory
- The greening of IR theory
- Case study
- Conclusion

Reader's guide

This chapter explores the ways in which environmental concerns have influenced International Relations (IR) theory. It provides a brief introduction to the ecological crisis and the emergence of green theorizing in the social sciences and humanities in general, noting its increasing international orientation, and then tracks the status and impact of environmental issues and green thinking in IR theory. It shows how orthodox IR theories, such as neorealism and neoliberalism,[1] have constructed environment problems merely as a 'new issue area' that can be approached through pre-existing theoretical frameworks. These approaches are contrasted with green IR theory, which challenges the state-centric framework, rationalist analysis, and ecological blindness of orthodox IR theories and offers a range of new green interpretations of international justice, development, modernization, and security. The case study of climate change is explored to highlight the diversity of theoretical approaches, including the distinctiveness of green approaches, in understanding global environmental change.

Introduction

Environmental problems have never been a central preoccupation in the discipline of International Relations (IR), which has traditionally focused on questions of 'high politics' such as security and interstate conflict. However, the escalation in transboundary ecological problems from the 1970s onwards saw the emergence of a dedicated sub-field of IR concerned with international environmental cooperation, which focused primarily on the management of common pool resources such as major river systems, the oceans, and the atmosphere. This scholarship has since grown apace with increasing global economic and ecological interdependence and the emergence of uniquely global ecological problems, such as climate change, the thinning of the ozone layer, and the erosion of the Earth's biodiversity. The bulk of research has focused on the study of environmental regimes, primarily from the evolving theoretical framework of neoliberalism, which has approached the environment merely as a new 'issue area' or new political problem, rather than a new theoretical challenge.

By the closing decades of the twentieth century, however, a growing body of green IR theory had emerged that called into question some of the basic assumptions, units of study, frameworks of analysis, and implicit values of the discipline of IR. Just as feminist discourses emerging from outside IR have exposed the gender blindness of much IR theory (discussed in **Chapter 10**), green IR theory, drawing on more radical green discourses from outside the discipline of IR, has helped to expose what might be called the ecological blindness of IR theory. Emerging primarily out of a critique of mainstream rationalist approaches (primarily neo- or structural realism as set out in **Chapter 4** and neoliberalism discussed in **Chapter 6**), green IR theory has simultaneously drawn upon, and critically revised and extended, neo-Marxist inspired **International Political Economy** (IPE) and normative international relations theories of a cosmopolitan orientation. This new wave of green scholarship has reinterpreted some of the central concepts and discourses in IR and global politics, and challenged traditional understandings of security, development, and international justice with new discourses of **ecological security**, **sustainable development** (and reflexive modernization), and **environmental justice**.

The complex problem of global warming provides an especially illuminating illustration of the diverse ways in which 'real-world' environmental problems are refracted through different theoretical lenses in the discipline of IR. As we shall see, realists typically dismiss the problem as peripheral to the main game of international politics unless the consequences of climate change can be shown to impinge directly on national security. Neoliberals, in contrast, are more likely to offer advice on how to adjust incentive structures in the climate change regime to induce inter-state cooperation. Critical theorists, however, tend to reject such piecemeal, 'problem-solving' approaches that fail to address social and economic structures of domination (as noted in **Chapter 8**). The green voices in the global climate change debate have extended this line of critical inquiry to include neglected areas of environmental domination and marginalization, such as the domination of non-human nature, the neglect of the needs of future generations, and the skewed distribution of ecological risks among different social classes, states, and regions. As we shall see, it is this overriding preoccupation with environmental justice that unites the IPE and normative wings of green IR theory.

After tracking the emergence of green theory in the social sciences and humanities in general, this chapter explores how green theory has itself become more transnational and global, while critical IR theory has become increasingly green. Green IR theory is shown to rest at the intersection of these two developments. The chapter will also point to the different ways in which environmental issues have influenced the evolution of traditional International Relations theory. The diversity of theoretical approaches, including the distinctiveness of green theories, will be further highlighted through the case study of global warming.

The emergence of green theory

Environmental degradation caused by human activity has a long and complex history. However, until the period of European global expansion and the industrial revolution, environmental degradation generally remained uneven and relatively localized. The 'modern ecological crisis' – marked by an exponential increase in the range, scale, and seriousness of environmental problems around the world – is generally understood to have emerged only in the latter half of the twentieth century. Likewise, the 1960s is typically taken to mark the birth of the 'modern' environment movement as a widespread and persistent social movement that has publicized and criticized the environmental 'side-effects' of the long economic boom following the Second World War. Rapid economic growth, the proliferation of new technologies, and rising population in this period generated increasing energy and resource consumption, new sources (and rising levels) of pollution and waste production, and the rapid erosion of the Earth's biodiversity. While some environmental indicators had improved in some countries by the closing decades of the twentieth century, the overall global environmental assessment for the twenty-first century remains bleak. The United Nations Environment Program's Millennium Ecosystem Assessment, completed in March 2005, found that approximately 60 per cent of the ecosystem services that support life on Earth are being degraded or used unsustainably (UNEP 2005).

The 'ecological crisis' is clearly an apt characterization of these developments although the phrase 'ecological predicament' probably best captures the peculiar conundrum facing policy-makers at all levels of governance, namely, that environmental problems remain persistent and ubiquitous even though nobody intended to create them. Unlike military threats, which are deliberate, discrete, specific, and require an immediate response, environmental problems are typically unintended, diffuse, transboundary, operate over long time-scales, implicate a wide range of actors, and require painstaking negotiation and cooperation among a wide range of stakeholders. Indeed, environmental problems are sometimes described by policy analysts as 'wicked problems' because of their complexity, variability, irreducibility, intractability, and incidental character. Most environmental risks have crept up, as it were, on a rapidly modernizing world as the unforeseen side-effects of otherwise acceptable practices. As Ulrich Beck has put it, 'they are "piggy-back products" which are inhaled or ingested with other things. They are *the stowaways of normal consumption*' (Beck 1992: 40).

However, it did not take long for radical voices within the environment movement, and critical voices in the social sciences and humanities, to question not just the side-effects of economic growth but also the phenomenon of economic growth itself and the broader processes of modernization. This debate became highly politicized with the 'limits-to-growth' debate of the early 1970s. Influential publications such as the Club of Rome's *The Limits to Growth* report (Meadows *et al.* 1972) and *The Ecologist* magazine's *Blueprint for Survival* (*Ecologist* 1972), offered dire predictions of impending ecological catastrophe unless exponential economic growth was replaced with 'steady-state' economic development. These debates coincided with the first United Nations Stockholm Conference on the Human Environment (1972), which formalized the emergence of the environment as a 'global issue'.[2]

From environmental issues to green theories

Environmental concerns, like feminist concerns, have left their mark on most branches of the social sciences and humanities. However, it was not until the late 1980s that a distinctly 'green' social and political theory emerged to give voice to the interrelated concerns of the new social movements (environment, peace, anti-nuclear, women's) that have shaped green politics. These movements also spearheaded the formation of a wave of new green parties in the 1980s at the local, national, and regional level (most prominently in Europe), based on the 'four pillars' of green politics: ecological responsibility, social justice, non-violence, and grass-roots democracy. These pillars have provided a common platform for new green party formations around the world, including in Africa, Latin America, and Asia. Indeed, green politics is the only new global political discourse and practice to emerge in opposition to neoliberal globalization.

While the term 'green' is often used to refer simply to environmental concerns, by the early 1990s green political theory had gained recognition as a new political tradition of inquiry that has emerged as an ambitious challenger to the two political traditions that have had the most decisive influence on twentieth-century politics – liberalism and socialism.[3] Like liberalism and socialism, green political theory has a normative branch (concerned with questions of justice, rights, democracy, citizenship, the state, and the environment), and a political economy branch (concerned with understanding the relationship between the state, the economy, and the environment). As we shall see, the international normative and political economy dimensions of this new green tradition are now discernible but they are less sharply etched than their domestic counterpart, largely because they are still in a formative phase of development.

In broad outline, the first wave of green political theory mounted a critique of both Western capitalism and Soviet-style communism, both of which were regarded as essentially two different versions of the same overarching ideology of industrialism, despite their differences concerning the respective roles of the market and the state. The green critique of industrialism formed part of a broader re-examination of taken-for-granted ideas about the idea of progress and the virtues of modernization inherited from the Enlightenment. Both liberalism and orthodox Marxism were shown to have developed on the basis of the same cornucopian premises, which assumed that the Earth's natural resource base could support unbridled economic growth, and that increasing growth and technological advancement were both highly desirable and inevitable. Both political traditions were shown to share the same optimism about the benefits of science and technology, and either explicitly or implicitly accepted the idea that the human manipulation and domination of nature through the further refinement of instrumental reason were necessary for human advancement. Green political theorists have taken issue with these Enlightenment legacies and highlighted the ecological, social, and psychological costs of the modernization process. They have criticized humanity's increasingly instrumental relationship with non-human nature, along with the subjugation of indigenous peoples and many traditional forms of agriculture. Drawing on the kindred disciplines of environmental ethics and environmental philosophy, which emerged in the late 1970s and early 1980s, green political theorists have called into question anthropocentrism or human chauvinism – the idea that humans are the apex of evolution, the centre of value and meaning in the world, and the only beings that possess moral worth. Rejecting such a posture as arrogant, self-serving, and foolhardy, many green theorists have embraced a new ecology-centred or 'ecocentric' philosophy that seeks to respect all life-forms in terms of their own distinctive modes of being, for their own sake, and not merely for their instrumental value to humans. From an ecocentric perspective, environmental governance should be about protecting not only the health and well-being of existing human communities and future generation but also the larger web of life, made up of nested ecological communities at multiple levels of aggregation (such as gene pools, populations, species, ecosystems). This perspective also draws attention to the limits to humanity's knowledge of the natural world, arguing that nature is not only more complex than we know, but possibly more complex than we shall ever know. Major technological interventions in nature are seen as invariably producing major social and ecological costs. Green theorists therefore generally counsel in favour of a more cautious and critical approach to the assessment of new development proposals, new technologies, and practices of risk assessment in general.

Some of these green themes – particularly the critique of the ascendancy of instrumental reason – were central to the first generation of Frankfurt school critical theorists (discussed in Chapter 8), who were the first Western Marxists to problematize the domination of nature and explore its relationship to the domination of humans. Whereas the mature Marx had adopted a Promethean posture towards nature and welcomed scientific and technological progress, the exploration by Theordor Adorno and Max Horkheimer of the 'dialectic of Enlightenment' pointed to the multiple costs to human and non-human nature that accompanied the increasing penetration of instrumental reason into human society and nature (Adorno and Horkheimer 1972). This general theme has been further developed (albeit in less pessimistic terms) by the second generation of Frankfurt school critical theorists, led by Jürgen Habermas. One of Habermas's enduring concerns has been to protect the 'lifeworld' from the march of instrumental rationality by ensuring that such rationality remains subservient to the practice of critical deliberation. Habermas's ideal of communicative rationality has served as a major source of inspiration in the development of green democratic theory and critical green explorations of the relationship between risk, science, technology, and society. Whereas orthodox Marxist theory had confined its critical attention to the relations of production, green theory has expanded this critique to include the 'forces of production' (technology and management systems) and what Ulrich Beck has called 'the relations of definition' that define, assess, distribute, and manage the risks of modernization.

There remains disagreement among green political theorists as to whether green politics should be understood as anti-modern, postmodern, or simply seeking more 'reflexive modernization', although the latter appears to have emerged as the most favoured approach. Indeed, the second wave of green political theory of the mid-1990s and beyond has been less preoccupied with critical philosophical reflection on humanity's posture towards the non-human world and more concerned to explore the conditions that might improve the 'reflexive learning capacity' of citizens, societies, and states in a world of mounting yet unevenly distributed ecological risks. The green critique of industrialism and modernization has not eclipsed the politics of 'left versus right', but it has certainly placed the traditional distributive struggles between labour and capital, and between rich world and poor world, in a broader and more challenging context. Indeed, improving distributive justice while simultaneously curbing ecologically destructive economic growth has emerged as the central political challenge of green theory and practice, both domestically and internationally.

The transnational turn in green theory

In exploring the relationship between environmental justice and environmental democracy, the second wave of green political theory has become more transnational and cosmopolitan in its orientation. The first wave of green political theory sought to highlight the ecological irrationality of core social institutions such as the market and the state and many green political theorists had extolled the virtues of grass-roots democracy and ecologically sustainable communities as alternatives. The second wave of green political theory has been more preoccupied with critically rethinking and, in some cases, 'transnationalizing' the scope of many core political concepts and institutions with environmental problems in mind. This scholarship has produced new, transnational, deterritorialized or global conceptualizations of environmental justice (e.g. Low and Gleeson 1998), environmental rights (e.g. Hayward 2005), environmental democracy (Doherty and de Geus 1996), environmental activism (Wapner 1998), environmental citizenship (Barry 1999; Dobson 2003), and green states (e.g. Eckersley 2004; Barry and Eckersley 2005). There has also been an increasing engagement by green political theorists with some of the core debates within normative IR theory, particularly those concerned with human rights, cosmopolitan democracy, transnational civil society, and transnational public spheres. This scholarship has also fed into, and helped to shape, a distinctly green branch of normative IR theory concerned with global environmental justice.

According to green theory, environmental injustices arise when unaccountable social agents 'externalize' the environmental costs of their decisions and practices to innocent third parties in circumstances when the affected parties (or their representatives) have no knowledge of, or input in, the ecological risk-generating decisions and practices. Environmental injustices also occur when privileged social classes and nations appropriate more than their 'fair share' of the environment, and leave behind oversized 'ecological footprints' (Wackernagel and Rees 1996). The basic quest of green theory is therefore a double one: to reduce ecological risks across the board, and to prevent their unfair externalization and displacement, through space and time, onto innocent third parties.

Ultimately, environment justice demands: (1) recognition of the expanded moral community that is affected by ecological risks (i.e. not just all citizens, but all peoples, future generations, and non-human species); (2) participation and critical deliberation by citizens and representatives of the larger community-at-risk in all environmental decision-making (including policy-making, legislating and treaty-making, administration, monitoring, enforcement, and adjudication); (3) a precautionary approach to ensure the minimization of risks in relation to the larger community; (4) a fair distribution of those risks that are reflectively acceptable via democratic processes that includes the standpoint of all affected parties and public interest advocacy groups; and (5) redress and compensation for those parties who suffer the effects of ecological problems.

Green scholarship on questions of political economy has likewise become more globally focused, although discourses of economy–environment integration have always had a global dimension – even before the emergence of a distinctly green theory that identified with the concerns of the new social movement and green parties. The early 'limits-to-growth' debate had generated calls for radical policy changes to bring about a curbing or even cessation of economic growth (and, in some cases, population growth) to put a break on rising global environmental degradation. However, these calls proved to be both controversial and politically unpalatable. By the late 1980s, the limits-to-growth debate was eclipsed by the more appealing discourse of sustainable development, which had been widely embraced following the publication of *Our Common Future* (the Brundtland Report) by the World Commission on Environment and Development (1987). The Brundtland Report challenged the idea that environmental protection and economic development stand in a simple zero-sum relationship and it pointed to the opportunities for 'decoupling' economic growth and environmental deterioration by pursuing an environmentally friendly or sustainable development path. Sustainable development, according to the Brundtland Committee's pithy and oft-quoted formulation is understood as development that meets the needs of present generations without sacrificing the ability of future generations to meet their own needs. A broad strategy of sustainable development was officially endorsed at the United Nation's Conference on Environment and Development ('the Earth Summit') in Rio de Janiero in 1992 and it continues to serve as the dominant meta-discourse of national and international environmental law and policy, despite the fact that it remains deeply contested.

However, from a green perspective, the Brundtland approach, while it represented an artful political compromise, rested on an instrumental orientation towards the non-human world and ignored the question of biodiversity preservation in focusing only on intra- and intergenerational equity. Even more problematically, the Report optimistically assumed that sustainable development could be achieved by increasing economic growth rates. In defending an alternative conception of *ecologically* sustainable development, green political economists have rejected the dominant framework of neoclassical economics in favour of the new theoretical framework of ecological economics. For ecological economists, while market mechanisms may provide an efficient allocation of resources they can neither ensure a fair distribution of wealth and income relative to present and future human need nor ensure that the scale of the economy operates within the ecological carrying capacity of ecosystems. These matters are beyond the capacity of markets and must be addressed politically, through environmental education, community cooperation, societal contestation and negotiation, state regulation, and international cooperation.

Nonetheless, the general argument that there are synergies between more efficient capitalist development and environmental protection has been reinforced by the more recent, and mostly European-led, discourse of **ecological modernization** (Hajer 1995). Proponents of ecoliberal modernization argue that economic competition and constant technological innovation produce economic growth that uses less energy and resources and produces less waste per unit of gross domestic product (GDP). Far from acting as a break on growth, proponents of ecological modernization maintain that stronger domestic environmental regulation can act as a spur to further environmental/technical innovation, which enhances national economic competitiveness and forces an upward ratcheting of environmental standards. This 'win–win' approach has been warmly embraced, if not systematically implemented, by many governments in the Organization for Economic Cooperation and Development (OECD), particularly in Western Europe, and it coincides with a shift towards the increasing use of market-based instruments in environmental policy.

While limits-to-growth advocates clearly underestimated the synergies between capitalist development and environmental protection, green critics maintain that the discourse of sustainable development, and especially the more technologically oriented discourse of ecological modernization, have overestimated them. Improving the environmental efficiency of production through technological innovation is welcomed but it does not reduce aggregate levels of resource consumption and waste production. Indeed, gains in environmental efficiency typically fuel further consumption and production. Moreover, not all environmental protection measures – such as biodiversity protection – are necessarily conducive to economic growth. In some cases, difficult political trade-offs are necessary. Finally, green critics argue that a strategy of technologically driven ecological modernization provides no means of addressing the deeply skewed distribution of ecological risks among different social classes and nations. In contrast, the Brundtland Report was concerned to promote intra- and intergenerational equity, but it relied on the 'trickledown' effect brought about by increasing growth (with faster growth recommended for the South to enable it to 'catch up' to the North). From a green perspective, these recommendations encapsulate the sustainable development paradox: that environmental protection is best achieved by pursuing more (albeit environmentally efficient) growth, which generates more *aggregate* environmental problems (albeit at a slower rate).

In grappling with this paradox (which also sheds light on why environmental problems are such 'wicked' problems), green political theorists and green political economists have drawn on the new field of environmental sociology, particularly the sub-branch dealing with modernization and the risk society, which provides a direct challenge to neoclassical economics and neoliberal political ideology. For sociologists of the risk society, such as Ulrich Beck (1992), ecological problems persist because they are generated by the very economic, scientific, and political institutions that are called upon to solve them. The paradox of sustainable development therefore cannot be solved simply by the pursuit of more environmentally efficient means to achieve given ends. Rather, it is necessary to pursue 'reflexive modernization', which entails reflecting critically and continuously on the means *and* the ends of modernization. Following Christoff (1996), many green theorists now draw a distinction between 'weak' and 'strong' versions of ecological modernization. The former represents the 'technical fix' interpretation favoured by many OECD governments, and the latter represents the more critical, green approach of reflexive modernization. It is here that green IPE and green normative theory join forces in advocating a more 'ecologically informed' democracy that provides extensive opportunities for citizens to represent long-range, generalizable interests and to challenge the settled practices of risk definition, generation, distribution, and management.

Nonetheless, there remain internal divisions within green circles over whether capitalist economies, states, or the state system are indeed capable of becoming ecologically reflexive to the degree required to avert significant and ongoing environmental degradation. However, all agree that the intensification of economic globalization and the ascendancy of neoliberal discourses at the national and international levels have made the general green case harder to pursue. Nor is the anarchic structure of the state system well suited to resolving transnational and global ecological problems, especially global warming, which is one of the most complex and challenging collective-action problems facing the international community. Of course, IR scholars working in the broad traditions of realism, liberalism, and Marxism have well developed (and diverging) views about the prospects of international environmental cooperation. As we shall see, green IR theory has largely defined itself in opposition to mainstream rationalist approaches to IR (principally neorealism and neoliberalism) while also taking on board green theory's critique of many elements of the Marxist tradition.

The greening of IR theory

Green IR theory shares many of the characteristics of the new IR theories emerging out of the so-called 'third debate' (also sometimes referred to as the 'fourth debate', see Chapter 1): they are generally critical, problem-oriented, interdisciplinary, and above all unapologetic about their explicit normative orientation. In their quest to promote global environmental justice, green IR scholars seek to articulate the concerns of many voices traditionally at the margins of international relations, ranging from environmental non-government organizations, green consumers, ecological scientists, ecological economists, green political parties, indigenous peoples, and, broadly, all those seeking to transform patterns of global trade, aid, and debt to promote more sustainable patterns of development in the North and South.

Green IR theory may be usefully subdivided into an IPE wing, which offers an alternative analysis of global ecological problems to that of regime theory, and a normative or 'green cosmopolitan' wing that articulates new norms of environmental justice and green democracy at all levels of governance. Both of these sub-fields remain indebted to critical theory, particularly the neo-Gramscian-inspired critical political economy of Robert Cox, and the cosmopolitan discourse ethics of Jürgen Habermas, and therefore can be located clearly on the critical/constructivist side of the rationalism versus constructivism debate in IR theory. (This debate is discussed in Chapters 1 and 9.)

Rationalist accounts and green alternatives

The two dominant rationalist approaches in IR theory – neorealism and neoliberalism – have tended to approach environmental problems as a 'new issue area' to be absorbed within their pre-existing theoretical frameworks rather as something that presents a new analytical or normative challenge. Whereas neo- or structural realists have been mostly dismissive of the 'low politics' of the environment, neoliberals have conducted extensive empirical work on regimes dealing with transboundary and global environmental problems. This scholarship has produced a range of insights that help to predict whether or not states are likely to cooperate or defect, along with a range of reforms for improving the effectiveness of environmental regimes. In general, dominant rationalist approaches have not explicitly engaged in normative theorizing, although neoliberals have openly acknowledged their problem-solving and reformist, rather than critical, orientation (Haas, Keohane, and Levy 1993: 7). Their primary research purpose has been to observe, explain, and predict the international behaviour of states.

Both the political economy and normative wings of green IR theory have challenged these dominant rationalist approaches on four levels. First, green critics have directed critical attention to the normative purposes that are served by rationalist approaches by exposing the problematic environmental assumptions and ethical values that are implicit in neorealist and neoliberal analyses. In this respect, green IR theorists take seriously Robert Cox's observation that 'theory is always for someone and for some purpose' (Cox 1981). Neorealism, in particular, is criticized for 'normalizing' rather than challenging the environmentally exploitative practices sponsored by states. From their Hobbesian universe, neorealists maintain that rivalrous state behaviour is inevitable owing to the anarchic structure of the state system, and that it would be foolhardy for states to pursue environmental cooperation that did not confer absolute gains. Of course, neorealist theorists do not personally endorse environmental exploitation but they remain unreflective about the political purposes served by their theories and therefore provide an apology for environmental exploitation and international non-cooperation. As we shall see, green IR theorists have also challenged the restrictive understanding of national security that has dominated realist theories of all persuasions and argued instead for a more comprehensive framework for understanding security that takes human well-being and ecosystem integrity, rather than states, as the fundamental moral and analytical reference point.

In contrast, neoliberals, from their Lockean universe, seek to create international regimes that optimize the 'rational exploitation' of nature, both as a 'tap' (in providing energy and natural resources) and as a 'sink' (via the waste assimilation services of the earth, oceans, and atmosphere) in ways that expand the menu of state development options. However, their rational choice framework implicitly sanctions an instrumental orientation towards the non-human world and leaves little room for understanding or promoting alternative 'green identities' of particular states or non-state actors. Whereas neoliberals implicitly accept capitalist markets and sovereign states as background 'givens' to international regime negotiations, green IR theorists are concerned to expose the ways in which these social structures serve to thwart the development of more effective environmental initiatives. They also seek to give voice to new forms of counter-hegemonic resistance to neoliberal economic globalization. Like all critical theorists, green IR theorists emphasize the role of agents in transforming social structures – in this case, to promote environmental justice and sustainability.

Second, green IR theorists have added their weight to the critique of rationalist approaches pioneered by critical theorists and constructivists, who have exposed the limitations in the analytical frameworks and explanatory power of positivist IR theories. For example, neorealists predict that inter-state environmental cooperation is highly unlikely unless it can be induced or coerced by a hegemonic state, and that such cooperation will always remain vulnerable to shifts in the distribution of power (understood as the distribution of material capability). For neorealists, such as Kenneth Waltz, the 'tragedy of the commons' is generated by the anarchic structure of the state system, which is essentially unchanging. The only changing variable in this system is the distribution of material capabilities among states. Non-state actors and normative discourses are considered peripheral. Green theorists point out that neorealism provides a crude and incomplete account of international environmental politics. Indeed, one of the biggest growth areas in international treaty-making is in the environmental field, yet realists are at a loss to explain why or how this has occurred.

Although neoliberals offer a more plausible account of the evolution of international environmental cooperation, their framework of analysis is unable to provide a satisfactory account of the normative dimension of environmental regimes. Instead, neoliberals typically reduce environmental regimes to the outcome of a set of interest-based bargaining positions held by states, usually unpacked in terms of relative environmental vulnerability, relative capacity to adjust to environmental change, and the relative costs of adjustments. By contrast, green theorists point out that environmental regimes embody moral norms that cannot be reduced to state interests or capacities. Understanding why regimes have emerged to protect endangered species (such as whales or elephants), the atmosphere, the oceans, or wilderness areas (such as Antarctica) requires an examination of not only state interests but also national cultures and values, the role of scientists and transnational environmental advocacy networks, and the persuasive practices of regimes negotiators and other 'norm entrepreneurs'. The deficiencies in rationalist regime theory have prompted some green IR theorists to develop alternative constructivist theoretical foundations for the study of environmental regimes (e.g. Vogler 2003).

More generally, however, green political economy scholarship has defined itself in opposition to rationalist regime theory. Indeed, the state-centric focus of rationalist regime theory is seen to deflect attention away from what is seen to be the primary driver of global ecological degradation and environmental injustices, namely the competitive dynamics of globalizing capitalism rather than the rivalry of states *per se*. A single-minded focus on states or 'countries' is also seen to be misguided because it disaggregates global production and consumption in arbitrary ways and therefore misidentifies where social power, social responsibility, and the capacity to adjust lie. Capitalism operates at a global level in ways that leave highly uneven impacts on different human communities and ecosystems, with some social classes and communities leaving much bigger 'ecological footprints' at the expense of others. Merely punishing those countries that are, say, heavy aggregate polluters ignores the fact that many consumers and financial interests located elsewhere benefit from the pollution without taking any responsibility for the costs. In this respect at least, states are not always the most meaningful units of consumption, and aggregate figures of wealth or pollution in particular states say nothing about the vast disparities of wealth, income, and risks within particular states. Instead of allocating blame and responsibility to particular states, green IPE theorists suggest that we should be monitoring and allocating responsibility to transnational commodity chains, from investment, resource extraction, production through to marketing, advertising, retailing, consumption, and disposal (Conca 2000: 149).[4] Indeed, one of the innovations of green IPE is that it focuses as much on global consumption as global investment and production (e.g. Princen, Maniates, and Conca 2002).

Third, green IR theorists have directed their critical attention to the social agents and social structures that have systematically blocked the negotiation of more ecologically enlightened regimes. These critical analyses have been applied not only to ineffective regimes (chief among which is the Tropical Timber Agreement that is dominated by the timber industry and states involved in the import and export of timber) but also to the relationship between overlapping regimes and to global governance structures in general. One prominent concern of green IR theorists is that international economic regimes, such as the global trading regime, tend to overshadow and undermine many international environmental regimes. This has sparked an ongoing green debate about the desirability and/or possibility of greening the World Trade Organization (WTO) versus setting up counter-institutions, such as a World Environment Organization, to balance the disciplinary power of the WTO.

Finally, green IR theorists have explored the role of non-state forms of 'deterritorialized' governance, ranging from the transnational initiatives of environmental NGOs (such as the Forest Stewardship Council, which has produced an influential certification scheme for forest products produced from sustainably managed forests) to the private governance practices of industrial and financial corporations, including the insurance industry. This new scholarship has produced a more complex and layered picture of global environmental governance that is able to recognize new, hybrid, and/or network patterns of authority that straddle state jurisdictional boundaries or, in some cases, bypass the traditional hierarchical forms of governance typical of nation-states.

In sum, green IR theory has self-consciously sought to transcend the state-centric framework of traditional IR theory and offer new analytical and normative insights into global environmental change. The case study of climate change provides a useful means of illustrating this contribution, from the critique of mainstream IR approaches through to the recommendation of alternative policy prescriptions.

Case study: the challenge of climate change

The problem of human-induced climate change represents one of the most challenging environmental problems confronting humankind. Atmospheric concentrations of greenhouse gases resulting from human activity have increased substantially from around 1750 and exponentially since the end of the Second World War, with the 1990s emerging as the hottest decade in instrumental record (IPCC 2001: 31). Scientists predict that if greenhouse gas emissions continue unchecked, the world will face mass extinctions, water, energy and food scarcity, the loss of reefs through coral bleaching, rising sea levels, coastal and infrastructural damage, and human death and suffering from a growing incidence of 'extreme weather'. While the incidence of climate change risks is expected to vary geographically, lower-income populations in developing countries are expected to suffer the most (IPCC 2001: 9, 13). Climate change will also exacerbate existing inequalities in access to basic necessities such as health care, adequate food, and clean water. The inhabitants of small islands and low-lying coastal areas are particularly at risk from sea-level rise and storm surges.

In response to the alarming predictions of the Intergovernmental Panel on Climate Change's (IPCC) First Assessment Report in 1990, the international community negotiated the United Nations Framework Convention on Climate Change (UNFCCC), which was signed at the Earth Summit at Rio de Janeiro in 1992. The basic objective of the agreement is to achieve a 'stabilization of greenhouse gas concentrations in the atmosphere at a level that would prevent dangerous anthropogenic interference with the climate system' (Article 2). The Framework Convention also established basic principles of equitable burden sharing in Article 3, the most significant of which are that the parties should protect the climate system in accordance with their 'common but differentiated responsibilities'; that developed countries should take the lead in combating climate change; and that full consideration should be given to the specific needs and special circumstances of developing countries, especially those that are particularly vulnerable to the impacts of climate change. No binding targets or timetables were included in the Framework Convention, partly at the insistence of the USA. However, by the first Conference of the Parties held in Berlin in 1995 it was agreed that a legally binding Protocol, containing mandatory emission reduction targets by industrialized countries, should be negotiated as a matter of urgency. This 'Berlin mandate' set in train the negotiations that eventually led to the signing of the Kyoto Protocol at the third Conference of the Parties (COP3) held in Kyoto, Japan, in 1997.

Under the Kyoto Protocol, industrialized countries agreed to reduce their aggregate levels of greenhouse gas emissions below 1990 levels by an average of 5.2 per cent by 2012, although different countries negotiated different targets. However, the 8 per cent target negotiated by the Clinton administration at Kyoto was repudiated in 2001 by the Bush administration, which (along with Australia) has steadfastly refused to ratify the Protocol. Despite the non-cooperation of the world's most powerful state, the Kyoto Protocol became legally binding in 2005 following Russia's ratification in late 2004.

The USA and Australia remain the only two industrialized countries that have declined to ratify the Protocol. Both countries have questioned climate change science and the seriousness of the predicted impacts of global warming, maintained that undertaking emission reductions would harm their economies, and argued that the Protocol is flawed because it does not require major developing countries, such as China, to undertake mandatory emission reductions. This is despite the fact that the negotiators at Kyoto introduced a range of 'flexibility mechanisms' to make it easier for industrialized countries to reach their targets. These include a carbon-trading scheme, carbon 'sinks' (such as the planting of forests to absorb carbon from the atmosphere), joint implementation (joint projects between industrialized countries), and the clean development mechanism (which enables industrialized countries to earn carbon credits by investing in emission reductions schemes in developing countries).

The USA has also sought to circumvent the Kyoto Protocol by concluding an alternative climate change agreement in 2004, known as the Asia–Pacific Partnership on Clean Development and Climate, with Australia, China, India, South Korea, and Japan that operates outside the United Nations framework. The pact does not contain any time-frames, targets, or compliance mechanisms and reflects the USA's preferred approach to tackling climate change, which is to promote voluntary technological development rather than mandatory emission reductions.

Even with the USA's full participation in the Kyoto Protocol, the negotiated aggregate target of around 5 per cent will do very little to stem the problem of global warming, given that atmospheric concentrations of greenhouse gases must be reduced by around 60–80 per cent to protect the Earth's atmosphere. The concerted local, national, and international action required to achieve targets of this magnitude is nothing short of monumental. Nonetheless, the Kyoto Protocol remains the 'only game in town' in the view of the 157 states that have ratified it. Given the enormity of the challenge, we can expect climate change negotiations to be a continuing feature of international politics for some time to come.

Given the scope of the climate change challenge, and the complexity of the issues involved, it is hardly surprising that it has elicited a diversity of theoretical analyses and responses from the discipline of International Relations. However, the contribution of green IR theory is distinctive in two respects. First, it has offered an alternative analysis and explanation of the political problem and of the international negotiating process to that of mainstream rationalist approaches. Second, green IR theories have promoted new normative discourses that have generated alternative policy proposals to those that have dominated the international negotiations thus far.

Alternative green explanations

While the theoretical parsimony of realism served it reasonably well in accounting for relations between the superpowers during the Cold War, it has struggled to make sense of complex international politics, including those associated with the climate change negotiations. The problem for neorealists, in particular, is that they allow no or little room for any diversity of state international responses to climate change, since all states are, to borrow Kenneth Waltz's phrase, 'like-units' and therefore respond in the same way to systemic pressures. However, this understanding cannot explain the significant differences between states, or particular groupings of states, let alone the significant differences between successive governments in the same state, such as between the Clinton and Bush administrations in relation to the Kyoto Protocol. Above all, neorealists cannot explain why 157 industrialized countries have agreed to ratify the Kyoto Protocol, and pursue a second round of negotiations to strengthen emissions reduction targets, despite the USA's defection and without extracting any binding commitments from developing countries.

Neoliberals are able to offer a more plausible account of the outcome to date based on their analyses of relative state interests and capacities. However, in focusing their attention on the hard bargaining among states over the distribution of benefits and burdens of adjustment, neoliberals tend to sideline the larger ideational context that shapes and drives the negotiations. This includes the scientific findings of the IPCC and the shared environmental justice norms embedded in the Framework Convention that provide the *raison d'être* and constant reference point for the negotiation of the more detailed, and legally binding, rules in the Kyoto Protocol. The principle of common but differentiated responsibility embedded in the Convention recognizes asymmetrical obligations based on differing capacities and levels of responsibility among states in the developed and developing world. It acknowledges that industrialized countries are primarily responsible for past emissions and that it is necessary that they 'cut some slack' for developing countries to pursue their legitimate aspirations to improve the quality of life of their peoples. This normative framework is essential to understanding why a majority of states have ratified the Protocol and agreed to a further round of negotiations to pursue further emission reductions. The idea that high-consumption societies should be the first to move away from a carbon-based economy has been central to the environmental justice arguments of green theorists.

Alternative green arguments

While green IR theorists give prominence to the role of justice norms in their analysis, along with the importance of critical discourse in transforming the modernization process (and the self-understanding of social actors), they are by no means starry eyed about progress to date on the climate change negotiations. Like all critical theorists, they are particularly attentive to the relationship between **knowledge and power** and concerned to expose exclusionary discourses and practices. They are also concerned to improve the communicative context of negotiations and expand the range of actors that may participate, and the range of arguments advanced, in regime negotiations. To this end, green Habermasians welcome the proliferation of transnational public spheres as key mechanisms for consensual social learning in response to new problems. More generally, they welcome the growing array of non-state actors who attend, criticize, and/or influence the climate regime negotiations as providing new forms of democratic accountability that transcend the limitations of 'executive multilateralism'. Indeed, some green theorists have suggested that regimes themselves may be regarded as public spheres insofar as they promote critical deliberation (Payne and Samhet 2004).

In addition to exposing distortions in the communicative context of the climate change negotiations, green IR theorists have also offered alterative ways of framing the global warming challenge, along with alternative policy prescriptions that they believe will provide a fairer and more lasting solution to the problem of human-induced global warming. For green theorists, the environmental injustices generated by climate change graphically illustrate the problem of environmental injustice in general. Poor communities (particularly in the South) produce relatively low per capita carbon emissions relative to the affluent, consuming classes in the North yet it is predicted that they will suffer the most from global warming and will be less able to afford insurance to protect them against climate-related damage. The green ideal of environmental justice argues that all individuals, irrespective of nationality or social class, should have an equal right to the energy resources and waste absorption services provided by the natural environment, provided the total use of resources and services remains safely within the ecological carrying capacity of the biosphere. This ideal cannot be realized by market mechanisms alone and it certainly cannot be realized by the USA's preferred strategy of weak ecological modernization, which fails to cap aggregate levels of carbon emissions and ignores the uneven production and distribution of risks associated with global warming. Rather, it requires extensive environmental regulation along with a significant redistribution of environmental allowances from the rich to the poor to ensure the simultaneous satisfaction of basic needs and environmental quality for all. In line with this ideal, the climate policy proposals of most appeal to green scholars, and many developing countries, are those based on the principle of equal per capita rights to the atmosphere. One such model is 'contraction and convergence' developed by the London-based Global Commons Institute, which proposes a major contraction of emissions by the rich countries and an eventual per capita convergence by all countries at a level that the atmosphere can safely absorb. This model provides developing countries with some room to grow, while also facilitating a considerable transfer of resources from the high per capita emitters to the low per capita emitters under carbon-trading schemes. In contrast, the Kyoto model is based on targets that individual industrialized countries are prepared to accept, which is a long way short of what is required to protect the Earth's atmosphere. Moreover, some green critics argue that the 'flexibility instruments' introduced into the Kyoto Protocol, such as carbon trading and tree planting, are simply too flexible to guarantee significant reductions of emissions at source, given the weak aggregate targets. They also enable rich nations to 'buy their way out of the problem' rather than set an example for developing countries to follow.

Conclusion

Green IPE initially formed the backbone of green IR theory. However, it has been increasingly complemented by green normative inquiry, particularly in the wake of the increasing transnationalization of green political theory, which has injected a distinctly green voice into the more general debates about international justice, cosmopolitan democracy, and the future of the state. At the same time, many well known cosmopolitan theorists, such as David Held, Andrew Linklater, Henry Shue, and Thomas Pogge, have turned their attention to the ethical and institutional implications of transboundary environmental harm.

While green political economists and green normative theorists remain united by their condemnation of environmental injustices, green IR theory is not without its internal tensions. First, green political economists are prone to adopt a stronger anti-statist position than green normative theorists, who tend to be more preoccupied with exploring how states and the state system might become more responsive to ecological problems. Whereas green political economists single out the competitive dynamics of global capitalism as the key driver of environmental destruction, green normative theorists argue that states represent the pre-eminent institution with the requisite steering capacity and legitimacy to impose ecological constraints on capitalism (Barry and Eckersley 2005). Democratizing states and the state system is thus a necessary step towards reflexive modernization, which is expected to yield a more ecologically constrained global capitalism.

Second, although most green IR theorists share the cosmopolitan idea that all those affected by decisions or risks should have some sort of say in making them (irrespective of nationality or locality), there remains a significant body of green communitarian theory (which includes bioregionalism, ecoanarchism, and ecofeminism) that emphasizes the virtues of place-based identity and ecologically sustainable local communities. For these theorists, extending an individual's sense of belonging to particular social and ecological communities, and cultivating a place-based identity (which includes an attachment to local flora, fauna, and landscapes), provides a far more potent political motivation to protect non-human species and victims of environmental injustice than does the more abstract idea of global citizenship or cosmopolitan democracy.

A further area of disagreement concerns the wisdom of conceptualizing ecological problems as security problems. Advocates of ecological security maintain that environmental problems – pre-eminent among which is global warming – should be considered a growing source of insecurity. Some environmental security scholars (who do not necessarily identify as green IR scholars) also argue that growing natural resource scarcity (particularly water), environmental degradation, and increasing numbers of ecological refugees are likely to generate increasing conflict and violence both with and between states, and that states should include an ecological dimension in their national security strategies.

However, more sceptical green IR theorists have argued that framing ecological problems as a security issue in order to raise their status to a matter of 'high politics' could backfire. Instead of leading to a broader and more enlightened security agenda that will also 'green' the military, they suggest that the new discourse of ecological security may end up merely playing on traditional security concerns and possibly facilitating militarized solutions to the sustainability challenge. According to the sceptics, led by Daniel Deudney (1990), environmental threats and military threats are of a different order, and they should therefore be addressed differently. Conceptualizing ecological problems as security problems also betrays the core green values of non-violence and anti-militarism and deflects attention away from the important task of promoting ecologically sustainable development. Sceptics have also pointed to the dangers of linking environmental deterioration and scarcity with conflict, arguing that it represents a crude form of environmental determinism (e.g. Barnett 2001). Other green IR theorists have emphasized the potential for shared ecological problems to present peace-making opportunities by providing a basis for conducting collaborative research, stimulating dialogue, building trust, and transcending differences by working towards common environmental goals and strategies (Conca and Dabelko 2003).

However, Deudney's critique is directed against those who argue for the development of national environmental security strategies. It does not address green arguments for a more comprehensive conceptualization of ecological security that seeks to widen the moral referent or unit of analysis of security as well as extend traditional understandings of the sources of insecurity, responses to insecurity, and the conditions for long-term security. Proponents of this more expansive understanding argue that it has the potential to undermine traditional ideas of state territorial defence (along with the logic of the zero-sum game presumed by realists) and promote international cooperation towards long-term sustainability. This broader conceptualization also directs attention to value-complexity in security policy-making, enables a more critical scrutiny of the role of the military as a source of insecurity, and seeks a diversion of military spending to sustainability spending.

The internal debate over environmental security is indicative of green IR theory's strong anti-militarist posture. This may partly explain why green IR theory has yet to develop a considered or clear ethical position on a range of security-related debates, such as the appropriate relationship between order and justice in world politics or the appropriate use of force for humanitarian intervention or environmental protection.

Nonetheless, green IR theory has undergone significant development in the last decade to the point where it is recognized as a significant new stream of IR theory. The new green discourses of environmental justice, sustainable development, reflexive modernization, and ecological security have not only influenced national and international policy debates. Taken together, they have also recast the roles of states, economic actors, and citizens as environmental stewards rather than territorial overlords, with asymmetrical international obligations based on differing capacities and levels of environmental responsibility. This recasting has important implications for the evolution of state sovereignty. If it is accepted that sovereignty is a derivative concept, the practical meaning of which changes over time in response to changes in the constitutive discourses of sovereignty, then to the extent that some of these discourses (on development, justice, and security) take on a greener hue, it is possible to point to 'the greening of sovereignty'. Moreover, to the extent that states – and citizens within states – become increasingly accountable to communities and environments beyond their own borders, then they may be characterized as transnational states and citizens rather than merely nation-states or national citizens. Of course, the society of states is a long way short of this ideal. However, green IR theorists have brought this ideal into view and made it thinkable.

? QUESTIONS

1. What are the core criticisms made by the first wave of green political theory against liberal and socialist theories? Is green political theory modernist or postmodernist?

2. What is the cause of the ecological blindness of traditional IR theories?

3. In what ways has the second wave of green political theory become more transnational?

4. Why are green IR theorists critical of dominant discourses of sustainable development and ecological modernization? What alternatives do they propose?

5. What normative and analytical criticisms have green IR theorists levelled against mainstream rationalist approaches (neorealism and neoliberalism)?

6. What does green IR theory have in common with critical theory and constructivism? How does it differ from them?

7. How would you describe the different preoccupations of green normative IR theory and green IPE? What unites these two strands of green IR theory?

8. In what ways does the green analysis of the climate change negotiations differ from mainstream approaches?

9. Why are green IR theorists internally divided over the wisdom of conceptualizing ecological problems in the language of security?

10. What do you consider to be the major contribution of green IR theory to IR theory in general?

11. Are environmental problems a security threat?

12. What consequences do green theory and ecological concerns have for the concept of sovereignty and the role of the state?

≋ FURTHER READING

■ **Bryant, R. and Bailey, S. (1997),** *Third World Political Ecology* **(London: Routledge).** Provides a systematic examination of green political economy questions from a Third World perspective.

■ **Gale, F. P. and M'Gonigle, R. M. (2000) (eds),** *Nature, Production, Power: Towards an Ecological Political Economy* **(Cheltenham: Edward Elgar).** An edited collection providing a good illustration of recent innovative research in green political economy.

■ **Paterson, M. (2000),** *Understanding Global Environmental Politics: Domination, Accumulation, Resistance* **(London: Palgrave).** Provides an excellent illustration of a neo-Gramscian approach to green political economy.

■ **Princen, T., Maniates, M., and Conca, K. (2002) (eds),** *Confronting Consumption* **(Cambridge MA: MIT Press).** Provides a path-breaking examination of the problem of over-consumption.

■ **Eckersley, R. (2004),** *The Green State: Rethinking Democracy and Sovereignty* **(Cambridge MA: MIT Press).** Develops a theory of the green state (and state system) from a critical constructivist perspective.

■ **LaFerrière, E. and Stoett, P. J. (1999),** *International Relations Theory and Ecological Thought: Towards a Synthesis* **(London: Routledge).** The first book to explore the intersection of IR theory and green political thought.

■ **Paehlke, R. C. (2003),** *Democracy's Dilemma: Environment, Social Equity and the Global Economy* **(Cambridge MA: MIT Press).** Examines the democratic challenge of achieving sustainability while improving social equity.

■ **Käkönen, J. (1994) (ed.),** *Green Security or Militarised Environment* **(Aldershot: Dartmouth).** An edited collection providing a good overview of the ecological security debate.

IMPORTANT WEBSITES

● Environmental Change and Security project. Part of the Woodrow Wilson International Center for Scholars, this site focuses on the relationship between peace, conflict, and environmental change.
www.wilsoncenter.org/index.cfm?topic_id=1413&fuseaction=topics.home

● Global Commons Institute. An independent London-based institute, directed by Aubrey Meyer, devoted to 'shrinking and sharing' future global greenhouse gas emissions.
www.gci.org.uk

● Third World Network. An independent non-profit international network of organizations and individuals involved in issues relating to development, the Third World and North–South issues, with a comprehensive environment link.
www.twnside.org.sg

 Visit the Online Resource Centre that accompanies this book for lots of interesting additional material. www.oxfordtextbooks.co.uk/orc/dunne/

14 International Relations Theory and Globalization

COLIN HAY

✔ **Reader's guide**

This chapter seeks to establish what is at stake in the globalization debate(s) for contemporary International Relations theory. There is no field (or sub-field) of social and political analysis that has more at stake than International Relations theory in adjudicating claims as to the extent to which we have witnessed, are in the process of witnessing, or have yet to witness, an epochal transition to globalization. Quite simply, the very term international relations is anachronistic if some variants of the globalization thesis are accurate. This chapter reviews both the existing debate on the extent and nature of globalization itself – What is it? Is it occurring? What are its consequences? How evenly distributed are they? What are its drivers? – and the stakes of these debates for a range of core theoretical perspectives in International Relations. It shows how the literature on globalization has developed over time, revealing how the nature of the debate has changed, and it illustrates this both theoretically and empirically by developing a case study of the impact of globalization on the development of the welfare state.

Introduction

It is difficult to conceive of a topic more controversial or one that has given rise to a greater proliferation of literature in recent years than the nature, extent, and consequences of globalization. Nor is it easy to think of a field of scholarly inquiry that has more invested in such controversies and that literature than International Relations theory. For, quite simply, whether the political landscape can meaningfully be said to comprise national units that one might credibly describe as engaged in inter-national relations (literally, 'relations *between* nations') is at issue. If globalization, as for many, characterizes the contemporary period and if, as again for many, the extent of globalization is the degree to which the national recedes in significance, then globalization may already have ushered in an age of *post*-international relations (Rosenau 1990; Youngs 1999).

That, of course, is an immensely controversial claim. It is, moreover, not one that I will defend in this chapter. And, as we shall see, it is one that is challenged both by those who question the degree to which the contemporary landscape of world politics has, indeed, been globalized and by those who argue that it has, but who see globalization and international relations as far less mutually exclusive. As this perhaps already serves to indicate, the stakes of 'the globalization debate', for International Relations theory in particular, could scarcely be higher. Yet, as it also serves to indicate, in entering this debate we embroil ourselves in both a semantic minefield – in which terms like globalization do not always mean quite what we might assume them to mean – and an area of considerable empirical dispute – in which it seems almost no evidential claim remains uncontested.

That provides some important contextualization for what is to follow. My aim in this chapter is to guide the reader through this battle-ground of evidential claim and counter-claim, conceptualization and reconceptualization, definition and redefinition. In so doing I hope to establish what is at stake for International Relations in the globalization debate and also to show how the debate itself has come at times to be distorted by the extraordinarily high stakes for the chosen theoretical perspectives of its principal protagonists. The chapter proceeds in four core sections. In the first of these I consider in a little more detail the extent to which globalization itself might be seen to pose a challenge to the defining assumptions of International Relations theory, calling into question the very identify of International Relations as a field of scholarly inquiry. In the second I seek to unpack the semantics of the globalization debate. I show how both the extent to which we can credibly describe contemporary trends in terms of globalization and the implications of so doing depend crucially on what globalization is taken to imply. Define globalization inclusively and, while there is plenty of evidence of globalization, its identification is of no great consequence. Conversely, set the definitional threshold higher and the significance of identifying globalization trends or tendencies is all the greater, but the evidence to substantiate such a description all the more difficult to find. Having dealt with the semantics of globalization in the second section, we turn to the empirics of globalization in the third. This section deals separately with the extent and character of the process of economic globalization on the one hand, and its implications on the other. Here I advance a sceptical position showing that, with respect to economic globalization at least, it is only if we adopt the least exacting of definitional standards that the term globalization is easily reconciled with the available empirical evidence. Indeed, the more we examine the empirical evidence, the less globalization appears a self-evident empirical fact and the less it seems to constrain domestic policy-making autonomy. This latter point is illustrated in the fourth section in which I develop a case study of the future of the welfare state in the advanced liberal democracies in an era of globalization.

What's at stake in the globalization debate?

It may seem somewhat odd to seek to establish what is at stake for International Relations theory in the globalization debate before considering what the term globalization might be taken to imply. The reasons for this are, however, simply stated. They are principally two-fold. First, as we shall see presently, there is no commonly accepted conception, far less definition, of globalization in the existing literature. Indeed, as much as anything, the debate about globalization is a debate about what we understand by the term. As a consequence we cannot turn to the definition of globalization to provide a simple point of access to the debate, for the question of definition is a far from innocent one theoretically. As this perhaps already suggests, we need to understand the nature of the debate before we can see what is at stake in defining globalization. Second, the debate about globalization within International Relations theory is, in fact, merely the latest incarnation of a longer running dispute between state-centric and non-state-centric theorists. It is important, then, that we understand the character of that evolving debate before we consider the language of globalization within which it is conducted today.

Perhaps more so than for any other field (or sub-field) of social and political analysis, International Relations theory's globalization debate is a negative rather than a positive one. That this is so is not difficult to explain. For arguably it is realism and neo- or structural realism (see Chapters 3 and 4), for so long the dominant perspectives in International Relations theory and the perspectives around which contemporary International Relations theory has arguably been built, that have most invested in the globalization debate – and most to lose. It is perhaps unremarkable, given this, that it is realists and neorealists who have tended to be most persistently dismissive of globalization's extent, its qualitative novelty, and its system redefining qualities – indeed, invariably all three. And it is not difficult to see why realists might have something of a natural disposition to scepticism when it comes to globalization. For, as is described in rather greater detail in Chapter 4, the neorealist worldview is one that sees international politics through the eyes of the self-interested, self-contained, and above all sovereign state-as-actor. Realism, in other words, is predicated on a state-centric ontology. It is this state, according to realists, that is the dominant and, in many accounts, the only significant actor on the international stage. Yet, according to the globalization thesis, the days of the nation-state are over.

This already tells us much about the character of the globalization debate in International Relations theory – and it also serves to explain, in part, the rather traditional theoretical focus of this chapter. It might seem odd that a chapter on a topic as both controversial and contemporary as globalization should focus so much attention on the seemingly almost timeless debate between neorealists and their critics. Yet, a little further reflection reveals that this is not quite as odd as it might first appear. For International Relations theory's globalization debate is, in effect, an ontological dispute – between state-centrism and non-state centrism. As a consequence much – arguably too much – of its content is about the continuing relevance or the contemporary irrelevance (depending on one's worldview) of realism and neorealism as theoretical perspectives. But this is not to suggest that other theoretical perspectives – notably feminism (**Chapter 10**), constructivism (**Chapter 9**), critical theory (**Chapter 8**), poststructuralism (**Chapter 11**), and green theory (**Chapter 13**) – do not have a stake in the globalization debate or, indeed, much to contribute to our understanding of globalization itself. The key point, however, is that none of these alternative perspectives is predicated on ontological assumptions about the centrality or non-centrality of the state in International Relations. As such they have rather less invested in the globalization debate than neorealism, neoliberalism, and, indeed, **cosmopolitanism**. Each offers an analytical/theoretical perspective which can be brought to bear on the world system independently of its degree of globalization; each has relevance and critical purchase in both a state-centric and a non-state-centric world alike; and each perspective contains, among its advocates, globalists and sceptics.

The stakes are, by contrast, significantly higher for neorealists, neoliberals, and cosmopolitans. For each, the degree of globalization is an index of the degree of relevance/irrelevance of their theoretical perspective. For neoliberals and cosmopolitans, globalization challenges practically all of realism's most cherished analytical assumptions. Their critique of realism's continued relevance can be summarized in a series of core claims:

1. The **sovereignty** and policy-making capacity of the nation-state, on which realism is predicated, are both compromised to a very significant extent (if in slightly different ways) by the proliferation of cross-border flows beyond the purview and control of the state.

2. Globalization is associated with (or arises out of) a proliferation of issues that are global in scope and scale (such as climate change and the threat of global pandemics); these, arguably, nation-states never had the capacity to deal with.

3. In response to such challenges, and whether at the behest of nation-states or not, a range of genuinely trans-national institutions of global governance has developed which have changed fundamentally the character of world politics – taking us, as it were, beyond the era of the nation-state.

4. This new multi-layered and multi-level political landscape is populated by a rather more disparate range of potentially consequential actors and, while this may include some (though by no means all) nation-states, the nation-state is no longer the principal, far less the sole significant, actor in world politics.

5. The emergent trans-national arena of political deliberation associated with globalization has served to increase the relative salience of matters of 'low politics' while relegating those of 'high politics' with which realism was principally concerned.

6. The process of economic globalization, in increasing the mobility of capital and hence its capacity to flit from national jurisdiction to national jurisdiction, has enhanced the

power of capital relative to the state, with the effect that whole areas of domestic policy-making have essentially been depoliticized.

7. Taken together, these globalization-engendered challenges to realist assumptions constitute not only a refutation of realism as a theoretical doctrine but the passing of the era of the nation-state with which it was inextricably linked.

Unremarkably, each of these claims has given rise to considerable debate and controversy – not all of which has been confined to International Relations theory. It is first important, however, that we differentiate between sovereignty and policy-making capacity at the domestic level (see also Hay 2007a). For, as indicated in the very first point, though frequently conflated they are in fact significantly if nonetheless subtly different. Arguably it is the former that is of greatest importance to realism and neorealism. Sovereignty refers to the capacity or characteristic (of nation-states) to be independent of external influence in the management of their internal affairs, where the distinction between internal and external is in turn delimited by the territorial boundaries of a state's claim to (sovereign) authority (see also Krasner 1999). As Anthony McGrew usefully puts it, sovereignty can be said to exist when, 'within its borders the state or government has an entitlement to supreme, unqualified, and exclusive political and legal authority' (2005: 29). The key point is that sovereignty is no guarantee of policy-making capacity, just as policy-making capacity is no guarantee of sovereignty. Indeed, it is a core contention of the neoliberal literature that rational states may benefit from pooling (in effect, sacrificing) elements of their sovereignty in the design and development of institutions of trans-national governance. Their motive in so doing is precisely to enhance their ability to manage issues that they lack the policy-making capacity to deal with domestically. As this suggests, the politics of globalization is bound up with the complex trade-off between sovereignty and policy-making capacity. We simply cannot afford to conflate the two.

The above discussion pits realism and neorealism squarely against globalization and the proponents of theories of globalization. And, indeed, for the most part that is precisely how the debate has developed, with realists/neorealists and their critics exchanging blows from either side of a rather deep theoretical chasm over the extent and implications of globalization. Yet this is by no means unproblematic as we shall see, and it has led to a fair amount of confusion and conflation that has certainly not helped to sharpen our analytical purchase on either the empirical or theoretical issues involved here.

Let me explain. The point is that there has been something of a tendency in International Relations theory to reduce the debate about globalization to a debate about the relevance of the realist/neorealist worldview (or ontology). That is unfortunate, for it has given rise to a further tendency to conflate a series of empirical, analytical, and theoretical claims that might usefully be separated and assessed independently of one another. In effect, a series of empirical issues about the extent of globalization and a series of analytical questions about the implications of globalization for the nature of the world system have been used to provide a theoretical test of realism's relevance and the validity of the ontological assumptions (about the nature of the state and its centrality) on which it is predicated. This has resulted in an at times confusing debate which does justice neither to the analytical strengths and weaknesses of realism/neorealism nor to the complex empirical issues involved in adjudicating the extent of globalization and its implications for the character of world politics. Realists, it seems, feel almost duty bound to deny the significance of globalization, just as their critics feel obliged to embrace it, seizing upon theories of globalization as if they provided an empirical refutation of realism. In fact, as we shall see presently, neither reaction respects the complexity and indeterminacy of the world system today. Realism/neorealism, (neo)liberal intergovernmentalism, and cosmopolitanism are perhaps best seen as lenses through which contemporary trends might be interpreted. Each is selective in what it considers and what it excludes from view. But the point is that world politics today is sufficiently multi-layered and multi-faceted for each to bring interesting and important issues into focus. It is wrong, then, to think that the world system can deliver a knock-down blow to the analytical assumptions on which any of these contending theories are predicated. As Richard Ned Lebow points out in his introduction to Chapter 3 on classical realism, 'neorealism is unfalsifiable, and its rise and fall has had little to do with conceptual and empirical advances'. Nor, it might be added, has it much more to do with the changing character of the world system. Moreover, even were we to conclude that the empirical evidence of globalization's extent and impact was sufficient to invalidate the realist paradigm, we would be quite wrong to infer from this that realism was never valid theoretically, nor that any of its contemporary challengers are thereby vindicated. By the same token, were we to conclude that realist assumptions had by no means been rendered anachronistic by the process of globalization to date, we would be just as wrong to infer from this that realism is the most appropriate way to analyse such trends. Empirical evidence cannot adjudicate ontological differences and theoretical choices of this kind, though it is all too often assumed that it can (see also Hay 2002).

If much of International Relations theory's globalization debate has pitted realist/neorealist 'sceptics' against neoliberal/cosmopolitan 'globalists' in the manner described above, then it is important to note that there are exceptions. Particularly interesting in this respect is an extremely respectful and temperate exchange between Barry Buzan (defending a particular conception of neorealism) and David Held (the key proponent of cosmopolitanism), published in the *Review of International Studies* almost a decade ago (Buzan, Held, and McGrew 1998). Buzan's position is especially interesting here. For, unlike many realists, he concedes much to the globalists while nonetheless resolutely defending the continued relevance of realism – at least in certain policy domains. The core elements of this qualified defence of realism/neorealism are summarized in Table 14.1.

What is particularly interesting is that Buzan accepts almost all of the points seen by globalists as posing fundamental challenges for realism. He concedes that trans-national flows compromise the ease with which one might speak of nation-states as sovereign; he concedes the growing salience of trans-national processes of governance while emphasizing the role of states in the promotion of such developments; he concedes the importance – indeed, the growing importance – of non-state actors on the international stage; and he concedes the higher salience of low politics relative to high politics, especially in those more interdependent parts of the world system. Moreover, though more implicit than explicit, his remarks would also seem compatible with the idea that world politics today is characterized by a proliferation of issues with which the nation-state never had the capacity to deal effectively and that the constraints imposed by economic globalization have greatly diminished the capacity for domestic policy-making autonomy. Yet, despite all this, he manages to defend an (albeit qualified) form of realism. This he does, not by

Table 14.1 Buzan's qualified defence of realism in a context of globalization

1. The position Buzan seeks to defend	'the state is . . . the key political unit in the international system' (387); 'as long as the international system is divided into states the relations between states will have the characteristic of being about power politics' (388).
2. The concessions to the globalists	'in relation to the emergence of a world economy, and to some extent the development of a world society, and even in terms of transportation and communication systems, it is clearly naive now to think of a world made up of sovereign states which 'contain' everything' (390); 'where states have become very open and interdependent, then some of the realist theorising about the balance of power (and all that) is clearly less relevant . . . thinking about states in terms of traditional power politics is unhelpful' (390); 'states . . . get together sometimes with other actors, sometimes just with other states, to discuss issues of joint concern and sometimes they can hammer out a set of policies, a set of rules of the game, which enable them to coordinate their behaviour' (392).
3. The qualification of the concessions	'there are plenty of parts of the world in which the realist rules of the game still apply . . . the world is really divided into two or three spheres in which the rules of the game are quite different because the level of globalisation is very differently distributed' (390); 'in most areas of world politics . . . states are still the principal authorities' (391); 'globalisation is primarily an economic phenomenon. It is also in part a logistical phenomenon to do with transportation and communication and the ability to move goods, peoples, ideas, etc. around the world much faster and much more easily than before' (394); 'it is not clear what the alternative political structure to the state is, or how indeed we would make the transition from the current order to another' (394).

Note: All references are from Buzan, Held, and McGrew (1998)

challenging the globalization thesis itself, but effectively by departmentalizing it. In so doing he makes four core claims:

1. In essence, globalization is an economic phenomenon whose implications as such are largely confined to certain (low political) domains – domains that realism was never especially concerned with.

2. Although the salience of such domains has undoubtedly increased, a significant proportion of international politics retains its realist character.

3. Often independently of the process of economic globalization, states have increasingly, but only under certain highly specific conditions, effectively pooled their sovereignty in developing mechanisms of trans-national governance (whether regional or global) that reflect their mutual self-interest.

4. Both economic globalization and the involvement of states in such mechanisms of trans-national governance are extremely unevenly distributed, with the effect that the lion's share of the content of international politics remains essentially statist and hence realist in character in spite of globalization.

This is a neat and self-contained position which, while ceding certain terrain to cosmopolitans like Held (2002, 2003) and neoliberals like Joseph Nye and Robert O. Keohane (see, for instance, Keohane and Nye 1977; Nye and Donahue 2000), suggests the core contribution that realism can make to International Relations theory even in a context of presumed globalization. Moreover, it indicates the potentially highly fruitful character of the interparadigm debate that globalization is capable of generating within International Relations theory – at least, once the attempt to use globalization to adjudicate between paradigms is put to one side. Yet there is still one problem with the position Buzan seeks to defend. For, however credible it may seem, and however creditable his concessions to the globalists are, they rest on a series of assumptions about economic globalization in particular that are of an empirical kind – assumptions which are simply not tested empirically. Ironically, Buzan may go too far in his concessions to the globalists. For, as we shall see in the third section of this chapter, for many so-called 'sceptics' evidence of the kind of economic globalization he seems to presume here is rather less forthcoming than one might think. Yet, before considering such evidence directly, and having established the high stakes for International Relations theory of the globalization debate, it is first important that we establish quite what we mean by the term globalization anyway. It is to this potential conceptual minefield that we now turn.

The semantics of globalization

Thus far we have assumed that all protagonists in the globalization debate know exactly what they are talking about when they refer to the term 'globalization'. Moreover, we have assumed that, basically, they are all talking about the same thing. As will become clear presently, this is dangerously presumptuous on both counts. To be fair to them, they may in fact know precisely what they are referring to when they refer to the term globalization, but if that is the case they are seemingly exceedingly reluctant to share that with the reader. As a consequence protagonists in the same globalization debate repeatedly talk past one another, simply because they are talking about different things. This is not helped by the great many things that have been referred to in terms of globalization. As David Held and his co-authors suggest, globalization is 'the cliché of our times: the big idea which encompasses everything from global financial markets to the Internet but which delivers little substantive insight into the contemporary human condition' (Held *et al.* 1999: 1). And, recall, Held is an unapologetic if sophisticated globalist who in fact goes on to provide a rather exacting and extremely useful definition of globalization to which we will return in due course.

The simple point is that globalization has come to mean a variety of rather different things to a range of different authors. Moreover, given the vast array of processes and practices to

Table 14.2. Potential indices of globalization

1. Cross-border flows of goods, investment, and information
2. Trans-national processes of political deliberation and decision-making
3. Inter-dependence between states
4. The development of a world system whose dynamic and developmental trajectory is not reducible to the simple product of the units (states) which comprise it
5. The proliferation of problems to which global solutions are required
6. The development of institutions charged with responsibility for fashioning genuinely global public policy

which it is often (legitimately) used to refer even by the same author, it is perhaps hardly surprising that it has come so often to prove a source of confusion rather than clarity.

This can be seen even in the relatively brief exchange between Barry Buzan and David Held discussed above. For, in the space of a few pages, a great variety of rather different things is referred to in terms of globalization. (See Table 14.2).

There is, of course, nothing wrong with referring to any of these processes in terms of globalization. Yet it is actually very difficult to think of some common property of factor that they all share by virtue of which we might label them instances of the same thing (globalization). Moreover, with respect to each and every item in the list there are choices involved; choices which need to be defended if the term globalization is not to obscure more than it reveals.

Take the first, for instance. Globalization is commonly associated with a variety of cross-border flows – typically flows of goods, investment, and information, but also holiday-makers, migrant workers, asylum seekers, environmental pollutants, infectious agents, and so forth. But the existence of such flows, and in some cases even the magnitude of such flows, is by no means unprecedented historically. So what is it precisely about the magnitude or scope of such flows that might lead us to identify the contemporary period as one characterized by globalization where that which preceded it was not? Oddly, this is a question which is very rarely posed. Each of these flows may be more or less global in character – and, presumably, we would want to know that such flows were really quite global in character before we would be happy referring to them as instances of globalization. But quite how global do they have to be? And what does global mean here anyway?

Consider the flow of infectious agents. These are, of course, not exactly diligent observers of national borders and so the cross-border transmission of infection is clearly as old as the existence of nominal borders that infectious agents might cross. Yet at what point might we legitimately start talking about the possibility of their globalization? When a farmer in Alsace sneezes and their neighbour in Germany catches a cold, is this globalization? When the Crusaders took their Western European viruses and bacteria to the Holy Lands, was this an early form of globalization? When the crew of Christopher Columbus passed their pathogens to the people of North America, was this globalization? Or is globalization a term we should reserve to describe the (contemporary) era of mass public transportation across continents and the prospect of the proliferation of global pandemics that this threatens?

There are, of course, no 'correct' answers to questions like these; but there are choices which can be defended – and which *should* be defended if the concept of globalization is to increase our analytical purchase on such matters. In particular, we need to ask ourselves whether all cross-border flows, for instance, are by definition instances of globalization, or whether such flows need to be trans-regional, trans-continental, or, indeed, genuinely global before they count as evidence of globalization. Similarly, we need to ask ourselves whether the question of globalization merely relates to the geographical character (the 'extensivity' in Held *et al.*'s (1999) useful terms) of such flows, or whether it also relates to their prevalence (or 'intensivity'). In other words, should the identification of processes of globalization just be about identifying *some* flows that are global in their geographical character or should it also be about identifying an increasing propensity for flows to be of that kind?

The point is that whether globalization is happening or not depends on what globalization is taken to imply – and there are fairly substantial differences among International Relations theorists on this point. Unremarkably, sceptics tend to adopt more exacting definitional standards than their globalist counterparts, taking some delight in pointing to the disparity between the real evidence (such as it is) and the rigours of such an exacting definitional standard. Globalists by contrast set for themselves a rather less discriminating definitional hurdle, with the effect that they interpret the very same evidence that often leads sceptics to challenge the globalization thesis as seemingly unambiguous evidence *for* the thesis. What makes this all the more confusing is something that I have already referred to – the seeming reluctance of authors on either side of the exchange to define clearly and concisely their terminology.

Yet, though frustrating, this is hardly surprising. For, as in Table 14.2, a great variety of rather different things is referred to, often by the same author, in terms of globalization – and, as already noted, it is often extremely difficult to put one's finger on a single factor in respect of which each might be labelled an instance of globalization. As this suggests, we might well excuse the absence of a simple definition of globalization on the grounds that the phenomena to which it refers are multi-faceted and complex. Yet our generosity cannot extend to absolving International Relations theorists of their responsibility to be clear about how and why they are using the term. If globalization is multi-dimensional, then authors who deploy the term need to be able to specify the dimensions of globalization to which they are referring.

Pointing to potential *dimensions* of globalization may help us out here. No less helpful is one further factor – that like so many contested terms in the social sciences, globalization is perhaps better understood in negative rather than positive terms. In other words, we can learn quite a lot about what globalization *is*, by considering what it is not. In fact a review of the literature on globalization rapidly reveals a number of globalization's 'others' – terms presented alongside globalization but starkly counterposed to it. Among such oppositional pairings the following are perhaps the most obvious:

1. National versus global. Referring to the level at which the centre of gravity of the world system might be seen to lie and the primary character of the cultures, economies and polities within that system.

2. International versus global. Referring to the character of supra-national decision-making processes and, specifically, to the extent to which these might be seen as trans rather than merely inter-national in form.

3. Regionalization versus globalization. Referring to the precise geographical scope and character of any particular process of integration.

4. Protectionism/isolationism versus globalization/internationalism. Referring to the internal or external orientation of domestic level policy-making.

This is immediately instructive, revealing a range of rather different senses of globalization or, better perhaps, a range of *dimensions* of the term. Each is worthy of a brief commentary.

In the first of these conceptual pairings, globalization is counterposed and contrasted to the nation and the state (indeed, to the nation-state). This distinction and contrast clearly lies at the heart of International Relations theory's globalization debate. Sceptics, typically realists and neorealists, continue to privilege the national level, conceptualizing world politics in terms of the interaction of distinct and nationally embedded political cultures. Globalists, by contrast, point to the transcendence of the national and its dissolution in a proliferation of cross-border flows. This, they suggest, generates a new global arena of political struggle and contestation that is, literally, *supra*-national – above the level of the national.

The second conceptual opposition follows almost logically from the first. Yet the emphasis here is subtly different, the focus falling less on the constituent units of the world system than on the character of supra-national decision-making that follows. Here the global is counterposed to the international, globalization to internationalization. This opposition is equally central to the globalization debate in contemporary International Relations theory. Realist and neorealist sceptics continue to view world politics in state-centric and inter-national terms, denying in so doing the existence of a distinct realm of trans-national political deliberation that is not a simple aggregation of state-level preferences. By contrast, globalists, typically neoliberals and cosmopolitans, point to the increasing salience of trans-national institutions of governance and to the existence of a distinct political process and dynamic at this level that is not reducible to the preferences of states.

The third conceptual opposition is rather different and takes us into issues that we have yet to discuss in any detail. It refers less to the character of the politics of the world system itself, than to how we might most accurately describe those cross-border flows we witness. In short, it takes us from largely conceptual/ontological issues to largely empirical matters. Here, as we shall see in more detail in the next section, trade economists and a range of critical international political economists challenge the extent to which the term globalization captures well contemporary trends in economic integration. They suggest that it is important that we differentiate very clearly between regionalization and globalization and that, if we do so, we see rather clearer evidence of the former than the latter. This dispute is more empirical than theoretical and it is one to which we return in the next section.

Finally, globalization is also counterposed to protectionism and isolationism in the rather more specialist literature characterizing the orientations of domestic policy-makers and the choices they make. Policy-makers may embrace globalization by, for instance, promoting a global regime of free trade and free capital mobility both domestically and on an international stage; or they may resist globalization, shoring up their national defences against trade penetration and other trans-border economic flows through a series of protective tariffs and other restrictions.

As the above discussion serves to indicate, globalization is indeed a multi-dimensional concept in that there is a variety of rather different senses of the term to which authors appeal, often in the same breath. Yet, while this might seem to lessen the importance somewhat of specifying precisely a definition of globalization, it does not diminish the significance of the question 'How global does it have to be to count as evidence of globalization?' – indeed, it merely projects this question into a number of different dimensions. But sadly this is a question that is very rarely posed and on which it is difficult to find any consensus. Yet, if it is expecting too much of the existing literature to provide an answer to this question, we can at least be clear about how the term globalization will be employed in what follows. The definition I prefer is a relatively specific and exacting one; it is one that can be operationalized empirically (as we shall see presently) and it is one that differentiates very clearly between processes of regionalization and processes of globalization. All these requirements are satisfied by the definition advanced by David Held and his colleagues. For them, 'globalisation is a process (or set of processes) that embodies a transformation in the spatial organisation of social relations and transactions, generating trans-continental or inter-regional flows and networks of activity, interaction and power' (1999: 16).

The empirics of globalization: its extent and consequences

What counts as evidence of globalization is, as I have suggested, a semantic issue. Yet whether or not globalization is occurring and what, if any, consequences it has remain, in essence, empirical matters. It is appropriate, then, that having discussed the semantics of globalization in the previous section we now turn, albeit more briefly, to the empirics of globalization.

There is a vast and at times quite technical literature here which we cannot hope to survey in any depth in the space of a few pages (for far more detailed reviews, see Hay 2005, 2007b). And, what is more, it is a literature in which almost every claim is a contested one – at least in the sense that almost every empirical claim made is either a refutation or an attempted refutation of a claim made somewhere else in the literature. There is, nonetheless, a distinct pattern to the empirical evidence and to the debate that it has generated. In particular, as the debate has become more and more empirical in character – as, in effect, we have acquired greater and greater knowledge of the extent and consequences of globalization – so the balance of opinion has become more and more sceptical of the often hyperbolic character of the early globalist literature. Globalization, it seems, is less self-evidently a fact, rather more unevenly developed, and potentially rather less consequential for domestic policy-making autonomy than was once assumed. This is certainly not to suggest that the world has not changed; but it is to suggest that the period of restructuring of the international system since the 1960s that we invariably label globalization is rather less unprecedented historically, rather less well described in terms of globalization, and rather less corrosive of state autonomy than many had tended to assume.

What follows, then, is an unmistakably sceptical view of globalization – yet one which is, as I hope to show, well substantiated empirically. I suggest that there is a significant and, indeed, a growing disparity between the simple presumption of globalization in much of the existing literature and the nature and trajectory of developments in the world system. The literature on which I draw in seeking to defend that claim is primarily economic in focus, and the contents of this section reflect that focus. The reasons for this privileging of the economic in the existing literature and in this section are relatively simple. They are principally four-fold. First, it is far more difficult to gauge empirically the extent of political globalization than the extent of economic globalization. Economic flows, unlike their political equivalents, are recorded and quantified and their significance relatively easy to gauge. Political flows, by contrast, can really be assessed only qualitatively. Second, if we are interested in the extent to which the policy-making autonomy and capacity of the state have been eroded then it is vital that we consider the extent and consequences of economic globalization – since this is invariably seen as the most significant constraint on such autonomy. Third, many accounts depict globalization as, if not a purely economic

Table 14.3. The empirical case against the globalization thesis

The extent of globalization	The consequences of globalization
1. The integration of the world economy since the 1960s has yet to reach unprecedented levels, returning the international system to levels of economic integration last seen in the period between 1870 and 1914.	1. In contrast to the expectations of globalists, the relationship between public spending and globalization (economic openness) continues to be positive rather than negative; that positive correlation has, if anything, strengthened since the 1960s and 1970s.
2. Globalization is a poor description of the current phase of international economic integration, which is more accurately characterized as one of regionalization and so-called 'triadization'.	2. In contrast to the expectations of globalists, there is no inverse relationship between levels of inward foreign investment and a variety of indices of public spending taxation, and labour-market, environmental, and other standards.
3. The current phase of financial integration has yet to produce either the convergence in interest rates across the globe or the divergence in rates of domestic savings and domestic investment anticipated in a fully integrated global capital market.	3. While the liberalization of financial markets has increased the potential impact of speculative attacks on currencies, capital market participants are far less prone to penalize high levels of public spending and market-regulating interventions by the state than is conventionally assumed.

phenomenon, then at least a principally economic phenomenon. It is, then, more plausible to extrapolate from the economic sphere than it is to extrapolate from any other. Fourth, and relatedly, if it can be shown that claims about economic globalization are exaggerated, considerable damage is done to the globalization thesis since it is the economic sphere which is invariably presented as the most globalized of all social realms.

The empirical evidence assembled in the recent literature deals really with two different, if closely related issues – the extent and geographical character of the process of economic globalization (if we can call it that) on the one hand, and the consequences of economic globalization (or, as much of this literature would prefer, 'complex economic interdependence') for the policy-making autonomy of the state domestically on the other. In the pages that follow we will review each in turn. The findings of this literature are summarized in Table 14.3.

The extent of globalization

As indicated in Table 14.3, the empirical case against the standard depiction of the process of economic globalization comes in three parts. Perhaps the best known aspect of the sceptics' case is their observation that current levels of global economic integration, though far greater than at any point during the postwar period, are by no means unprecedented historically. In fact, as they show both for levels of trade and capital flows, the world economy today is more closely integrated than at any point since the Second World War, but it is in fact no more integrated in aggregate terms than it was in the latter part of the nineteenth century and the early years of the twentieth century (Bairoch 1996; Hirst and Thompson 1999; Lewis 1981).

Though this is perhaps the most widely discussed aspect of the sceptics' case, it is probably also the least significant – and it is also the most misunderstood. In the end, this is little more than the statement of an empirical fact – or, insofar as it is contentious, an empirical claim. The sceptics are often misunderstood as suggesting that the world economy has simply not changed. That is, in fact, a considerable distortion of the argument they present. What they are suggesting is that the current and ongoing reintegration of the world economy still has some way to go before it is, in quantitative terms, unprecedented historically. This is certainly an important finding, but it is by no means a definitive refutation of the globalization thesis in itself. It suggests, in particular, that we should be somewhat cautious of those accounts which infer historically unprecedented degrees of constraint on domestic policy-making autonomy from the quantitative force of globalization alone. Yet, we cannot conclude from this that globalization is not an unprecedented constraint on policy-making autonomy. For, as authors like Hirst and Thompson (1999: 27ff.) freely concede, in qualitative if not quantitative terms, there are very significant differences between the contemporary period and the last time the world economy was so closely integrated.

The second pillar of the case against the globalization thesis is rather more significant, though as yet rather less widely acknowledged. Trade economists have, for decades, mapped in detail trends in the global distribution of trade, differentiating in so doing between processes of trade integration that are intra-regional and those that are inter-regional in character. In recent years the techniques used in this literature have been taken up by a number of international political economists to map trends in the geographical distribution of trade and foreign direct investment (Frankel 1997, 1998; Hay 2006; Hirst and Thompson

1999; Petrella 1996). This literature shows that the term globalization is both a poor description and an *increasingly* poor description of the current trajectory of patterns of international economic integration. Their findings can be summarized as follows:

1. In almost all regions within the world economy, the pace of intra-regional integration currently exceeds that of inter-regional integration and has done so for some time; this is true for both trade and foreign direct investment.

2. As a consequence, the most powerful dynamic in the world economy today is regionalization, not globalization.

3. In addition to such regionalizing tendencies, there is evidence of some regions within the world economy becoming ever more closely integrated with one another.

4. Such inter-regionalization processes are, however, very unevenly distributed.

5. Accordingly, for the world economy as a whole the most accurate description of such trends is not globalization, but triadization, where the triad comprises the North American, South-East Asian, and European regional economies.

Taken together, these are extremely important findings, suggesting that the contemporary characterization of the international economy in terms of globalization is not only inaccurate but increasingly so. When it is considered that a significant proportion of contemporary policy-making, at both the national and trans-national levels, is predicated on the assumption that economies must increasingly demonstrate themselves globally competitive, the potential policy relevance of such findings is revealed.

The final pillar in the case against the standard globalization thesis is the most technical. Again, however, it has a potentially significant bearing on the responses of policy-makers to the world of globalization they invariably presume they inhabit. The stylized algebraic models of the world economy which now guide economic policy-making in almost all national capitals invariably assume the existence of a fully integrated world financial market. Indeed, in essence, their contribution to economic policy-making is to derive from such assumptions an optimal set of policy settings appropriate for an era of globalization.

Yet such models also make a series of predictions about the world economy that are, in principle, testable empirically (see, for instance, Bayoumi 1990, 1997; Feldstein and Horioka 1980; Watson 2001). The problem is that such predictions are not borne out by the available empirical evidence.

The technical details need not concern us here (though see Hay 2005 and Watson 2001 for more detailed reviews). Suffice it to note that two predictions, in particular, have troubled economists. These are:

1. In an ever more globally integrated financial market, interest rates should converge and, in a perfectly integrated world financial market, interest rate differentials should be eliminated – the persistence of interest rate differentials providing a simple index of the lack of global financial market integration.

2. In an ever more globally integrated financial market the correlation between domestic savings and investment should fall and, in a perfectly integrated capital market, it should fall to zero – the persistence of savings–investment correlations being an equivalent index of the lack of financial market integration.

The problem is that there is evidence of neither, with interest rate differentials and domestic savings–investment correlations proving rather more resilient than economists anticipated they should. The most obvious conclusion to draw from these results is that financial markets are not as well integrated globally as we tend to assume. That is an important point in its own right. More important still, however, is the point that financial markets are not as well integrated globally as policy-makers using (now) standard economic models assume them to be.

The consequences of globalization

As we have seen, there is a fairly robust case to be made against the highly influential globalization thesis. Yet the case against the presumed corrosive impact of globalization on domestic policy-making autonomy is, if anything, stronger still.

Again, the sceptics' case comes in three parts (summarized in Table 14.3 above). The first of these is the simplest. Since the 1970s, when it was first reported by David Cameron in a highly influential paper (1978), a strong and persistently positive statistical correlation has been shown between the openness of an economy (the proportion of trade it conducts expressed as a share of GDP) and various indices of public spending. In other words, the most integrated economies in the world are also the biggest public spenders. In 1978, though even then an important finding, this was perhaps less significant than today. But the point is that the positive correlation first revealed by Cameron has, if anything, only strengthened in the intervening decades (Garrett 1998; Rodrik 1996, 1997). In short, in aggregate terms at least, there is no evidence of globalization exerting a downward pressure on public spending and state autonomy.

The second and third pillars of the case against the corrosive impact of globalization on the viability of the welfare state go together. They relate to the behaviour of international investors. Most conventional treatments of globalization explore the implications of stylized models of the behaviour of such market participants in a borderless economy (i.e. under conditions of globalization). These models typically predict that investors will use their heightened mobility in a context of globalization to flee from economies characterized by high levels of domestic regulation and high levels of corporate and personal taxation, relocating in more ostensibly conducive investment environments. But such models are all based upon assumptions about the preferences of international investors and are highly sensitive to variations in those assumptions. It is at this point that a new body of literature enters the fray. Rather than deriving the implications of globalization from a series of *untested* assumptions about market participants' behaviour, this literature examines the exhibited preferences of such actors in the decisions they make. It challenges, quite fundamentally, many previous orthodoxies about the impact of globalization.

Two findings of this research are particularly significant. The first is that levels of inward foreign investment are in fact correlated positively not negatively with public and welfare expenditure, levels of both personal and corporate taxation, and an array of indices of labour, environmental, and other regulatory standards (Cooke and Noble 1998; Swank 2002; Traxler and Woitech 2000; Wilensky 2002). By and large the most comprehensive welfare states the world has ever known continue to attract a disproportionate share of inward foreign investment, belying the notion that the welfare state is an unsustainable burden on competitiveness in an era of globalization.

The second finding is arguably more significant still. This shows that investment decisions of financial market actors are in fact far less well informed and far less discriminating in terms of economic policy content than is often assumed. In other words, although economic policy-makers often seem to fear the wrath of international investors, choosing economic policies so as to minimize the risk that they incur such wrath, the evidence suggests that such investors are rather more easily satisfied than is often assumed. Indeed, as Layna Mosley's (2003) detailed analysis of investors' preferences and their investment decisions shows, in monitoring economic policies, market participants are generally interested only in levels of inflation and budget deficits. Provided both are kept under control, there is no evidence that expansive social policy, generous welfare states, and exacting regulatory standards are likely to be penalized by financial markets (Mosley 2003; Swank 2002).

 # Case study: from the welfare state to the competition state?

The previous section suggests, very strongly, that the era of the nation-state as an effective policy-making instrument is far from over. Indeed, it is almost certainly the case that the state today consumes a greater share of global GDP than at any previous point in its history. Yet it would be wrong to infer from evidence like that reviewed in the previous section that the nation-state is entirely unconstrained by globalization and that globalization has played no part in its contemporary transformation. Here International Relations theorists have also had much to say. In particular, Philip G. Cerny, in a series of important interventions (1995, 1997, 2000), has pointed to the role of globalization in the transition that he identifies from the era of the welfare state to that of the competition state in the advanced liberal democracies. His argument is worth considering in a little more detail, and by way of a case study, in the light of the evidence discussed above.

But, before considering this literature, it is perhaps first important to justify such a case study in a book such as this. For, it might be argued, important though the future of the welfare state may be, this is surely more a matter for social-policy analysts than it is for International Relations theorists? Though perhaps understandable, such a reaction would be both premature and problematic. For, as I aim to show, the specific question of the future of the welfare state and the more general question of the transformation of the nation-state is of great consequence to International Relations theorists. Three points might here usefully be made.

First, as we have seen, International Relations theory's globalization debate pits realists and neorealists against globalists. And, as we have also seen, the former stress the continued sovereignty and policy-making autonomy of the nation-state, while the latter see these as having both been profoundly compromised by globalization. The point is that there is no more direct test of the extent of the state's sovereignty and policy-making capacity than its ability to provide for the welfare of its citizens. As such, the question of the future of the welfare state and, in particular, the assessment of the thesis that the state's role as a guarantor of its citizens' welfare has been subordinated to that of promoting competitiveness, is a core concern for International Relations theory.

Second, this is not just a question of the state's sovereignty or of its capacity to provide for its citizens. It is also, crucially to International Relations theory, a question of the relative power and influence of state actors and non-state actors – most obviously, trans-national corporations. For, if Cerny is right to identify the emergence of a competition state which subordinates all other policy imperatives to that of promoting the competitiveness of the national economy in a global environment, then the state today has become little more than a relay for the interests of capital. And, to the extent that this is accepted, it is surely with those interests and not with those of the state that International Relations theorists should now be principally concerned. Again, the consequences for state-centred International Relations theory are potentially considerable, the stakes of the debate considerable indeed.

Finally, and as already noted, International Relations theorists, like Ian Clark (1999) and Philip G. Cerny, have contributed much to our understanding of the development of the state. It is to this work of the latter that we now turn directly.

Competition state versus welfare state

Cerny's seminal contribution starts, like many before it, from the premise that in an era of heightened economic integration (or globalization), competitiveness becomes ever more central to economic performance. As trade and investment flows increase, so national economies are increasingly pitted against one another in an ever more intense competitive struggle. Those economies which are either innately uncompetitive or whose states impose upon them burdensome regulatory restrictions and unnecessary levels of direct and indirect taxation will lose ground – unless, that is, they reform their practices imposing on each and every form of state intervention an exacting competitive audit. Any such audit, Cerny suggests, reveals the welfare state to be an indulgent luxury of a bygone era – normatively desirable in its own terms, certainly, but an unsustainable burden on competitiveness in an era of globalization that can now no longer be afforded.

The argument here is simple and, in all likelihood, familiar. Faced with a choice between national jurisdictions, mobile investors seeking to maximize profits will choose lightly regulated environments characterized by low levels of corporate and personal taxation over densely regulated environments with high levels of corporate and personal taxation. All things being equal, they will relocate their productive activities from economies with burdensome welfare states to those more committed to the free play of market mechanisms. In so doing they will serve to summon the passing of the era of the welfare state in the advanced liberal democracies. In its place, Cerny suggests, a new form of the state – the 'competition state' – is developing. Where the welfare state's principal priority was the promotion of the welfare of its citizens through the insulation of 'key elements of economic life from market forces', the competition state's principal strategy is one of 'marketisation in order to make economic activities located within the national territory . . . more competitive in international and trans-national terms' (1997: 258, 259). The competition state, he goes on, is a minimal or residual state when compared to its welfare state predecessor. It promotes the flexibility and dynamism of the economy through a series of fine-grained (microeconomic) interventions (typically on the supply-side, typically designed to incentivize competitive practices). In so doing it resists the (Keynesian) tendency to manage demand within the economy as a whole. It places competitiveness above all other priorities of government, subordinating social and labour-market policies to the promotion of a flexible economy capable of adapting rapidly to the changing pressures imposed upon it by the global marketplace. Finally, it promotes welfare only to the extent to which this contributes unambiguously to the flexibility, productivity, and, above all, competitiveness of the economy as a whole.

Cerny's account is cogent and compelling and it certainly seems to describe extremely well the reform trajectory on which many advanced liberal democracies are currently embarked. Yet it is not easily reconciled with the evidence considered in the previous section and, even if it describes well the development of the competition state, can it credibly explain its emergence? A number of points might be usefully made here.

Weaknesses in the competition state thesis

First, Cerny in fact relies upon a rather simple conception of the determinants of competitiveness in an open or integrated world economy. It is, moreover, one that is arguably at increasing odds with the available empirical evidence. Cerny assumes that competitiveness is to be gauged solely (or certainly primarily) in terms of the cost for which a business or economy can supply a good to market. As a consequence, all forms of taxation and all regulatory restrictions are burdens on competitiveness since they increase the costs of production (or, at least, the costs incurred by the business in the process of production). Couched in such terms it is not at all difficult to see how and why the welfare state might be seen as a burden on competitiveness. But cost is not the sole, or arguably even the principal, determinant of consumer choice in a complex marketplace. The quality, performance, and pedigree of the goods on offer are just as important, arguably more so. Moreover, by and large economies characterized by the highest levels of social welfare expenditure tend to compete in markets which are less price-sensitive than quality-sensitive. As the Swedes would have it, consumers do not buy Saabs and Volvos because they are cheap. The point is that if we concede that there is more to competitiveness in international markets than cost minimization, then the competitive audit of the welfare state becomes far more complex than Cerny assumes it to be. High levels of societal welfare, though expensive in terms of high non-wage labour costs, may well be associated with a healthy and dedicated workforce, with cooperative rather than adversarial industrial relations, with high levels of human capital and product innovation, and with high domestic levels of consumer demand – all of which might be seen to correlate positively with economic performance.

Second, it is presumably for this reason that foreign direct investment continues to be attracted in disproportionate levels to the highest aggregate welfare spenders in the world economy and why levels of trade integration are positively and not negatively correlated with state and welfare expenditure. In short, there is little evidence to substantiate the thesis that the welfare state is, indeed, a drain on competitiveness.

These are crucial points. For they suggest that the trade-off that Cerny simply assumes between welfare expenditure/the welfare of citizens, on the one hand, and economic performance in an era of economic interdependence, on the other, is more imagined than real. As a consequence, the state's capacity to care for the welfare of its citizens may be less eroded by globalization than we, or indeed it, have tended to assume. Moreover, insofar as this is the case, it is the perceived interest of political actors in developing competition state-like entities, rather than the needs of capital *per se*, that is driving the development of the state today.

Third, as the above discussion already begins to indicate, Cerny's rather dualistic distinction between the competitive-corrosive welfare state on the one hand, and the competitive-enhancing competition state on the other is crude and overly simplistic. It is certainly the case that the welfare state can – and to some extent is being – reformed so as to increase its potential contribution to international competitiveness, but it is important not to lose sight of the considerable contribution to competitiveness that it has arguably always made. Indeed, the archetypal high-public-spending Nordic welfare states were, throughout the postwar period, among the most open economies in the world. The welfare state has always gone hand-in-hand with economic openness; there is no evidence of that symbiotic relationship being eroded today. This, too, is an important point. For it reminds us of the need for International Relations theorists to consider the historically variant but always important relationship between political and economic interests in understanding the development of the world system. Though it has often failed to attract much attention from International Relations theorists, the state has always played a crucial role in determining domestic economic prospects. Arguably in this respect the era of globalization is no different.

Fourth, Cerny's account of the development of the competition state both assumes and, indeed, attributes causality to, a fully integrated world economy. As the previous section serves to indicate, that assumption is in fact increasingly problematic. The European economies which both pioneered the development of the welfare state and in which the majority of advanced welfare states are still located are ever more tightly integrated regionally. But, by virtue of this fact, they are arguably less exposed to the pressures of seeking competitive advantage in the global economy. The determinants of competitiveness for them are increasingly regional in character and, indeed, less global in character than at any point in the postwar period.

Finally, however accurate descriptively Cerny's account of the development of the competition state may be, it provides no credible explanation for this development – attributing causality rather vaguely to a fairly amorphous conception of globalization. The closest we get to a mechanism is the appeal to a neo-Darwinian process of natural selection in which the competitive advantage conferred by the development of the competition state ensures that it is emulated. Yet the problem with this is that there is no real evidence to suggest that competition states are more globally competitive than the welfare states they purportedly replaced. And, while this remains the case, the argument that we have witnessed a decisive sea change in the relative balance of power between the state and capital, is unconvincing. Altogether more likely is that, in the absence of compelling evidence one way or the other, a series of largely neoliberal reforms has successfully been presented and promoted as determinants of economic prosperity – and implemented as such. In this respect the proliferation of competition state-like entities is less a confirmation of Cerny's thesis than it is an indication of the influence of many of the assumptions on which his thesis is predicated.

If that is indeed the case, much of the policy-making autonomy of the state and its capacity to care for the needs of its citizens remains intact – though whether it is perceived to remain intact is perhaps another matter.

Conclusion

This chapter has covered a fair amount of ground. Yet its conclusions can be relatively simply stated. As we have seen, globalization is often presented as a profound challenge to the very field of International Relations itself, calling into question the appropriateness and contemporary relevance of a continued focus on the relations between nations. Yet, as any sanguine assessment of the empirical evidence of globalization reveals, the current level of interdependence within the world system though considerable is not easily reconciled with the stronger variants of the globalization thesis. Nor is the term globalization necessarily a very accurate description of current realities and contemporary trends. Accordingly, while there is certainly much to be gained from a focus on processes of transnational interdependence and global governance, there are still profound insights to be had from a more traditional focus on the state as a key if not the only actor on both the domestic and international stage. In the end neither focus is mutually exclusive. And while that remains the case talk of post-international relations is somewhat premature.

? QUESTIONS

1. What is globalization?

2. Is globalization good for us?

3. To what extent, if any, does globalization invalidate realism and neorealism?

4. Are globalization and International Relations anathema?

5. How intensive and how extensive do processes have to be before we can happily refer to them as globalized?

6. What is meant by 'triadization', and is it occurring?

7. Are globalization and regionalization antagonistic or mutually reinforcing trends?

8. Assess the sceptics' case against the globalization thesis.

9. Does the welfare state have a future in an era of globalization?

10. What is a competition state and how might it confer a competitive advantage upon a national economy in an era of globalization?

11. Is globalization compatible with democratic deliberation?

12. Is the state a victim or an agent of globalization – or both?

≋ FURTHER READING

■ **Buzan, B., Held, D., and McGrew, A. (1998), 'Realism versus Cosmopolitanism',** *Review of International Studies,* **24: 387–98.** A fascinating exchange about the consequences of globalization for International Relations theory between a defender of a (qualified) realism and the key proponent of cosmopolitanism.

■ **Cerny, P. G. (1997), 'Paradoxes of the Competition State: The Dynamics of Political Globalisation',** *Government and Opposition*, **32/1: 251–74.** A clear and accessible statement of Cerny's influential 'competition state' thesis.

■ **Clark, I. (1999),** *Globalisation and International Relations Theory* **(Oxford: Oxford University Press).** An excellent, careful, and judicious assessment of the implications of globalization for International Relations theory.

■ **Held, D. (2003), 'Cosmopolitanism: Globalisation Tamed?',** *Review of International Studies*, **29/4: 465–80.** A clear and accessible statement of the cosmopolitan position by its principal advocate.

■ **Youngs, G. (1999),** *International Relations in a Global Age: A Conceptual Challenge* **(Cambridge: Polity).** A cogent if perhaps somewhat overstated critique of the limitations of state-centred International Relations theory in an age of globalization.

 IMPORTANT WEBSITES

● Globalisation guide. A globalization resource for students.
www.globalisationguide.org

● The Globalization Website. A resource for students and researchers compiling debates about the consequences of globalization.
www.sociology.emory.edu/globalization

● One Europe or Several? Research project investigating the link between globalization, Europe, and the viability of social models.
www.one-europe.ac.uk/cgi-bin/esrc/world/db.cgi/proj.htm?id=26

Visit the Online Resource Centre that accompanies this book for lots of interesting additional material. www.oxfordtextbooks.co.uk/orc/dunne/

INTERNATIONAL RELATIONS THEORY AND GLOBALIZATION

15 Still a Discipline After All These Debates?

OLE WÆVER

✔ **Reader's guide**

This concluding chapter reflects on the aggregate picture produced by the preceding chapters. What discipline do these theories sum up to? To avoid discussion at the same level as the previous chapters – that is speaking from one theory observing itself and the world – the discussion will now be located at the level of the discipline as such, and it will link examination of the intellectual pattern with the social pattern and discuss the discipline as a social system, its relations of power, privilege, and careers. For this it draws on theories from the sociology of science. It argues among other things that the discipline of International Relations (IR) is likely to continue whether or not 'international relations' ('i.r.') remains a distinct or delineable object, that the central social mechanism of organization and control is the control by theorists of the leading journals, and that the core of the intellectual structure is recurring 'great debates'. However, both contextual factors and observable patterns in debate among the theories point to a loosening of the grip of great debates. This does not mean more agreement but less – we do not even agree on what to discuss any more. Nevertheless, the ultimate evaluation of the state and outlook of IR is positive about its ability to stay committed to the world and theory simultaneously, and therefore be of some occasional benefit.

Introduction

After visiting thirteen different theories, it would be nice to know how this all sums up. Is the whole more or less than the parts – do the theories challenge or support each other – and where is it all heading? The preceding authors have been tasked to look at the world through their own theory, and not surprisingly it all looks very promising for each of them. But, most likely, some are going to fare better than others, some will change, and we would like to know what debates become pivotal in the future.

It would be a (common) illusion to discuss this as if it were either decided by 'reality' or by 'debate' about pure ideas. Most stock-taking exercises approach this task in one of two ways. Many point to i.r. reality, to important questions or challenges and predict that the discipline will change in relay fashion (terrorism and therefore non-state actors, terrorism and therefore realism, terrorism and therefore liberal theories of cooperation, etc.). Histories of the disciplines are written in retrospect viewing the events through the theories that won the debate, and it therefore looks as if the events caused the theories (Wæver 1998: 691–2). The second version of prediction is to assume that the best argument wins, and therefore by checking in the debate who is right and wrong one knows how it will go (Katzenstein, Keohane, and Krasner 1998), but I do not feel in a position to judge the contributions of all the wise colleagues in the preceding chapters. In any case, there is no reason to assume that the discipline will suddenly – and for the first time – develop according to the power of the better arguments, because like any social system it is a structured field permeated by relations of power. A theory from the USA is more likely to gain influence than one made in Nigeria, and if it comes from an Ivy League university that again increases its chances, and then there is gender and meta-theoretical bias, and so forth.

The preceding chapters asked what the discipline has to say about various theories. In this concluding chapter I want in the first part to turn this question on its head. What do all these theories tell us about IR? From this in turn it is possible to see each theory in a new light, and gain a deeper understanding of the world which we approach with their help.

The founder of the Copenhagen School, nuclear physicist Niels Bohr, in the 1920s, argued that after carrying out an experiment it is impossible to talk about its results in terms of knowledge about the object in itself. The description has to include a description of the experimental set-up (Bohr 1957). Not: real world factors are connected A $\Rightarrow$ B $\Rightarrow$ C. But, in an experiment like X, we see a $\Rightarrow$ b $\Rightarrow$ c. What we know about i.r. is always contingent on the theory used – one cannot subtract the theory afterwards and get 'clean' knowledge of reality. Therefore, one only knows i.r. when one knows IR. And one only knows the separate theories of IR, when one understands what they are doing to each other. The portrait of the discipline is not an aim in itself, but it is necessary to understand the past, present, and future of the theories which in turn is necessary to understand the world we study.

This exercise helps to answer another puzzle from the volume: in what sense are these different theories *International Relations theories*? Some of them come from other fields – from economics (game theory and neoliberal institutionalism), cultural studies (post-colonialism), philosophy (poststructuralism), political economy (Marxism), and from various sources (feminism) – and some of the theories even resist the concept of IR. Are they IR theories, nevertheless? The answer is yes, and this becomes clear when under-standing the discipline as an institution.

The previous question provokes a follow-up. Why does the volume present this set of theories? Are there any limits to the number of theories one could choose? A selection can be justified because the theories are not living alone in the world; they play a relational game of recognition and mutual interest. When looking at the whole they form, it becomes possible to see what theories make up the discipline.

There is a further and even more basic follow-up. Does IR exist? In what sense can we talk any more about a discipline of International Relations when most of the chapters here argue that the world is in significant respects post-international, globalized, or character-ized by 'world politics' rather than international relations? When furthermore a number of the main theories refuse the label of IR theory themselves, and increasingly argue in favour of interdisciplinarity, what then becomes of the discipline of IR?

Therefore, the first question has to be whether IR is (still?) a discipline, and whether it is likely to remain one (or whether you wasted your time reading those preceding chapters about the theories of a disappearing discipline).

The discipline question

Conceptions of the discipline of IR

It is often discussed whether IR is a discipline or has been overtaken by fragmentation, multi-disciplinarity, hybridity, or – as argued most forcefully by rational choice theorists – by method-based (re-)integration of at least all of political science and potentially all social sci-ences (or more). Most ubiquitous are probably arguments pointing to the obsolescence of the domestic/international distinction, interestingly argued by both rationalists and many critical theorists and poststructuralists (Milner 1998; Katznelson and Milner 2002; George 1994). Others emphasize more – and typically lament – the proliferation of theories, approaches, and sub-fields that makes it harder and harder for a research community to recognize itself and its members (a question covered by Steve Smith in the Introduction to this volume). Much of the anxiety (and hope) about disciplinary demise rests on a false premise that it is possible and necessary to have agreement over objects or definitions in a discipline.

Such debates assume that, to exist, a discipline demands (1) a clear and distinct object, or (2) agreement on a definition. The most widespread view is probably (1), in other words, disciplines exist because and to the extent that their *object exists*. There are living organisms, therefore biology; an economy and therefore economics; and people have psychological disorders and therefore psychology exists. From at least 1969 onwards, it should have been difficult to view things this way. Michel Foucault showed convincingly in the *Archeology of Knowledge* how disciplines do not mirror given objects – they constitute them or are formed together with the formation of their objects. The notions of 'economy' or 'psyche' as distinct objects form only at specific points in time and replace other ways to delineate and differentiate the world (Foucault 1972 [1969]).

Enter (2): if the basis of a discipline is not in the object as such, because objects can be constituted and delineated in different ways, the basis must be in the *constant reproduction of a consensus* according to which the object exists. It would seem that the ability to continue to generate agreement in a community of researchers is the key to being and surviving as a discipline.[1] However, this is empirically as unfounded as (1): the history of science is full of disciplines that did not agree at all on their self-definition, subject matter, or methodology, and continued nevertheless. A recent example is organization studies (Knudsen 2003), to which one could add psychology and sociology which have been in this situation for most of their lives.

Strangely missing from the normal 'to be or not to be' discussions of the discipline is a third approach: (3) a conception of the discipline as focused on *power and institutions*. Strange for the reason that (3) is what one would expect to find in a discipline dominated by realists and institutionalists. (This approach can even be recast as political economy for the critically minded.)

The discipline is real and reproducing – even in the absence of a clear and given object (i.r.) and a shared agreement (IR). This becomes visible through a more external, sociological glance on our activity as IR scholars.[2] The usual discussion commits the fallacy of fairness, of assuming that existence has to be deserved or earned. The result is a naivety we usually do not exhibit in relation to other things we study, only when we talk about the academic world. It goes generally for reflections on the discipline – the many stock-taking exercises about 'the state of the discipline' – that they are in the prescriptive key. For instance, it is common to lament the widespread practice of describing IR in terms of 'great debates' as if this is just some kind of 'bad habit', which 'we' can stop doing if we so decide. But, as I will be demonstrating in the next section, it is actually a part of the *structure* of the discipline; it serves purposes and removing it would have far-reaching effects. So change would affect relations of power and privilege, and therefore just to point out that 'we' should do differently, is slightly naive. It is idealistic in the good old moralistic sense of the word (Carr 1946). Prescription is fine, but when talking about 'the world out there' we usually assume that reform will turn out better if we first try to understand the patterns, structures, interests, and dynamics of a field, whereas when discussing the discipline, because it is about 'doing our job', we tend to assume that one can talk directly about 'what we want to do'. In this section the example is that disciplines reproduce for reasons better explained by sociology of science than because of the state of the world or the practices of disciplinary cultivation.

Sociological explanation for the reproduction of disciplines

Thinking in terms of disciplines emerged gradually as the medieval university gave way to the modern research university, but what explains the staying power of disciplines is the relationship between them and the practical and social organization of the universities, a system that emerged at the turn of the twentieth century in the USA. Disciplines became more than categories in the organization of *knowledge*, and also crucial in the organization of *scholars* and *universities* (Abbott 2001; Clark and Youn 1976; Clark 1983; Geiger 2005: 55f.). Since at least the 1920s, the narrowness, over-specialization, and confinement of disciplines has been criticized, and new patterns predicted.[3] Waves of inter-disciplinarity and large multidisciplinary projects came – and went (Campbell 1969; Abbott 2001: 122,

131–6). The disciplinary system proved surprisingly resilient. The main explanation for this is the departmental structure invented in the USA: 'academic disciplines in the American sense – groups of professors with exchangeable credentials collected in strong associations – did not really appear outside the United States until well into the postwar period' (Abbott 2001: 123; 2002: 207; for a comparative description of the situation in Germany, France, and the UK, see Abbott 2001: 123–5; 2002: 207–8). The system with 'departments of equals' and a Ph.D. 'in something' was part of the solution to an administrative problem of a lack of internal structure in a rapidly expanding university system. It proved highly durable. The duality of internal organization and a system for structured career mobility externally – backed up by national disciplinary societies such as the American Political Science Association (APSA) – became self-reinforcing because it is self-penalizing to challenge the discipline (Abbott 2001: 126; cf. Hammond 2004). It becomes hard for single universities to challenge the disciplinary system, because their Ph.D. graduates would lose their career options: they would no longer qualify as Ph.D.s 'in xx'. Abbott further underpins this argument by mechanisms related to undergraduate education and 'the college major', which we do not need to go into here. The main point is that the system of disciplines as invented in the USA proved highly self-reinforcing. With the postwar dominance of US universities, the model spread. American universities often were the pinnacle of career prospects for foreigners too, so global disciplines became replicas of US ones, in turn leading to local accommodation in most countries to this format.

Disciplines, therefore, generally do not die, merge, or split just because their subject appears in a new light. Occasionally, splits happen, typically if a field receives generous funding for a long period (biology), and mergers can happen if an area is gradually losing influence (classics). But disappearance of a field is unlikely, and even more unlikely is a general reorganization of, say, all of the social sciences according to a new and better format, to get away from the nineteenth-century assumptions about society, state and international built into the current disciplines (Wallerstein 2001 [1991]), or because the success of a specific approach (rational choice) makes it better to reorganize according to the different branches of rational choice theory than according to the disciplines, which are anyway all applying the same rational choice theories (or ought to).

Waves of change have swept through the various disciplines, major **paradigms** have come and gone and the dominant format of research has changed in many disciplines, and yet the general map has been surprisingly constant. Why is it important that disciplines are more unshakeable than widely assumed? Because it refocuses our attention on the internal structure of the discipline, rather than assuming that its survival is all the time at stake. For instance, boundary drawing is usually less about ensuring the continuation of political science/IR than it is part of power struggles within the disciplines about who are to be included/excluded and who are more central than others (cf. Gunnell 1991; Guzzini 1998). Rather than mirroring the picture of precarious disciplinary existence, it is more interesting to take IR as a continuing condition – for better and worse – and study its internal organization.

IR and political science

So disciplines reproduce. But an obvious objection could be that IR is a *sub*-discipline within political science. It is true that political science is a discipline, and it reproduces for the reasons given by Abbott and others. IR is not in an immediate sense a discipline of this kind – it is, in the vast majority of universities, political science that plays this dual institutionalization role of being a unit in each university and a (trans)national scene for careers. However, a conception of political science as made up of a few sub-fields is endemic. In the USA it is typically the quartet of American politics, comparative politics, political theory, and IR; and in some European systems, comparative politics, political theory, public administration, and IR. This structure is neither necessary, natural, nor very old (Kaufman-Osborn 2006), but when the current fourfold structure finally emerged in the late 1950s (after a number of very different structures in the first half of the twentieth century), it quickly became stable and self-reproducing. Abbott's explanation can be extended down to the sub-disciplinary level. To prepare for careers in a discipline organized around these four sub-fields, one needs to have credentials in these terms.[4] Therefore, the four became self-reproducing and IR has staying power as a sub-discipline.

Among the four, it seems that IR (and possibly political theory) has a stronger sense of independent disciplinarity (cf. the common use of the term discipline for both IR and political science in places like this volume). Part of the reason for this is that IR emerged with separate chairs and institutes partly independently of political science (especially in the UK and the European continent, see Goodwin 1951; Manning 1954), and leading orgnizations such as the International Studies Association (ISA) and its British counterpart (BISA) officially see themselves as interdisciplinary, despite the reality of overwhelming political science dominance. IR has its own journals and independent organizations/conferences, and therefore many tend to think of themselves as 'international relationists' rather than 'political scientists'. IR is a discipline within a discipline.

A lot of the relevant challenges and dynamic factors influencing the discipline are noticed in the ongoing discussions in the discipline, but often the factors are linked to the wrong questions due to the constant underestimation of the staying power of disciplines. Globalization in its many senses does upset the standard categories of domestic/international, medialization challenges the conception of politics, and so forth. But this is not likely to lead (all of) us beyond the discipline to new fields defined to mirror 'new realities' – rather these are important challenges that the discipline and its theories will try to make sense of in different ways. Similarly, the degrees of agreement and diffusion in the discipline are not likely to make it disappear, nor should it be a reason for idealistic lamentation and calls for improvement; we should look systematically at the changes in the structure of the discipline and what this means for the kinds of knowledge it produces and can produce.

Finally, the reluctance to celebrate the durability of disciplines is probably strengthened by the connotations of 'discipline' where poststructuralists and especially postmodernists (terms used as defined by Campbell, Chapter 11) play on the social control sense of 'discipline'. (Compare the discussion of 'disciplinarity' in Messer-Davidow, Shumway, and Sylvan 1993.) This mock-etymology – fun as it is – should probably give way to the real origins of 'discipline' in Latin *discere*, to learn. Since 'there are far more research problems than there are disciplines . . . a university organized around problems of investigation would be hopelessly balkanized' (Abbott 2001: 135; cf. Campbell 1969), and, due to lack of abstraction, knowledge defined by a specific problem will constantly lose out to 'problemportable knowledge'. Therefore, 'disciplinary boundaries are, after all, necessary for the growth of knowledge' (Fuller 2002 [1988]: 197).

It is not that everybody should be doing IR theory, or that disciplinary knowledge is somehow privileged or finer than inter-disciplinary, multi-disciplinary, or post-disciplinary work; only that there will *also* be IR theory. There are often good reasons to focus on a given issue, problem, or question and develop theory specifically for the purpose and at the interface between different disciplines. However, there will be a discipline called IR for the above reasons, and most likely a set of theories known as IR theories will go together with this field. Notably, there will be a certain premium on being recognized as a theory of a recognized field, because these constitute the largest and most stable market for candidates. New theories typically emerge not at the core of the discipline but at the interstices between disciplines, but they then face strategic choices about whether to cultivate an identity as co-founder of a new field (start founding journals and associations for it, as done by development research, feminism, communication studies, and many other fields in the early stages) or celebrate their radical homelessness, or stake a claim to being an IR theory (and possibly simultaneously make similar claims in other disciplines; compare, for example, feminism and poststructuralism). Even new and radical theories of IR fall back on the same institutional infrastructure – using the same techniques of persuasion at the conferences, writing for the top journals, gaining major research council grants, etc. So, while they may claim to be 'post IR', to others this looks like a contestation *within* IR.

For instance, it is increasingly often observed that the discipline's Western (and especially American) perspective and categories often make it rather useless for Third World concerns (Tickner 2003). However, when attempting to develop 'post-Western IR' that takes into account more adequately the concepts and issues that matter in other parts of the world, a new dilemma immediately emerges: this kind of IR will be stronger if recognized by the discipline as being part of the discipline of IR (Tickner and Wæver 2004).

There is and most likely will remain a discipline of IR and theories of IR too. That was step number one. The remaining questions are as follows. What kind of discipline is it? What is it doing? How is it changing? More specifically, I will in the next section look at the *social structure* of the discipline in order to describe in general how it is organized, and whether this organization is changing. It is not possible to understand the development in theories without understanding how the discipline is constituted and how it is changing. The following section looks at the *intellectual structure* of the discipline. This leads into a discussion of the pattern within and among the specific theories: which ones are around and especially what pattern do they form in combination? What are the main axes of debate and are they changing? The conclusion addresses questions about relevance, cumulation, and progress.

What kind of discipline is IR? Changes in social structure

Social and intellectual structure

Academic disciplines have both social and intellectual structures. The *social* structures include institutions from the large and formal organization of disciplines grouped in faculties within universities, to smaller and often more informal ones such as procedures of refereeing in key journals. The discussion here will focus on the central question of how researchers within a given field relate to each other – how dependent they are on each other and through this how they are coordinated and 'ruled'. This is central because it is in the nature of science to be a relationship among colleagues: 'scientific fields are a particular work organisation which structure and control the production of intellectual novelty through competition for reputations from national and international audience for contributions to collective goals' (Whitley 1984: 81). 'They reward intellectual innovation – only new knowledge is publishable – and yet contributions have to conform to collective standards and priorities if they are to be regarded as competent and scientific' (Whitley 1986: 187). The publication system has become the central institution, and competition for influencing and directing other researchers through publications a central mechanism. In contrast to professions, individual autonomy is very low, and a scientist continues to depend 'on colleagues for approval and recognition throughout one's research career' (Whitley 1984: 25). Recognition is the central medium, but recognition from some colleagues counts more than from others – authority is concentrated with those who achieve power over knowledge goals and procedures.

Intellectual structures include how the knowledge in the field hangs together – to what degree over-arching systems or paradigms encompass the different contributions or unify them through clear methods or techniques, and thus the degree to which it is predictable to practitioners whether their work will count as novel and meaningful. (Social and intellectual structures are closely connected, but I will present them in this chapter separately for purposes of clarity.)

The variations among the sciences do not – as is often assumed – derive from the subject matter of the different disciplines as in the standard contrast between natural and social/humanistic sciences. It is not a sufficient explanation that the social world is more complex, or natural phenomena in their nature more mechanical and thus predictable. A good illustration of this is the difference between physics and chemistry. In physics, you need expensive equipment and decisions are made by a few, whereas, in chemistry, most apparatus is available in university departments. Chemistry then shows much less concern with theoretical unification and much less coordination, and its sub-fields are not ordered into a single hierarchy of importance (Whitley 1984: 108 – see also pp. 89–90 and 256–7). This example shows that it is not a question of 'natural scienceness' – much more a question of specific conditions that shape the organization of a field which in turn influences the kind of research output. Similarly, social sciences such as sociology, political science, and economics vary in their internal structure, not necessarily reflecting their subject matter but as a combination of a number of factors relating to their organization.

Disciplinary structures change over time. Christian Knudsen (2003) tells the story of organization studies as going through quite different formations, from a single paradigm situation in the late 1950s to mid-1970s, to two different kinds of more diverse formations in later decades. The shift was largely explained by the rapid growth of the field, which undermined the previous hegemony of one dominant research programme. Whitley (1984) often uses the example of the bio-medical field, where dramatic increases in funding meant a fragmentation, because scholars were no longer dependent on a few gate-keepers but could get funding from many different sources more easily.

So what is the social structure of IR?

First, the global structure: IR is 'an American social science' (Hoffmann 1977). Modern IR theory was born in the USA after the Second World War when IR first became a general and widespread discipline. The Cold War meant generous funding, and the US research community became by far the largest and therefore most attractive to succeed in. American journals were seen as leading 'international journals', despite often publishing less than 10 per cent from scholars not at US universities (Wæver 1998; Breuning, Bredehoft, and Walton 2005). In this situation, US scholars could afford to ignore work done outside the USA, and it was up to others to bring their work to the attention of US-based universities, journals, and publishers – dominance through neglect. Recent years have witnessed increased attention to this pattern and to the marginalized voices – from the most articulate ones like the English school (see Chapter 7 in this volume) to the almost silenced Third World scholars. There has been discussion about whether this is 'only' a social injustice where non-US and especially non-Western scholars are underprivileged or whether there is a qualitative difference and IR would look different if written from elsewhere. One should recognize both the significant differences between IR in say Germany, the UK, the USA, and Japan (Wæver 1998; Kinvall 2005; Inoguchi and Bacon 2001), and simultaneously the omni-presence of US-style IR all over the world. The IR world is best viewed as a mix of a US/global system and national/regional ones with varying degrees of independence (Wæver 2003). The US scene is both national and the central global one (consider the status of the ISA as both a North American organization and de facto global IR convention) but, although others relate to this scene, they simultaneously operate on different conditions dependent on whether their home is in India, Germany, or Brazil. I cannot go into detail about the other ones here. In line with the book, I focus on the US/global discipline and only occasionally note the limits and problems of this model, but will not cover the variations as such.

The second layer of social structural analysis is then to understand the US-based/centred one. What are the institutions, degree of coherence, and forms of power? A key category here is 'mutual dependence' (Whitley 1984, 1986, 2000).[5] Mutual dependence 'refers to scientists' dependence upon particular groups of colleagues to make competent contributions to collective intellectual goals and acquire prestigious reputations which lead to material rewards' (1984: 87). Increased dependence generally leads to increased competition, increased cooperation/coordination, and stronger organizational boundaries and identity.

IR has some clear 'symptoms' of strategic dependence. Why? Why should International Relations scholars be dependent on colleagues? '[T]he more limited access to the necessary means of intellectual production and distribution, the more dependent do scientists become upon the controllers of such channels and the more connected and competitive are their research strategies likely to be'(Whitley 1984: 84f.). In some disciplines, this is a question directly about resources such as equipment. This is usually not the case in IR, although it matters who controls (or advises) the various (private) foundations and (public) research councils. To most researchers in the discipline, dependence is more a question of access to publications which, in turn, influences resource allocation.

Researchers are dependent upon those 'colleagues who dominate reputational organizations and set standards of competence and significance'(Whitley 1984: 86). In fields where you can contribute to a number of distinct problem areas and seek reputations from different audiences by publishing results in different journals this dependence is much lower than in disciplines such as particle physics where journals form a clear hierarchy and audiences are clearly defined.

IR has a hierarchy of journals. In the USA there is a big market for academic posts and scholars are highly mobile. There is a hierarchy of universities, and the way to climb up the ladder is via publications, meaning that the lead journals are the most important hurdle. And it is a high one, because the leading journals in the social sciences have acceptance rates as low as 11–18 per cent (compared to 65–83 per cent in the natural sciences) (Hargens 1988: 150). Conversely, access to expensive equipment is a scarce resource in the natural sciences. This makes evaluation by foundations and hiring at leading and wealthy institutions relatively more central compared to evaluation on the basis of journal publications that take absolute priority in most social sciences. In most human sciences and some social sciences there are many journals and it is easy to get published. In IR too, given the proliferation of journals, almost any article can be published but there is a relatively clear intersubjective understanding of the value of different journals and publishing houses (Peterson, Tierney, and Maliniak 2005; Goodson, Dillman, and Hira 1999). Lead journals become absolutely central. Thus, the key to IR's relatively high strategic dependence is concentration of control over the means of intellectual distribution.

Articles about theory as such do not rank higher than empirical, application ones. On the contrary, there is a fatigue with more new theories or meta-theories and a premium (not least for *International Organization* which is often thought of as the pre-eminent journal in IR) on theory testing. However, the journals are mainly defined, structured, and to a certain extent controlled by theorists. You become a star only by doing theory. The highest citation index scores all belong to theorists. Thus the battle among theories/theorists defines the structure of the field, but the practice it stimulates is one where all sub-fields compete for making it into the lead journals. This is in contrast to the situation in economics, where there is a closed system dominated by pure theory (and the different specializations have their own journals, and an article of an applied nature usually cannot make it into the leading journals at all).

In IR, the result is a two-tiered discipline. To get into the lower tier, you have to become accepted as competent in a sub-field. Most sub-fields are relatively tolerant, welcome new members, and are not terribly competitive. They are hierarchical, but the hierarchy is not settled internally, so there is not much to fight over. Top positions are gained by making it into the upper tier, i.e. publishing in the leading all-round journals; this means convincing those at the centre about relevance and quality (you still have to prove technical competence to your fellow-specialists because some of them will most likely be reviewers).

This specific structure explains the most-often noticed peculiarity of IR: its fondness of 'great debates'. Debates ensure that theorists remain central but empirical studies important (in contrast to economics).[6] Without recurrent debates, empirical work would break off and just apply the accepted theory. Debates are possible – and necessary – in the USA because of the one big national 'market'. The decisive resources for careers have moved out of local control and up to the national, disciplinary level. In the USA it is possible to compete for definition of the whole field; in Europe and elsewhere it is easier to maintain local peculiarities.

It is important to note that IR has historically been relatively coherent compared to e.g. sociology, which has tended to diversify into numerous kinds of sociology, has had less agreement on the hierarchy of journals, and has had less correspondence between what is discussed in one sub-field and another. Many of the leaders typically did not establish themselves through theories of direct transferability, but through exemplary empirical works (books) that left a less clear message for the discipline at large. So for IR the infamous great debates actually constitute a form of coherence.

Change in social structure

If we turn from statics to dynamics, what does this kind of theory tell us about changes? What are the factors that could upset the structure? This is of course a large subject in itself, but to list a few strong candidates:

- The social boundary is important not because of a likely dissolution of the discipline as an institution but because changes in boundary drawing transform the internal set-up of the discipline. Does authority over IR rest only with IR (and over political science only with political science)? Recent years have shown two rather different challenges. One is the hegemony of rational choice. Since this is a supra-disciplinary movement it means that scholars across the sub-fields and across disciplines have views on who should be hired in, say, an IR position in a department.

- The second challenge to the social boundary is 'audience plurality and diversity' (Whitley 1984: 111). In many human sciences lay audiences have strong opinions, and positions within the field can therefore be built through success with these audiences. This has not usually been the case for IR – you could become a star in the media, but that does not necessarily count academically. However, increasingly, hiring criteria start to include not only research but teaching and public performances in the media. This too weakens the hold of a disciplinary elite that controls the leading journals. Notably, status in the policy world does not correlate or follow from intra-academic debates (in which case this new factor would not shift much; the ultimate source of authority would be the same). Often theories can be highly successful academically and without policy influence, and increasingly policy research in think-tanks happens without anchorage in IR theory (see Kahler 1993, 1997; Peterson, Tiemey, and Maliniak 2005; Wæver and Buzan 2006).

- In the same direction pulls a general change in the nature and status of science related to the 'knowledge society'. One might at first think, the 'knowledge society' means increased status to academics. Not so. Science has become too important to be left to scientists (Gibbons et al. 1994; Fuller 2000). Politics is scientificized, but science becomes politicized. The effects of much natural science in particular are too momentous (genetic manipulation for instance) to be left to intra-scientific decisions. Ulrich Beck's theory of the risk society (Beck 1992) also includes the argument that risks related to science-based developments mean that science can be only one voice in science-related decisions – economic and political voices count inside academe too.

The main factors influencing the social structure are, in the case of IR, pointing towards a loosening of central control and less forceful coordination through the combined mechanism of leading journals and theorists in mutual debate.

This kind of structural–institutional approach to the discipline does not imply that one should accept everything as unchangeable (or a given change as inevitable). There are lots of reasons to argue about how we would like to change our academic world (for example the Perestroika movement, 2000; see Monroe 2005[7]), and the most useful are probably those that focus on process or culture, i.e. what kind of attitude and forms of interaction we should cultivate in order to generate a more productive and searching discipline (Lapid 2002, 2003), rather than direct description of better end-states. However, all such 'reformism' – and even revolutionary approaches – usually fare better when they have analysed the setting first, to understand the kind of social system they are trying to change, including its structures and relations of power.

Changes in intellectual structure? The end of great debatism?

Task uncertainty

A key technical term from the sociology of science is here 'task uncertainty' (Collins 1975; Whitley 1984). The basic paradoxical combination in science of novelty and conformity creates a high level of uncertainty about what will count and succeed. Research cannot aim at repetitious and predictable results. Novelty is constituted in relation to background expectations and assumptions; and the more systematic, general, and precise these are, the clearer the results will be. There is less uncertainty where work techniques are well understood and produce reliable results and/or clarity about the most significant topics. If you have followed the rules in most natural sciences and done something not done before, this is almost by definition a contribution to knowledge especially if it has taken place in an important area. If criteria are more diffuse, you might get your submission back with evaluations like 'nothing new', 'too idiosyncratic and not comprehensible', 'not IR', or 'the question is not interesting and important enough'. IR neither has agreement on very strict techniques nor clear priorities. Great debates have served to organize the discipline instead.

The set-up in IR with periodic great debates has been part of the structure of our discipline. It corresponds to a situation with a relatively high degree of integration but far from a complete, hierarchical integrated structure where every piece has its place in the larger architecture of collective knowledge. The debates serve to focus the discipline and to define both a hierarchy of forms of work – the leading journals concentrating on presenting and not least elaborating and testing the main theories – and to give a meaningful role to larger parts of what goes on.

Stop the great debates?

'Great debates' are decried these days and most commentators hope we are getting away from them. This is problematic for three reasons:

1. Critics of the great debates implicitly assume that the alternative is a more coherent discipline. By contrast, a more likely outcome is that the field will be less integrated if the narrative of great debates were lost.

2. The debatism is part of the structure, so we must take it seriously to understand how our discipline works, and there are power and privileges at stake.

3. These debates help us in important ways to understand the theories themselves.[8]

Studying (and teaching) the great debates helps not only to understand the pattern, not only to track *what theories* are in the field, but also to understand what is *in those theories*, i.e. how they are structured. And by understanding *why* they look the way they do, it also becomes easier to get deeper into their inner logic and thereby also to work with them, not least for a student.

Theories are shaped by their immediate social setting, that is the academic scene (and only to a much lower degree by external factors relating to political developments). Theories are not developed in an ideal process of 'learning' and adjusting to the anomalies or weaknesses (Kuhn, Lakatos) – the academic scene is much more combative, and there are always a number of theories competing. Therefore, the landscape or 'fronts' explain to a very large extent what a given theory is 'up to', i.e. why particular challenges are seen as decisive for this theory. To prove A or redefine B is important because of what this will mean in the current main fights. Therefore, a contemporary student of a given theory can best get to the nerve of this theory by understanding what it was designed to do originally – and therefore the student needs to have a good, graphic depiction of the scene as it was. Or as Peter Berger notes – in a phrase attributed to a 'somewhat cynical colleague – "the goal of every scholarly enterprise is to blow someone's theory out of the water"' (2002: 1).

To understand a theory implies to know why it was created that way. In other words, to understand neorealism, it helps to have the IR scene of the 1970s as a setting, and see how Waltz intervened most cleverly into that by his strategic move of a structural relaunch of realism. Similarly, Keohane constructs his neoliberalism on the basis of rational egoists and as a theory that says a few important things. This is a strategic move given Waltz's triumph and the standards of evaluation that have transformed accordingly. That certain elements of poststructuralism came to be defining in an IR context (different from poststructuralism elsewhere) had a lot to do with the battle lines and constellations among IR theories (Wæver 1996). Wendt's theory is state-centric, both for theory-internal reasons (having to do with the structure–agency debate), but surely also for relational reasons – thereby it becomes a parallel to Waltz and Keohane, the third book on that top shelf. The result is the pattern of transformation of the discipline from the third to fourth debate – illustrated in Figure 15.1.

Out of the triangle of realism, liberalism, and Marxism/radicalism, emerges what I have labelled the 'neo-neo synthesis' between neorealism and neoliberalism, which in turns stimulates the radicalization of an all-out reflectivist critique. The long diagonal axis (upper left to lower right) became the main debate in the 1980s, while the remaining narrow intra-rationalist debate between neorealists and neoliberals (short arrow) became the other constitutive element of the fourth debate.

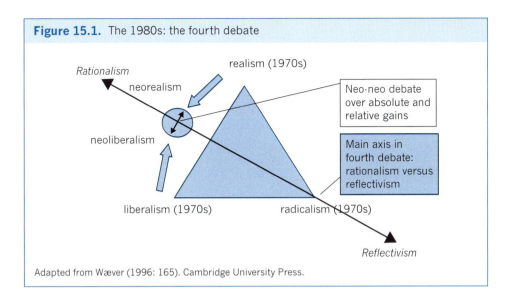

Figure 15.1. The 1980s: the fourth debate

Rationalism

neorealism

realism (1970s)

Neo-neo debate over absolute and relative gains

Main axis in fourth debate: rationalism versus reflectivism

neoliberalism

liberalism (1970s)

radicalism (1970s)

Reflectivism

Adapted from Wæver (1996: 165). Cambridge University Press.

This argument about the importance of debates exists in the shape of a much more general (and far-reaching) version. In his remarkable book *The Sociology of Philosophies: A Global Theory of Intellectual Change* (1998) Randall Collins develops a general theory of how intellectual work can be understood through the networks of – in his case – philosophers. This allows him to trace philosophical thought in ancient Greece, China, Japan, India, medieval Islamic, Jewish, and Christian traditions, and modern Europe. Not 'only' that, he explains it all in a conception that covers both the micro-level of the movements and moves of individuals and the macro-level of the large patterns. The core is intellectual conflict, which is 'always limited by focus on certain topics, and by the search for allies' (Collins 1998: 1) and produces 'the law of small numbers' (1998: 38, 81). The number of positions that succeed in gaining general attention (and constitute active schools of thought which reproduce themselves for more than one or two generations) is typically *three to six*. There have to be rival positions, thus at least two, and then it is always easy to define a third in contrast to both. The upper limit is around six, because the need for allies and the scarcity of attention tend to make processes of multiplication beyond this self-defeating.

Probably Collins generalizes too lightly (even with the nuances made possible by 1,100 pages). The theory is mostly applicable to philosophy and sociology, not as easily to natural science. Therefore, we need to supplement Collins's magisterial grand theory with a differentiation among disciplines *à la* Whitley. However, when mapping IR in more detail (Wæver 2003), it turns out that we happen to be rather like philosophy (and some parts of sociology) in this respect, so Collins *is* actually quite applicable to IR. The intellectual law of small numbers works on us. Or at least it used to.

Great debates – did they stop after all?

Great debates with shifting fronts and axes is the general long-term picture. But what about the current situation? Examining leading US journals, one finds little debate among general theories in the journals that are dominant in the IR discipline. In these – and *the* leading one, *International Organization* (IO), in particular – IR theory has become marginalized and great debate references have almost disappeared. *International Security*, the leading journal on the security side of US IR, has had some limited discussion along the main axis of discussion in the fourth debate (rationalism versus reflectivism) in the form of a discussion about moderate constructivism, while a debate over demo-cratic peace largely followed the axis of the neo-neo debate (small arrow in Figure 15.1). The most vigorous debates have been intra-realist and hardly count as 'great debates' for the discipline as a whole. *International Studies Quarterly* and *World Politics* who share with *IO* the status as the top IR journals (Breuning, Bredehoft, and Walton 2005) confirm the picture of very limited orientation in relation to any general map of IR.

A few years back, almost all articles in the USA fitted into a few main orientations and posi-tioned themselves in relation to these, whereas the 'other' category, that is non-traditional theories, was much larger in several European and especially British journals (Wæver 1998). This underlines the general point that the discipline is organized with a US centre, and the great debates that focus the discipline therefore find their most complete representation in the leading US journals. Also, the journals do not want to publish new theories all the time – the idea is that we should have a relatively limited set of theories (produced by the scholars at the top of the pyramid), and then others are supposed to use, test, and modify mildly. Therefore, many articles were either extensive applications of one theory or competitive tests of several. However, this kind of preferred article a decade ago is actually hard to find these days. Today, articles use lots of theory, and apply or test it – only it is not *IR* theory! The IR theory map lurks in the background as meta-references, but the operative theory in a typical *IO* article is a branch of sociological institutionalism, then a theory from economics, and then an ad hoc home-made model of norms or institution building. These are not derived directly from any general debates within IR.

Specific theories – what axes of debate?

The picture of no single great debate framing the entire field today is reinforced by the chapters of this volume. The picture of debates changes chapter by chapter. We seem to witness separate developments within each 'family'. Optimistic interpretation would be that each 'research programme' is trying to develop its own potential by internally settling the remaining issues, and the programmes are in parallel trying to do as well as possible – thus leading up to a grand comparison of IR theories. Some (including me) have previ-ously summed up the situation as a period of debate within each, i.e. a period where all theories turn inward and discussion runs among competing branches of each theory. However, this is too generalized and systematic a picture.

The theories are broad, parallel streams but their internal activity differs. How they are integrated and how participants interact varies. The brief survey below draws on the preceding chapters (and therefore gives no separate documentation or sources). I start with the theories that define the main debate among themselves. A little later I turn to the remaining theories/chapters:

- Structural realism is structured by competing theories within itself. The main debates are among offensive and defensive realism (and neoclassical and postclassical realism, all developments of neorealism). The typical kind of study uses not quantitative methods or formal modelling but historical case studies to explore the very abstract general theoretical questions about causal relations between a few key variables (Walt 1999). Because structural realism is the core of US security studies, this form of debate characterizes all security studies (Wæver 2004; Wæver and Buzan 2007). So not only the structural realist discussions but also other debates in security studies such as those on the democratic peace or 'constructivism' understood as 'ideational variables' have used the same format.

- Neoliberalism has a quite different pattern. The typical *IO* article does not put the general theory in play (as the structural realist does), but draws on a specific theory or model from organization theory or economics. It is then tested or explored with one or more IR cases, as summarized in Chapter 6 in this volume and in Moravcsik (2003). Optimistically, one could say the research programme adds more and more variables in a maturing construct. However, it is doubtful whether this really lives up to being a research programme in a Lakatosian sense, at least not a 'progressive' one, which would demand that the different theories are drawn from the same 'hard core' and are developing this (Lakatos 1970). Neoliberalism is not spreading out from a common core and filling out different niches, building a common construct. It is more a family of like-minded attempts that are not easily compatible, additive, or cumulative. This broad family shares a general perspective on institutions and rational choice, but it is not a unified framework. Neoliberalists have no great debate internally like the one among structural realists, but they have a sense of working on mid-range theories with shared premises.

- Hard rational choice is absent from this book. It seems that it has lost some of its previous centrality – compared to especially the days of the relative/absolute gains debate – and it has found its place in various sub-settings (see Katznelson and Milner 2002). It has done so less as a unified research project than it was, probably because the core of theory development is outside the discipline – in economics – which makes it hard to keep together as an IR theory.

- Constructivism is marked first of all by debate between different 'degrees' of constructivism and some *vis-à-vis* the most approachable parts of the establishment (neoliberals) and some with poststructuralists. There is much less debate between the extremes, the 'rationalism versus reflectivism' debate often characterized by a focus on neorealism as the quintessential rationalist theory. Also, much soft constructivist work has been published in leading journals where it has followed a pattern like the one outlined for neoliberalism above (cf. Sterling Folker 2000) – not developing one core theory (maybe because constructivism is not an IR theory but a meta-theory; Onuf 2002), but drawing on different middle-range theories from, typically, sociology or organization theory to introduce specific mechanisms not found in constructivism *per se*.

- Poststructuralism shows a somewhat surprising tendency (despite Campbell's welcome plea for abstractions) to engage primarily with specific subjects (famine, migration, exceptionalism), and engage less with general theory debates both *vis-à-vis* the establishment and internally. This is especially the case for British poststructuralists who are hegemonic in this part of the discipline.

- Feminism, critical theory, and neo-Marxism tend to follow the pattern of poststructuralism and in this sense keep the category of 'reflectivism' somewhat valid. They

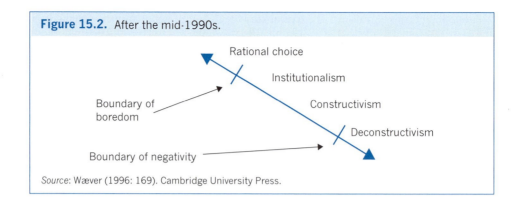

Figure 15.2. After the mid-1990s.

Source: Wæver (1996: 169). Cambridge University Press.

position themselves against the 'establishment', but have less faith in the chance of getting anybody there to listen (Tickner 1997), so less is invested in any great debate.

The overall pattern remains in line with my prediction from the last survey of the discipline (Wæver 1996, 1997; and Figures 15.1 and 15.2 in this chapter): the fourth debate is being transformed into a continuum, a series of debates along the same axis. Most strikingly, along the rationalism–reflectivism axis, we have several relatively similar debates at various points. For example, within constructivism it is evident that there are lively debates between mainstream and moderate constructivists (*International Organization* and *International Security*), conventional and consistent constructivists (Chapter 9 in this volume), as well as ongoing debates over Wendt's contribution to constructivism.

Andrew Abbott (2001) has noticed how many debates in social science exhibit a fractal pattern, or 'self-similarity'. The debate over constructivism has taken on the same form and is repeated at any step along the axis. Any position can be attacked by a more radical constructivist or a more whole-hearted materialist one. Or, to put it more fractally, within each position, the same debate reappears.

Compared to the 1996–7 prediction, we do not have a new axis (the line has the same end points and the same location), but the pattern has shifted from debate to continuum – a dichotomy (reflectivism/rationalism) has changed to a range of possibilities, but defined in the same terms. The important article by Fearon and Wendt on 'rationalism vs constructivism: a sceptical view' (2002) is in this respect both a symptom of this evolution and an instructive intervention showing how to proceed in this newly opened land. 'In short, we believe the most fruitful framing of "rationalism vs. constructivism" is a pragmatic one, treating them as analytical lenses for looking at social reality. . . . This prompts a concluding suggestion: that the rationalism–constructivism issue be seen not as a debate but as a conversation' (Fearon and Wendt 2002: 68).

Pinpointing our position in the genealogy of debates, we are still 'after the fourth debate'. Orientation still operates via the categories from the fourth debate as witnessed by most of the chapters in the present volume. There is not a lively and intense debate as in the late 1980s and early 1990s, but the categories are still around as the main signposts in the landscape. We are neither in a total interregnum, nor in a fifth debate. Neorealists and neoliberals each follow their own guiding pattern and spend little time explicitly on the fourth debate. They do not even debate much with each other. However, neoliberals and neorealists form internal debates simulating their classical first debate axis. The intra-realist debate follows the classical axis *vis-à-vis* liberals: defensive realism is closer to liberalism than offensive realism. Also the neoliberal debate is along the classical axis *vis-à-vis* realists: power versus institutions (very clear in Chapter 6 in this volume). Also this debate is 'self-similar' or 'fractal': you can at any step take a discussion between a more and a less tough *Realpolitik* interpretation.

The optimistic interpretation would be that each research programme in parallel tries to optimize itself and we are thereby about to have all the theories measured, preparing for the grand conclusion. This is not likely. This view overestimates both the parallelism of what happens within each, and assumes a non-existing agreement on the criteria for assessment. More likely, the meaning of this pattern is less coherence, less agreement.

A final alternative interpretation could be that diversity is temporary, because one theory is about to win. Each theory is to some extent internally relatively coherent. So, if one would come to control the whole, we would have coherence. The only serious candidate for this is rational choice. But there are two objections to the claim that it dominates the field. First, it is dominant only in the USA, not in Europe, or the rest of the world (Wæver 1998; Kinnvall 2005); and, second, it faces quite stiff and possibly increasing resistance 'at home' in the USA as the so-called Perestroika movement in political science attests (Perestroika 2000; Monroe 2005).

If we are then left with the diagnosis of less integration, why did this happen? Because of reality? Complexity? The end of the Cold War, the 'War on Terror', or globalization? Dissolution of disciplinary boundaries? Probably none of these. This is again the realist fallacy assuming the discipline reflects its object. A sociological explanation would return to the factors discussed above:

- the ironic effect of an attempted take-over by rational choice, which weakened the boundaries of control systems;

- politicization of knowledge in general which diversifies control;

- marketization which increases the relevance of different kinds of arena and thereby multiple career criteria: not only research in main journals and publishing houses but also teaching and public visibility.

If we look at the other chapters of the volume, much of the implicit or explicit disciplinary mapping takes the form of contrasting itself to all of modern IR theory, a kind of general dissatisfaction with all of Figure 15.1 (the fourth debate). The dissatisfied either emphasize the value of classical, more enduring approaches such as classical realism, classical liberalism, political theory, or Marxism; or they see a temporal move beyond this constellation into post-international theory as with postcolonialism, globalization theory, and green theory. Is the fifth debate to be found in this emerging pattern?

Conclusion: What are we doing? How are we doing?

On the basis of the preceding chapters, I have taken stock of where, what, and how IR is today, and in doing this use some of the theories from the sociology of science in order to obtain the necessary distance and not become one more article in defence of, and located in, a given IR theory.

This volume is introduced by an argument about the necessity of theory for the understanding of relevant political questions. Interestingly, this claim comes close to being a consensus in the discipline. It agrees on both the following points:

- We should not do IR for IR's sake. IR should be relevant in some sense – not necessarily in the classical instrumental 'adviser to the Prince' sense of useful empirical knowledge which policy-makers draw on; it can also be the poststructuralist political approach to discussing academic practices. Stephen Walt (1999) has as a neorealist attacked rational choice in security studies, primarily because it is not helpful.

- We should not give up theory for the sake of immediate relevance, because IR without theory (or method) is not really helpful in the long run. There are intense discussions between problem-driven and method-driven approaches but this is not about being theoretical or not; more it is a question of different sequences of theory, method, and issue according to different meta-theories. We see occasional appeals for the discipline to be less esoteric and more directly useful (Lepgold and Nincic 2001; Jentleson 2002; cf. Büger and Gadinger 2006), but most often the discipline refuses this trade-off (Peterson, Tiemay, and Maliniak 2005; Wæver and Buzan 2007). Its avoidance is assisted through a division of labour where institutes and think-tanks such as the American Enterprise Institute in Washington or the Royal Institute of International Affairs in London focus exclusively on immediate policy.

The ideal in the discipline is relevance through theory, not excessive policy orientation. This rules out the route taken by many disciplines (both natural, humanistic, and social ones) of treating the discipline as an end in itself. In Fuller's harsh words, a discipline 'forms *not* by staking out a clear domain *for itself*, but rather by successively failing to control some *other* body of knowledge' (Fuller 2002 [1998]: 191). Not IR. There is a general sense that the subject matter is too important for that – that IR is ultimately justified by the severity of its issues.

Many student readers of this book will be exasperated by the amount of theory, but it is a red herring to construct a debate for and against theory. Perhaps there is a more significant question. Are we getting better at theory? This is often discussed as progress or 'cumulation'. 'A good indicator for a noncumulative field is that it has a debate on whether cumulation is possible or not' (Fuchs 1993: 947). This debate on progress in IR often gets trapped because it is unfavourably compared with the process of cumulation that takes place in the natural sciences. However, Stephan Fuchs among others has argued that different specialties with different structures change through different processes. Some of the indicators associated with 'progress' – a fiercely competitive 'research frontier' especially – are not indicative of progress *per se*, but of a specific *kind* associated with the natural sciences. And the social sciences are unlikely to become this kind of 'high consensus, rapid discovery science' (Collins 1994). Not because there will be no discoveries, a lack of empiricism, or too much ideological controversy, but because modern science since Galileo became organized around 'the practice of adapting or inventing technologies for purposes of research' (Collins 1994). Since new equipment is not central to social sciences, they are unlikely to get the same pattern of development.

This does not spell 'no improvement' in a general sense. Only through misleading standards of natural science (and labelling all else as relativism and 'anything goes') does the discipline fear that no judgements can be passed and nothing deemed better than anything else (Kratochwil 2003, 2006). In practice, we evaluate and value all the time – in the classroom, at the exam table, reviewing for journals, hearing a lecture – all the choices aim at improving the situation from our perspective. Naturally we often produce progress according to the practical criteria relevant today. (It would not necessarily have been progress seen from the perspective of a colleague doing what he did fifty or seventy-five years ago.) It is our progress.

As a young discipline, the evergrowing layers of reflection on predecessors produce increasing depth and sophistication not least of self-reflection. Self-reflection grows both meta-theoretically (Lapid 2002, 2003; Chapter 1 in this volume), through sociology of science-based self-examinations, and politically (Smith 2004). IR increasingly understands itself and, as the case studies in the preceding chapters show:[9] all the theories can tell us a lot about the world of 'i.r.'. In a diverse discipline like IR, the challenge is not to achieve knowledge, but how to understand the multiplicity of it, and this is only possible when we understand both the world and the processes through which our understanding of it came about.

? QUESTIONS

1. Why does a discipline not die or change if its subject matter changes shape in the real world?

2. When more and more important questions do not fit within the boundaries of distinct disciplines, should we not reorganize ourselves in interdisciplinary units defined by the things we study? What would be the advantages and disadvantages of this?

3. What are the most important resources to control in order to have influence within the discipline of IR?

4. The chapter mentions three factors whose change influences the social structure of the discipline. Can you think of other actual or potential changes in either society at large or academe that would change the discipline, and in what directions?

5. What are the main advantages and disadvantages of seeing the discipline in terms of 'great debates'?

6. Why has the narrative of great debates been so influential in IR?

7. If there is to be a fifth debate in IR what do you think it would look like?

OLE WÆVER

■ **Walter Carlsnaes, Thomas Risse, and Beth, A. Simmons (2002) (eds),** *Handbook of International Relations* **(London: Sage).** Comprehensive overview of the discipline with articles covering theories, issue areas, concepts, and meta-theory. It succeeds surprisingly well in covering both American and European debates. Looking up any specific field, the article is likely to be a treasure trove of references and ideas for further research, but often very compact.

■ **Ira Katznelson and Helen V. Milner (2002) (eds),** *Political Science: State of the Discipline* **(New York and London: Norton).** The latest 'authoritative' handbook sponsored by the American Political Science Association. Gives the same kind of dense overview as the previous text (although for all of political science), but interestingly it attempts to avoid the sub-field structure and defines fields cutting across e.g. an IR/comparative politics divide.

■ **Donald J. Puchala (2002) (ed.),** *Visions of International Relations: Assessing an Academic Field* **(Columbia: University of South Carolina Press).** Eight prominent scholars from very different approaches assess the field and present their visions for the discipline.

■ **Arlene B. Tickner (2003), 'Seeing IR Differently: Notes from the Third World',** *Millennium: Journal of International Studies,* **32/2: 295–324.** Seminal article re-examining key categories, including war and conflict, the state, sovereignty/autonomy, and nationalism, showing the value of Third World perspectives.

■ **Jörg Friedrichs (2004),** *European Approaches to International Relations Theory: A House with Many Mansions* **(London: Routledge).** This ambitious, short book contains, among other things, a report on Italian, French, and Scandinavian IR, their interpretation in terms of centre–periphery relationship to the USA, and a discussion of lessons about strategies to adopt for a more unified European IR.

■ **Knud Erik Jørgensen and Tonny B. Knudsen (2006) (eds),** *International Relations in Europe* **(London: Routledge).** This collection studies developments in the International Relations discipline in Europe including factors influencing theory development and options *vis-à-vis* the American centre.

■ **Arlene B. Tickner and Ole Wæver (2007) (eds),** *The World of International Relations Scholarship: Geocultural Epistemologies,* **Vol 1 (London: Routledge).** The state of IR in all parts of the world is surveyed and explained, which makes quite concrete what the tensions and difficulties are for articulating new IR insights from the periphery.

■ **Jennifer Sterling-Folker (2006) (ed.),** *Making Sense of International Relations Theory* **(Boulder CO: Lynne Rienner).** All the main IR theories make sense out of 'Kosovo' (the crisis and NATO intervention in 1998–9), and the book is an excellent occasion for students to see (and compare) the theories in action. A unique and very informative exercise.

 Visit the Online Resource Centre that accompanies this book for lots of interesting additional material. www.oxfordtextbooks.co.uk/orc/dunne/

Notes

Introduction

[1] This phrase could be found, at one time, on the office wall of Nicholas J. Wheeler, my former colleague in Aberystwyth.

Chapter 1

[1] We have used the terminology of International Relations (IR) only as a matter of convenience and convention. We do not mean to imply that this restricts the discipline to the study of relations between international actors. We prefer the term 'global' since we think the discipline does, and should, study the totality of global interactions among a vast range of actors.

[2] Some other authors in this volume follow Lapid (1989), and refer to this as the third debate. However, we follow Wæver's (1996) distinction between the interparadigm and the fourth debate.

[3] It may be that many so-called 'positivists' within the discipline are 'naive' realists, since they are often unreflective about the philosophy underpinning their research practices. However, positivism, as a philosophy of science, is clearly not realist in a 'naive' sense.

[4] This type of theory can also be interpreted as causal if causal analysis is equated with analysis of causal powers carried within objects. Because many critical realists see causal analysis as analysis of causal powers, they would not necessarily see constitutive theory as a form of non-causal theorizing, as many other post-positivists do.

[5] Importantly, this provides yet another point of critique through which critical theories might be constructed. For the critical theorist can take these views of the social actor and be critical of them. Hence if a group of social actors has the view that X group needs to be eradicated because of belief Y, and if the social theorist shows belief Y to be false, then the theorist must necessarily be critical of both belief Y and the view that group X needs to be eradicated.

[6] The dominant theories of truth are the 'correspondence theory', the 'coherence theory', the 'conventionalist, or consensus, theory', and the 'pragmatic theory'. The correspondence theory of truth sees truth as correspondence with objective reality. Thus, a sentence is said to be true if it refers to a state of affairs that exists in the world. Most scientists and many philosophers hold some version of the correspondence theory of truth. It is the dominant theory of truth for most positivists in IR. The coherence theory sees truth as coherence with some specified set of sentences or, more often, of beliefs. For example, belief held by an individual is true if it is coherent with all or most of their other beliefs. Usually, coherence is taken to imply something stronger than mere consistency: justification, evidence, and comprehensiveness of the belief set are common restrictions. The consensus theory holds that truth is whatever is agreed upon or, in some versions, might come to be agreed upon, by some specified group. This tends to be the theory of truth adopted by many of the postpositivists who argue that truth is constructed by social processes, which are historically and culturally specific, and shaped through the power struggles within a community. Pragmatism sees truth as the success of the practical consequences of an idea, i.e. its utility.

Chapter 2

[1] I am grateful to the editors and to David Boucher for comments on an earlier draft of this chapter. The usual disclaimers apply.

[2] For a useful overview, see David Boucher and Paul Kelly (1994).

[3] A central figure here is Quentin Skinner; see his collected papers *Visions of Politics: Regarding Method* (2002) and James Tully's *Meaning and Context: Quentin Skinner and His Critics* (1988). For an overview placing Skinner's work alongside other approaches to the interpretation of texts see Terence Ball (2004).

[4] The most influential study of the rise of civic republicanism is J. G. A. Pocock (2003); for a pithier study, Quentin Skinner (1997).

[5] See www.un.org/millenniumgoals/ for details of the UN programme. The impressive list of sponsors of the Trade Justice Movement can be found at www.tjm.org.uk/.

[6] For a fuller discussion of the putative shift from international to global justice, see Chris Brown (2006).

[7] See Boucher and Kelly (1994) for a fuller account of Rawls's conceptual apparatus.

[8] See Jagdish Baghwati (2004) for a neo-liberal perspective, and Meghnad Desai (2002) for a (surprisingly similar) Marxist viewpoint.

[9] David Miller is the best source for this reading of nationalism; see his *On Nationality* (1995) and David Miller and Michael Walzer, *Pluralism, Justice and Equality* (1995).

Chapter 3

[1] See Lebow (2003: 68–70, 217–20) for brief biographies.

[2] Morgenthau and Hannah Arendt were friends and colleagues, and their extensive correspondence suggests that they drew on each other's insights in their work. Morgenthau was favourably impressed by Arendt's *Eichmann in Jerusalem: A Report on the Banality of Evil* (1964).

Chapter 4

[1] The presence of a preponderant power is not the same as unipolarity, because a preponderant power is not the only great power in the system. In unipolarity, there is a single great power.

Chapter 5

[1] While Andrew Moravcsik's own contribution to International Relations theory remains in the upper-left box of actor-centred rationalist liberalism, his 1997 review article discusses 'ideational liberalism' as a constructivist version of liberalism.

[2] Russett's book *Grasping the Democratic Peace* (1993) is hard to group here, since he discusses different explanations for the 'democratic peace' that rest on both rationalist and constructivist assumptions.

[3] For good narratives of the case, see e.g. Woodward (2004) and Pond (2004).

[4] But please note once again that the applicability of democratic peace theory to this particular case is questionable.

Chapter 6

[1] Neoliberalism is often referred to as 'neoliberal institutionalism'. In this chapter, I am using the former but without implying any difference between the two labels.

[2] This work built on Keohane and Nye (1977), who had studied international cooperation, by introducing a more rigorous and parsimonious theoretical framework.

[3] The terms of trade are the relative price of imports to exports. A country improves its terms of trade by increasing the price it gets for its exports, or by paying less for its imports. Obviously, a shift in these terms will benefit one side while hurting the other. Thus, as long as trade agreements must be approved by all parties, they must hold the terms of trade constant, otherwise one side will veto the agreement.

[4] Nevertheless, nearly all enforcement cases at the WTO come from interested parties, not from the WTO's own efforts.

Chapter 7

[1] This chapter benefited significantly from input from my fellow editors, and from Jocelyn Vaughn in the graduate school at Exeter. I would like to thank Colin Wight for his inspired guidance and also the postgraduates in politics at the University of Sheffield for their gentle criticisms. Thank you also to Penny Stanley for providing shelter from the storm.

[2] It is important, at an early stage in the chapter, to discuss the difficulties attached to the label 'English school'. If the label is taken literally, then it is highly misleading: many of the founding members and leading lights were not English (Charles Manning was a South African and Hedley Bull was an Australian). However, it is fairly routine to sever the connection between scholarly identity and territoriality. As one Canadian defender of the English school put it, those who are in the English school 'are as likely to reside outside of England: in Wales, Australia, Canada, Norway, Germany, even the US' (Epp 1999: 48). It is worth noting that this distinction between people and place is relatively uncontroversial in the case of those critical theorists in IR who associate with the 'Frankfurt school', even though the closest they are likely to come to the famous Institute for Social Research is Frankfurt airport.

[3] In his work on humanitarian intervention, Nicholas Wheeler has developed and applied both of these insights (2000).

[4] Despite the centrality of the concept, one can find in the English school literature several usages. It exists either 'as a set of ideas to be found in the minds of statesmen' (Manning being an exponent), or 'as a set of ideas to be found in the minds of political theorists' (which he likens to a Wightean approach), or 'as a set of externally imposed concepts that define the material and social structures of the international system'. These contending usages of international society are mapped out by Buzan (2004: 12–15) and subjected to scrutiny in Dunne (2005).

[5] This section draws heavily on the following sources: Dunne and Wheeler (1999), Foot (2000), and Risse, Ropp, and Sikkink (1999).

[6] The entire Helsinki Final Act document can be read at the HR Net website. See http://www.hri.org/docs/Helsinki75.html.

Chapter 8

[1] This chapter is not using capital C and T for Critical Theory. This goes somewhat against the grain in terms of the often-made distinction between Critical Theory which has its roots in Marxism and Frankfurt school social theory, and critical theories which embrace a wide range of non-mainstream positions in the field. This convention has been abandoned in part because we have reservations about its merits but also because none of the theoretical positions in this volume appears in upper case (unless they relate to a proper noun such as Marxism). For a contrasting view of the merits of the upper case/lower case distinction, see Chris Brown (1994).

[2] Marx's language here betrays an historical context prior to the women's movement and feminist theorizations of the political economy of the household and culture of gendered privilege (see Sayer 1991: 31–2). This should not be misunderstood as implying that Marxist or socialist feminisms are inconceivable: for a striking example of this kind of work, see Barrett (1980).

[3] Again, we may note in Marx's language the historically prevailing Eurocentric cultural norms of which he was himself not innocent (see Sayer 1991: 14–20). Whether Eurocentrism is intrinsic to Marxism as such is a matter of controversy. My own view, in a nutshell, is that this is not necessarily the case, especially as regards those versions of Marxism which eschew economic determinism and teleological understandings of history (Rupert 2005).

[4] For a more fully developed version of these arguments, see Rupert and Solomon (2006), ch. 5.

Chapter 9

[1] A note is in order about my use of the term positivism, which is as 'essentially contested' as constructivism and is also associated with a range of philosophical traditions, many of which have been discredited in the larger scientific world. For a more detailed discussion of the meaning of positivism within IR, see Chapter 1.

[2] It should be noted that 'emancipation' is a concept associated with the Frankfurt school of critical theory (see Chapter 8) which is distinct from poststructuralism. Poststructuralists do not generally embrace this concept. The two schools of thought tend, however, to be conflated in the contrast with conventional constructivism.

[3] The linguistic turn in philosophy introduced language to the relationship between logic and world. The phrase 'linguistic turn' is often associated with Wittgenstein's later work, and particularly his *Philosophical Investigations*

(1958), but it actually originated with his earlier *Tractatus Logico-philosophicus* (1922). This work influenced the logical positivism of the Vienna Circle and its conception of verification. By contrast, *Philosophical Investigations* influenced a number of different philosophers, from the constructivism of Anthony Giddens and John Searle, to the critical theory of Jurgen Habermas, as well as the poststructuralism of Richard Rorty and Jean François Lyotard.

[4] The material interest in expansion did become more obvious after 2001, and the global threat of terrorism, so the phenomenon to be explained is the initial wave of expansion prior to that time.

[5] For a more extended analysis of this process, see Fierke (1999).

Chapter 10

[1] Jacqui True (2003) made the distinction that first-generation feminist work in IR was theory-building, where second-generation work does empirical research investigating the implications of those theories for global politics (see Moon 1997; Prügl 1999).

[2] Harding (1986) points out that the problem with purported 'objective' knowledge is that only a small percentage of voices is represented in the production of that knowledge. Specifically, most knowledge is produced by white, Western men, while the voices most often excluded from the knowledge-production process are those of women and minorities.

[3] Jean Elshtain (1992) explains that the just war tradition produces a narrative of heroic, masculine soldiers (just warriors) protecting innocent, female civilians (beautiful souls), justifying violence *for* women while neglecting violence against women.

[4] See UN Security Council Resolution 687; S/RES/687, 1991. Resolution 687 included demands that Iraq recognize and respect Kuwait's independence; allow a demilitarized zone between Iraq and Kuwait; surrender all nuclear, biological, chemical, and long-range weapons, weapons research, and weapons-related material; accept liability for the First Gulf War in its entirety; return all Kuwaiti possessions stolen during occupation; repatriate all Kuwaiti prisoners of war; and renounce terrorist activities as legitimate politics.

Chapter 11

[1] In addition to the editors, I am grateful to Martin Coward, Marieke de Goede, Debbie Lisle, and Simon Philpott for critical commentaries on drafts of this chapter. All responsibility for the final version nonetheless remains mine.

2 See the entry on de Saussure and semiotics on the Communication, Cultural and Media Studies website (www.ccms-infobase.com) for a good discussion with examples of this approach.

3 The list could include Jean Baudrillard, Helene Cixous, Gilles Deleuze, Jacques Derrida, Luce Irigaray, Jacques Lacan, Emmanuel Levinas, Jean-François Lyotard, Paul Virilio, and many, many others. It would be wrong to argue their philosophies are identical, and it would be a mistake to ignore the many differences between them. For good introductions to the range of poststructuralist philosophy, see Descombes (1981), Culler (1982), White (1991), Edkins (1999), and Hoy (2004).

4 A number of media studies demonstrate the pervasiveness of this negative imagery and its effects on understandings of the global South. For downloadable copies of studies by the UK Department for International Development, the International Broadcasting Trust, 3WE, and the VSO, see http://www.imaging-famine.org/gov_ngo.htm. The figure of 80% of UK respondents comes from the 2001 VSO report, *The Live Aid Legacy*.

Chapter 12

1 I say a place called Europe because I do not believe that Europe has a fixed identity and fixed traditions. I also wish to underscore historical codependencies among regions of the world.

2 One witnesses defections today from the international regime on nuclear weapons during the February 2006 vote on Iran. It was the first time in its history that the International Atomic and Energy Agency could not reach a consensus on condemning a clear violation of the non-proliferation treaty. Of the thirty-five governors, who represent countries, twenty-seven supported the measure, three opposed it, and five abstained. While it may be argued that the votes of the dissenters were to be expected, the abstention of South Africa and Brazil was a significant indicator of a certain sentiment of injustice.

3 On modernity, subjectivity, and violence, see for instance, Richard Ashley (1987), David Campbell and Michael Dillon (1993), and Chris Brown (1988).

Chapter 13

1 In common with other chapters in the textbook, I am using neoliberalism as a shorthand for neoliberal institutionalism, and using neorealism as being synonymous with what John Mearsheimer (in Chapter 4) calls structural realism.

2 This period also saw the formation of the world's first proto-green parties in Australasia and Europe in direct response to the publication of *A Blueprint for Survival* (1972).

3 While the description 'green political theory' is widely used in Europe and Australasia, in North America it is more typically referred to as 'environmental political theory'.

4 For example, Mathew Paterson (2000) has provided an innovative green neo-Gramscian study that tracks the power of, and ecological shadow cast by, the global automobile industry, which includes a critique of 'car culture'.

Chapter 15

1 Classical examples of diagnoses of the discipline (of political science or IR) which pronounce a condition of disintegration and lack of coherence are Holsti (1985); Almond (1990); Katznelson and Milner (2002); Laitin (2004). For reflections on the discipline, see Gunnell (2002); Grant (2005). Put in more critical terms: hegemonic actors in the discipline carry out constant practices of boundary-drawing and exclusion to ensure a hegemonic conception of the discipline. However, this critical observation should not lead one uncritically to believe in an actual risk to the survival of the discipline. This boundary maintaining practice is primarily power politics *within* it.

2 See also the concluding section of Chapter 1 which stresses the importance of the internal structure of disciplines, and the importance of the academic world as the immediate social setting for the actions of theorists. See also Collins (1975, 1998).

3 It is widely believed that we are currently in or heading towards a novel situation in which the traditional disciplines are out of synch with major issues and concerns, and so many claim there is more room for multi-disciplinary work. This, however, is far from a new perception. '[T]he emphasis on interdisciplinarity emerged contemporaneously with, not after, the disciplines. There was no long process of ossification; the one bred the other almost immediately' (Abbott 2001: 312).

4 A recent survey of the hiring criteria used by department chairs supports this interpretation: 'First and foremost, the survey results establish "fit" as the most important factor across school types. Whether a job candidate works in the sub-field of the available position is of greater importance than anything else' (Fuerstman and Lavertu 2005: 734).

5 Whitley distinguishes between two kinds of mutual dependence, 'functional dependence' and 'strategic dependence'; for explanation and a detailed application of these concepts to IR, see Wæver (1998, 2003).

6 This showed statistically (in Wæver 1998: fig. 3) that a high proportion of articles in American journals fitted

into the dominant categories compared to especially the British journals.

7 'Perestroika' was a revolt – probably led by graduate students – in political science. It started in 2000 with an anonymous email signed 'Mr. Perestroika', attacking especially the dominance and privileging of rational choice and quantitative approaches in the journals and governance structure of the American Political Science Association. Much of the debate can be followed in the journal *PS: Political Science and Politics* and Monroe (2005).

8 There has been much criticism of the accuracy of the debates as history writing (Wæver 1997; Wilson 1998; Schmidt 1998) – plus some rebuttals (Vigneswaran and Quirk 2005). Irrespective of their historical accuracy as general portrait, these powerful images had real effects as they structured key moves, which decisively shaped the discipline.

9 See Sterling-Folker (2006) for a similar exercise in which the different theories speak to the *same* case – Kosovo. The book shows that all have something important to say.

Bibliography

Abbott, A. (2001), *Chaos of Disciplines* (Chicago: University of Chicago Press).

—— (2002), 'The Disciplines and the Future', in S. Brint (ed.), *The Future of the City of Intellect: The Changing American University* (Standard CA: Stanford University Press).

Adler, E. (1997), 'Seizing the Middle Ground: Constructivism in World Politics', *European Journal of International Relations*, 3/3: 319–63.

—— (2002), 'Constructivism and International Relations' in W. Carlsnaes, T. Risse, and B. A. Simmons (eds), *Handbook of International Relations* (London: Sage), 95–118.

Adorno, T. and Horkheimer, M. (1972), *The Dialectic of Enlightenment* (New York: Herder).

Alderson, K. and Hurrell, A. (2000), *Hedley Bull on International Society* (Basingstoke: Macmillan).

Almond, G. (1990), *A Discipline Divided* (Newbury Park CA: Sage).

Angell, N. (1913), *The Great Illusion: A Study of Military Power to National Advantage* (New York: G. P. Putnam's Sons, Knickerbocker Press).

Anzuldúa, G. (1999), *Borderlands/La Frontiera*, 2nd edn (San Francisco: Aunt Lute Books).

Appadurai, A. and Breckenridge, C. (1990), *The Making of a Transnational Culture: Asians in America and the Nature of Ethnicity* (New York: Berg Publishers).

Arendt, H. (1964), *Eichmann in Jerusalem: A Report on the Banality of Evil* (New York: Viking).

Aristotle (1984), *The Complete Works of Aristotle: The Revised Oxford Translation*, edited by J. Barnes (Princeton NJ: Princeton University Press).

Armstrong, D. (1999), 'Law, Justice and the Idea of World Society', *International Affairs*, 75/3: 547–61.

Asad, T. (1993), *Genealogies of Religion: Discipline and Reasons of Power in Christianity and Islam* (Baltimore MD: Johns Hopkins University Press).

Ashcroft, B., Giffiths, G., and Tiffin, H. (1990), *The Empire Writes Back: Theory and Practice in Post-colonial Literatures* (New York: Routledge).

Ashley, R. (1981), 'Political Realism and Human Interests', *International Studies Quarterly*, 25/2: 204–36.

—— (1984), 'The Poverty of Neorealism', *International Organization*, 38/2: 225–86.

—— (1986), 'The Poverty of Neorealism', in R. Keohane (ed.), *Neorealism and Its Critics* (New York: Columbia University Press), 255–300.

—— (1987), 'The Geopolitics of Geopolitical Space: Towards a Critical Social Theory of International Politics', *Alternatives*, 12/4: 403–34.

—— (1988), 'Untying the Sovereign State: A Double Reading of the Anarchy Problematique', *Millennium: Journal of International Studies*, 17/2: 227–62.

—— (1989), 'Living on Boarder Lines: Man, Poststructuralism and War', in J. Der Derian and M. Shapiro (eds), *International/Intertextual Relations: Postmodern Readings of World Politics* (Lexington KY: Lexington Books), 259–322.

Ashley, R. and Walker, R. B. J. (1990) (eds), 'Conclusion: Reading Dissidence/Writing the Discipline: Crisis and the Question of Sovereignty in International Studies', *International Studies Quarterly*, 34/3: 367–416.

Baghwati, J. (2004), *In Defence of Globalization* (Oxford: Oxford University Press).

Bagwell, K. and Staiger, R. (1999), 'An Economic Theory of GATT', *American Economic Review*, 49/1: 215–48.

Bain, W. (2003), *Between Anarchy and Society: Trusteeship and the Obligations of Power* (Oxford: Oxford University Press).

Bairoch, P. (1996), 'Globalisation Myths and Realities: One Century of External Trade and Foreign Investment', in R. Boyer and D. Drache (eds), *States Against Market: The Limits of Globalisation* (London: Routledge), 173–92.

Baldwin, D. (1985), *Economic Statecraft* (Princeton NJ: Princeton University Press).

Ball, T. (2004), 'History and the Interpretation of Texts', in G. Gaus and C. Kukathas (eds), *Handbook of Political Theory* (London: Sage Publications).

Banks, M. (1984), 'The Evolution of International Relations', in M. Banks (ed.), *Conflict in World Society: A New Perspective on International Relations* (Brighton: Harvester Press), 3–21.

Barbieri, K. (2002), *The Liberal Illusion: Does Trade Promote Peace?* (Ann Arbor: University of Michigan Press).

Barnett, J. (2001), *The Meaning of Environmental Security: Ecological Politics and Policy in the New Security Era* (London: Zed Books).

Barnett, M. and Finnemore, M. (2004), *Rules for the World: International Organizations in Global Politics* (Ithaca NY: Cornell University Press).

Barrett, M. (1980), *Women's Oppression Today: The Marxist/Feminist Encounter* (London: Verso).

Barry, B. (1998), 'International Society from a Cosmopolitan Perspective', in D. Mapel and T. Nardin (eds), *International Society* (Princeton NJ: Princeton University Press), 144–63.

Barry, J. (1999), *Rethinking Green Politics* (London: Sage Publications).

Barry, J. and Eckersley, R. (2005), *The State and the Global Ecological Crisis* (Cambridge MA: MIT Press).

Bayoumi, T. (1990), 'Savings–Investment Correlations', *IMF Staff Papers*, 37: 360–87.

—— (1997), *Financial Integration and Real Activity* (Manchester: Manchester University Press).

Beck, U. (1992), *The Risk Society: Towards a New Modernity*, translated by M. Ritter (London: Sage Publications).

Beitz, C. R. (1979/2000), *Political Theory and International Relations*, 1st/2nd edns (Princeton NJ: Princeton University Press).

Beitz, C. R., Lawrence, A. A., and Scanlon, T. (1985) (eds), *International Ethics* (Princeton NJ: Princeton University Press).

Bensmaïa, R. (2003), *Experimental Nations: Or, the Invention of the Maghreb* (Princeton NJ: Princeton University Press).

Benthall, J. (1993), *Disasters, Relief and the Media* (London: I. B. Tauris).

Berger, Peter L. (2002), 'Introduction: The Cultural Dynamics of Globalization', in P. L. Berger and S. P. Huntington (eds), *Many Globalizations: Cultural Diversity in the Contemporary World* (Oxford: Oxford University Press), 1–16.

Bernstein, R. (1979), *The Restructuring of Social and Political Theory* (London: Methuen).

—— (1983), *Beyond Objectivism and Relativism* (Oxford: Blackwell).

Bhabha, H. (1994), *The Location of Culture* (New York: Routledge).

Bhaskar, R. (1978), *A Realist Theory of Science* (Hassocks: Harvester Press).

—— (1979), *The Possibility of Naturalism: A Philosophical Critique of the Contemporary Human Sciences* (Atlantic Highlands NJ: Humanities Press).

Biswas, S. (2001), ' "Nuclear Apartheid" as Political Position: Race as a Postcolonial Resource?', *Alternatives*, 26/4: 485(38).

Bleiker, R. (1997), 'Forget IR Theory', *Alternatives*, 22/1: 57–85.

—— (2000), *Popular Dissent, Human Agency and Global Politics* (Cambridge: Cambridge University Press).

—— (2001), 'The Aesthetic Turn in International Political Theory', *Millennium: Journal of International Studies*, 30/3: 509–33.

—— (2005), *Divided Korea: Toward a Culture of Reconciliation* (Minneapolis: University of Minnesota Press).

Bohr, N. (1957), *Atomfysik og menneskelig erkendelse* (Copenhagen: J. H. Schultz Forlag).

Booth, K. (1995), 'Dare Not Know: International Relations Theory versus the Future', in K. Booth and S. Smith (eds), *International Relations Theory Today* (Cambridge: Polity).

—— (1997), 'Discussion: A Reply to Wallace', *Review of International Studies*, 23/2: 371–7.

Börzel, T. A. (1999), 'Towards Convergence in Europe? Institutional Adaptation to Europeanization in Germany and Spain', *Journal of Common Market Studies*, 37/4: 573–96.

Boucher, D. (1998), *Political Theories of International Relations* (Oxford: Oxford University Press).

Boucher, D. and Kelly, P. (1994) (eds), *The Social Contract from Hobbes to Rawls* (London: Routledge).

Breuning, M., Bredehoft, J., and Walton, E. (2005), 'Promise and Performance: An Evaluation of Journals in International Relations', *International Studies Perspectives*, 6/4: 447–61.

Brewer, A. (1990), *Marxist Theories of Imperialism: A Critical Survey*, 2nd edn (London: Routledge).

Brown, C. (1988), 'The Modern Requirement? Reflections on Normative International Theory in a Post-Western World', *Millennium: Journal of International Studies*, 17/2: 339–48.

—— (1994), ' "Turtles All the Way Down": Antifoundationalism, Critical Theory and International Relations', *Millennium: Journal of International Studies*, 23/2: 213–38.

—— (1997), *Understanding International Relations* (Basingstoke: Macmillan).

—— (2002), *Sovereignty, Rights and Justice* (Cambridge: Polity).

—— (2006), 'From International to Global Justice?', in J. S. Dryzek, B. Honig, and A. Philips (eds), *The Oxford Handbook of Political Theory* (Oxford: Oxford University Press).

Brown, C., Nardin, T., and Rengger, N. J. (2002) (eds), *International Relations in Political Thought: Texts from the Ancient Greeks to the First World War* (Cambridge: Cambridge University Press).

Brown, M. E., Coté Jr, O. R., Lynn-Jones, S. M., and Miller, S. E. (2004) (eds), *Offense, Defense, and War* (Cambridge MA: MIT Press).

Brown, M. E., Lynn-Jones, S. M., and Miller, S. E. (1996) (eds), *Debating the Democratic Peace* (Cambridge MA: MIT Press).

Brown Weiss, E. and Jacobson, H. K. (1998), *Engaging Countries: Strengthening Compliance with International Accords* (Cambridge MA: MIT Press).

Bryant, R. and Bailey, S. (1997), *Third World Political Ecology* (London: Routledge).

Bueno de Mesquita, B. J., Jackman, W. A., and Silverson, R. M. (1991) (eds), 'Democracy and Foreign Policy: Community and Constraint', *Journal of Conflict Resolution* (special issue), 35/2.

316

Bueno de Mesquita, B. J. and Lalman, D. (1992), *War and Reason* (New Haven CT: Yale University Press).

Büger, C. and Gadinger, F. (2006) 'Große Gräben, Brücken, Elfenbeintürme und Klöster? Die Wissensgemeinschaft Internationale Beziehungen und die Politik – Eine kultur-theoretische Neubeschreibung', in G. Hellmann (ed.), *Forschung und Beratung in der Wissensgesellschaft*, (Baden-Baden: Nomos).

Bull, H. (1977/1995), *The Anarchical Society: A Study, of Order in World Politics* (London: Macmillan).

—— (2000), 'International Relations as an Academic Pursuit', in K. Alderson and A. Hurrell (eds), *Hedley Bull on International Society* (Basingstoke: Macmillan).

Bull, H. and Watson, A. (1984), *The Expansion of International Society* (Oxford: Clarendon Press).

Busch, M. L. (2000), 'Democracy, Consultation, and the Paneling of Disputes Under GATT', *Journal of Conflict Resolution*, 44/4: 425–46.

Busch, M. L. and Reinhardt, E. (2003), 'Developing Countries and General Agreement on Tariffs and Trade/World Trade Organization Dispute Settlement', *Journal of World Trade*, 37/4: 719–35.

Butler, J. (1993), *Bodies that Matter: On the Discursive Limits of 'Sex'* (New York: Routledge).

Bütler, M. and Hauser, H. (2000), 'The WTO Dispute Settlement System: A First Assessment from an Economic Perspective', *Journal of Law, Economics, and Organization*, 16/2: 503–33.

Butterfield, H. and Wight, M. (1966) (eds), *Diplomatic Investigations: Essays in the Theory of International Relations* (London: Allen & Unwin).

Buzan, B. (2001), 'The English School: An Underexploited Resource in IR', *Review of International Studies*, 27/3, 471–88.

—— (2004), *From International to World Society* (Cambridge: Cambridge University Press, 2004).

Buzan, B., Held, D., and McGrew, A. (1998), 'Realism versus Cosmopolitanism' *Review of International Studies*, 24/3: 387–98.

Buzan, B., Jones, C. A., and Little, R. (1993), *The Logic of Anarchy: Neorealism to Structural Realism* (New York: Columbia University Press).

Buzan, B. and Little, R. (2000), *International Systems in World History: Remaking the Study of International Relations* (Oxford: Oxford University Press).

Bybee, J. S. (2002), 'Memo 14 – Re: Standards of Conduct for Interrogation', in K. J. Greenberg, J. L. Dratel, and A. Lewis (2005), *The Torture Papers: The Road to Abu Ghraib* (Cambridge: Cambridge University Press).

Cameron, D. R. (1978), 'The Expansion of the Public Economy: A Comparative Analysis', *American Political Science Review*, 72/4: 1243–61.

Campbell, D. (1992), *Writing Security: United States Foreign Policy and the Politics of Identity* (Manchester: Manchester University Press).

—— (1998a), *Writing Security: United States Foreign Policy and the Politics of Identity*, 2nd edn (Minneapolis: University of Minnesota Press).

—— (1998b), *National Deconstruction: Violence, Identity and Justice in Bosnia* (Minneapolis: University of Minnesota Press).

—— (2005), 'The Biopolitics of Security: Oil, Empire and the Sports Utility Vehicle', *American Quarterly*, 57/3: 943–72.

Campbell, D. and Dillon, M. (1993), *The Political Subject of Violence* (Manchester: Manchester University Press).

Campbell, D. T. (1969), 'Ethnocentrism of Disciplines and the Fish-scale Model of Omniscience', in M. Sherif and C. W. Sherif (eds), *Interdisciplinary Relationships in the Social Sciences* (Chicago: Aldine Publishing), 328–48.

Caprioli, M. and Boyer, M. (2001), 'Gender, Violence, and International Crisis', *Journal of Conflict Resolution*, 45/4: 503–18.

Carlsnaes, W. (2002), 'Foreign Policy', in W. Carlsnaes, T. Risse, and B. A. Simmons (eds), *Handbook of International Relations* (London: Sage), 331–49.

Carlsnaes, W., Risse, T., and Simmons, B. A. (2002) (eds), *Handbook of International Relations* (London: Sage).

Carr, E. H. (1946), *The Twenty Years' Crisis 1919–1939: An Introduction to the Study of International Relations*, 2nd edn (London: Macmillan).

—— (1987), *What Is History?*, 2nd edn (London: Penguin).

Cerny, P. G. (1995), 'Globalisation and the Changing Logic of Collective Action', *International Organisation*, 49/4: 595–625.

—— (1997), 'Paradoxes of the Competition State: The Dynamics of Political Globalisation', *Government and Opposition*, 32/1: 251–74.

—— (2000), 'Political Globalisation and the Competition State', in R. Stubbs and G. R. D. Underhill (eds), *Political Economy and the Changing Global Order* (Oxford: Oxford University Press).

Césaire, A. (2000), *Discourse on Colonialism*, translated by J. Pinkham (New York: Monthly Review Press).

Chakrabarty, D. (2000), *Provincializing Europe: Postcolonial Thought and Historical Difference* (Princeton NJ: Princeton University Press).

Chase, K. (2003), 'Economic Interests and Regional Trading Arrangements: The Case of NAFTA', *International Organization*, 57/1: 137–74.

Chatterjee, P. (1986), *Nationalist Thought and the Colonial World: The Derivative Discourse?* (Minneapolis: University of Minnesota Press).

Chayes, A. and Chayes, A. H. (1993), 'On Compliance', *International Organization*, 47/2: 175–205.

Checkel, J. T. (1997), 'International Norms and Domestic Politics: Bridging the Rationalist–Constructivist Divide', *European Journal of International Relations*, 3/4: 473–95.

—— (1998), 'The Constructivist Turn in International Relations Theory', *World Politics*, 50/2: 324–48.

—— (1999), 'Social Construction and Integration', *Journal of European Public Policy*, 6/4: 545–60.

—— (2001), 'Why Comply? Social Learning and European Identity Change', *International Organization*, 55/3: 553–88.

Cheyfitz, E. (1997), *The Poetics of Imperialism: Translation and Colonization from the Tempest to Tarzan* (Philadelphia: University of Pennsylvania Press).

Chin, C. (1998), *In Service and Servitude: Foreign Female Domestic Workers and the Malaysian 'Modernity' Project* (New York: Columbia University Press).

Chowdhry, G. and Nair, S. (2002) (eds), *Power, Postcolonialism and International Relations; Reading Race, Gender and Class* (London: Routledge).

Christoff, P. (1996), 'Ecological Modernisation, Ecological Modernities', *Environmental Politics*, 5/3: 476–500.

Clark, B. R. (1983), *The Higher Education System: Academic Organization in Cross-national Perspective* (Berkeley: University of California Press).

Clark, B. R. and Youn, T. I. K. (1976), *Academic Power in the United States: Comparative Historic and Structural Perspectives* (Washington DC: American Association for Higher Education).

Clark, I. (1999), *Globalisation and International Relations Theory* (Oxford: Oxford University Press).

—— (2005), *Legitimacy in International Society* (Oxford: Oxford University Press).

Cohn, B. S. (1996), *Colonialism and Its Forms of Knowledge: The British in India* (Princeton NJ: Princeton University Press).

Collins, R. (1975), *Conflict Sociology: Towards an Explanatory Science* (New York: Academic).

—— (1994), 'Why the Social Sciences Won't Become High-consensus, Rapid-discovery Science', *Sociological Forum*, 9/2, 155–77.

—— (1998), *The Sociology of Philosophies: A Global Theory of Intellectual Change* (Cambridge MA: Belknap).

Conca, K. (2000), 'Beyond the Statist Frame: Environmental Politics in a Global Economy', in F. P. Gale and R. M. M'Gonigle, *Nature, Production, Power: Towards an Ecological Political Economy* (Cheltenham: Edward Elgar), 141–55.

Conca, K. and Dabelko, G. (2003), *Environmental Peacemaking* (Washington DC: Woodrow Wilson Center Press).

Connolly, W. E. (2004), 'Method, Problem, Faith', in I. Shapiro, R. M. Smith, and T. E. Masoud (eds), *Problems and Methods in the Study of Politics* (Cambridge: Cambridge University Press).

Constantinou, C. M. (1995), 'NATO's Caps: European Security and the Future of the North Atlantic Alliance', *Alternatives*, 20/2: 147–64.

—— (1996), *On the Way to Diplomacy* (Minneapolis: University of Minnesota Press).

Cooke, W. N. and Noble, D. S. (1998), 'Industrial Relations Systems and US Foreign Direct Investment Abroad', *British Journal of Industrial Relations*, 36/4: 581–609.

Copeland, D. C. (2000), *The Origins of Major War* (Ithaca NY: Cornell University Press).

Coward, M. (2002), 'Community as Heterogeneous Ensemble: Mostar and Multiculturalism', *Alternatives*, 27/1: 29–66.

Cowles, M. G., Caporaso, J., and Risse, T. (2001) (eds), *Transforming Europe: Europeanization and Domestic Change* (Ithaca NY: Cornell University Press).

Cox, R. (1981), 'Social Forces, States and World Orders: Beyond International Relations Theory', *Millennium: Journal of International Studies*, 10/2: 126–55.

—— (1986), 'Social Forces, States and World Orders: Beyond International Relations Theories', in R. Keohane (ed.), *Neorealism and its Critics* (New York: Columbia University Press), 204–54.

Cox, R. and Sinclair, T. (1996), *Approaches to World Order* (Cambridge: Cambridge University Press).

Crawford, N. C. and Klotz, A. (1999), *How Sanctions Work: Lessons from South Africa* (New York: Palgrave Macmillan).

Culler, J. (1982), *On Deconstruction: Theory and Criticism after Structuralism* (Ithaca NY: Cornell University Press).

Czempiel, E.-O. (1986), *Friedensstrategien, Systemwandel durch Internationale Organisation, Demokratisierung und Wirtschaft* (Paderborn: Schöningh).

Daalder, I. H. and Lindsay, J. M. (2005), *America Unbound: The Bush Revolution in Foreign Policy*, revised edn (Hoboken NJ: Wiley).

Dam, K. W. (1982), *The Rules of the Game: Reform and Evolution in the International Monetary System* (Chicago: University of Chicago Press).

Darby, P. (2000), *At the Edge of International Relations: Postcolonialism, Gender and Dependency* (Cambridge: Continuum International Publishing Group).

Davis, C. (2003), *Food Fights Over Free Trade: How International Institutions Promote Agricultural Trade Liberalization* (Princeton NJ: Princeton University Press).

Debrix, F. (1999), *Re-envisioning Peacekeeping: The UN and the Mobilization of Ideology* (Minneapolis: University of Minnesota Press).

de Goede, M. (2003), 'Beyond Economism in International Political Economy', *Review of International Studies*, 29/1: 79–97.

—— (2005), *Virtue, Fortune and Faith: A Genealogy of Finance* (Minneapolis: University of Minnesota Press).

—— (2006), *International Political Economy and Poststructural Politics* (Basingstoke: Palgrave).

BIBLIOGRAPHY

Deitelhoff, N. and Müller, H. (2005), 'Theoretical Paradise: Empirically Lost? Arguing with Habermas', *Review of International Studies*, 31/1: 167–79.

Deleuze, G. (1988), *Foucault* (Minneapolis: University of Minnesota Press).

Dell, S. (1981), *On Being Grandmotherly: The Evolution of IMF Conditionality* (Princeton NJ: Princeton University Press).

Der Derian, J. (1987), *On Diplomacy: A Genealogy of Western Estrangement* (Oxford: Blackwell).

—— (1992), *Antidiplomacy: Spies, Terror, Speed, and War* (Oxford: Blackwell).

—— (1994) (ed.), *Critical Investigations* (London: Macmillan).

—— (2001), *Virtuous War: Mapping the Military–Industrial–Media–Entertainment Network* (Boulder CO: Westview).

—— (2003), 'Hedley Bull and the Case for a Post-Classical Approach', in H. Bauer and E. Brighi (eds), *International Relations at LSE: A History of 75 Years* (London: Millennium Publishing Group).

Der Derian, J. and Shapiro, M. J. (1989) (eds), *International/Intertextual Relations: Postmodern Readings of World Politics* (Lexington KY: Lexington Books).

Desai, M. (2002), *Marx's Revenge: The Resurgence of Capitalism and the Death of Statist Socialism* (London: Verso).

Descombes, V. (1981), *Modern French Philosophy*, translated by L. Scott-Fox and J. M. Harding (Cambridge: Cambridge University Press).

Deudney, D. (1990), 'The Case Against Linking Environmental Degradation to National Security', *Millennium: Journal of International Studies*, 19/3: 461–76.

Deutsch, K. W. (1957), *Political Community and the North Atlantic Area* (Princeton NJ: Princeton University Press).

Devetak, R. (1995), 'Critical Theory', in S. Burchill, A. Linklater, *et al.* (eds), *Theories of International Relations* (New York: St Martin's), 145–78.

—— (2001), 'Postmodernism', in S. Burchill, A. Linklater, *et al.* (eds), *Theories of International Relations*, 2nd edn (London: Palgrave), 181–208.

Diamond, L. (2004), 'What Went Wrong in Iraq?', *Foreign Affairs*, 83/September–October: 9–22.

Diani, M. (1996), 'Linking Mobilization Frames and Political Opportunities: Insights from Regional Populism in Italy', *American Sociological Review*, 61/6: 1053–69.

Dickinson, G. L. (1916), *The European Anarchy* (New York: Macmillan Company).

Diels, H. and Kranz, W. (1956), *Die Fragmente der Vorsokratiker*, 7th edn (Berlin: Weidmanische Verlansbuchhandlung).

Dillon, M. (1996), *The Politics of Security: Towards a Political Philosophy of Continental Thought* (London: Routledge).

—— (2000), 'Poststructuralism, Complexity and Poetics', *Theory, Culture and Society*, 17/5: 1–26.

—— (2003), 'Virtual Security: A Life Science of (Dis) Order', *Millennium: Journal of International Studies*, 32/3: 531–8.

Dillon, M. and Reid, J. (2001), 'Global Liberal Governance: Biopolitics, Security and War', *Millennium: Journal of International Studies*, 30/1: 41–66.

Dirks, N. B. (2001), *Castes of Mind: Colonialism and the Making of Modern India* (Princeton NJ: Princeton University Press).

Dobson, A. (2003), *Citizenship and the Environment* (Oxford: Oxford University Press).

Doherty, B. and de Geus, M. (1996) (eds), *Democracy and Green Political Thought: Sustainability, Rights and Citizenship* (London: Routledge).

Doty, R. L. (1993), 'Foreign Policy as Social Construction: A Post-positivist Analysis of US Counterinsurgency Policy in the Philippines', *International Studies Quarterly*, 37/3: 297–320.

—— (1996), *Imperial Encounters: The Politics of Representation in North–South Relations* (Minneapolis: University of Minnesota Press).

Downs, G. W. and Rocke, D. M. (1995), *Optimal Imperfection? Domestic Uncertainty and Institutions in International Relations* (Princeton NJ: Princeton University Press).

Downs, G. W., Rocke, D. M., and Barsoom, P. N. (1996), 'Is the Good News about Compliance Good News about Cooperation?', *International Organization*, 50/3: 379–406.

Doyle, M. (1983), 'Kant, Liberal Legacies, and Foreign Affairs', *Philosophy and Public Affairs*, 12 (3/4).

—— (1986), 'Liberalism and World Politics', *American Political Science Review*, 80/4: 1151–9.

—— (1997), *Ways of War and Peace: Realism, Liberalism, and Socialism* (New York and London: Norton).

Dreher, A. and Vaubel, R. (2004), 'The Causes and Consequences of IMF Conditionality', *Emerging Markets Finance and Trade*, 40/3: 26–54.

Dreyfuss, R. (2003), 'The Thirty-year Itch', *Mother Jones*, (March–April): 41–5.

Du Bois, W. E. B. (1999), *The Souls of Black Folk* (New York: Norton).

Dunne, T. (1998), *Inventing International Society: A History of the English School* (Houndmills: Macmillan).

—— (2005), 'System, State and Society: How Does It All Hang Together', *Millennium: Journal of International Studies*, 34/1, 157–70.

Dunne, T. and Schmidt, B. (2004), 'Realism', in J. Baylis and S. Smith (eds), *The Globalization of World Politics*, 3rd edn (Oxford: Oxford University Press).

Dunne, T. and Wheeler, N. J. (1999), *Human Rights in Global Politics* (Cambridge: Cambridge University Press).

Dunning, J. H. (1988), 'The Eclectic Paradigm of International Production: An Update and Some Possible Extensions', *Journal of International Business Studies*, 19/1: 1–32.

Easterly, W. (2001), *The Elusive Quest for Growth: Economists' Adventures and Misadventures in the Tropics* (Cambridge MA: MIT Press).

Eckersley, R. (2004), *The Green State: Rethinking Democracy and Sovereignty* (Cambridge MA: MIT Press).

The Ecologist, reprinted as Goldsmith, E. (1972), *A Blueprint for Survival* (Harmondworth: Penguin).

Edkins, J. (1999), *Poststructuralism and International Relations: Bringing the Political Back In* (Boulder CO: Lynne Reinner).

—— (2000), *Whose Hunger? Concepts of Famine, Practices of Aid* (Minneapolis: University of Minnesota Press).

Edkins, J., Pin-Fat, V., and Shapiro, M. J. (2004) (eds), *Sovereign Lives: Power in Global Politics* (New York: Routledge).

Elshtain, J. (1992) (ed.), *Just War Theory* (New York: Blackwell).

Elster, J. (1992), 'Arguing and Bargaining in the Federal Convention and the Assemblée Constituante', in R. Malnes and A. Underdal (eds), *Rationality and Institutions: Essays in Honour of Knut Midgaard* (Oslo: Univeritetsforlaget), 13–50.

Enloe, C. (1990), *Bananas, Beaches and Bases: Making Feminist Sense of International Politics* (Berkeley: University of California Press).

—— (2000), *Maneuvers: The International Politics of Militarizing Women's Lives* (Berkeley: University of California Press).

Epp, R. (1999), 'The English School on the Frontiers of International Relations', in T. Dunne, M. Cox, and K. Booth (eds), *The Eighty Years Crisis: International Relations 1919–1999* (Cambridge: Cambridge University Press).

Epstein, J. and Stannard, M. (2005), 'Tally of Civilian Deaths Depends on Who's Counting', *San Francisco Chronicle*, 12 May.

Evans, P. B. (1993), 'Building an Integrative Approach to International and Domestic Politics', in P. B. Evans, H. K. Jacobsen, and R. D. Putnam (eds), *Double-edged Diplomacy: International Bargaining and Domestic Politics* (Berkeley CA: University of California Press), 397–430.

Evans, P. B., Jacobson, H. K., and Putnam, R. D. (1993) (eds), *Double-edged Diplomacy: International Bargaining and Domestic Politics* (Berkeley CA: University of California Press).

Everest, L. (2004), *Oil, Power, and Empire* (Monroe ME: Common Courage Press).

Fanon, F. (1968), *Wretched of the Earth*, translated by C. Farrington (New York: Grove Press).

Fearon, J. and Wendt, A. (2002) 'Rationalism *v.* Constructivism: A Skeptical View', in W. Carlsnaes, T. Risse, and B. A. Simmons (eds), *Handbook of International Relations*, (London: Sage), 52–72.

Featherstone, K. and Radaelli, C. (2003) (eds), *The Politics of Europeanization* (Oxford: Oxford University Press).

Feldstein, M. and Horioka, C. (1980), 'Domestic Savings and International Capital Flows', *Economic Journal*, 90/358: 314–29.

Ferguson, K. and Turnbull, P. (1998), *Oh, Say, Can You See? The Semiotics of the Military in Hawaii* (Minneapolis: University of Minnesota Press).

Fetter, B. (1979), *Colonial Rule in Africa: Readings from Primary Sources* (Madison: University of Wisconsin Press).

Fierke, K. M. (1999), 'Dialogues of Manoeuvre and Entanglement: NATO, Russia and the CEECs', *Millennium: Journal of International Studies*, 28/1: 27–52.

—— (2002), 'Links Across the Abyss: Language and Logic in International Relations,' *International Studies Quarterly*, 46/3: 331–54.

Fierke, K. M. and Jorgensen, K. E (2001), *Constructing International Relations: The Next Generation* (Armonk NY: M. E. Sharpe).

Fierke, K. M. and Wiener, A. (1999), 'Constructing Institutional Interests: EU and NATO Enlargement', *Journal of European Public Policy*, 6/5: 721–42.

Finnemore, M. (1996), *National Interests and International Society* (Ithaca NY: Cornell University Press).

Fischer, F. (2003), 'Public Policy as Narrative: Stories, Frames, and Metanarratives', in F. Fischer (ed.), *Reframing Public Policy* (New York and London: Oxford University Press), 161–79.

Foot, R. (2000), *Rights Beyond Borders: The Global Community and the Struggle over Human Rights in China* (Oxford: Oxford University Press).

Foucault, M. (1972 [1969]), *The Archeology of Knowledge*, translated by A. M. Sheridan Smith (London: Tavistock Publishers).

—— (1977), 'Nietzsche, Genealogy, History', in D. F. Bouchard (ed.), *Language, Counter-memory, Practice: Selected Essays and Interviews* (Ithaca NY: Cornell University Press).

—— (1979), *Discipline and Punish: The Birth of the Prison*, translated by A. Sheridan (New York: Vintage Books).

—— (1982), 'Afterword: The Subject and Power', in H. L. Dreyfus and P. Rabinow, *Michel Foucault: Beyond Structuralism and Hermeneutics* (Brighton: Harvester Press), 208–26.

—— (1984a), 'What is Enlightenment?' in P. Rabinow (ed.), *The Foucault Reader* (New York: Pantheon Books), 32–50.

—— (1984b), 'The Order of Discourse', in M. Shapiro (ed.), *Language and Politics*, (Oxford: Blackwell), 108–38.

320

Foucault, M. (1988), *Politics, Philosophy and Culture: Interviews and Other Writings 1977–1984*, ed. with an introduction by L. D. Krittman, translated by A. Sheridan *et al.* (New York and London: Routledge).

Frankel, J. A. (1997), *Regional Trading Blocs: In the World Economic System* (Washington DC: Institute for International Economics).

—— (1998) (ed.), *The Regionalisation of the World Economy* (Cambridge MA: National Bureau of Economic Research).

Freund, C. and Rittberger, V. (2001), 'Utilitarian-liberal Foreign Policy Theory', in V. Rittberger (ed.), *German Foreign Policy since Unification: Theories and Case Studies* (Manchester: Manchester University Press), 68–104.

Friedrichs, J. (2004), *European Approaches to International Relations Theory: A House with Many Mansions* (London: Routledge).

Frost, M. (1996), *Ethics in International Relations* (Cambridge: Cambridge University Press).

Frost, M., Mayall, J., Rengger, N., and Lebow, R. N. (2003, 2005), Two Symposia on 'Tragedy, Ethics and International Relations', *International Relations*, 17/4: 480–503 and 19/4: 324–36.

Fuchs, S. (1993), 'A Sociological Theory of Scientific Change', *Social Forces*, 71/4, 933–53.

Fuerstman, D. and Lavertu, S. (2005). 'The Academic Hiring Process: A Survey of Department Chairs', *PS: Political Science and Politics*, 38/4: 731–6.

Fuller, S. (2000), *The Governance of Science: Ideology and the Future of the Open Society* (Buckingham: Open University Press).

—— (2002 [1988]), *Social Epistemology*, 2nd edn (Bloomington: Indiana University Press).

Gale, F. P. and M'Gonigle, R. M. (2000), *Nature, Production, Power: Towards an Ecological Political Economy* (Cheltenham: Edward Elgar).

Galeano, E. (1985), *Genesis*, Memory of Fire Trilogy, Part 1 (New York: Norton).

Gallarotti, G. M. (1991), 'The Limits of International Organization: Systematic Failure in the Management of International Relations', *International Organization*, 45/2: 183–220.

Garrett, G. (1998), *Partisan Politics in the Global Economy* (Cambridge: Cambridge University Press).

Garritsen De Vries, M. (1985), *The International Monetary Fund, 1972–1978* (Washington DC: IMF).

Garritsen De Vries, M. and Horsefield, J. K. (1969), *The International Monetary Fund, 1945–1965: Twenty Years of International Monetary Cooperation* (Washington DC: IMF).

Geiger, R. L. (2005), 'The Ten Generations of American Higher Education', in P. G. Altbach, R. O. Berdahl, and P. J. Gumport (eds), *American Higher Education in the Twenty-first Century: Social, Political and Economic Challenges*, 2nd edn (Baltimore MD: Johns Hopkins University Press), 58–70.

George, J. (1994), *Discourses of Global Politics: A Critical (Re)Introduction to International Relations* (Boulder CO: Lynne Reinner).

Gibbons, M., Limoges, C., Nowotny, H., Schwartzman, S., Scott, P., and Trow, M. (1994), *The New Production of Knowledge: The Dynamics of Science and Research in Contemporary Societies* (London: Sage).

Giddens, A. (1984), *The Constitution of Society: Outline of the Theory of Structuration* (Berkeley CA: University of California Press and Cambridge: Polity).

Gilroy, P. (2005), *The Black Atlantic: Modernity and Double-consciousness* (Cambridge: Harvard University Press).

Glaser, C. L. (1997), 'The Security Dilemma Revisited', *World Politics*, 50/1: 171–201.

Gold, J. (1984), *Legal and Institutional Aspects of the International Monetary System: Selected Essays*, vol. 2 (Washington DC: IMF).

Goldstein, J. and Keohane, R. O. (1993) (eds), *Ideas and Foreign Policy: Beliefs, Institutions, and Political Change* (Ithaca NY: Cornell University Press).

Goldstein, J., Kahler, M., Keohane, R. O., and Slaughter, A. (2000), 'Introduction: Legalization and World Politics', *International Organization*, 54/3: 385–99.

Gong, G. W. (1984), *The Standard of 'Civilization' in International Society* (Oxford: Clarendon Press).

Gonzalez-Pelaez, A. (2005), *Human Rights and World Trade: Hunger in International Society* (London: Routledge).

Goodson, L. P., Dillman, B., and Hira, A. (1999), 'Ranking the Presses: Political Scientists' Evaluations of Publisher Quality', *PS: Political Science and Politics*, 32/2: 257–62.

Goodwin, G. L. (1951) (ed.) *The University Teaching of International Relations* (Oxford: Blackwell; Paris: Presses Universitaires de France).

Gordon, J. (1999), 'Economic Sanctions, Just War Doctrine, and the "Fearful Spectacle of the Civilian Dead" ', *Cross Currents*, 49/3, http://www.crosscurrents.org.

Gould, E. R. (2003), 'Money Talks: Supplementary Financiers and International Monetary Fund Conditionality', *International Organization*, 57/3: 551–86.

Gourevitch, P. (1978), 'The Second Image Reversed: The International Sources of Domestic Politics', *International Organization*, 32/4: 881–912.

Gramsci, A. (1971), *Selections from the Prison Notebooks*, edited by Q. Hoare and G. N. Smith (New York: International Publishers).

Grant, J. T. (2005), 'What Divides Us? The Image and Organization of Political Science', *PS: Political Science and Politics*, 38/3: 379–86.

Gregory, D. (1995), 'Between the Book and the Lamp: Imaginative Geographies of Egypt, 1849–50', *Transactions of the Institute of British Geographers*, 20/1: 29–57.

Grossman, G. M. and Helpman, E. (1994), 'Protection for Sale', *American Economic Review*, 84/4: 833–50.

Grovogui, S. N. Z. (1996), *Sovereigns, Quasi Sovereigns, and Africans: Race and Self-determination in International Law* (Minneapolis: University of Minnesota Press).

—— (2006), *Beyond Eurocentrism and Anarchy: Memories of International Order and Institutions* (New York: Palgrave Macmillan).

Guha, R., Spivak, G. C., and Said, E. (1988) (eds), *Selected Subaltern Studies* (Oxford: Oxford University Press).

Gunnell, J. G. (1991), 'In Search of the State: Political Science as an Emerging Discipline in the U.S.', in P. Wagner, B. Wittrock, and R. Whitley (eds), *Discourses on Society: The Shaping of the Social Science Disciplines*, Sociology of the Sciences Yearbook (Reidel: Kluwer), 123–62.

—— (2002), 'Handbooks and History: Is It Still the American Science of Politics?', *International Political Science Review*, 23/4: 339–54.

Guzzini, S. (1998), *Realism in International Relations and International Political Economy: The Continuing Story of a Death Foretold* (London: Routledge).

Guzzini, S. and Leander, A. (2005) (eds), *Constructivism and International Relations* (London: Routledge).

Haas, P. M. (1992) (ed.), 'Knowledge, Power and International Policy Coordination', *International Organization* (special issue), 46/1.

Haas, P. M., Keohane, R. O., and Levy, M. A. (1993) (eds), *Institutions for the Earth: Sources of Effective International Environmental Protection* (Cambridge MA: MIT Press).

Haggard, S. and Simmons, B. A. (1987), 'Theories of International Regimes', *International Organization*, 41/3: 491–517.

Hajer, M. (1995), *The Politics of Environmental Discourse: Ecological Modernization and the Policy Process* (Oxford: Clarendon Press).

Hall, S. (1996), 'The Problem of Ideology: Marxism without Guarantees', in D. Morley and K. Chen (eds), *Stuart Hall: Critical Dialogues in Cultural Studies* (London: Routledge), 25–46.

Halliday, F. (1996), 'The Future of International Relations: Fears and Hopes', in S. Smith, K. Booth, and M. Zalewski (eds), *International Theory: Positivism and Beyond* (Cambridge: Cambridge University Press), 318–27.

Hammond, T. H. (2004), 'Herding Cats in University Hierarchies: Formal Structure and Policy Choice in American Research Universities', in R. G. Ehrenberg (ed.), *Governing Academia: Who Is in Charge of the Modern University?* (Ithaca NY: Cornell University Press).

Harding, S. (1986), *The Science Question in Feminism* (Ithaca NY: Cornell University Press).

Hargens, L. (1988), 'Scholarly Consensus and Journal Rejection Rates', *American Sociological Review*, 53/1: 139–51.

Harley, J. B. (1988), 'Maps, Knowledge, and Power', in D. Cosgrove and S. Daniels (eds), *The Iconography of Landscape: Essays on the Symbolic Representation, Design and Use of Past Environments* (Cambridge: Cambridge University Press), 277–312.

Harnisch, S. and Maull, H. (2001) (eds), *Germany as a Civilian Power? The Foreign Policy of the Berlin Republic* (Manchester: Manchester University Press).

Harvey, D. (1989), *The Condition of Postmodernity: An Enquiry into the Origins of Cultural Change* (Oxford: Blackwell).

Hay, C. (2002), *Political Analysis* (Basingstoke: Palgrave).

—— (2005), 'Globalisation's Impact on States', in J. Ravenhill (ed.), *Global Political Economy* (Oxford: Oxford University Press).

—— (2006), 'What's Globalisation Got to Do With It? Economic Interdependence and the Future of European Welfare States', *Government and Opposition*, 41/1: 1–22.

—— (2007a), 'The End of the Nation-state?', in D. Lee, J. Steans, C. Hay, D. Hudson, and M. Watson, *International Political Economy* (Oxford: Oxford University Press).

—— (2007b), 'Towards a Global Political Economy?', in D. Lee, J. Steans, C. Hay, D. Hudson, and M. Watson, *International Political Economy* (Oxford: Oxford University Press).

Hayward, T. (2005), *Constitutional Environmental Rights* (Oxford: Oxford University Press).

Headrick, D. (1981), *The Tools of Empire: Technology and European Imperialism in the Nineteenth Century* (Oxford: Oxford University Press).

Held, D. (2002), 'Cosmopolitanism: Ideas, Realities, Deficits', in D. Held and A. McGrew (eds), *Governing Globalisation* (Cambridge: Polity).

—— (2003), 'Cosmopolitanism: Globalisation Tamed?', *Review of International Studies*, 29/4: 465–80.

Held, D., McGrew, A., Goldblatt, D., and Perraton, J. (1999), *Global Transformations: Politics, Economics, Culture* (Cambridge: Polity; Stanford: Stanford University Press).

Herodotus (1998), *The Histories*, translated by R. Waterfield (Oxford: Oxford University Press).

Hersh, S. M. (2004), *Chain of Command: The Road from 9/11 to Abu Ghraib* (New York: Harper).

Herz, J. (1950), 'Idealist Internationalism and the Security Dilemma', *World Politics*, 2/2: 157–80.

Hesse, M. (1980), *Revolutions and Reconstructions in the Philosophy of Science* (Brighton, Sussex: Harvester Press).

Hirst, P. and Thompson, G. (1999), *Globalisation in Question*, 2nd edn (Cambridge: Polity).

Hoffmann, S. (1977), 'An American Social Science: International Relations', *Dædalus*, 106/3: 41–60.

Hollis, M. (1996), 'The Last Post?', in S. Smith, K. Booth, and M. Zalewski (eds), *International Theory: Positivism and Beyond* (Cambridge: Cambridge University Press), 301–8.

Hollis, M. and Smith, S. (1990), *Explaining and Understanding International Relations* (Oxford: Clarendon Press).

Holsti, K. J. (1985), *The Dividing Discipline* (Boston: Allen & Unwin).

—— (2002), 'Interview with Kal Holsti', A. Jones, *Review of International Studies*, 28/3: 619–33.

Hooper, C. (2001), *Manly States: Masculinities, International Relations, and Gender Politics* (New York: Columbia University Press).

Hopf, T. (1998), 'The Promise of Constructivism in International Relations Theory', *International Security*, 23/1: 171–200.

Hopkins, A. G. (1997), *The Future of the Imperial Past*, Inaugural lecture, delivered 12 March (Cambridge: Cambridge University Press).

Howard, P. (2004), 'Why Not Invade Korea? Threats, Language Games and US Foreign Policy', *International Studies Quarterly*, 48/4: 805–28.

Hoy, D. C. (2004), *Critical Resistance: From Poststructuralism to Post-critique* (Cambridge MA: MIT Press).

Hudec, R. E. (1993), *Enforcing International Trade Law: The Evolution of the Modern GATT Legal System* (Salem NH: Butterworth Legal Publishers).

Hughes, R. (1991), *The Shock of the New*, revised edn (New York: Knopf).

Hulme, P. (1992), *Colonial Encounters: Europe and the Native Caribbean, 1492–1797* (New York: Routledge).

Huntington, S. P. (1998), *The Clash of Civilizations and the Remaking of the World Order* (New York: Simon & Schuster).

Hutchings, K. (1999), *International Political Theory: Rethinking Ethics in a Global Era* (London: Sage).

Inoguchi, T. and Bacon, P. (2001), 'The Study of International Relations in Japan: Towards a More International Discipline', *International Relations of the Asia–Pacific*, 1/1: 1–20.

Intergovernmental Panel on Climate Change (IPPC) (2001), *Climate Change 2001 – Synthesis Report: Summary for Policymakers*, http://www.ipcc.ch/pub/un/syreng/spm.pdf.

Isaac, J. (1987), *Power and Marxist Theory* (Ithaca NY: Cornell University Press).

Jackson, J. H. (1998), *The World Trade Organization: Constitution and Jurisprudence* (London: Royal Institute for International Affairs).

Jackson, R. H. (1990), *Quasi-states: Sovereignty, International Relations, and the Third World*, Cambridge Studies in International Relations 12 (Cambridge and New York: Cambridge University Press).

—— (2000), *The Global Covenant: Human Conduct in a World of States* (Oxford: Oxford University Press).

Jackson, R. and Sørensen, G. (1999), *Introduction to International Relations* (Oxford, Oxford University Press).

James, C. L. R. (1989), *The Black Jacobins: Toussaint L'Ouverture and the San Domingo Revolution* (New York: Vintage).

Jameson, F. (1991), *Postmodernism, or, the Cultural Logic of Late Capitalism* (New York: Verso).

Jentleson, B. W. (2002), 'The Need for Praxis: Bringing Policy Relevance Back In', *International Security*, 26/4, 169–83.

Johnston, A. I. (2001), 'Treating International Institutions as Social Environments', *International Studies Quarterly*, 45/4: 487–515.

Jørgensen, K. E. and Knudsen, T. B. (2006) (eds), *International Relations in Europe*, (London: Routledge).

Kahler, M. (1993), 'International Relations: Still an American Social Science?', in L. B. Miller and M. J. Smith (eds), *Ideas and Ideals* (Boulder CO: Westview Press).

—— (1997), 'Inventing International Relations: International Relations Theory after 1945', in M. W. Doyle and G. J. Ikenberry (eds), *New Thinking in International Relations* (Boulder CO: Westview Press), 20–53.

—— (2000), 'Legalization as Strategy: The Asia–Pacific Case', *International Organization*, 54/3: 549–71.

Käkönen, J. (1994) (ed.), *Green Security or Militarised Environment* (Aldershot: Dartmouth).

Kant, I. (1795/1983), 'To Perpetual Peace: A Philosophical Sketch', in *Immanuel Kant: Perpetual Peace and Other Essays on Politics, History, and Morals*, edited by T. Humphrey (Indianapolis IN: Hackett Publishing), 107–43.

Katzenstein, P. (1996) (ed.), *The Culture of National Security: Norms and Identity in World Politics* (New York: Columbia University Press).

—— (2003), 'Same War – Different Views: Germany, Japan, and Counterterrorism', *International Organization*, 57/4: 731–60.

Katzenstein, P., Keohane, R. O., and Krasner, S. D. (1998), 'International Organization and the Study of World Politics', *International Organization*, 52/4: 645–85.

Katznelson, I. and Milner, H. V. (2002) (eds), *Political Science: State of the Discipline* (New York and London: Norton).

Kaufman-Osborn, T. V. (2006), 'Dividing the Domain of Political Science: On the Fetishism of Subfields', *Polity*, 38/1: 41–71.

Keck, M. and Sikkink, K. (1998), *Activists Beyond Borders: Advocacy Networks in International Politics* (Ithaca NY: Cornell University Press).

Keene, E. (2002), *Beyond the Anarchical Society: Grotius, Colonialism and Order in World Politics* (Cambridge, Cambridge University Press).

—— (2005), *International Political Thought: A Historical Introduction* (Cambridge: Polity).

Kellner, D. (1989), *Critical Theory, Marxism and Modernity* (Baltimore MD: Johns Hopkins University Press).

Keohane, R. O. (1982), 'The Demand for International Regimes', *International Organization*, 36/2: 325–55.

—— (1984), *After Hegemony: Cooperation and Discord in the World Political Economy* (Princeton NJ: Princeton University Press).

—— (1986) (ed.), *Neorealism and its Critics* (New York: Columbia University Press).

—— (1988), 'International Institutions: Two Approaches', *International Studies Quarterly*, 32/4: 379–96.

—— (1989), *International Institutions and State Power* (Boulder CO: Westview).

—— (1990), 'Multilateralism: An Agenda for Research', *International Journal*, 45/Fall: 731–64.

Keohane, R. O. and Nye, J. S. (1971) (eds), *Transnational Relations and World Politics* (Boston MA: World Peace Foundation; Cambridge MA: Harvard University Press).

—— (1974), 'Transgovernmental Relations and International Organizations', *World Politics*, 27/1: 39–62.

—— (1977), *Power and Interdependence: World Politics in Transition* (Boston MA: Little, Brown; Boulder CO: Westview).

Kern, S. (1983), *The Culture of Time and Space, 1880–1914* (Cambridge MA: Harvard University Press).

King, G., Keohane, R. O., and Verba, S. (1994), *Designing Social Inquiry: Scientific Inference in Qualitative Research* (Princeton NJ: Princeton University Press).

Kinnvall, C. (2005), 'Not Here, Not Now! The Absence of a European Perestroika Movement', in K. R. Monroe (ed.), *Perestroika! The Raucous Rebellion in Political Science* (New Haven CT: Yale University Press), 21–44.

Kinzer, S. (2003), *All the Shah's Men* (New York: Wiley).

Klare, M. (2004), 'Bush–Cheney Energy Strategy: Procuring the Rest of the World's Oil', *Foreign Policy in Focus Special Report*, January, http://www.fpif.org/papers/03petropol/politics_body.html.

Klein, B. (1994), *Strategic Studies and World Order* (Cambridge: Cambridge University Press).

Knorr, K. E. and Rosenau, J. N. (1969) (eds), *Contending Approaches to International Politics* (Princeton NJ: Princeton University Press).

Knudsen, C. (2003), 'Pluralism, Scientific Progress and the Structure of Organization Studies', in H. Tsoukas and C. Knudsen (eds), *The Oxford Handbook of Organization Theory* (Oxford: Oxford University Press), 262–86.

Knutsen, T. (1992), *A History of International Relations Theory* (Manchester: Manchester University Press).

Kodré, P. and Müller, H. (2003), 'Shifting Policy Frames: EU Equal Treatment Norms and Domestic Discourse in Germany', in U. Liebert (ed.), *Gendering Europeanization* (Brussels: P.I.E.-Peter Lang), 83–116.

Kolakowski, L. (1969), *The Alienation of Reason: A History of Positivist Thought*, translated by N. Guterman (New York: Anchor Books).

Koremenos, B. (2001), 'Loosening the Ties that Bind: A Learning Model of Agreement Flexibility', *International Organization*, 55/2: 289–325.

Koremenos, B., Lipson, C., and Snidal, D. (2001), 'The Rational Design of International Institutions', *International Organization*, 55/4: 761–99.

Korman, S. (1996), *The Right of Conquest: The Acquisition of Territory by Force in International Law and Practice* (Oxford: Clarendon).

Krasner, S. D. (1982), 'Structural Causes and Regime Consequences: Regimes as Intervening Variables', *International Organization*, 36/2: 185–205.

—— (1983) (ed.), *International Regimes* (Ithaca NY: Cornell University Press).

—— (1991), 'Global Communications and National Power: Life on the Pareto Frontier', *World Politics*, 43/3: 336–56.

—— (1996), 'The Accomplishments of International Political Economy', in S. Smith, K. Booth, and M. Zalewski (eds), *International Theory: Positivism and Beyond* (Cambridge: Cambridge University Press), 108–27.

—— (1999), *Sovereignty: Organized Hypocrisy* (Princeton NJ: Princeton University Press).

Kratochwil, F. (1989), *Rules, Norms and Decisions: On the Conditions of Practical and Legal Reasoning in International Relations and Domestic Affairs* (Cambridge: Cambridge University Press).

—— (2000), 'Constructing a New Orthodoxy? Wendt's "Social Theory of International Politics" and the Constructivist Challenge', *Millennium: Journal of International Studies*, 29/1: 73–101.

—— (2003), 'The Monologue of Science', *International Studies Review*, 5/1: 128–31.

—— (2006), 'History, Action and Identity: Revisiting the "Second" Great Debate and Assessing its Importance for Social Theory', *European Journal of International Relations*, 12/1: 5–29.

Kratochwil, F. and Ruggie, J. R. (1986), 'International Organization: A State of the Art or an Art of the State', *International Organization*, 40/4: 753–75.

Krishna, S. (1999), *Postcolonial Insecurities: India, Sri Lanka, and the Question of Nationhood*, Borderlines Series (Minneapolis: University of Minnesota).

Kuehls, T. C. (1996), *Beyond Sovereign Territory: The Space of Ecopolitics* (Minneapolis: University of Minnesota Press).

Kuhn, T. (1962), *The Structure of Scientific Revolutions* (Chicago: University of Chicago Press).

Laclau, E. and Mouffe, C. (1995), *Hegemony and Socialist Strategy* (London: Verso).

LaFerrière, E. and Stoett, P.J. (1999), *International Relations Theory and Ecological Thought: Towards a Synthesis* (London: Routledge).

Laffey, M. (2000), 'Locating Identity: Performativity, Foreign Policy and State Action', *Review of International Studies*, 26/3: 429–44.

Laitin, D. D. (2004), 'The Political Science Discipline', in E. D. Mansfield and R. Sisson (eds), *The Evolution of Political Knowledge: Theory and Inquiry in American Politics* (Columbus: Ohio State University Press), 11–40.

Lakatos, I. (1970), 'Falsification and the Methodology of Scientific Research Programmes', in I. Lakatos and A. Musgrave (eds), *Criticism and the Growth of Knowledge* (London: Cambridge University Press).

Lake, D. (1992), 'Powerful Pacifists: Democratic States and War', *American Political Science Review*, 20/1: 24–37.

Lapid, Y. (1989), 'The Third Debate: On the Prospects of International Theory in a 'Post-positivist' Era', *International Studies Quarterly*, 33/4: 235–54.

—— (2002), 'Sculpting the Academic Identity: Disciplinary Reflections at the Dawn of a New Millennium', in D. J. Puchala (ed.), *Visions of International Relations: Assessing an Academic Field* (Columbia: University of South Carolina Press), 1–15.

—— (2003), 'Through Dialogue to Engaged Pluralism: The Unfinished Business of the Third Debate', *International Studies Review*, 5: 128–31.

Lebow, R. N. (1994), 'The Long Peace, the End of the Cold War, and the Failure of Realism', *International Organization*, 48/1: 49–78.

—— (2003), *The Tragic Vision of Politics: Ethics, Interests and Orders* (Cambridge: Cambridge University Press).

Lepgold, J. and Nincic, M. (2001), *Beyond the Ivory Tower: International Relations Theory and the Issue of Policy Relevance* (New York: Columbia University Press).

Levy, J. S. (1982), 'Historical Trends in Great Power War, 1495–1975', *International Studies Quarterly*, 26/2: 278–301.

—— (2002), 'War and Peace', in W. Carlsnaes, T. Risse, and B. A. Simmons (eds), *Handbook of International Relations*, (London: Sage), 350–68.

Lewis, W. A. (1981), 'The Rate of Growth of World Trade, 1830–1973', in S. Grassman and E. Lundberg (eds), *The World Economic Order: Past and Prospects* (Basingstoke: Macmillan).

Liberman, P. (1996), *Does Conquest Pay: The Exploitation of the Occupied Industrial Societies* (Princeton NJ: Princeton University Press).

Linklater, A. (1990), *Men and Citizens in the Theory of International Relations*, 2nd edn (London: Macmillan).

—— (1995), 'Rationalism', in S. Burchill, A. Linklater, *et al.* (eds), *Theories of International Relations* (London: Macmillan), 93–118.

—— (1996), 'The Achievements of Critical Theory', in S. Smith, K. Booth, and M. Zalewski (eds), *International Theory: Positivism and Beyond* (Cambridge: Cambridge University Press), 279–98.

Linklater, A. and Suganami, H. (2006), *The English School of International Relations: A Contemporary Reassessment* (Cambridge: Cambridge University Press).

Lisle, D. and Pepper, A. (2005), 'The New Face of Global Hollywood: Black Hawk Down and the Politics of Meta-sovereignty', *Cultural Politics*, 1/2: 165–92.

Locke, J. (1980), *Second Treatise of Government* (New York: Hackett).

Low, N. and Gleeson, B. (1998), *Justice, Society and Nature: An Exploration of Political Ecology* (London: Routledge).

Lukes, S. (1973), *Individualism* (Oxford: Blackwell).

Mann, J. (2004), *Rise of the Vulcans: The History of Bush's War Cabinet* (New York: Penguin).

Manning, C. A. W. (1954), *The University Teaching of Social Sciences: International Relations*, a report prepared on behalf of the International Studies Conference, UNESCO.

—— (1962), *The Nature of International Society* (London: G. Bell & Sons).

Mansfield, E. and Reinhardt, E. (2003), 'Multilateral Determinants of Regionalism: The Effects of GATT/WTO on the Formation of Regional Trading Arrangements', *International Organization*, 57/4: 829–62.

Mansfield, E. D. and Snyder J. (2002), 'Democratic Transitions, Institutional Strength, and War', *International Organization*, 56/2: 297–337.

March, J. G. and Olson, J. P. (1989), *Rediscovering Institutions* (New York: Free Press).

Marchand, M. H. and Runyan, A. S. (2000) (eds), *Gender and Global Restructuring: Sightings, Sites, and Resistances* (London and New York: Routledge).

Martin, L. (1992), *Coercive Cooperation: Explaining Multilateral Economic Sanctions* (Princeton NJ: Princeton University Press).

Martin, L. and Simmons, B. (1998), 'Theories and Empirical Studies of International Institutions', *International Organization*, 52/4: 729–57.

Marx, K. (1977), *Capital*, vol. 1 (New York: Vintage).

—— (2000), *Selected Writings*, edited by D. McLellan, 2nd edn (Oxford: Oxford University Press).

May, E. (1993) (ed.), *American Cold War Strategy* (New York: St Martin's).

McCubbins, M. D. and Schwartz, T. (1984), 'Congressional Oversight Overlooked: Police Patrols Versus Fire Alarms', *American Journal of Political Science*, 28/1: 165–79.

McGrew, A. (2005), 'Globalisation and Global Politics', in J. Baylis and S. Smith (eds) *The Globalisation of World Politics: An Introduction to International Relations*, 3rd edn (Oxford: Oxford University Press).

Mead, W. R. (2001), *Special Providence: American Foreign Policy and How It Changed the World* (New York: Knopf).

Meadows, D. H., Meadows, D. L., Randers, J., and Behrens, W. W. (1972), *The Limits to Growth: A Report to the Club of Rome's Project on the Predicament of Mankind* (New York: Universe Books).

Mearsheimer, J. J. (1990), 'Back to the Future: Instability in Europe after the Cold War', *International Security*, 15/1: 5–56.

—— (1994–5), 'The False Promise of International Institutions', *International Security*, 19/3: 5–49.

—— (2001), *The Tragedy of Great Power Politics* (New York: Norton).

Megill, A.(1994) (ed.), *Rethinking Objectivity* (Durham OH: Duke University Press).

Memmi, A. (1965), *The Colonizer and Colonized* (Boston MA: Beacon Press).

Messer-Davidow, E., Shumway, D. S., and Sylvan, D. J. (1993) (eds), *Knowledges: Historical and Critical Studies in Disciplinarity* (Charlottesville: University Press of Virginia).

Mignolo, W. (2000), *Local Histories/Global Designs: Coloniality, Subaltern Knowledges, and Border Thinking* (Princeton NJ: Princeton University Press).

—— (2003), *The Darker Side of the Renaissance: Literacy, Territoriality, and Colonization* (Ann Arbor: University Michigan Press).

Mill, J. S. (1998), *On Liberty and Other Essays* (Oxford: Oxford University Press).

Millennium Forum, (2005), 'Barry Buzan's *From International to World Society?*', 34/1, 156–99. Contributions by Emmanuel Adler, Tim Dunne, Barry Buzan.

Miller, D. (1995), *On Nationality* (Oxford: Oxford University Press).

Miller, D. and Walzer, M. (1995) (eds), *Pluralism, Justice and Equality* (Oxford: Oxford University Press).

Milner, H. (1997), *Interests, Institutions, and Information. Domestic Politics and International Relations* (Princeton NJ: Princeton University Press).

—— (1998), 'Rationalizing Politics: The Emerging Synthesis of International, American, and Comparative Politics', *International Organization*, 52/4: 759–86.

Milner, H. V. and Keohane, R. O. (1996) (eds), *Internationalization and Domestic Politics* (Cambridge: Cambridge University Press).

Moeller, S. (1999), *Compassion Fatigue: How the Media Sell Disease, Famine, War and Death* (New York: Routledge).

Mohanty, C. T. (1988), 'Under Western Eyes: Feminist Scholarship and Colonial Discourse', *Feminist Review*, 30/3: 61–88.

Monmonier, M. (1996), *How to Lie with Maps*, 2nd edn (Chicago: University of Chicago Press).

Monroe, K. R. (2005) (ed.), *Perestroika! The Raucous Rebellion in Political Science* (New Haven CT: Yale University Press).

Montesquieu, C. L. S. (1973), *The Persian Letters* (New York: Penguin).

Moon, K. H. S. (1997), *Sex Among Allies: Military Prostitution in U.S.–Korea Relations* (New York: Columbia University Press).

Moravcsik, A. (1993a), 'Introduction: Integrating International and Domestic Theories of International Bargaining', in P. B. Evans, H. K. Jacobson, and R. D. Putnam (eds), *Double-edged Diplomacy: International Bargaining and Domestic Politics* (Berkeley CA: University of California Press), 3–42.

—— (1993b), 'Preferences and Power in the European Community: A Liberal Intergovernmentalist Approach', *Journal of Common Market Studies*, 31/4: 473–524.

—— (1997), 'Taking Preferences Seriously: A Liberal Theory of International Politics', *International Organization*, 51/4: 513–53.

—— (1998), *The Choice for Europe: Social Purpose and State Power from Rome to Maastricht* (Ithaca NY: Cornell University Press).

—— (2003), 'Theory Synthesis in International Relations: Real Not Metaphysical', *International Studies Review*, 5: 131–6.

Moreiras, A. (2001), *The Exhaustion of Difference: The Politics of Latin American Cultural Studies* (Durham OH: Duke University Press).

Morgan, C. T. and Campbell, S. H. (1991), 'Domestic Structures, Decisional Constraints, and War: So Why Kant Democracies Fight?', *Journal of Conflict Resolution*, 35/2: 187–211.

Morgan, T. C. and Schwebach, V. L. (1997), 'Fools Suffer Gladly: The Use of Economic Sanctions in International Crises', *International Studies Quarterly*, 41/1: 27–50.

Morgenthau, H. J. (1947), *Scientific Man vs. Power Politics* (London: Latimer Press).

—— (1948a), *Politics among Nations: The Struggle for Power and Peace* (New York: Alfred A. Knopf).

—— (1948b), 'Letter to Michael Oakeshott, 22 May 1948' *Morgenthau Papers*, B-44.

—— (1958), *Decline of Domestic Politics* (Chicago IL: University of Chicago Press).

—— (1960), *Politics among Nations*, 3rd edn (New York: Alfred A. Knopf).

—— (1966), 'The Purpose of Political Science', in J. C. Charlesworth (ed.), *A Design for Political Science: Scope, Objectives and Methods* (Philadelphia PA: American Academy of Political and Social Science).

—— (1972), *Politics among Nations: The Struggle for Power and Peace*, 5th edn (New York: Alfred A. Knopf).

—— (1978), *Politics among Nations: The Struggle for Power and Peace*, 5th edn, revised (New York: Alfred A. Knopf).

326

Morgenthau, H. J. and Thompson, K. W. (1985), *Politics among Nations: The Struggle for Power and Peace*, 6th edn (New York: Alfred A. Knopf).

Morrison, T. (1993), *Playing in the Dark: Whiteness and the Literary Imagination* (New York: Vintage).

Morrow, J. (1994), 'Modelling the Forms of International Cooperation: Distribution Versus Information', *International Organization*, 48/3: 387–423.

Mosley, L. (2003), *Global Capital and National Governments* (Cambridge: Cambridge University Press).

Mueller, J. and Mueller, K. (1999), 'Sanctions of Mass Destruction', *Foreign Affairs*, 78/3: 43–53.

Müller, H. (2002), 'Antinomien des demokratischen Friedens', *Politische Vierteljahresschrift*, 43/1: 46–81.

Nardin, T. (1983), *Law, Morality and the Relations of Nations* (Princeton NJ: Princeton University Press).

Nardin, T. and Mapel, D. (1992) (eds), *Traditions of International Ethics* (Cambridge: Cambridge University Press).

Neumann, I. B. (1996), *Russia and the Idea of Europe: A Study in Identity and International Relations* (London: Routledge).

Nevzat, S. (1999), *States and Strangers: Refugees and Displacements of Statecraft* (Minneapolis: Minnesota University Press).

Nicholson, M. (1996), *Causes and Consequences in International Relations: A Conceptual Study* (London: Pinter).

Nielson, D. L. and Tierney, M. J. (2003), 'Delegation to International Organizations: Agency Theory and World Bank Environmental Reform', *International Organization*, 57/2: 241–76.

Nye, J. S. and Donahue, J. D. (2000) (eds), *Governance in a Globalising World* (Washington DC: Brookings Institute Press).

Oatley, T. and Nabors, R. (1998), 'Redistributive Cooperation: Market Failure, Wealth Transfers, and the Basle Accord', *International Organization*, 52/1: 35–54.

Onuf, N. (1989), *World of Our Making: Rules and Rule in Social Theory and International Relations* (Columbia SC: University of South Carolina Press).

—— (1998), 'Constructivism: A User's Manual,' in V. Kubalkova, N. Onuf, and P. Kowert (eds), *International Relations in a Constructed World* (Armonk NY: M. E. Sharpe), 58–78.

—— (2002), 'Worlds of Our Making: The Strange Career of Constructivism in International Relations', in D. J. Puchala (ed.), *Visions of International Relations: Assessing an Academic Field* (Columbia SC: University of South Carolina Press), 119–41.

Osiander, A. (1994), *The State System of Europe 1640–1990: Peacemaking and the Conditions of International Stability* (Oxford: Clarendon Press).

Østerud, Ø. (1996), 'Antinomies of Postmodernism in International Studies', *Journal of Peace Research*, 33/4: 385–90.

Owen, J. M. (1996), 'How Liberalism Produces Democratic Peace', in M. E. Brown, S. M. Lynn-Jones, and S. E. Miller (eds), *Debating the Democratic Peace* (Cambridge MA: MIT Press).

—— (1997), *Liberal Peace, Liberal War: American Politics and International Security* (Ithaca NY: Cornell University Press).

Paehlke, R. C. (2003), *Democracy's Dilemma: Environment, Social Equity and the Global Economy* (Cambridge MA: MIT Press).

Palan, R. (2000), 'A World of Their Making: An Evaluation of the Constructivist Critique in International Relations', *Review of International Studies*, 26/4, 575–98.

Paterson, M. (2000), *Understanding Global Environmental Politics: Domination, Accumulation, Resistance* (London: Palgrave).

Patomäki, H. and Wight, C. (2000), 'After Post-Positivism? The Promises of Critical Realism', *International Studies Quarterly*, 44/2: 213–37.

Payne, R. A. (2001), 'Persuasion, Frames and Norm Construction', *European Journal of International Relations*, 7/1: 37–61.

Payne, R. A. and Samhat, N. H. (2004), *Democratizing Global Politics: Discourse Norms, International Regimes, and Political Community* (Albany NY: State University of New York Press).

Perestroika, Mr. (2000), 'To the Editor, PS and APSR, On Globalization of the APSA: A Political Science Manifesto', posted on the Perestroika list serve, 26 October; reprinted in K. R. Monroe (ed.), *Perestroika! The Raucous Rebellion in Political Science* (New Haven CT: Yale University Press), 9–11.

Peterson, S., Tierney, M. J., and Maliniak, D. (2005), *Teaching and Research Practices, Views on the Discipline, and Policy Attitudes of International Relations Faculty at the US College and Universities* (Williamsburg VA: College of William and Mary).

Peterson, V. S. and Runyan, A. S. (1999), *Global Gender Issues*, 2nd edn (Boulder CO: Westview Press).

Petrella, R. (1996), 'Globalisation and Internationalisation: The Dynamics of the Emerging World Order', in R. Boyer and D. Drache (eds), *States Against Market: The Limits of Globalisation* (London: Routledge).

Phillips, D. L. (2005), *Losing Iraq: Inside the Postwar Reconstruction Fiasco* (Boulder CO: Westview Press).

Philpott, S. (2001), *Rethinking Indonesia: Postcolonial Theory, Authoritarianism and Identity* (London: Palgrave Macmillan).

Pillay, S. (2004), 'Anti-colonialism, Post-colonialism, and the "New Man"', *Politikon: South African Journal of Political Studies*, 31/1: 91–104.

Pocock, J. G. A. (2003), *The Machiavellian Moment: Florentine Political Thought and the Atlantic Republican Tradition* (Princeton NJ: Princeton University Press).

Pogge, T. (2002), *World Poverty and Human Rights* (Cambridge: Polity).

Pollard, R. (1985), *Economic Security and the Origins of the Cold War* (New York: Columbia University Press).

Pond, E. (2004), *Friendly Fire: The Near-death of the Transatlantic Alliance* (Pittsburgh PA and Washington DC: European Union Studies Association and Brookings Institution Press).

Poovey, M. (1998), *A History of the Modern Fact: Problems of Knowledge in the Sciences of Wealth and Society* (Chicago: University of Chicago Press).

Popper, K. R. (1959), *The Logic of Scientific Discovery* (London: Hutchinson).

Posen, B. R. (1984), *The Sources of Military Doctrine: France, Britain, and Germany between the World Wars* (Ithaca NY: Cornell University Press).

Prakash, G. (1994), *After Colonialism: Imperial Histories and Postcolonial Displacement* (Princeton NJ: Princeton University Press).

—— (1999), *Another Reason: Science and the Imagination of Modern India* (Princeton NJ: Princeton University Press).

Princen, T., Maniates, M., and Conca, K. (2002) (eds), *Confronting Consumption* (Cambridge MA: MIT Press).

Prügl, E. (1999), *The Global Construction of Gender: Home-based Work in the Political Economy of the 20th Century* (New York: Columbia University Press).

Puchala, D. J. (2002) (ed.), *Visions of International Relations: Assessing an Academic Field* (Columbia: University of South Carolina Press).

Putnam, R. (1988), 'Diplomacy and Domestic Politics: The Logic of Two-level Games', *International Organization*, 42/2: 427–60.

Rasmussen, M. V. (2001), 'Reflexive Security: NATO and International Risk Society', *Millennium: Journal of International Studies*, 30/2: 285–309.

Rauchhaus, R. W. (2001) (ed.), *Explaining NATO Enlargement* (London: Frank Cass).

Rawls, J. (1971), *A Theory of Justice* (Oxford: Oxford University Press).

—— (1999), *The Law of Peoples* (Cambridge MA: Harvard University Press).

—— (2005), *Political Liberalism*, expanded edn, Columbia Classics in Philosophy (New York and Chichester: Columbia University Press).

Ray, J. L. (1995), *Democracy and International Conflict: An Evaluation of the Democratic Peace* (Columbia SC: University of South Carolina Press).

Rein, M. and Schön, D. (1993), 'Reframing Political Discourse', in F. Fischer and J. Forester (eds), *The Argumentative Turn in Policy Analysis and Planning* (Durham NC: Duke University Press)

Reinhardt, E. (2001), 'Adjudication Without Enforcement in GATT Disputes', *Journal of Conflict Resolution*, 45/2: 174–95.

Reiss, H. (1970) (ed.), *Kant's Political Writings* (Cambridge: Cambridge University Press).

Reus-Smit, C. (1999), *The Moral Purpose of the State: Culture, Social Identity, and Institutional Rationality in International Relations* (Princeton NJ: Princeton University Press).

Review of International Studies (2001), Forum on the English school 27/3: 465–513.

Rieger, E. and Leibfried, S. (2003), *Limits to Globalization: Welfare States and the World Economy* (Cambridge: Polity).

Risse, T. (2000), ' "Let's Argue!": Communicative Action in World Politics', *International Organization*, 54/1: 1–39.

—— (2002), 'Transnational Actors and World Politics', in W. Carlsnaes, T. Risse, and B. A. Simmons (eds), *Handbook of International Relations* (London: Sage), 255–74.

—— (2003a), 'Beyond Iraq: The Crisis of the Transatlantic Security Community', *Die Friedens-Warte*, 78/2–3: 173–93.

—— (2003b), 'Konstruktivismus, Rationalismus und die Theorie Internationaler Beziehungen – Warum empirisch nichts so heiß gegessen wird, wie es theoretisch gekocht wurde', in G. Hellmann, K. D. Wolf, and, M. Zürn (eds), *Forschungsstand und Perspektiven der Internationalen Beziehungen in Deutschland* (Baden-Baden: Nomos Verlagsgesellschaft), 99–132.

Risse, T., Ropp, S. C., and Sikkink, K. (1999) (eds), *The Power of Human Rights: International Norms and Domestic Change* (Cambridge: Cambridge University Press).

Risse-Kappen, T. (1995a) (ed.), *Bringing Transnational Relations Back In: Non-state Actors, Domestic Structures, and International Institutions* (Cambridge: Cambridge University Press).

—— (1995b), 'Democratic Peace – Warlike Democracies? A Social Constructivist Interpretation of the Liberal Argument', *European Journal of International Relations*, 1/4, 489–515.

Robichek, W. E. (1984), 'The IMF's Conditionality Re-examined', in J. Muns (ed.), *Adjustment, Conditionality, and International Financing* (Washington DC: IMF), 67–83.

Robinson, F. (1999), *Globalising Care: Ethics, Feminist Theory and International Relations* (Oxford: Westview Press).

Robinson, W. I. (2004), *A Theory of Global Capitalism* (Baltimore MD: Johns Hopkins University Press).

Rodman, P. W. (1995), 'NATO's Role in a New European Security Order', Working Paper 95, Old Dominion University Graduate Program in International Studies, Norfold VA, 2 October.

Rodrik, D. (1996), 'Why Do More Open Economies Have Bigger Governments?', *NBER Working Paper*, 5537 (Cambridge MA: National Bureau of Economic Research).

Rodrik, D. (1997), *Has Globalisation Gone Too Far?* (Washington DC: Institute for International Economics).

Rorty, R. (1967) (ed.), *The Linguistic Turn* (Chicago: University of Chicago Press).

Rose, G. (2001), *Visual Methodologies* (London: Sage).

Rosenau, J. N. (1967), *Domestic Sources of Foreign Policy* (New York: Free Press).

—— (1969), *Linkage Politics: Essays on the Convergence of National and International Systems* (New York: Free Press).

—— (1990), *Turbulence in World Politics: A Theory of Change and Continuity* (Princeton NJ: Princeton University Press).

Rosenberg, J. (1994), *Empire of Civil Society* (London: Verso).

Rosendorff, B. P. and Milner, H. V. (2001), 'The Optimal Design of International Trade Institutions: Uncertainty and Escape', *International Organization*, 55/4: 829–58.

Roy, A. (1998), 'The End of Imagination', *The Guardian* (UK), 1 August.

Ruggie, J. G. (1998), 'What Makes the World Hang Together? Neo-utilitarianism and the Social Constructivist Challenge', *International Organization*, 52/4: 855–85.

Rummel, R. J. (1983), 'Libertarianism and International Violence', *Journal of Conflict Resolution*, 27/1: 27–71.

Rupert, M. (1995), *Producing Hegemony* (Cambridge: Cambridge University Press).

—— (2005), 'Reading Gramsci in an Era of Globalising Capitalism', *Critical Review of International Social and Political Philosophy*, 8/4: 483–97.

Rupert, M. and Smith, H. (2002) (eds), *Historical Materialism and Globalisation* (London: Routledge).

Rupert, M. and Solomon, S. (2006), *Globalisation and International Political Economy* (Lanham MD: Rowman & Littlefield).

Russett, B. (1993), *Grasping the Democratic Peace* (Princeton NJ: Princeton University Press).

Russett, B. and O'Neal, J. R. (2001), *Triangulating Peace: Democracy, Interdependence, and International Organizations*, Norton Series in World Politics (New York: Norton).

Said, E. (1979), *Orientalism* (New York: Vintage).

Sayer, D. (1991), *Capitalism and Modernity* (London: Routledge).

Scharpf, F. W. and Schmidt, V. A. (2000) (eds), *Welfare and Work in the Open Economy, Vol. I: From Vulnerability to Competitiveness; Vol. II: Diverse Responses to Common Challenges* (Oxford: Oxford University Press).

Schimmelfennig, F. (1999), 'NATO Enlargement: A Constructivist Explanation', *Security Studies*, 8/2–3: 198–234

Schmidt, B. (1998), *The Political Discourse of Anarchy: A Disciplinary History of International Relations* (Albany: State University of New York Press).

Schmitt, C. (2003), *The Nomos of the Earth in the International Law of the Jus Publicum Europaeum*, translated and with an introduction by G. L. Ulmen (New York: Telos Press).

Schmitt, R. (1997), *Introduction to Marx and Engels: A Critical Reconstruction*, 2nd edn (Boulder CO: Westview).

Scott, D. (1999), *Refashioning Futures: Criticism after Postcoloniality* (Princeton NJ: Princeton University Press).

Searle, J. R. (1995), *The Construction of Social Reality* (London: Allen Lane; New York: Free Press).

Sending, O. L. (2002), 'Constitution, Choice and Change: Problems with the "Logic of Appropriateness" and Its Use in Constructivist Theory', *European Journal of International Relations*, 8/4: 443–70.

Shannon, T. (1992), *An Introduction to the World-system Perspective*, 2nd edn (Boulder CO: Westview).

Shapiro, I. and Brilmayer, L. (1999) (eds), *Global Justice* (New York: New York University Press).

Shapiro, M. J. (1988), *The Politics of Representation: Writing Practices in Biography, Photography and Policy Analysis* (Madison: University of Wisconsin Press).

Shapiro, M. J. and Alker, H. R. (eds), *Challenging Boundaries: Global Flows, Territorial Identities* (Minneapolis: University of Minnesota Press).

Sikkink, K. (1993), 'Human Rights, Principled Issue Networks, and Sovereignty in Latin America', *International Organization*, 47/3: 411–41.

Simmons, B. A. (2000), 'International Law and State Behavior: Commitment and Compliance in International Monetary Affairs', *American Political Science Review*, 94/4: 819–35.

Singer, P. (1985), 'Famine, Affluence and Morality', in C. R. Beitz, M. Cohen, T. Scanlon, and A. J. Simmons (eds), *International Ethics* (Princeton NJ: Princeton University Press).

Skinner, Q. (1997), *Liberty Before Liberalism* (Cambridge: Cambridge University Press).

—— (2002), *Visions of Politics: Regarding Method* (Cambridge: Cambridge University Press).

Smith, A. (1993), *Wealth of Nations*, edited by K. Sutherland (Oxford: Oxford University Press).

Smith, S. (1987), 'Paradigm Dominance in International Relations: The Development of International Relations as a Social Science', *Millennium: Journal of International Studies*, 16/2: 189–206.

—— (1997), 'Power and Truth: A Reply to William Wallace', *Review of International Studies*, 23/4: 507–16.

—— (2004), 'Singing Our World into Existence: International Relations Theory and September 11 Presidential Address to the International Studies Association, February 27, 2003, Portland, OR', *International Studies Quarterly*, 48/3: 499–515.

Smith, S., Booth, K., and Zalewski, M. (1996) (eds), *International Theory: Positivism and Beyond* (Cambridge: Cambridge University Press).

Snow, D. A. and Benford, R. D. (1992), 'Master Frames and Cycles of Protest', in A. D. Morris and C. M. Mueller (eds), *Frontiers in Social Movement Theory* (New Haven CT: Yale University Press), 133–55.

Snyder, J. L. (1991), *Myths of Empire: Domestic Politics and International Ambition* (Ithaca NY: Cornell University Press).

Soguk, N. (1999), *States and Strangers: Refugees and Displacements of Statecraft* (Minneapolis: University of Minnesota Press).

Spivak, G. C. (1987), *In Other Worlds; Essays in Cultural Politics* (New York: Routledge).

—— (1999), *A Critique of Postcolonial Reason: Toward a History of the Vanishing Present* (Cambridge MA: Harvard University Press).

Stein, A. A. (1982), 'Coordination and Collaboration: Regimes in an Anarchic World', *International Organization*, 36/2: 299–324.

Steinberg, R. H. (2002), 'In the Shadow of Law or Power? Consensus-based Bargaining and Outcomes in GATT/WTO', *International Organization*, 56/2: 339–74.

Sterling-Folker, J. (2000), 'Competing Paradigms or Birds of a Feather? Constructivism and Neoliberalism Institutionalism Compared', *International Studies Quarterly*, 44/1, 97–119.

—— (2006) (ed.) *Making Sense of International Relations Theory* (Boulder CO: Lynne Rienner).

Stone, R. W. (2004), 'The Political Economy of IMF Lending in Africa', *American Political Science Review*, 98/4: 577–91.

Strange, S. (1973), 'IMF: Monetary Managers', in R. W. Cox and H. K. Jacobson (eds), *The Anatomy of Influence: Decisionmaking in International Organizations* (New Haven CT: Yale University Press), 263–97.

Surel, Y. (2000), 'The Role of Cognitive and Normative Frames in Policy-making', *Journal of European Public Policy*, 7/4: 495–512.

Swank, D. (2002), *Global Capital, Political Institutions and Policy Change in Developed Welfare States* (Cambridge: Cambridge University Press).

Thacker, S. C. (1999), 'The High Politics of IMF Lending', *World Politics* 52/2: 38–75.

Thomas, D. C. (1999), 'The Helsinki Accords and Political Change in Eastern Europe', in T. Risse, S. C. Ropp, K. Sikkink (eds), *The Power of Human Rights: International Norms and Domestic Change* (Cambridge: Cambridge University Press).

Thucydides (1954), *History of the Pelopennesian War*, translated by R. Warner (New York: Penguin).

Thucydides (1996), *The Landmark Thucydides: A Comprehensive Guide to the Peloponnesian War*, edited by R. B. Strassler (New York: Free Press).

Tickner, A. B. (2003), 'Seeing IR Differently: Notes from the Third World', *Millennium: Journal of International Studies*, 32/2: 295–324.

Tickner, A. B. and Wæver, O. (2004), *Geo-cultural epistemologies and IR: Montreal follow-up memo*, unpublished paper.

Tickner, A. B. and Wæver, O. (2007) (eds), *The World of International Relations Scholarship: Geocultural Epistemologies, Vol. 1* (London: Routledge).

Tickner, J. A. (1997), 'You Just Don't Understand: Troubled Engagements Between Feminists and IR Theorists', *International Studies Quarterly*, 41/4: 611–32.

—— (2001), *Gendering World Politics: Issues and Approaches in the Post-Cold War Era* (New York: Columbia University Press).

Todorov, T. (1993), *On Human Diversity: Nationalism, Racism, and Exoticism in French Thought*, translated by C. Porter (Cambridge MA: Harvard University Press).

Tormey, S. (2004), *Anti-capitalism: A Beginner's Guide* (Oxford: Oneworld).

Toulmin, S. (1972), *Human Understanding* (Oxford: Clarendon Press).

Traxler, F. and Woitech, B. (2000), 'Transnational Investment and National Labour Market Regimes: A Case of "Regime Shopping"?', *European Journal of Industrial Relations*, 6/2: 141–59.

Trouillot, M.-R. (1997), *Silencing the Past* (Boston MA: Beacon Press).

True, J. (2003), *Gender, Globalization, and Post-socialism: The Czech Republic after Communism* (New York: Columbia University Press).

Tsebelis, G. (1990), *Nested Games: Rational Choice in Comparative Politics* (Berkeley: University of California Press).

Tuck, R. (2001), *The Rights of War and Peace: Political Thought and the International Order from Grotius to Kant* (Oxford: Oxford University Press).

Tully, J. (1988) (ed.), *Meaning and Context: Quentin Skinner and his Critics* (Cambridge: Polity).

United Nations Environment Program (UNEP) (2005), *Millennium Ecosystem Assessment*, Conclusion: Main Findings, www.greenfacts.org/ecosystems/millennium-assessment-3/99-main-findings.htm.

van der Gaag, N. and Nash, C. (1987), *Images of Africa: The UK Report*, www.imaging-famine.org/images_africa.htm.

van der Pijl, K. (1984), *The Making of an Atlantic Ruling Class* (London: Verso).

van der Veer, P. (2001), *Imperial Encounters: Religion and Modernity in India* (Princeton NJ: Princeton University Press).

Van Evera, S. (1999), *Causes of War: Power and the Roots of Conflict* (Ithaca NY: Cornell University Press).

Vaubel, R. (1986), 'A Public Choice Approach to International Organization', *Public Choice*, 51/1: 39–57.

Vigneswaran, D. and Quirk, J. (2005), 'The Construction of an Edifice: The Story of a First Great Debate', *Review of International Studies*, 31/1: 59–74.

Vincent, R. J. (1986), *Human Rights in International Relations* (Cambridge: Cambridge University Press).

Vogler, J. (2003), 'Taking Institutions Seriously: How Regime Analysis Can Be Relevant to Multilevel Environmental Governance', *Global Environmental Politics*, 3/2: 25–39.

Vreeland, J. R. (2003), *The IMF and Economic Development* (Cambridge: Cambridge University Press).

Wa Thiong'o, N. (1986), *Decolonizing the Mind: The Politics of Language in African Literature* (Portsmouth: Heinemann).

Wackernagel, M. and Rees, W. (1996), *Our Ecological Footprint: Reducing Human Impact on the Earth* (Gabriola Island BC: New Society Publishers).

Wæver, O. (1996), 'The Rise and Fall of the Interparadigm Debate', in S. Smith, K. Booth, and M. Zalewski (eds), *International Theory: Positivism and Beyond* (Cambridge: Cambridge University Press), 149–85.

—— (1997), 'Figures of International Thought: Introducing Persons Instead of Paradigms', in I. B Neumann and O. Wæver (eds), *The Future of International Relations: Masters in the Making?* (London: Routledge).

—— (1998), 'The Sociology of a Not so International Discipline: American and European Developments in International Relations', *International Organization*, 52/4: 687–727.

—— (2003), 'The Structure of the IR Discipline: A Proto-comparative Analysis', ISA paper, Portland.

—— (2004), 'Aberystwyth, Paris, Copenhagen: New "Schools" in Security Theory and their Origins between Core and Periphery', paper presented at the annual meeting of the International Studies Association, Montreal, 17–20 March.

Wæver, O. and Buzan, B. (2006), 'After the Return to Theory: The Past, Present, and Future of Security Studies', in A. Collins (ed.), *Contemporary Security Studies* (Oxford: Oxford University Press), 383–402.

Waldman, P. (2004), 'A Historian's Take on Islam Steers U.S. in Terrorism Fight', *Wall Street Journal* (3 February): A1.

Walker, R. B. J. (1987), 'Realism, Change and International Political Theory', *International Studies Quarterly*, 31/1: 65–86.

—— (1993), *Inside/Outside: International Relations as Political Theory* (Cambridge: Cambridge University Press).

Wallace, W. (1996), 'Truth and Power, Monks and Technocrats: Theory and Practice in International Relations', *Review of International Studies*, 22/3: 301–21.

Wallerstein, I. (2001[1991]), *Unthinking Social Science: The Limits of Nineteenth-century Paradigms*, 2nd edn (Philadelphia PA: Temple University Press).

Walt, S. M. (1987), *The Origins of Alliances* (Ithaca NY: Cornell University Press).

—— (1998), 'International Relations: One World, Many Theories', *Foreign Policy*, 110: 29–35.

—— (1999), 'Rigor or Rigor Mortis? Rational Choice and Security Studies', *International Security*, 23/4: 5–48.

Waltz, K. N. (1959), *Man, the State, and War: A Theoretical Analysis* (New York: Columbia University Press).

—— (1979), *Theory of International Politics* (London: McGraw-Hill; New York: Random House; Reading MA: Addison-Wesley).

—— (1984), 'The Origins of War in Neorealist Theory', in R. I. Rotberg and T. K. Rabb (eds), *The Origin and Prevention of Major Wars* (Cambridge: Cambridge University Press), 39–52.

—— (1993), 'The Emerging Structure of International Politics', *International Security*, 18/1: 5–43.

—— (1998), 'Interview', *Review of International Studies*, 24/3: 371–86.

Walzer, M. (2000), *Just and Unjust Wars*, 3rd edn (New York: Perseus Publishers).

Wapner, P. (1998), *Environmental Activism and World Civic Politics* (Albany: State University of New York Press).

Warrior, R. A. (1994), *Tribal Secrets: Recovering American Indian Intellectual Traditions* (Minneapolis: University of Minnesota Press).

Watson, A. (1992), *The Evolution of International Society* (London: Routledge).

Watson, M. (2001), 'International Capital Mobility in an Era of Globalisation: Adding a Political Dimension to the "Feldstein–Horioka Puzzle" ', *Politics*, 21/2: 81–92.

Weber, C. (1994), *Simulating Sovereignty: Intervention, the State and Symbolic Exchange* (Cambridge: Cambridge University Press).

—— (1999), *Faking It: US Hegemony in a Post-phallic Era* (Minneapolis: University of Minnesota Press).

Welsh, J. M. (1995), *Edmund Burke and International Relations* (Basingstoke: Macmillan).

Wendt, A. (1987), 'The Agent–Structure Problem in International Relations', *International Organization*, 41/3: 335–70.

—— (1992), 'Anarchy Is What States Make of It: The Social Construction of Power Politics', *International Organization*, 46/2: 391–425.

—— (1998), 'Constitution and Causation in International Relations', *Review of International Studies*, 24/5: 101–17.

—— (1999), *Social Theory of International Politics* (Cambridge and New York: Cambridge University Press).

Wheeler, N. J. (2000), *Saving Strangers: Humanitarian Intervention in International Society* (Oxford: Oxford University Press).

White, S. (1991), *Political Theory and Postmodernism* (Cambridge: Cambridge University Press).

White House (2002), *National Security Strategy of the United States* (17 September), www.whitehouse.gov/nsc/print/nssall.html.

Whitley, R. (1984), *The Intellectual and Social Organization of the Sciences* (Oxford: Clarendon Press).

—— (1986), 'The Structure and Context of Economics as a Scientific Field', in W. J. Samuels (ed.), *Research in the History of Economic Thought and Methodology*, Vol. 4 (Greenwich CT and London: JAI Press), 179–209.

—— (2000), 'Introduction [to the second edition]. Science Transformed? The Changing Nature of Knowledge Production at the End of the Twentieth Century', in R. Whitley, *The Intellectual and Social Organization of the Sciences*, 2nd edn (Oxford: Oxford University Press), ix–xliv.

Whitworth, S. (1994), *Feminism and International Relations: Towards a Political Economy of Gender in Interstate and Non-governmental Institutions* (Basingstoke: Macmillian).

Wiener, A. (2003), 'Constructivism: The Limits of Bridging Gaps', *Journal of International Relations and Development*, 6/3: 252–75.

Wight, C. (1996), 'Incommensurability and Cross Paradigm Communication in International Relations Theory: What's the Frequency Kenneth?', *Millennium: Journal of International Studies*, 25/2: 291–319.

Wight, M. (1966), 'Why Is There No International Theory?', in H. Butterfield and M. Wight (eds), *Diplomatic Investigations* (London: Allen & Unwin).

—— (1977), *Systems of States*, edited by H. Bull (Leicester: Leicester University Press).

—— (1978), *Power Politics*, edited by H. Bull and C. Holbraad (Leicester: Leicester University Press).

—— (1991), *International Theory: The Three Traditions* (Leicester: Leicester University Press for the Royal Institute of International Affairs).

Wilensky, H. L. (2002), *Rich Democracies: Political Economy, Public Policy and Performance* (Berkeley CA: University of California Press).

Williams, H., Wright, M., and Evans, T. (1992) (eds), *A Reader in International Relations and Political Theory* (Buckingham: Open University Press).

Williams, M. C. (2001), 'The Discipline of the Democratic Peace: Kant, Liberalism and the Social Construction of Security Communities', *European Journal of International Relations*, 7/4: 525–53.

Wilson, P. (1998), 'The Myth of the "First Great Debate" ', *Review of International Studies*, 24/Special Issue: 1–15.

Wittgenstein, L. (1922), *Tractatus Logico-philosophicus* (London: Kegan Paul; New York: Harcourt, Brace).

—— (1958), *Philosophical Investigations* (Oxford: Blackwell).

Wohlforth, W. C. (1994–5), 'Realism and the End of the Cold War', *International Security*, 19/1: 91–129.

—— (1999), 'The Stability of a Unipolar World', *International Security*, 24/1: 5–41.

Wood, E. M. (2003), *Empire of Capital* (London: Verso).

Woodward, B. (2004), *Plan of Attack* (New York: Simon & Schuster).

World Commission on Environment and Development (1987), *Our Common Future: The Report of the World Commission on Environment and Development* (Oxford: Oxford University Press).

Young, O. R. (1991), 'Political Leadership and Regime Formation: On the Development of Institutions in International Society', *International Organization*, 45/3: 281–308.

Youngs, G. (1999), *International Relations in a Global Age: A Conceptual Challenge* (Cambridge: Polity).

Zangl, B. and Zürn, M. (1994), 'Theorien des rationalen Handelns in den Internationalen Beziehungen', in V. Kunz and U. Druwe (eds), *Rational Choice in der Politikwissenschaft: Grundlagen und Anwendungen* (Opladen: Leske + Budrich), 81–111.

Zehfuss, M. (1997), 'Constructivism in International Relations. The Approaches of Wendt, Onuf and Kratochwil', in K. E. Jørgensen (ed.), *The Aarhus-Norsminde Papers: Constructivism, International Relations and European Studies*, Papers collected at the Workshop 10–12 October 1997, in Norsminde/Aarhus, Denmark, University of Aarhus, pp. 151–67.

Zehfuss, M. (2002), *Constructivism in International Relations: The Politics of Reality* (Cambridge: Cambridge University Press).

Glossary

Explanatory note. This glossary has been compiled by the editors, although it draws upon the definitions of key concepts provided by the contributors. In a small number of cases, different theories contest the meaning of key terms: where significant interpretive differences exist, we have endeavoured to make this clear in the descriptions below.

agency – intentional actors or their actions. The role of 'agency' in social life is traditionally contrasted to the role of 'structures', such as institutions or norms. The agency–structure debate refers to the debate over the priority to be accorded to agents (individuals or states) as opposed to structures in shaping social life.

balance of power – a dominant idea within realist and English school traditions of thought. For most classical realists, the balance of power was something that was contrived (i.e. actors had to cooperate to maintain the balance) whereas for neorealists the balance of power is akin to a natural equilibrium. For neorealists, states within the international system will automatically balance against any dominant state power. In English school thought, the balance of power is an 'institution' which requires not only cooperation but a shared belief that a balance of power is crucial if international order is to be achieved.

balancing – where a threatened state accepts the burden of deterring an adversary and commits substantial resources to achieving that goal. The threatened state can mobilize its own resources or join with other threatened states to form a balancing coalition.

bandwagoning – when a weaker states joins a stronger or dominant alliance in the context of the balance of power in the international system.

behaviourism – a school of thought that, drawing on empiricist theory of knowledge and positivist philosophy of science, seeks to study human behaviour in reference to observable and measurable behavioural patterns. In IR the term behaviouralism is more commonly used.

bipolarity – a system in which there are only two great powers.

bounded communities – political communities, as bounded communities, tend to define loyalties and moral obligations as belonging to the people seen to exist within the bounds of the political community. States, for example, can be seen as the classic form of territorially and normatively bounded communities. See also 'inside/outside'.

buck-passing – where threatened states try to get another state to check an aggressor while they remain on the sidelines.

capitalism – an historically particular form of social life in which social means of production are privately owned, and labour is commodified. Entailing a constellation of political, economic, and cultural aspects, capitalism involves a relation of class power in which the owning class controls the process of labour and appropriates its product. Marx respected the historic achievements of capitalist society, especially its enhancement of human productive powers, but was scathingly critical of the ways in which capitalism disempowered and dominated human beings, preventing them from realizing the potential for freedom which its historic achievements made possible.

central wars – conflicts that involve all or almost all the world's great powers. The French Revolutionary and Napoleonic Wars (1792–1815), the First World War (1914–18), and the Second World War (1939–45) were all central wars.

civic republicanism – a tradition of thought that emphasizes civic virtue and the notion of a common good as opposed to liberal neutrality. Influential with respect to both the American and French Revolutions.

classical approach – an alternative to behaviourism advocated by Hedley Bull. The classical approach eschews positivist commitments to a fact/value distinction, and their expectation that hypotheses should be testable. In its place, the English school puts an interpretive mode of inquiry that tries to understand historical and normative change by engaging with 'texts' such as legal treaties, speeches, and diplomatic discourses. Other characteristics of a classical approach include the inescapability of ethical considerations and a realization that the study of world politics must engage with (and interpret) the dilemmas faced by practitioners.

communitarianism – a political theory that sees political obligations and allegiances to be defined in reference to a distinct and discrete political community, not in reference to universal ('cosmopolitan') norms. In IR, many realists have adopted (often implicitly) a communitarian position, defending the ethical primacy of state as the definer of valid moral and political rules.

competition state – used by Cerny and others to refer to those states which subordinate all other policy imperatives to that of promoting the competitiveness of the national economy in a global environment.

constructivist feminism – a branch of feminism in IR that focuses on the way that ideas about gender shape and are shaped by global politics, studying how states and other international actors' perceptions of their own and others' gender identities shape their behaviour in global politics.

correspondence theory of truth – defines truth as correspondence with facts. For an advocate of correspondence theory of truth, the observer can capture truth in statements that are true if they correspond to the facts and false if they do not.

cosmopolitanism – an ethical theory which holds that all individuals are of equal moral standing and that it would be desirable for universal ethical codes, such as human rights, to be upheld globally. While they are united in their advancement of normative commitments that cross state boundaries, cosmopolitans disagree on the institutional arrangement which is best suited to promoting cosmopolitan values. Cosmopolitanism is often contrasted with 'communitarianism' and is challenged by some poststructuralist and postcolonialist theorists.

critical feminism – a branch of feminism in IR that addresses the ideational and material manifestations of gendered identities and gendered power in global politics, committed to understanding the world in order to try to change it.

defensive realists – structural realists or neorealists who argue that systemic factors put significant limits on how much power states can gain, which works to dampen security competition.

democratic peace – advocates of democratic peace explain war and peace in the international system with reference to domestic-level variables. Their basic claim is that regime types (defined by institutional features, e.g. elections, decision-making structures, and culture) shape foreign-policy inclinations of national decision-makers and their interactions on the international level. Democratic peace theorists, following Kant, argue that democratic domestic institutions are conducive to producing peace on the international level, especially among democracies.

deterrence – persuading an opponent not to initiate a particular action because the perceived benefits are outweighed by the anticipated costs and risks.

dialectical understanding of history – an understanding of social life central to Marxism and critical theory that examines humans as embedded in social relations, which are themselves in process. Humans are seen as historical beings, simultaneously the producers and the products of historical processes. Accordingly, politics is understood in a relatively expansive sense as struggles affecting the direction of these processes of social self-production, rather than narrowly distributive struggles over who gets what. In contrast to the liberal conception of freedom as individual choice, a dialectical view suggests that freedom involves a process of social-self-determination.

discourse – the language and representations through which we describe and understand the world, and through which meanings, identities, and social relations are produced. According to social theorists who believe that social reality is constituted by and through discourse, claims to pre-discursive reality are unwarranted. Borrowing from the French philosopher Michel Foucault, discourse theorists recognize that power is at work in defining the terms of debate (see also 'knowledge and power'). Discourse is a term closely associated with poststructuralism and also postcolonialism.

ecological modernization – refers to a strategy of continuous innovation in environmental technological development and environmental management systems, encouraged or forced by governments and pursued by firms, to increase the efficiency of energy and resource use and reduce waste production and pollution. This strategy is defended as both good for business and good for the environment.

ecological security – there are numerous conceptualizations of ecological security, ranging from conservative to radical. Conservatives maintain that ecological problems are a new source of insecurity and inter-state conflict that require the development of national ecological security strategies. Radicals seek to widen the traditional state-centric approach to security questions, arguing that ecological problems challenge the very idea of territorial defence and demand inter-state cooperation over common environmental problems.

economic determinism – the idea that processes intrinsic to the economy (narrowly understood) are the primary determinants of social and political life. Economic determinism was a predominant tendency among Marxists well into the twentieth century. Western Marxism and critical theory reacted against this tendency, insisting that dialectical processes could not be understood without active human agents, and that the ideological and political conditions of human social agency were essential to an understanding of the limits and possibilities of particular social orders.

economic sanctions – import or export barriers or restrictions imposed on one state or international actor by another state or group of states for the purpose of obtaining political or economic concessions.

empiricism – a theory of knowledge (an epistemology) that holds that knowledge should be grounded in empirical experience. Empiricist epistemology has been influential in informing positivist philosophies of science and is often seen to underlie positivist theories in IR theory.

environmental justice – environmental justice advocates seek to reduce ecological risks and also prevent their unfair externalization and displacement, through space and time, onto innocent third parties. Green theorists have approached this challenge by exploring new and more extensive forms of democratic account-ability by risk generators and more extensive forms of representation and participation by classes and communities (including non-human species and ecosystems) affected by ecological risks, irrespective of their nationality, social class, or geographic location.

epistemic realism – the view in the social sciences that there is an external world, the existence and meaning of which is independent of ideas, beliefs and theories, or the actions of an observer. Although underpinned by an empiricist theory of knowledge and the positivist philosophy of science, it is not synonymous with either.

epistemology – a branch of philosophy that seeks to theorize how we gain knowledge about the world. One of the most influential theories of knowledge in modern philosophy has been empiricism, which has emphasized the centrality of empirical observation in obtaining and justifying knowledge (see 'empiricism').

essentialism – a term used to describe the result of simplifying or organizing people on the basis of 'natural' or 'general' characteristics. Constructivism, feminism, and critical theory emphasize that differences among people are not natural or timeless, but some of the most vehement critics of essentialism tend to be found among the poststructuralists and postcolonialists.

explaining and understanding – a distinction introduced into IR theory by Hollis and Smith (1990). 'Explanatory' theories seek to emulate natural sciences and explain general causes, while 'understanding' approaches aim to account for agents actions 'from within' through interpreting actors' meanings, beliefs, and reasons for action.

foundationalism – a term used to describe theories that believe that our knowledge can have foundations, either in reason and rationality (rationalism), systematic empirical observation (empiricism), or independent existence of reality (realism). Foundationalist theories are criticized by the so-called anti-foundationalist theorists, typically associated with poststructuralist perspectives.

gender – a set of socially constructed characteristics describing what men and women ought to be. Feminists, who have pioneered the study of gender, contrast differences ascribed by society (gender variations) with differences that are biologically 'given' (sexual differences). While individual men and women may not embody all the socially ascribed characteristics, expectations about gender roles serve to empower men and disempower women.

gendered lens – the use of gender as a category of analysis through which to filter understandings of global politics. This is a term famously used by Cynthia Enloe (1990).

global distributive justice – the notion that wealth and resources should be distributed justly on a global basis. Instead of taking states as reference points of moral and political obligations, global distributive justice aims to establish global justice between individuals and/or societies.

great debates – a disciplinary narrative that describes the historical development of IR scholarship. The first debate is said to have taken place between idealists and realists, the second debate between traditionalists and modernizers. The interparadigm debate in the 1970s and 1980s pitted realist, liberal, and Marxist theoretical viewpoints against each other. Finally, the debate between metatheoretical positions variously described as a contest between explaining and understanding, positivism and postpositivism, and rationalism and reflectivism, engaged theorists from the 1980s onwards. This debate has been referred to as the 'third debate' by some (Lapid 1989) and as the 'fourth debate' by others who see it as a debate beyond the interparadigm debate (Wæver 1996).

hegemonic war – a war between two dominant or 'leading' powers (hegemons) within the international system.

hegemony – in realist thought used to refer to an international system dominated by a hegemon that dominates the system through its military and economic might. In Gramscian and critical theory thought, hegemony refers to a situation in which socially dominant groups secure their power by getting subordinate social groups to subscribe to their ideological vision, thereby effectively consenting to their social power and making

the widespread use of direct (and obviously oppressive) coercive power unnecessary.

'how possible' question – knowledge claims are sometimes categorized as answering one of three kinds of question: the 'what', the 'why', or the 'how possible' questions. 'How possible' questions differ from the other two in that they do not ask for knowledge of causes of an event (why) or about the constitution of an object (what) but rather about the 'conditions of possibility' under which certain things/events/meanings can exist.

imperialism – as seen by the Marxists, imperialism involves the deployment of (primarily coercive) state power in the service of capital accumulation. Classical theories of imperialism, developed in the early twentieth century, tended to emphasize economic determinism as the motor of imperial expansion, but contemporary recastings of the concept have framed it in more dialectical terms, emphasizing the integral roles of agency, ideology, and politics in the construction of capitalist world orders.

incommensurability – a term associated with Thomas Kuhn's (1962) work referring to the incomparability of theoretical positions. A term widely used, perhaps unjustifiably, in the interparadigm debate in IR to characterize the mutually exclusive nature of theoretical views of the world by realist, pluralist, and globalist approaches.

inside/outside – a distinction pioneered by R. J. B. Walker (1993) used to refer to the division of modern political life into discrete territorial units, which divide political identities according to an insider/outsider logic. The modern nation-state, for example, is defined by distinctions set between the insiders and outsiders through territorial boundaries and requirements of formal citizenship. See also 'bounded communities'.

international institutions – sets of norms and rules designed by states to structure and constrain their behaviour and to facilitate cooperation. International institutions have traditionally been the focus of analysis of the neoliberal school of thought that has challenged realists' scepticism of their significance. Increasingly constructivism has also analysed the role of institutions in international politics.

international justice – the notion that justice can exist in the relations between states (rejecting the realist belief that justice is simply a matter of domestic concern). However, advocates of international justice have prioritized the recognition of sovereignty norms and, hence, have seen justice as existing between states rather than between individuals or societies (cf. 'global distributive justice'). Also, justice has been seen as largely 'procedural' consisting in the correct application of international legal rules, rather than as 'substantive', ensuring just outcomes between actors on the ground.

international organizations – also known as intergovernmental organizations. Entities created by states to carry out activities on the international level. States have delegated authority for autonomous action, within constraints, to some international organizations. International organizations embody the norms and rules that constitute international institutions.

International Political Economy (IPE) – a branch of political inquiry that studies the intersection of international relations and political economy. Rather than privileging states over markets, as traditional IR has tended to, IPE examines both states *and* markets.

International Political Theory – political theory that engages with traditional political theory themes, such as justice and community, within the international political realm. Associated with normative theorizing at an international level on questions of ethics and political obligation. Debates within International Political Theory can be seen to have been centred around the dichotomies universal/particular, inside/outside, and system/society.

international regimes – defined famously by Stephen Krasner (1983) as 'sets of principles, norms, rules, and decision-making procedures around which actors' expectations converge'. The notion of regimes was useful in opening up the study of international institutions away from focus on formal international organizations towards recognition of more informal regimes.

international society – closely associated with the English school, international society describes an institutional arrangement for promoting order. It can be said to exist when there are criteria for membership, and when those belonging to international society have shared values and believe themselves to be bound by the agreed rules. The values that are shared could be minimal (toleration) or maximal (highly interventionist to promote universal values).

international system – a term widely used to describe the totality of state actors in global politics. While realists believe that the anarchical character of the system leads to self-help behaviour, both liberals and English school theorists have pointed to the possibility of 'societal' characteristics among states (see 'international society'). In classical English school thinking the term 'international system' refers to patterns of contact between the units (states in the modern period) which may be structured but are not rule-governed.

justice – in European international society of the seventeenth and eighteenth centuries, justice was defined by sovereignty norms: what was just was the recognition of other states and granting them independence and respecting their territorial integrity. Yet sovereign states have never been able to contain justice claims. Questions about minority rights, the rights of non-European peoples enslaved during the colonial period, the rights of prisoners of war, and, increasingly, the call for equality and democracy, all presuppose a realm of justice beyond the domain of the society of states. A feature of late modern international relations is the growing sensitivity of all international actors to transnational justice claims. See also 'international justice' and 'global distributive justice'.

just war – associated with the tradition of thought instigated initially by medieval thinkers such as Augustine and Aquinas who sought to establish legitimate basis for the conduct of war. While acknowledging that peace was the preferred state when social justice was served, they recognized the possibility that violent means might have to be used to restore just peace. Just War tradition, while controversial, still retains its influence in international political theory.

knowledge and power – Many positivist IR theorists believe in the possibility of objective and value-neutral knowledge. Many postpositivists have, however, emphasized the importance of reflection on the social context of knowledge generation, which is often embedded in power relations. The relations of power and knowledge is emphasized especially by poststructuralists and postcolonialists who, following the work of Michel Foucault, emphasize the inevitable and mutually constitutive nexus of knowledge and power. Indeed, the poststructuralists and postcolonialists go beyond many other postpositivists in emphasizing that all knowledge is embedded in discursive constructions and strategies of power. In so arguing, these theorists are following Foucault's concept of power, which emphasizes the dispersal of power and its location in the techniques and practices of power rather than in a power centre.

liberal feminism – a branch of feminism in IR that addresses the various material manifestations of women's subordination in global politics, usually through empirical analysis.

logic of appropriateness – a term associated with March and Olsen (1989), used to describe the logic-informing actions that are taken in reference to rules and norms that define what constitutes legitimate behaviour. This term is contrasted to the 'logic of consequences' (see next entry).

logic of consequences – a term used to describe the logic through which rational actors come to make decisions. When acting through the logic of consequences, actors conduct themselves on the basis of a rational calculation of which action produces an outcome that maximizes their interests. See 'logic of appropriateness'.

meta-theory – inquiry into the underlying philosophical assumptions that inform theoretical approaches. Meta-theoretical inquiry engages with philosophical questions of ontology, epistemology, and methodology. Often referred to as 'theory about theory'.

methodology – methodological schools of thoughts debate how we best gain evidence about the nature of the natural and the social world. Different theoretical approaches in the social sciences have contrasting understandings of the validity and hierarchy of social science methods. Key methodological avenues in the social sciences include quantitative, qualitative, discursive, and historical methods.

moral hazard – a term associated with neoliberal theory to describe the situation in which institutions unwittingly generate incentives for actors to behave in a reckless or short-sighted manner. For example, if a state is undergoing a severe financial crisis and it knows it will be bailed out by the IMF, then it is likely to behave more recklessly by adopting inappropriate policies and over-borrowing.

multilateralism – while this is a contested concept, a straightforward definition is cooperation among three or more states. Keohane (1990) brought the concept of multilateralism back into the neoliberal approach to the study of institutions.

multipolarity – a world in which there are three or more great powers.

mutually constituted – a phrase used to refer to the dialectical relationship of two concepts or forces that simultaneously co-determine each other. For example, in the agency–structure debate some argue that agents and structures 'mutually constitute' each other (Giddens 1984), and thus have to be understood in reference to each other, rather than in isolation from each other.

offence–defence balance – indicates how easy or difficult it is to conquer territory or defeat a defender in battle. If the balance favours the defender, conquest is difficult and war is therefore unlikely. The reverse is the case if the balance favours the offence.

offensive realists – structural realists who maintain that states should attempt to gain as much power as possible, which works to intensify security competition.

ontology – a branch of philosophy that studies the nature of being and existence. In International Relations all theorists make assumptions about the kinds of objects they conceive to exist in and to shape international politics. While many realists tend to argue that states are the key ontological units in international politics (see 'state-centric'), constructivists, feminists, and Marxists, for example, emphasize 'social ontologies' where emphasis is on examining the social interaction and social relations between states or other actors (such as genders or classes).

order – a concept which both realists and English school theorists consider pivotal. For realists, order is generally considered to consist in the absence of war. While they accept that order can be achieved, for example, through balance of power or deterrence politics, given the anarchical nature of the international system, order in the eyes of realists is always precarious. For the English school, given the specific context of international anarchy, the achievement of order is the only purpose that culturally diverse, sovereign 'units' can agree upon. The institutions of international society – diplomacy, the balance of power, peace conferences, great power management, international law – were primarily designed to achieve the goal of order upon which the liberty of the units depends.

paradigm – a term associated with Thomas Kuhn's (1962) work referring to theoretical schools, or sets of principles, concerning the nature of science, that are accepted as exemplary in any given historical period.

pluralist international society – a term associated with the English school that describes an institutional arrangement designed to sustain international order. R. J. Vincent (1986) used an 'egg-box' metaphor to explain pluralism. International society is the box and the eggs are states: we can assume that the eggs are valuable but also fairly fragile. The task of the box is to separate and cushion the eggs. Pluralism is defended by those who attach a premium to cultural diversity, and who are suspicious of particular states that regard themselves as ethical states with a duty to impose their values on others.

positivism – a contested term in the philosophy of science and in International Relations theory. Generally understood to refer to a philosophy of science that is founded on (1) the empiricist theory of knowledge (which argues that sensory experience provides the only legitimate source of knowledge); (2) an assumption of 'naturalism' (the belief in unity of natural and social sciences); and (3) the belief in the possibility of making fact–value distinctions (separation of normative, political, and ethical beliefs from 'factual' statements).

postcolonial feminism – a branch of feminism in IR that is interested in the intersection of gender and cultural subordination, addressing the way that dominant gender and political relations are entrenched both in global politics and between feminists, depending on their class, race, and geographic location.

post-empiricism – refers to debates in the philosophy of science which challenge the empiricist theory of knowledge by identifying how the social constitution of meaning, the linguistic construction of reality, and the historicity of knowledge are important for an understanding of science.

postpositivism – an umbrella term for a number of approaches that criticize positivist approaches to knowledge generation. Postpositivists can be seen to include a heterogeneous group of theorists critical of the positivist approach to studying world politics, such as interpretive/hermeneutic theorists, poststructuralists, feminists, critical theorists, scientific/critical realists, and some, although not all, constructivists.

poststructuralist feminism – a branch of feminism in IR that is particularly concerned with the way dichotomized linguistic constructions, such as strong/weak, rational/emotional, and public/private, serve to empower the masculine over the feminine.

principal-agent theory – an approach to studying institutional relationships that focuses on the delegation of authority from principals, who have the right to make decisions, to their agents. Authority is delegated within specified constraints, and principals can change the structure of delegation if it is not operating to their satisfaction. Neoliberal scholars apply principal-agent theory to understand the autonomy of international organizations (IOs), treating member states as the principals and the IO's management and staff as agents.

Prisoners' Dilemma – a game in which two players try to get rewards by cooperating with or betraying the other player. In this game, one of the most influential examples in game theory, it is assumed that the only concern of each individual player ('prisoner') is to maximize their own advantage, with no concern for the well-being of the other player. Because of the structure of the game, no matter what the other player does, one will always get a greater pay-off by defecting. However, the rewards of mutual cooperation are greater than those of mutual defection. Since in any situation playing defect is more beneficial than cooperating, rational players will defect even though they would be better off cooperating, creating the dilemma.

rationalism/rationalist theory – form of theorizing that utilizes rational choice explanation in its explanatory framework (see also 'rationality' and 'Prisoners' Dilemma'). Keohane (1988) used this term to highlight the similarities between the neorealist and neoliberal theorists, who shared with each other the assumption of rationality and, further, tended to apply the rules of the positivist model of science in their research. Keohane contrasted rationalism with 'reflectivism' (see below).

rationality – a rational actor calculates the costs and benefits of different courses of action and chooses the course of action that provides the highest net pay-off. Rational actors also behave strategically, meaning that they take into account the likely reactions of others to their choices and how those reactions will influence their own pay-offs. The rationality of state behaviour is an important assumption in neorealist and neoliberal theories.

Realpolitik – associated with the realist school of thought in IR. *Realpolitik* is a term arising from Bismarck's foreign policy and is used to describe policies that concern themselves solely with the singular pursuit of the national interest.

reason – a justification given by an actor for an action. Many argue that there is a difference between reasons and causes such that investigation of 'reasons' of an action makes social inquiry distinct from causal analysis in the natural sciences. This is because reasons, for these interpretive scholars, cannot be said to act in a (causal) 'when A, the B' manner but have to be understood in reference to the complex social meanings that they are embedded in.

recognition – refers to the act of acknowledging others as actors and as particular kinds of actors. States, for example, mutually recognize each others as states, thus constituting each other and themselves as such. They can also recognize each other as different kinds of states, for example, as democratic or autocratic states. Recognition is treated as a socially constructed category and is deemed important by many social constructivists and English school theorists in the construction of identity of actors.

reflectivism – a term used initially by Robert Keohane (1988) to refer to theorists that reject the rational choice methods and the positivist approach to knowledge generation of the 'rationalist theorists' in the study of world politics. Reflectivism is often interpreted to incorporate various 'postpositivist' schools such as feminism, critical theory, but especially poststructuralism.

regionalization – trend towards increasing and intensifying interaction between actors within a given geographical region.

revisionist states – states looking for opportunities to use military force to alter the balance of power.

rule – a philosophical term associated with social constructivist literature referring to a (set of) meaning(s) that is transmitted through language in social interaction and in reference to which actors formulate their thoughts and actions.

scientific realism – philosophy of science that aims to overcome the limitations of the positivist philosophy of science. The key assumption that informs scientific realism, and its close associate 'critical realism', is the belief in the independent existence of reality (however, not in accordance with 'epistemic realism' of the positivists, see above). Scientific and critical realists advocate deep ontological inquiry through conceptualization and epistemological and methodological pluralism.

second image – second-image approaches focus neither on the international system, nor on individual actors, in explaining international politics. The major explanatory variable of second-image approaches is the state. Second-image approaches are also called 'inside-out approaches', because they theorize how state characteristics (e.g. formal institutions, culture, and domestic actors) influence inclinations towards cooperation and discord, or war and peace, on the international level.

second image reversed – second-image-reversed approaches focus on the impact of the international system on domestic structures and processes. They examine how international politics (e.g. human-rights regimes) and processes (e.g. globalization) affect states in their polity, politics, and policy.

security dilemma – the paradox that occurs when a state seeks to improve its own security resulting in the decreased security of other states. Providing assurances to the contrary is not effective, realists argue, given the lack of trust between actors in a self-help world. At the heart of the security dilemma is the idea that security is a relative concept: all actors cannot have more of it.

social construction – the process of bringing to existence objects or subjects through the process of social interaction and transmission of social meanings. Social constructions do not exist in nature but have come about through acts of human creation (see 'social facts').

social contract theory – an influential strand of political theory that holds that the basis of a political community and political obligations can be framed in the terms of a contract. Social contracts can be formed either between rulers and ruled (Locke) or between potential citizens so as to give rise to a ruler or a system of laws (Hobbes, Rawls).

social facts – facts that, unlike so-called brute facts (Searle 1995), require social institutions or norms for their existence. Social facts, such as money or states, exist by the virtue of their social construction by actors.

sociology of science – a field of inquiry that seeks to understand scientific knowledge and scientific practices in relation to the historical, social and political environment of the practice of science.

solidarist international society – a term associated with the English school, referring to the collective enforcement of international rules. Collective security, for example, could be considered a solidarist security architecture. In his original formulation, Bull associated solidarism, not only with collective enforcement, but beyond it, the guardianship of human rights. This is primarily why a great deal of solidarist literature in the 1990s was liberal in orientation. However, there is no a priori reason why solidarism needs to be thought of in liberal terms. It is quite possible for key actors in international society to use multilateral institutions to spread conservative values (as the Concert of Europe did in the early nineteenth century).

sovereignty – a key characteristic or a norm in the international system/society denoting the independent, territorially self-standing and self-determining qualities of states. There are many conceptions of the nature and role of sovereignty in international political life. Realists tend to see sovereignty as an expression of the power and autonomy of states. Postpositivists theorists, such as constructivist and poststructuralist theorists, seek to demonstrate the socially constructed nature of the assumption of sovereign states. Many theorists have also pointed to the erosion of the sovereignty of states in the context of globalization.

speech act – a category of language that does not only describe or convey information but can be thought of as an act. For example, actions such as 'to promise' or 'to threaten' function through language and, hence, can be seen as speech acts.

state-centric – theories that take as their key ontological objects state actors. Mainstream IR theories such as realism, neorealism, and neoliberalism take the state-as-actor as their point of departure. In addition, variants of constructivism can also be conceived of as state-centric, especially Wendt (1999).

status quo states – states satisfied enough with the balance of power that they have no interest in using military force to shift it in their favour. Status quo powers are sometimes referred to as security seekers.

structural violence – the violence done to people when their basic needs are not met. This includes the effects of malnutrition, domestic violence, gender subordination, poor education, poor health care, and so on.

sustainable development – according to the Brundtland Report published by the World Commission on Environment and Development in 1987, sustainable development is development that meets the needs of the present generation without sacrificing the needs of future generations. However, the term remains deeply contested on ethical, political, and economic grounds. Much of this disagreement can be ultimately traced to different assumptions about what should be sustained, for whom, and by what means.

system/society – an important fault-line especially in International Political Theory and English school theory demarcating mere interaction in the case of the former, but the presence of social relations among sovereign states in the latter. See the individual entries on 'international system' and 'international society'.

theory – a central but contested term in natural and social sciences and in IR. In IR explanatory theorists tend to see theory as sets of statements that explain particular events, either in reference to a series of prior events or in reference to one or more causal variable. Critical theorists point to the role of theory in, not only explaining, but also in simultaneously critiquing social systems. Constitutive theory examines the way in which social structures are internally constituted or how ideas or discourses constitute social objects. Normative theory examines the plausibility of ethical arguments about what 'ought to be'.

Theory can also be seen to refer, more generally, to the frameworks of thought or knowledge through which we engage and give meaning to the world.

triadization – trend towards increasing and intensifying interactions between actors in a triad, where the triad comprises the North American, South-east Asian, and European regional economies.

two-level game – an approach that assumes that domestic and foreign policy are not two distinct spheres and highlights the interrelatedness of interactions on the international and the domestic levels. In the domestic level 'game', decision-makers seek to build winning coalitions that would ratify bargaining outcomes achieved in the international negotiation 'game'.

understanding – see 'explaining and understanding'.

unilateralism – when a state conducts its actions and reaches its foreign-policy decisions without consulting or cooperating with other international actors.

unipolarity – a world in which there is only one great power. Global hegemony is synonymous with unipolarity.

universal/particular – a conceptual pairing used to refer to the debate about whether frames of reference for political obligation should be understood to be local, based on the will and beliefs of particular political communities, or universal, defined in reference to rights that are seen to encompass humanity as a whole. See also 'cosmopolitanism' and 'communitarianism'.

welfare state – a state whose principal domestic priority is the promotion of the welfare of its citizens through the provision of social and medical services.

world society – shared values and common interests among the society of human kind. Depending on the degree to which values and interests converge, there will be an institutional dimension to world society: in the late-twentieth and early-twenty-first centuries, these institutions are primarily international non-governmental organizations that are prone to cajole and embarrass states into upholding their transnational commitments. It is important to note that world society is not the exclusive domain of actors with liberal values – the content of the transnational values (and action) may be extremely illiberal.

Index